NEURO-PSYCH

Mastery

IN BOWLING

Unveil The Impact Of Psychological Transitions On
Bowling Performance, Empowered By Neuroscience

MOHAMED JANAHI

NEURO-PSYCH MASTERY IN BOWLING
Copyright © 2024 by Mohamed Janahi

ISBNs
Hardback: 978-1-963351-04-0
Ebook: 978-1-963351-08-8
Paperback: 978-1-963351-01-9

Printed in the United States of America

Within every life journey lies deep purpose. My parents introduced the essence of embracing uniqueness and selfless service. With their support, I embarked on this transformative three-year endeavor, completing three books not just for personal growth, but to uplift and inspire others. The joy that makes me knowing these words may kindle a flame of hope. This literary dedication is not just about making a positive impact but about being an example of inspiration. May it ignite your true potential, bringing help and encouragement. Journey from good to great, creating a flow of positive change. Wishing everyone the best on their remarkable journey.

MJ

"I am certain that bowling, bowlers, and coaches around the world will benefit hugely from Mo's inspirational work in this book and others."

Coach Mark Heathorn, EBF L3 Coach, Team England Coach

"I applaud the publication of your fantastic book on the sport of bowling. It is an excellent source of information to look at, learn, and remember for our daily challenges as coaches. Writing about the challenges we face in our daily training takes a lot of spirit and courage. Thank you for sharing this wonderful gift you have worked so hard to perfect."

Pedro Merani, Qatar National Team Head Coach

CONTENTS

PHSYCHLOGICAL OPTIMIZATION / CORRECTION OF TECHNIQUE IN ELITE BOWLERS   297

ABOUT THE AUTHOR

Mohamed's journey through the world of bowling is a tapestry woven with tenacity, hard work, and an insatiable quest for knowledge. In the 1990s, Mohamed emerged as a bright star in the Gulf region's youth bowling scene. His journey was unique; he had no formal coach and a distinctive self-taught approach. As he set out on his quest for excellence, he explored the technical and psychological aspects of the sport in a way that sets him apart.

In the pursuit of excellence, Mohamed was a self-forged bowler, a solitary figure who, devoid of formal coaching, embarked on a personal odyssey to master the art of bowling. His journey was one of both a physical and psychological nature, constantly pushing the boundaries of his mental fortitude. His style, unique and idiosyncratic, evolved from the blend of traditional and contemporary power tactics, bearing witness to a keen mind always in search of the perfect equation. He was haunted by the enigma of the professional bowlers from the Professional Bowlers Association (PBA) and other luminaries of the sport, ceaselessly pondering what made them excel and how they managed to thrive in a game that demanded not just skill but profound mental resilience.

Yet, amid his successes, a persistent question lingered in his mind like a ghost from the past — why couldn't he shake off his old bowling habits and fully embrace the new techniques he worked so hard to learn? His commitment to learning and mastering the sport is evident in his impressive collection of over 22 professional qualifications, including those in sport psychology, nutrition, conditioning, and more.

The struggle was real for Mohamed. Despite dedicating himself to breaking free from the clutches of his former style, whether it was the physical execution or the mental aspects, the old habits would resurface at the most challenging times, especially during high-stakes tournaments. In the 1990s, Mohamed achieved remarkable success in the Asian Bowling Tour, consistently ranking among the top 7 bowlers from 2011 to 2016 out of a field of 500 Asian bowlers.

The question of why he clung to these habits, even when he consciously sought to move beyond them, fueled his determination to explore the psychological dimensions of the sport. Yet, there's more to his story than just technique. His emotional connection to bowling is profound. Bowling became his lifeline, especially during his formative years. The day he scored a remarkable 82 in his first game, a momentous transformation occurred. It was the first time he felt socially accepted, and bowling became more than just a sport; it became a means of connecting with others.

This introspection became the catalyst for Mohamed's latest endeavor — a book delving into the core mental and psychological challenges that most bowlers encounter on their journeys. In 2017, a pivotal realization altered his course. He recognized that becoming a true professional bowler required a robust support system, superior coaching, and more resources than he currently possessed.

The book, the second in a series, aimed to unravel the mysteries behind why bowlers, including Mohamed himself, grapple with their past habits and how these challenges can be overcome. It promised to be a comprehensive guide, drawing not only from Mohamed's experiences but also from the collective wisdom of his friends and colleagues in the coaching community. Balancing international competition with his responsibilities as a banker, a father, a coach, an entrepreneur, and a part-time ABF tournament bowler was unsustainable.

This wasn't just a book about technique; it was a narrative about the mental fortitude required to navigate the complexities of the sport. His legacy is defined by a commitment to the psychological aspects of the game, transforming how bowlers approach their performance. Mohamed's commitment to learning and mastering the sport is evident in his impressive collection of over 22 professional qualifications, including those in sport psychology, nutrition, conditioning, and more. He didn't just excel as a bowler; he also became a coach, inspiring the next generation of bowlers.

In the grand tapestry of Mohamed's bowling legacy, this chapter represented a crucial exploration into the inner workings of a bowler's mind. It was a contribution that went beyond technique, offering a roadmap for bowlers worldwide to navigate the intricate intersection of skill, psychology, and the relentless pursuit of excellence. Today, Mohamed's contributions to the bowling community extend beyond his playing days. He's deeply involved in scholarly and scientific research, striving to uncover the secrets of skill acquisition in bowling. His story continues to inspire and guide the bowling community towards new horizons in skill acquisition and performance.

THANK YOU

I would like to extend my heartfelt gratitude to two organizations whose unwavering commitment to the sport of bowling has been nothing short of exceptional: The United States Bowling Congress Academy and the European Bowling Federation Academy. Their dedication to the development and promotion of bowling, as well as their tireless efforts in providing education and training, have had a profound impact on countless players and coaches around the globe.

In the spirit of excellence and technical mastery, this book draws inspiration from the rich tapestry of knowledge and expertise offered by the USBC and EBF academies. Their mission to provide top-notch bowling instruction, coach training, and support to bowling centers has elevated the standard of the sport.

The USBC Academy and EBF Academy are not just organizations; they are beacons of hope for the future of bowling. Their goal to develop innovative promotional programs for bowling centers reflects a deep commitment to the grassroots of the sport. By actively engaging with bowling centers, they aim to ignite and sustain the enthusiasm of both seasoned players and newcomers.

The true essence of their work lies in nurturing the next generation of bowlers. They understand that the key to the longevity of this sport rests in the hands of the youth. Through these initiatives, they empower young bowlers to take ownership of their journey in bowling.

Ownership, as they rightly believe, breeds loyalty. When bowlers feel a sense of belonging and responsibility within a program, they are more likely to stay, learn, and thrive. It is this forward-thinking approach that ensures the continued growth and vitality of bowling as a sport.

In conclusion, the pages of this book stand as a testament to the invaluable contributions of these academies. Their wisdom, passion, and dedication have shaped the content within, making it a valuable resource for those seeking to master the technical intricacies of bowling.

As we move forward on our collective journey to foster the love of bowling, let us remember that it is organizations like these that serve as the guiding stars, illuminating our path and paving the way for a brighter future for this cherished sport.

FOREWORD

We are all aware that, overall, athletics may not be of utmost importance. Although it provides entertainment and distraction, it does not control life or death. "Sports is the most important of the unimportant things in life." - Arrigo Sacchi, Famed football manager.

Beyond just being a form of exercise and pleasure, sports can help us better understand who we are. It let us understand why some players succeed, even under pressure, but others struggle.

This book examines how we may all work to be the best versions of ourselves through a cutting-edge investigation of what I now refer to as sports psychology. The book takes us on a tour through the intriguing worlds of the human mind by first examining why younger siblings frequently outperform their older counterparts.

Sport has become a more important cultural institution recently, which is intriguing to observe. Few countries have escaped the accomplishments of outstanding bowlers, whether it be the imposing steps of Jason Belmonte or EJ Tackett on the PBA Tour, the resounding displays of Choi Bok or Park Jong in championship matches, or Anthony Simonsen's capacity to use bowling as a medium for artistic expression. These players will continue to cherish the ever-evolving and inspiring field of bowling.

The ESPN documentary series "The Last Dance," which details the incredible career of NBA legend Michael Jordan, has me spellbound as I type these words. A sportsman who single-handedly turned around a failing basketball team into one of the finest teams in history is depicted in this engrossing story. The example Jordan sets for others around him, along with his continuous pursuit of perfection, shows the power of character. Given the reality that he could have possibly come across as demanding or perhaps dictatorial, there is no disputing his relentless brilliance on the court.

In the world of sports, people are constantly interested in what makes someone truly remarkable. Questions like "How does one develop such extraordinary skill?" It is sometimes wondered, "What drove them to such dizzying heights?" This book makes an effort to shed light on the subject, despite the fact that it is almost hard to fully address such intricate and bordering on supernatural questions.

This sports psychology-focused book, offers a thorough examination of the elements that go into achieving peak performance through psychology. It provides insightful advice on how to reach our maximum potential in the game of bowling by drawing on a wide range of research, personal experiences, and interviews with elite bowlers and instructors from around the world.

You will investigate the complex interactions between physical prowess, mental toughness, tactical decision-making, and the psychology of game mastery as you set out on this instructive trip. You will obtain a greater grasp of what it takes to maximize your mental game performance in bowling through engrossing anecdotes, academic studies, and useful advice.

Also acknowledged in this book are the significant contributions of many people who kindly contributed their knowledge and experiences. This book's pages are enhanced by the insights and viewpoints of top bowlers and coaches around the world.

Finally, this book provides his book thoroughly explores the crucial role of psychological skills in a bowler's journey to peak performance. It covers topics like flow in bowling, mental attributes of top bowlers, personality traits, motivations, mindset, and practical applications. The book emphasizes the interconnectedness of psychological skills and successful performances. It concludes by examining motivations, performance dynamics, and the healthy role of perfectionism in pursuit of excellence. Ultimately, it aims to be a valuable resource for bowlers, coaches, and enthusiasts, helping them unlock their full potential in this captivating sport.

PROLOGUE:

As I immerse myself in bowling, I see the top bowlers' extraordinary abilities and accomplishments every day. My desire to join their ranks is stoked by their astounding performances on my television, in my social media feeds, and in the newspaper pages. What are my odds of doing the same? Even after spending quite a good amount of time on this subject, the resolution is equally depressing and perceptive.

One in 2000 high school bowlers has a chance of becoming a professional bowler. These probabilities are enormously increased, though, on the path to winning the sport. The International Bowling Federation (IBF) estimated that there were more over 100 million registered bowlers globally as of September 2021. Jason Belmonte, is the only one bowler among them has pulled off the incredible accomplishment of winning 15 major championships in the course of just 10 years. There are 67 million bowlers in the United States, yet only one, Walter Ray Williams Jr., has won more than 100 PBA titles and PBA regional titles combined.

I'm excited to announce that, I've written a trilogy of books that explore the subject of peak performance and flow state in bowling. These publications are the result of my in-depth research and personal experiences, and they attempt to give thorough insights into all facets of bowling, whether they be technical, psychological, or the development of talent.

The first book in the trilogy is titled "The Bowling Flow Blueprint - Nurturing talent and decoding the science of Elitism" This book discusses the critical function of identifying and developing bowling talent. It offers a guide for developing an atmosphere that promotes growth, skill development, and achieving the coveted flow state in bowling by drawing on the knowledge of great instructors and the most recent studies.

The Technical Mastery of Bowling Progression - Path to Ultimate Motor Skills Development," the second book in the series, is a comprehensive manual for learning how to develop superior motor skills when bowling. This book decodes the mysteries of technique, form, and precision through in-depth research and useful exercises, providing bowlers with useful tools to hone their abilities and reach their maximum potential.

This book is the third " The Neuro-Psych Mastery in Bowling " explores the complex connection between the mind and performance as we move on to the psychological aspect of bowling. This book provides bowlers with tools to harness the power of their brains and make seamless transitions toward their best performance on the lanes by examining subjects like mental toughness, focus, motivation, and managing pressure.

These three volumes provide a thorough and all-encompassing analysis of the bowling's art and science when taken together. This trilogy will be a priceless resource on your road to success in bowling. Whether you're an expert pro aiming to improve your techniques, a coach seeking to bring out the best in your athletes, or a passionate bowler longing to deepen your knowledge of the sport.

CHALLENEGS:

Before we dig into the world of bowling, I want to express my gratitude. While working on this book, I faced some unexpected challenges in reaching out to renowned bowlers and coaches. Despite my hopes of tapping into their vast knowledge and experiences, I encountered limited cooperation from some individuals.

This was indeed surprising and somewhat depressing. I had envisioned a book filled with insights from these legends of the sport, but sometimes, life unfolds differently. However, this did not deter me. My commitment to delivering a valuable resource for bowlers, coaches, and enthusiasts remained steadfast.

I want to be candid with you all. While I've strived for accuracy in every detail presented here, there may be moments where information were not strong enough. Please understand that I meticulously researched and analyzed every aspect, aiming to bring you fresh perspectives and insights that have not previously appeared in any other resource. My unique blend of expertise as a sport psychologist, sports coach, national team bowler, and a well-traveled participant within the sport has influenced my approach.

My primary goal is to offer you knowledge that's not only valuable but also inspirational. As we explore the technical and psychological aspects of bowling, rest assured that my analyses derive from both professional experience and my personal journey through the sport.

WHAT'S IN THIS BOOK

This book presents a comprehensive exploration of the profound role of psychological skills in the journey of a bowler towards achieving peak performance. Each chapter has been carefully crafted to build upon the central theme of mental attributes and strategies that are essential for excellence in this sport.

I began my journey by introducing the concept of "flow" in bowling, emphasizing the delicate balance between athletic self-concept and psychological skills. From there, I explored into the mental features that distinguish top-level bowlers, highlighting qualities such as unwavering focus, resilience, confidence, and mental toughness—skills that form the bedrock of success in professional bowling.

The exploration continued with an examination of personality traits in athletes, underscoring the importance of psychological adaptability and resilience. I provided a framework for bouncing back from setbacks through self-forgiveness and discussed the diverse motivations that drive bowlers, emphasizing the critical role of motivation as a psychological cornerstone.

I then explored into the significance of mindset and attitude, exploring the neuroscience of elite bowlers and the intricate workings of the bowler's brain. My journey took me deep into the neuroanatomical science of elite bowlers and the specific brain processes that underpin their exceptional skills.

Shifting the focus to practical applications, I guided bowlers in developing a winning mindset, and addressed the psychological transitions they experience at different career stages. I explored the impact of psychosocial factors on the development of young bowlers and outlined the psychological factors essential for competence in bowling competition.

Pre-performance routines, repeatability theories, and motivational differences between bowlers were dissected to underscore the interconnectedness of psychological skills and consistent, successful performances. I emphasized the strategic importance of anticipating and predicting future shots and the optimization of technique through programs like ICC.

The journey concluded by exploring the motivations that drive elite bowlers and the dynamics of performance plateaus, challenges, and breakthroughs in skill development. I provided insights into how perfectionism, when managed healthily, can be a powerful motivator in the pursuit of excellence.

In essence, this book has illuminated the intricate web of psychological skills that underlie greatness in bowling. It is my hope that the insights and knowledge shared within these chapters will serve as a valuable resource for bowlers, coaches, and enthusiasts, helping them unlock their full potential and attain the peak of their performance in this captivating sport.

I am honored and appreciative of the chance to educate and enlighten the bowling community. My objective is that these publications will inspire and equip bowlers of all skill levels to achieve new levels of performance and fulfillment on the lanes, in addition to informing and educating them.

DEFINING SPORT PSYCHOLOGY IN BOWLING

Sport psychology shows itself to be a complex and valuable science in the bowling world, providing deep insights into the complex mental processes of bowlers. As we begin this investigation, we hope to clarify the complex aspects of bowling-specific sport psychology, set it apart from other subfields of psychology, and highlight its essential connection to the larger field of sport sciences.

Sport psychology is a complex field that is ideally suited to analyze the psychological nuances inherent in bowling when it is applied to the complex dynamics of the sport. Although there are several definitions of sport psychology in the archives of psychology, a widely acknowledged description that is unique to bowling is still lacking. We, therefore, set out on a quest to ascertain the fundamentals of sport psychology in this particular setting, highlighting its salient features relative to other domains of psychology.

Sport psychology in bowling, at its core, explores the psychological underpinnings, mechanisms, and outcomes associated with the mental control of actions that are fundamental to the sport. One or more bowlers may participate in these activities, each of them acting as the main subject(s) involved in the pursuit.

Sport psychology, when combined with the complex world of bowling, seeks to understand the long-term effects of continued involvement in the sport on the psychological resources and personal growth of bowlers under the controlled environment of competitive play.

Remarkably, the word "sport" here refers to a broad category that includes a variety of sports, including bowling. This term has a broader definition that goes beyond bowling competitions to include other physical activities, workout routines, and active hobbies. These activities frequently take place in a variety of situations, such as structured physical education programs, leisure activities, and even therapeutic rehabilitation settings.

A unique feature that sets sport psychology apart in the context of bowling is its dual nature. The sport provides a unique setting for examining the complex psychological dynamics of individuals, but it also serves as a fundamental component of psychology as a whole. However, there is a strong symbiotic relationship between its core knowledge base and the specialized field of sport sciences. With a focus on bowling as a particular sport, these sport sciences aim to provide a thorough understanding of human behavior.

In real-world settings, the combination of these two knowledge bases—sport sciences and psychology—acts as a pillar supporting a greater understanding of the bowler, their surrounding environment, and the crucial elements of the sport. This synergy helps to improve our understanding of the psychological processes at work in bowling as well as the bowler's overall development and performance, both on the lanes and in the larger context of their athletic journey.

The Major Focus On Competitive Bowling: An In-Depth Examination

When we restrict our attention to the setting of competitive bowling, a more complex and specialized terrain within the field of sport psychology appears. Sport psychology explores the immediate and long-term effects of psychological variables on bowlers' performance as well as the possible consequences of regular engagement in the sport in this field.

Competitive bowling provides an engaging environment for analyzing the psychological aspects that affect the performance of athletes because of its distinctive combination of skill, strategy, and mental agility. Sport psychology examines various key concepts in this context, each of which adds to a comprehensive understanding of the bowler's journey and is skillfully adapted to the needs of bowling:

1. **Athletic Excellence:** The goal of athletic excellence is at the forefront of sport psychology in competitive bowling. This involves a thorough investigation of the psychological and cognitive components that support outstanding performance on the lanes. Together with bowlers, sport psychologists work to uncover the mental secrets of regularly hitting bowling pinnacle performance.

2. **Performance-Related Subjective Experiences:** A bowler's mental landscape is extremely important. Sport psychology explores the feelings, thoughts, and subjective experiences that come with bowling at the top levels of competition. To illuminate the complex interactions between the mental and emotional aspects of sports, this investigation seeks to understand how these aspects affect performance outcomes.

3. **Individual Resources (Psychological Strengths):** Just like athletes in every other sport, bowlers have a special combination of psychological resources and strengths. These natural qualities can be developed and used to improve performance and build perseverance in the face of difficulties. Sport psychologists and bowlers collaborate to find and develop these unique resources, which help bowlers succeed in competitive bowling.

Beyond the immediate context of being prepared for individual tournaments and attaining performance excellence in certain events, the athletic ability in competitive bowling is examined. Sport psychology broadens its scope to include the long term and explores the areas of career growth and bowlers' sustained brilliance. The goal of this long-term approach is to comprehend the complex path of a bowler's career, from the beginning to the end, and any possible modifications in between.

A Brief Historical Perspective: The Evolution Of Sport Psychology

The history of sport psychology begins with the turn of the 20th century when innovative projects laid the groundwork for the future development of the discipline. Norman Triplett, an Indiana University psychologist, is one of the visionaries who is recognized for carrying out one of the first studies on sports performance in 1898. Still, Coleman Griffith is regarded as the founding father of sport psychology.

Coleman Griffith

A key figure in the development of sport psychology is University of Illinois psychologist Dr. Coleman Griffith. He founded the first sport psychology laboratory, entered the coaching profession, and wrote seminal books including "The Psychology of Coaching" (Griffith 1926) and "The Psychology and Athletics" (Griffith 1928). His contributions to the discipline were revolutionary. Griffith's legacy includes an array of research done in partnership with the University of Illinois and the Chicago Cubs baseball team, as well as conversations with well-known players from his day.

Two major groups of practitioners emerged in sport psychology during the course of the twentieth century. Treating psychological issues and disorders is a common area of specialization for clinical sport psychologists, who are usually licensed in applied psychology fields like clinical, counseling, and personality psychology. Conversely, educational sport psychologists—who are not licensed psychologists—acclaim training in kinesiology, physical education, exercise and sport science, and the psychology of human movement. Their knowledge encompasses human behavior psychology, particularly as it relates to sports.

The Holistic Perspective

Sport psychology's complex relationship to competitive bowling weaves together a comprehensive view that highlights the interaction between the mental and physical aspects of the sport. This viewpoint encompasses the experiences, goals, and quest for perfection of the bowler and goes beyond the walls of the bowling alley into the larger life environment.

Fundamentally, this holistic perspective acknowledges the mind as an essential component in the bowler's toolbox. Athletes must possess mental toughness, fortitude, and sharpness in addition to physical skill if they hope to succeed in their sport. The bowler's psychological state, which includes their feelings, ideas, and mental techniques, has a direct impact on how well they perform.

The psychological aspects of bowling are closely intertwined with the physical aspects of the sport within its competitive environment. Think about the split second of focus before releasing the ball, the tactical choices made during play, or the emotional reaction to a crucial strike or split. These examples highlight the mutually beneficial interaction between the bowler's mental and physical performance.

Moreover, the holistic viewpoint goes beyond the boundaries of the bowling lanes, acknowledging the interdependence of the bowler's experiences both inside and outside of the sport. Their entire well-being, self-esteem, and self-perception are all impacted by the struggles and victories they undergo on the lanes.

The significance of sport psychology in competitive bowling is highlighted by this complex network of interactions. Together with bowlers, sport psychologists go on a complex journey that includes several crucial dimensions:

1. **Performance Enhancement**: Sport psychology aims to improve a bowler's performance by giving them the mental tools they need to perform well under the stress of competition. In the bowler's pursuit of perfection, concentration, visualization, and mental practice techniques become vital tools.

2. **Mental Resilience**: Bowling competitions sometimes involve challenges and setbacks. Sport psychology cultivates a philosophy of constant growth and improvement in bowlers, giving them the resilience to recover from setbacks.

3. **Emotional Regulation**: Bowlers experience a wide range of emotions, from joy after a strike to annoyance at a split. Sport psychologists help bowlers develop emotional intelligence so they can handle the highs and lows of the game with poise and calm.

4. **Goal-Setting**: Goal-setting is a crucial step in the development of a bowler. Setting attainable goals is made easier with the help of sport psychology, which also offers the drive and guidance needed to advance.

5. **Life Skills**: In addition to the game, sport psychology gives bowlers life skills that apply to many different facets of their lives. For both personal and professional development, effective communication, time management, and stress management techniques become invaluable tools.

The long-lasting influence of competitive bowling on a bowler's personal growth is further highlighted by the comprehensive viewpoint. Engaging in bowling can help develop a person's character, impart virtues like self-control and determination, and create a feeling of camaraderie among bowlers.

It becomes clear that sport psychology illuminates the route to success as we navigate the lanes of competitive bowling. The journey of a bowler involves much more than just hitting the ball; It also involves constant mental development, emotional mastery, and reaching peak performance.

Competitive bowling becomes more than just a physical activity in this mind-body synergy; it becomes a profound psychological and emotional adventure. We set out on a mission to realize the bowler's full potential as we dig further into the complex field of sport psychology in this particular context. We honor the bowler's accomplishments on the lanes as well as the extraordinary development and resiliency that define their overall athletic journey.

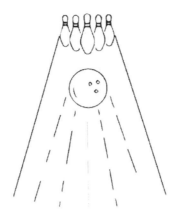

FLOW BOWLING: THROUGH ATHLETIC SELF-CONCEPT AND PSYCHOLOGICAL SKILLS

In the subject of applied sport psychology, investigating the complicated interactions between psychological variables and good athletic performance is crucial. It is necessary to dig deeply into particular psychological concepts that are pertinent to this achievement in order to comprehend the mental processes leading to such outstanding performance. This investigation reveals the underlying workings of the psychological systems that influence an athlete's ability to perform. In this book, we embark on the challenging work of disentangling the connections among psychological techniques and strategies, self-concept, and the elusive mental state referred to as "flow." It was covered in "The Bowling Flow Blueprint," our very first book. We also set out on a quest to discover the relationships between peak performance in sports and flow. We hope to gain further insight into the causes of a flow state in sports and shed light on the fascinating connection between this mental state and the caliber of athletic performance through this extensive study.

In bowling, as in many other sports, the idea of "flow" is crucial. A state of mind known as flow is defined by an ideal harmony between the abilities needed for a given task and the perceived challenges involved. The bowler is fully submerged in this state of extreme concentration, which enables them to play at their peak.

Mihaly Csikszentmihalyi's groundbreaking work has influenced a lot of studies on flow in sports and fitness. His original research focused on flow in physical activities, and his conclusions set the stage for future investigations into the relationship between flow and athletic performance.

Mihaly Csikszentmihalyi

Attaining flow can have a significant effect on a bowler's performance in the game. Bowlers who are in a state of flow exhibit increased attention and concentration, which can result in more precise and reliable throws. A sensation of effortless control over the game might result from the careful balancing act between the difficulty of hitting the pins precisely and the bowler's skill level, helping to boost scores.

A flow state involves seamlessly aligning mental stability, physical well-being, the perfection of technical movements and overall joy. Allowing athletes to achieve optimal and flawless performance.

It's important to understand that although flow and peak performance are frequently linked, they are not the same thing. The immersive nature of the activity and intrinsic enjoyment are what define the flow, whereas reaching ideal outcomes is the main focus of peak performance. Optimal performance in bowling could be defined as hitting strikes frequently or getting a high score.

Hypothetical example

Experienced professional bowler Alex, who is known for his skill, goes into a deep state of flow during his last games:

Hyper-Awareness: *Alex's senses become hyper-attuned to the environment. He not only sees the pins and the lane but can sense the results that he will positively achieve. This heightened awareness allows him to make successful and accurate adjustments in his approach and release, adapting seamlessly to the ever-changing conditions.*

Perfect Synchronization: *He has perfect coordination between his thoughts and body. Everything about this move is perfectly orchestrated, right down to the second he scoops up the ball and lets go. He appears to be dancing with the pins, and the movement of his ball corresponds with his goals.*

Consistent Shots: *Nearly all shots end in strikes. Alex is quite precise. He can predict the pin action remarkably well because he reads the lane so well. The game has an almost symphonic, rhythmic aspect due to the captivating patterns in which the pins fall.*

Timelessness and Focus: *Time becomes less significant. Alex gets lost in the game entirely. He's not considering the prize money, the audience, or the trophy. He is focused on the present moment, frame by frame, shot by shot.*

Effortless Mastery: *No sense of strain or effort is present. Alex is at the level of effortless proficiency. He is aware that he has the ability and mental clarity to respond appropriately to everything the lane throws at him. It feels really good to have this level of influence over his game.*

In the Zone: *When everything is just right, Alex feels as though he is in the zone. He enjoys the challenge of making accurate hits to the pocket, making easy adjustments to difficult spares, and playing with total focus throughout.*

In the world of professional bowling, an almost superhuman degree of attention, precision, and performance can result from experiencing flow at the greatest levels. This is demonstrated by the below hypothetical example.

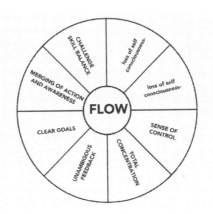

THE NINE DIMENSIONS OF FLOW STATE

The state of flow is characterized by a harmony between perceived problems or possibilities for action that stretch but do not overwhelm existing skills, as well as by clear goals and immediate feedback about the progress being made. Flow is made up of cognitive, physiological, and affective elements. When someone experiences flow, he is extremely happy and joyful, and he wants to recreate this feeling. The following nine dimensions can be used to describe the sense of flow: (1) a challenge-skills balance that makes one feel engaged but not overwhelmed; (2) clear objectives that allow one to concentrate on the current task and know what will come next, reducing distractions and stress; (3) an action-awareness merging that makes the person completely consumed by the situation; (4) concise and unambiguous feedback, which suggests that when in flow, the person is always aware of what he is doing; (5) a high level of task-related concentration; (6) an absolute sense of control; (7) a loss of self-consciousness, which results in the person being so absorbed in the activity that there is a lack of ego-oriented protection; (8) the transformation of time, which indicates that the time elite Performers feel completely involved in the activity and as though no effort is necessary after experiencing these dimensions; and (9) autotelic experience is where the activity itself is inherently satisfying and enjoyable, independent of external rewards, and elite players may exemplify this by deriving fulfillment from the game's mechanics, challenges, skill demands, and their own sense of progress and mastery.

Myth: Flow State Is A Guarantee Of Success.

Reality: The myth that flow state guarantees success is debunked by the understanding that there are various factors that contribute to outcomes in bowling. While flow state can significantly enhance a bowler's performance, it is not an absolute guarantee of success. Other factors such as technical skill, strategic decision-making, and external circumstances also play a crucial role.

Flow state is characterized by heightened focus, complete immersion, and the seamless integration of abilities and challenges. It can undoubtedly elevate a bowler's performance by facilitating precise execution and effortless decision-making. However, external factors like lane conditions, the performance of competitors, and unforeseen events can influence the outcome of a game.

Elite bowlers recognize that flow state is a dynamic process that requires continuous adaptation and refinement. While being in flow enhances their performance, they understand the importance of skill development, strategy implementation, and remaining adaptable to changing circumstances.

By dispelling the myth of guaranteed success in flow state, we gain a more accurate understanding of the complexity of bowling. Flow state is a valuable mental state that can enhance performance, but it is not the sole determinant of success. Elite bowlers embrace the potential of flow state while acknowledging the multifaceted nature of the sport and the importance of other factors that contribute to achieving their goals.

The ambiguity of the flow notion has drawn criticism from certain academics. The revised multidimensional description of flow, as given above within the framework of the nine dimensions, depicts flow as a less frequent and more particular event, which closely resembles the reality of the phenomenon and may be easier to quantify and assess.

For both experienced bowlers and newcomers, the descriptions and illustrations of each flow condition in the context of bowling are provided below:

Balancing Challenges And Skills For Engaging Flow: When the amount of challenge in the bowling game meets the player's skill level, a feeling of equilibrium results, and a flow state develops. Elite athletes may exhibit this when they take part in competitive events or face opponents that challenge them to use their cutting-edge abilities and plans to succeed.

For instance, a skilled bowler might experience flow while competing in a championship match with high stakes where his abilities are put to the test to the maximum.

The difficulty, though, may come from trying to raise one's technical proficiency or beat one's previous best score for novices. For instance, when a novice bowler effectively employs a new bowling technique he has been practicing and the challenge level corresponds to his present ability level, he may feel flow.

CLEAR OBJECTIVES: Accurate goals or objectives help the bowler into a state of flow because he provides his activities a sense of direction and purpose.

When elite players have specific goals in a game, such as hitting a certain score or winning a certain match, this may be shown. A great bowler, for instance, might feel flow if he sets out to consistently hit the pocket—the best place on the lane to strike—and execute his throws expertly in order to do so.

For newcomers, specific goals could be more centered on improving their fundamental abilities, such as hitting the pins reliably or increasing their accuracy. For instance, when they set a goal to regularly hit a particular number of pins with each stroke and concentrate their efforts towards accomplishing that objective, a novice bowler may feel flow.

Merging Action And Awareness For Immersive Flow: The bowler is fully present in the moment and feels completely absorbed in the activity when he is in a flow state, where his actions and awareness mix. When exceptional athletes are completely concentrated on their movements, breathing, and mental processes without being diverted by other factors, this may be seen in them.

A top bowler could experience flow, for instance, when he is totally focused on his pre-shot routine, conscious of his body motions and alignment, and precise in his shot execution.

Comparable to experienced bowlers, beginners who are fully focused on their technique and not sidetracked by outside variables may feel flow. For instance, when a rookie bowler is totally present in his approach, concentrating on his stance, grip, and release, and executing his shots with concentration, he may experience flow.

Receiving Clear And Precise Feedback For Enhanced Awareness And Engagement: Receiving rapid, precise feedback on one's performance helps one into a state of flow. Elite athletes may exhibit this when they hear evaluation from coaches, teammates, or even when they evaluate themselves in the heat of battle.

Getting immediate, accurate feedback on one's performance aids in entering the state of flow. When elite athletes receive criticism from coaches or teammates, or even when they evaluate themselves in the heat of combat, they may display this behavior.

Seeing the outcomes of their shots, such as the pins that were knocked over or the ball's trajectory down the lane, can provide beginners with unambiguous feedback. For instance, a novice bowler could feel flow if he can immediately assess the effects of his shot and modify his technique accordingly.

Skills For Sustaining High Levels Of Concentration On The Task At Hand: The likelihood of entering a flow state increases when the bowler has a high level of task-related skills and confidence in his abilities. Elite athletes can display this through their high levels of technical proficiency, strategic thinking, and decision-making.

A top bowler could feel flow, for instance, if he can hit his goal consistently, modify his ball speed and rotation to suit shifting lane circumstances, and plan when to apply various bowling adjustments or approaches.

For novices, improving their fundamental bowling techniques, such as a consistent approach, release, and targeting, may fall under the category of high task-related skills. An amateur bowler could experience flow, for instance, if he can regularly hit the pocket, modify his approach to suit various oil patterns, and improve his accuracy and pin carry.

Cultivating A Strong Sense Of Control And Mastery Over The Activity: A feeling of mastery and control over the task is a defining feature of the flow state. When exceptional players feel in control of their skills, techniques, and strategies and are able to execute them with accuracy and confidence, this may be apparent.

For instance, an expert bowler may be in flow when he can consistently strike his target, modify his technique for various lane conditions, and make judgments with confidence to increase his score.

Similar to this, novice bowlers may experience flow when they sense control and growth in their game. A rookie bowler, for instance, might experience flow when he can consistently strike his target, manage the speed and spin of his ball, and show improvement in his accuracy and pin carry, giving him a sense of mastery over the game.

Myth: Flow State Is Always Positive And Enjoyable.

Reality: The myth that flow state is always positive and enjoyable is debunked by the nuanced nature of the experience. While flow state is often associated with positive emotions like joy and satisfaction, it can also encompass moments of struggle, frustration, and intensity.

Elite bowlers, despite being in flow state, may encounter a range of emotions, both positive and negative, as they navigate challenges, difficult lane conditions, or fierce competition. The key distinction is their ability to channel these emotions constructively, utilizing them as motivation and focus to enhance their performance.

Flow state is a dynamic state of consciousness characterized by deep absorption in the task at hand and a seamless alignment of skills and challenges. It is not solely about feeling good but rather about being fully present and immersed in the moment. Elite bowlers understand that the intense and demanding nature of flow state can bring forth a mix of emotions, and they embrace these challenges as opportunities for growth and self-improvement.

Loss Of Self-Consciousness: A person in a flow state is wholly immersed in the task and has little self-consciousness. When exceptional athletes are completely focused on their performance and are not sidetracked by self-doubt, outside expectations, or other distractions, this may be apparent.

An exceptional bowler might feel flow, for instance, when he is completely focused on his shots, strategy, and the game's dynamics and aren't unduly worried about how he is performing or what other people might think.

Comparable to this, novice bowlers who can let go of self-consciousness and concentrate only on their game may experience flow. An amateur bowler, for instance, might experience flow when he is completely focused on his approach, release, and targeting without being unduly self-conscious or comparing himself to others.

Time Transformation In Elite Flow: A bowler may experience a warped sense of time in a flow state, believing that time is moving either too rapidly or too slowly. Elite players may exhibit this when they are really immersed in the game; hours may fly by as they are caught up in the action.

During a key match, for instance, when they are totally focused on their performance and time seems to be passing quickly, a top-tier bowler could experience flow.

A rookie could also notice a change in the passage of time while in a flow state, where he might become so engrossed in his bowling performance that he loses sight of time. For instance, a novice bowler may experience flow when he is completely concentrated on his approach, release, and targeting, with time appearing to pass more slowly.

Autotelic Experience: When someone is in a flow state, he is frequently describing an autotelic experience, which means that regardless of any external rewards or results, the activity itself is intrinsically satisfying and delightful. Elite players may demonstrate this when they find enjoyment and fulfillment in the game's mechanics, the difficulties and abilities required, and the sense of development and mastery.

An expert bowler, for instance, might experience flow when he is totally immersed in the game, loving the act of planning, carrying out shots, and competing rather than being purely concerned with the result or external benefits.

A newbie might also have an autotelic experience while in a flow state, where he takes pleasure in the act of playing the game, improving his skills, and making advancements. For instance, when a novice bowler is completely immersed in the game, enjoying the challenge of improving his technique, hitting his targets, and watching his scores rise without being primarily concerned with succeeding or receiving external benefits, he may be in flow.

The Skill-Challenge Balance And Flow

The skill-challenge balance is of particular relevance since it is a fundamental component of bowling, even though there are other antecedents associated with the creation of flow. With highly competitive fields, complex oil patterns, and difficult tournament structures, the difficulty of the game increases in all successful bowling competitions as the players' ability levels rise. The "channel model" is a traditional way to conceptualize the relationship between skill-challenge balance and optimal flow. The model claims that when a game's difficulty fits a bowler's abilities, optimal flow results. According to numerous research, flow occurs when skill and challenge are roughly equal. The talent and challenge level of the bowlers are irrelevant in the channel model. Even for inexperienced players who are playing simple games, flow should be felt because their limited competence is matched by the game's limited difficulty. Additionally, if being in flow is a very motivating mood, then even somewhat inexperienced bowlers should be encouraged to continue playing straight away using handicap points.

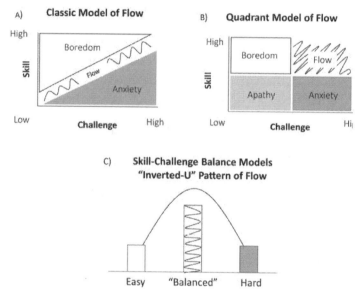

Fig. 1. Models of Flow based on the skill-balance.

(A) Classic Model of Flow showing optimal flow emerges with a matching of challenge and skill (Csíkszentmihályi, 1975)

(B) Quadrant Model of Flow showing optimal flow emerging with high skill and high challenge (Csikszentmihalyi, 1992)

(C) Inverted-U pattern of flow as posited by the skill-challenge balance models

(A) Classic Model of Flow showing optimal flow emerges with a matching of challenge and skill

(B) Quadrant Model of Flow showing optimal flow emerging with high skill and high challenge

(C) Inverted-U pattern of flow as posited by the skill-challenge balance models

Within bowling, delving into the psychology of flow and its interaction with skill and challenge brings forth a profound understanding of optimal performance. Let's explore this dynamic interplay using the Classic Model of Flow, the Quadrant Model of Flow, and the Inverted-U pattern of flow, all in the context of a bowler.

The Classic Model of Flow (Fig 1 -A) comes to life as we envision a skilled bowler entering a competition. Their years of practice and experience have honed their skills to a point where they can effectively read lane conditions, control their release, and adjust their approach. As the competition unfolds, they encounter a level of challenge that aligns seamlessly with their skillset. The rhythm of their movements, the precision of their shots, and the strategic decisions they make converge harmoniously. Their focus is unwavering, and the act of bowling becomes an immersive experience. This equilibrium between their skill and the challenge presented on the lane epitomizes the Classic Model of Flow in action.

Transitioning to the Quadrant Model of Flow (Fig 1 -B), consider a bowler who seeks to enhance his performance further. He deliberately embarks on rigorous training regimes, working with coaches to refine his technique and master advanced techniques. As he continues to elevate his skill level, he also embraces increasingly challenging lane conditions and enters higher-stakes tournaments. In this example, the Quadrant Model comes into play when the bowler's newfound skills are met with the heightened challenges of the competitive landscape. As he stands at the approach, facing a complex oil pattern and a formidable opponent, heightened skills empower them to conquer these challenges. The exhilarating state of flow emerges as he navigates the synergy between his elevated skills and the intensified challenges they willingly embrace.

The Inverted-U pattern of flow (Fig 1 -C) becomes evident when observing a bowler who has embarked on an exceptional journey of growth. As he diligently trains and elevates his skill level, he continuously seeks out more challenging competitions. However, there comes a point when the challenges become exceedingly formidable, surpassing his perceived skill level. Initially, as the challenges escalate, his flow experience intensify, leading to remarkable performances. However, as the challenges continue to mount beyond a certain threshold, his flow experiences start to wane. The stress of the overpowering challenges begins to eclipse his ability to perform optimally. This represents the Inverted-U pattern, emphasizing the importance of finding the delicate balance where challenges foster growth without overwhelming the athlete.

A high-stakes competition or a demanding competitive setting may induce a flow state in a highly competent and experienced bowler who has mastered advanced technical skills and has a thorough comprehension of the sport. A perfect balance between the degree of complexity and the bowler's skill level can be achieved thanks to his confidence in his abilities and the game's difficulty, resulting in a state of flow. The bowler might feel totally absorbed in the game, in complete control of his actions, and completely focused. He might also feel more delight and satisfaction from playing his best. Given that the game's difficulty is in line with the bowler's high skill level in this instance, the quadrant model, which takes both the challenge level and skill level into account, may provide a more accurate explanation of the bowler's flow state.

However, a casual, recreational game with a low degree of difficulty may be more favorable to experiencing flow for a novice or less experienced bowler who is still improving his technical skills and understanding of the game. The game may be quite simple for the bowler, with a low bar that fits his level of proficiency, enabling him to play effectively without experiencing stress or anxiety. The bowler might also be in a peaceful frame of mind, free from the strain of competition or high stakes, which might help him achieve a state of flow. Given the low challenge level and the bowler's developing skill level in this situation, the quadrant model, which considers both the challenge level and skill level, may also offer a better explanation for the bowler's flow state.

In order to perform at their highest level in an effortless and joyful way, bowlers are said to be in the flow experience, a state in which they are pushed to their limits while believing they have the ability to handle these demands. Additionally, bowlers who experience flow report being wholly focused on the action to the point of becoming completely involved in it and feeling in control of what they are doing. Peak performance is linked to flow states, which are also thought to provide beneficial psychological effects like greater wellbeing, improved self-concept, and good subjective experience. Because of this, bowlers and coaches can benefit much from understanding flow and how it occurs. Numerous factors have reportedly been linked to flow in sports up to this point. The precise manner in which those elements can affect its prevalence, however, is less clear.

The Myth Of Harder Is Better – Cases With National Teams

The pursuit of excellence in competitive bowling necessitates a meticulous and strategic training approach, particularly when national teams prepare for tournaments marked by elevated difficulty levels. As elite athletes engage in arduous practice sessions, the physiological and psychological impacts on bowlers assume critical importance. The intricate interplay between the challenges encountered in practice and the skill levels of the bowlers gives rise to a spectrum of effects that reverberate far beyond the confines of the bowling lanes.

When national bowling teams embark on rigorous practice sessions ahead of high-difficulty tournaments, bowlers may undergo a diverse range of psychological and physiological effects. The intensified challenges during these practice conditions can, on occasion, lead to an array of adverse psychological outcomes. Bowlers may grapple with a loss of hope and trust in their abilities, nurturing self-doubt and eroding confidence. Moreover, the demanding nature of these practice regimens may precipitate burnout, characterized by emotional exhaustion and dwindling motivation. The stress and anxiety induced by the extreme difficulty can contribute to an overall negative impact on self-esteem, as bowlers persistently confront challenging conditions.

Physiologically, the taxing nature of these practices can manifest in physical fatigue, given that bowling is a sport demanding both strength and endurance. This fatigue not only impairs performance but also heightens the risk of injuries, as bowlers may push their physical limits to meet formidable challenges. Sleep disturbances may further compound these issues, as the stress and anxiety associated with demanding practice sessions can disrupt adequate rest.

In light of the skill-challenge balance and the psychological concept of flow, a complex recommendation for practice emerges. A balanced approach, commencing with challenges aligned with the team's current skill levels and gradually intensifying, proves advantageous. This progression allows bowlers to focus on skill development without overwhelming pressure, fostering confidence and mitigating the risk of injuries associated with abrupt challenges. While this approach necessitates meticulous planning and consideration, its benefits in skill enhancement and psychological well-being outweigh potential drawbacks. In essence, cultivating a measured and progressively challenging practice environment aligns with the principles of optimal performance and athlete well-being.

Examples Of Extreme Skill Challenges Unbalances

Unrealistic Lane Conditions:

Example Scenario: During practice, the national bowling team faces lane conditions deliberately altered to be extremely challenging. The oil patterns change dynamically, making it nearly impossible for bowlers to predict ball reactions. Bowlers consistently leave splits and struggle to find a consistent line.

Psychological Impact: Bowlers become frustrated and demoralized as they face constant failure during practice. This erodes their confidence and creates a sense of helplessness, impacting their mental resilience.

Neurological Impact: The persistent frustration and demoralization can lead to increased stress levels, activating the body's stress response over time. Chronic stress may negatively affect neuroplasticity, hindering the brain's ability to adapt and learn from challenges.

Excessive Pressure from Coaches:

Example Scenario: Coaches set unrealistically high performance expectations during every practice session, emphasizing perfection and flawless execution. Any deviation from the expected standard is met with harsh criticism and disappointment.

Psychological Impact: Bowlers feel immense pressure to meet the coach's standards, leading to heightened stress and anxiety. The fear of failure diminishes their enjoyment of the sport, affecting their intrinsic motivation.

Neurological Impact: Prolonged exposure to high-pressure situations can contribute to the development of anxiety disorders. The persistent activation of stress pathways may lead to alterations in neurotransmitter levels, affecting mood regulation and cognitive function.

Time-Pressured Practice Sessions:

Example Scenario: Bowlers are subjected to drills where they have a limited time to analyze lane conditions, make strategic decisions, and execute shots. The rushed nature of the practice sessions increases tension and anxiety.

Psychological Impact: Bowlers experience heightened stress during time-pressured sessions, impacting their decision-making abilities. The anxiety associated with time constraints diminishes their overall sense of control.

Neurological Impact: Chronic exposure to time pressure can contribute to sustained elevated cortisol levels, affecting neural structures involved in decision-making and executive function. This may lead to impaired cognitive performance over time.

Inconsistent Coaching Feedback:

Example Scenario: Coaches provide conflicting feedback on bowlers' techniques and strategies. One coach emphasizes a particular adjustment, while another suggests the opposite. This inconsistency leaves bowlers uncertain about their strengths and weaknesses.

Psychological Impact: Bowlers become unsure about their abilities, leading to self-doubt. The lack of clarity in feedback erodes their confidence and prevents them from fully embracing and refining their skills.

Neurological Impact: The ambiguity in feedback can contribute to heightened cognitive dissonance, impacting the brain's reward system. The lack of clear reinforcement hinders the formation of neural pathways associated with skill acquisition and refinement.

Intense Competitive Drills:

Example Scenario: Coaches organize highly competitive drills that foster an environment of individual rivalry. Bowlers are encouraged to outperform each other, leading to heightened tension and resentment within the team.

Psychological Impact: The constant comparison and rivalry among teammates create a toxic team environment. Insecurities develop, hindering effective collaboration. The negative team dynamics persist, affecting the overall cohesiveness during actual competitions.

Neurological Impact: Prolonged exposure to a competitive and hostile environment may activate the brain's threat detection systems, leading to chronic stress. This stress can influence neural circuits related to social cognition, potentially impacting teamwork and interpersonal relationships.

Overbearing Physical Demands:

Example Scenario: The national bowling team engages in physically demanding training sessions that exceed the typical duration and intensity. Bowlers are pushed to their physical limits, leading to fatigue, muscle soreness, and heightened physical stress.

Psychological Impact: Bowlers experience physical exhaustion, contributing to mental fatigue. The constant strain on the body reduces their enthusiasm for practice, making them more susceptible to frustration and negative emotions.

Neurological Impact: Prolonged physical exhaustion can impact neurotransmitter balance, affecting mood regulation and cognitive function. The brain's ability to efficiently process information and sustain attention during competitions may be compromised over time.

Isolation Drills with Minimal Social Interaction:

Example Scenario: Practice sessions are structured to involve minimal interaction between bowlers. Each bowler is isolated, focusing solely on individual performance without the camaraderie of team support.

Psychological Impact: The lack of social interaction diminishes the sense of team spirit and support. Bowlers may feel isolated, leading to a decline in morale and a sense of loneliness during practice and, subsequently, during competitions.

Neurological Impact: Social isolation can contribute to feelings of loneliness and affect neural pathways associated with social reward. Over time, this may impact the release of neurotransmitters related to mood regulation and motivation, potentially affecting overall mental well-being.

Excessive Number of Games in a Single Day:

Example Scenario: The national bowling team implements a training regimen where bowlers are required to play an unusually high number of games, such as 12 games, in a single day. This extended play aims to enhance their endurance and overall fitness for handling the standard 6-game blocks in competitions.

Psychological Impact: The demanding schedule puts immense pressure on bowlers, leading to mental fatigue and increased stress. Bowlers may struggle to maintain focus and enthusiasm as they navigate through the extended series of games.

Neurological Impact: Prolonged mental exertion without adequate breaks can lead to cognitive fatigue and a decline in attentional resources. This may impact decision-making, concentration, and reaction time during the later stages of the training day and potentially in subsequent competitions.

The 5% (Skill – Challenge) Prep Theory

Finding the right balance between skill and challenge in competitive bowling is more than just understanding the basics. While it's commonly known that a good balance is key for optimal performance and getting into a flow state, taking a closer look at this balance reveals its nuanced nature. It's not just about the recommended 5-8% increase in training difficulty; there are additional factors like oil pattern difficulty and mental readiness that play a crucial role. Looking at the bigger picture, this approach recognizes the various aspects of the skill-challenge balance, turning tournament preparation into a delicate dance that requires a deep understanding.

This story places the bowler's well-being front and center, moving beyond the technical aspects of the game. A tailored and gradual training approach becomes even more crucial, understanding that reaching top performance is a process, not a straightforward journey.

As we unpack the layers of this balance, we begin to see a tapestry woven with different elements that shape a bowler's experience. The mental side of the game takes the spotlight, revealing the different mental states that push bowlers to bring out their best. However, within this tapestry, potential challenges emerge, especially when dealing with extremely tough practice conditions. Understanding this balance means taking a closer look at the psychological impacts of overly challenging practice sessions.

The journey towards excellence in competitive bowling becomes a narrative that goes beyond the ordinary. It's a story that guides the way to long-term growth and success, where mastering skill and facing challenges come together in a dance. This exploration encourages a shift away from fixed ideas, prompting coaches and bowlers to see the skill-challenge balance as something dynamic. In this evolving story, the bowler's experience transforms into a canvas painted with adaptability, resilience, and a profound understanding of the subtle aspects that make bowling an exciting and rewarding sport.

The table below outlines key strategies and examples for a 5% challenge in bowling, focusing on diverse aspects for improvement. Tactics include modifying lane conditions, incorporating biomechanical readiness exercises, creating pressure situations in practice, and adjusting environmental factors. The goal is to enhance adaptability, improve psychological and neurological advantages, and employ specific methods tailored to each challenge, fostering a well-rounded approach to skill development.

Example	5% Benefit	Psychological Advantage	Neurological Advantage	Tactics/Methods for 5% Challenge
Lane Conditions	Enhanced adaptability	Improved stress management	Increased pattern recognition	Strategically alter oil patterns during practice sessions, introducing subtle variations in length or volume. Observe and analyze bowlers' adaptability, providing targeted feedback on adjustments.
Biomechanical Readiness	Improved endurance	Mental resilience	Enhanced neuromuscular coordination	Integrate targeted strength and conditioning exercises into warm-up routines before training sessions. Monitor the impact of fatigue on biomechanics, adapting training plans accordingly.
Comfort Zone	Better focus under unpredictable conditions	Increased adaptability	Improved sensory adaptation	Sporadically alter settings during training, changing lighting conditions or introducing ambient noise. Observe how bowlers cope with alterations to gauge adaptability and mental fortitude.
Pressure Situations	Enhanced stress tolerance	Improved concentration	Efficient stress response	Orchestrate friendly competitions or timed drills during practice. Create an environment that mimics the inherent pressure of actual events. Provide guidance to enhance mental resilience and maintain precision under time constraints.
Temperature	Adaptation to varying physiological conditions	Resilience to discomfort	Improved thermoregulation	Subtly adjust ambient temperatures during practice. Evaluate bowlers' responses to temperature variations to ensure optimal performance under different physiological conditions.
Equipment Adjustments	Increased adaptability	Confidence in equipment changes	Enhanced motor control	Introduce variations in equipment, such as different ball weights or grip configurations. Analyze how bowlers adjust techniques to accommodate changes, tailoring training plans accordingly.
Distractions	Improved focus in noisy environments	Sharpened concentration	Enhanced attentional control	Intentionally introduce controlled disruptions during training, such as intermittent noise or simulated crowd reactions. Observe bowlers' ability to maintain focus and composure in the face of distractions.
Skill Variety	Broadened skill set	Increased creativity	Enhanced skill integration	Integrate advanced techniques and trick shots into practice sessions. Encourage bowlers to broaden their skill set, providing tailored guidance to enhance versatility.

Example	5% Benefit	Psychological Advantage	Neurological Advantage	Tactics/Methods for 5% Challenge
Shot Accuracy	Precision improvement	Increased confidence	Improved motor accuracy	Narrow down target zones during training, designating smaller areas for precision. Provide focused feedback on improving accuracy, a crucial skill in competitive environments.
Posture and Balance	Enhanced stability	Increased poise under pressure	Improved proprioception	Incorporate balance-challenging exercises into warm-ups, introducing controlled instability. Observe how bowlers adapt to these challenges and tailor exercises to enhance stability.
Mental Toughness	Strengthened mental resilience	Improved stress regulation	Enhanced cognitive flexibility	Incorporate visualization and mindfulness exercises into training. Simulate high-pressure scenarios to build mental toughness, providing targeted guidance on developing coping mechanisms.
Decision-Making	Sharpened strategic thinking	Improved decision speed	Enhanced cognitive processing	Introduce unexpected lane changes or alter game formats during training. Challenge bowlers to make swift and strategic decisions, providing insights into their decision-making processes.
Consistency Challenges	Improved performance stability	Enhanced mental fortitude	Increased adaptive learning	Inject variability into practice conditions, varying lane conditions or introducing sporadic challenges. Provide tailored feedback on maintaining consistency amid unpredictability.
Post-Game Analysis	Quick adaptability	Improved self-awareness	Enhanced analytical thinking	Encourage bowlers to engage in real-time analysis during training. Prompt them to assess performance frame by frame, facilitating immediate adjustments.
Competitive Edge	Heightened tournament readiness	Increased motivation	Improved competitive mindset	Foster a culture of friendly competition during training. Encourage bowlers to push each other, creating an environment that mirrors the intensity of actual events.
Pre-Event Mini-Tournaments	Better preparation for official events	Enhanced focus under pressure	Improved performance under stress	Organize pre-event mini-tournaments that mirror the intensity and dynamics of actual competitions. Observe how bowlers respond to the intensified environment and provide targeted feedback.
Time-Pressured Practice Sessions	Quick decision-making under stress	Improved time management	Enhanced attention allocation	Structure drills where bowlers have limited time for analysis and execution. Observe how bowlers maintain composure and make effective decisions under time pressure.
Inconsistent Coaching Feedback	Improved decision-making autonomy	Enhanced self-reliance	Increased cognitive adaptability	Deliberately provide conflicting feedback on techniques and strategies. Challenge bowlers to trust their instincts and make decisions independently.
Isolation Drills	Improved focus in solitary conditions	Enhanced concentration	Increased self-motivation	Structure practice sessions with minimal interaction between bowlers. Observe how individuals cope with the lack of social interaction, assessing their ability to maintain focus.
Excessive Number of Games	Improved stamina	Increased mental endurance	Enhanced fatigue resistance	Implement training regimens with an unusually high number of games in a single day. Evaluate bowlers' ability to maintain focus and enthusiasm throughout extended play.
Overbearing Physical Demands	Increased endurance	Improved mental toughness	Enhanced physiological resilience	Introduce physically demanding training sessions that exceed typical durations and intensity levels. Monitor the impact on bowlers' performance, recognizing the delicate balance between pushing boundaries and avoiding burnout.
Excessive Crowd Simulation	Improved concentration amid distractions	Sharpened focus under pressure	Enhanced attentional control	Implement drills with excessive crowd simulation, including loud cheers and distracting elements. Train bowlers to maintain concentration and focus amid external disruptions.
Dynamic Lane Changes During Practice	Enhanced adaptability to varying circumstances	Improved decision-making in dynamic environments	Increased cognitive flexibility	Add unpredictability to practice by dynamically changing lane conditions. Observe how bowlers navigate sudden changes, providing insights into their ability to read and adjust to varying circumstances.

Participation Prior The Big Event

Engaging in significant events before the intended championship is a multifaceted strategy that holds immense benefits for national bowling teams. This approach unfolds as a pivotal phase in the team's holistic preparation, contributing to their overall readiness and competitive edge in the forthcoming championship. Here are several ways in which participating in substantial events beforehand can prove to be invaluable:

Adaptation to Tournament Environment: Competing in big events ahead of a major championship offers national bowling teams a valuable opportunity for acclimatization. Familiarity with the tournament environment, including the venue, crowd, and overall atmosphere, can significantly benefit bowlers. Reduced anxiety and an enhanced comfort level contribute to optimal performance. Stepping onto the championship lanes with confidence, bowlers can focus better on their game without being overwhelmed by unfamiliar surroundings. However, it's essential to strike a balance, as excessive familiarity may lead to overconfidence, potentially undermining the team's competitive edge.

Pressure Testing Decision-Making Strategies: One of the advantages of participating in big events prior to a championship is the pressure testing of decision-making strategies. Real-time application of strategies under high-stakes situations helps refine them for optimal performance. Successfully managing pressure scenarios during these events enhances the team's confidence in their decision-making abilities. However, there are potential drawbacks, including the stress induced by high-pressure scenarios, which may negatively impact decision-making. Bowlers might also risk overthinking their moves, leading to hesitation at critical moments.

Experience in High-Stakes Scenarios: Participating in big events provides national teams with invaluable experience in handling high-stakes scenarios. Exposure to intense competition closely simulates the pressure that comes with a championship, fostering mental resilience. Bowlers become better prepared to manage the psychological demands of crucial moments during the main event. However, some players may experience heightened anxiety in high-stakes scenarios, and there's a risk of burnout if they are frequently exposed to such situations.

Identifying Areas for Improvement: Another benefit of participating in big events is the opportunity for coaches to identify specific areas for improvement. Analyzing team performance, strengths, and weaknesses during these events allows for targeted training and the development of adaptive strategies. However, there's a risk of potential demoralization if weaknesses are emphasized without constructive feedback. A balanced approach that focuses on improvement rather than dwelling on negatives is crucial.

Team Building and Chemistry: Competing in big events fosters team building and enhances team chemistry. Shared experiences of overcoming challenges together strengthen the bond among team members. Effective communication and a unified approach to competition are positive outcomes. However, there's a need for careful management to prevent conflict escalation arising from shared experiences. Additionally, overreliance on shared experiences may limit the team's adaptability to new challenges.

Real-Time Feedback and Analysis: Participation in big events allows for immediate feedback from actual tournament play. Coaches can observe bowlers in action, analyze their performance, and provide real-time feedback. This feedback loop is crucial for making timely adjustments and improvements. However, there's a risk of adding pressure on players through real-time scrutiny, potentially affecting their confidence. Coaches must strike a balance in providing constructive feedback without overwhelming the players.

Fine-Tuning Tactics and Approaches: Big events offer teams the opportunity to fine-tune tactical approaches and game plans. Adjustments can be made based on how the team performs against a diverse field of competitors, optimizing strategies for the championship. However, constant adjustments may lead to strategic fatigue, affecting decision-making. It's essential to find the right balance between refining tactics and allowing players to execute their skills with confidence.

Boosting Confidence: Successful participation in big events boosts the confidence of individual bowlers and the team as a whole. Positive outcomes, even in non-championship settings, contribute to a positive mindset and belief in their capabilities. Nevertheless, there's a risk of overestimating competence if too much reliance is placed on past successes. Bowlers should be prepared to learn from failures and maintain a balanced perspective on their performance.

Oil Condition Variation: An often overlooked aspect is the potential variation in oil conditions between big events and the main championship. The oil pattern on the lanes, which significantly affects ball movement and strategy, may differ. Bowlers who judge themselves and get accustomed to a specific body adjustment based on one oil condition during pre-events might face challenges when encountering a different pattern during the championship. This shift can impact their performance negatively, highlighting the importance of adapting quickly to varying conditions for sustained success.

Participating in big events prior to the intended championship is a multifaceted approach that offers numerous benefits. From acclimatization to real-time feedback, each aspect contributes to the team's overall readiness and competitive edge. However, careful consideration of potential drawbacks and effective management is crucial to ensuring that the experience is beneficial rather than detrimental to the team's preparation.

The Psychology Of Flow State And Pre-Championship Participation

Engaging in substantial events before a major championship emerges as a multifaceted strategy, holding immense benefits for national bowling teams in their holistic preparation for upcoming competitions. This pivotal phase contributes significantly to their overall readiness and competitive edge. Firstly, participating in these events allows teams to acclimatize to the tournament environment, fostering familiarity with the venue, crowd, and atmosphere. Reduced anxiety and enhanced comfort levels contribute to optimal performance on the championship lanes, promoting focused gameplay. However, a delicate balance must be maintained, as excessive familiarity may lead to overconfidence, potentially undermining the team's competitive edge. Furthermore, engaging in big events facilitates the pressure testing of decision-making strategies, refining them for high-stakes situations. Real-time application of strategies under such conditions enhances the team's confidence in their decision-making abilities. Yet, there is a potential drawback as stress induced by high-pressure scenarios may negatively impact decision-making, risking overthinking and hesitation at critical moments. Moreover, these events provide invaluable experience in handling high-stakes scenarios, fostering mental resilience for the championship. Despite the positive outcomes, some players may experience heightened anxiety, and there is a risk of burnout if they are frequently exposed to such situations. Another advantage lies in coaches identifying specific areas for improvement through the analysis of team performance during these events, allowing targeted training and adaptive strategies. Nevertheless, there's a risk of potential demoralization if weaknesses are emphasized without constructive feedback. The process of participating in big events also fosters team building and enhances team chemistry, with shared experiences strengthening the bond among team members. However, there's a need for careful management to prevent conflict escalation arising from shared experiences, and overreliance on these experiences may limit the team's adaptability to new challenges. Additionally, participation allows for immediate feedback from actual tournament play, aiding coaches in making timely adjustments and improvements. However, coaches must strike a balance in providing constructive feedback without overwhelming the players with real-time scrutiny, potentially affecting their confidence. Furthermore, big events offer teams the opportunity to fine-tune tactical approaches and game plans based on their performance against a diverse field of competitors. The challenge lies in finding the right balance between refining tactics and allowing players to execute their skills with confidence, as constant adjustments may lead to strategic fatigue, affecting decision-making. Successful participation in big events boosts the confidence of individual bowlers and the team as a whole, contributing to a positive mindset and belief in their capabilities. Nevertheless, there's a risk of overestimating competence if too much reliance is placed on past successes. Bowlers should be prepared to learn from failures and maintain a balanced perspective on their performance. An often overlooked aspect is the potential variation in oil conditions between big events and the main championship, impacting ball movement and strategy. Bowlers accustomed to specific adjustments based on one oil condition during pre-events might face challenges when encountering a different pattern during the championship. This shift can negatively impact their performance, highlighting the importance of adapting quickly to varying conditions for sustained success. Participating in significant events before the intended championship is a comprehensive approach that offers numerous benefits, from acclimatization to real-time feedback. Each aspect contributes to the team's overall readiness and competitive edge, although careful consideration of potential drawbacks and effective management is crucial to ensuring that the experience is beneficial rather than detrimental to the team's preparation.

Psychological And Neurological Differences In Practice Vs Simulation Sessions Vs Pre-Event Preparation Vs Main Event

Aspect	Practice Sessions	Simulation Sessions	Pre-Event Preparation	Main Event
Psychological States	- Focus on technique improvement.	- Emphasis on mimicking real-game scenarios.	- Transition to event-specific focus.	- Peak psychological readiness.
	- Comfort in a familiar setting.	- Stress exposure and management.	- Manage anxiety and increase confidence.	- Focus on performance execution.
	- Moderate arousal levels.	- Moderate to high arousal levels.	- Moderate to high arousal levels.	- High arousal levels, controlled excitement.
	- Moderate comfort, low pressure.	- Moderate to high comfort, increased pressure.	- High comfort with anticipation, moderate pressure.	- High comfort, heightened pressure.
	- High concentration, skill reinforcement.	- Increased concentration, stress resilience.	- Enhanced concentration, increased stress resilience.	- Peak concentration, stress resilience.
	- Moderate resilience, intrinsic motivation.	- Variable motivation, optimistic with some self-doubt.	- High motivation, optimistic outlook.	- High motivation, optimistic mindset.
	- Optimism with minimal self-doubt.	- Moderate to high fear of failure.	- Some self-doubt, controlled fear of failure.	- Minimal self-doubt, managed fear of failure.
	- Low fear of failure.	-	-	-
Neurological States	- Routine-based, procedural memory activation.	- Exposure to stressors for improved stress response.	- Fine-tuning motor memory for specific event conditions.	- Optimal neurological activation for peak performance.
	- Lower stress response.	- Incorporation of stress management techniques.	- Activation of stress-response systems.	- Enhanced synchronization of motor and cognitive functions.
	- Skill reinforcement.	- Cognitive and emotional engagement.	- Neurological priming for optimal performance.	- Controlled stress response for heightened alertness.
	- Normal neurological activation, minimal impact.	- Variable neurological activation, stress response impact.	- Impact on neurological activation, controlled stress response.	- Peak neurological activation, managed stress response.
Physical Readiness	- Skill development and conditioning.	- Integration of physical and mental aspects.	- Fine-tuning for specific event conditions.	- Peak physical condition for extended performance.
	- Standard physical readiness, minimal stress impact.	- Variable physical readiness, stress impact.	- Simulation of event-specific physical demands.	- Optimal physical readiness, managed stress impact.
		- Increased physical readiness, controlled stress impact.	- Increased physical readiness, controlled stress impact.	
Team Dynamics	- Collaboration, skill-sharing, team building.	- Routine team dynamics, minimal external stress.	- Stress test team cohesion, communication.	- Unified team front, strategic cohesion, mutual support.
	- Routine team dynamics, minimal external stress.	- Variable team dynamics, increased stress.	- Enhanced team cohesion, controlled stress.	- High team cohesion, managed stress.
Coach's Role	- Technical guidance, skill refinement.	- Standard coaching role, minimal stress impact.	- Stress management coaching, scenario analysis.	- Game strategy reinforcement, morale boost, in-game support.
	- Standard coaching role, minimal stress impact.	- Varied coaching role, increased stress impact.	- Mental preparation, confidence-building.	- Peak coaching impact, managed stress.
			- High coaching impact, controlled stress.	
Why It Feels Different	- Emphasis on skill improvement, less external pressure.	- Simulated pressure and stressors, increased cognitive engagement.	- Stressors introduction, heightened psychological elements.	- Transition to event-specific conditions, heightened anticipation.

Aspect	Practice Sessions	Simulation Sessions	Pre-Event Preparation	Main Event
Psychological Factors	- Comfort, routine, skill development.	- Exposure to stress, scenario analysis, mental toughness.	- Confidence-building, stress management, positive visualization.	- Event-specific mental elements, heightened psychological readiness.
Thought Process	- Skill-focused, routine-driven.	- Strategic, stress-exposure scenarios.	- Transition to event-specific conditions, heightened anticipation.	- Event-specific, positive visualization.
Pre-Shot Routine Difference	- Focused on skill execution.	- Standard routine, minimal stress impact.	- Incorporates stress management elements.	
Flow State	- In the flow, effortless concentration. Stable due to a balance between skill and challenge.	- Seamless integration of skills and challenges. Stable with moderate stress for enhanced focus.	- Effortless adaptation to event-specific conditions. Stable with controlled excitement.	- Sustained peak performance, total immersion. Stable with managed stress and optimal conditions.

Table 1 - This table provides a comprehensive overview of the psychological and neurological dynamics across different stages of athletic preparation and performance. Comparing practice sessions, simulation sessions, pre-event preparation, and the main event, the table delves into various aspects such as psychological states, neurological activation, physical readiness, team dynamics, coach's role, and the overall experiential differences. It outlines how each stage influences the athlete's mindset, skill execution, and the achievement of a flow state, offering valuable insights into the nuanced progression from training to peak performance.

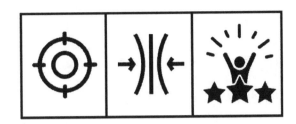

MENTAL FEATURES OF TOP LEVEL BOWLERS

Coaches who want their students to become champions must take a therapeutic metaphorical approach, similar to that of a gardener. Every bowler has distinct needs for maximum development, just as plants have various needs. Numerous scholars have underscored the complex and enduring character of preparing to be a great champion.

Certain traits immediately come to mind when examining outstanding bowlers: complete focus, fearlessness in the face of failure, absolute immersion in the activity, absence of performance-related thoughts, complete control, effortless performance, and a sense of oneness with the cosmos. Prominent bowlers often have certain mental traits.

Therapeutic metaphorical approach in Bowling

In bowling, a therapeutic metaphorical approach could involve drawing parallels between the act of releasing a bowling ball and the process of letting go of life's challenges. The physical action of releasing the ball symbolizes releasing stress or negativity, promoting a sense of catharsis. Additionally, the strategic aspects of aiming for a target on the lane could serve as a metaphor for setting and achieving personal goals. This approach aims to use the bowling experience as a therapeutic tool for personal growth, stress relief, and goal setting.

One characteristic of high-performance bowlers is confidence. In comparison to amateur bowlers, they frequently think about bowling while engaging in daily activities, have dreams about the sport in the future, tend to blame external reasons less for failures, exhibit fewer worried states before competitions, and have some pre-competition worry.

Motivational characteristics have also been connected to family birth order. Firstborns typically have a strong desire to succeed, but other children may be more motivated to avoid failure.

Bowlers have discovered eight mental and physical states that define their peak performances in their pursuit of outstanding performance. These include a sense of automatic control, mental and physical ease, self-assurance, present-focused concentration, high vitality, increased awareness, and a cocoon-like experience. Elite bowlers frequently experience the paradox of control, in which they feel in control but are not consciously aware of it since they are totally focused on the activity at hand.

Chris Barnes

To perform better, careful preparation and pre-competition training that addresses potential distractions is essential. Bowlers are urged to put more emphasis on effective competition planning and the process rather than the outcome. Bowlers are greatly impacted by their emotional-affective experiences, both good and bad, as well as their emotional stability and attitudes. These factors are arbitrary and rely on each person's evaluation of themselves.

Chris Barnes, a PBA Hall of Famer and multiple medalist, offers advice on how to handle mental stress when competing. Barnes has established particular behavioral methods for each event and can visualize plans for various scenarios. Elite bowlers are also concerned about coping with depression and use a variety of coping mechanisms.

A unique mix of cognitive, psychomotor, and personality characteristics distinguish elite bowlers from other athletes. These qualities are developed over years of practice and are crucial for excelling at the sport of bowling.

The Cognitive/Intellectual Traits Of Elite Bowlers:

Bowlers who compete at the highest levels of the sport share a unique combination of traits that help them perform so well. Their unshakable focus is one of their distinguishing characteristics, allowing them to ignore outside distractions and keep their attention on the game at hand. They are able to maintain total focus and control over their game because of their ability to concentrate so hard. Additionally, professional bowlers have the ability to think strategically, allowing them to assess how the ball responds on the lane and change their game strategy as appropriate. They formulate a plan that increases their chances of success by taking into account the lane conditions, the motion of the ball, and the speed of the ball. These bowlers also have fast decision-making abilities, which enable them to select the best option in a couple of seconds. Bowling is a fast-paced activity, therefore having the ability to think quickly is essential. The ability to overcome obstacles, such a difficult game or a poor shot, is another trait shared by exceptional bowlers. When confronted with difficulty, they possess the ability to remain composed and focused. Bowlers like Kelly Kulick, Pete Weber, and Jason Belmonte, who have all attained significant success and gained a lot of respect in the sport, are notable examples of bowlers that exhibit these qualities.

"Concentrate so hard !!"

Refers to the intense and solid focus that exceptional bowlers exhibit during their performance. Concentrating hard involves the ability to direct one's attention fully to the task at hand, ignoring distractions and maintaining a high level of mental engagement.

To concentrate harder than others, individuals often need to develop and hone their mental discipline. This may involve practicing mindfulness techniques, improving attention control, and building mental resilience. Athletes who excel in concentration often go through rigorous mental training, which can include visualization exercises, meditation, and specific drills to enhance their focus.

A professional bowler who exemplifies exceptional concentration is Jason Belmonte. Belmonte, a highly successful and respected bowler in the sport, is known for his intense focus during competition. He has the ability to block out external factors, analyze lane conditions, and make split-second decisions to optimize his performance. His mental toughness and concentration contribute significantly to his success in the fast-paced and competitive world of professional bowling.

Focus:

A young bowler who is able to maintain his focus during competition and not get distracted by the crowd or other external factors.

A bowler who is able to keep his mind on the game, even when his opponents are trying to psych him out.

Strategic Thinking:

A bowler who can quickly analyze the lane conditions and make adjustments to his ball speed, angle of approach, and release technique to optimize his performance.

A bowler who can read the ball motion and adjust his targeting based on the ball's reaction to the lane surface.

Decision Making:

A bowler who is able to make quick decisions about which ball to use and where to target based on the lane conditions.

A bowler who is able to decide whether to play aggressively or conservatively based on the situation, such as when trying to make a comeback or maintain a lead.

Mental Toughness:

A bowler who is able to stay composed and focused, even after a series of bad shots or a tough game.

A bowler who is able to maintain his confidence and positive attitude, even when facing a challenging opponent or unfavorable lane conditions.

Parents and coaches are key players in helping young athletes develop the mental and intellectual qualities of elite bowlers. These actions and strategies can be used from an early age to assist a bowler in becoming a top bowler.

Cognitive/ Intellectual Trait	Childhood (Ages 6-12)	Adolescence (Ages 13-18)	Adulthood (Ages 19+)
Solid Focus	**Parents**	**Parents**	**Parents**
	- Create a dedicated practice space	- Attend matches and provide reinforcement	- Promote ongoing mindfulness practices
	- Encourage regular focused practice	- Support mindfulness or meditation programs	- Discuss strategies for maintaining focus
	- Teach basic relaxation techniques	- Encourage goal-setting for focus-related goals	- Encourage self-assessment and adjustments
	Coaches	**Coaches**	**Coaches**
	- Introduce basic concentration exercises	- Incorporate mindfulness into training	- Use video analysis to assess and improve focus
	- Foster a supportive learning environment	- Conduct focus-enhancement drills	- Support mental toughness development
	- Teach basic pre-shot routines for learning how to focus	- Provide feedback on concentration levels	- Emphasize mental routines and visualization

Cognitive/ Intellectual Trait	Childhood (Ages 6-12)	Adolescence (Ages 13-18)	Adulthood (Ages 19+)
Strategic Thinking	**Parents**	**Parents**	**Parents**
	- Teach basics of lane conditions, ball motion, and ball speed	- Attend coaching sessions to understand strategy	- Promote ongoing learning about new lane conditions
	- Encourage curiosity and observation	- Encourage discussions about match strategies	- Attend matches to provide feedback on strategy
	- Play strategy-based games	- Support the use of a bowling journal	- Encourage self-assessment of strategic decisions
	Coaches	**Coaches**	**Coaches**
	- Introduce strategic concepts in coaching	- Offer structured lessons on lane conditions	- Use video analysis to assess strategic decisions
	- Provide simple strategies for adjustments	- Analyze outcomes of strategic choices	- Help bowlers understand psychology of decision-making
	- Incorporate discussions about lane conditions	- Use video analysis to help understand ball motion	- Teach advanced strategic concepts and adjustments

Cognitive/ Intellectual Trait	Childhood (Ages 6-12)	Adolescence (Ages 13-18)	Adulthood (Ages 19+)
Quick Decision-Making	**Parents**	**Parents**	**Parents**
	- Encourage critical thinking skills	- Promote confidence in quick decisions	- Support decision-making in high-pressure situations
	- Create scenarios for quick decision-making	- Encourage practice under time constraints	- Encourage bowlers to refine decision-making processes
	- Support decision-making exercises	- Discuss the importance of trusting instincts	- Discuss strategies for maintaining composure
	Coaches	**Coaches**	**Coaches**
	- Simulate fast-paced game scenarios	- Provide feedback on decision-making skills	- Continuously expose bowlers to high-pressure situations
	- Emphasize adaptability to changing situations	- Refine mental process for quick decisions	- Use video analysis to assess and improve decisions

Cognitive/Intellectual Trait	Childhood (Ages 6-12)	Adolescence (Ages 13-18)	Adulthood (Ages 19+)
Mental Toughness	Parents	Parents	Parents
	- Foster a growth mindset	- Support participation in mental toughness training	- Emphasize maintaining composure under pressure
	- Teach resilience and positive attitude	- Discuss the importance of mental resilience	- Promote a mindset that thrives on challenges
	- Encourage perseverance after setbacks	- Foster self-belief and composure	- Encourage a mindset that embraces adversity
	Coaches	Coaches	Coaches
	- Conduct mental toughness training sessions	- Help set and work toward mental toughness goals	- Foster a team culture of emotional resilience
	- Use relaxation and visualization techniques	- Provide mental preparation techniques	- Promote self-belief and self-regulation

Table 2 - This table charts the developmental path of cognitive traits in bowling, illustrating how parents and coaches shape solid focus, strategic thinking, quick decision-making, and mental toughness. From childhood basics to advanced adult concepts, it provides a concise guide for fostering essential skills at each stage of a bowler's journey.

The Psychomotor Characteristics Of Elite Bowlers:

A special blend of mental and physical abilities enable elite bowlers to compete at a high level in their sport. These bowlers have remarkable physical stamina that enables them to maintain their intensity of play for the duration of a game. In addition, they have excellent hand-eye coordination, which helps them make accurate and reliable shots. Furthermore, exceptional bowlers possess perfect timing; they know instinctively when to release the ball to achieve maximum accuracy. They can also produce a good amount of ball speed and power, which contributes to their remarkable ability to knock down more pins every shot. Elite bowlers have a laser-like mental focus that allows them to fully concentrate on the task at hand and block out outside distractions. They have an innate ability to scan lanes, assess ball reflexes, and modify their game plan as needed. They may also think quickly and make snap decisions when faced with pressure. These bowlers also demonstrate mental fortitude, which enables them to recover from trying circumstances and keep their composure and concentration throughout the game, no matter what. When combined, these abilities make top bowlers extremely strong competitors on the alleys.

Another essential component of a top bowler's arsenal is the ability to estimate speed and hook accurately. Pro bowlers gain an instinctive sense of the exact speed and hook needed to deliver a perfect shot through years of experience and unrelenting practice. Their ability to make appropriate modifications based on their understanding of ball motion and lane circumstances is a vital skill that guarantees consistent success.

It takes the full development of both mental and physical talents to become an exceptional bowler. From childhood until elite status, these are the strategies and actions for each of the psychomotor traits of elite bowlers:

Myth: The Bowling Prodigy

The myth of the "Bowling Prodigy" suggests that elite bowlers are those who started bowling from an incredibly young age and showed exceptional talent and skills almost immediately. According to this myth, these prodigies were born with a natural gift for the sport, and their success was predestined.

This myth can be misleading because it downplays the importance of hard work, dedication, and continuous improvement in the journey to becoming an elite bowler. While starting early can provide an advantage, it's not the sole determinant of success.

In reality, most elite bowlers have put in countless hours of practice and training to reach their level of skill, regardless of when they started bowling. Talent may provide a head start, but it's the commitment to improvement that ultimately leads to excellence in the sport.

Physical Stamina:

An elite bowler like Walter Ray Williams Jr. has exceptional physical endurance, able to maintain his performance level over the course of a tournament that lasts several days.

Coordination:

An elite bowler like Chris Barnes possesses excellent hand-eye coordination, allowing him to make precise shots with consistency.

Timing:

An elite bowler like Liz Johnson has impeccable timing, able to release the ball at the perfect moment for maximum accuracy.

Speed and Power:

An elite bowler like EJ Tackett can generate high ball speed and power, allowing him to knock down more pins with each shot.

Psychomotor Characteristic	Childhood (Ages 6-12)	Adolescence (Ages 13-18)	Adulthood (Ages 19+)
	Parents	Parents	Parents
	- Encourage active play and games	- Support joining school sports teams	- Maintain a balanced fitness regimen
	- Promote fitness through outdoor activities	- Encourage training programs for endurance	- Adapt training routines for bowling-specific muscles
Endurance	- Participate in stamina-building activities	- Design longer practice sessions	- Continue aerobic and strength training
	Coaches	Coaches	Coaches
	- Promote fitness components in practice	- Incorporate interval training	- Adapt practice sessions for fitness
	- Design fun drills for stamina development	- Focus on endurance during training	- Provide guidance for bowling-specific fitness

Psychomotor Characteristic	Childhood (Ages 6-12)	Adolescence (Ages 13-18)	Adulthood (Ages 19+)
	Parents	Parents	Parents
	- Engage in hand-eye coordination games	- Play sports requiring precision	- Practice hand-eye coordination exercises
	- Introduce basic hand-eye coordination drills	- Incorporate coordination drills into practice	- Use technology for precision refinement
Hand-Eye Coordination	- Encourage activities that improve coordination	- Practice regularly for precision	- Maintain precision through consistent practice
	Coaches	Coaches	Coaches
	- Include coordination drills in early training	- Work on refining hand-eye coordination	- Provide advanced coordination exercises
	- Monitor and assess coordination progress	- Offer precision drills in practice	- Use video analysis to refine accuracy

Psychomotor Characteristic	Childhood (Ages 6-12)	Adolescence (Ages 13-18)	Adulthood (Ages 19+)
Timing	**Parents**	**Parents**	**Parents**
	- Teach timing fundamentals in the approach	- Support timing adjustments with practice	- Monitor and adjust timing during practice
	- Practice basic timing drills	- Encourage timing refinement	- Seek advanced timing techniques
	- Begin with the basics of timing	- Continuously practice timing skills	- Focus on refining timing as a key element
	Coaches	**Coaches**	**Coaches**
	- Introduce timing concepts during coaching	- Refine timing through repetition	- Offer advanced timing drills
	- Incorporate timing drills into practice	- Work with bowlers on timing adjustments	- Use video analysis to fine-tune timing

Psychomotor Characteristic	Childhood (Ages 6-12)	Adolescence (Ages 13-18)	Adulthood (Ages 19+)
Ball Speed and Power	**Parents**	**Parents**	**Parents**
	- Build core strength and coordination	- Transition to heavier bowling balls	- Maintain strength and conditioning routines
	- Start with a lighter ball to develop fundamentals	- Develop a powerful delivery technique	- Explore advanced ball speed strategies
	- Focus on muscle coordination	- Work on building strength	- Adapt training routines to maintain power
	Coaches	**Coaches**	**Coaches**
	- Incorporate strength-building exercises	- Help bowlers develop powerful techniques	- Provide guidance for advanced power training
	- Teach the importance of proper technique	- Monitor and assess power development	- Offer strategies for maintaining power

Table 3 - This table outlines the developmental progression of psychomotor characteristics in bowling, emphasizing endurance, hand-eye coordination, timing, and ball speed/power across childhood, adolescence, and adulthood. It provides succinct guidance for parents and coaches, highlighting the evolution of physical skills from basic play and coordination games to advanced techniques and training, ensuring a comprehensive approach at each life stage.

The Personality Characteristics Of Elite Bowlers:

Elite bowlers are driven to succeed in their sport by a special combination of abilities and characteristics. Their mental and emotional abilities are what really distinguish them, even though physical attributes like strength, endurance, coordination, and timing are important. One such quality is their laser-like attention, which allows them to stay focused on the work at hand even under duress. Another quality is strategic thinking, which enables them to assess the situation, decide carefully, and hit exact shots. Their capacity to make decisions quickly also helps them quickly adjust to changing conditions. Furthermore, professional bowlers have extraordinary mental toughness, which enables them to overcome obstacles, recover from failures, and perform well under duress. Together with their self-confidence, which gives them a strong sense of self-worth, they possess a ferocious competitive spirit that motivates them to continuously push the boundaries and pursue perfection. Another important quality is perseverance. Pro bowlers see failures as chances to learn and utilize that as fuel to get even better. Lastly, by treating their opponents with respect and maintaining the integrity of the game, they exemplify sportsmanship. Great bowlers are able to continuously improve their skills and reach new heights in the sport because of this combination of mental and emotional attributes.

Competitive Spirit:

An elite bowler like Sean Rash has a fierce competitive spirit, driving him to constantly improve and strive for excellence on the lanes.

Confidence:

An elite bowler like Shannon O'Keefe has a strong sense of self-confidence, allowing her to trust in her abilities and make bold decisions during competition.

Perseverance:

An elite bowler like Marshall Kent has a strong sense of perseverance, willing to put in the hard work and dedication required to achieve his goals in the sport.

Sportsmanship:

An elite bowler like Kelly Kulick has a high level of sportsmanship, respecting her opponents and the game, and displaying humility and respect towards her fellow competitors.

The ultimate in bowling success is attained by adding critical elements that winners value. Being at the top of one's game as a bowler demands a careful balancing act between mental, technical, and physical aspects. It's critical to maintain laser-like focus, unshakable concentration, and unwavering confidence during a match or competition. In addition, top bowlers need to be exceptionally resilient against mental exhaustion, have accurate speed and rev prediction skills, and allocate their attention well.

For professional bowlers, mental exhaustion presents a serious obstacle as they manage the game's repetition, the need for unwavering focus, and the pressure of competition. They use a variety of mental strategies, like visualization, relaxation, and encouraging self-talk, to combat this. During crucial times, these techniques help maintain mental clarity and a laser-like focus.

The capacity of exceptional bowlers to focus their concentration is essential to their success. Their laser-like concentration enables them to thoroughly examine lane circumstances, ball movement, and their opponents' play. They also become experts at dividing their focus between different aspects of the game, such as self-analysis, tracking their opponents, and subtle technical details. Their ability to allocate their attention in multiple ways enables them to make well-informed decisions and modify their tactics accordingly.

For elite bowlers, confidence is a fundamental component of optimum performance. Having steadfast faith in one's own skills and maintaining composure under duress are distinguishing traits. The development and maintenance of confidence are facilitated by years of committed training, consistent practice, and exposure to competitive contexts. This crucial quality can be developed and reinforced by mental practices including goal-setting, vivid imagery, and positive self-talk.

Personality Characteristic	Childhood (Ages 6-12)	Adolescence (Ages 13-18)	Adulthood (Ages 19+)
Combatting Mental Fatigue	Parents	Parents	Parents
	Teach the importance of fun and enjoyment in the game.	Support participation in competitive leagues.	Promote a balanced lifestyle beyond bowling to prevent burnout.
	Introduce simple relaxation techniques like deep breathing.	Advocate for access to a sports psychologist or mental coach.	Encourage the bowler to continue working with a mental coach.
	Encourage short breaks during practice to maintain enthusiasm.	Encourage journaling for self-reflection and mental strategies.	Emphasize the importance of mental preparation in training.
	Coaches	Coaches	Coaches
	Keep practice sessions engaging and diverse to prevent monotony.	Introduce advanced mental techniques like visualization.	Collaborate with sports psychologists for tailored mental training.
	Teach basic mental relaxation techniques suitable for young bowlers.	Provide resources for maintaining focus during long tournaments.	Continuously assess and address mental fatigue challenges individually.

Personality Characteristic	Childhood (Ages 6-12)	Adolescence (Ages 13-18)	Adulthood (Ages 19+)
Effective Attention Allocation	Parents	Parents	Parents

Personality Characteristic	Childhood (Ages 6-12)	Adolescence (Ages 13-18)	Adulthood (Ages 19+)
	Teach young bowlers to observe and enjoy the technical aspects of the game.	Emphasize the importance of focus and self-assessment in skill improvement.	Advocate for lifelong learning and skill refinement.
	Encourage self-assessment during practice to enhance focus.	Support participation in technical workshops or seminars.	Encourage bowlers to mentor younger players, promoting attention management skills.
	Promote a love for learning and attention to detail.	Encourage journaling for tracking progress and technical insights.	Emphasize the importance of being a student of the game.
	Coaches	Coaches	Coaches
	Incorporate basic attention management exercises into training.	Provide advanced attention management techniques and drills.	Offer access to resources for continued learning and development.
	Foster an environment that values curiosity and observation.	Create a learning environment that encourages questioning and experimentation.	Promote a culture of continuous improvement and innovation.

Personality Characteristic	Childhood (Ages 6-12)	Adolescence (Ages 13-18)	Adulthood (Ages 19+)
	Parents	Parents	Parents
	Celebrate small successes and progress.	Emphasize the importance of self-belief and composure during play.	Provide a balanced approach to sports and life.
	Encourage positive self-talk and a belief in their abilities.	Create a supportive and encouraging atmosphere.	Advocate for ongoing mental preparation.
	Create a supportive and encouraging atmosphere.	Foster a fun and positive team culture.	Collaborate with sports psychologists to reinforce mental resilience.
Confidence as a Cornerstone	Coaches	Coaches	Coaches
	Provide praise and constructive feedback to boost self-esteem.	Teach the importance of self-belief and composure under pressure.	Offer access to advanced mental techniques and technology.
	Introduce goal-setting to build confidence and motivation.	Encourage goal-setting for personal and team success.	Collaborate with sports psychologists to fine-tune mental strategies.
	Foster a growth mindset that embraces challenges as opportunities to grow.	Reinforce the value of a strong self-belief system.	Continuously assess and address confidence challenges at the elite level.

Table 4 - This table traces the evolution of mental attributes in bowling from childhood to adulthood. Parents initiate with fun and relaxation, advancing to mental coaching support. Coaches diversify practice and introduce advanced techniques. The second trait, confidence, begins with praise, progresses through goal-setting, and matures into collaboration for elite-level refinement. The concise guide ensures comprehensive mental skill progression in bowling.

To put it simply, becoming an exceptional bowler requires combining mental toughness, technical skill, and physical strength. Crucial skills include the capacity to keep concentration, fight mental exhaustion, precisely estimate speed and rev, and allocate attention. The unwavering confidence they have earned through mental approaches helps them perform even better. Bowling pros who master these characteristics reach the highest level of their sport and leave an everlasting mark.

Bowler Name	Notable Characteristics and Traits	Cognitive/ Intellectual Traits	Psychomotor Characteristics	Personality Characteristics
Tim Mack	Immense power, precision, substantial hook, influential	Analytical thinker, strategic planner, adaptability	Precise release, timing, ability to read lane conditions	Confident, determined, influential in the sport
Mohamed Al Qubaisi	Exceptional technical skills, strong mental game, championship wins	Analytical mindset, focus, game strategy	Smooth approach, excellent spare shooting, consistent shot execution	Disciplined, focused, competitive, resilient
Shalin Zulkifli	Resistance to mental fatigue, long career with focus	Mental endurance, concentration, self-awareness	Consistent delivery under pressure, adjustments over long tournaments	Resilient, persistent, calm under pressure
Cherie Tan	Attention concentration, versatile skills, international success	Strategic thinking, pattern recognition, versatility	Adaptable release, manipulation of ball motion, pattern adjustments	Versatile, adaptive, competitive, detail-oriented
Shusaku Asato	Confidence, mental toughness, multiple titles under pressure	Mental resilience, positive self-talk, visualization	Composure in high-pressure situations, consistent shot execution	Confident, resilient, composed, unshakeable mindset
Kim Moon-jung	Hand-eye coordination, impeccable timing, gold medalist	Spatial intelligence, precision, impeccable timing	Consistency in shot placement, ability to adapt to changing conditions	Focused, precise, determined, gold medal-winning mindset
Wu Siu Hong	Competitive spirit, perseverance, multiple international medals	Competitive drive, determination, adaptability	Strong work ethic, ability to overcome setbacks, consistent delivery	Tenacious, persistent, adaptive, driven
Jesper Svensson	Explosive power, accuracy, emotional control, PBA success	Analytical approach to lane conditions, mental composure	Explosive delivery, accuracy in challenging conditions, emotional control	Composed, analytical, focused, high level of emotional control
Dom Barrett	Smooth release, flawless repetition, PBA success	Analytical approach to lane conditions, consistency	Smooth and consistent release, accuracy in spare shooting	Methodical, precise, disciplined, calm under pressure
Laura Beuthner	Consistent performance, accuracy, international representation	Strategic thinking, adaptability, pattern recognition	Consistency in shot execution, adaptability to lane conditions	Persistent, adaptable, competitive, focused on consistent performance
Francois Lavoie	High accuracy, emotional control, PBA success	Analytical mindset, mental composure, game strategy	Exceptional accuracy, emotional control under pressure	Analytical, composed, focused, cool under pressure
Mika Koivuniemi	Smooth release, shot anticipation, PBA success	Analytical thinker, adaptability, anticipation	Smooth and consistent release, anticipation of lane conditions	Analytical, adaptable, anticipatory, focused on shot planning
Shaker Al-Hassan	Strong mental game, focus, accuracy	Analytical approach to lane conditions, mental resilience	Accurate delivery, focus on execution, confidence under pressure	Analytical, focused, confident, mentally strong
Marcelo Suartz	Accurate speed and hook, adjustments based on lane conditions	Analytical thinker, adaptability, knowledge of lane conditions	Precise adjustments to lane conditions, adaptation to ball motion	Analytical, adaptable, knowledgeable, keen on strategic adjustments
Rocio Restrepo	Mental toughness, confidence, international success	Positive self-talk, visualization, mental resilience	Emotional control, performance under pressure, confidence	Mentally tough, confident, resilient, focused on mental preparation
Arturo Quintero	Attention concentration and distribution, international success	Analytical mindset, adaptability, lane condition analysis	Focus on lane conditions, ball motion control, distribution of attention	Analytical, adaptable, focused, attention to detail
Tommy Jones	Consistent performance, multiple titles, longevity	Strategic thinking, adaptability, experience	Precise shot placement, adaptability to lane conditions, versatility	Experienced, adaptable, competitive, calm under pressure
E.J. Tackett	Young talent, PBA success, versatile skills	Analytical thinker, adaptability, pattern recognition	Versatile release, adaptability to changing conditions, consistency	Ambitious, adaptable, versatile, determined

Bowler Name	Notable Characteristics and Traits	Cognitive/ Intellectual Traits	Psychomotor Characteristics	Personality Characteristics
Kyle Troup	Unique appearance, entertaining style, accuracy	Creative problem-solving, adaptability, showmanship	Unconventional style, accuracy in spare shooting, crowd engagement	Charismatic, creative, entertaining, confident
Bill O'Neal	Consistent performance, major championships, veteran	Analytical mindset, adaptability, experience	Consistency in execution, adaptability to lane conditions, resilience	Experienced, adaptable, resilient, focused under pressure
Parker Bohn	Longevity, left-handed advantage, accurate shots	Strategic thinking, adaptability, experience	Precise left-handed delivery, adaptability to lane conditions	Experienced, adaptable, focused, accuracy under pressure

Table 5 - This table provides concise insights into notable bowlers' characteristics, focusing on cognitive/intellectual traits, psychomotor characteristics, and personality traits. From Tim Mack's influential precision to Laura Beuthner's international adaptability, the concise guide highlights the unique attributes and strengths that define each bowler's approach, mindset, and success in the sport.

PERSONALITY IN SPORT: EVERYONE IS DIFFERENT

Personality is a complex concept with many facets that make it difficult to define. Still, "everyone is different" is a commonly accepted fact, particularly when it comes to coaching and athletics. Coaches must comprehend the characteristics of their bowlers in order to communicate effectively and maximize output. It's also critical that bowlers understand how their personalities affect their game.

Personality is frequently linked to particular characteristics that people display. Numerous psychological theories have addressed these characteristics that make an individual who they are. One of the frameworks that are most frequently utilized is the Five Factor Model of Personality (FFM). The FFM includes extraversion, neuroticism, conscientiousness, agreeableness, and openness to experience as major characteristics determining personality, according to the APA Dictionary of Psychology.

Extraversion: An extrovert, gregarious, and vivacious bowler is typically extraverted. They enjoy interacting with both rivals and teammates, they are comfortable in social situations, and they exhibit energy and enthusiasm when competing. Additionally, they aggressively cultivate relationships with other players and frequently take on leadership responsibilities within their squad.

Chris Barnes is a bowler who demonstrates extraverted qualities. American bowler Barnes is a professional who has won multiple championships and honors in his short career. His friendly disposition and eagerness to engage with both fans and other bowlers are well-known traits. During the Weber Cup competition, Barnes captained the US squad, demonstrating his leadership abilities within his teams. His social butterfly tendencies have also been noted; he frequently strikes up discussions with other players and exhibits excitement and vigor when competing. He may be able to connect with people and build lasting relationships in the bowling community because of his extraverted nature.

Neuroticism: Bowlers with high neuroticism are more prone to negative feelings such as worry, anxiety, and mood swings. They could find it harder to control their emotions and stay stable during competitions because they are more susceptible to pressures both on and off the bowling lane.

Hypothetical Example

Consider a bowler who exhibits high neuroticism. This bowler often experiences heightened worry and anxiety, making it challenging to maintain emotional stability during competitions. The fear of not meeting personal expectations intensifies these negative emotions, impacting shot accuracy and decision-making. Off the bowling lane, the anticipation of upcoming competitions and the desire for perfection contribute to mood swings. This high neuroticism poses a unique psychological challenge, requiring targeted interventions to enhance emotional regulation, stress management, and overall resilience for improved performance.

Myth: Personality Is Fixed

One common myth in sports is that a person's personality is fixed and unchangeable. This myth suggests that if a bowler possesses certain personality traits, they are destined to perform in a certain way, and there's nothing that can be done to alter their personality characteristics.

In reality, personality is not entirely fixed. While individuals may have predispositions toward certain traits, they can work on developing and improving aspects of their personality. Coaches and athletes can engage in psychological training and interventions to enhance specific traits or learn to manage and harness their personality traits more effectively for improved performance.

Conscientiousness: Bowlers who are conscientious exhibit responsibility, organization, and diligence. They follow strict practice schedules, approach training and preparation with steadfast dedication, and pay close attention to technique and approach nuances. Furthermore, their commitment to their team and competitive activities demonstrates their dependability and dependability.

Martin Larsen

Sweden's Martin Larsen is one bowler from Europe who demonstrates a high level of conscientiousness in his game. Larsen is renowned for his meticulousness, self-control, and strong work ethic. He is renowned for following an intense training and practice schedule and for being methodical in both his approach and technique. Having competed internationally for Sweden, Larsen is also renowned for his dependability and dedication to his squad.

Agreeableness: Friendship, cooperation, and compassion are the top priorities for cooperative bowlers. They appreciate getting along well with coaches, rival teams, and teammates. They also appreciate making concessions and working together for the good of the team as a whole. Additionally, they provide teammates with support and empathy, lending a helping hand and offering encouragement when required.

Shusaku Asato

According to the book, Japan's Shusaku Asato is an example of a bowler from Far East Asia. Asato is renowned for his ability to collaborate well with others on his team and for having a pleasant disposition. He is frequently characterized as a cooperative and friendly player who values good ties with both his opponents and teammates. Asato is also well-known for being sympathetic and helpful, frequently lending a hand and encouraging his fellow players whenever they need it. His ability to get along with others makes him an asset to any team and fosters a productive work atmosphere.

Openness: Bowlers who are open to new experiences demonstrate imagination, curiosity, and a willingness to try new things. They approach their bowling tactics and methods with inventiveness and imagination, welcoming a diversity of viewpoints and views. Additionally, they welcome the chance to improve their performance through cutting-edge training approaches.

Clara Guerrero

Bowler Clara Guerrero, a Colombian, has won multiple medals in international events. She is renowned for her originality and inventiveness in the lane, frequently experimenting with different methods and strategies to enhance her performance. She is inquisitive and broad-minded, always eager to try new things and pick up insights from others.

Aumi Guerra, a Dominican Republic bowler, has won numerous medals in international competitions. She is renowned for her creative and inventive approach to the game, frequently experimenting with various methods and approaches.

Given that the FFM's qualities are interrelated, it is plausible that no single trait exists in a vacuum and that an individual's personality is the product of their interaction with one another. Personalities impact people subconsciously, which means that they generate actions that a person cannot control with their cognitive abilities.

Aumi Guerra

Consequently, it is evident how crucial it is for a coach to value a bowler's personality because personality factors might lead to behavior that the bowler finds incomprehensible.

The degree to which a bowler exhibits one of the traits listed in FFM can influence how well they perform in sports. For instance, bowlers who compete internationally are more likely to exhibit higher levels of conscientiousness and lower levels of neuroticism. A competition is preceded by increased conscientiousness after excellent preparation.

In addition to the types of objectives people create, personality also has a big impact on goal-setting. There is a strong correlation between goal setting and personality; objectives are often created to either enhance or compensate for a person's inherent traits. A major and vast topic in itself, goal-setting is a crucial part of sports. But typically, objectives are tailored to the personality of the person setting them. If this is the case, their objective might be to increase their extroversion. It is imperative to acknowledge that goal planning necessitates a thorough consideration and comprehension of the individual's personality in order to fully comprehend the rationale behind a particular goal.

Coping behaviors and techniques are another component of athletic performance that is related to personality. This has to do with a bowler's capacity or strategies for handling mental strain like nervousness. Various trait dominances have been explored as leading to the manifestation of various coping mechanisms. This may be significant from a coaching standpoint since it allows for the customization of bowlers' coping instructions by knowing their dominant traits and the coping mechanism that yields the best outcomes for that attribute. It follows that a bowler who can handle the mental strain of competition will probably be more successful. Additionally, in his capacity as a coach, he is able to identify when a bowler is utilizing an unfavorable coping mechanism and can take steps to enhance the mechanism in order to increase its efficacy and enhance subsequent performance.

Myth: Personality Determines Goals

Some may believe that a bowler's personality dictates the type of goals they should set. For example, an introverted bowler may be assumed to have more conservative or inward-focused goals, while an extroverted bowler should have more ambitious and outgoing goals.

In reality, while personality can influence goal-setting preferences, it doesn't prescribe specific goals. Individuals have the autonomy to set goals based on their personal aspirations, regardless of their personality traits. Coaches and athletes should encourage bowlers to set goals that align with their individual motivations and desires rather than making assumptions based on personality alone.

Example in PWBA:

PWBA professional bowler, Danielle McEwan, is well-known for her extraversion and agreeableness. She enjoys engaging with people in social situations and is cooperative and friendly with both her opponents and teammates. McEwan has been seen to utilize an emotion-focused coping approach when dealing with psychological pressures, putting more emphasis on controlling her emotional reaction to stressors than on attempting to solve problems. She has found that using this coping mechanism helps her stay emotionally stable throughout contests and perform better on the lanes.

Danielle McEwan

Beyond the world of athletics, personality has a significant impact on both physical and mental health. Elite bowlers in the sport of bowling have certain qualities and attributes that help them advance in the sport. While some of these qualities are intrinsic, bowlers can grow and improve them through a variety of events in life, including as involvement in sports and young physical training programs, familial influences, and other experiences.

Personality Trait	Causes or Factors Since Early Stage of Bowler's Career
Extraversion	1. Social Exposure: Bowlers who were exposed to social and team-based activities from a young age may develop extraverted tendencies as they enjoy interactions with teammates and competitors. 2. Supportive Environment: A supportive and encouraging family, including parents, can foster confidence and sociability in young bowlers. 3. Team Dynamics: Being part of a bowling team with positive team dynamics and camaraderie can enhance extraversion, as it encourages socialization and team spirit.
Neuroticism	1. High Expectations: Young bowlers subjected to excessively high expectations from parents or coaches may develop neurotic tendencies due to the pressure to perform exceptionally well. 2. Lack of Emotional Support: A lack of emotional support or understanding during challenging moments in early bowling experiences can contribute to neuroticism, as bowlers may not have learned effective coping mechanisms. 3. Previous Failures: Early failures or setbacks in a bowler's career, especially without proper emotional guidance, can lead to neuroticism if the bowler does not learn to manage disappointment and anxiety effectively.
Conscientiousness	1. Discipline and Training: Bowlers who receive disciplined training and practice regimes from a young age tend to develop conscientiousness as they learn the value of hard work and attention to detail. 2. Parental Influence: Parents who emphasize responsibility and discipline in all aspects of life can instill conscientiousness in their children, which may carry over into their bowling careers. 3. Coaching Style: Coaches who prioritize structured training and meticulous technique often influence bowlers to adopt conscientious habits in their approach to the sport.
Agreeableness	1. Sportsmanship: Young bowlers who are taught the importance of sportsmanship and fair play are more likely to develop agreeable personalities as they value cooperation and positive interactions with others. 2. Team Sports Experience: Participation in team sports like bowling, where teamwork is essential, can cultivate agreeableness as bowlers understand the significance of working harmoniously with teammates. 3. Role Models: Having positive role models, such as coaches or experienced bowlers, who exhibit agreeable behaviors and attitudes can influence young bowlers to adopt similar traits.
Openness	1. Exposure to Diversity: Exposure to diverse experiences and cultures from an early age can promote openness, as it encourages curiosity and a willingness to explore new ideas and approaches. 2. Innovative Coaching: Coaches who introduce innovative techniques, strategies, and approaches to bowling can foster openness in their bowlers, encouraging them to explore new methods and adapt to different challenges. 3. Curious Nature: Bowlers with an inherently curious nature may naturally develop openness as they seek out new information and approaches to improve their skills and performance in the sport.

Table 6 - This table explores the origins of bowlers' personality traits from early career influences. Extraversion arises from social exposure and positive team dynamics, while neuroticism may result from high expectations and a lack of emotional support. Conscientiousness develops through disciplined training, parental influence, and coaching styles. Agreeableness is cultivated through sportsmanship, team sports experience, and positive role models. Openness stems from exposure to diversity, innovative coaching, and a naturally curious nature. The concise guide unveils the key factors shaping the distinct personalities of successful bowlers.

It's crucial to remember that these are broad influences and aspects that may have an impact on how bowlers' personalities develop. The true process of personality development involves a complicated interaction between a person's genetic makeup, early experiences, environment, and personal traits. Individual variances are important since different bowlers may have various paths to obtaining these features.

OVERCOMING SETBACKS IN SPORTS: A FRAMEWORK FOR SELF-FORGIVENESS (MOVE ON)

Within the world of competitive sports, there is an intense cultural emphasis on performance and winning. Even for the most successful sportsmen, failure is an unavoidable aspect of being a bowler, and this must be acknowledged. In order to better grasp this, let's examine two instances.

Let us first take a look at a double elimination event similar to the USBC, in which 64 bowlers participate. Most of the contestants will inevitably lose at some time. It's fascinating to notice that bad events typically leave a bigger emotional impression than good ones. According to research, in order to maintain emotional equilibrium, people should have at least three times as many happy experiences as negative ones.

Let's now focus on bowlers who are professionals. Seven bowlers in the top 50 rankings in 2022 had more losses than victories. There are just three bowlers who have won three times as many games as they have lost. These figures demonstrate how losses in competition are an inevitable aspect of sports. These results, meanwhile, run counter to the popular belief that one should always be the greatest and win. It is a conundrum that bowlers have to acknowledge and come to terms with. Athletes who can efficiently recover from setbacks are more likely to succeed in sports.

Understanding Failure

Various bowlers may interpret failure differently based on their own experiences and social pressures. The dramatic difference between the thrill of winning and the misery of losing defines failure for some people. Some might see failure as a personal experience related to their performance level, reaching their objectives, or how it affects their reputation and sense of self. Bowlers experience failure when they feel they can't achieve a competitive performance standard that they view as a sign of success, such winning a match or feeling like they made too many unintentional mistakes.

Understanding the Impact of Failure and How Bowlers Cope

Bowlers who compete in the sport may experience a great deal of stress if they don't do well. Bowlers who fail not only lose confidence and feel less worthy of themselves but their psychological health is also compromised. A series of negative feelings, including guilt, rage, and anxiety, are set off by this sense of failure. Their motivation, actions, ideas, and even bodily reactions are influenced by it. Bowlers use a variety of coping techniques that can be classified into different categories according to their nature and function in order to manage this stressful experience and the associated negative feelings.

> ### Pete Weber" EVERY SHOT IS A FAILURE"
>
> The statement "Every shot is a failure" by Pete Weber, a prominent professional bowler, reflects the incredibly high standards and expectations that top-level bowlers place on themselves. In the world of professional bowling, perfection is the ultimate goal. Even a single pin left standing or a slight deviation from the intended path can be seen as a failure to achieve that perfection. This mindset drives bowlers to continually strive for improvement, pushing themselves to deliver the most precise and accurate shots possible. It's a testament to the dedication and pursuit of excellence that characterizes the sport at its highest levels.

Bowlers use a variety of coping mechanisms to manage the difficulties of losing. These coping mechanisms can be divided into several groups according to their method, purpose, and mode of operation. Some bowlers, for instance, choose an approach-oriented coping method, which entails confronting the feelings and experiences connected to failure head-on. They actively work to address issues and control their emotions. Studies indicate that engagement-oriented coping strategies, which include problem- and emotion-focused tactics, are generally more successful. Bowlers who use these techniques frequently report increased performance satisfaction and improved coping skills. Indicators of objective performance, like qualifying for a bowling event, validate the benefits of engagement-oriented coping strategies.

Bowlers' coping mechanisms aren't all that flexible, though. While certain tactics could offer short-term comfort, they might not satisfy the psychological requirements at their core, especially the need for competence. Additionally, bowlers might not have the coping mechanisms needed to handle failure and the pressures of competitive sports. Their coping mechanisms may therefore be unproductive or even harmful to their wellbeing. Therefore, it is essential to investigate different coping mechanisms that can promote well-being and personal development.

Self-Forgiveness

Genuine self-forgiveness is one strategy that has gained traction in the field of forgiveness studies. Historically, self-forgiveness has been associated with a favorable emotional state by substituting pleasant emotions with negative self-oriented ones. Recent research, however, has shown that alternate reactions, such as absolving oneself or placing the blame elsewhere, can also support a constructive emotional change. However, these answers fail to acknowledge the crucial step of owning up to one's mistakes and owning up to oneself. Particularly in the context of bowling, this process is essential for personal development and advancement.

Failure is an inevitable part of the road when it comes to bowling. When faced with disappointment and losses, bowlers frequently experience unpleasant feelings like as guilt, humiliation, and rage. A potent technique for overcoming these emotional obstacles and promoting personal development is sincere self-forgiveness.

Pseudo-self-forgiveness techniques could provide brief comfort, but true self-forgiveness transcends sentimental states. Bowlers go through an eudaimonic process in which they examine their deeds and faults, take ownership of their mistakes, and respond constructively in order to regain positive self-esteem. Encouraging growth and mental well-being both on and off the bowling alley are promoted by this transforming process.

Aspect	Pseudo Self-Forgiveness	Genuine Self-Forgiveness
Definition	Superficial or temporary forgiveness where the bowler may appear to forgive himself but doesn't genuinely let go of negative feelings or self-blame.	A deep and authentic process of forgiving oneself for mistakes or failures, leading to inner peace and self-acceptance.
Steps	1. Denial: The bowler may deny responsibility or downplay the mistake. 2. Rationalization: They might provide excuses or external factors to justify the error. 3. Suppression: Suppressing negative emotions without addressing them.	1. Acknowledgment: Recognizing the mistake or failure. 2. Acceptance: Taking responsibility for the actions. 3. Self-Compassion: Showing understanding and kindness to oneself. 4. Learning: Identifying lessons and areas for improvement.

Aspect	Pseudo Self-Forgiveness	Genuine Self-Forgiveness
Strengths	1. Provides short-term relief from guilt or negative emotions. 2. May help maintain self-esteem in the short run.	1. Promotes genuine personal growth and development. 2. Enhances emotional well-being and self-acceptance. 3. Improves long-term mental resilience.
Weaknesses	1. Temporary relief leads to recurring guilt and self-blame. 2. Doesn't address the underlying issues or promote personal growth.	1. Can be a challenging and time-consuming process. 2. Requires confronting and processing difficult emotions. 3. May not come naturally and requires practice.

Table 7 - This table contrasts pseudo self-forgiveness (temporary relief, denial, rationalization, and suppression) with genuine self-forgiveness (acknowledgment, acceptance, self-compassion, and learning). Pseudo forgiveness provides short-term relief but perpetuates guilt, while genuine forgiveness fosters authentic personal growth, emotional well-being, and self-acceptance by addressing underlying issues.

Pseudo Self-Forgiveness

During a critical tournament match, a bowler faces a challenging spare in the final frame that could secure victory for the team. Unfortunately, the bowler misses the spare, resulting in the team's defeat.

Pseudo Self-Forgiveness Process:

Step 1: Denial:

- *Instead of acknowledging the miss, the bowler immediately denies personal responsibility. They attribute the mistake solely to external factors, insisting that the lane conditions were unfavorable and significantly impacted the ball's trajectory.*

Step 2: Rationalization:

- *Seeking to mitigate guilt, the bowler rationalizes the miss by emphasizing the inherent difficulty of the spare. They point out how unexpected changes in lane conditions made it nearly impossible to execute a perfect shot.*

Step 3: Suppression:

- *In an attempt to quickly move past the mistake, the bowler suppresses negative emotions associated with the miss. They maintain a composed exterior, pretending that the loss doesn't affect him and deflecting any self-blame.*

Outcome:

- *The bowler experiences momentary relief from immediate guilt, preserving a semblance of self-esteem in the short term.*
- *However, the underlying issues, such as personal responsibility for the mistake and potential areas for improvement, remain unaddressed.*
- *The pseudo self-forgiveness process provides only temporary comfort, and unresolved emotions may resurface later, hindering long-term personal and athletic development.*

In this scenario, the bowler's utilization of pseudo self-forgiveness offers a fleeting sense of relief but fails to foster genuine growth or address the factors contributing to the missed spare. The superficial nature of this approach can potentially impede future performance and emotional well-being.

True self-forgiveness results in a significant emotional transformation. Bowlers who actually forgive themselves become less distressed and let go of heavy emotions like guilt, shame, and rage. Bowlers can release themselves from the unpleasant emotional fallout of failure by letting go of self-deprecating ideas like self-blame and rumination. Emotional self-control is essential for preserving mental well-being and building resilience in the face of hardship.

Examples

Example 1: Missing a Single Pin
A bowler who should have been able to spare easily misses a single pin during a friendly game of bowling with friends. The bowler pauses, initially frustrated. He admits his error, takes ownership of it, and mentally notes how to do better at spare shooting going forward. He can release his aggravation and enjoy the remainder of the game without thinking back on his mistake, thanks to this small act of self-forgiveness.

Example 2: Low Scoring Game
A bowler has an exceptionally poor scoring game in a league match, far below his norm. Rather than being unduly judgmental, he engages in sincere self-forgiveness. He understands that bad days are common and aren't exclusive to any one sport. He embraces his performance and concentrates on the opportunities it offers for learning. He is able to let go of his guilt and sense of failure by doing this, which gives him the energy and resolve to play better in the following game.

Moreover, true forgiveness of oneself has a wider effect on bowlers' general welfare. Subjective measures of happiness and fulfillment, such as a greater sense of life satisfaction and quality of life as well as a more profound sense of meaning and purpose, are linked to it. Bowlers set off on a path of personal development by owning up to their transgressions, practicing restorative practices, and accepting who they are. Self-forgiveness gives individuals the ability to grow, reflect, and transform in a constructive way in addition to helping them to overcome failure.

Honest self-forgiveness has tremendous promise. It gives bowlers the opportunity to mend emotional scars, regain self-assurance, and improve their game. Bowlers can develop a positive internal atmosphere that fosters resilience and well-being in the face of upcoming difficulties by practicing self-forgiveness. Bowlers can leverage the power of self-acceptance, self-improvement, and personal progress by embracing the eudaimonic process of self-forgiveness, which will ultimately lead to a successful and rewarding bowling journey.

The Importance Of Self-Forgiveness In Bowling

The idea of self-forgiveness has mostly been used in relation to interpersonal transgressions, where people ask for forgiveness for the wrongs they have done to other people. Nonetheless, the idea of self-forgiveness holds just as much weight in intrapersonal contexts, such as when bowlers encounter setbacks or inadequacies that affect their own standards and objectives.

Interpersonal offenses, such as mistreating a colleague or breaking training guidelines, can occur during bowling. Bowlers might also occasionally exhibit intrapersonal failings, such skipping practice or not putting in their best effort in the gym. With regard to bowlers' assessments of their own shortcomings in competitive performance, this article concentrates specifically on the intrapersonal side of self-forgiveness.

The process of forgiving oneself can be impacted by outside forces, even when bowlers' mistakes may be internal in origin. In order to facilitate self-forgiveness, prior research has emphasized the significance of social support, forgiveness from others, and the perception of forgiveness from a higher power. When it comes to bowling, players frequently go to friends and coaches for assistance, as well as others outside of their personal athletic community. When these networks of support are in line with true self-forgiveness instead of fake self-forgiveness, they can be very helpful in the process of developing self-forgiveness.

Examples

Teammate Mistreatment: After arguing with a teammate during a pivotal game, a bowler in a bowling league gets into a furious confrontation. He acknowledges he was incorrect when he looks back on what he did. He asks for forgiveness for his actions and offer an apology to his teammate. The team's harmony is restored through this process of interpersonal self-forgiveness.

Missed Practice Sessions: A committed bowler has to skip multiple practice sessions for personal reasons. At first, he feels bad for not using himself fully during exercise. But he learns that everyone has difficulties, with the help and encouragement of his coach and other bowlers. He offers himself grace for skipping practices and concentrate on getting the most out of his upcoming workouts.

External Support: A bowler in competition goes through a run of poor outings. He seeks advice and support from his coach and close friends by confiding in him. He is able to forgive himself for his previous setbacks and restore faith in his skills, thanks to the kind comments and encouragement he gets. This outside assistance supports his performance recovery and is consistent with sincere self-forgiveness.

Myth: Self-Forgiveness Is a Sign of Weakness

One common myth surrounding self-forgiveness in competitive bowling is that it's a sign of weakness or lack of competitiveness. Some may believe that bowlers who engage in self-forgiveness are not driven to win or lack the necessary competitive spirit.

In reality, self-forgiveness is not a sign of weakness but rather a valuable coping strategy. It allows bowlers to take responsibility for their performance shortcomings, learn from their mistakes, and address their emotional responses to

---

failure. It's an essential part of the psychological resilience that enables athletes to bounce back from setbacks and perform at their best in future matches.

Myth: Self-Forgiveness Means Excusing Failure

Another myth is that self-forgiveness is synonymous with excusing or justifying failure. Some may fear that by forgiving themselves, bowlers are essentially letting themselves off the hook and not holding themselves accountable for their mistakes.

In reality, self-forgiveness does not mean excusing or ignoring failures. It involves acknowledging one's role in the failure and taking appropriate responsibility. Self-forgiveness is a way to move forward constructively by learning from errors and making improvements. It does not absolve bowlers of accountability but rather helps them grow and develop as athletes.

Accepting personal responsibility for poor performance and making an effort to improve are necessary components of true self-forgiveness. Rather than only looking for approval from others or assigning blame, it entails owning up to one's mistakes and making the necessary corrections. Bowlers who want to grow personally and navigate the path of self-forgiveness might benefit greatly from support networks that promote sincere self-forgiveness.

It's crucial to remember, though, that not all types of support might be advantageous. The process of forgiving oneself might be hampered by support that downplays accountability or places an unduly harsh blame on the victim. Bowlers want a well-rounded approach that accepts their responsibilities and provides them with support, understanding, and direction. Support networks can help bowlers move past their mistakes and resume their concentration on getting better by finding this balance.

A Framework For Self-Forgiveness: Coping With Failure In Competitive Bowling

The idea that self-forgiveness is a positive response when people don't uphold social-moral ideals is supported by a wealth of research. When it comes to competitive bowling, self-forgiveness is a purposeful coping technique that enables bowlers to own up to their performance flaws, validate their value, and deal with any arising uncomfortable feelings, including guilt.

Taking Personal Responsibility For Failure

In order to preserve their sense of self-worth, people frequently attempt to avoid acknowledging their part in a failure. But this defensive reaction impedes learning and personal development. It is impossible to truly forgive oneself if one does not accept some degree of personal accountability for the subpar performance in the competition. There's nothing to forgive if one does not take responsibility. Even though it is uncommon, there are times when an opponent outperforms a bowler with a remarkable display of expertise. Since bowlers typically bear some of the blame for their own performance shortfalls, it is essential to acknowledge this fact in order to truly be able to forgive themselves.

It is crucial to remember, though, that bowlers might occasionally react to failure by placing an undue amount of blame on themselves and elevating their sense of accountability. This may result in severe self-punishment and self-loathing. According to academics, self-compassion can assist in preventing these self-punitive reactions. Self-compassion entails looking inward and embracing without passing judgment and treating oneself with respect and understanding, no matter what flaws one may have. Reduced self-criticism, rumination, and humiliation are examples of maladaptive reactions to failure that are linked to self-compassion.

However, it is important to note that self-compassion does not always translate into a reduction in defensiveness or an acceptance of one's own shortcomings when it comes to competitive performance. Perhaps this is because accepting responsibility is not a prerequisite for practicing self-compassion. As such, depending exclusively on self-compassion could omit the crucial phase of admitting one's part in the setback, which could restrict prospects for individual development. True forgiveness for oneself, on the other hand, finds a middle ground between self-reproach and self-exoneration. While encouraging self-compassion and personal growth, it also acknowledges the bowler's accountability for the defeat in the competition.

Embracing Personal Responsibility for Failure:

Hypothetical Example: An elite bowlers realizes that certain technical mistakes throughout the tournament led to his downfall after a poor showing in a national bowling championship. He admits personal responsibility for his errors and acknowledge that he didn't execute this shots as intended.

Steps for Coping:

a) Acknowledge the Mistake: The bowler admits that errors were made during the competition, including forgetting to bring extra spares and failing to adjust for changing lane circumstances.

b) Take Ownership: The bowler accepts responsibility for his errors without offering explanations or placing blame elsewhere. He acknowledges that improved shot execution could have led to better performance.

c) Learn from the Mistake: The bowler reflects on his technical mistakes and identifies areas that need improvement. Understanding what went wrong and how to prevent it from happening again becomes a crucial aspect of the learning process.

Restoring Self-Worth And Embracing Growth In Competitive Bowling

The sport of bowling requires both mental and physical toughness. Bowlers may have flaws or failures despite their greatest efforts, which can be emotionally upsetting and damage their self-esteem. Bowlers typically look for ways to reaffirm their value when they are going through difficult times, and true self-forgiveness is viewed as an essential step that entails reaffirming their basic beliefs. Bowlers should address the ideals their actions reflect and accept appropriate responsibility for their part in their team's poor performance in competition.

Stages:

1. **Acknowledgment Stage:** Acknowledge emotional impact and recognize setbacks.

2. **Reaffirmation Stage:** Reflect on fundamental beliefs and reconnect with core values.

3. **Responsibility Acceptance Stage:** Accept responsibility for team performance.

4. **Evaluation Stage:** Assess whether failure violates moral principles.

5. **Indirect Affirmation Stage:** Redirect focus to other life aspects for indirect affirmation.

6. **Restoration Stage:** Engage in activities to restore self-integrity.

7. **Emotional Nurturing Stage:** Cultivate positive emotions and counteract negativity.

8. **Affirmation Practice Stage:** Regularly practice self-affirmations for emotional stability.

9. **Contemplation Stage:** Step back to holistically evaluate the entire match.

10. **Objective Analysis Stage:** Analyze errors objectively with less defensiveness.

11. **Information Utilization Stage:** Utilize failure as a source of useful information for improvement.

Nevertheless, there are times when bowlers experience failure that does not inherently violate their moral principles, or when there appear to be few prospects for quick progress. An indirect method of reaffirming ideals may be helpful in certain circumstances. Bowlers are encouraged by indirect self-affirmations to refocus on other important areas of their lives and highlight their value in relation to their identity as a whole. This procedure improves several facets of self-worth, such as self-esteem and self-integrity, and makes it possible to restore overall self-integrity.

Rebuilding one's self-esteem is especially important when bowlers lose in tournaments that have a string of games or matches. Bowlers can nurture good emotions like happiness and joy and lessen negative emotional tension by practicing self-affirmations, which help them separate the failure from their identity. As a result, bowlers are more equipped to handle defeat and regain emotional stability when they practice self-forgiveness, which is accomplished through value affirmation and self-affirmation. This, in turn, improves bowlers' performance in subsequent games.

The restoration of self-regard creates an opportunity for holistic contemplation for bowlers who are confronting failure. Bowlers can stand back and evaluate the entire match rather than focusing on one particular situation or result. This impartial method makes it possible to analyze one's own errors and limitations more objectively. Moreover, bowlers who approach failure with less defensiveness and bias are more likely to be able to use the useful information that comes with it (such as concentration errors) to pinpoint areas where they can improve technically, strategically, or psychologically.

Restoring Self-Worth

Hypothetical examples:

Example 1: John is a professional bowler who is competing in a big event. He puts his all into a crucial match but fails, it damages his confidence and makes him angry and nervous. In order to manage his feelings, John uses self-affirmation and value affirmation to start the process of self-forgiveness. Acknowledging his part in the loss, he upholds the moral principles that his behavior transgressed and directs his attention towards other noteworthy facets of his existence. John's positive emotional states grow, his negative emotional stress reactions decrease, and his sense of self-worth is restored as a result. Then, he is able to consider the matter objectively and holistically, which aids in helping him pinpoint areas that need work and make appropriate use of the knowledge gained from the setback.

Example 2: Bowler Jane goes through a string of setbacks in a competition. Her self-esteem is put in jeopardy as she experiences frustration and discouragement. Jane utilizes self-affirmation and value affirmation as a means of self-forgiveness. She acknowledges that she contributed to the failures, upholds the moral principles that her behavior transgressed, and refocuses her attention on other important facets of her life. Consequently, Jane boosts her good feelings, decreases her negative emotional stress responses, and regains her sense of self-worth. After that, she is in a position to evaluate the circumstances objectively and holistically, which enables her to pinpoint areas in need of development and make flexible use of the knowledge gleaned from the mistakes. With this fresh viewpoint, Jane may now compete more successfully and accomplish more in the future.

Coping Strategy: Restoring Self-Worth and Embracing Growth in Competitive Bowling

Steps:

1. **Acknowledge Emotional Impact:**
   - **Cue:** *Recognize the emotional impact of failures or flaws.*
   - **Explanation:** *Acknowledge that setbacks can be emotionally upsetting and potentially damaging to self-esteem.*

2. **Reaffirm Basic Beliefs:**
   - **Cue:** *Reflect on fundamental beliefs about oneself.*
   - **Explanation:** *Reconnect with core values and beliefs to reaffirm personal identity.*

3. **Accept Responsibility:**
   - **Cue:** *Identify one's role in team performance.*
   - **Explanation:** *Take appropriate responsibility for any contribution to the team's poor performance in competition.*

4. **Evaluate Moral Principles:**
   - **Cue:** *Assess whether failure violates moral principles.*
   - **Explanation:** *Distinguish between failures that challenge moral principles and those that are part of the sport's inherent challenges.*

5. **Indirect Self-Affirmations:**
   - **Cue:** *Redirect focus to other life aspects.*
   - **Explanation:** *Use indirect self-affirmations to highlight personal value outside of bowling, fostering a broader sense of self-worth.*

6. **Restore Self-Integrity:**
   - **Cue:** *Engage in activities that rebuild self-integrity.*

- *Explanation:* Address self-worth issues by restoring integrity through positive actions and affirmations.

7. *Nurture Positive Emotions:*

- *Cue:* Cultivate positive emotions like happiness and joy.
- *Explanation:* Counteract negative emotional tension through intentional practices that nurture positive emotions.

8. *Practice Self-Affirmations:*

- *Cue:* Regularly affirm positive aspects of oneself.
- *Explanation:* Use self-affirmations to separate failure from personal identity, promoting emotional stability.

9. *Holistic Contemplation:*

- *Cue:* Step back to evaluate the entire match.
- *Explanation:* Adopt an impartial perspective to analyze the overall performance rather than fixating on specific situations.

10. *Objective Analysis:*

- *Cue:* Approach failure with less defensiveness.
- *Explanation:* Analyze errors and limitations objectively, allowing for a more constructive assessment.

11. *Useful Information Utilization:*

- *Cue:* Embrace failure as a source of useful information.
- *Explanation:* Identify areas of improvement, such as concentration errors, with a focus on technical, strategic, or psychological aspects.

The Interpersonal Context Of Self-Forgiveness In Competitive Bowling

In competitive bowling, self-forgiveness has been shown to be an effective reaction to failure. Bowling, however, is a team sport that requires a variety of interpersonal ties with coaches, teams, and organizations. As a result, self-forgiveness in the bowling context deals with bigger picture elements of the sport experience rather than just the person. Thus, it's critical to create assessment instruments that adequately reflect the complex dynamics of self-forgiveness in athletics.

Although self-forgiveness is largely influenced by the interpersonal setting, failure itself may be an internal experience. When bowlers bowl poorly in a team event, they may feel more guilty because they think they let their teammates down. The way victims—such as teammates or other people impacted by the setback—respond is essential to self-forgiveness. Victims who appropriately answer back and participate in the healing process are more likely to forgive themselves. On the other hand, self-forgiveness may be impeded by victimization and social rejection experiences. This emphasizes how crucial understanding and support from others are in helping bowlers forgive themselves.

Examining bowling-specific scenarios that either facilitate or obstruct self-forgiveness is crucial to developing a greater knowledge of self-forgiveness in the sport. For example, in team sports environments, bowlers who are unfairly singled out or held responsible for losing matches may find it more difficult to overcome their inclination toward self-loathing. However, bowlers are more likely to develop self-forgiveness in team cultures that find a balance between encouraging and supporting one another while also holding themselves accountable.

Restoring Self-Worth and Resolving Emotional Discomfort:

Hypothetical Example: A talented bowler is upset and disappointed with her performance in a local bowling tournament since she didn't meet her own goals. Her performance frustrates and upsets her, which lowers her sense of value.

Steps for Coping:

a) Practice Self-Compassion:

- **Description:** *Demonstrate self-compassion by accepting feelings and allowing oneself to experience disappointment.*
- **Explanation:** *Be compassionate and empathetic toward oneself instead of being critical or judgmental.*

b) Reframe Failure as a Learning Opportunity:

- **Description:** *Change perspective to see failure as a teaching opportunity rather than a reflection of personal value.*
- **Explanation:** *Understand that failure is a necessary component of competitive sports and a chance for personal development.*

c) Seek Support:

- **Description:** *Look to coaches, teammates, and friends for support; they provide perspective, encouragement, and assurance.*
- **Explanation:** *Discuss ideas and feelings with others to ease emotional distress and gain valuable insights.*

Developing a Growth Mindset:

Example: A skilled bowler loses in a high-stakes bowling match, and despite best efforts, is not able to advance to the finals. Understanding that adopting a growth mindset is essential for effectively handling failure.

Steps for Coping:

a) Embrace Challenges as Opportunities:

- **Description:** *Welcome challenges as chances for development.*
- **Explanation:** *View failure not as a permanent setback but as an opportunity to grow and learn.*

b) Cultivate a Positive Attitude:

- **Description:** *Reinterpret failure as a necessary step on the path to success.*
- **Explanation:** *Foster a positive outlook by concentrating on lessons learned rather than flaws.*

c) Develop Resilience:

- **Description:** *Gain resilience by persevering through setbacks and staying dedicated to objectives.*
- **Explanation:** *Work hard to improve skills, refusing to let failure define personal identity.*

Faults And Fixes Of Self Forgiveness

The journey of athletes in the world of sports is often marked by triumphs, challenges, and the continuous pursuit of excellence. However, the inability to forgive oneself can cast a shadow over this path, giving rise to various emotional challenges. The roots of these challenges often trace back to early experiences, societal expectations, and the pressure to meet high standards. In this exploration of faults and fixes in self-forgiveness, we dig into the multifaceted aspects of shame, guilt, anger, anxiety, low self-esteem, overwhelm, frustration, insecurity, and resentment. Each of these emotions has its origins, often stemming from early age experiences, and understanding these roots is the first step towards finding effective coping mechanisms. The following discussion offers insights into the causes of these emotions, the factors and people contributing to them, and practical steps and strategies to overcome these hurdles on the path to self-forgiveness and personal growth in the world of competitive bowling.

Shame:

Shame, a pervasive emotional experience in the lives of dedicated bowlers, emerges as a consequence of their unwavering commitment to the pursuit of perfection and triumph in their sport. This emotional burden is often rooted in the early socialization of these athletes, instilling a belief that winning is paramount, and any deviation from these expectations elicits a profound sense of shame. The intricate web of causation extends to the high expectations imposed on bowlers, be it by their own aspirations, parental influences, or the standards set by coaches. The fear of disappointing significant others, including loved ones and teammates, further intensifies this emotional response. Coping with shame necessitates the cultivation of self-acceptance and self-compassion, critical components in the journey towards overcoming this deeply ingrained emotion. Seeking support from empathetic individuals, such as friends, teammates, or mental health professionals, becomes instrumental in managing and alleviating these complex feelings. The pathway to overcoming shame involves adopting a growth-oriented perspective, prioritizing continual improvement over the unattainable pursuit of perfection—a nuanced approach that diverges from the detrimental effects of perfectionism-driven coping mechanisms.

Guilt:

The genesis of guilt among bowlers can be traced back to an early age when the perception crystallizes that personal failures are indicative of intrinsic shortcomings. This belief system, ingrained from youth, renders them susceptible to the pervasive emotion of self-blame. The factors and individuals contributing to this emotional tapestry include a pronounced tendency towards self-critical assessments, engendering a perpetual loop of guilt. To cope with this profound sense of culpability, it is imperative to divert from fixating on one's perceived shortcomings. Instead, a strategic coping mechanism involves confronting and overcoming self-defeating thoughts. Seeking the guidance of a mental health specialist emerges as a potentially advantageous avenue for those grappling with the complexities of guilt. Effectively overcoming guilt demands a shift in perspective, recognizing that the relentless pursuit of victory and perfection is a primary instigator of this emotional burden. Actively endeavoring to alter one's mindset from a perpetual cycle of self-blame, and acknowledging even the smallest victories, becomes a pivotal step towards emancipation from the shackles of guilt.

Anger:

The genesis of anger within bowlers often traces its roots to their early experiences in the sport, where frustration with the inability to meet personal or external standards manifests. The initial encounters with bowling may serve as the wellspring of this persistent frustration. Factors contributing to the development of anger encompass unmet expectations and a perceived sense of letting down coaches or teammates. Additional triggers may involve unfavorable criticism from coaches or an unjust sense of accusation. Coping with rage requires a multifaceted approach, including the utilization of relaxation techniques to exert control over emotional outbursts and fostering open communication with teammates or coaches. In cases of persistent anger issues, the implementation of anger management techniques may prove beneficial. Overcoming anger necessitates a deliberate exploration of the sources provoking this emotion. Concentrating on emotional control becomes imperative, prompting a shift in perspective on competition—one that prioritizes personal development over the often burdensome pursuit of meeting external expectations. This nuanced approach serves as a transformative step towards emancipation from the grip of anger, fostering a healthier and more constructive relationship with the sport.

Anxiety:

The roots of anxiety in the world of competitive bowling often extend back to early experiences, where coaches, teammates, or the bowlers themselves become frequent targets of this pervasive emotion. The specter of anxiety, perhaps ingrained since childhood bowling endeavors, persists as a significant aspect of their sporting journey. Contributing factors to anxiety involve external pressures from classmates, parents, or coaches, urging bowlers to excel. Another dimension of this emotional landscape is the apprehension of failing the team or falling short of one's personal expectations. Effectively coping with anxiety requires a holistic approach, beginning with the cultivation of mindfulness to address worrisome thoughts. Seeking mental health assistance becomes essential when needed. Shifting the focus from the final result to the process and enjoyment of the sport serves as a valuable strategy to alleviate anxiety. Overcoming anxiety involves a systematic approach, incorporating regular practice of relaxation methods, confronting irrational thoughts, and gradually acclimating oneself to competitive environments. This comprehensive strategy not only enhances self-esteem but also contributes to more effective anxiety management, fostering a healthier and more fulfilling engagement with the sport of bowling.

Low Self-Esteem:

The genesis of low self-esteem among bowlers often finds its roots in a prolonged association between performance outcomes and self-worth, a connection that may have taken shape during their early forays into bowling. A myriad of factors contributes to this complex emotional state, including negative feedback, early experiences, and the detrimental habit of comparing oneself to others. Coping with low self-esteem necessitates a multifaceted strategy, beginning with the regular practice of self-affirmation and self-compassion. Seeking encouraging feedback from a supportive network and setting realistic goals further forms integral components of this coping mechanism. To overcome the shackles of poor self-esteem, it becomes imperative to disentangle self-worth from performance results. Redirecting the focus towards personal development and cultivating an environment surrounded by positive and encouraging individuals marks a transformative step in fostering a healthier self-perception. This nuanced approach to overcoming low self-esteem not only facilitates a more constructive relationship with the sport but also lays the foundation for enduring personal growth and fulfillment.

Overwhelm:

The pervasive sense of overwhelm experienced by bowlers often traces its origins to an early adoption of a relentless pursuit of perfection and a persistent fear of falling short of either personal or external expectations. This motivation, possibly ingrained during the nascent stages of their bowling careers, manifests as overwhelming feelings in the face of demanding standards. The emotional burden is compounded by high expectations placed upon the bowlers, whether by instructors, parents, or self-imposed pressures. Overindulgence in training and the intense competitiveness prevalent in the sport further contribute to this sense of overload. Coping with overwhelm demands a strategic approach, involving the setting of priorities for obligations and effective time management. Establishing boundaries and seeking assistance from mentors or coaches to develop a balanced schedule emerges as crucial in alleviating this complex emotion. Practical steps to overcome overwhelm include the incorporation of self-care practices, such as breathing exercises, and the cultivation of the ability to say no when necessary. Redirecting attention towards establishing reasonable objectives and recognizing the indispensable role of balance in long-term success represents a transformative step in overcoming the challenges posed by overwhelm and fostering a more sustainable and fulfilling engagement with the sport of bowling.

Frustration:

Frustration, a prevalent emotional state among bowlers, often finds its roots in early experiences characterized by earnest efforts that did not yield the intended outcomes. This frustration may stem from a foundational inclination toward success, encountering obstacles that impede progress. The persistence of this emotional response is fueled by ongoing attempts that fail to deliver the desired results. Factors contributing to frustration include unresolved technical or strategic concerns in bowling and a perceived stagnation in skill improvement. Effectively coping with frustration involves the establishment of reasonable goals and a deliberate shift in focus from the outcome to the process. Seeking advice from instructors or seasoned bowlers to identify specific areas requiring improvement becomes integral in alleviating this emotional state. Overcoming frustration demands the cultivation of patience, the adoption of a growth mentality, and the recognition of failures as valuable opportunities for improvement. Embracing the continuous process of self-improvement, with an acknowledgment that hard work and perseverance are inherent to the journey, forms the bedrock for overcoming frustration and fostering enduring success in the world of competitive bowling.

Insecurity:

The origins of insecurity among bowlers often trace back to early experiences marked by unfavorable comparisons to more accomplished peers or the internalization of inadequacy stemming from a perceived failure to meet the lofty standards set by parents or coaches. These feelings of insecurity can be compounded by a continuous pattern of comparing oneself to others, coupled with instances of undervaluation or criticism in past performances. Unfavorable comments and apparent criticism from coaches or classmates may further exacerbate this emotional landscape. Effectively coping with insecurity necessitates a deliberate effort to enhance self-assurance through the use of affirmations and constructive self-talk. Seeking mentorship or guidance from seasoned bowlers becomes a valuable resource, emphasizing personal development over the pursuit of external approval. The steps to overcome insecurity involve a focused commitment to boosting self-worth, confronting self-doubt, and setting attainable goals. Surrounding oneself with positive influences who believe in one's potential and provide unwavering support throughout the journey toward improvement is pivotal in overcoming the pervasive challenges posed by insecurity in the competitive world of bowling.

Resentment:

Resentment, a complex emotional state prevalent among bowlers, often originates from early experiences characterized by unjust treatment, criticism, or unmet expectations from coaches, peers, or even oneself, marking the inception of their bowling careers. The persistence of resentment is fueled by unresolved disputes, relentless criticism, or a pervasive sense of being underappreciated. Past perceived injustices in the sport can further fan the flames of this emotionally charged response. Coping with resentment requires a multifaceted approach, entailing the crucial components of forgiveness, open communication to address underlying problems, and a transformative shift in perspective from blame to personal development and progress. Seeking support from mentors or mental health specialists becomes instrumental in managing the complex terrain of anger. Overcoming this emotional hurdle involves engaging in productive conversations to settle disputes and redirecting focus toward aspects of the bowling journey that are within one's influence. The transformative process includes learning to forgive and adopting an optimistic mindset for a more rewarding and less bitter experience in the sport, fostering personal growth and resilience.

Emotion	How It Started Since Early Age	Responsible Factors and People	How to Solve It
Shame	Rooted in dedication to perfection and triumph in bowling, often socialized to believe winning is everything.	High expectations from oneself, parents, or coaches, fear of disappointing loved ones and teammates.	Cultivate self-acceptance and self-compassion. Seek support from friends, teammates, or mental health professionals. Adopt a growth-oriented perspective, emphasizing improvement over unattainable perfection.
Guilt	Belief that failures reflect personal shortcomings from an early age.	Self-blame and critical self-assessment, perpetuating a loop of guilt.	Confront and overcome self-defeating thoughts. Seek assistance from mental health specialists. Recognize that the focus on winning and perfection is the primary cause. Change perspective from constant self-blame, acknowledge even modest victories.
Anger	Originates from frustration with not meeting personal or external standards in early bowling experiences.	Unmet expectations, perceived letdown of coaches or teammates, unfavorable criticism.	Use relaxation techniques to control outbursts, share problems with teammates or coaches. Consider anger management techniques if needed. Determine sources of anger, concentrate on emotional control, shift perspective to personal development over meeting external expectations.
Anxiety	Targets coaches, teammates, or bowlers themselves, possibly ingrained since childhood bowling experiences.	Pressure to excel from classmates, parents, or coaches, fear of failing the team or falling short of personal expectations.	Practice mindfulness, seek mental health assistance when needed. Refocus on the process and enjoyment of the sport. Practice relaxation methods, confront illogical thoughts, gradually acclimate to competitive environments.
Low Self-Esteem	Results from a persistent link between performance outcomes and self-worth, formed in early bowling adventures.	Low self-esteem from early experiences, negative feedback, comparisons to others.	Practice self-affirmation and self-compassion. Look for encouraging feedback, make realistic goals. Detach self-worth from performance results. Concentrate on personal development, surround oneself with positive and encouraging individuals.
Overwhelm	Arises from a relentless pursuit of perfection and fear of falling short, possibly ingrained in early bowling careers.	High expectations from instructors, parents, or self-imposed pressures, overindulgence in training and competitiveness.	Set priorities, manage time effectively. Establish boundaries, seek assistance from mentors or coaches. Practice self-care, develop the ability to say no. Focus on reasonable objectives, realize the importance of balance for long-term success.

Emotion	How It Started Since Early Age	Responsible Factors and People	How to Solve It
Frustration	Originates in early experiences of putting forth effort without intended outcomes.	Constant attempts without desired results, unresolved technical or strategic concerns, perceived lack of improvement.	Set reasonable goals, emphasize the process over the result, seek advice from instructors or seasoned bowlers. Practice patience, maintain a growth mentality, see failures as chances to improve. Accept the process of self-improvement, acknowledge the role of hard work and perseverance.
Insecurity	Traces back to early experiences comparing oneself to accomplished peers or feeling inadequate by parental or coach standards.	Constant comparison to others, undervaluation or criticism, unfavorable comments from coaches or classmates.	Enhance self-assurance with affirmations and constructive self-talk. Seek mentorship from seasoned bowlers, prioritize personal development over external approval. Focus on boosting self-worth, confront self-doubt, set attainable goals. Surround oneself with positive influences who believe in potential.
Resentment	Originates from unjust treatment, criticism, or unmet expectations in early bowling career.	Unresolved disputes, relentless criticism, a sense of being underappreciated, past perceived injustices.	Practice forgiveness, engage in open communication to address underlying problems. Shift perspective from blame to personal development. Seek support from mentors or mental health specialists. Have productive conversations to settle disputes, redirect focus toward aspects within one's influence. Learn to forgive, adopt an optimistic mindset for a more rewarding experience.

Table 8 - This table delves into bowling-related emotions—shame, guilt, anger, anxiety, low self-esteem, overwhelm, frustration, insecurity, and resentment—outlining their origins and influencing factors. Solutions encompass self-compassion, seeking support, adopting a growth mindset, mindfulness, realistic goal-setting, and fostering an optimistic perspective. The concise guide underscores proactive emotional well-being strategies, emphasizing addressing issues, seeking assistance, and prioritizing personal growth.

IT MEANS LIFE TO ME - BALANCING SACRIFICE AND WELL-BEING

Children's dreams have always been the source of their aspirations, as they see themselves developing into the people they want to be. For individuals who are enthralled with bowling, the journey to fulfilling their aspirations can be difficult. In addition to talent and commitment, it also necessitates favorable circumstances and a readiness to endure setbacks.

I had the honor of speaking with ten bowlers from all over the world for my research on the sport of bowling. These interviews highlight the difficulties and early sacrifices they had to make, as well as the significant impact bowling has had on their lives.

Young bowlers encounter several challenges throughout their path, from joining school sports teams to rising through regional and representative squads and, eventually, aiming for high-performance selection. It's important to investigate how a top bowler develops in order to comprehend the sacrifices that bowlers make. Understanding the sustainability and long-term growth of a successful sporting career has become an international enterprise, with governments all over the world placing an increasing emphasis on international sporting success. By identifying the important influences and contributions to bowlers' development, we can obtain insight into the enormous sacrifices they make to achieve their unique lifestyle.

When bowlers are developing, a number of elements play a major influence. Strong social support networks, the benefit of being based in large cities, later specialization—in which bowlers participate in other sports during adolescence—and the pursuit of a university degree are some of these aspects. There is a consistent path that the majority of good bowlers follow when their lives and traits are examined. To better prepare on the court or the field, bowlers are urged to forgo social opportunities and occasionally even family obligations, which means that following this route frequently requires sacrificing one's freedom of choice. Institutions provide sports scholarships to guarantee their continuous involvement in the educational system, but the expectation that they maintain a balance between their academics and competition poses additional expectations. This delicate balancing act turns their lives into a perpetual juggling act, with attending postsecondary schools for sport becoming more than a choice, but an obligation.

Myth: Sacrificing Everything Leads to Success

This myth suggests that for bowlers to achieve success, they must be willing to sacrifice all aspects of their life, including personal relationships and well-being. In reality, a balanced approach that prioritizes well-being and maintains a healthy work-life balance is often more sustainable and effective.

Myth: Over-conformity Equals Sporting Excellence

This myth implies that bowlers who conform entirely to the "sporting ethic" and engage in extreme sacrifice will automatically achieve excellence in their sport. However, over-conformity can lead to negative consequences, including health issues and isolation, and does not guarantee success.

Surprisingly, the expectation for bowlers to forego social chances contradicts the results of sports psychologists, who emphasize the importance of social influences on sporting engagement. The degree of participation in sports is mostly determined by a variety of social ties. Youngsters who have favorable opinions of their coaches, teammates, and bowling as a sport typically participate at higher levels in the following seasons. On the other hand, people who have negative associations with these elements have higher dropout rates. It's important to remember that a bowler's performance is more heavily influenced by their favorable relationships with the sport and its participants than it is by their return rates or dropout rates. Bowlers are primarily motivated by social reasons, of which the coach's actions are just one important aspect of a broader social impact matrix. Participation rates and the incidence of dropouts in a variety of sports are influenced by factors such as strong bowler-coach connections, social control within the sport, prevention of burnout, fear of failure, and emotional and mental resilience.

A closer look at the underlying reasons of burnout reveals that it is rooted in the social structure of high-performance sports and is entwined with control and identity concerns. These social issues, which are sometimes called "sporting politics," include prejudices that exist within organizations, including coaches who favor certain players over others. Reforming the social structure of high-performance sport is essential to preserving the health of young bowlers and avoiding burnout. This involves rebuilding the dynamics of connections between bowlers and important people in their path, like coaches, teammates, and support personnel, as well as rethinking how sports are experienced and incorporated into the lives of young bowlers. This method places an emphasis on bowlers' overall health, which goes beyond how effectively they bowl. In the field of high-performance sport management, providing bowlers with possibilities to succeed in numerous spheres of life, such as friendships, family, and employment, has just lately become more important.

Effective recovery from rigorous training loads is crucial to success or failure in the hard world of competitive bowling. Bowlers are at serious risk from fatigue, both mental and physical. It can be harmful to push bowlers beyond their limitations of physical and psychological exhaustion, since this can result in over-conformity or excessive sacrifice of their personal life outside of the game. The question of whether excessive sacrifice might reduce performance in the same way that excessive training can arises from the delicate balance between sacrifice and performance.

Achieving the ideal balance is crucial. For bowlers to succeed in their athletic careers, they must manage a complex web of responsibilities, personal sacrifices, and well-being. Maintaining a healthy work-life balance and understanding the value of relaxation and recuperation are essential for long-term success. Bowlers cannot achieve their maximum potential without sacrificing their general well-being and contentment unless they comprehend the intricate relationship between psychological and physical demands.

The welfare of bowlers must be given top priority by the bowling community, which includes coaches, administrators, and support personnel. We can make sure that bowlers may pursue their goals with fervor and determination while leading happy, balanced lives by establishing an atmosphere that values their overall well-being and offers chances for growth and development both on and off the lanes.

Myth: Sporting Success Requires Defying All Boundaries

This myth suggests that successful bowlers must be willing to defy all boundaries and norms in their pursuit of excellence. In truth, a more balanced approach that respects personal boundaries and promotes holistic well-being is crucial for long-term success.

Myth: Sacrificing Personal Growth for Sport Is Necessary

This myth implies that bowlers must sacrifice personal growth, education, and career aspirations to excel in bowling. However, fostering personal growth and pursuing interests outside of the sport can contribute to a more fulfilling and balanced life, which can, in turn, enhance sporting performance.

The Dangers Of Over-Conformity In Bowling: Balancing Sacrifice And Well-Being

In the bowling world, there's a well-known notion called the "sporting ethic." This ethic emphasizes risk-taking, pushing boundaries, pursuing distinction, and making sacrifices for the sake of the game. It distinguishes the "real bowlers"—those who are prepared to give up anything in order to follow these rules. This ethic seeks to instill moral principles in the sport, but it also poses a special problem: the problem of over-conformity and its aftereffects on bowlers' lives outside of the lanes.

Positive deviance, sometimes known as over-conformity, is the practice of bowlers exceeding the standard boundaries with a degree of intensity and extensibility that deviates from the norm. The dominant "power and performance" paradigm in sports frequently places emphasis on putting in "whatever it takes" to prevail. Uncritical acceptance of this model, however, may encourage bowlers to engage in a number of behaviors that are harmful to their health. For example, eating problems have tragically claimed the lives of men and female bowlers in their unwavering quest for a professional sporting career. This harsh reality shows that bowlers who practice positive deviance are prepared to push the boundaries and put their personal welfare at risk in order to achieve their unwavering goals.

Over-conformity is not just a physical health issue. It seeps into and controls bowlers' social lives when they're not practicing or competing. There can be intense pressure to uphold the sporting ethic, which leaves little time for relationships, personal development, and other facets of life. Bowlers could find themselves forgoing important social and family time, putting off pursuing their educational or professional goals, or even jeopardizing their mental and emotional health. Bowlers may unintentionally become isolated from the world outside of the bowling alley due to their quest of athletic greatness.

It is critical to acknowledge and confront the risks associated with over-conformity. A multimodal strategy is necessary to strike a balance between the pursuit of athletic performance and the preservation of well-being. A loving and encouraging environment that prioritizes bowlers' overall growth must be actively fostered by coaches, administrators, and support personnel. Fostering strong relationships within the sport, encouraging a healthy work-life balance, and offering resources and guidance for maintaining mental and physical health are all part of this.

Bowlers also have a vital responsibility to protect their own health. In addition to advocating for their own needs and boundaries, it is imperative that they understand the possible risks associated with conforming. Creating a solid support system of friends, family, and mentors can help you get the direction and insight you need to face the difficulties of striking a balance between sacrifice and personal accomplishment. Furthermore, following pursuits and hobbies outside of bowling can provide a much-needed feeling of purpose and identity outside of the game.

Positive deviance in bowling is best illustrated by bowlers who continue to practice in spite of severe pain and injury, disruptions to their family life, the risk to their health and safety, and a dogged pursuit of meaningless and impossible athletic goals.

Factors of Over-Conformity	Description	Example	Steps to Stop It
Fear of Judgment	Bowlers may conform excessively due to fear of being judged or criticized by peers or coaches.	Mike always imitates his teammates' bowling styles to avoid criticism, even if it doesn't suit him.	Encourage open communication and constructive feedback. Create a supportive team environment where mistakes are seen as opportunities for growth.
Lack of Confidence	Low self-esteem or self-doubt can lead to over-conformity as bowlers may not trust their own decisions.	Sarah constantly seeks validation from her coach and changes her approach based on their opinions.	Build self-confidence through skill development, mental training, and positive reinforcement. Encourage self-trust and decision-making.
Pressure to Fit In	Peer pressure within the bowling community can lead to conformity, as bowlers want to fit in and be accepted.	Tom feels compelled to use the same equipment as his teammates, even if it doesn't suit his playing style.	Promote individuality and diversity of styles within the team. Emphasize the importance of finding what works best for each player.
Coaching Authority	Over-reliance on coaching advice can stifle creativity and lead to over-conformity to the coach's methods.	Emily follows her coach's instructions to the letter, even when it feels unnatural for her.	Encourage a two-way dialogue between coaches and players. Coaches should adapt their guidance to suit individual strengths.
Fear of Failure	The fear of making mistakes and failing can lead to over-conformity as bowlers play it safe to avoid errors.	Jake always plays a conservative line, avoiding riskier shots, to prevent embarrassing mistakes.	Promote a growth mindset where failure is seen as a valuable learning experience. Encourage calculated risk-taking and experimentation.
Sporting Ethic Pressure	Pressure to adhere to the traditional values and norms of the sport, even at the expense of personal well-being.	Example: A bowler feeling compelled to practice excessively to meet societal expectations of dedication.	1. Promote a balanced approach that values well-being alongside success. 2. Encourage open discussions about the realities of the sport's demands.
Fear of Being Judged	Fear of being seen as not committed enough or "less than" other bowlers who conform to established norms.	Example: A bowler pushing through an injury to avoid being perceived as weak or not dedicated.	1. Create a culture where bowlers feel safe expressing their concerns and limitations. 2. Emphasize the importance of injury prevention and self-care.
Extreme Dedication Belief	Belief that extreme dedication and sacrifice are the only paths to success in the sport.	Example: A bowler believing that they must train every day, neglecting other life responsibilities.	1. Educate bowlers about the potential hazards of over-conformity and the importance of balance. 2. Encourage rest and recovery as essential parts of training.
External Recognition	Seeking external validation and recognition, often through conforming to societal or peer expectations.	Example: A bowler making sacrifices in their personal life to gain approval and admiration from others.	1. Promote intrinsic motivation and self-fulfillment as primary sources of satisfaction. 2. Celebrate achievements beyond the bowling alley to reduce the need for external validation.
Lack of Awareness	Bowlers may not realize the extent of their over-conformity and its impact on their health and life outside of bowling.	Example: A bowler unaware of the toll overtraining is taking on their mental and physical health.	1. Provide education and resources on recognizing the signs of over-conformity and its negative effects. 2. Encourage self-reflection and self-awareness through regular check-ins.
Social Pressure	Pressure from peers, coaches, or the bowling community to conform to established norms and expectations.	Example: A bowler feeling obligated to conform to teammates' training habits to fit in.	1. Foster a supportive environment that values holistic development and individuality. 2. Encourage open communication about the negative impacts of social pressure.

Table 9 - This table explores factors contributing to over-conformity in bowling, such as fear of judgment, lack of confidence, peer pressure, coaching authority, fear of failure, sporting ethic pressure, fear of being judged, extreme dedication belief, external recognition, lack of awareness, and social pressure. Each factor is exemplified, and practical steps to mitigate over-conformity are outlined. Solutions include promoting open communication, building self-confidence, embracing individuality, fostering a balanced approach, and encouraging intrinsic motivation. The concise guide emphasizes proactive measures to address over-conformity and foster a supportive bowling environment.

An all-encompassing strategy that incorporates communication, education, and a shift in the sport's culture is needed to end over-conformity among bowlers. Encouraging wellbeing, self-awareness, and the value of a balanced bowling strategy should be the main goals of this strategy.

The Attraction Of Positive Deviance In Bowling: Sacrifices, Identity, And The Dark Side

In bowling, positive deviance is a term used to characterize the tendency of players to follow rules and regulations without question out of a never-ending quest for achievement. Regretfully, their physical and emotional health are frequently sacrificed in the process. The positive deviance phenomenon has been exacerbated by recent headlines exposing instances of abusive behavior by instructors, who have authority over bowlers. Such behaviors can be harmful to bowlers, especially in their early adolescent years, when social, psychological, and physical development are greatly influenced by their contact with peers in sports. This raises questions regarding the potential repercussions of positive deviance as well as the sacrifices made by bowlers.

Three main motivations lie at the root of bowlers' positive deviance: the attraction of sensation, enjoyment, and experience. Bowlers may develop an addiction to the powerful feelings and pleasure that come from the adrenaline rush of competition or practice. Their universe can be consumed with bowling-related dreams, objectives, and aspirations, making it difficult for them to see beyond the sport's confines. Training and competition can provide a highly fulfilling physical and mental stimulus. For example, engaging in physical activity causes the brain to release endorphins, which enhance feelings of well-being. In addition, playing sports gives young bowlers a feeling of self-worth, improves their social interactions, and gives them a means of achievement. Driven by the heightened sensations and satisfaction they gain from the sport, many aspiring high-performance bowlers find that being a bowler becomes an integral part of who they are. The cultural elements, the relationships made with others, the pure joy of the activity, and the demanding stages of training and competition are all part of the all-encompassing experience. In a high-performance setting, positive deviation becomes the norm and becomes the way of life. But in sports, positive deviance frequently passes for devotion and commitment, making it difficult to distinguish between what is normal and abnormal. This is the point at which giving up important facets of life outside of sports, including family, friends, and even one's own health, can be dangerous. In the unique setting of high-performance sports, bowlers start to feel that their identity as bowlers would vanish if they didn't have their teammates, the rigorous training regimen, and the excitement of competition. They discover a feeling of purpose in pushing the boundaries of their bodies and develop close relationships with their peers via shared challenges. Their identity is shaped by their bowling, which becomes their defining feature. In the world of high-performance sports, where it's necessary to survive and reaffirm one's identity as a bowler, sacrifices become inevitable.

A careful balance is needed to navigate the intricacies of positive deviation. Support personnel, administrators, and coaches are essential in establishing an atmosphere that promotes bowlers' well-being. This means encouraging open communication, offering advice on how to preserve a healthy work-life balance, and swiftly and effectively handling any abusive actions. Encouraging bowlers to prioritize their overall growth and to identify the possible dangers of over-conformity is equally vital. Creating a support system that embraces hobbies and goals outside of bowling can help people feel like they have a purpose and identity that goes beyond achieving physical achievement.

Hypothetical examples

After years of training, Sarah has become a high-performance bowler. Her addiction to the sport is driven by the immense pleasure and sensation she derives from practicing and competing. She frequently sacrifices other aspects of her life, like her relationships and wellness, in order to pursue her lofty ambitions, which take up the majority of her time.

Michael, a young bowler, has recently entered high-level competitions. As he advances in rank and develops his abilities, he feels a sense of satisfaction and accomplishment. As a bowler, he has a strong sense of self, and his peers and instructors view his devotion to the game as beneficial qualities.

Over the course of several years, Emily has been a competitive bowler. She considers her fellow bowlers to be her second family because of the strong bonds they have formed. Though she feels that being a professional bowler is essential to her identity and sense of self-worth, she finds it difficult to give up other aspects of her life, such as spending time with her real family or engaging in other activities.

The Intersection Of Sport And Religion: Exploring Sacrifice And Devotion

In the thought-provoking book "If Christ Came to the Olympics," an intriguing comparison between religion and sport is used to explore the idea of over-conformity in sports. The statement implies that whereas religion instructs people to commit their lives to a higher force and make compromises in order to have a "normal life," the same principle applies to sports. In many ways, individuals devote their time, effort, and emotion to sport, which turns it into a dominant false deity. Since both religion and athletics are structured institutions with their own set of rules and customs, there is a close bond between them. Furthermore, they are both capable of imbuing their adherents with religious attributes from the heart and soul. Many bowlers have replaced conventional ideas of deity and religion with sport and the goal of victory. It develops into an ingrained, fundamental idea that serves as a motivator for them to identify their ultimate objectives and to form their wants. Star and superstar bowlers are like gods in the world of sports, controlling large crowds with their great charm and power. Furthermore, just like religious objects, sport has its own sacred symbols. These could include trophies, shields, titles, championships, or even the highly revered game balls.

Hypothetical examples

Good Example: Emily - The Devoted Bowler

Similarity to Religion: Emily has a strong passion for bowling. She sees the game as a means of achieving personal development and self-improvement, in the same way that people give their life to a greater power in religion. She views bowling as a means of fostering self-control, drive, and focus.

Description: Emily sticks to a rigorous training schedule, practices frequently, and actively seeks advice from mentors and coaches. She treats the sport with seriousness, appreciating its traditions and disciplines. In addition, Emily competes in events not only to win but also to push herself and gain a deeper understanding of her own strengths. Trophy and title are representations of her hard work and devotion, in her opinion.

Bad Example: Jason - The Fanatic Bowler

Similarity to Religion: Jason has developed an unhealthy obsession with bowling. It's similar to religious fanaticism, in which people lose sight of other facets of life and become too dedicated. He forgoes personal fulfillment, professional prospects, and even his health in order to further the sport.

Description: Jason ignores his friends and family in favor of bowling, which takes up all of his time and energy. He disregards his obligations and is prepared to go to any lengths to succeed, even lying or using unethical tactics. He no longer enjoys bowling because of his obsession with winning; instead, it's more important to him to keep up his reputation as a successful bowler. Like religious zealots whose lives center around their beliefs to an extreme and sometimes dangerous degree, his entire identity is enmeshed with bowling.

Understanding The Psychological And Emotional State Of Bowlers

In bowling, resilience is an essential quality because of the high failure rate and non-linear career development. Bowlers frequently have disappointments, such as dealing with injuries or not being selected for teams, squads, or trials. The resilience of bowlers' bodies and minds are crucial when they consistently push themselves to the limit. Bowlers often struggle with physical weariness, but emotional and mental exhaustion can also be very harmful to their general health. Young bowlers often live in constant fear of failing, which can negatively affect many aspects of their lives and cause stress and burnout that impedes their ability to advance in the sport. Anxiety in particular can be evoked by fear and cause negative feelings that might impair performance. There is a dearth of study on the fear of failure among children and adolescents, despite the critical role that sports play in their lives. According to studies, kids between the ages of 14 and 17 believe that failure will harm their sense of self-worth, ability to succeed, and emotional health. Additionally, emotions have a big impact on how well athletes perform in competitive sports. If young bowlers experience negative feelings like fear and anxiety due to sport, which are known to hinder performance, then putting their health first and avoiding unnecessary pressure could be the key to developing high-achieving bowlers.

Hypothetical example

Example 1: Sarah has been bowling for four years, at the age of sixteen. She trains for several hours nearly every day because she is incredibly dedicated to her sport. Sarah has a strong technical skill set and is in good physical shape. She does, however, frequently feel anxious before competitions and battles with her dread of failing. Since mental toughness is important, Sarah's coach has been helping her create techniques to control her anxiety and strengthen her resilience.

Sacrifices And Challenges In Bowling

The majority of social science study in the field of sport concentrates on adults and professional players, frequently ignoring the sacrifices made by younger people who are still improving their abilities. Early in life, when they are still learning the sport and developing their skills, bowlers must make the sacrifices necessary to become professional bowlers. Although youth bowling has drawn attention to stress and burnout, the particular sacrifices made by these young people have not yet been thoroughly investigated.

Bowlers give up things, especially when it comes to excessive conformity or positive deviation. Nevertheless, these are more often health-related sacrifices than they are giving up social life, education, or other social facets. It is important to prioritize bowlers' well-being for both short- and long-term results, as we may learn more about by delving deeper into the concept of sacrifice. Sports systems will be better able to meet the needs and goals of young bowlers if they have a greater understanding of their motivations, desires, and willingness to make sacrifices. More junior bowlers may be kept in high-performance programs for longer periods of time as a result, which will increase provincial teams' competitiveness and success. Sporting systems can adjust and cater to the specific demands of these bowlers by understanding why they play the sport and what motivates them to give up things in order to achieve their objectives.

It's critical to acknowledge the complex nature of bowlers' lives outside of the game. With this knowledge, sports organizations will be able to give young bowlers' well-being top priority while also considering the different facets of their lives that their bowling commitment may affect. We can assist young bowlers in finding a balance between their athletic endeavors and other significant areas, including education, family, and personal growth, by offering extensive support networks and fostering a supportive atmosphere. Promoting a holistic way of living will improve their performance on the lanes in addition to their general well-being.

In addition, it is necessary to reinterpret and reevaluate the concept of sacrifice in athletics. High-performance sports need sacrifice, but it's crucial to make sure that young bowlers make fair sacrifices that won't endanger their physical or mental well-being or hinder their overall development. Sports organizations can create an environment where bowlers may develop and reach their full potential as athletes and people by encouraging a healthier and more balanced attitude.

Social networks exist, as bowlers realized, both inside and outside of the game. Even so, they made it clear that high-performance sport was the center of most of their social networks. Bowlers entrenched in the high-performance lifestyle bonded with shared experiences at tournaments and intense training sessions, which helped to establish these connections. These relationships were important to the social life of Interviewees One and Three, for example.

Interviewee nine stated:

The same holds true for mingling. Being very involved in training and bowling obviously interferes with your social life. There's hardly any time left for anything else. Your life is taken over by sport, particularly when you're competing at a high level of performance. Simply said, there is less time for other facets of life.

My teammates and I get out a lot, and they've grown to be my best friends. In the sport, training full-time with them forges close bonds. We laugh together, and support one another through difficulties, and yet we also compete with one another. We have comparable difficulties and share the same ambitions, which makes our group close-knit. Among us, there is a strong sense of acceptance and comprehension.

Interviewee ten stated:

I met my boyfriend through bowling. He was my coach once, so he really knows the demands on time and effort. He understands the sacrifices I make for the sport, unlike my pals. I have to concentrate on my training and games, while others can party every weekend. My parents and boyfriend both genuinely get how committed I am.

High-performance sports demand sacrifices to be made in order to succeed, and bowling is no exception. It's interesting to note that bowlers frequently have to give up social possibilities in order to devote themselves entirely to their sport. Bowlers' engagement in the sport depends heavily on social contacts, which may be why a lot of them view their training sessions as their main socializing opportunities. Moreover, social variables have been found to be bowlers' main sources of motivation, highlighting the significance of social networks and well-being for their overall success and tenacity in the sport.

Many bowlers express the opinion that having additional time away from their demanding training and competition schedule would be extremely beneficial to their social life and personal relationships. High-performance sports inevitably include social compromises; bowlers frequently bemoan the lack of time they have for social events. This does not imply, however, that bowlers completely give up on social lives. Because they have little time for other things outside of bowling, many ambitious bowlers actually create social circles and friendships within their sport by combining their social interactions with their training. Fascinatingly, deviation is defined as behaviors, characteristics, or concepts that defy societal norms, according to the philosophy of positive deviance and over-conformity to sport. Social life are important to bowlers, especially those between the ages of 18 and 21, and they may see their classmates partaking in parties, drinking, and other common social activities. However, because their social lives are centered more around their sport and less around traditional social activities, bowlers who prioritize their sport may be seen as breaking from these social standards. Sporting systems can improve bowlers' performance and long-term results by prioritizing their well-being and acknowledging the social sacrifices they make. Sporting systems may effectively retain junior bowlers within high-performance programs for extended periods of time by providing for their needs and fostering an atmosphere that fosters their social and emotional well-being. This will boost the competitiveness and success of provincial teams.

Hypothetical examples

John is a twenty-year-old pre-elite bowler. He has been working diligently to become a professional bowler because he has always had a strong enthusiasm for the game. John is aware of the role that societal circumstances have had in his sporting success and tenacity, despite his advanced age. The majority of his time is spent practicing and interacting with his pals who bowl. John thinks that his drive and mental health are greatly influenced by his close bonds with his fellow bowlers. John recognizes that his commitment to the sport demands him to make social sacrifices, even if he occasionally feels left out when he observes his peers attending parties and other social events.

Sarah is a bowler who has competed at the highest level professionally for a number of years. She loves to spend time with her friends and family and has always been outgoing. Sarah is aware, nevertheless, that her dedication to the sport demands that she put her training and tournaments ahead of social events. Sarah has succeeded in striking a balance between her social life and her athletic responsibilities in spite of many obstacles. She makes time to spend with her friends and family after her tournaments and frequently invites them to see her compete. Sarah feels that her achievements and mental health as a professional bowler are largely due to her great support network.

Bowlers' families are also very important in their life. Their families help them in many ways, but the most important way is definitely the emotional support they give them. This assistance is a sharp contrast to the demands that bowlers frequently encounter from trainers and the sports world. Parents have a significant impact on their children's healthy athletic development, and bowlers are aware of the critical role parents may play in their achievement. Examining the effects of "pushy parents" on sport is crucial because bowlers all agree that their parents provided them with understanding and steadfast support.

This sentiment was echoed by three bowlers:

My folks are very kind and helpful. They have no expectations of me and don't place any pressure on me. They unconditionally support me no matter what, knowing that I set my own objectives and dreams. My happiness and wellbeing are their top priorities. Although they would be thrilled to see me succeed in bowling and represent my nation, they are more interested in my character than in my sporting prowess. They put my general well-being and happiness above anything else if the sport gets to the point where it becomes too much for me or negatively impacts me.

"My parents are concerned about my rigorous training schedule. My dad believed I was pushing myself too hard when I told him about my daily regimen, which included jogging, working out at the gym, swimming, and more running. I respectfully disagree, though, as their training isn't at the same level as mine. Even while I respect their viewpoints, I make choices based on what I think will benefit my own performance. Their opinion counts to me, even though they might advise against running or taking a break, but it doesn't change how I train."

Since my family was very involved in sports, even though I hadn't participated with them myself, I was exposed to the athletic world at a young age. But it wasn't until I was twelve or thirteen years old that I began to pursue athletics with my family as a serious hobby.

In high-performance sports, bowlers are held to extremely high standards due to the significant time commitment needed for both training and competition. Performance and concentration throughout practice and competition are also held to this degree of expectation. Building on the socializing aspect we covered before, bowlers often report feeling pressured to engage in less social activities. Many bowlers still experience pressure to avoid social interaction, even in situations where it may be appropriate or even permitted. This is a prime example of the impact of the sport ethic, which tells bowlers to over-conform social norms in order to succeed in their sport. They are frequently advised to give up everything in order to pursue their athletic goals. These aspiring bowlers are often subjected to expectations since outside factors and people's perceptions put pressure on them to pursue and stay dedicated to the sport. For example, "you sort of know what is expected of you" or "the expectation is that you want to be there to represent your country and be the best" are statements that bowlers frequently hear. One bowler stated :

> *My coach expects us to give the sport our full attention, therefore I frequently feel bad when I engage in hobbies other than bowling. I find it particularly challenging to meet this requirement as a young person and a university student.*

Beyond the training sessions, instructors have a lasting effect on the lives of bowlers. The goal of a coach-player relationship is to build a solid social link based on mutual respect for each other's professional and personal qualities. A bowler emphasized the impact of their coach and the demands made of them, saying:

> *Alcohol, partying, and energy-sapping pursuits like sunbathing must be avoided by athletes. After a day at the beach, coaches advise against players training because it might cause dehydration and hinder performance. Complete dedication is required for high-performance sports, and any hint of carelessness is met with criticism.*

Bowlers' lives are greatly influenced by their coaches, not just in terms of their overall lifestyle choices but also in terms of their technical and strategic growth. The relationship between a coach and player extends beyond the lanes; coaches take on the role of mentors and role models, impacting different facets of a bowler's life. Coaches try to provide bowlers the support and direction they need to overcome obstacles because they understand the sacrifices bowlers make and the demands put on them. One bowler stated:

> *According to my coach, I am always better than other bowlers. He continually searches for an explanation when I lose, thinking I must have erred. He never thinks about the potential that my rivals might just be superior. He'll look for any reason, such as if I was sick or trained too much. This is his way of handling defeat. Thus, it's never my fault if I lose—not because someone else could be better.*

Shaping Life Paths in Bowling

Athletes who want to compete at the highest levels must make enormous sacrifices in bowling. Their personal life and goals for the future are significantly impacted by these sacrifices. Many bowlers find themselves at a turning point in their lives, where big changes are made to their non-sporting trajectory. This is especially true for pre-elite bowlers who are considering post-secondary schooling options after leaving secondary school. During this critical time, their bowling commitments may have an impact on the decisions they make regarding their course of study.

Take the example of a bowler who at first thought he would like to become an engineer. But a seasoned national team player gave some insightful counsel, pointing out that it would be difficult to reconcile the demands of competitive bowling with such a demanding scholastic program. Following this advice, she thoughtfully decided to change her concentration and get a degree in sports coaching. She tried to achieve a balance by selecting a field that provided more latitude for training sessions and tournaments. Many pre-elite bowlers can relate to this story since they are going through a critical time in their lives, usually between the ages of 17 and 23. This is the time when the majority of young people finish their postsecondary education and start thinking about their future job prospects.

This transitional phase requires bowlers to maintain a delicate balance as they expertly negotiate the confluence of their academic and athletic goals. Key elements that allow them to succeed intellectually and athletically are flexibility and adaptability. The decisions individuals make during this pivotal time have a lasting impact on how their lives unfold and how they develop both personally and professionally.

Bowlers' steadfast dedication to their sport is embodied by the sacrifices and changes that come with this journey. It demonstrates their deep comprehension of the difficulties and requirements involved in rising to the top of the sport of bowling elites. Bowlers demonstrate their unwavering passion and steadfast desire to succeed in their chosen sector by reevaluating their educational choices and looking for alternatives that correspond with their athletic aspirations. These choices perfectly capture their fortitude and readiness to adjust to the particular requirements of their sporting career.

This sentiment was echoed by one bowler:

When I think back on my life in the ninth grade, before I started playing sports, I see how easily I could have gotten into trouble or, worse, ended up in jail. I would have taken the same route as many other teenagers, engaging in frivolous activities without any goals or direction.

Once again, the coach is the main figure and has a big say in how this bowler is expected to perform. Furthermore, a pair of bowlers reflected on a pivotal choice they made a full two years prior that had a significant influence on their athletic career and future opportunities.:

The speaker is not sure if she would have picked her current degree if she hadn't taken up bowling and gotten the scholarship to attend Wichita State University. Her mother persuaded her to apply to the university even though she wasn't initially interested in doing so. After being awarded the scholarship, she had to adjust to several changes in her field of study. Had it not been for bowling, the speaker probably would have followed through on her original intention to travel after graduating from college and possibly study landscape architecture—a course she had originally enrolled in but was discouraged from taking on top of her bowling obligations.

Bowlers need to understand that playing sports can have a significant impact on their goals and future results. For bowlers in particular, this knowledge is crucial because their life is shaped by the choices they make now, even after their athletic careers are over. This is particularly valid when bowlers have to move for the sake of their sport.

Financial Considerations

Financially speaking, it has been noted in a number of sports as well as among bowlers that monetary assistance is typically scarce in their respective activities. The only exception to this rule are some competitions, when teams or individual bowlers may get funds to help with travel costs:

Bowling presents hurdles to one's means of subsistence; one must be financially stable to survive. Making ends meet becomes essential; without it, it becomes hard to survive. Those around me suffer because of my incapacity to earn.

Financial strains frequently affect bowlers' parents and families in addition to themselves, especially if they are still living at home while transferring from high school to college. With their rigorous training schedules making it difficult for many bowlers to find time for work, the financial burden eventually falls on their parents. Interviewee Three brought this to light by outlining the difficulties bowlers and their families experience:

There are expenses associated with attending camps and competitions, which are usually borne by the people or their families. Whether it's age group competitions or traveling abroad to represent my nation, my parents pay for all of my costs. Our families also pay for our travel expenses.

In order to achieve their educational and professional objectives, bowlers frequently have to make substantial sacrifices, which can take many different forms. Devoting time to their sport is among the most frequent sacrifices. The arduous task of managing camps, competitions, and everyday training falls on this age group, potentially leading to extended absences from school. One bowler, for example, talked about how he missed a whole month of school because of the World Cup. He also had to take a week or two off school for the preparatory camps before competitions like the World Cup. Certain bowlers have turned to dropping or skipping classes in an attempt to better balance the demands of their school and sport. This puts them behind their colleagues in terms of graduating and earning a degree.

It was difficult to plan my final exam before Nationals. It's inconveniently located and falls on the day I'm leaving. To reduce the stress of flying, I intend to take the test in a school. But my job flexibility is hampered by the majority of my time being spent on bowling training. Financial hardship results from this, particularly in the summer when full-time employment is unfeasible. It is tough to obtain a work from 10 to 2 p.m. with training and gym sessions. Weekend competitions severely restrict my capacity to work, which makes paying the rent challenging and requires help from relatives. It becomes imperative to put money before social interactions. With the bowling championship in September three and a half weeks away and a return immediately before a test, things get worse, making it difficult to study and keep on top of things.

Bowlers frequently put their sports above everything else in their lives, with college coming in second. Their athletic careers are pursued concurrently with tertiary education, with the primary academic objective being to "just pass." But this emphasis on athletics has come at the expense of academic achievement. The difficulty of balancing sport and education is sometimes blamed for poor educational outcomes, and bowlers themselves admit that their sporting priorities have impacted their academic success.

Other sports

There comes a time when it's important to reflect and consider what one is doing. Making a choice when it appears that development is slow is difficult. Still, I have no regrets about the decision I made. I used to be banned from bowling, but now I enjoy it. I'm eager to work out freely now.

Relocating

A lot of bowlers and their families have chosen to move away from home in order to pursue chances in the field or in sports. Bowlers may experience stress, injuries, and mental illness as a result of such relocations. Nearly half of the study participants reported having symptoms of mental illness, which suggests that there may be a higher likelihood of mental disease among bowlers who have relocated for their sport, according to the results of the interviews. This emphasizes how important it is to have the right kind of support and expert guidance when moving for sports. Respecting bowlers' decisions if they don't feel ready to move is also essential, as this may be a difficult and daunting step for novice bowlers:

To enhance the bowling environment, I switched to a new club, becoming my sole training ground. Commuting between school and training entailed six daily trips, which became too burdensome. To ease the strain, my family decided to relocate closer to the club.

Goals vs. Injuries

As they provide bowlers the drive to keep going and pursue their sport, goals are essential in the life of pre-elite and perhaps all bowlers. Goals, however, are especially difficult to maintain when misfortune occurs, as in the case of accidents. Interviewee One talked about their experience dealing with injuries:

I have different goals now that I'm injured. My previous goal was to pursue the trail and get into the top team, but that never happened. I don't have any goals right now. Though the likelihood of my hope to serve my country is dubious, I still hold onto it.

Pre-elite bowlers, and perhaps all bowlers, have goals in their lives because they give them the drive to keep going and excel in their sport. But goals get especially hard to stick with when misfortune hits, such in the case of accidents. Interviewee One discussed his experience dealing with an injury.

The bowlers in this study learned that getting hurt could actually help them become stronger and more focused athletes. It gave them time for introspection and helped them identify their actual goals. Interviewee Six shared his experience:

I'm still committed to pursuing a career in high-performance sports, despite my injury. The injury, in fact, has strengthened my resolve to make a comeback and inspired me to put in more effort to reach my objectives.

Every respondent stated that they wanted to compete internationally, especially in the World and European Championships. Interviewee Four stated:

My main goal is to compete in Kuwait during the IBF World Championship in 2023. In addition, I have more modest but more urgent objectives for the upcoming year, such as competing in the Asian Championship in Thailand, which I believe will be a worthwhile experience.

Participants disclosed that life coaches and other support personnel are available to high-performance bowlers. These experts help bowlers develop a plan for their career, identify objectives, and set deadlines for reaching those objectives. Bowlers are able to maintain focus and have a clear understanding of the purpose and intent of their training with this methodical technique. Interviewee Four emphasized how this assistance marked a substantial advancement from the amateur to the pre-elite ranks.

Positive Deviance

Bowlers can lose sight of what is regarded as healthy drive and desire due to their extreme focus on their sport. To measure the amount of dedication and commitment among bowlers, all participants in the study were asked to list the sacrifices they would be willing to make for their sport. Interviewee One shared his perspective:

Attending nationals in 2018 meant I had to miss my best friend's wedding.

During the research, Interviewee One passionately exclaimed:

All the training and work I put in would have been for nothing if I had quit before nationals. The Nationals are the only way to get a chance to try out and advance in bowling. It was therefore imperative that I do well at nationals; otherwise, my efforts would have been in vain.

Interviewee One explains how positive deviance is strongly depicted:

Nothing else took precedence over it when I was bowling in Christchurch. My primary objective took up the majority of my time and energy, and that was bowling. I turned down everything that tried to get in the way of my commitment. It wouldn't make sense to give up or put anything else first after the sacrifices made.

This sentiment was echoed by Interviewee Two:

Everything is subordinate to sports, including my family. It's unquestionably my top priority, in line with interviewee three's declaration that bowling is their primary emphasis.

Although the sacrifices made by bowlers have been the main emphasis of this research, it's vital to remember that they also highlighted the numerous advantages and benefits of participating in high-performance sport. Interviewee No. 2 looked back on their childhood and educational experiences:

I was directionless at first and frequently got into problems at school. That being said, I sharpened my attention after learning about athletics. I started to use school as an escape, and sports gave me a way to let my energy out. My grades went up as a result, and I even won an award for making great academic progress.

Interviewee Four shared a similar outlook on sport:

My education has been considerably enhanced by sports, which have helped to balance academics and athletics. It has also resulted in university scholarships.

This sentiment was reinforced by Interviewee Three:

Playing sports has improved my organizing abilities since I put doing homework, internals, and school tasks ahead of football games. My objective is to complete my schoolwork as soon as possible, ideally on Sundays or after school, avoiding late evenings to guarantee enough sleep and avoid fatigue.

Interviewee Four stated that while high-performance sports put more financial hardship on athletes and cut down on time for professional development, they were not interested in the business side of sports:

My motivation is not money. I'm happy that bowling isn't a very profitable sport. Not for financial gain, but rather out of passion and fun.

Interviewee Four discussed the lessons she has learned in life and the exposure to high-performance sports:

I'm more interested in growing personally and gaining useful life skills than I am in winning only at sports. Bowling success is useless on its own, but when combined with personal development, it has substantial significance. My style is not idleness; I aim for significant achievements. Given my desire to succeed, sports looked to be the ideal way for me to achieve my goals.

Similarly, Interviewee Five commented on her determined and high-achieving personality:

Being a high-performance bowler is a way of life rather than just a sport. If I didn't bowl, I would focus on being a better student and leading a healthy lifestyle. Being fit is essential to who I am.

These quotations imply that leading an elite sporting lifestyle requires a particular personality type. These people seem to have a natural willingness to make sacrifices, as seen by the fact that they gladly accept the requirements of this way of life.

Interviewee Four provided a positive outlook on the life of a pre-elite bowler by sharing a range of unbiased thoughts and observations and emphasizing the benefits of making the sacrifices required to succeed:

I've learned useful skills that I can use on a daily basis because of my adventure. Being a committed and diligent person, which are traits valued in sports and other endeavors, I am always learning new things.

It can be challenging to comprehend why these people stick with their sport in the face of hardship when you first read about the costs and sacrifices involved in being a bowler. Interviewee Five described her personal periods of introspection and contemplation:

I ask myself why I put myself through such hard training sessions when I'm feeling discouraged and tired. However, I'm propelled onward by my love of bowling. I can get past problems by reminding myself why I enjoy the sport.

Interviewee Seven adds:

My identity has been fashioned by sports, which have also given me priceless connections and memories.

Athletes frequently have to make compromises in order to pursue a career in bowling, especially those who are not yet exceptional. Through interviews with pre-elite bowlers, researchers investigated the scope and motivations for these sacrifices. The results showed that these bowlers were prepared to sacrifice their social life, their family ties, and their future professions in order to succeed in their sport. Their financial status was also affected by this. Their own aspirations, coaches, and athletic organizations increased the pressure they were under. These bowlers were aware of the possible hazards, yet they were committed to their sport because they enjoyed training and competition, even if it meant defying expectations.

It's critical to create clear paths for high-performance growth and to offer post-sport career support in order to assist these bowlers. Pathway to Podium and similar programs can support bowlers' psychological well-being as part of their holistic growth. Enabling them to have access to life coaches and mental skills training will help them make better decisions, maintain their mental health, and strike a better balance between their personal and athletic lives. The financial and scholastic difficulties these bowlers endure, as well as the sacrifices they make, should be recognized and addressed by high-performance sports organizations. Some of these difficulties and the financial burden can be lessened by increasing financing and resources for pre-elite bowlers. Furthermore, providing bowlers with greater academic support as they pursue their sporting careers can help avoid dropout rates following high school.

"WANTING TO WIN" AND "NOT WANTING TO BE BEATEN"

In competitive settings, like bowling, the human will to prevail and avoid loss is common and natural. It's important to keep a healthy perspective on competition, though, and to stay clear of the boundary that separates constructive rivalry from unhealthy fixation. Anxiety, tension, and a loss of enjoyment in the competitive process might result from an obsession with winning. On the other side, the fear of losing may originate from a need for approval or a fear of failing, both of which can produce unfavorable feelings and actions. A more positive strategy may be to put more emphasis on personal development and progress rather than winning or not losing. In the long term, this strategy can help people improve their performance by allowing them to grow from their mistakes and acquire new abilities. Those who embrace this viewpoint can concentrate on their own growth and development, which increases happiness and cultivates a more positive outlook.

In terms of bowling, a bowler's psychological health can be significantly impacted by their will to succeed and their fear of failing. Psychology research has demonstrated the close relationship between these two ideas and how they influence people's behavior in competitive environments. Bowlers may be highly motivated to work harder, push themselves outside their comfort zones, and accomplish their objectives by the desire to win. It may have its roots in the desire for approval and acknowledgment, which can be a powerful source of inspiration for people to work hard to achieve their goals.

Furthermore, the feeling of satisfaction, confidence, and success that comes with winning can have a good effect on a bowler's self-worth and general well-being. But when the urge to win turns into an obsession, it can have unfavorable effects like tension, worry, and a loss of interest in the competition itself. An exclusive concentration on winning can also result in a restricted perspective on competition, where people may act unethically, compromise their morals, or cheat in order to succeed. A bowler's mental and physical health may suffer as a result of burnout, worry, and stress brought on by this pressure to succeed.

It's critical to place more emphasis on personal development and improvement than winning when bowling in order to keep a positive mindset. In the long run, this strategy can assist bowlers in improving their performance by helping them learn from their errors and acquire new abilities. Regardless of the competition's outcome, putting more of an emphasis on self-improvement might lead to a more fruitful and satisfying experience than an obsessive obsession with winning.

However, not wanting to be defeated by anyone can be the result of a need for control, a fear of failing, or a need for approval and recognition. The fear of failing can be a strong motivator for people to put in more effort and pursue their objectives. But it may also become troublesome if it causes one to focus too much on succeeding at all costs and avoid failure at all costs. This may cause people to adopt a risk-averse mindset in the face of competition, where they refrain from taking chances or attempting novel experiences out of fear of failing. Furthermore, unpleasant feelings like tension, anxiety, and low self-esteem can result from the fear of losing and can negatively affect a person's mental and physical health. It can also result in a bad attitude toward competition, where people start to disdain the advantages of competition altogether or grow resentful of others who succeed. Ultimately, how people approach competitive circumstances can be greatly influenced by both their drive to win and their fear of losing. While it is human nature to desire to succeed and avoid failure, it is crucial to keep a balanced view of competition and place a higher value on personal development and advancement than on winning or staying out of trouble. In the long run, this can help people learn from their mistakes, adopt a growth mindset, and produce better outcomes.

Myth: Winning at All Costs

This myth suggests that winning should be the sole focus of competitive bowlers, even if it means engaging in unsportsmanlike behavior or compromising values. In reality, ethical and sportsmanlike conduct should always be prioritized over winning.

Myth: Fear of Losing Equals Weakness

This myth implies that having a fear of losing or a fear of failure is a sign of weakness in competitive bowlers. In truth, these fears are natural and can be motivating factors, as long as they are managed in a healthy and constructive way.

Myth: Perfectionism Leads to Success

This myth suggests that perfectionism, driven by a fear of being beaten, is necessary for success in bowling. While striving for excellence is important, an excessive focus on perfectionism can lead to negative consequences such as stress and anxiety.

Myth: Winning Is the Only Measure of Competence

This myth implies that a bowler's competence is solely determined by their ability to win. In reality, competence in bowling encompasses various skills and aspects, and success should be measured by personal growth and improvement, not just winning.

Traits And Characteristics In Bowlers

Two psychological characteristics common among bowlers are the want to win and the fear of losing. Extremely competitive and driven, bowlers with a strong desire to win are often inspired by the rush of winning and the tangible sense of achievement it brings. They frequently have strong goals in mind and are prepared to put in a lot of effort and make sacrifices in order to get them. Bowlers who are afraid of losing are frequently fierce competitors as well, but their motivation comes from their dread of losing rather than their desire to win. They frequently have a strong sense of perfection, are extremely critical of their own work, and fear making mistakes or disappointing their team. They might also feel that they have to be in charge of every part of their performance in order to succeed, which could lead to a high desire for control. For bowlers, both of these qualities can be quite helpful because they can give them the drive and incentive to play better. If they are applied excessively, though, they may potentially have unfavorable effects. Overly competitive bowlers run the risk of acting unsportsmanlikely or aggressively, which can result in fines, suspensions, or even disqualification. Additionally, they can experience excessive tension or anxiety, which could harm their physical and emotional health.

A bowler's performance may suffer if they are unduly worried or stressed out due to their excessive focus on not losing. They could also start criticizing themselves or their teammates excessively, which might damage the trust within the team. In the end, bowlers need to find a way to balance their need to succeed with their fear of losing.

Bowlers are more likely to succeed in the long run and preserve their mental and physical health if they can keep a balanced view of competition and concentrate on bettering their own performance rather than just the final result.

Hypothetical examples:

John is an extremely motivated and competitive bowler. He is driven by the rush of winning and the sense of achievement it brings, and he has a great desire to succeed. He is very focused on his goals and is prepared to put in a lot of effort and make sacrifices in order to reach them. He approaches the game strategically, assessing the advantages and disadvantages of his rivals to maximize his own chances of winning. John has to learn how to use his competitiveness constructively, though, as he occasionally exhibits excessive aggression.

When it comes to bowling, Sarah is a perfectionist. She constantly aspires to perfection, is extremely critical of her own performance, and fears being defeated. Instead of being driven by a desire for success, she is driven by a fear of failing. She feels that in order to succeed, she needs to be in complete control of every aspect of her performance. Although Sarah is a really good bowler, she occasionally lets her fear of failing get in the way. She must learn to have faith in her abilities and put more emphasis on her own performance than on the game's result.

Neurological Responses: A Bowler's Journey Between The Pursuit Of Victory And The Avoidance Of Defeat

The general relationship between "Wanting to Win" and "Not Wanting to be Beaten" in a bowler is intricately woven into the neurological fabric, significantly influencing their long-term trajectory and performance outcomes. When a bowler harbors a fervent desire to win, the neurological response is marked by elevated stress, yet it is often adaptive. The activation of reward pathways, particularly the release of dopamine, propels the bowler with a positive motivational force, enhancing focus on goals and outcomes. Over time, this adaptive stress response fosters a growth mindset, resilience to setbacks, and an ability to view failures as opportunities for improvement. In contrast, the bowler grappling with an intense fear of losing experiences a chronic stress condition, triggering persistent activation of threat-related neural pathways, notably the release of cortisol. This chronic stress not only affects decision-making, emotional regulation, and cognitive functions but also hampers the consolidation of positive learning experiences and memories. Over time, the bowler's susceptibility to negative spirals and risk aversion may impede their adaptive response to challenges, hindering personal growth and diminishing overall well-being. Coaches and mentors play a pivotal role in guiding bowlers to maintain a balanced neurological state, ensuring that the desire to win remains a positive force for motivation while mitigating the detrimental impacts of an overwhelming fear of defeat. Tailored interventions, including stress reduction strategies and cognitive restructuring, can contribute to a more sustainable and adaptive neurological profile, fostering enduring success and fulfillment in the competitive world of bowling.

Aspect	"Wanting to Win"	"Not Wanting to be Beaten"
Stress Response	Elevated stress due to high stakes	Persistent stress due to fear of failure
Neural Pathways	Activated reward pathways (dopamine release)	Activated threat pathways (elevated cortisol)
Cognitive Impact	Enhanced focus on goals and outcomes	Heightened vigilance, potential cognitive overload
Brain Regions	Increased activity in reward-related areas	Over-activity in fear-related regions
Performance Impact	Improved performance under moderate stress	Performance fluctuations due to chronic stress
Adaptive Response	Positive stress adaptation, growth mindset	Difficulty adapting, risk aversion
Learning and Memory	Enhanced memory consolidation of successes	Impaired memory consolidation due to anxiety
Decision-Making	Willingness to take calculated risks	Tendency to avoid risks, decision hesitancy
Emotional Regulation	Balanced emotional responses	Difficulty regulating emotions, susceptibility to negative spirals
Resilience	Resilient to setbacks, views failures as opportunities	Vulnerable to setbacks, struggles to bounce back

Table 10 - This table explains the psychological aspects of "Wanting to Win" and "Not Wanting to be Beaten." The former involves elevated stress, enhanced focus, and positive stress adaptation. In contrast, the latter leads to persistent stress, potential cognitive overload, and difficulty adapting. Balancing emotional responses and fostering resilience are crucial for optimal performance.

Additional Context:

- **Wanting to Win:** The desire to win triggers a stress response, but it's often adaptive and performance-enhancing. Dopamine release in reward-related brain areas motivates the bowler, fostering a positive approach to challenges. Cognitive impact involves focused attention on goals, leading to improved decision-making under moderate stress.

- **Not Wanting to be Beaten:** The fear of losing induces chronic stress, affecting neural pathways associated with threat perception. Elevated cortisol levels may hinder cognitive functions, leading to difficulties in decision-making and emotional regulation. The brain's fear-related regions may dominate, impacting memory consolidation and resilience.

Understanding the nuanced neurological responses associated with these mindsets can aid in tailoring coaching strategies. For bowlers wanting to win, reinforcing positive stress adaptation and resilience is key. For those fearing defeat, interventions focusing on stress reduction and cognitive restructuring may be beneficial, fostering a more balanced and adaptive neurological state.

Theories And Differences

Researchers have researched the psychological issues of wanting to win and being afraid of losing a lot. Numerous ideas endeavor to elucidate the distinctions between these two motives. The achievement motivation theory, which was created by psychologists David McClelland and John Atkinson, is one idea that explains the drive to succeed. According to this hypothesis, people are driven by a different demand for achievement in order to feel motivated. Individuals who have a strong need for achievement are frequently driven by a strong desire to succeed and reach difficult objectives, such as taking first place in a competition. However, those who don't feel the need to succeed could be more driven by other things, like social standing or money gain, than by the desire to succeed. On the other hand, the Self-Determination Theory, which was created by psychologists Richard Ryan and Edward Deci, explains why people fear beatings. According to this idea, people have three basic psychological needs: relatedness, competence, and autonomy. People feel bad emotions like worry and anxiety when these demands are not satisfied. The fear of failing, which jeopardizes people's feeling of competence and autonomy, may be the root cause of the fear of being defeated. The emphasis on the result rather than the process is another distinction between the will to win and the fear of losing. The goal of winning is frequently centered on the result and the benefits that follow, such approval and recognition. On the other hand, the fear of losing is frequently concentrated on preventing failure and the bad effects that accompany it, such as humiliation and guilt. Different attitudes to competition can result from this difference in focus; those who place more emphasis on the outcome are more likely to act in an unsportsmanlike manner, while those who place more emphasis on the process are more likely to rise to the occasion and learn from their mistakes.

Hypothetical example 1 - "Wanting to Win"

Jessica is a competitive bowler with a strong drive for success. Her drive to succeed and reach difficult objectives drives her very hard. She is driven to succeed in every competition she enters and will stop at nothing to get there. Jessica dedicates hours of her day to practicing, improving her skills and assessing the advantages and disadvantages of her rivals. She is very motivated and competitive, and she enjoys nothing more than the rush of winning and the sense of success it brings. Jessica is largely concerned with the result, and in order to win, she is prepared to act aggressively in the lanes. She may face fines and disqualifications as a result of this, but it has also helped her win numerous competitions and establish herself as one of the world's top bowlers.

Hypothetical example 2 - "Not Wanting to Be Beaten"

As a professional bowler, Jack doesn't feel pressure to do well. His motivation comes from other sources, such as the social standing that comes with being a professional bowler, rather than from a strong desire to win. He is terrified of losing and getting defeated, though. Jack is quite critical of his own performance, and his main goal is to avoid failing. He gets extremely nervous and stressed out before tournaments because he fears making mistakes or disappointing his team. In order to avoid making mistakes, he plays it cautiously in the lanes and is not willing to take chances. The outcomes of this strategy have been average.

Theory	Description	Example of a Bowler
Achievement Motivation Theory	The Achievement Motivation Theory, developed by psychologists David McClelland and John Atkinson, digs into the innate desire to win. According to this theory, individuals possess varying levels of a need for achievement. Those with a high need for achievement are profoundly motivated by the pursuit of success and the challenge of accomplishing difficult goals, such as winning competitions. On the contrary, individuals with a low need for achievement may prioritize factors like social status or financial gain over the desire to win.	An excellent example of a bowler embodying the principles of the Achievement Motivation Theory whose outstanding performance can be attributed to a strong need for achievement.
Self-Determination Theory	The Self-Determination Theory, developed by psychologists Edward Deci and Richard Ryan, focuses on the fear of being beaten. This theory posits that individuals harbor three intrinsic psychological needs: autonomy, competence, and relatedness. When these fundamental needs are left unfulfilled, individuals often experience negative emotions such as anxiety and stress. The fear of being beaten may stem from a fear of failure, which directly threatens individuals' sense of competence and autonomy. To mitigate this fear, it becomes crucial to address these basic psychological needs.	A real-world example of a bowler grappling with the fear of being beaten, as described in the Self-Determination Theory is when they encounters situations where autonomy and competence are not met, they tend to experience heightened levels of anxiety and stress, impacting their performance.
Outcome vs. Process Focus	Another important distinction between the desire to win and the fear of being beaten lies in their focus. The desire to win tends to be outcome-oriented, placing heavy emphasis on the end result and the rewards that accompany it, such as recognition and validation. In contrast, the fear of being beaten adopts a process-oriented approach, concentrating on the avoidance of failure and the adverse consequences that it may entail, including embarrassment and shame. This disparity in focus often leads to different approaches to competition, with individuals who are outcome-focused potentially being more inclined to engage in unsportsmanlike behavior, while those who are process-focused tend to embrace challenges and use failures as learning experiences.	A bowler epitomizes the outcome-focused mindset, consistently striving for victories and the associated recognition. Conversely, they are is predominantly process-focused, eagerly tackling challenges and utilizing failures as valuable stepping stones towards improvement.

Table 11 - This table delves into psychological theories shaping a bowler's mindset. The Achievement Motivation Theory explores the innate drive to win, with examples of high and low achievement needs. The Self-Determination Theory focuses on the fear of defeat, linking it to unmet psychological needs. Lastly, the Outcome vs. Process Focus highlights distinct approaches, with an example of a bowler embodying both outcome and process orientations.

Personalities

Bowlers who have a strong desire to win are frequently motivated by a competitive spirit that stems from a desire for accomplishment and acknowledgment. These bowlers typically have a strong sense of purpose, exude confidence, and aren't afraid to take chances to accomplish their goals. They are driven by the rush of adrenaline that accompanies victory and flourish in high-stress environments. Bowlers who are motivated to win often possess a strong sense of self-efficacy or the conviction that they can succeed. These bowlers don't hesitate to take on new challenges since they have a strong belief in their own talents. Additionally, they frequently exhibit high levels of self-motivation since they are driven to raise their game and accomplish their objectives. In addition to being fiercely competitive, winning bowlers may come out as aggressive to their opponents. They can occasionally take chances that others might consider too risky and are eager to push themselves to their absolute limits. They also have a propensity to be overly preoccupied with the result and the benefits of victory, such as approval and recognition.

Conversely, bowlers who are afraid of losing are frequently driven by a fear of failing and a wish to stay away from bad outcomes. These bowlers may not have confidence in their skills and have a tendency to be quite critical of themselves. They could be extremely critical of their own work and perfectionists who worry a lot about making mistakes. They might therefore find it tough to take chances and reluctant to step outside of their comfort zone. Bowlers who have a fear of losing could also have trouble delegating and having trust. They could be reluctant to rely on teammates to assist them in achieving their objectives since they have a strong need for control. Additionally, they could be extremely sensitive to criticism and could react negatively to criticism. Because of this, it could be challenging for teammates and coaches to offer helpful feedback and collaborate to achieve a common objective.

Hypothetical Examples

Jane is a highly skilled bowler who is driven to succeed. She takes calculated risks to reach her objectives and does well under duress. She has a great sense of self-worth and faith in her own abilities. The acclaim and validation that come with victory are what drive Jane the most. She is goal-oriented and prepared to go above and beyond to accomplish her goals.

As a bowler, Tom worries about losing. He has little faith in his own abilities and is very critical of himself. Being a perfectionist, he takes great care to prevent errors. He can therefore find it challenging to take chances and step outside of his comfort zone. Tom has a strong need for control and has trouble with delegation and trust. He is quite sensitive to criticism, and when given criticism, he could react negatively.

Category	Wanting to Win	Not Wanting to Be Beaten
Motivation	Driven by a desire for achievement and recognition	Motivated by a fear of failure and a desire to avoid negative consequences
Personality	Highly goal-oriented, self-confident, and willing to take risks	Highly self-critical, may lack confidence in abilities, and hesitant to take risks
Approach to Competition	Focus on the outcome and the rewards that come with winning	Focus on avoiding failure and the negative consequences that come with it
Performance	Highly competitive and can be aggressive	May struggle with trust and delegation and may have a difficult time taking risks
Perception of Mistakes	View mistakes as opportunities to learn and improve	View mistakes as failures and may be overly critical of their own performance
Need for Control	May be willing to delegate and rely on teammates	May have a strong need for control and may be hesitant to rely on others
Sensitivity to Criticism	May be open to constructive criticism and feedback	May be highly sensitive to criticism and may become defensive
Mental and Physical Health	May become overly stressed or anxious	May become overly stressed or anxious
Long-term Success	More likely to achieve long-term success and maintain mental and physical well-being	May struggle with achieving long-term success and maintaining mental and physical well-being
Psychological Theory	Driven by a need for achievement (Achievement Motivation Theory)	Fear of failure (Self-Determination Theory)

Table 12 - This table explores contrasting motivations in bowling. "Wanting to Win" bowlers are goal-oriented, confident, and embrace risks for achievement. Conversely, "Not Wanting to Be Beaten" bowlers fear failure, leading to hesitancy and critical self-perception. Their competition approach, response to mistakes, and need for control differ. Mental and physical health challenges may arise, influencing long-term success and aligning with psychological theories of achievement and fear of failure.

Generally, distinct motivations and attitudes to competition distinguish the mindsets of bowlers who dread losing from those who want to win. Bowlers who are driven to win are typically fiercely competitive, self-assured, and driven by a desire for success; conversely, bowlers who are afraid of losing may have difficulties with trust, confidence, and delegation. Coaches and teammates can collaborate with bowlers to create methods for enhancing performance and succeeding in the competitive setting by being aware of these distinctions.

THE GOLDEN ATTITUDE TO START WINNING

Sports: The Winning Attitude

Before bowlers can start acquiring the necessary mental abilities to compete at the elite level, they must adopt the proper mindset toward their bowling activities. This mindset concentrates on two things. First, their perspective on competition: their thoughts and feelings about it. Secondly, their perspective on winning and losing: how they interpret these terms and whether they are aware of the crucial responsibilities they each play in improving as a bowler. They will be more equipped to succeed in the mental game and reach Elite level when they make these two aspects of their mindset clear.

Attitude Toward Competition

They might be interested in sports. They might invest a lot of energy in their preparation and competitive endeavors. As a result, each time they compete, they risk damaging their ego. They get frustrated when they don't bowl well. While this may not feel pleasant, it makes sense because it shows that they are passionate about their sport.

But there comes a point where their attitude toward their sport can become toxic and affect their bowling. The term "too zone" is the main warning sign. Although they don't want to care "too" much, they do want to be concerned about their bowling involvement. They want to work hard to accomplish their goals, but they don't want to try too hard; they want their bowling technique to matter to them, but not too much.

In the "too zone," people's self-esteem is unduly correlated with their performance, meaning that their bowling performance has an excessive impact on how they feel about themselves as people. They have lost perspective on the significance of bowling as a sport in their lives if they find themselves in the "too zone." They ought to reconsider the significance of bowling for them and the ways it affects their quality of life. They'll likely discover that it affects their self-perception too much. When this occurs, individuals may discover that their sport is no longer enjoyable for them in addition to bowling poorly (because of the excessive pressure they feel when their self-esteem is at stake).

A competitive mindset at the elite level necessitates maintaining perspective when bowling. They must maintain healthy bowling participation in their lives in order to bowl their best and have pleasure. Although it might be crucial to them, it shouldn't be a life-or-death decision. Their lives should revolve around sports, not around life itself. Recall their motivations: it's enjoyable, they enjoy the exercise, the companionship, the sense of accomplishment upon mastering a new skill, and, yes, they enjoy competing and taking first place. They will enjoy competing more, bowl better, and have a higher chance of succeeding if they have fun, work hard, love the process of their sport, and don't care too much about winning or losing.

Mental Plan: Attitude Toward Competition for Bowler

Stage 1: Self-awareness and Recognition

Drills: Reflective Journaling: Encourage the bowler to maintain a journal, noting emotions and thoughts after each competition.

Steps: Example: Write down feelings of frustration after a subpar performance.

Cues: Internal Cues: Pay attention to emotional responses and thoughts post-competition.

Stage 2: Identifying the "Too Zone"

Drills: Mindfulness Meditation: Practice mindfulness to observe thoughts and emotions without judgment.

Steps: Example: During meditation, notice when thoughts about performance start dominating.

Cues: Awareness Cues: Recognize when thoughts shift from healthy concern to excessive preoccupation.

Stage 3: Shifting Perspective

Drills: Values Clarification Exercise: Define the broader values associated with bowling beyond winning.

Steps: Example: List reasons why bowling is enjoyable, including exercise, companionship, skill mastery, and competition.

Cues: Motivational Cues: Remind themselves of the intrinsic joys associated with the sport.

Stage 4: Fun and Process-Oriented Mindset

Drills: Visualization Techniques: Imagine a successful and enjoyable bowling experience.

Steps: Example: Visualize a competition where enjoyment and process take precedence over winning or losing.

Cues: Positive Affirmation Cues: Use affirmations focusing on enjoyment, improvement, and the pleasure of the process.

Stage 5: Balanced Competition Perspective

Drills: Goal Setting: Establish performance-based goals that emphasize improvement rather than just winning.

Steps: Example: Set a goal to focus on improving a specific aspect of their technique rather than winning.

Cues: Goal-oriented Cues: Redirect emphasis from outcomes to personal development goals.

Stage 6: Maintaining Joy and Perspective

Drills: Gratitude Practice: Express gratitude for the positive aspects of bowling after each competition.

Steps: Example: Acknowledge the enjoyment of the exercise, camaraderie, and personal growth.

Cues: Gratitude Cues: Cultivate a mindset of appreciation for the holistic experience of the sport.

Stage 7: Integration and Reflection

Drills: Periodic Review: Schedule regular reviews to assess mindset and make adjustments.

Steps: Example: Reflect on whether the balanced mindset was maintained and if adjustments are needed.

Cues: Reflection Cues: Evaluate the ongoing balance between competition, joy, and personal growth.

Note: This mental plan is designed to guide the bowler through a progressive journey of self-awareness, perspective shift, and the cultivation of a balanced mindset toward competition. Regular practice of these drills, steps, and cues will contribute to a healthier, more enjoyable, and successful competitive bowling experience.

Hypothetical examples

Example 1: The Overzealous Competitor

Bowler A, deeply passionate about the sport, inadvertently enters the "too zone." Their self-esteem becomes excessively tied to bowling performance, turning each match into a high-stakes endeavor for validation. To regain a healthier perspective, Bowler A should reassess the role of bowling in their life, reconnect with the joy and intrinsic motivations, and ensure that winning doesn't overshadow the enjoyment of the sport.

Example 2: The Perfectionist Undermined

Bowler B, driven by a perfectionistic mindset, sees bowling as a relentless quest for flawlessness. This pursuit diminishes the joy of the game, as every mistake becomes a personal failure. To break free from the "too zone," Bowler B must shift their focus to embrace the process, find fulfillment in incremental progress, and understand that perfection is not the sole measure of success. This mindset shift will rekindle the enjoyment in bowling and contribute to a healthier attitude toward competition.

Attitude Toward the Ups and Downs of Sport

They also need to acknowledge and embrace bowling's ups and downs if they want to reach the Elite level. Very few bowlers in bowling history have had a perfect or nearly perfect season: Parker Bohn, Norm Duke, Earl Anthony, Walter Ray William, and Jason Belmonte. It happens to even the best bowlers. They ought to anticipate having them as well, given that they do. What matters in bowling is not if they experience ups and downs, but rather the magnitude of those fluctuations and their reaction to them. This blog series is actually dedicated to helping them minimize the highs and lows associated with sports.

It's simple to become irritated, hostile, and despondent over a rough patch. They could feel incredibly frustrated with their performance and powerless to alter it. Maybe they just want to give up. Still, none of these emotions will enable them to achieve their main objectives: ending the slump and playing at a high level once more. It is this ability that distinguishes the elite bowlers. The top bowlers know how to swiftly regain their form.

What is their method for doing this? First of all, they maintain their composure during the slump, understanding that it is a normal and expected aspect of bowling. They don't feel as pressured to come back to their previous level of play right away, which actually keeps them in the hole longer, and they also don't get too agitated. Additionally, it keeps people upbeat and inspired. Above all, no matter how hard things get, never give up and always put forth your best effort. Outstanding bowlers seek out the reason behind their slump and then work to solve it. Their down periods will be shorter and they will return to an up phase faster if they keep this mindset regarding the ups and downs of bowling.

Hypothetical examples

Example 1: The Adaptive Competitor

In pursuit of Elite status, Bowler A, inspired by the experiences of bowling legends, approaches the sport with a keen understanding of its inherent ups and downs. Rather than being disheartened by challenges, Bowler A anticipates them, recognizing that resilience is key. This adaptive mindset focuses not on the occurrence of fluctuations but on managing their magnitude and responding effectively.

When faced with a rough patch, Bowler A avoids succumbing to irritation or despondency. Instead, they maintain composure, understanding that slumps are a normal aspect of bowling. The pressure to immediately return to peak performance is eschewed, allowing for a more measured and effective recovery. This approach not only keeps Bowler A upbeat and inspired but also shortens the duration of their down periods, ensuring a quicker return to an upward trajectory.

Example 2: The Resilient Performer

Bowler B, recognized for resilience in the bowling community, acknowledges the inevitability of ups and downs on the journey to Elite level. Drawing inspiration from the experiences of bowling icons, Bowler B sees challenges as opportunities for growth. The resilient performer understands that success in bowling is not defined by the absence of setbacks but by the ability to swiftly overcome them.

When encountering a challenging phase, Bowler B avoids giving in to frustration or hostility. Maintaining composure, they recognize that slumps are a normal and expected aspect of the sport. The pressure to immediately return to previous performance levels is rejected, ensuring a more thoughtful recovery. This resilient mindset not only keeps Bowler B optimistic and motivated but also facilitates shorter down periods, allowing for a quicker return to the pinnacle of their bowling performance.

Mental plan for managing the ups and downs:

1. Embracing the Rollercoaster:

Drills: Reflection *Journaling: Regularly journal about your bowling experiences, noting both successes and challenges. Weekly Reflection Sessions: Dedicate time each week to reflect on your overall bowling journey.*

Steps: *Schedule dedicated reflection time. Be honest and open in your reflections.*

Cues: *Establish a cue, like setting a reminder on your phone, to prompt reflection sessions. Develop positive affirmations to reinforce acceptance of the sport's fluctuations.*

2. Resilience Building:

Drills: Resilience Training *Visualization Exercises: Picture yourself overcoming obstacles and bouncing back from setbacks. Controlled Adversity: Intentionally expose yourself to controlled challenges to build resilience.*

Steps: *Incorporate visualization exercises into your routine. Gradually increase the difficulty of challenges to build resilience.*

Cues: *Create a visual cue, like a resilience symbol, to remind yourself of your ability to overcome challenges. Develop a mantra or phrase to boost resilience during tough moments.*

3. Maintaining Composure:

Drills: Mindfulness Techniques *Deep Breathing: Practice deep breathing exercises to stay calm under pressure. Body Scan Meditation: Perform a body scan to release tension and maintain composure.*

Steps: *Integrate mindfulness exercises into your pre-game routine. Use mindfulness techniques during high-stress situations.*

Cues: *Associate a specific breathing pattern with maintaining composure. Develop a mental checklist for a quick body scan during challenging moments.*

4. Understanding Slumps:

Drills: Performance Analysis *Video Analysis: Record and analyze your performance to identify technical issues. Data Tracking: Keep statistics to recognize patterns during slumps.*

Steps: *Regularly review performance recordings. Track key performance metrics consistently.*

Cues: *Develop a checklist for performance analysis to ensure a systematic approach. Associate a specific cue, like reviewing stats, when entering a slump analysis mode.*

5. Never Give Up Mentality:

Drills: Goal Setting for Persistence *Process-Oriented Goals: Set goals focused on consistent effort and improvement. Long-Term Vision: Define your long-term vision to reinforce persistence.*

Steps: *Establish a mix of short-term and long-term goals. Emphasize continuous effort in goal setting.*

Cues: *Create visual cues, such as goal-oriented symbols, to reinforce persistence. Develop a mantra that embodies the spirit of never giving up.*

6. Swift Recovery Mindset:

Drills: Visualization for Quick Recovery *Mental Rehearsal: Visualize successful comebacks in detail. Positive Affirmations: Use affirmations to cultivate a positive recovery mindset.*

Steps: *Integrate visualization sessions into your routine. Practice positive affirmations daily.*

Cues: Associate a specific cue, like a recovery phrase, with visualizing successful comebacks. Develop a routine of affirmations during challenging periods.

These detailed drills, steps, and cues aim to provide a comprehensive framework for bowlers to enhance their mental resilience, composure, and persistence, ultimately managing the ups and downs of competitive bowling with a positive and proactive mindset.

Attitude Toward Love and Fun

It's simple to forget why they compete. There's the rivalry, recognition, accolades, and focus. However, they risk losing sight of the more significant internal motivations behind their training and competitiveness if they become fixated on the outside advantages of bowling. They won't bowl as well and they might not have as much fun. They must remind themselves of the fundamentals of bowling when this occurs. Participating in bowling should focus on two things. Let's start with love: love for the game, love for other people, and love for oneself. They have an opportunity to reach the elite level if they have a passion for their sport.

Secondly, athletics ought to be enjoyable. It should be enjoyable to work hard, improve, compete fiercely, and take pleasure in the process whether you win or lose. They will love playing and probably bowl their best if they never forget that sports are about love and having fun.

Hypothetical examples

Example 1: The Passionate Competitor

Bowler A, driven by a passion for the sport, understands the importance of maintaining the right attitude toward love and fun in bowling. Amidst the pressures of rivalry, recognition, and accolades, Bowler A guards against losing sight of the internal motivations that fuel his training and competitiveness. He recognizes that fixation on external advantages may compromise his performance and diminish the joy he derive from the game.

In moments of distraction, Bowler A refocuses on the fundamentals of bowling, emphasizing love for the game, for others, and for oneself. This love becomes the foundation for reaching the elite level. Bowler A understands that a genuine passion for the sport is a powerful driving force, contributing not only to skill development but also to sustained enjoyment on the lanes.

Example 2: The Joyful Athlete

Bowler B, embodying the spirit of enjoyment in athletics, prioritizes love and fun in his approach to bowling. Amidst the competitive pressures and the pursuit of excellence, Bowler B recognizes the risk of forgetting the fundamental reasons for participating in the sport. The reminder is clear: bowling is about love and having fun.

When the allure of external rewards tempts distraction, Bowler B grounds himself in the idea that sports should be enjoyable. The pleasure derived from hard work, improvement, and fierce competition, regardless of victory or defeat, becomes the driving force. By never losing sight of the fundamental joy in playing, Bowler B not only loves the game but also consistently bowls at his best, achieving a harmonious balance between competitiveness and pure enjoyment.

Mental plan for managing winning and losing:

1. *Understanding Control and Redefining Success:*

Drills: Self-Reflection and Goal-Setting Reflect on past performances and emotions associated with winning and losing. Set performance-oriented goals within their control (effort, focus, enjoyment).

Steps: Regularly engage in self-reflection to understand personal perceptions of success. Establish clear, controllable goals for every practice session and competition.

Cues: Develop a cue, like a deep breath, to refocus on controllable aspects during a match. Use a specific phrase, such as "My best effort is my success," to reinforce the new definition of success.

2. *Shifting Focus from Outcome to Effort:*

Drills: Mindfulness and Performance Journaling Practice mindfulness to stay present during matches. Maintain a performance journal to track efforts, regardless of outcomes.

Steps: Integrate mindfulness techniques into pre-game routines. Regularly journal about the positive efforts made during training and competition.

Cues: Establish a cue word or gesture to bring attention back to the present moment. Use a specific cue, like a reflective phrase, to appreciate efforts over outcomes.

3. *Embracing Both Wins and Losses for Development:*

Drills: Growth Mindset Visualization Visualize success as continuous improvement and overcoming challenges. Mentally embrace both victories and losses as opportunities for growth.

Steps: Include growth-oriented visualization in mental preparation. Celebrate small victories in development, not just match outcomes.

Cues: Develop a cue to redirect focus to personal growth during moments of frustration. Use a phrase, such as "Every challenge is a step forward," to reinforce the growth mindset.

4. *Balancing Success and Guarding Against Complacency:*

Drills: Performance Review and Goal Adjustment Regularly review performances, identifying areas for improvement. Adjust goals based on continuous improvement rather than just winning.

Steps: Set aside time for post-match performance reviews. Update goals to maintain challenge and prevent complacency.

Cues: Use a cue to prompt a critical evaluation of performance after each competition. Develop a phrase, like "Challenge breeds improvement," to encourage goal adjustment.

5. *Learning from Losses and Building Resilience:*

Drills: Loss Analysis and Resilience Exercises Analyze losses to pinpoint areas for improvement. Engage in resilience-building exercises to bounce back from setbacks.

Steps: Conduct a thorough analysis after each loss, focusing on learning opportunities. Integrate resilience exercises into regular mental training routines.

Cues: Establish a cue to prompt a positive mindset shift after a defeat. Use a phrase, such as "Learn and grow," to reinforce the resilience-building process.

6. *Appreciating the Journey:*

Drills: Gratitude Practices and Reflection Cultivate gratitude for the journey, regardless of specific outcomes. Reflect on personal growth and enjoyment derived from the sport.

Steps: Regularly practice gratitude for the privilege of participating in competitive bowling. Reflect on the positive aspects of the journey after each competition.

Cues: Develop cues to bring attention to the broader journey during challenging moments. Use phrases like "Grateful for the journey" to reinforce a positive perspective.

This mental plan aims to help bowlers cultivate a balanced attitude toward winning and losing, emphasizing personal development, effort, and resilience over solely outcome-based success. By incorporating these stages, drills, steps, and cues into their mental preparation, bowlers can foster a healthier mindset, leading to sustained success and enjoyment in competitive bowling.

They will get perspective on their sport that will enable them to play at an elite level, bowl their hardest, and have a great time if they can cultivate these attitudes regarding their sports lives.

Attitude	Description	Good Attitude Example	Bad Attitude Example	Building the Attitude
Attitude Toward Competition	This attitude reflects a bowler's perspective on the importance of competition in their sport. It involves finding a balance between valuing competition and not letting it become all-consuming.	Chris values competition but doesn't make it life-or-death. He enjoys the competitive aspect of bowling and recognizes it as a path for personal growth.	Becoming overly obsessed with winning to the point of extreme anxiety. A focus on winning that negatively impacts overall well-being.	Encourage a balanced view of competition. Emphasize the enjoyment of the game, camaraderie with teammates and opponents, and personal growth. Promote a mindset where winning is a goal but not the sole measure of success.
Attitude Toward the Ups and Downs of Sport	This attitude pertains to how a bowler deals with the inevitable challenges and setbacks in their sport, including performance slumps and difficult periods.	Dave approaches ups and downs with resilience. He remains positive, seeks opportunities for improvement, and uses setbacks as valuable learning experiences.	Getting frustrated, angry, and considering giving up when facing difficulties. Allowing setbacks to negatively impact motivation and self-esteem.	Teach the importance of maintaining perspective during downs. Encourage a growth mindset where challenges are seen as opportunities for learning and improvement. Provide strategies for staying resilient and seeking solutions during tough times.
Attitude Toward Love and Fun	This attitude relates to a bowler's emotional connection to the sport. It emphasizes the importance of love for the game and the fun aspects of participation.	James has a deep love for bowling and finds joy in the process. He values the social aspect and actively seeks ways to make the game enjoyable.	Losing sight of the love and fun aspects, focusing solely on external benefits like awards and recognition. Neglecting the enjoyment of the game and the social bonds formed through bowling.	Encourage bowlers to reflect on their initial passion for the sport. Create a positive and inclusive team environment that fosters camaraderie and shared enjoyment of the game. Emphasize that success includes both love for the sport and having fun during every aspect of participation.
Attitude Toward Winning and Losing	This attitude determines how a bowler defines success and failure. It encourages focusing on controllable aspects like effort and personal growth rather than just winning.	Lindsay values the process and learning from both wins and losses. She doesn't let outcomes define her self-worth and prioritizes effort, improvement, and enjoyment.	Defining success solely by winning, leading to complacency when winning frequently. Neglecting personal growth and learning opportunities from losses.	Teach that success is in effort, personal improvement, and enjoyment, not just winning. Emphasize the learning opportunities presented by both winning and losing. Encourage a mindset that views both outcomes as part of the journey towards becoming a better bowler.

Table 13 - This table explains bowlers' attitudes and their impact on performance. Positive examples include valuing competition without obsession and embracing ups and downs with resilience. Negative attitudes involve becoming overly obsessed with winning and letting setbacks impact motivation. Building a positive attitude includes emphasizing the enjoyment of the game, fostering resilience during challenges, and defining success beyond mere victories.

BOWLERS' BRAIN PERFORMANCE OPTIMIZATION

One can't improve what one can't measure.

There has never been more rivalry and a desire to succeed than there is right now in human history. In most competitive sports, the science of maximizing athletes' physical performance is the first priority and it excels in this area. To maximize an athlete's performance, it is simpler to apply exact sciences like chemistry, physics, anatomy, physiology, and bio-kinetics.

The mental aspect of performance optimization is where the majority of elite athletes and sports teams still struggle. Sportspeople competing in world championship events continue to exhibit a lack of emotional control, exhibit a lack of big match temperament, fail to work as a team, miscommunicate, cost their teams penalties for breaking the rules, show disrespect for the referees, become demotivated, and the list goes on.

Sports organizations and coaches may not be aware of what constitutes a winning mental strategy, which could explain why they pay less attention to their athletes' mental optimization. It is also thought to be "fuzzy" and less precise.

Sporting individuals and teams may only get a greater competitive edge in the sports world by outwitting, outlearning, and out-creating their rivals. The brain's primary functions include thought, learning, and creativity. This puts emotional intelligence and mental toughness at the top of the success ladder and puts neuroscience at the core of professional sport.

Every athlete has a unique method of thinking, learning, and producing. An effective mental strategy for enhancing athletes' mental performance should include a thorough grasp of their individual neurological makeup, an awareness of the factors influencing their brain function, and the emotional intelligence skills required to comprehend and effectively manage both others and oneself. This is the secret to optimizing performance and maximizing potential.

6 Drivers That Optimize Brain Performance

The capacity of the brain to learn, think, and create is limitless. World-class bowlers sometimes don't seem to be performing at their best because they lack certain qualities, such as brain fitness, the ability to handle stress, appropriate eating habits, adequate mobility, optimistic mindsets, and restful sleep patterns. It is imperative that coaches and bowlers understand how these drivers affect their bowler's neurological design and brain function in order to teach them how to optimize it.

A bowler who is not brain-fit may experience issues with hand-eye coordination or experience a brief decrease in their natural muscular speed. Just as vital as physical fitness is mental fitness. Even if a bowler is mentally fit, exhaustion (from inadequate stress management, poor sleep habits, a negative mindset, or eating the wrong foods) will counteract that mental fitness and cause certain brain regions to "switch off" (become less sensitive).

Driver	Description	Benefit Neurologically to the Brain	Good Example	Bad Example
Brain Fitness	Maintaining cognitive health and mental agility.	Improved neural plasticity and faster processing speed	A bowler regularly engages in brain-training exercises.	A bowler neglects mental exercises and becomes mentally sluggish.
Stress Coping Skills	Managing and reducing stress effectively.	Reduced cortisol levels, decreased anxiety, and better focus	A bowler practices relaxation techniques before competitions.	A bowler becomes overwhelmed by stress and performs poorly under pressure.
Good Sleeping Patterns	Consistently getting quality sleep.	Enhanced memory consolidation, improved mood, and increased alertness	A bowler ensures 7-9 hours of uninterrupted sleep before tournaments.	A bowler frequently stays up late and suffers from sleep deprivation.
Sufficient Movement	Regular physical activity and exercise.	Increased blood flow to the brain, enhanced mood, and reduced stress	A bowler incorporates regular workouts into their training routine.	A bowler leads a sedentary lifestyle and experiences decreased cognitive function.
Positive Mind-Sets	Cultivating a positive and growth-oriented mindset.	Elevated dopamine and serotonin levels, improved motivation	A bowler maintains a resilient attitude and views failures as opportunities to learn.	A bowler has a defeatist mindset and easily gives up after setbacks.
Healthy Eating Habits	Nourishing the body with proper nutrition.	Improved brain function, enhanced focus, and reduced inflammation	A bowler follows a balanced diet rich in brain-boosting nutrients.	A bowler frequently consumes processed foods and sugary snacks, affecting cognitive performance.

Table 14 - These drivers are essential for bowlers to maximize brain function. Developing positive habits in each of these areas will help you make better decisions, think more clearly, and perform better all-around the bowling alley.

Fit is essential. A bowler becomes intensely committed and naturally driven to compete when their inherent brain makeup and style of play are in harmony. From a neuroscience standpoint, bowlers' excitement fuels their bodies and minds by producing essential neurotransmitters that promote energy health and enhanced performance. Playing a sport in accordance with their neural makeup will consequently enhance their mental well-being and capabilities, making them more competitive and productive.

The conditions are right for a bowler's performance to suffer when there is a mismatch between their neurological makeup and style of play. From a neurology standpoint, this will lead individuals to create inhibitory substances, which will function as poor brain fuel and consequently weaken their immune system and sap their vitality.

For instance, a right-handed bowler who dominates with his left eye may experience a visual neurological impairment due to insufficient brain function or exhaustion, which could have a major adverse impact on his game performance and possibly result in a loss for the team.

Bowlers and their coaches need to be fully aware of their lateral dominance, expressive/receptive preference, rational/emotional preference, figurative brain language preferences, genetic combination of brain hemisphere dominance, eye, ear, and hand dominance, and intelligence preferences in today's competitive world. Few bowlers and instructors genuinely comprehend this about themselves and how to maximize their brains' special neurological makeup.

Emotional Intelligence

Advances in brain science have led to a greater understanding of the role emotions play in poor performance, thought, and action. More knowledge is known regarding the relationship between the emotional, social, and cognitive regions of the brain as well as the consequences of their being out of synchrony.

Emotional intelligence appears to be more important than ever, according to research. Because of the significant advancements in the world of competitive bowling in recent years, personal qualities like optimism, resilience, and motivation have become increasingly crucial. Cognitive capacities are inhibited in the absence of certain emotional intelligence traits.

For example, a bowler's capacity to digest information and make wise decisions decreases as he grows agitated. Three qualities set one bowler's performance apart from another: self-motivation, self-management, and realistic self-confidence.

These are the elements and proficiencies of emotional intelligence that are essential for success in sports. Cognitive aptitude is necessary for thinking, learning, and creativity. These cognitive capacities degrade in the absence of emotional intelligence. The basis for optimal mental and physical health, cognitive aptitude, and physical performance is emotional intelligence.

Emotional intelligence (EI), not cognitive intelligence (IQ), appears to be one of the most significant indicators of human potential, according to brain studies. Outstanding bowlers are distinguished not only by their individual accomplishments but also by their ability to function successfully in groups. As a bowler climbs the success ladder, all facets of emotional intelligence become increasingly important.

Importance Of Emotional Intelligence (Ei) For Elite Bowlers:

<u>Managing frustration and disappointment:</u> Even professional bowlers feel disappointment and frustration when they don't perform to their full potential because the sport may be difficult. But those with high EI can control their emotions in these kinds of circumstances, remaining composed, optimistic, and focused. Negative emotions don't have an impact on their work or the dynamics of the team.

<u>Building and maintaining team cohesion:</u> Teams play bowling a lot, and good bowlers know how important team dynamics are. By showing their teammates sympathy, empathy, and support, they are excellent at fostering and preserving team cohesion. They are adept at settling disputes, communicating clearly, and creating a supportive team environment, all of which improve the performance of the team as a whole.

<u>Adapting to changing situations</u>: Lane-to-lane variations in bowling conditions mean that top bowlers must modify their game plans accordingly. People with high emotional intelligence (EI) are more adaptive and flexible; they can swiftly evaluate the situation and modify their strategy accordingly. Even under duress, they maintain composure and concentration, which enables them to make wiser choices and give their best work.

<u>Demonstrating self-awareness:</u> Strong self-awareness and an understanding of their own emotions, strengths, and shortcomings characterize elite bowlers with high EI. They have good emotional control, which helps them to control their anxiety before an important shot. They may also set reasonable goals and strive for ongoing growth since they have a realistic view of their own talents.

<u>Exhibiting empathy and social skills:</u> Empathy and social skills are important for productive teamwork, and elite bowlers with high EI score highly in these areas. They are able to empathize with and comprehend the feelings and viewpoints of their teammates, offering encouragement, inspiration, and support when required. They also establish positive relationships, listen intently, and communicate well, all of which improve team cohesion and performance.

> **Myth: Elite athletes are born with their mental attributes.**
>
> Reality: Mental attributes, including emotional intelligence and cognitive skills, can be developed and honed through training and practice, just like physical abilities.
>
> **Myth: There's a one-size-fits-all approach to optimizing mental performance.**
>
> Reality: Each athlete has a unique neurological design and emotional intelligence profile. Tailoring mental training to an individual's specific attributes is essential for success.

Intrapersonal Intelligence Of Elite Bowlers

An expansion of interpersonal (social) and intrapersonal (personal) intelligence is emotional intelligence.

Howard Gardner

Intra-personally intelligent bowlers are able to effectively manage their own emotional lives and carry out independent tasks. It has to do with being strong within. What is intelligence? Intrapersonal intelligence. It denotes having self-awareness.

Being interpersonally intelligent is what's meant by this term. It is the intelligence to recognize and comprehend the feelings, wants, and openness to communication of others. Those who bowl with this intelligence preference are generally regarded as team players since they appreciate social interaction. They have relationship skills.

Understanding oneself, including one's feelings, ideas, and motives, is referred to as intrapersonal intelligence in Howard Gardner's theory of multiple intelligences. Here are a few bowlers that demonstrate potential intrapersonal intelligence in the context of bowling:

Self-reflective Bowler: Upon finishing a game or frame, the bowler might take some time to evaluate his performance, noting his advantages, disadvantages, and places for development. With time, he may use his acute awareness of his own bowling style, preferences, and tactics to refine and elevate his technique.

Emotionally aware Bowler: The bowler may possess a high degree of emotional intelligence since he is aware of his own feelings and use that knowledge to control how to behave on the lanes. He could be able to efficiently control his anger, stress, or worry and keep an optimistic outlook despite difficulties. Additionally, he could utilize his feelings as fuel for his ambition and desire for achievements.

Self-motivated Bowler: The bowler in question exhibits a strong sense of intrinsic desire, as seen by his persistent pursuit of personal challenges and goals. His in-depth awareness of his own advantages and disadvantages may enable him to create reasonable goals for growth. Along with his strong will and self-control, he can also drive himself to train frequently and perform at a constant caliber.

Intuitive Bowler: When making judgments on the lanes, the bowler may have a strong sense of intuition and trust his gut. He might have a thorough awareness of his own habits and bowling style, and he may make fast and wise decisions during play based on their knowledge. Additionally, he might possess a keen sense of situational awareness, accurately interpreting the lane conditions, the actions of his rivals, and his own emotional and physical states.

Self-driven Bowler: The bowler might be extremely driven, goal-oriented, and has a strong sense of purpose. He can have a distinct idea of what he wants to accomplish in his bowling career and move proactively to make his dreams come true. A high degree of self-efficacy, or confidence in one's own performance and talents, may also be present in him, enabling him to push himself to reach greater success.

Myth: Emotional intelligence is a soft skill that doesn't impact sports outcomes.

Reality: Emotional intelligence, encompassing self-awareness, self-management, and empathy, has a quantifiable impact on an athlete's performance, including decision-making under pressure and team dynamics.

Myth: Intrapersonal intelligence is less critical than interpersonal intelligence in sports.

Reality: Intrapersonal intelligence, involving self-understanding and emotional regulation, is equally crucial as interpersonal intelligence for athletes to manage their own emotions and maximize their potential.

In general, bowlers who possess intrapersonal intelligence are those who have a profound awareness of their own feelings, drives, and strengths and make use of this self-awareness to enhance their performance on the lanes. They can be introspective, emotionally conscious, self-driven, natural, and self-motivated, and they can use their inner intelligence to succeed in bowling.

Dimensions Of Emotional Intelligence

According to Daniel Goleman, emotional intelligence is a multifaceted construct that includes the ability to recognize, analyze, and regulate emotions in both oneself and others. The following are hypothetical instances for each dimension, followed by examples of how these dimensions could appear in the context of bowling:

Daniel Goleman

Accurate Self-Awareness: Bowlers who possess accurate self-awareness have a profound comprehension of their own emotions, strengths, and shortcomings, as well as how these aspects affect their bowling performance. They can identify how their feelings, such as anxiety or displeasure, may impact their games and are conscious of them when they are playing. For instance, a bowler may discover that he becomes nervous while under pressure, which can lead him to hurriedly deliver their shots and make errors. The bowler may efficiently manage his emotions and stay focused on his play by developing proper self-awareness.

Accurate Self-Awareness:

Hypothetical Example: Being a competitive bowler, Sarah possesses precise self-awareness. She understands that when she misses a spare, she becomes irritated easily, which can impair her focus and effectiveness. Sarah has created a technique to help cope with this, which involves taking a deep breath, refocusing, and visualizing her next shot. This helps her maintain her composure and play better under pressure.

Self-Management: The capacity to control one's own emotions and conduct in a positive way is known as self-management. A bowler who practices self-management is able to restrain their emotions, handle tension, and maintain composure under pressure. For instance, a bowler may experience frustration and disappointment if he consistently receives low scores. Instead of allowing negative emotions to negatively impact his performance, a bowler with self-management abilities can stand back, take deep breaths, refocus their attitude, and strategically alter his strategy.

Self-Management:

Hypothetical Example: John is a skilled professional bowler who possesses tremendous self-control. He knows that his performance depends on his ability to keep an optimistic outlook. At a tournament, John maintains his composure in the face of difficult lane conditions. He practices deep breathing and visualization during the gaps between frames, which helps him control his emotions, maintain focus, and make tactical changes to his game.

Social Awareness: The term "social awareness" describes the capacity to comprehend and feel other people's feelings and viewpoints. This might include being aware of the feelings and responses of opponents, teammates, and even spectators when bowling. A bowler with social awareness, for instance, might see that a teammate is dejected following a string of missed shots and offer words of support to lift their spirits. Additionally, he could be able to detect clues from rivals, such as agitation or anxiety, and modify his approach accordingly.

Social Awareness:

Hypothetical Example: Lisa is a socially conscious team bowler. She is aware of her colleagues' needs and feelings. Lisa observes that her teammate Mike is upset following a string of poor scores during a league game. During a break, she walks over to him, gives him encouraging words, and pays close attention to his worries. Mike gains confidence thanks to her understanding and encouragement, and he performs better in the next frames.

Social Skills: The capacity to cooperate, communicate, and form wholesome bonds with people is referred to as social skills. This can show up in bowling interactions with coaches, opponents, teammates, and even spectators. A bowler with excellent social skills, for instance, might be able to organize tactics, interact with teammates during a team event, and offer support and encouragement to raise morale. Regardless of the result of the game, he can still demonstrate good sportsmanship by being respectful to their opponents, keeping an optimistic outlook, and recognizing good shots.

Social Skills:

Hypothetical Example: An experienced bowler, Alex has amazing interpersonal skills. With both opponents and teammates, he has excellent interactions. He keeps a cordial and courteous manner on the lanes while sharing techniques and pointers with other bowlers. Along with giving constructive criticism and seeking advice when necessary, Alex also interacts well with his coach. His exceptional interpersonal abilities cultivate a positive environment and promote good sportsmanship among all participants.

Ultimately, a bowler's ability to negotiate social situations, better understand and control their own emotions, and develop wholesome relationships can all be greatly impacted by emotional intelligence. In bowling, correct self-awareness, self-management, social awareness, and social skills are a few examples of emotional intelligence that can help in games and overall performance in the sport.

Dimension of Emotional Intelligence	Brief Description	Benefits for the Bowler	How to Build This Dimension (Steps and Drills)	Neurological Advances	Psychological Advances
Accurate Self-Awareness	Bowlers with this dimension comprehend their own emotions, strengths, and weaknesses, recognizing how these aspects influence their game. They can efficiently manage emotions and stay focused.	- Improved focus and performance under pressure. - Enhanced ability to cope with emotions like anxiety.	1. Reflection: Encourage bowlers to reflect on their emotional responses after each game. 2. Journaling: Maintain a bowling journal to track emotional patterns and triggers. 3. Mindfulness: Introduce mindfulness exercises to increase self-awareness during play.	- Enhanced neural connections related to emotional regulation and self-awareness.	- Increased emotional resilience. - Greater self-understanding.
Self-Management	This involves controlling emotions positively, handling tension, and maintaining composure under pressure. Bowlers with self-management skills can strategically alter their approach in challenging situations.	- Consistent performance despite challenges. - Ability to make tactical changes for better results.	1. Breathing Techniques: Teach deep-breathing exercises to manage frustration. 2. Visualization: Guide bowlers to visualize success to maintain composure. 3. Coping Strategies: Develop personalized coping strategies for various emotions.	- Strengthened neural pathways related to emotional regulation and self-control.	- Improved stress management. - Enhanced decision-making under pressure.
Social Awareness	Social awareness entails understanding others' feelings and perspectives, crucial in interactions with teammates, opponents, and spectators. It involves adapting to others' emotional states.	- Improved team dynamics and communication. - The ability to adapt strategies based on opponents' emotions.	1. Observation: Train bowlers to observe body language and expressions. 2. Empathy Building: Encourage discussions on understanding teammates' feelings. 3. Role Play: Practice situational scenarios to enhance social awareness.	- Strengthened neural circuits related to empathy and social cognition.	- Enhanced interpersonal relationships. - Improved team cohesion.
Social Skills	Social skills involve cooperation, communication, and building positive relationships. A bowler with excellent social skills can contribute positively to team dynamics and sportsmanship.	- Effective teamwork and camaraderie. - Good sportsmanship and positive interactions.	1. Communication Training: Provide workshops on effective communication. 2. Team-Building Exercises: Engage in activities that foster teamwork. 3. Peer Support: Encourage bowlers to support and encourage teammates.	- Development of neural pathways associated with communication and collaboration.	- Improved leadership skills. - Positive team culture and support system.

Table 15 - By addressing emotional intelligence in these dimensions, bowlers not only enhance their performance but also experience positive neurological and psychological advances that contribute to their overall well-being and success in the sport.

A Comprehensive 6-Month Emotional Intelligence Blueprint

Stage 1: Foundation (Month 1-2) - Continuous

1. *Accurate Self-Awareness:*

- *Psychological Drills:*
  - *Reflection Journaling:* Bowlers are provided with a journal to document emotions after each game, encouraging self-reflection.
  - *Emotion Tracking:* Develop a personalized system where bowlers track emotional patterns and triggers during practice sessions.

- *Neurological Advances:*
  - *Increased neural connections related to emotional regulation.*
  - *Enhanced activity in brain regions associated with self-awareness.*

2. *Self-Management:*

- *Psychological Drills:*
  - *Breathing Techniques:* Conduct workshops on deep-breathing exercises to manage frustration and enhance focus.
  - *Visualization:* Guide bowlers in creating mental images of successful shots, helping maintain composure.

- *Neurological Advances:*
  - *Strengthened neural pathways related to emotional regulation and self-control.*
  - *Improved connectivity between emotional and decision-making areas of the brain.*

Example for Stage 1: John, a dedicated bowler, notices that he often feels nervous during crucial moments of a game, affecting his performance. Through reflection journaling, he identifies that missed spares trigger irritation and anxiety. Implementing deep-breathing techniques helps him regain composure and focus during these situations. Visualization exercises further solidify his ability to manage emotions, creating a foundation for improved self-management.

Stage 2: Understanding (Month 3-4) Continuous

3. *Social Awareness:*

- *Psychological Drills:*
  - *Observation Training:* Conduct sessions where bowlers learn to observe body language and facial expressions, enhancing social awareness.
  - *Empathy Building Discussions:* Facilitate team discussions on understanding teammates' feelings to build empathy.

- *Neurological Advances:*
  - *Strengthened neural circuits related to empathy and social cognition.*
  - *Increased activity in brain regions associated with understanding others' perspectives.*

4. *Social Skills:*

- *Psychological Drills:*
  - *Communication Workshops:* Organize workshops focusing on effective communication strategies.
  - *Team-Building Exercises:* Engage in activities that require teamwork and cooperation.

- *Neurological Advances:*
  - *Development of neural pathways associated with communication.*
  - *Enhanced connectivity in brain regions related to social interaction.*

Example for Stage 2: Lisa, an experienced bowler, realizes the importance of understanding her teammates' emotions. During a league game, she observes that her teammate Mike is visibly upset after a series of poor scores. Lisa engages in an empathy-building discussion during a break, providing words of encouragement. Mike gains confidence due to Lisa's understanding, leading to improved performance in the next frames. Lisa's excellent interpersonal skills contribute to a positive team culture and sportsmanship.

Stage 3: Application (Month 5-6) Continuous

5. **Integrated Practice:**

- **Psychological Drills:**
  - **Role Play:** *Simulate scenarios where bowlers apply social awareness and social skills.*
  - **Peer Support Initiative:** *Encourage bowlers to actively support and encourage teammates.*
- **Neurological and Psychological Advances:**
  - *Consolidation and reinforcement of learned skills.*
  - *Improved leadership skills and positive team culture.*

6. **Reflect and Adjust:**

- **Psychological Drills:**
  - **Continuous Journaling:** *Maintain the reflection journal, ensuring ongoing self-awareness.*
  - **Feedback Sessions:** *Regularly discuss and adjust strategies based on continuous reflection.*
- **Neurological and Psychological Advances:**
  - *Continued growth and adaptation of emotional intelligence.*
  - *Enhanced connectivity in brain regions related to adaptive learning and self-reflection.*

Example for Stage 3: In a team event, John applies role-playing techniques to adapt his strategies based on opponents' emotions. During a challenging match, he actively supports a struggling teammate using the peer support initiative. Continuous reflection in the journal helps John refine his emotional intelligence strategies. Feedback sessions with teammates contribute to a positive team culture. John's overall enhanced emotional intelligence leads to consistent high-level performance and positive team dynamics.

This 6-month plan emphasizes continuous development, integrating psychological drills and neurological advances at each stage, creating a comprehensive approach to building emotional intelligence in advanced bowlers.

12 EMOTIONAL INTELLIGENCE COMPETENCIES

In the highly competitive world of bowling, success goes beyond technical prowess; it extends into the realm of emotional intelligence. Recognizing the paramount importance of mental acuity in the sport, Neuro-Link has meticulously developed a comprehensive 12 Emotional Intelligence Competencies Profile tailored specifically for bowlers. This profile digs into crucial abilities that significantly impact a bowler's mental performance, ultimately influencing their success on the lanes.

Find Your Purpose: Understanding the true meaning and motive for engaging in the sport of bowling is necessary to discover one's purpose in the game.

When it comes to her bowling, Sarah's goal is very clear: she wants to keep getting better and encourage her teammates to get better too. She uses her own objectives, like raising her strike or spare conversion rate, as motivation to remain dedicated and focused on her bowling adventure.

Mind Power: The capacity to efficiently use one's mind to control emotions, ideas, and concentrate is referred to as mind power. Mind strength in bowling is demonstrated by players who possess high levels of mental toughness, focus, and concentration.

A bowler named James encounters several difficult circumstances during a pivotal match, such as a split and a missed spare. But he keeps his cool, concentrates on his strategy, and employs encouraging self-talk to bolster his self-esteem, all of which help him bounce back and play well in the closing frames.

Coping with Change, Managing Stress, and Maintaining Wellness: Bowlers need to possess emotional intelligence competencies such as stress management, change adaptation, and wellbeing maintenance because the activity may be physically and mentally taxing.

Lisa is aware of how crucial stress reduction and self-care are to her work. She manages her stress levels and preserves her physical and emotional well-being through regular exercise, adequate sleep, and the use of relaxation techniques like mindfulness and meditation, all of which improve her bowling performance.

Coping and Resilience Skills: Being resilient and able to overcome obstacles are key components of coping and resilience abilities. Whether it's unexpected lane conditions, equipment malfunctions, or challenging opponents, bowlers frequently encounter difficulties.

Through his bowling experience, Michael has achieved tremendous resilience and coping abilities. A bad shot or a game lost doesn't deter him; instead, he sees them as chances to grow, adjust, and improve for the next attempt.

Social Awareness: The capacity to comprehend and sense the needs and feelings of others is known as social awareness. Bowlers who possess social awareness are able to understand the emotions of their teammates, communicate clearly, and offer assistance when needed.

After several missed spares, Rachel is irritated, and Emily observes this. In order to help Rachel regain her confidence and perform better, Emily approaches her with empathy, gives her words of encouragement, and assists her in refocusing on the next frame.

Interpersonal Communication and Conflict Resolution: Effective interpersonal communication and conflict resolution abilities are essential in team bowling since they can improve team cohesion and performance.

Jake has strong interpersonal and conflict-resolution skills. He respectfully and clearly states his own beliefs, actively listens to the worries and viewpoints of his coworkers, and works with them to settle any problems. His ability to communicate effectively facilitates the development of a supportive team atmosphere and strong bonds between team members, all of which eventually lead to increased team performance.

Social Cohesion and Team Functioning: The terms "social cohesion" and "team functioning" describe the capacity to get along with people, develop a sense of camaraderie, and create a cohesive, encouraging work atmosphere. In order to plan, encourage, and celebrate victories, bowlers must collaborate as a team.

Chris is aware of the value of cohesive social groups and effective teamwork. He supports and stimulates his teammates, actively engages in team activities, and fosters a supportive environment. His work fosters a supportive and cohesive team atmosphere where each member feels appreciated and supported, which enhances team performance.

Servant Leadership: A leader who practices servant leadership puts the needs of others above their own and leads by empowering and serving others.

Servant leadership is best shown by Jessica. She assumes a leadership role within her team and concentrates on fostering the success of her peers. She pays attention to their worries, offers direction and encouragement, and cultivates a welcoming and cooperative team atmosphere. Her approach to servant leadership fosters a healthy team dynamic and improves the group's overall performance and well-being.

Winning Mind-set of a Champion: A champion's winning mindset is their capacity to be upbeat and self-assured in the face of obstacles and disappointments.

Mark has the winning mentality of a victor. He keeps a positive outlook, has faith in his skills, and imagines himself succeeding. Missed shots and lost games don't depress him; instead, he sees them as chances to grow. He performs consistently at a high level because of his winning mindset, which keeps him resilient, driven, and focused.

Big Match Temperament for the Big Moments: Big match temperament is the capacity to function successfully under duress and under high-pressure circumstances. Players in bowling frequently have to make decisions in close games or frames.

Samantha's competitive bowling experience has helped her establish a solid big-match temperament. She uses calming strategies to control her anxiety and maintains her composure under pressure while staying focused on her strategy. Her success in crucial matches is a result of her capacity to execute well under duress.

Optimism: A key emotional intelligence competency, involves cultivating and sustaining a positive and hopeful perspective, especially when confronted with challenges or adversity. Bowlers who possess a high level of optimism are better equipped to handle setbacks, persevere through tough times, and maintain a constructive approach to their sport.

Sarah, a dedicated bowler, exemplifies the power of optimism in the face of adversity. Despite encountering a series of challenging tournaments where her performance didn't meet expectations, Sarah consistently maintained a positive and hopeful outlook. Instead of letting setbacks demoralize her, she used them as learning opportunities. Sarah focused on areas of improvement, worked closely with her coach, and approached each practice session with a determined and optimistic mindset.

Her optimism not only helped her bounce back from defeats but also positively influenced her team. Sarah's teammates admired her resilience and positive attitude, turning her into a source of inspiration during challenging times. By embracing optimism, Sarah not only improved her own performance but also contributed to the overall positive atmosphere within the team. The capacity to maintain hope and positivity, even in the face of adversity, allowed Sarah to navigate the ups and downs of competitive bowling with a steadfast and constructive mindset.

Effective Personal Management to Cope with Stress and Fatigue: The ability to properly handle stress, exhaustion, and other issues that could affect performance is a necessary component of effective personal management.

Tim understands that in order to meet the physical and psychological demands of the sport, good personal management is essential. He leads a healthy lifestyle that includes frequent exercise, enough sleep, and a balanced diet and hydration. In order to deal with stress and exhaustion, he also employs time management strategies and deep breathing exercises. His ability to maintain good self-management helps him remain mentally and physically fit, which improves his bowling performance.

Emotional Intelligence Competence	Brief Description	Benefits for the Bowler	How to Build This Competence (Steps and Drills)
Find Your Purpose	Discovering the true meaning and motive for engaging in bowling.	Clear motivation and dedication, fostering commitment and focus.	1. Self-Reflection: Encourage bowlers to explore their personal motivations for participating in the sport. 2. Goal Setting: Develop specific and meaningful goals to provide direction. 3. Team Discussions: Engage in team discussions to understand shared purposes and motivations.
Mind Power	Efficiently using the mind to control emotions, ideas, and concentration.	Enhanced mental toughness, focus, and concentration for consistent performance.	1. Visualization Techniques: Teach bowlers to visualize success and maintain focus. 2. Positive Self-Talk: Encourage the use of positive affirmations to boost self-esteem. 3. Mindfulness Practices: Introduce mindfulness exercises for improved concentration.
Coping with Change, Managing Stress, and Maintaining Wellness	Developing competencies in stress management, change adaptation, and overall well-being.	Improved physical and mental resilience, ensuring consistent performance.	1. Stress Management Workshops: Conduct workshops on stress reduction techniques. 2. Change Adaptation Exercises: Practice adapting to unexpected situations in training. 3. Wellness Programs: Promote a healthy lifestyle with exercise, sleep, and relaxation techniques.
Coping and Resilience Skills	Building resilience and overcoming obstacles in the face of challenges.	Greater ability to bounce back from setbacks and learn from experiences.	1. Resilience Training: Integrate resilience-focused drills into regular practice. 2. Post-Game Reflection: Encourage bowlers to reflect on challenges and identify growth opportunities. 3. Problem-Solving Scenarios: Simulate challenging situations to enhance coping skills.
Social Awareness	Comprehending and sensing the needs and feelings of others, crucial for teamwork.	Improved team dynamics, communication, and assistance when needed.	1. Body Language Observation: Train bowlers to observe body language and expressions. 2. Empathy Building: Conduct sessions to enhance empathy and understanding of teammates. 3. Role Play: Practice situational scenarios to enhance social awareness.
Interpersonal Communication and Conflict Resolution	Effective communication and conflict resolution abilities for team cohesion.	Stronger team bonds, improved communication, and conflict resolution.	1. Communication Workshops: Provide workshops on effective communication techniques. 2. Conflict Resolution Training: Develop skills in resolving conflicts respectfully. 3. Team-Building Exercises: Engage in activities that foster teamwork and collaboration.

Emotional Intelligence Competence	Brief Description	Benefits for the Bowler	How to Build This Competence (Steps and Drills)
Social Cohesion and Team Functioning	Creating a cohesive, encouraging work atmosphere for team success.	Positive team culture, support, and celebration of victories together.	1. Team-Building Activities: Organize activities that encourage collaboration. 2. Encourage Celebrations: Foster a culture of celebrating both individual and team achievements. 3. Open Communication: Establish an open communication channel within the team.
Servant Leadership	Leading by empowering and serving others, putting their needs above one's own.	Healthy team dynamic, improved performance, and support for each team member.	1. Leadership Workshops: Provide training on the principles of servant leadership. 2. Peer Support Encouragement: Promote a culture of supporting and empowering teammates. 3. Lead by Example: Demonstrate servant leadership through actions and behaviors.
Winning Mind-set of a Champion	Maintaining positivity and self-assurance in the face of challenges.	Resilience, focus, and consistency in performance with a positive outlook.	1. Positive Visualization: Guide bowlers to visualize success and winning outcomes. 2. Positive Self-Talk: Encourage a positive internal dialogue during challenges. 3. Goal-Setting with Positivity: Set goals framed in a positive and optimistic context.
Big Match Temperament for the Big Moments	Functioning successfully under duress and high-pressure circumstances.	Consistent decision-making in crucial moments, contributing to team success.	1. Simulated Pressure Scenarios: Create scenarios that replicate high-pressure moments. 2. Visualization under Pressure: Practice visualizing success in challenging situations. 3. Mindfulness Techniques: Train bowlers to stay present and focused during critical frames.
Optimism	Cultivating and sustaining a positive and hopeful perspective.	Better handling of setbacks, perseverance through tough times, and constructive approach.	1. Positive Affirmations: Develop personalized affirmations to foster optimism. 2. Optimism Reflection: Discuss and share optimistic perspectives in team settings. 3. Learn from Setbacks: Emphasize the learning opportunities in every setback and challenge.
Effective Personal Management to Cope with Stress and Fatigue	Handling stress, exhaustion, and other issues affecting performance.	Improved mental and physical fitness, contributing to enhanced performance.	1. Time Management Techniques: Teach effective time management for stress reduction. 2. Physical Well-being Programs: Promote a healthy lifestyle with exercise and balanced nutrition. 3. Stress Reduction Drills: Integrate drills that focus on stress reduction and mental recovery.

Table 16 - This table explains emotional intelligence competencies for bowlers. Building these skills benefits bowlers with enhanced focus, resilience, and team dynamics. Steps include self-reflection, visualization techniques, stress management workshops, resilience training, social awareness exercises, communication workshops, team-building activities, servant leadership training, and optimism cultivation. These competencies contribute to consistent performance, positive mindset, and effective teamwork.

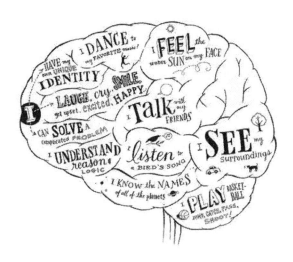

NEUROANATOMICAL SCIENCE OF ELITE BOWLERS (BRAIN ARCHITECTURE)

In bowling, elite players frequently achieve incredible accomplishments by showcasing extraordinary ability and accuracy in their shots. An intricate web of neuroanatomical processes interacts to produce these remarkable performances, which add to their extraordinary skills. Recent developments in neuroimaging methods have illuminated the ways in which the brains of great bowlers differ neuro-biologically from those of average players. In the neuroanatomical science of top bowlers, let's examine more closely several instances of how various brain regions are involved.

Reviewing all terminology relating to brain structure is essential to comprehending the neurological differences between amateurs and elites:

Gm Volumes Research has demonstrated a connection between athletic performance and the quantity of gray matter in specific brain regions. This association raises the possibility that a bowler's prowess in the sport may be correlated with the quantity of gray matter in brain areas connected to perception, memory, and motor control. A bowler may have an edge when it comes to performing precise and correct motions in their bowling technique if he has a greater quantity of gray matter in the cerebellum, which is involved in motor control and coordination. Similar to this, a bowler may be better able to recall and duplicate effective bowling tactics if he has more gray matter in their hippocampal region, which is involved in memory and learning.

It is crucial to remember that the precise nature of the complicated interaction between hereditary, environmental, and training factors likely affects the link between gray matter volume and athletic performance. Those who are inherently gifted in some domains, like motor control or memory, might, for instance, have more gray matter overall in those locations. Furthermore, research indicates that specific exercise regimens may enhance the volume of gray matter in brain regions linked to motor control and cognitive function, hence influencing the quantity of gray matter in the brain.

GM VOLUMES: Professional bowlers may have more gray matter in their motor control, memory, and perceptual regions of the brain. These higher volumes could be linked to enhanced motor abilities, memory for bowling tactics and plans, and enhanced awareness of the lane's characteristics and the trajectory of the ball.

Decreased Wm Diminished white matter (WM) in a specific brain region has drawn attention from neuroscientists because of possible effects on cognitive performance. Connecting and facilitating effective communication between the various brain regions is the job of white matter. Cognitive functions may be impacted by delayed information transmission resulting from decreased white matter (WM) in specific brain regions. Since motor skills and coordination are crucial for success in bowling, bowlers' performance may be impacted by this decline in WM. The brain regions in charge of motor control, including the PMD proper, were found to be active during a study on professional athletes. This shows that complicated motor tasks like bowling may require the normal functioning of WM in these locations. Upcoming studies on this subject might clarify how reduced WM affects bowlers' performance and offer suggestions for treatments that could enhance their cognitive abilities.

A reduction in the volume of white matter in a specific area of the brain, like the inferior occipitofrontal fasciculus, could be linked to a decline in the integration of vision and the ability to plan movements accordingly. This may have an impact on a bowler's capacity to precisely interpret visual cues from the lane and modify their motions accordingly.

Technique To Detect Gm & Wm

The Voxel-Based Morphometry (Vbm) Voxel-based morphometry (VBM) is a powerful neuroimaging technique that allows researchers to analyze the structure of the brain and detect changes in gray matter (GM) and white matter (WM) volumes. In the context of bowlers, this technique can be used to investigate how the brain structure is related to their performance in this sport. By segmenting brain images into different tissue types, such as GM, WM, and cerebrospinal fluid, and comparing these volumes between groups of bowlers with different skill levels, researchers can identify specific brain regions that may be associated with better performance. For example, bowlers with higher skill levels had larger GM volumes in the PPC, a brain region involved in processing spatial information. Similarly, decreased WM volumes in specific brain regions, such as the corpus callosum, have been associated with poorer motor performance in bowlers. By A strong neuroimaging method called voxel-based morphometry (VBM) enables researchers to examine the anatomy of the brain and identify variations in the volumes of the white matter (WM) and gray matter (GM). This method can be applied to bowlers to study the relationship between brain shape and bowling performance. Researchers can pinpoint particular brain regions that might be linked to improved performance by segmenting brain scans into distinct tissue types, including GM, WM, and cerebrospinal fluid, and then comparing these volumes between groups of bowlers with varying skill levels. For instance, in the PPC, a part of the brain involved in processing spatial information, bowlers with greater skill levels had bigger GM volumes. Likewise, lower motor performance in bowlers has been linked to reduced white matter quantities in particular brain regions, like the corpus callosum. Researchers can learn a great deal about the neurological mechanisms underpinning sports and find possible targets for training and rehabilitation programs by utilizing VBM to study the link between brain anatomy and athletic performance. using VBM to investigate the relationship between brain structure and sport performance, researchers can gain valuable insights into the neural mechanisms underlying this sport and identify potential targets for training and rehabilitation programs.

VBM is a method that can be used to examine the structural alterations in bowlers' brains by detecting changes in gray and white matter volumes in brain pictures. To detect potential changes in brain structure linked with expertise, it may be utilized, for instance, to compare the gray and white matter volumes between amateur and professional bowlers.

The Role Of Genetics And Brain Differences In Bowling Performance

Pmd Proper, It's become more and more crucial to comprehend how the brain functions when it comes to movement planning and execution in bowling. The Proper Dorsal Premotor Cortex (PMD Proper), which is in charge of organizing and carrying out motor movements, is one specific area of study. The PMD Proper is a motor area situated in the frontal lobe of the brain. It is related to the primary motor cortex and the supplementary motor area. Research has demonstrated that an athlete's capacity to perform motions with accuracy and precision can be strongly influenced by the size and activation of the PMD Proper. Moreover, studies have discovered a favorable association between an athlete's ability in activities requiring intricate motor planning and execution, like bowling, and the quantity of gray matter detected in the PMD Proper. Thus, gaining a deeper comprehension of the PMD Proper's function in bowlers' motor control may enhance training regimens and athletic performance.

A professional bowler may have a more active and well-developed correct dorsal premotor cortex since it is involved in the planning and execution of movement. Better timing, accuracy, and coordination in the player's bowling technique could arise from this, as well as quicker decision-making when it comes to altering their actions in response to shifting lane conditions.

The Posterior Parietal Cortex (Ppc): The processing of sensory data, particularly spatial data, is greatly aided by the PPC, a vital brain region. Situated in the parietal lobe, its principal role is to amalgamate visual, auditory, and somatosensory data to construct an all-encompassing depiction of the external surroundings. The PPC plays a role in how bowlers perceive the spatial arrangement of the bowling alley, particularly where the pins are located. Bowlers need to know this information in order to properly aim and release the ball toward the target.

Furthermore, the PPC plays a role in both motor control and attention. PPC helps direct attention between various parts of the bowling lane, like the pin positions and lane oil patterns. For bowlers to make correct and timely adjustments during a game, they must possess the ability to change their focus quickly. Precise movement of the arm and hand during the ball release is an example of a planned and executed movement that the PPC is involved in. To provide precise and well-coordinated motions, the PPC gets input from many motor regions of the brain, including the primary motor cortex and the supplementary motor area.

Furthermore, current research indicates that individual variations in bowlers' ability levels and PPC anatomy may be connected. Researchers have discovered, for instance, a positive correlation between athletes' skill level and the volume of gray matter in the PPC. This implies that mastery of bowling requires the PPC's structural integrity. PPC may also be connected to shot accuracy and ball release precision. This emphasizes how crucial the PPC is to the execution of deft bowling motions.

A bowler's brain may contain important functions related to the posterior parietal cortex, which processes both spatial and sensory information. In order to attain the intended result, the player may find it useful to process the spatial arrangement of the bowling lane, calculate the trajectory and speed of the bowling ball, and modify their motions accordingly.

The Hemisphere An important component of our ability to engage in physical sports like bowling is the brain, an extraordinarily complex organ. It is split into the left and right hemispheres, each of which has a distinct role. While the right hemisphere is in charge of creativity, intuition, and spatial awareness, the left hemisphere is mostly in charge of language, logical reasoning, and analytical work. Communication between the two hemispheres occurs via the corpus callosum, a dense network of fibers that facilitates information flow. Both hemispheres are used when bowlers examine lane circumstances, modify their release and approach, and make snap decisions regarding their shot. The right hemisphere is utilized to visualize the shot and make modifications based on spatial awareness, while the left hemisphere analyzes and computes the angle and speed of the ball. Bowling success requires the capacity to use both hemispheres of the brain properly.

A bowler's brain may use both hemispheres—the left and right—to coordinate their motor actions. To release the bowling ball, for instance, the movements of the right hand may be controlled by the left hemisphere, and the right hemisphere may be responsible for processing visual and spatial information about the lane conditions and ball trajectory.

Spatial Information Human perception relies heavily on spatial information, which is critical for managing, interacting with our surroundings, and performing difficult motor activities like grabbing, reaching, and tossing a ball. The brain uses multiple areas, including the parietal lobe's posterior parietal cortex (PPC), to analyze spatial information. The PPC integrates sensory data from several modalities to provide a coherent representation of space. It is linked to other brain regions involved in perception, attention, and motor control. The fine motor motions needed to bowl, among other complicated motor activities, are mostly planned and carried out by this area of the brain. For the purpose of precisely positioning themselves on the approach, aiming the ball, and modifying their motions in reaction to shifting lane circumstances, bowlers primarily depend on their capacity to receive and process spatial information. Because of this, the PPC is probably a significant brain region for bowlers and could be a factor in performance variations between individuals.

A bowler needs to be aware of spatial information such as the pins' locations and movements, the player's body position in respect to the lane, and the bowling ball's position. Multiple brain regions, including those involved in attention and spatial processing, such as the precuneus, intraparietal sulcus, posterior parietal cortex, and superior parietal lobule, are involved in precisely and rapidly processing this information.

The Dorsal Premotor Cortex (Dpmc) A bowler must be aware of spatial information, which includes the positions and movements of the pins, their body's orientation in relation to the lane, and the position of the bowling ball.

This information is processed accurately and quickly by a number of brain regions, including the precuneus, intraparietal sulcus, posterior parietal cortex, and superior parietal lobule. These regions are also involved in attention and spatial processing.

When a bowler prepares and executes a bowling shot, his dorsal premotor cortex, which is involved in movement planning and execution, may be quite active in their brain. To produce a precise and fluid shot, it could aid in coordinating the several motor movements used in bowling technique, such as the swing, release, and follow-through.

The Role Of The Primary Motor Cortex In Bowling Performance

The Motor Cortex The brain region that is primarily in charge of regulating voluntary movement is the motor cortex. The frontal lobe is home to it, and it is well known to be crucial to how movements are carried out. Working together to coordinate movements, the supplementary motor area (SMA) and primary motor cortex (M1) are two components of the motor cortex. Direct movement control is the domain of the primary motor cortex, while complicated movement planning and organization is the domain of the supplementary motor region. Additionally, the premotor cortex and the somatosensory cortex are linked to the motor cortex and other brain areas that are involved in motor control. In order to precisely and effectively control movement—which is crucial for athletes like bowlers who depend on their motor abilities for success—these regions work together to form a complicated network.

Bowlers' brains may be particularly important for the motor cortex, which controls voluntary movement. It might assist in producing the motor commands that regulate the muscles used in the bowling method, such as the hand and arm muscles that swing and release the bowling ball.

Primary Motor Cortex (M1)

The primary motor cortex (M1) is a critical component of the performance of professional bowlers, as it influences both accuracy and speed. The M1 is in charge of organizing and carrying out voluntary motions, and motor skill performance is directly impacted by the M1's neuronal activity. Prominent bowlers display distinct neurophysiological modifications in M1, which enhance their outstanding abilities.

M1 affects high-level bowlers in terms of speed by increasing brain activity and coordination. Compared to novice bowlers, elite bowlers have higher neuronal activation in M1 during bowling movements. Years of experience and motor learning have resulted in more efficient and coordinated motor patterns inside M1, which is the cause of this improved activation. Additionally, the synchronization of brain activity inside M1 is better in elite bowlers, which facilitates faster and more fluid motor control during bowling. These elements play a part in the elite players' reported gain in speed.

M1 helps elite bowlers with accuracy because it improves their motor coordination and planning. Proficient bowlers exhibit accurate and synchronized motions, which improves ball placement and targeting accuracy. Expert bowlers are able to make accurate modifications based on lane conditions, ball weight, and other factors because they have highly developed motor planning and coordination inside M1. Years of experience and training have enhanced motor planning and coordination, which has led to optimized neural pathways in M1 for precise and accurate bowling actions.

Hypothetical examples

Speed: Alex is a professional bowler who has spent years improving his craft and has become incredibly fast. Alex's M1 exhibits enhanced neuronal activation and synchronization as he gets ready to release the ball. Alex's M1 demonstrates improved motor patterns and coordinated brain activity, which enables him to bowl at a very high speed. Alex can send the ball faster down the lane than inexperienced bowlers because of the increased neuronal activation in M1, which enables Alex to generate the appropriate muscle force and coordination.

Accuracy: Emily is another outstanding bowler who has been competing at a high level for a number of years. Her bowling accuracy is remarkable. During Emily's bowling actions, her M1 demonstrates enhanced motor planning and coordination. Emily's M1 shows more advanced motor planning and coordination, which enables her to precisely modify her motions in response to different stimuli, including her target, the weight of the ball, and the lane conditions. Emily's M1's improved brain pathways allow her to move with great precision and accuracy, which enables her to reliably strike her target on the lane and produce high-accuracy bowling shots.

Primary motor cortex (M1) neurophysiological changes are responsible for the extraordinary speed and accuracy of elite bowlers. Its higher bowling ability is largely attributed to these changes, which include increased motor planning, synchronization, and brain activation. As a result of years of focused training and experience, these neurocognitive processes mature, improving M1 motor control and raising the performance levels of elite bowlers overall.

Three stages of the Fitts pattern—cognitive, associative, and autonomous—are frequently used in cognitive psychology to characterize competent performance. Automaticity development is the key idea behind these levels. Skilled acts are initially laborious, attention-grabbing, and somewhat inefficient. They also demand conscious control. Yet with continued practice and refinement, skills develop into automatic abilities that execute quickly and smoothly, requiring little conscious thought and resisting conscious disturbance.

Hypothetical example

Sarah, a new bowler who has just begun to learn the game, as an example. Sarah's performance is marked by conscious effort and attention-demanding procedures during the cognitive stage. She must deliberately consider how she is holding the ball, how she is standing, how she is aiming, and how she will release the ball. She can struggle to strike her target on the lane consistently and make mistakes in technique. Since Sarah is still learning and improving her motor abilities, her movements may be clumsy, slow, and ineffective. She is very focused on every aspect of bowling and needs her coach to give her constant feedback.

Sarah moves on to the associative level as she keeps practicing and gains experience. Sarah's performance becomes more polished and fluid at this point. She begins to gain muscle memory and familiarize herself with the proper technique. She starts to move less consciously and more instinctively. Sarah is now able to more fluidly and reliably modify her stance, grip, aim, and release. Her performance gains overall as she becomes better at anticipating and correcting technical faults.

Sarah eventually achieved the independent level with further training and experience. Sarah's performance has become incredibly automatic and effective at this point. She does not have to deliberate over each step to execute the bowling technique with ease and precision. She moves quickly, fluidly, and with little conscious thought or effort. Sarah's performance becomes dependable and steady, and she easily adjusts to various lane conditions, ball weights, and other variables.

Sarah's bowling performance in this instance demonstrates how the Fitts pattern works, progressing from cognitive to associative to autonomous. Her performance grows more automatic, and efficient, and requires less attentional capacity as she acquires experience and practice, which is consistent with the Fitts pattern's main idea of growing automaticity.

Somatosensory Cortex

THE SOMATOSENSORY CORTEX For bowlers, the somatosensory cortex—which processes touch and proprioceptive information—is an essential part of the brain. Players can feel the ball and their grip thanks to tactile information, while proprioceptive information gives them feedback on where their bodies are in relation to one another during a game. For precise and reliable shots, this information is crucial.

The processing of tactile and proprioceptive information involves the somatosensory cortex, which may be heavily activated in the brain of a bowler when his hand makes physical touch with the bowling ball. It might facilitate the player's ability to perceive the ball's tactile feedback, such as its weight, texture, and grip, and to combine this knowledge with other sensory cues to modify their motions.

The Superior Parietal Lobule (SPL)

THE SUPERIOR PARIETAL LOBULE (SPL), Important parietal lobe regions for bowlers also include the precuneus, intraparietal sulcus, and superior parietal lobule (SPL). Accurate targeting and spatial awareness during gameplay depend on these brain areas' involvement in the processing of spatial information and attention. The integration of sensory and motor information for action planning is a function of the IPS, whereas the perception of body position and movement is mostly handled by the SPL.

Additionally, significant parietal lobe regions for bowlers are the precuneus, intraparietal sulcus, and superior parietal lobule (SPL). Accurate targeting and spatial awareness during gameplay depend on these brain areas' involvement in the processing of spatial information and attention. The integration of sensory and motor information for action planning is a function of the IPS, whereas the perception of body position and movement is mostly handled by the SPL.

The Inferior Occipitofrontal Fasciculus (IOFF)

The **Inferior Occipitofrontal Fasciculus (Ioff)** The occipital lobe, which is engaged in visual processing, and the frontal lobe, which is involved in motor control and cognitive processing, are connected by a white matter tract called the inferior occipitofrontal fasciculus (IOFF). It is believed to be involved in the integration of visual and motor skills as well as the planning of motions based on visual data. This is crucial for bowlers because they target the ball and modify their actions based on visual cues. That's why having a strong IOFF is essential for precise and reliable shots.

The occipital lobe, which is involved in visual processing, and the frontal lobe, which is involved in motor control and cognitive processing, are connected by the IOFF, a white matter tract. The IOFF may have a function in visual-motor integration in the bowler's brain, enabling the player to plan and carry out exact motions of the arm, hand, and fingers during the ball release by using visual cues such as pin positions and lane circumstances.

Intraparietal Sulcus (IPS)

Intraparietal Sulcus (Ips): IPS is a well-known fissure in the brain's parietal lobe. It is significant to activities like bowling since it is known to play a crucial role in the processing of spatial information and motor planning. The IPS is involved in a number of cognitive processes that are connected to sensorimotor integration, attention, and spatial perception. A professional bowler may find the assessment of object placement and velocity in space to be useful, as the IPS has been linked to this process. For instance, the player may be able to modify their approach and release by using the IPS to estimate the bowling ball's lane performance in relation to the lane condition. Additionally, the IPS participates in attentional processes, specifically in the distribution of attention to pertinent visual stimuli. The IPS may assist the bowler in focusing on the aim, removing environmental distractions, and staying focused on the task at hand when they are bowling. By connecting visual information with motor planning and execution, the IPS is involved in sensorimotor integration. It might make it easier for the player to combine their motor motions during the bowling approach and release with visual signals, like pin positions and lane conditions. This would enable more accurate and synchronized movements.

Bowling-related spatial information processing may take place in the parietal lobe, home of the IPS. The ball's revolutions, direction, and speed in relation to the lane and the pins can be estimated by the player with its assistance. The sensorimotor integration process, which connects visual data to motor planning and execution of the player's motions during the bowling approach and release, may also involve the IPS.

PRECUNEUS:

PRECUNEUS: It is a section of the brain that is found at the posterior end of the cingulate gyrus in the parietal lobe. It is engaged in many different cognitive processes, some of which may be pertinent to a professional bowler, such as attention, self-awareness, and visuospatial processing. The precuneus may be involved in the player's mental visualization of the bowling ball's trajectory and course in terms of visuospatial processing. It might assist them in mentally simulating the ball's movement, modifying their approach position, and projecting the throw's result. Additionally, the precuneus is linked to self-awareness, which may be important for keeping an eye on one's own actions during bowling. By being more conscious of their body alignment, arm motions, and release technique, the player may be able to make necessary corrections and enhance their bowling performance. The precuneus also plays a role in attentional functions, such as directing attention toward pertinent cues. It might assist the player in focusing on their performance, blocking out distractions, and keeping their mind on the bowling job.

A professional bowler's brain may also engage the precuneus, another area of the parietal lobe. It is linked to self-awareness, attention, and visuospatial processing. This could potentially impact the player's capacity to mentally picture the trajectory and route of the ball, modify their positioning during the approach, and keep an eye on their own motions while bowling.

Brain-Derived Neurotrophic Factor (BDNF)

Investigating the intricate functions of the brain has become more important as we try to understand how it affects the preparation and performance of motions. We are particularly interested in the Brain-Derived Neurotrophic Factor (BDNF), which is one specific area of the brain. Within the intricate web of brain activities, BDNF is recognized as being essential to cognitive functioning and the development of motor skills. This protein has drawn interest because it may have an effect on a person's capacity to learn and perform well in bowling, providing insight into the genetic component of performance.

When it comes to bowling ability, one gene that has been closely studied is called Brain-Derived Neurotrophic Factor, or BDNF. a particular BDNF gene variant that has been linked to a decreased ability to learn new bowling skills. It seems that over time, this genetic diversity affects a person's capacity to pick up new skills and improve their bowling game. These genetic variables support the theory that our genes might significantly influence both our starting skill level and our ability to improve our skills in the game of bowling.

Hypothetical examples

Two competitive bowlers, John and Mark, have received the same amount of coaching and practice time. But while Mark does not have this polymorphism, John does have a BDNF polymorphism that has been linked to a lower ability for skill acquisition. Mark's bowling prowess steadily improves over time as he hits more of his targets and achieves higher total scores. Conversely, John finds it difficult to advance significantly; he has trouble modifying his grip, aim, and release, and he finds it tough to hit his targets consistently. This implies that the inter-individual variation in John and Mark's capacity to acquire new skills in bowling may be influenced by their genetic differences in BDNF polymorphism.

Term	Description	Example	Role	Strength	Weakness	Technique to Enhance
Spatial Information	Refers to the perception and processing of information related to space and location	Judging the placement of the pins, adjusting the angle of the ball based on lane conditions	Helps with accurate targeting and spatial awareness during shots	Improves accuracy and consistency in shots	Difficulty in adjusting to changes in the environment	Practicing spatial awareness and sensory integration tasks during training
White Matter (WM)	A type of brain tissue that contains nerve fibers responsible for communication between different brain regions	Maintaining coordination between different brain regions involved in motor planning and control	Facilitates communication between brain regions for improved motor control	Helps with consistent and accurate shots	Decreased white matter volume or connectivity may lead to motor control issues	Engaging in physical exercise and practicing coordination tasks during training
Motor Cortex	A region of the brain responsible for planning, coordinating, and executing voluntary movements	Controlling the movement and trajectory of the ball during a shot	Plays a crucial role in the control of movements and coordination	Helps with consistent and accurate shots	Damage or dysfunction can lead to motor control issues	Practicing drills and exercises that target the motor cortex for improved coordination and control
Somatosensory Cortex	A region of the brain responsible for processing tactile and proprioceptive information from the body	Sensing the position and movement of the body during a shot	Provides feedback on body position and movement for improved motor control	Helps with consistent and accurate shots	Damage or dysfunction can lead to sensory deficits or motor control issues	Practicing exercises that target somatosensory processing for improved body awareness
Superior Parietal Lobule (SPL)	A region of the brain involved in spatial cognition and sensory integration	Judging the placement of the pins and tracking the path of the ball down the lane	Plays a role in visual-spatial processing and integrating sensory information for motor planning and control	Helps with accurate targeting and spatial awareness during shots	Damage or dysfunction can lead to difficulty in adjusting to changes in the environment	Practicing spatial awareness and sensory integration tasks during training

Term	Description	Example	Role	Strength	Weakness	Technique to Enhance
Inferior Occipitofrontal Fasciculus (IOFF)	A white matter tract connecting the occipital and frontal lobes, involved in visual-spatial processing and attention	Tracking the path of the ball down the lane and adjusting the angle of the ball based on lane conditions	Facilitates communication between brain regions involved in visual-spatial processing and attention	Helps with accurate targeting and spatial awareness during shots	Decreased connectivity may lead to attention deficits or difficulty in adjusting to changes in the environment	Engaging in physical exercise and practicing attentional tasks during training
Intraparietal Sulcus (IPS)	A region in the parietal lobe of the brain involved in spatial processing	Identifying the location of bowling pins	Processing of spatial information	Improved accuracy in targeting	Difficulty in visualizing complex spatiotemporal patterns	Practice visualizing complex spatiotemporal patterns
Precuneus	A region located in the parietal lobe of the brain, situated at the posterior part of the cingulate gyrus. It is involved in a wide range of cognitive functions, including visuospatial processing, self-awareness, and attention	Cognitive functions, visuospatial processing, self-awareness, attention	Relevant for mental simulation, self-awareness, attentional focus	Enhances mental visualization and self-monitoring	Not specified in the provided information	Not specified in the provided information

Table 17 - This table elucidates essential cognitive terms for bowlers. Understanding spatial information aids in precise shots, involving brain regions like the motor cortex and somatosensory cortex. White matter facilitates communication, while the SPL contributes to visual-spatial processing. The IOFF and IPS play roles in attention and spatial processing, enhancing accuracy. Practicing spatial awareness exercises and attentional tasks improves cognitive functions for better performance.

World Class Bowlers Potential Neuroanatomical Features And Genetic Factors

The players' probable neuroanatomical characteristics and genetic makeup that are thought to be responsible for their exceptional bowling ability are displayed in the table below. It is noteworthy that these theories have their foundation in theoretical and exploratory research, which integrates insights from video analysis, interviews with the bowlers during their television appearances, and the author's personal correspondence. Their personas, techniques of training, and mental processes both on and off the track at championship events are revealed by these conversations and exchanges. **It is imperative to acknowledge that these results are broad and might not accurately encompass the distinct experiences and characteristics of every professional bowler.** To verify and hone these theories, more investigation would be necessary.

Bowler Name	Possible (Main Neuroanatomical Feature)	Possible Genetic Factor	How it Helps Them
Mika Koivuniemi	GM Volumes (Cerebellum)	BDNF Polymorphism	Enhanced motor control and skill acquisition
E J Takett	Decreased WM in Motor Regions	GM Volumes (Hippocampus)	Improved cognitive function and memory for strategy
Walter Ray Williams Jr.	Posterior Parietal Cortex	Hemisphere Communication	Enhanced spatial awareness and decision-making
Jesper Svensson	Dorsal Premotor Cortex	GM Volumes (PPC)	Precise and coordinated movements for accuracy
Osku Palermaa	Primary Motor Cortex (M1)	GM Volumes (M1)	Increased speed and accuracy in bowling
Dominic Barrett	Somatosensory Cortex	IOFF	Enhanced tactile feedback and visual-motor integration
Norm Duke	Superior Parietal Lobule (SPL)	IPS	Improved spatial perception, attention, and sensorimotor integration
Paeng Nepomuceno	Inferior Occipitofrontal Fasciculus	Precuneus	Visual-motor integration, self-awareness, and attention

Bowler Name	Possible (Main Neuroanatomical Feature)	Possible Genetic Factor	How it Helps Them
Pete Weber	Brain-Derived Neurotrophic Factor	BDNF Polymorphism	Enhanced capacity for skill acquisition and learning
Kelly Kulick	Spatial Information Processing	Hemisphere Communication	Improved spatial awareness and decision-making
Chris Barnes	Primary Motor Cortex (M1)	Decreased WM in Motor Regions	Enhanced motor control and cognitive function
Liz Johnson	Posterior Parietal Cortex	GM Volumes (PPC)	Accurate targeting and precise movements
Jason Belmonte	Dorsal Premotor Cortex	GM Volumes (M1)	Precise and coordinated movements for accuracy
Shannon O'Keefe	The Hemisphere	Hemisphere Communication	Effective analysis and spatial awareness
Marshall Holman	Spatial Information Processing	BDNF Polymorphism	Improved spatial awareness and learning capacity
Choi Bok Em	Somatosensory Cortex	Decreased WM in Motor Regions	Enhanced tactile feedback and motor coordination
Park Jong	Superior Parietal Lobule (SPL)	Hemisphere Communication	Enhanced spatial perception and attention
Parker Bohn III	Inferior Occipitofrontal Fasciculus	Precuneus	Visual-motor integration, self-awareness, and attention
Clara Guerrero	Brain-Derived Neurotrophic Factor	BDNF Polymorphism	Enhanced capacity for skill acquisition and learning
Diandra Asbaty	Spatial Information Processing	GM Volumes (PPC)	Improved spatial awareness and decision-making
Rafiq Ismail	The Hemisphere	Hemisphere Communication	Effective analysis and spatial awareness
Brian Voss	Dorsal Premotor Cortex	Decreased WM in Motor Regions	Precise and coordinated movements for accuracy
Robert Smith	Primary Motor Cortex (M1)	GM Volumes (M1)	Increased speed and accuracy in bowling
Tim Mack	Posterior Parietal Cortex	BDNF Polymorphism	Enhanced spatial awareness and learning capacity
Arturo Quantiro	Somatosensory Cortex	GM Volumes (Hippocampus)	Enhanced tactile feedback and memory for strategy
Shalin Zulkifli	Superior Parietal Lobule (SPL)	Hemisphere Communication	Improved spatial perception and attention
Tore Torgersen	Inferior Occipitofrontal Fasciculus	Precuneus	Visual-motor integration, self-awareness, and attention
Amleto Monacelli	Brain-Derived Neurotrophic Factor	BDNF Polymorphism	Enhanced capacity for skill acquisition and learning
Wu Siu Hong	Spatial Information Processing	Decreased WM in Motor Regions	Improved spatial awareness and motor coordination
Marshall Kent	The Hemisphere	Hemisphere Communication	Effective analysis and spatial awareness
Kelly Kulick	Dorsal Premotor Cortex	GM Volumes (M1)	Precise and coordinated movements for accuracy
Shogo Wada	Primary Motor Cortex (M1)	GM Volumes (PPC)	Increased speed and accuracy in bowling
Anthony Simonsen	Somatosensory Cortex	Brain-Derived Neurotrophic Factor	Enhanced tactile feedback and capacity for skill development
Bill O'Neal	Superior Parietal Lobule (SPL)	Hemisphere Communication	Improved spatial perception and attention
Tommy Jones	Inferior Occipitofrontal Fasciculus	Precuneus	Visual-motor integration, self-awareness, and attention

Bowler Name	Possible (Main Neuroanatomical Feature)	Possible Genetic Factor	How it Helps Them
Ildemaro Ruiz	Brain-Derived Neurotrophic Factor	BDNF Polymorphism	Enhanced capacity for skill acquisition and learning
Joonas Jehkinen	The Hemisphere	Hemisphere Communication	Effective analysis and spatial awareness
Pontus Andersson	Dorsal Premotor Cortex	GM Volumes (M1)	Precise and coordinated movements for accuracy
Ahmed Shaheen	Somatosensory Cortex	Inferior Occipitofrontal Fasciculus	Enhanced tactile feedback and visual-motor integration
Mohamed Khalifa Qubaisi	Spatial Information Processing	Brain-Derived Neurotrophic Factor	Improved spatial awareness and capacity for skill development

Table 18 - This table unveils neurological features and potential genetic factors influencing bowlers. Mika Koivuniemi's enhanced motor control links to cerebellar GM volumes and BDNF polymorphism. E J Takett's cognitive function benefits from hippocampal GM volumes. Each bowler's unique neurological profile contributes to their specific strengths, fostering precise movements, improved cognitive function, and heightened spatial awareness.

Note: Please keep in mind that these assumptions are based only on the information that has been presented; further research is needed to validate the precise neuroanatomical and genetic traits of these bowlers.

Decoding The Neurological Progression Of A Bowler's Skill Evolution

The development of a bowler's competences progresses through several stages, from unconscious incompetency to unconscious competence, with each stage marked by distinct neurological and genetic factors influencing the individual's motor skills and overall performance. **In the cognitive stage**, the bowler may be unaware of the intricacies of the sport, lacking both knowledge and skills. Neurological factors, such as the quantity of gray matter in brain regions linked to perception, memory, and motor control, play a vital role. A greater quantity of gray matter in the cerebellum aids in precise motor control, while the hippocampal region contributes to effective memory and learning of bowling tactics. Genetic factors may also predispose individuals to excel in certain domains, influencing gray matter distribution. As the bowler progresses to the **Associative stage**, they start recognizing and refining their skills but may still experience inconsistencies. White matter (WM) in specific brain regions becomes crucial, as it facilitates communication between brain areas responsible for motor control. Decreased WM may result in delayed information transmission, impacting cognitive functions and, consequently, motor skills. The Proper Dorsal Premotor Cortex (PMD Proper), a region responsible for organizing and executing motor movements, gains prominence. The size and activation of the PMD Proper influence a bowler's accuracy and precision in executing motions. The posterior parietal cortex (PPC) becomes essential for spatial awareness, motor control, and attention, contributing significantly to the bowler's ability to aim and release the ball accurately. **In the autonomous stage**, competences become more refined, and the bowler can perform with consistency. Both hemispheres of the brain actively engage in examining lane conditions, modifying approach and release, and making quick decisions. Spatial information, processed by areas like the somatosensory cortex, plays a pivotal role, enabling the bowler to feel the ball and receive proprioceptive feedback. The superior parietal lobule (SPL) and the inferior occipitofrontal fasciculus (IOFF) contribute to accurate targeting and planning of motions based on visual data. The motor cortex, particularly the primary motor cortex (M1), undergoes neurophysiological changes, enhancing both speed and accuracy in elite bowlers. The transition from conscious control to automaticity is observed, with neural pathways in M1 optimized for precise and efficient bowling actions. Spatial information processing remains critical in the advanced stages, involving areas like the precuneus, intraparietal sulcus (IPS), and precuneus. The integration of visual and motor skills, facilitated by the inferior occipitofrontal fasciculus (IOFF), supports the bowler in targeting and adjusting actions based on visual cues. The Brain-Derived Neurotrophic Factor (BDNF) emerges as a genetic factor influencing cognitive functioning and motor skill development. Specific gene variants, like those related to BDNF, may impact a bowler's ability to learn and enhance their skills over time. Understanding these neurological and genetic factors enhances the comprehension of a bowler's journey from novice to elite, emphasizing the intricate interplay between the brain, genes, and skill development in the context of competitive bowling.

Impact Of Medical Conditions On Bowling Neurological Competencies

In the highly competitive world of bowling, where precision, focus, and mental acuity are paramount, the physical and mental well-being of a player plays a pivotal role in determining success. Various medical conditions can significantly impact a bowler's neurological factors, potentially influencing the percentages associated with each stage of skill development. Conditions such as anxiety disorders, concussions, and neurodevelopmental disorders can alter neurotransmitter levels, sensory processing, and cognitive function. Beyond these, players may grapple with depression, attention-deficit/hyperactivity disorder (ADHD), migraines, multiple sclerosis (MS), and substance abuse, each posing unique challenges to a bowler's emotional, cognitive, and motor competencies. These conditions not only underscore the intricate interplay between physical and mental health but also emphasize the necessity of a holistic approach to athlete well-being. Understanding the potential effects of these conditions on a bowler's performance underscores the importance of tailored support, medical intervention, and a comprehensive approach to foster an environment conducive to optimal athletic achievement.

Examples of Medical Conditions that affect bowlers neurological factors

Concussion or Traumatic Brain Injury (TBI): Symptoms:

Headaches, dizziness, memory problems, difficulty concentrating.

Impact: Reduced gray matter volume, impaired cognitive function, altered motor control.

Effect on Percentages: Gray matter quantity may decrease, and both cognitive and associative stages may be affected.

Bowling Impact: During development, a bowler may struggle to learn new techniques, and in a tournament, compromised cognitive function may lead to difficulty adapting to changing lane conditions.

Chronic Stress or Anxiety Disorders: Symptoms:

Elevated stress levels, persistent worry, muscle tension.

Impact: Altered white matter functionality, increased cortisol levels affecting cognitive function.

Effect on Percentages: White matter functionality may decrease, particularly in the cognitive stage.

Bowling Impact: Persistent stress may hinder the bowler's ability to focus during development and can lead to poor decision-making under pressure in a tournament.

Genetic Factors affecting BDNF Production: Symptoms:

Variability in learning ability, difficulty in skill acquisition.

Impact: Altered BDNF levels affecting cognitive and associative learning.

Effect on Percentages: BDNF influence percentage may be affected across all stages.

Bowling Impact: Genetic factors may influence a bowler's learning capacity, potentially affecting skill acquisition and development.

Degenerative Neurological Disorders (e.g., Parkinson's Disease): Symptoms:

Tremors, bradykinesia, cognitive decline.

Impact: Changes in motor cortex functionality, reduced gray matter over time.

Effect on Percentages: Primary motor cortex changes may be affected, impacting all stages.

Bowling Impact: Tremors and motor control issues can significantly impact a bowler's accuracy and performance during both practice and tournament play.

Sleep Disorders (e.g., Insomnia or Sleep Apnea): Symptoms:

Difficulty falling asleep, disrupted sleep patterns.

Impact: Impaired memory consolidation, altered cognitive function.

Effect on Percentages: Cognitive and associative stages may be affected due to impaired memory and concentration.

Bowling Impact: Poor sleep can lead to reduced focus during practice sessions and impact decision-making and accuracy during tournaments.

Depression:

Symptoms: Persistent sadness, loss of interest, fatigue.

Impact: Altered neurotransmitter levels, particularly serotonin, affecting mood and cognitive function.

Effect on Percentages: Cognitive and associative stages may be affected due to changes in mood and motivation. **Bowling Impact:** In both development and tournaments, depression can lead to decreased motivation, impacting practice consistency and tournament performance.

Attention Deficit Hyperactivity Disorder (ADHD): Symptoms:

Inattention, hyperactivity, impulsivity.

Impact: Altered dopamine levels affecting attention and cognitive function.

Effect on Percentages: Cognitive stage may be affected due to difficulties in sustained attention.

Bowling Impact: ADHD may pose challenges during development, making it harder for a bowler to focus on refining techniques, and in tournaments, impulsivity may affect decision-making.

Traumatic Experiences or Post-Traumatic Stress Disorder (PTSD): Symptoms:

Intrusive memories, hypervigilance, emotional numbness.

Impact: Altered amygdala and hippocampal function, affecting emotional regulation and memory.

Effect on Percentages: Cognitive and emotional stages may be affected due to heightened stress responses. **Bowling Impact:** Trauma may hinder a bowler's ability to concentrate during development and trigger stress responses during tournaments.

Addiction to Pornography: Symptoms:

Obsessive consumption of pornography, Compulsive behaviors, Altered perceptions of intimacy and relationships

Impact: Psychological struggles, Distorted perceptions, Altered focus on interpersonal connections

Effect on Percentages:, Potential decrease in mental focus and team cohesion

Bowling Impact: Impaired mental focus during practice and tournaments, Difficulty forming healthy interpersonal connections within the team

Addiction to Electronic Games: Symptoms:

Excessive gaming leading to addiction, Time management issues, Potential mental health issues

Impact: Reduced practice and training time, Sedentary behaviors affecting physical health

Effect on Percentages: Potential decrease in skill development and overall performance

Bowling Impact: Hindered physical fitness and skill execution, Strained relationships affecting team dynamics and performance

Addiction to Drugs: Symptoms:

Substance addiction, Impaired cognitive function, Altered behavior

Impact: Physical and mental health issues, Reduced focus and coordination,

Effect on Percentages: Compromised performance in various aspects

Bowling Impact: Impaired focus and coordination during practice and tournaments, Strained relationships affecting team collaboration and performance

Neurocognitive Basis Of Skill Development

When it comes to developing skills, we frequently concentrate on physical aptitudes like motor coordination. Nevertheless, the neurocognitive elements of learning a skill—like perception and judgment—are crucial. Long-term cognitive growth in games like chess and language is important to take into account, even if the majority of study has focused on immediate gains in perception and motor skills.

Bowlers' brains experience notable modifications in the sensory cortex as they advance and hone their skills. In order to process pertinent sensory inputs like lane conditions and ball trajectory more effectively, this requires expanding the brain map. Bowlers can make better decisions and perform better on the lanes if they have an improved cortical representation, which improves their ability to comprehend sensory information.

Neural tuning is also linked to improved bowling perceptive ability. In the sensory cortex, neurons exhibit heightened selectivity towards particular sensory attributes. The sensitivity and discrimination of bowlers increase as they grow more skilled because their neurons are more precisely tuned to pertinent stimuli. To help bowlers better sense and understand their environment, for example, visual cortical neurons can have an increased ability to recognize small visual cues connected to the lane or ball.

Additionally, as bowling skill increases, so too may the temporal response characteristics of neurons in the sensory brain. As one gains experience, the timeliness and dynamics of the brain's reactions to sensory stimuli improve. This means that there will be improvements in synchronization with other neural networks involved in motor planning and execution, as well as faster response times and accurate timing. The bowler's capacity to interpret and integrate sensory data is greatly impacted by these changes, which leads to more precise and efficient motor motions during play.

Hypothetical example

Consider a young bowler named Sarah who has been improving her craft for a few months by practicing on a daily basis. Sarah has improved her ability to perceive and analyze sensory clues from the bowling alley, such as the lane conditions and ball trajectory, via constant practice and experience.

Sarah's primary sensory cortex—that is, the visual cortex, which processes visual information—may expand its map as her perceptual ability advances. This indicates that when Sarah's brain commits more cerebral resources to processing these crucial cues, the cortical representation of pertinent visual cues, such as the lane conditions and ball trajectory, may get larger. Sarah may be able to make better decisions when bowling if she is able to recognize and understand minor visual cues from her surroundings, such as variations in the lane's oil patterns or the angle of the ball's trajectory, thanks to this map enlargement in the visual cortex.

Sarah may also be able to sharpen neuronal tuning in the visual cortex as a result of her improved perceptual abilities. This suggests that some visual cues associated with bowling may be detected by the neurons in the visual cortex with greater selectivity. Sarah might be able to distinguish between various sensory cues and alter her bowling approach more accurately if, for instance, her neurons become more sensitive to changes in lane conditions or ball trajectory.

Furthermore, the features of the temporal response of the neurons in Sarah's visual cortex may also vary with improved perceptual ability. Her neurons might, for example, respond more quickly, time things more precisely, and synchronize more with other neural networks that are involved in motor planning and execution. Sarah may be better able to receive and integrate sensory data in real time as a result of these modifications in the temporal response properties of neurons, which would help her make prompt and accurate decisions when bowling.

Myth: Left brain dominance is always advantageous for bowlers.

Reality: While left brain dominance may provide certain advantages, such as analytical thinking and technical expertise, it's not the sole determinant of bowling success. Bowlers can excel with a variety of cognitive styles, and a balanced approach that combines both left and right brain functions can be beneficial.

Myth: Right brain dominant bowlers lack strategic planning and analytical skills.

Reality: Right brain dominant bowlers may have a different approach to strategy and decision-making, relying more on intuition and creativity. However, this doesn't mean they lack the ability to analyze situations or make strategic adjustments. Their strengths lie in adaptability and improvisation.

Left And Right Brain Dominant Bowlers

The human brain is an intricate and interesting organ that governs all mental and physiological activities. It is separated into the left and right hemispheres, and the corpus callosum, a dense network of nerve fibers, connects them. Studies have demonstrated that, while both hemispheres are involved in different cognitive activities, top athletes, like bowlers, may have a hemispheric specialization, in which some brain regions are more developed and active in one hemisphere than the other.

Left Brain: Sequential processing, language processing, and logical and analytical thought processes are generally linked to the left hemisphere of the brain. According to research, athletes' left hemisphere's pre-motor cortex (PMd), supplementary motor area (SMA), and primary motor cortex (M1) all have larger gray matter volumes. These regions are important in synchronization, motor planning, and execution; exceptional athletes, like bowlers, may have developed these areas more due to their significant training and experience.

For instance, a study on golfers revealed that top athletes, which might apply to both professional bowlers and non-bowlers, had considerably more gray matter volume in the left M1 and PMd compared to non-athletes. While the left PMd is involved in the organizing and preparatory stages of movement, the left M1 is in charge of initiating and carrying out voluntary movement. Elite bowlers have undergone substantial motor training and experience, which may be reflected in the increased gray matter volume in these regions as they establish specialized neural networks for motor planning and execution.

Furthermore, research indicates that when doing motor activities, exceptional athletes' left hemisphere is more active than their right. Using functional magnetic resonance imaging (fMRI), Hwang et al. (2019) discovered that elite athletes activated their left M1 and SMA more during a movement task than did non-athletes. The dominance of the left hemisphere in bowlers may be due to a more specialized and effective neural network for motor planning and execution.

Right Brain: Generally speaking, creativity, visual-spatial processing, and spatial reasoning are attributed to the right hemisphere of the brain. According to studies, the right posterior parietal cortex (PPC) and other right hemisphere regions may have more gray matter volume in exceptional athletes. In visual-spatial processing, the PPC is essential for hand-eye synchronization when performing motor activities.

For instance, compared to non-athletes, elite athletes had a noticeably larger gray matter volume in the right PPC in research on basketball players. Because accurate and consistent bowling requires substantial visual-spatial processing and hand-eye coordination, there may be an increase in gray matter volume in this region.

It's crucial to remember that both hemispheres are still involved in motor control and other cognitive processes, even in excellent bowlers who have a left hemisphere specialization. Actually, prior studies have indicated that whilst the right hemisphere may be more dominant in left-handed people, the left hemisphere may be more dominant in right-handed people. Thus, it's plausible that handedness has an impact on the neuroanatomical variations seen in professional bowlers.

Examples of how these terms could be related to a bowler's brain:

Left Brain Dominant Bowler:

Strengths:

Analytical and logical: A bowler who uses his left brain more often might be skilled at evaluating the lane conditions, figuring out the angles, and making accurate modifications depending on the information.

Strategic planning: In order to maximize their bowling performance, he might be adept at creating a plan of attack, establishing objectives, and carrying it out.

Technical expertise: Through meticulous practice and repetition, a left-brain dominant bowler may succeed in understanding the technical components of the game, such as follow-through, release, and accurate footwork.

Data-driven decision making: He might be adept at evaluating ball speed, rev rate, and other statistical data to help them choose the right equipment and make modifications as the game progresses.

Weaknesses:

Lack of creativity: Being more dependent on pre-established methods and routines, left brain dominant players may find it difficult to be creative and improvise.

Limited adaptability: They could be more inflexible in their approach, making it difficult for them to swiftly adjust to sudden changes in lane conditions or opponents' tactics.

Difficulty adapting to changing conditions: In reaction to shifting lane conditions or opposing strategies, they could find it difficult to immediately adjust their strategy and technique.

Over-analysis: The tendency to overanalyze circumstances, decision paralysis, or being overly cautious might be symptoms of a left-brain dominant athlete, which can result in missed opportunities.

Right Brain Dominant Bowler:

Strengths:

Creativity and intuition: By using their imagination and improvisational abilities, a right-brained bowler may be adept at instinctively modifying their approach and adjusting to shifting lane conditions.

Emotional intelligence: He may have an acute awareness of both his own and other people's emotions, which can aid in pressure management and good performance in demanding situations.

Natural feel for the game: An individual who bowls predominantly using his right brain may possess an innate sense of intuition and feel for the game, which he can use to modify and adjust to shifting circumstances.

Creative shot-making: His ability to improvise and devise original strategies for attacking the pins, utilizing various ball routes and angles to generate scoring opportunities, maybe his strongest suit.

Weaknesses:

Lack of structure and planning: A player who is right brain dominant could find it difficult to plan strategically and might depend more on instinct than on gathering information.

Difficulty with details: He could find it difficult to focus on minute technical aspects, and he might have trouble performing consistently.

Lack of consistency: Because of his improvisational style may result in variances in the way he executes shots, players that are right brain dominant may find it difficult to perform consistently.

Difficulty with structure: He can find it difficult to create an organized strategy or stick to a set schedule since he would rather trust his gut feelings than examine information or figures.

Types Of Potential Neuroimaging Techniques For Future Bowling Research:

We're studying the science to find out how our brains work when we drive on the lanes. Imagine a future in which we have figured out what makes a great bowler. This voyage is based on actual research that the author has performed; it is not just a hypothesis. We are actively attempting to understand the part our brains play in this complex process, as bowling requires accuracy, coordination, and acute mental acuity. The use of cutting-edge brain-scanning methods that allow us to see inside our minds is the key to these discoveries. Nevertheless, **given the lack of specialized research facilities for bowling neuroscience, it is imperative to recognize the limitations in this subject. However, these methods and their results may offer insightful information to researchers and coaches, leading to further developments in this area.**

Voxel-Based Morphometry (VBM):

A neuroimaging method called Voxel-Based Morphometry (VBM) quantifies variations in brain anatomy, specifically in gray matter volume, between various groups or circumstances.

Example 1: VBM in Elite Bowlers

With VBM, differences in gray matter volume between leisure and professional bowlers might be examined. Elite bowlers may have greater gray matter volumes than amateur bowlers in regions like the cerebellum and premotor cortex which are important to motor planning and coordination. This could be an indication of more developed neural networks for motor control and coordination.

Example 2: VBM in Amateur Bowlers

The technique may assist in demonstrating that amateur bowlers have greater gray matter volume in visuospatial processing and motor planning regions in their brains than do non-bowlers, indicating that bowling may have an impact on the structure of the brain, particularly in regions connected to spatial awareness and motor skills.

Diffusion Weighted Imaging (DWI)

Diffusion Weighted Imaging (Dwi) Water molecule mobility in brain tissue is measured using a magnetic resonance imaging (MRI) method called DWI. Because sports carry a significant risk of head injuries, it is frequently employed in elite athletes to evaluate and track brain health. Damage to the brain can alter the diffusion of water molecules, and DWI is sensitive to these alterations. Swelling, inflammation, and cellular damage are examples of minor alterations in the microstructure of brain tissue that it can identify that might not be picked up on traditional MRI scans. The acute and long-term effects of head trauma, such as concussions, sub-concussive impacts, and repetitive head injuries, can be assessed in elite athletes using DWI. It can be used to determine the location, degree, and severity of brain injuries as well as monitor the course of healing over time. In elite athletes, DWI can also be used to evaluate the long-term consequences of recurrent head trauma, such as chronic traumatic encephalopathy (CTE), a neurodegenerative condition linked to repeated brain trauma. DWI can provide important information about how recurrent head injuries affect elite athletes' brain health by identifying changes in the microstructure of brain tissue.

Diffusion Weighted Imaging (DWI) And Tractography:

By measuring the diffusion of water molecules in brain tissue, a neuroimaging technique called DWI can be used to infer the structure and integrity of white matter tracts. Utilizing DWI data, Tractography is a technique for recreating and visualizing the brain's white matter tract routes.

Example 1: DWI and Tractography in Elite Bowlers

The arrangement and integrity of white matter tracts connected to motor planning and execution in the brains of professional bowlers could be studied using Tractography and DWI. Elite bowlers may have higher fractional anisotropy (FA), a measure of white matter integrity, in tracts like the cerebellar peduncles and the corticospinal tract, according to the technique. This could indicate more effective neural communication and coordination between various brain regions involved in motor skills.

Example 2: DWI and Tractography in Amateur Bowlers

The method may assist in demonstrating that amateur bowlers have less developed brain connection and coordination linked to motor control and planning than elite bowlers, which may help explain their lower skill level in the game. Amateur bowlers also appear to have lower FA values in some white matter tracts compared to elite bowlers.

DWI And Tractography In Bowling Acquisition:

Regardless of ability level, DWI and Tractography can also be utilized to look into changes in white matter integrity during the learning and acquisition of bowling skills.

Example 1: DWI and Tractography in Elite Bowlers during Skill Acquisition

Tractography and DWI could be used to look into how professional bowlers' brains evolve in terms of white matter integrity as they learn new bowling approaches or talents. Once training or practice is completed, the technique may help reveal that specific white matter tracts, like the arcuate fasciculus involved in language and motor planning, show increased FA values, suggesting improved neural connectivity and coordination related to the learned bowling skills.

Example 2: DWI and Tractography in Amateur Bowlers during Skill Acquisition

Through practice, the approach may assist in demonstrating how some white matter tracts, including the superior longitudinal fasciculus, which is involved in visuospatial processing and motor planning, show changes in FA values, suggesting brain adaptations connected to learning bowling abilities.

Structural Magnetic Resonance Imaging (MRI):

A non-invasive imaging method called structural magnetic resonance imaging (MRI) gives researchers precise pictures of the anatomy of the brain, enabling them to assess the dimensions, integrity, and form of various brain regions.

For instance, one could use structural MRI to look into how the brain structure of professional and recreational bowlers differs. The method may serve to show that, in comparison to amateur bowlers, elite bowlers have greater gray matter volumes in areas linked to motor planning and coordination, such as the cerebellum and prefrontal cortex, suggesting possible structural differences connected to bowling expertise.

Functional Magnetic Resonance Imaging (FMRI):

Functional magnetic resonance imaging (fMRI) provides information on brain activity during various tasks or activities by measuring changes in blood flow and oxygenation in the brain. It can assist researchers in determining which parts of the brain are engaged in particular motor or cognitive functions.

Example, fMRI might be used to study bowlers' brain activity while they are performing a bowling task. The method may aid in revealing enhanced activity in areas such as the parietal, premotor, and motor cortex during the performance of bowling motions, offering insights into the brain mechanisms behind visuospatial processing, motor planning, and coordination during bowling.

Positron Emission Tomography (PET):

PET is a functional imaging modality that measures brain activity and metabolism using radioactive tracers. It can offer details regarding neurotransmitter activity and brain function during various tasks or activities.

Example: Using PET, researchers could look into how the brain's metabolism and neurotransmitter activity alter when bowling. Insights into the neurochemical underpinnings of bowling performance and motor skills may be gained by using this technique to identify variations in glucose metabolism or neurotransmitter levels in areas such the motor cortex, basal ganglia, and cerebellum between professional and recreational bowlers.

Electroencephalography (EEG):

Electrodes are applied to the scalp to assess brain activity electrically using EEG, a non-invasive method. It can give researchers real-time information regarding brain activity, enabling them to examine the dynamics of brain functions throughout various tasks or activities.

For instance, an EEG could be used to look at how the brain connects and activates as a bowler performs. By comparing elite and amateur bowlers' event-related potentials (ERPs) or functional connectivity patterns in various frequency bands, like alpha, beta, and gamma, the technique may help shed light on the neural dynamics of bowling performance and motor skills.

Technique	Description	Example on Bowler	Advantages	Disadvantages
Voxel-Based Morphometry (VBM)	A neuroimaging technique that measures differences in gray matter (GM) concentration or volume in different brain regions.	Comparing the GM volumes of elite and amateur bowlers to identify differences in brain regions associated with skill.	Can identify specific brain regions associated with expertise.	Only measures GM volume and cannot provide information about white matter connections or brain function.
Diffusion Weighted Imaging (DWI)	A neuroimaging technique that measures the diffusion of water molecules in brain tissue, providing information about the brain's white matter connections.	Examining the integrity of white matter connections in the brain of an elite bowler compared to an amateur bowler.	Can provide information about the strength and organization of white matter connections in the brain.	Limited to measuring white matter connections and cannot provide information about brain function or gray matter volume.
Structural Magnetic Resonance Imaging (MRI)	A neuroimaging technique that uses a strong magnetic field to create detailed images of the brain's structure, including gray and white matter.	Examining the overall structure of the brain of a professional bowler compared to an amateur bowler.	Can provide high-resolution images of the brain's structure, including both gray and white matter.	Does not provide information about brain function or the strength of white matter connections.
Functional Magnetic Resonance Imaging (fMRI)	A neuroimaging technique that measures changes in blood flow in the brain, providing information about brain activity during different tasks.	Measuring brain activity in the motor cortex of bowlers while they perform a bowling task.	Can provide information about the brain regions involved in a specific task, and how they interact with each other.	Limited to measuring brain activity during specific tasks, and may not accurately reflect brain function during other tasks.
Positron Emission Tomography (PET)	A neuroimaging technique that measures changes in brain metabolism, providing information about brain function.	Examining changes in brain metabolism in professional bowlers during the execution of a bowling task.	Can provide information about the brain regions involved in a specific task, and how they interact with each other.	Invasive procedure that requires injection of a radioactive tracer into the bloodstream.

Technique	Description	Example on Bowler	Advantages	Disadvantages
Electroencephalography (EEG)	A neuroimaging technique that measures electrical activity in the brain, providing information about brain function.	Measuring electrical activity in the brain of bowlers while they perform a bowling task.	Non-invasive and can provide real-time information about brain function.	Limited to measuring electrical activity on the surface of the scalp, and may not accurately reflect activity in deeper brain regions.

Table 19 - This table outlines various neuroimaging techniques and their applications in understanding bowlers' brain function. For instance, Voxel-Based Morphometry (VBM) highlights differences in gray matter concentration, revealing brain regions associated with expertise. While techniques like Diffusion Weighted Imaging (DWI) provide insights into white matter connections' strength, each method has its advantages and limitations, offering a comprehensive yet nuanced understanding of bowlers' neural profiles.

THE DYNAMIC NATURE OF BOWLING

Bowlers sometimes struggle with the difficulty of reliably repeating exact actions in the game of bowling. Given the erratic nature of bowling scenarios, bowlers should understand why this challenge exists. It is uncommon for bowlers to begin a game at precisely the same spot, and lane conditions might vary from frame to frame. Striking a moving target is analogous to this. But neuroscience offers a fascinating revelation that may help us clarify this conflict.

Studies have revealed that neurons in the main motor cortex (M1), the area of the brain that controls motor function, are more concerned with assisting bowlers in reaching a steady state of motion than they are with the finer points of their starting stance. This notion has been expanded upon by ideas such as the unconstrained manifold hypothesis and the minimum intervention principle. In essence, these ideas imply that the brain is more concerned with reaching the intended result than with the precise route traveled when performing a skill, such as throwing a bowling ball.

> **Adaptability is key.** Consider a top-tier bowler facing ever-changing lane conditions due to factors like humidity and lane wear. Each shot presents a unique challenge.
>
> What sets this bowler apart is their focus on the outcome, not rigidly replicating the same motion. They embrace the minimum intervention principle, understanding that what matters is knocking down all the pins consistently. This mindset allows them to explore different techniques, release angles, and speeds during practice.
>
> Their approach mirrors how songbirds learn. Just as birds use variability to find the most effective songs, this bowler's motor exploration helps them adapt to the dynamic bowling environment. This adaptability is their secret to staying at the top of their game.

What does this signify, then, for bowlers? It implies that while having a solid technical basis is crucial, bowlers should also be able to vary their actions to some extent. Rigid, highly stereotyped actions can hinder a bowler's capacity to adjust and take in new information from various situations. To improve one's bowling game, one must experiment with various tactics and allow for some variety in their approach, much like a bird learning to sing. Bowlers who embrace this idea can develop a distinctive style while maintaining a high standard of performance.

Defining Bowling Skill

What precisely is the definition of bowling skill? If compared to non-bowlers, is it only about quicker ball rotation and better accuracy, or is there a higher order of perceptual and planning involved? How particular is bowling skill, furthermore? Is there a sport like table tennis where a bowler might excel?

The performance level acquired in a given task via consistent practice is referred to as skill. Professionals with exceptional dedication—who have practiced for a minimum of ten years, or 10,000 hours—are considered skilled in any discipline. A power law can be used to roughly represent the relationship between practice trials and skill, as determined by task completion speed in a variety of tasks. This suggests that performance improves forever with appropriate practice, albeit at a decreasing rate. It is significant to remember that the majority of the data that is currently accessible is derived from laboratory tasks that have brief learning periods.

Optimizing Bowling Skills And Motor Learning Through Computational Principles

The optimization of bowling abilities is largely dependent on computational concepts in motor learning. One such idea is called "execution noise," which describes the intrinsic unpredictability or randomness in the motor activities used to carry out a skill. Variations in release angle, speed, and ball spin in bowling are indicative of execution noise, which can be attributed to various factors such as grip pressure, muscle activation, and ambient conditions. Bowlers can improve the precision and consistency of their skill execution by accounting for these variances by incorporating computational models that take execution noise into account. Bowlers, for instance, can optimize their approach and release method by using a reinforcement learning (RL) framework with a policy, reward function, and value function. This allows them to dynamically alter their actions in response to intrinsic execution noise and obtain desired ball reactions on the lane.

Execution Noise: To maximize the execution of their skills, bowlers can utilize a computational model that takes execution noise into account. Based on the intrinsic variety in their motor actions—which can be influenced by grip pressure, lane conditions, and muscle activation patterns—they might, for instance, modify the release angle, speed, and spin of the ball. The bowler can produce more accurate and consistent shots by using the computational model to assist them in discovering the best release strategy that minimizes the effect of execution noise.

The Power Of Adaptation And Rotation

Bowling has an application for rotation adaptation, a crucial computational concept in motor learning. It entails adjusting to variations in rotation dynamics, such as shifts in the bowling ball's spin or rotation axis. For example, the ball rotation dynamics and lane reactivity are significantly altered when the ball is drilled asymmetrically instead of symmetrically. Bowlers can adjust their methods based on changes in the ball's rotation by using computational models of motor learning to add rotation adaptation. This involves changing the policy, reward function, and value function to account for these changes. To adjust to the changed rotation dynamics and produce the required ball reaction on the lane, it could be necessary to make changes to your grip, release technique, and *targeting*.

Computational principles are becoming instrumental in elevating bowling skills. One critical principle in motor learning is "execution noise," representing the natural variability in motor actions during skill execution. In bowling, this noise materializes as inconsistencies in release angle, ball speed, and spin, influenced by factors such as muscle activation, grip tension, and environmental conditions.

To harness the power of computational principles, bowlers can integrate models that account for execution noise. This integration aids in addressing these variations, ultimately refining the precision and consistency of their performance. For instance, bowlers may adopt a reinforcement learning (RL) framework, encompassing a policy, reward function, and value function. Through this approach, they adapt their approach and release technique dynamically, responding to inherent execution noise, and thereby achieving the desired ball reactions on the lane.

Hypothetical Examples

Example 1: Release Adjustment for Execution Noise

Imagine a bowler who has been consistently practicing for years and has developed a high level of skill. However, during a particular game, the bowler notices that the lane conditions have changed due to factors like ambient temperature and humidity. These variations in the environment create execution noise, leading to unpredictable changes in the ball's release angle, speed, and spin.

In response to this challenge, the bowler employs a computational model that takes execution noise into account. Using a reinforcement learning framework with a policy, reward function, and value function, the bowler dynamically adjusts their release angle and spin to counteract the effects of execution noise. By doing so, the bowler maximizes the precision and consistency of their shots, adapting to the intrinsic variability in motor actions influenced by factors like grip pressure and environmental conditions.

Stage 1: Observation and Assessment

- **Step 1:** *Observe the current lane conditions, including factors like ambient temperature, humidity, and any other environmental variables.*
- **Step 2:** *Assess the impact of these conditions on the ball's release angle, speed, and spin during warm-up shots.*

Stage 2: Policy Development

- **Step 3:** *Develop a policy within the reinforcement learning framework to dynamically adjust release parameters in response to observed changes in execution noise.*
- **Step 4:** *Specify different release strategies based on variations in grip pressure, lane conditions, and muscle activation patterns.*

Stage 3: Skill Execution and Feedback Loop

- **Step 5:** *Execute shots during practice, focusing on implementing the defined release strategies.*
- **Step 6:** *Gather real-time feedback on shot accuracy and consistency.*

Stage 4: Adaptation and Refinement

- **Step 7:** *Analyze the feedback to understand how well the chosen release strategies countered execution noise.*
- **Step 8:** *Refine the policy based on the effectiveness of different release adjustments.*

Example 2: Rotation Adaptation for Changed Dynamics

Consider a skilled bowler facing a scenario where the rotation dynamics of the bowling ball have undergone a significant change. This change could be a result of having the ball drilled asymmetrically instead of symmetrically, altering the spin or rotation axis of the ball.

To address this challenge, the bowler leverages computational models of motor learning to incorporate rotation adaptation. The bowler adjusts the policy, reward function, and value function in the reinforcement learning framework to account for the new rotation dynamics. This adaptation might involve modifying the grip, release technique, and targeting to align with the altered ball rotation.

In essence, the bowler harnesses the power of adaptation and rotation by using computational principles to optimize his bowling skills. By dynamically adjusting his approach based on changes in execution noise and rotation dynamics, the bowler achieves a higher level of precision, consistency, and control over the ball's reaction on the lane.

Stage 1: Identification of Rotation Dynamics Change

- **Step 1:** *Identify the specific changes in rotation dynamics, such as alterations in spin or rotation axis, resulting from having the ball drilled asymmetrically.*

Stage 2: Policy Adjustment for Rotation Adaptation

- **Step 2:** *Modify the existing policy within the reinforcement learning framework to incorporate rotation adaptation.*
- **Step 3:** *Define new actions in the policy related to grip adjustments, release techniques, and targeting.*

Stage 3: Skill Execution and Feedback Loop

- **Step 4:** *Implement shots using the adapted policy, considering the changes in rotation dynamics.*
- **Step 5:** *Collect feedback on how well the adjustments align with the desired ball reaction on the lane.*

Stage 4: Iterative Refinement

- **Step 6:** *Analyze the feedback to determine the effectiveness of the rotation adaptation.*
- **Step 7:** *Iteratively refine the policy, reward function, and value function based on the observed outcomes.*

The Actor-Critic Approach

Reinforcement learning (RL) makes extensive use of the actor-critic approach to improve motor abilities in a variety of domains, including bowling. The performer and the critic are the two primary parts of this method.

It is the actor's responsibility to decide what to do given the circumstances at hand. It makes use of a policy, which is a collection of guidelines for choosing which course of action to take. The actor, for example, depicts the bowler's decision-making process when it comes to deciding the ball's release angle, speed, and spin throughout the approach and delivery phases of the game. The policy can be stochastic, in which the actor chooses actions based on a probability distribution, or deterministic, in which the actor chooses the action with the highest probability.

By evaluating the current state or state-action pair, on the other hand, the critic evaluates the actor's actions. It assesses how well the performer performed and gives an indication of how effective they were. The value estimate provided by the critic is used as a feedback signal to modify the actor's policy. For instance, while evaluating a release technique for bowling, a critic can consider how well it hits the target or produces the intended ball reaction on the lane. To maximize the bowler's performance, the reviewer and the performer collaborate. The critic provides input on the acts' worth while the actor chooses actions based on the policy. Over time, the actor improves performance by updating the policy and refining its decision-making process in response to criticism.

> **The Actor-Critic approach** is a reinforcement learning technique used in machine learning and artificial intelligence. It's a type of model that combines elements of both value-based methods (Critic) and policy-based methods (Actor) to optimize decision-making in sequential tasks. Here's a brief overview of each component:
>
> Actor: The actor is responsible for making decisions or choosing actions. In reinforcement learning, this corresponds to the policy function, which determines the probability distribution over actions given a particular state.
>
> Critic: The critic evaluates the actions taken by the actor. It provides feedback in the form of a value function, which estimates the expected cumulative reward of being in a particular state and following a certain policy. The critic helps the actor by providing information on how good or bad the chosen actions are in the long run.

An example of the actor-critic architecture in bowling

There is one such bowler in the world of elite bowling who really gets the actor-critic method and applies it to his game. This is how he goes for it:

Step 1: Understanding the Game

Our top bowler examines the condition, the lane, and his mood for the day before he even begins to play. He is curious about his opponents.

Step 2: Making Decisions

He then employs a tool known as a "policy" to decide. It resembles a set of guidelines for gameplay. In bowling, this entails determining the ideal release angle, speed, and spin for the ball.

Step 3: Adapting as Needed

Bowlers are shrewd since they have the flexibility to instantly alter their policy. Depending on the circumstance, individuals can either attempt new things or cling to what they know works.

Step 4: Being Your Own Judge

This is where the critic enters the picture. This is analogous to having a court observe your actions. In bowls, the way things are going is how you determine whether or not your movements are effective.

Step 5: Learning and Getting Better

The purpose of the critic is to guide your improvement. When it notices that something is particularly effective, it notifies you so that you can continue. If not, it assists you in determining what needs to be altered.

Step 6: Making Smarter Choices

You can make more informed decisions with the help of this input. You change your strategy if something isn't working. You become very proficient at it over time.

Step 7: Getting Great Results

Our bowler constantly puts up exceptional performances thanks to this dynamic interaction between the critic and the actor. His choice and use of strategies are expertly calibrated, similar to the faultless musical performance of a master.

Scenario: Extreme Breakdown Patterns and Lofting Strategy

Situation: *In a professional bowling competition, the lane conditions undergo extreme breakdown patterns, resulting in a depleted oil pattern in the standard playing areas. Many bowlers struggle to find a consistent reaction on the worn-out lane surface. However, one skilled bowler recognizes the opportunity to exploit the unplayed area with remaining oil by lofting the ball high and playing deep inside.*

Actor-Critic Approach:

Step 1: Understanding the Game

The bowler carefully observes the extreme breakdown patterns, noting the depletion of the oil pattern in the traditional playing zones. Understanding that the unplayed area might still have some oil, the bowler sees an opportunity.

Step 2: Making Decisions

Using the "policy," the bowler decides to employ a lofting strategy, aiming to send the ball high in the air to reach the un-played area. The decision includes determining the ideal release angle, loft height, speed, and spin to optimize the ball's reaction.

Step 3: Adapting as Needed

Recognizing the need for immediate adaptation, the bowler adjusts his approach to loft the ball effectively. This may involve modifying the release technique, adjusting the loft height, and experimenting with different speeds.

Step 4: Being Your Own Judge

The critic comes into play as the bowler assesses the effectiveness of the lofting strategy. How well the ball travels through the air, hits the target in the un-played area, and reacts on the lane surface are critical evaluation points.

Step 5: Learning and Getting Better

The critic provides feedback on the lofting strategy. If it proves successful in reaching and utilizing the un-played area, the bowler learns from this experience. If adjustments are needed, the critic helps identify areas for refinement.

Step 6: Making Smarter Choices

Armed with feedback from the critic, the bowler can make more informed decisions. If the lofting strategy is effective, it becomes a part of the bowler's toolkit for similar breakdown patterns. If not, adjustments are made to enhance the lofting technique.

Step 7: Getting Great Results

Through this dynamic interaction between the critic and the actor, the bowler not only navigates the challenges of extreme breakdown patterns but also capitalizes on the un-played area, consistently achieving great results by lofting the ball high and playing deep inside the lane. This strategic adaptation sets the bowler apart in competitions with challenging lane conditions.

Scenario: Timing Issues and Lane Adjustment

Situation: *In the middle of a high-stakes tournament, a skilled bowler experiences an unexpected loss of timing, leading to inconsistent shots. The bowler, who generally struggles with timing issues in the outside lane area (around the 1st and 2nd arrow), finds himself playing in Zone 1 due to the lane conditions or strategic reasons.*

Actor-Critic Approach:

Step 1: Understanding the Game

The bowler recognizes the sudden loss of timing and acknowledges the inconsistency in shots while playing in Zone 1. Understanding the importance of timing in his game, the bowler evaluates whether external factors or strategic decisions led to this challenging situation.

Step 2: Making Decisions

Using the "policy," the bowler decides whether to persist in Zone 1 or to make a strategic adjustment. This decision involves considering potential changes to the release technique, footwork, or overall approach to regain and maintain proper timing.

Step 3: Adapting as Needed

Recognizing the urgency of the situation, the bowler adapts his approach by making real-time adjustments to correct the timing issues. This may involve experimenting with different release points, altering the footwork, or modifying the overall timing of the shot.

Step 4: Being Your Own Judge

The critic comes into play as the bowler assesses the effectiveness of the timing adjustments. The bowler observes how well the adapted approach aligns with the desired timing and consistency.

Step 5: Learning and Getting Better

The critic provides feedback on the timing adjustments. If the changes result in improved consistency, the bowler learns from this experience. If the adjustments are not effective, the critic helps identify areas for further refinement.

Step 6: Making Smarter Choices

Armed with feedback from the critic, the bowler can make more informed decisions. If the adapted approach works well in Zone 1, it becomes part of the bowler's repertoire for handling timing challenges. If not, adjustments are made to enhance the timing technique.

Step 7: Getting Great Results

Through this dynamic interaction between the critic and the actor, the bowler overcomes the unexpected timing issues, either by successfully adjusting to Zone 1 or by making strategic decisions that play to his strengths. Consistency is regained, allowing the bowler to perform at his best even in challenging situations during the tournament.

Myth: Elite Bowlers Have Identical Movements:

There's a common misconception that elite bowlers perform identical movements in every shot, resulting in consistent trajectories. In reality, they adapt and adjust joint angles to achieve desired outcomes, allowing for variations in their approach.

Myth: Consistency Equals Predictability:

It's a myth that consistency in elite bowlers' outcomes makes their shots predictable. While they aim for consistency, variations in joint angles and other factors keep opponents guessing and add an element of surprise to their game.

Myth: Optimal Control Means Fixed Movements:

There's a misconception that achieving optimal control in bowling means following fixed and unchanging movements. In reality, it means maintaining consistent outcomes while allowing flexibility in the path taken to reach those outcomes, adapting to the dynamic nature of the sport.

The Fascinating Freedom Of Movement In Bowling

It's natural to presume that the motions of bowlers at the top of *his* game follow predictable patterns from trial to trial. Variations in ultimate postures and early movement components may nonetheless coexist with consistent end results, thanks to the numerous degrees of freedom of the motor system. When the intended result—like the trajectory of a bowling ball—depends on the action rather than being an inherent component of it—like the swing's shape—this complexity increases even more. Simple movements have clear regularities, but with repetition, movement patterns tend to consolidate. Still, other elements are rather changeable, and this stabilization is mostly seen in features of posture that directly contribute to the desired result. At different phases of the movement, joint angles are important.

In bowling, freedom of movement refers to the bowler's ability to move smoothly and comfortably during his approach to the foul line, enabling him to deliver the ball effectively. Several key components contribute to freedom of movement in a bowler:

1. **Stance:** *The bowler's starting position before taking steps in the approach. A balanced and comfortable stance sets the foundation for a smooth delivery.*

2. **Grip:** *How the bowler holds the bowling ball is crucial. The grip should be firm enough to control the ball but not too tight, allowing for a natural and relaxed hand position.*

3. **Steps and Stride:** *The bowler's approach involves a series of steps leading up to the release of the ball. A consistent and well-timed series of steps contribute to a smooth approach. The length and timing of the steps can vary between bowlers based on their personal style and preferences.*

4. **Swing:** *The motion of the bowler's arm and the path of the bowling ball during the backswing and forward swing are critical. A controlled and smooth swing helps in maintaining balance and accuracy.*

5. **Release:** *The moment when the bowler lets go of the ball. The release should be controlled and well-timed, allowing the ball to roll smoothly off the hand.*

6. **Follow-through:** *The continuation of the bowling motion after the release. A good follow-through helps maintain balance and can provide feedback on the quality of the shot.*

7. **Balance:** *Throughout the entire approach and delivery, maintaining balance is crucial. Proper weight distribution and body alignment contribute to a fluid and controlled motion.*

8. **Timing:** *The coordination of all the components mentioned above is essential for proper timing. The bowler needs to synchronize his steps, swing, and release for an effective and accurate shot.*

9. **Flexibility and Fitness:** *Physical condition and flexibility play a role in a bowler's ability to move freely. Regular exercise and stretching can contribute to improved freedom of movement.*

10. **Equipment:** *Properly fitted bowling shoes and a well-maintained bowling ball can also impact a bowler's ability to move comfortably on the approach.*

Put more simply, optimum control implies that while elite bowlers consistently produce the results they want, the routes they choose to get there can differ. Bowlers must comprehend and become proficient in these ranges of motion in order to succeed in their sport.

Below are a few examples of joint angles that a bowler can change at various stages during his motion:

Approach: In order to maximize the bowler's balance, stability, and power production, joint angles like the knee, hip, and ankle angles can be changed during the approach, which is the first portion of the bowler's movement towards the foul line. For example, to have a steady foundation and provide the required amount of power for their shot, bowlers might slightly bend or stretch their ankle, hip, and knee joints.

Release: The moment the bowler releases the ball is known as the release. At this point, the spin, speed, and direction of the ball can be controlled by adjusting the joint angles in the wrist, fingers, and elbow. For instance, the fingers can be positioned to control the rotational axis, and the wrist can be stretched or flexed to impart more or less spin on the ball. Additionally, the elbow joint can be extended or flexed to change the ball's trajectory and speed.

Follow-through: Joint angles can also be used to modify the bowler's follow-through, which is the arm and body movement made after the ball is released. Various configurations of the wrist, elbow, and shoulder joints can be used to maximize follow-through consistency and precision. To regulate the ball's trajectory and precision, a bowler can, for instance, fully extend his arm or keep it slightly flexed during the follow-through.

Body Alignment: To maximize bowling technique overall, joint angles in the bowler's body alignment—such as the hips, shoulders, and spine—can be changed. The accuracy, force, and consistency of the bowler's shots can be significantly impacted by maintaining proper body alignment during approach, release, and follow-through. To align the ball with the intended target point and produce the correct ball reaction on the lane, for example, a bowler might modify the tilt and rotation of his spine, hips, and shoulders.

Balance: For optimal balance to be maintained throughout the bowling motion, joint angles are essential. It is possible to modify the alignment and placement of the knees, ankles, and hips to maximize the bowler's stability and balance during the approach, release, and follow-through. This is necessary to keep possession of the ball and make accurate shots.

THE ADVANTAGE OF ANTICIPATORY SKILLS IN EXPERT BOWLERS

In the high-stress setting of bowling, skilled players exhibit an amazing capacity to predict and respond to particular situations with seeming ease. This ability is especially clear when making difficult decisions, including selecting the perfect ball type based on the bowler's abilities, the lane circumstances, and the bowling center.

The fundamental skill of this ability is the expert's ability to use their in-depth understanding of situational probabilities to forecast the most likely course of action in a bowling scenario. According to one theory, specialists estimate based on prior knowledge and trends they have noticed in comparable circumstances.

Examples anticipatory information

Example 1: An excellent bowler adapts his game according to the conditions of the lane by using probabilistic expectations and anticipatory information pick-up. The bowler, for example, expects the ball to hook more, or hook sharply, as it goes down the lane if it is dry or breakdown. The bowler may decide to utilize a ball with a less friction coverstock or modify his throw technique to account for the expected hook based on this awareness of situational possibilities. In order to maximize his chances of hitting the pins with the greatest force, they can also set probabilistic expectations about the particular board or target region on the lane where the ball is least likely to hook.

Example 2: To read the pins and make changes for pin carry, a skilled bowler uses probabilistic expectations and anticipatory information pick-up. For example, when a throw is made, the bowler predicts how the pins will move and interact depending on the ball's angle and speed. He estimates the probability of a specific pin-fall or the potential pin carry. The bowler may decide to modify his next throws, such as changing the ball or pin they aim for (Focal Point), in order to increase his chances of earning a greater pin count, based on his comprehension of situational probabilities.

Apart from novices and less experienced bowlers, expert bowlers have the distinct ability to collect and apply information even prior to the ball being released. They are especially good at assessing how their bowling arm moves in relation to their hand in the final step before the ball is released. Their superior information processing is one of their unique selling points and a major element in their exceptional standing.

Skilled bowlers also show a benefit in producing the exact movements they must predict. For example, in research involving basketball players, experts outperformed professional viewers and novices in their ability to anticipate the result of a shot based just on the kinematics of the throwing motion prior to ball release. According to neuroimaging research, the way elite athletes use kinematic information from finger motions to anticipate ball trajectories is correlated with a unique modulation of corticospinal excitability, reflecting activity in the motor cortex.

Expert bowlers may do well on certain general sensory tasks, but their performance on tests unique to bowling, such as those measuring anticipation, search, and memory, is a better indicator of their total bowling ability. This implies that a key component of bowlers' competence is the development of domain-specific memory structures and decision-making skills.

Forward Models In Bowling

The idea of forward models is central to computational motor control. The brain can forecast expected changes in the status of an object or a bodily component as a result of an outgoing command thanks to these internal simulations. Forward models allow more accurate state estimates, allow precise actions that are too quick to rely exclusively on sensory feedback delays and can be improved through learning. The brain may approximate a hand's new location, for instance, even before it receives sensory feedback. An ideal estimate of the hand's location can be achieved by combining the forward model's prediction with real-world visual and proprioceptive feedback. In order to minimize prediction errors, forward models can also adjust when differences occur between feedback and predictions, such as while wearing prism glasses.

Here are the steps involved in utilizing the forward model for elite bowlers in bowling:

Gathering Information: *Pro bowlers collect data regarding ball varieties, bowling lane conditions, and their own body mechanics. They evaluate things like lane texture, oil patterns, and their own physical prowess.*

Building the Forward Model: *Skilled bowlers create a forward model that mimics the anticipated trajectory and behavior of the bowling ball based on their experience and knowledge. Variables including release angle, spin, pace, lane circumstances, and ball properties are taken into consideration by this model.*

Anticipation and Prediction: *Elite bowlers use the forward model to predict how their actions will turn out in advance. They create an accurate mental simulation of the ball's trajectory, including interactions with the lane surface, oil patterns, and pin layout. They forecast the ball's trajectory as it approaches the pins.*

Technique Adjustment: *Skilled bowlers make the required modifications to their technique based on the forward model's projections. To maximize the ball's trajectory and raise the possibility of reaching the intended pin impact, they could alter their release angle, speed, or spin.*

Strategic Decision-making: *Throughout the game, skilled bowlers use the forward model to guide their judgments. They take into account things like pin placement, ball changes, and lane transitions. They select the best tactics to optimize their scoring potential by taking into account their expectations and forecasts.*

Continuous Refinement: *Pro bowlers make ongoing improvements to their forward model in response to immediate feedback and outcomes. They modify their model in accordance with their comparison of the expected and actual ball behavior. Over time, the quality and dependability of their forward model are enhanced by this iterative process.*

Does the idea of forward models—which forecast the sensory effects of an individual's actions—have anything to do with anticipating other people's bowling strokes? The idea of the forward model must be demonstrated to apply to external things in the outside world in order to make this connection. One could assume that a bowler could estimate how their ball will move and how it would affect ball trajectory. One last query: What connection is there between the **mirror system** and forward models of other people's actions? For further motor planning, it is possible that the cerebellum receives a directive from the mirror system and subsequently relays predictions to the premotor cortex.

Examples:

Predicting ball trajectory: *In a bowling alley, a bowler can use a forward model to forecast the ball's trajectory based on the force and direction of their throw. The forward model allows the bowler to make real-time adjustments to their aim and technique to achieve the intended outcome by simulating the outcome of the outgoing command (the ball's release) and predicting the impending change in the ball's condition (the trajectory).*

Adjusting body posture: *Another instance would be if a bowler were to change his body alignment as he approached the lane and then release the ball. The forward model may forecast an impending shift in the body's state, such as balance and alignment, and simulate how the outgoing command to alter body posture will be carried out. In order to maximize his throw and raise* *his odds of striking the mark precisely, the bowler can then make small adjustments to their body position, weight distribution, and timing.*

Mirror System In Bowling

The mirror system, a fascinating neural mechanism discovered through research involving macaque monkeys in the 1990s, is now recognized for its significant role in both the execution and comprehension of actions. This neural network is characterized by the activation of mirror neurons, specialized nerve cells that fire not only when an individual performs a specific action but also when they observe someone else engaging in a similar movement. While the initial studies were conducted in monkeys, subsequent research has suggested the presence of analogous mechanisms in humans, making the mirror system a compelling area of exploration in various disciplines.

In the context of bowling, the mirror system finds intriguing applications, shedding light on how bowlers not only execute their own shots but also understand and anticipate the actions of fellow bowlers. The activation of mirror neurons during the execution of a bowling stroke could contribute to the internal simulation of the movement, allowing the bowler to refine and adjust their technique for optimal performance.

Mirror neurons, integral to the mirror system, play a pivotal role in motor simulation. As a bowler observes the movements and actions of another bowler preparing for their shot, mirror neurons may simulate the neural patterns associated with that specific bowling technique. This internal simulation aids in the understanding of the observed action and could potentially influence the observer's own motor planning and execution.

The mirror system's connection to social cognition and empathy is particularly relevant in the social context of bowling. As bowlers engage in friendly competition, the mirror system may contribute to the recognition and understanding of the intentions, emotions, and expressions of fellow players. This heightened social awareness fosters a sense of camaraderie and enhances the overall bowling experience.

Moreover, the mirror system's role in imitation and observational learning is noteworthy in the context of skill development in bowling. Novice bowlers may benefit from observing and internally simulating the techniques of more experienced players, utilizing the mirror system's capacity for motor simulation to enhance their own skills.

Scenario 1: The Perfect Strike

As a professional bowler steps up to the lane during a high-stakes competition, the pressure is palpable. The crowd watches in anticipation as the bowler begins their approach. The mirror system comes into play as the bowler's brain engages mirror neurons, internally simulating the precise movements required for the perfect strike. With a fluid swing, expert release, and spot-on aim, the bowler executes a flawless shot. The mirror system not only enhances the bowler's own motor planning and execution but also contributes to the audience's engagement as they vicariously experience the thrill of the well-executed strike.

Scenario 2: Observing a Competitor's Technique

During a professional bowling competition, a seasoned player observes a rival bowler who consistently scores high. The mirror system is activated as the observing player's mirror neurons fire, internally simulating the observed bowler's technique. The experienced bowler mentally replicates the movements, assessing the subtleties of the approach, release, and follow-through. This internal simulation facilitated by the mirror system allows the observing player to gain insights into the competitor's strategy. Subsequently, armed with this newfound understanding, the seasoned bowler adapts their own approach, demonstrating the mirror system's role not only in self-performance but also in learning and strategic decision-making based on the actions of others.

Aspect	Mirror System	Forward Models
Description	Neural mechanism involving mirror neurons; activates when observing or performing actions.	Computational models predicting sensory consequences of actions.
	During a competition, a professional bowler closely watches a rival's flawless delivery, and their mirror neurons fire, internally simulating the observed technique.	A player employs forward models by mentally calculating the anticipated path of the bowling ball based on their planned release and the lane conditions.
Advantages	- Facilitates motor imitation and learning.	- Enables accurate prediction of sensory outcomes of actions.

Aspect	Mirror System	Forward Models
	After observing a fellow competitor's unique spin technique, a bowler incorporates elements into their own game for improved versatility.	Anticipating the impact of a power throw, a player adjusts their approach to optimize the angle and speed for a more controlled outcome.
Weaknesses	- Limited in providing explicit details about the physics of actions.	- Highly dependent on accurate knowledge of the physical environment.
	While observing an opponent's finesse in spare conversions, the bowler might lack detailed insights into the exact physics governing those movements.	In rapidly changing lane conditions, a bowler's forward models may struggle if their predictions are not aligned with the actual behavior of the ball.
Strategic Process	- Observing and imitating other bowlers.	- Planning and adjusting actions based on predicted sensory outcomes.
	A bowler, inspired by a peer's consistent strikes, incorporates elements of their approach into their own strategy.	In response to challenging lane conditions, a player strategically adjusts their release angle based on the predicted ball path.
Thought Process	- Internal simulation of observed actions.	- Calculation of anticipated sensory effects of one's actions.
	While watching a competitor's powerful hook, a bowler mentally replicates the motion, attempting to understand and incorporate elements into their own game.	A player calculates the expected hook and pin action, adjusting their aim and release to optimize the sensory outcome on the lane.
Application in Bowling	- Understanding and replicating opponent's techniques.	- Adjusting the approach for optimal release and ball trajectory.

Table 20 - This table explores the Mirror System and Forward Models, two cognitive aspects crucial in bowling strategies. The Mirror System, involving mirror neurons, aids in motor imitation and learning, while Forward Models enable precise prediction of sensory outcomes. Bowlers benefit by observing and incorporating techniques, strategically adjusting actions based on sensory predictions, fostering adaptability in dynamic game scenarios. However, limitations exist, emphasizing the need for a nuanced understanding of observed actions and accurate environmental knowledge.

Motivation In Bowling

In bowling, motivation is essential for improving performance and making decisions. It can be characterized as the relationship between results and their worth. This concept covers many decision-making levels in bowling and is based on reinforcement theory. Either implicit or explicit motivation—which is sparked by outside rewards—is determined by an unconscious evaluation of the benefit-cost trade-off. When there is an implicit or explicit hierarchy of rewards, there is a chance for disputes that can be successfully handled under a coach's supervision.

Examples

General arousing effect: An intense desire to win a match or break a personal best may cause a bowler to become more aroused and excited. His improved physical preparedness, attention, and concentration as a result of this elevated drive may have a beneficial effect on his motor skills, including his accuracy, speed, and force when throwing the ball.

Goal-specific component: A bowler with a strong desire to increase his rate of spare conversion may make personal goals and strive to meet him. This goal-specific incentive might push the player to practice frequently, ask a coach for criticism, and evaluate his play to find areas for growth. Through directing his drive towards a particular objective, the player can concentrate his energies and intentionally modify his motor control techniques to maximize his performance in that specific domain.

There are two basic ways that motivation improves motor performance: a general energizing effect and a goal-specific component. Reinforcement learning provides insight into bowling motivation by teaching agents—whether they be artificial intelligence systems or humans—how to maximize cumulative rewards through decision-making. According to recent research, the benefits bowlers receive for specific tasks, like making a solid shot, may make "teaching signals"—which depend on dopamine, a crucial neurotransmitter linked to motivation and reward processing—more significant.

Phasic dopaminergic signals, or the reward's prediction error, are necessary for the dopamine-dependent weighting of instructional signals. Positive dopamine signals are produced when the actual reward meets or surpasses expectations; negative signals are produced when it does not. Task-specific rewards are received by bowlers who hit the pocket precisely, which leads to greater scores or strikes. By modifying dopamine-dependent teaching signals, these rewards have the ability to affect how people learn.

By comprehending the significance of motivation and how it relates to task-specific incentives and dopamine-dependent instructional cues, bowlers can reach their maximum potential. Bowlers can generate continual progress, improve their performance, and succeed more on the lanes by utilizing motivation and directing it toward their objectives.

Positive Reward Prediction Error: Imagine if a bowler modifies one aspect of his game, like aiming for a different pin or changing the speed of the ball, and he is able to hit more pins and score higher on a regular basis. Positive dopamine signals would be produced by the brain's reward prediction error system, suggesting that the actual reward—a higher score—was greater than anticipated. An higher weighting of the "teaching signal" associated with the particular adjustment made by the bowler would result from this positive reward prediction error strengthening the link between the adjustment and the good outcome. The bowler is therefore more likely to make the same modification in subsequent trials, which will result in better performance.

Singapore National Team

Negative Reward Prediction Error: In contrast, the brain's reward prediction error mechanism would produce negative dopamine signals if a bowler made a specific technique adjustment but it did not produce the expected rewards, like consistently missing the pins or receiving lower scores. This would suggest that the actual reward was less than anticipated, which would result in the "teaching signal" linked with that adjustment being given less weight. The fact that the modification did not produce the intended result may make the bowler less inclined to make it again in subsequent tries.

Reinforcement learning is mediated via the brain's reward prediction error system, which is governed by dopamine-dependent weighting of "teaching signals." Through this process, bowlers are able to adjust and improve their motor control methods in real time based on how their actions perform. Bowlers can improve their performance over time by using this approach to learn from their mistakes, modify their techniques, and get new insights.

Malaysia National Team

While motivation can have a good effect on learning and performance related to immediate rewards, it is important to consider what kind of motivation is responsible for the thousands of practice hours needed to become a top bowler. Studies indicate that even the most committed practitioners might not always find the most fulfillment in their work. Rather, they are driven by the desire for long-term benefits, with the most importance placed on future achievements.

Nature Versus Nurture: Exploring Skill Acquisition

It has long been a contentious topic to discuss the nature vs. nurture argument. According to one view, the amount of intentional practice (DP) done determines how well a person acquires skills, including elite performance. Working with optimized training tactics, focused effort, and feedback are what set deliberate practice apart from work and play. But factors including the need for recovery, personal drive, and the availability of resources all affect participation in DP.

Intentional practice is important, as evidenced by studies looking at the practice histories of successful bowlers. Bowlers from Malaysia and Singapore compete on a worldwide scale teams from other countries begin intentional practice early in the season and exceed their peers from other countries in terms of total practice hours. Training obviously has a big impact on the physiological characteristics related to bowling. Still, different interpretations and doubts regarding the validity of autobiographical and retrospective practice histories may result. Not only does concentrating on top performers overlook those who have practiced but have not achieved significant success, but it also breaks the link between practice and skill acquisition.

Bowlers can maximize their learning curve and game by comprehending the complex interactions among reinforcement, motivation, and skill gain. Bowlers can develop their skills, succeed in the sport, and realize their full potential by adhering to the principles of reinforcement learning, creating goals that are in line with long-term incentives, and practicing purposefully.

Myth: "Intensive Training Always Leads to Improvement"

Reality: While intensive training is essential for skill development, excessive training can lead to overtraining syndrome or the development of conditions like the "yips." Overtraining can harm performance, lead to burnout, and negatively affect both novices and elite bowlers. It's crucial to strike a balance between rigorous training and adequate rest to prevent these detrimental outcomes. Recognizing the signs of overtraining and taking steps to address them is essential for sustained performance at the highest level.

Myth: "Bowling Skill Development Has No Age Limit"

Reality: While skill development in bowling can occur at various ages, there are limits to how quickly and effectively one can progress. Young bowlers may have advantages in terms of physical adaptability and learning speed, but older individuals can still make significant strides with the right training and commitment. However, there may be a point where age-related factors, such as physical limitations, make it more challenging to achieve high-level performance. It's important to set realistic goals and expectations based on individual circumstances.

Nature Perspective:

a) Player A, a 10-year-old kid prodigy, shows remarkable bowling abilities from a young age without much formal instruction or focused effort. Player A is an exceptionally accurate and precise pin-hitter who routinely performs well in bowling events despite having no exposure to formal coaching or training programs.

b) Born into a family of accomplished bowlers, Player B is a professional bowler with a track record of success. Player B shows remarkable innate ability and aptitude in bowling without a strong focus on methodical, planned practice. Rather than being the result of prolonged intentional practice, Player B's talents appear to be mostly impacted by hereditary variables and innate abilities.

Nurture Perspective:

a) Player C, a beginner who has never bowled before and has no family history of bowling, begins bowling on a regular basis and participates in organized coaching and training programs. Player C practices purposefully, devoting a lot of time and energy to improving his skills, increasing his accuracy, and picking up sophisticated tactics. Player C's performance gradually becomes better over time, leading to higher scores and more reliable pin hits.

b) Player D, a casual bowler who is passionate about the game, begins routine bowling practice and engages in focused, in-depth sessions with a certified coach. Player D's performance gradually improves and finally he becomes a skilled bowler, participating at a high level in local bowling leagues despite having no prior natural aptitude or innate qualities in bowling.

The Psychological Toll: Understanding Choking And Burnout In Bowling

For bowlers, this "choking" phenomenon can be very frustrating. It describes the unanticipated drop in performance that occurs in competitive settings. The Fitts pattern of skill development offers one reason for choking. An earlier stage of skill learning is characterized by extensive self-analysis, which might impede performance as skills become highly practiced and routine. It's interesting to note that performance is typically negatively impacted by experimental interventions that direct attention toward internal movements rather than external stimuli, but primarily for proficient bowlers.

Neuro-anatomically speaking, after motor sequence training, people's attention is refocused on *his* movements, activating specific brain regions. This mechanism involves the right anterior cingulate cortex and left dorsal prefrontal cortex. Furthermore, activity in the rostral prefrontal cortex, linked to switching between internally directed and externally focused thought processes, may have an impact on the capacity to sustain a suitable focus.

Additionally, severe disorders like burnout or overtraining syndrome might result from intense training. Repetition can often lead to aberrant changes in highly practiced movements, which over time may have detrimental effects on other limb movements. It is thought that extended exposure to the motions practiced during practice causes aberrant alterations in the basal ganglia and sensorimotor cortical areas. Although bowlers call this illness the "yips," people frequently are left with no option except to give up professional bowling.

It is vital for bowlers to comprehend the elements that lead to a breakdown in performance, such as choking and the negative consequences of heavy training. Bowlers can reduce the dangers and maintain peak performance by identifying potential hazards and putting methods in place to keep a correct focus and avoid overtraining.

Example

A very good bowler who has trained hard could struggle with burnout or overtraining syndrome during a bowling competition. This could show itself as a general feeling of tiredness, diminished performance, and physical and mental exhaustion. The bowler might find it difficult to execute at his typical level and might exhibit symptoms of diminished accuracy, focus, and drive.

Another example in a bowling tournament may be a bowler who has been practicing a specific method a lot for a long time, which causes focal dystonia, which is often known as the "yips" in bowlers. The bowler's accuracy and performance may be significantly impacted by uncontrollably occurring muscle spasms, tremors, or jerking movements in the muscles used to hold or release the bowling ball. The bowler may find it challenging to perform his desired technique because of the aberrant plastic changes in the basal ganglia and sensorimotor cortical areas generated by continuous sensory input associated with the practiced actions.

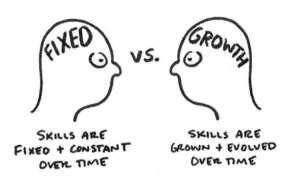

SKILLS ARE
FIXED + CONSTANT
OVER TIME

SKILLS ARE
GROWN + EVOLVED
OVER TIME

DEVELOPING THE WINNING
MINDSET IN BOWLING

Possessing the proper mindset is essential for both success and personal development in the bowling industry. Your beliefs, attitudes, and perceptions of your own skills are all part of your mindset. It has a big impact on how you approach practice, competition, and self-improvement. It can be either growth or fixed. With the use of real-world examples, let's examine the ideas of growth and fixed mindsets in bowling and see how adopting a growth mindset can accelerate your progress as a bowler.

Growth Mindset: This is the idea that you can improve your intelligence and skills by working hard, being committed, and being persistent. Growth mentality People view obstacles and failures as chances for growth and development. They accept that making mistakes is a necessary part of the growing process. Here's one instance:

Consider yourself a bowler who has trouble hitting the mark with consistency and accuracy. If you had a growth mentality, you would see this as an opportunity to improve your abilities. To fix your errors, you would examine your technique, ask your coach or teammates for comments, and put in a lot of practice. You would not view the issue as a setback, but as a worthwhile educational opportunity.

In bowling, adopting a growth mindset has multiple advantages for your own growth. First of all, it promotes perseverance in the face of difficulties and disappointments. Failures don't depress you; rather, you view them as chances to grow and learn. This perseverance enables you to recover quickly, maintain your motivation, and carry on with your goal of greatness. Secondly, having a growth mindset promotes openness to learning and asking for criticism. You're receptive to advice and criticism from teammates, coaches, and more seasoned bowlers. Feedback is not personal; rather, it is a tool for self-evaluation and growth. Your progress is accelerated and your potential is realized when you adopt this mindset of continuous learning and improvement.

Fixed Mindset:

A fixed mindset, on the other hand, is the conviction that IQ and skill levels are unchangeable and fixed. Those with fixated perspectives are more likely to shy away from new experiences, be afraid of failing, and oppose change. They can believe that *his* skills are fixed, viewing failures as evidence of their incapacity rather than as chances for improvement. Let's look at an illustration:

Consider a bowler who does well in training but finds it difficult to compete. If one has a fixed perspective, there might be a tendency to blame outside variables like bad luck or difficult lane circumstances for failures. If one thinks they're not good enough, motivation could be lost, and future participation in competitions might be avoided. Accepting responsibility for performance and making improvements becomes challenging due to this stuck thinking.

The ability to improve as a bowler is hampered by a fixed mindset in several ways. First of all, it restricts the ability to take chances and move beyond the comfort zone. Challenges are shied away from due to fear of failure and concerns about its impact on self-worth. This hinders talents, performance, and stalls advancement. Second, resistance to criticism and feedback is a sign of a rigid worldview. Criticism is interpreted as a personal slight against one's value. This defensive mindset prevents the recognition of feedback as an important tool for personal development, leading to missed opportunities to grow and develop.

Furthermore, persistence and motivation are impacted by a fixed perspective. When faced with obstacles or failures, motivation is quickly lost, and giving up becomes a likely response. Failure is viewed not as a roadblock to improvement but as a reflection of innate skills. The ability to bounce back and persevere becomes a major hindrance to long-term success in bowling or any other sport.

On the other hand, adopting a growth attitude will significantly benefit bowling progress. Believing that skills can be acquired with work and commitment, individuals take a proactive and optimistic approach to problems. They are prepared to try new things, ask for criticism, and grow from mistakes. This type of thinking facilitates reaching goals and realizing potential by accelerating learning and development as a bowler.

Strategic Plan To Cultivate A Growth Mindset In Bowling

Stage 1: Mindset Awareness and Education

Step 1: Understand the Difference

- Explain to bowlers the difference between a fixed and development attitude.
- Give lessons or workshops on how mentality affects bowling performance.
- Give concrete instances of how adopting a growth mindset might help someone succeed at bowling.

Step 2: Self-Assessment

- Assist bowlers in considering their present state of mind.
- Give bowlers a self-assessment tool or questionnaire to help them determine their prevailing mindset.
- Provide tailored advice and help in accordance with the findings of the assessment.

Stage 2: Embracing Challenges and Learning from Failure

Step 3: Challenge Acceptance

- Foster an environment where bowlers welcome difficulties and see them as chances to improve.
- Assign tasks or objectives to the team that call for moving outside of comfort zones.
- Honor and recognize efforts rather than just results.

Step 4: Failure as Feedback

- Help bowlers understand that failing is a great way to get feedback.
- Motivate them to examine their errors and create plans for growth.
- Tell tales of well-known bowlers who overcame adversity to further their careers.

Stage 3: Seeking and Using Feedback

Step 5: Feedback Culture

- Encourage a culture of feedback-giving among team members.
- Teach teammates and coaches how to give constructive criticism.
- Encourage bowlers to seek and provide feedback through open channels of communication.

Step 6: Self-Reflection

- Encourage bowlers to regularly reflect on their game.

- Tell them to record their analysis of their bowling performance in a journal.
- Instruct them in establishing goals for personal growth based on self-evaluation.

Stage 4: Setting and Pursuing Goals

Step 7: Goal Setting

- Assist bowlers in establishing realistic yet difficult objectives.
- Divide big objectives into more manageable benchmarks.
- Stress the value of establishing both outcome- and process-oriented goals (e.g., raising average score) in addition to one another.

Step 8: Goal-Driven Practice

- Arrange practice sessions in accordance with the objectives of bowlers.
- Include activities and drills that concentrate on particular areas that need work.
- Track developments and offer suggestions for achieving objectives.

Stage 5: Developing Mental Toughness and Resilience

Step 9: Mental Training

- Include mental training in your practice regimen on a regular basis.
- Instruct students in mental toughness-boosting methods like mindfulness, positive self-talk, and visualization.
- Provide bowlers with resources (books, courses, or experts) to help them hone their mental skills.

Step 10: Resilience Building

- Equip bowlers to handle hardship and failure.
- Create practice scenarios that test bowlers' ability to handle difficult circumstances.
- Promote a network of support among coworkers to keep one another resilient.

Stage 6: Cultivating Growth Mindset in All Aspects

Step 11: Comprehensive Growth Mindset

- Make sure that your bowling technique, strategy, and mental game are all incorporated into the growth mindset concept.
- Keep reinforcing the notion that progress is an ongoing process.
- Give instances of how a growth mindset might be used in different bowling situations.

Step 12: Continuous Learning

- Create an environment where learning and development are ongoing.
- To improve their knowledge and abilities, bowlers should be encouraged to attend training camps, seminars, and workshops.
- Make materials and bowling experts accessible.

Stage 7: Assessment and Monitoring

Step 13: Progress Evaluation

- Evaluate the bowlers' mental growth on a regular basis.
- To assess progress, use performance measures, one-on-one interviews, and surveys.
- Modify the coaching and support strategy in light of the assessment's findings..

Step 14: Celebrate Growth

- Celebrate and recognize achievements in both team and individual growth.
- Acknowledge and honor bowlers who exhibit a strong growth mentality.
- Encourage others by sharing your team's accomplishments.

Step 15: Continuous Improvement

- Iterate the strategy plan frequently in response to input and outcomes.
- Adjust to the changing demands and difficulties faced by the bowlers.
- Remain current on the most recent findings and applications concerning the formation of a bowling mindset.

Bowlers can improve their performance, resilience, and the bowling environment by progressively changing from a fixed mindset to a growth mindset by adhering to this strategic plan.

The Impact Of Mindset, Grit, And Self-Determination On Bowling Progression

Bowlers encounter significant influences from a variety of sources, including mentality, grit, and self-determination, on their self-efficacy and learning growth. Let us examine the ways in which these psychological factors influence their progress toward enhancement.

1. The Power of a Growth Mindset: A growth mindset has enormous potential for boosting self-efficacy and encouraging productive learning practices. It is characterized by the conviction that skills and talents can be developed through effort, practice, and learning. A growth mentality makes bowlers more likely to take on new challenges, aim high, actively seek out criticism, and evaluate their performance. These characteristics greatly aid in their education and growth, allowing them to keep getting better at bowling.

2. Unleashing Grit and Resilience: Grit is essential for fostering self-efficacy and the growth of learning since it is typified by resolute persistence, constant effort, and a positive outlook on obstacles and disappointments. Players who possess a high degree of grit demonstrate an exceptional degree of perseverance and resolve in their pursuit of objectives. Their unwavering drive for achievement boosts their self-efficacy and solidifies their conviction that they can succeed in spite of challenges. These bowlers exhibit exceptional dedication to purposeful practice and worthwhile educational opportunities, which further their entire development.

3. Nurturing Self-Determination: Bowlers' learning growth and self-efficacy are greatly influenced by their sense of self-determination, which includes relatedness, autonomy, and competence. Bowlers are more likely to feel driven, involved, and committed to their own growth when they have the authority to make decisions about their practices and competitions and are able to control their emotions and behavior. Their growth is greatly impacted by this innate motivation as they take charge of their bowling experience.

4. Embracing the Creative Mindset: Bowlers' self-efficacy and learning growth are significantly influenced by their perspective and sense of self-worth in relation to creativity and innovation. Individuals who possess a growth creativity mentality and high self-efficacy in creativity are more likely to believe that they are capable of coming up with novel ideas, adjusting to changing circumstances, and coming up with creative solutions to issues. Their self-efficacy is raised by this belief in their creative potential, which encourages them to actively participate in creative endeavors that advance their growth and learning.

Example 1: A bowler with a lot of grit puts forth constant effort and endures through training and matches. Despite obstacles or disappointments, he is prepared to invest the time and energy needed to advance their abilities. For instance, he may not give up easily and may practice consistently even in the face of unsatisfactory outcomes. He keeps an optimistic outlook and see setbacks as transient challenges that can be solved with perseverance and willpower.

Example 2: An additional illustration of grit in bowling is a player who consistently shows enthusiasm in the game in spite of a variety of obstacles, including setbacks, financial difficulties, or injuries. Even in the face of challenges, he never waver from his love of bowling or his dedication to his long-term objectives. He don't allow failures stop him from following his love of the game, and he is prepared to sacrifice and put in the required work to get over obstacles and meet his bowling objectives.

Self-determination: A key component in the growth of bowlers' learning and self-efficacy is self-determination. Autonomy, competence, and relatedness are the three psychological requirements that make up Self-Determination Theory (SDT), which was developed by psychologists Edward Deci and Richard Ryan. Competence is the conviction in one's own skills, relatedness is a feeling of kinship with others, and autonomy is the capacity to make decisions on one's own. Self-determination affects bowlers' motivation, engagement, and general well-being in the game, all of which have an impact on their self-efficacy and learning progress.

Through fostering competence, relatedness, autonomy, and self-determination, self-determination influences learning growth and self-efficacy. Bowlers are more likely to be motivated, interested, and dedicated to their learning and growth when they feel connected to others, empowered to make decisions about their training, and confident in their abilities. Bowlers with autonomy can make objectives and participate in activities that suit their interests. Relatedness promotes a nurturing environment for development, whereas competence builds self-assurance and belief in one's abilities. Bowlers are more likely to have better levels of self-efficacy and to participate in productive learning behaviors like goal-setting, getting feedback, and performance reflection when these psychological demands are satisfied, which eventually improves their learning and growth as bowlers.

Example 1: A bowler who possesses a high degree of self-determination feels empowered to make decisions about their practice and competitive bowling training. He is driven by his inner desire rather than outside constraints or expectations, and he feels that he has control over their bowling path. For instance, based on his own values and interests, he may decide on his own competition timetable, practice drills, and goal-setting. His motivation, involvement, and general dedication to his bowling objectives are increased by this autonomy in decision-making.

Example 2: A bowler who concentrates on improving his skill level in the game is another illustration of self-determination in the sport. He actively looks for ways to advance his abilities, know-how, and tactics via training, mentoring, and constructive criticism. He establishes difficult but attainable objectives and track his advancement toward them, which aids in the development of his perception of proficiency and effectiveness as bowlers. His self-efficacy is increased by this sense of competence since he thinks he can bowl well and will keep trying to get better.

Creativity Mindset: Bowlers' self-efficacy and learning growth are significantly impacted by having a creative mindset, which includes beliefs and attitudes toward creativity and invention. It includes being open to taking chances, embracing ambiguity, and using unconventional thinking for problem-solving and decision-making in the bowling setting.

Example 1: In both practice and competition, a bowler with a growth innovation mentality shows a willingness to take chances and try out novel strategies. He sees setbacks or errors as chances for improvement and are willing to try new methods, approaches, and bowling style modifications. He is not scared to step outside of his comfort zone in order to acquire new abilities or approaches, and he actively seeks out problems that call for innovative problem-solving techniques. His self-efficacy is increased by this growth-creativity mentality because he thinks he can adapt and perform well in many bowling scenarios.

Example 2: A bowler who subscribes to the growth-internal control theory is another illustration of a creative mentality in action. Instead of seeing creativity as an innate quality that someone either possesses or lacks, he sees it as an internal quality that can be developed with work, practice, and learning. He actively participates in creatively stimulating activities like brainstorming, experimenting, and contemplation because he feels that creativity is something he can control. Because kids believe they can come up with creative ideas and solutions when bowling, this internal locus of control belief increases his creativity self-efficacy, which in turn supports his learning and growth.

The development of learning is significantly influenced by creativity and self-efficacy. It molds bowlers' confidence in their capacity to come up with original solutions in a variety of bowling scenarios. Bowlers who possess a high level of creativity and self-efficacy have faith in their ability to come up with novel ideas, adjust to shifting conditions, and come up with inventive solutions to issues during practice and competition. Since they are more likely to participate in creatively stimulating activities, this conviction in their creative ability has a favorable impact on their learning and development. For instance, they might try out novel approaches or plans and actively look for problems that call for original problem-solving abilities.

The impact that self-determination, grit, growth mindset, and fixed mindset have on bowlers' self-efficacy and learning progress is significant. Bowlers' behaviors, attitudes, and beliefs are shaped by these characteristics, which also affect their learning results and sense of self-efficacy. For example, a growth mindset is essential for improving self-efficacy since it promotes the idea that skills can be acquired by work, experience, and education. Bowlers who have a growth mindset think they can overcome obstacles and get better at what they do by working hard. Additionally, bowlers who adopt a growth mindset are more likely to embrace obstacles, actively seek out criticism, and practice purposefully to improve their game. All of these behaviors are known to foster learning and development.

Conversely, a fixed perspective might impede bowlers' growth in terms of learning and self-efficacy. It imparts the idea that aptitudes are set and unchangeable. This idea may cause resistance to criticism or challenges, a fear of failing, and a lack of desire to learn. As a result, bowlers who have a fixed attitude could feel less confident in their abilities and be less likely to take part in learning activities. This may hinder their development as bowlers overall and hinder their progress.

PSYCHOLOGICAL TRANSITIONS TO HIGHER LEVEL IN BOWLING: FROM JUNIOR TO SENIOR (ELITE) AND ACADEMY TO FIRST ON TOUR

Understanding Transitions In Bowling Careers

In particular for young athletes, the road to becoming a professional bowler can be emotionally and physically taxing. Transitions can upset a bowler's social and personal balance and can happen as a result of a variety of events or circumstances. These crucial transitional phases in a bowler's career typically entail adjusting to new attitudes, behaviors, and the difficulties that come with dedication, hard effort, and personal sacrifice. In the last twenty years, studies have concentrated on the junior-to-senior stage, which is a critical turning point in the developmental model of sports involvement as it signifies the change from years of specialization to years of investment. Age and the organizational structure of the sport might have an impact on the transition to elite sport.

Challenges during the Transition Phase

There are many obstacles in the way of bowlers moving up to more competitive levels of play. The degree to which bowlers utilize their knowledge and abilities during this critical time will determine how successfully this shift goes depending on their own traits.

1. Effective Coping Strategies

It has been underlined that young bowlers must learn coping mechanisms to handle the pressures and adversities they face. The success or failure of the bowling transition from junior to senior levels can often be determined by how well one can handle these obstacles. Problem-focused coping, emotional-focused coping, appraisal-focused coping, and avoidance-focused coping are the four basic types of coping techniques. Here are some examples:

Problem-Focused Coping:

a) *Consulting a coach for technical guidance on increasing ball speed and accuracy.*

b)   *Experimenting with various bowling strategies to accommodate to shifting lane circumstances, such as modifying foot positioning or ball release.*

c)   *Creating a mental checklist and pre-shot ritual to help you stay focused and consistent throughout the tournament.*

Emotional-Focused Coping:

a)   *Calming nervousness and calming down with deep breathing exercises prior to a high-stakes match.*

b)   *Discuss feelings of frustration or disappointment following a low-scoring game with a coach or supportive teammate.*

c)   *During competition, using visualization and positive affirmations to increase self-confidence and keep an optimistic outlook.*

Appraisal-Focused Coping:

a)   *Rather than obsessing over a missed spare, consider it a teaching moment to sharpen your spare shooting techniques.*

b)   *Relying on prior achievements, such as a personal best or high score, to boost motivation and self-assurance.*

c)   *During the competition, engaging in mindfulness exercises by remaining in the present and avoiding becoming unduly preoccupied with previous or future results.*

Avoidance-Focused Coping:

a)   *Maintaining concentration on the present shot during a tournament while ignoring self-doubt or distracting thoughts.*

b)   *Recharging and de-stressing by taking a break from bowling practice or competition when feeling overburdened.*

c)   *To lessen pre-competition tension, refrain from talking about or thinking about impending competitions or opponents.*

A bowler's ability to effectively transition from junior to senior level in sport depends on their understanding of their personal resources. Several research investigations have found crucial human resources that are associated with exceptional performance in the future.

2. Personal Resources

Make reference to the internal and external components that bowlers need in order to advance to higher levels of competition. Common traits of the junior-to-senior level transition have been found in these studies. All things considered, psychological characteristics like confidence and self-belief, in addition to intrinsic motivation, are essential for bowlers to advance to the senior level. The environment also contributes significantly by offering the required support and encouragement. This approach is significantly aided by coaches and bowlers having a trustworthy relationship. Throughout the change, social support—especially from teammates, family, and friends—has been repeatedly shown to be essential. It's crucial to remember, though, that applying too much pressure can have negative consequences. It is also believed that equipment and facility access are essential for a smooth transition. It is simpler for bowlers to make the move to the senior level when they have the option to pursue two careers.

Additionally, personal resources like drive, dedication, and physical preparedness for the higher demands of the top level are important factors in determining the success of a move within a career. The importance of social support cannot be overstated, particularly the practical and emotional assistance that parents, significant others, and colleagues can provide.

It is clear that a variety of personal and environmental factors can have a favorable impact on a transition's result. It is imperative to emphasize, nonetheless, that there is no set route to success and that the transition process is very personalized. As a result, it's critical to acknowledge and resolve any obstacles or requests bowlers could encounter. This knowledge will make it easier to spot possible hazards that can result in a bad transition or even a sport-related dropout.

3. Demands And Barriers

3.1. Crisis Transition

When bowlers start competing in adult events, they often go through the junior-to-senior phase. This change, which might take one to four years to complete, signifies the beginning of the master stage. It's commonly accepted as the hardest adjustment, and it has a big effect on a bowler's future career. Bowlers invest a lot of money in their sport during the move to elite sport. **This change separates bowlers into two groups. The greater portion finds it difficult to handle the demands of the shift and either stays at a steady level, moves to recreational sports, or perhaps quits completely. Bowlers who make the transition and advance to higher levels of competition are in the second category.**

When a bowler uses the tools at their disposal to get through the difficulties while coping, the shift goes well. On the other hand, a crisis transition happens when a bowler is unable to handle the demands of the change and needs help or psychiatric intervention. The three sorts of interventions that Stambulova's model (2003) specifies are 1) crisis-coping interventions, 2) preventive interventions, and 3) interventions to address negative outcomes.

Preventive transitions:

Example 1: By making plans for their ultimate retirement from competitive bowling, a bowler in an educational setting can undertake a preventive shift. After bowling, he may choose to continue his school or get training in order to get ready for a different line of work. For instance, in order to acquire abilities that will be helpful in a new profession, the player can enroll in a business or marketing course.

Example 2: A bowler who sets goals to go to higher levels of competition might prepare for changes in their athletic career. For instance, he may choose to begin participating in local, regional, or national competitions with the intention of progressively raising the bar on his competitiveness over time. The athlete may also prepare for changes to different positions within the game, including coaching or mentoring younger athletes.

Crisis coping transitions:

Example 1: If an injury unexpectedly prevents a bowler from playing, he may go through a crisis-coping transition. In this situation, individuals might have to rely on their networks of support and coping mechanisms to get through the psychological and physical difficulties of the change. In order to maintain his motivation and optimism during the healing process, the player may choose to collaborate with a physical therapist to create a recovery plan and ask friends and family for support.

Example 2: If a bowler unexpectedly loses a coach or trainer, or another important member of his support system, he may go through a crisis coping shift. In this situation, he might have to look for a substitute right away and become used to working with a different coach or trainer. During this shift, the player may also need to rely on his own assets and knowledge to stay inspired and concentrated.

Reactive/negative transitions:

Example1: If a bowler gets a doping ban from competition, he can go through a reactive or negative transition. In this situation, the athlete can struggle with losing his sense of self as a sportsperson and go through a lot of emotional distress. A therapist may be consulted in order to treat any underlying issues that may have contributed to the doping, and a plan for restoring the player's credibility and reputation within the sport may need to be developed.

Example 2: If a bowler is suddenly eliminated from the team for subpar play, he may go through a reactive or negative shift. To get back on the squad in this situation, the player might have to focus on developing his abilities and enhancing his output. In order to stay upbeat and motivated throughout this trying time, the athlete may also need to rely on his network of friends and family.

The goal of preventive interventions is to assist bowlers in comprehending and becoming ready for the impending challenges of the shift. They will be able to overcome the obstacles they will encounter by building the necessary resources. Bowlers can analyze and handle problems more skillfully with the help of crisis coping strategies. The "costs" of a bad transition—which could include accidents, overtraining, psychosomatic disorders, dropout rates, drug abuse, or even criminal activity—are the main target of negative consequences interventions. In cases where bowlers have already suffered the effects of failing to effectively navigate a crisis shift, psychological treatment is frequently required. Getting ready for the change can help remove obstacles and make it easier for them to adjust to the next phase of *his* careers.

A significant number of junior bowlers who participated in competitive sports as children gave up throughout adolescence, and most of them stopped competing when they entered adulthood. As such, the move to professional sport is generally acknowledged as a difficult time for bowlers. Therefore, it is critical to comprehend the typical expectations and obstacles that prevent bowlers from advancing to higher levels or even prompt them to give up on the sport.

3.2. Common Demands and Barriers

This change brings with it a number of demands and difficulties for the bowlers in their daily life as well as in practice and competition. Finding a balance between sport and life goals, handling the pressure of selection, gaining recognition from peers, and handling relationship problems are the main difficulties during the move to the senior level. Bowlers who view the shift as a crisis frequently admit they require psychiatric support since they are unable to handle these obligations on their own. Bowlers also rank the most taxing tasks as rising physical demands, better performance goals, mental skill development requirements, and financial challenges (like decreased playing time, outside pressures, rigorous training schedules, juggling two careers, adjusting to new environments and competition levels, and low funds). The transition process becomes more difficult for bowlers who do not have access to the required resources and support systems. This might result in an unsuccessful transfer or even dropout. As examined here, a number of important obstacles can have a substantial impact on bowlers' growth and the way their transfer turns out.

Preventive Coping:

a) *Maintaining physical energy and avoiding exhaustion during competitions by eating a balanced diet and drinking plenty of water.*

b) *Regularly practicing mental training techniques to build resilience and avert psychological crises linked to performance, such as self-reflection or visualization.*

c) *Planning frequent relaxation and rest days to prevent burnout and enhance general well-being.*

Crisis Coping:

a) *Managing acute tension or anxiety during a crucial period in a competition by using relaxation techniques like progressive muscle relaxation or mindfulness.*

b) *Seeking out quick assistance from a coach or fellow player in the event that, during practice or a tournament, one suddenly loses confidence or motivation.*

c) *Reframing negative ideas and using constructive self-talk to help one recover concentration and confidence following a breakdown linked to performance.*

Negative-Consequences Coping:

a) *Thinking back on and examining performance data, like scorecards or video recordings, to pinpoint problem areas and avoid repeating the same errors.*

b) *Taking part in self-evaluation and self-care activities, such as journaling or speaking with a mental health specialist, to address any unfavorable effects of continuous stress or performance-related pressure.*

c) *Creating a stress management strategy that includes coping mechanisms, realistic expectations, and asking coaches or teammates for assistance in order to stop negative impacts on mental health and performance from getting worse.*

3.2.1 Self-Identity and Development.

People go through a number of developmental challenges during adolescence, a time marked by high dropout rates. These challenges include making new friends, becoming emotionally independent from parents, and figuring out who they are in society. A young person's life is largely shaped by the process of developing their sense of self, and competitive bowling can have an impact on this process. For bowlers, the degree of self-identity development can have both advantages and disadvantages. Adolescents who participate in competitive sports heavily may develop a strong sense of self-based on their athletic accomplishments.

"Bowlers may inadvertently neglect other facets of their lives, such as educational and professional prospects when they concentrate only on their sports endeavors. Identity foreclosure is a condition that can negatively impact an athlete's capacity to adjust and manage different changes during their sports career. Bowlers need to understand the value of leading a well-

rounded, balanced lifestyle in order to create useful coping mechanisms that will help them through the highs and lows of their sports careers."

3.2.2 Social Relationships.

Children learn how to interact with their peers in their early years, but as they become older and become more independent from their parents psychologically, they work to build more sophisticated and intricate friendships. They want to establish solid social and familial ties as adults. Relationships and the social environment are very important to bowlers' growth in the sport. Bowlers may experience detrimental effects on their general well-being in addition to their performance when they become socially isolated. A bowler's social network usually consists of classmates, parents, and coaches. Often referred to as the athletic triangle or the primary family of sport, the ties between bowler-coach, coach-parents, and parents-bowler have been highlighted as critical for effective development towards elite sports status.

A young bowler feels excluded from team events and finds it difficult to establish friends on his squad. His confidence in the lanes and general pleasure of the sport are being negatively impacted by this. Developing social skills with teammates can be facilitated by the player collaborating with his coach or parents. This can entail organizing team-building exercises or motivating the athlete to strike up discussions with his teammates.

An adolescent bowler's involvement in the sport is causing him to have arguments with his parents. The player's parents are not in favor of the player spending time and energy on bowling and instead want him to concentrate more on his studies. The family is experiencing stress and strain as a result, which is demotivating the player to keep playing the sport. Working with a coach or counselor can help the player improve his communication abilities and negotiation techniques with his parents. The athlete might also profit from reaching out to other members of the bowling community for social support, such as mentors or teammates who can offer guidance and inspiration.

3.2.3 Education.

Most people work toward their career and educational goals. It can be difficult, though, to strike a balance between the development of your academic career and your athletic career, particularly in nations where schooling is required until the age of 16. For young bowlers, the move to higher education is crucial since it's during this time that their focus on their academic and professional growth must coexist with the growing importance of high-performance sport. Furthermore, depending on the situation, the importance of role models and sport development in higher education institutions might change dramatically. For instance, university sports may not be as intense in the UK as they are in North America, where they are highly competitive and regarded seriously. Student-bowlers may face difficulties juggling two careers at this time.

3.2.4 Previous Development Experiences and Talent Identification.

In addition to obstacles that directly affect transitions within a bowler's career, a bowler's trajectory can also be impacted by prior growth experiences. Bowlers' growth is greatly influenced by talent identification and development (TID) models; development rates, the relative age effect, and an early emphasis on performance can all have an impact on how well a bowler performs when faced with difficult career transitions. Understanding the nature of TID programs and their impact on bowlers' development is crucial throughout their journey to become great players, as it acknowledges that transitions are a process rather than a single event.

4. Psychological Transition In Talent Identification And Development

4.1. Challenges with Traditional TID Models

For a number of reasons, talent identification methods that evaluate young bowlers' performances within age-specific groups based on physiological, anthropometric, or technical factors have proven to be problematic. Four steps are usually involved in discovering young bowlers with talent: detection, identification, development, and selection. In addition to relying on the gifted individual, talent development is a long-term process that needs a strong support network to help overcome obstacles as they come up. Talented bowlers develop at varying rates, which causes variances in the ages at which they perform at their best. While some bowlers may show signs of talent as early as age 12, others might not show signs of talent until age 17 or 18. Traditional talent assessment and development programs suffer substantially from these individual variances, which renders them unreliable. At the top level of bowling, success is not always guaranteed by strong performances in young championships. Bowlers' effective development and progression can be hampered by a number of factors, including disparities in maturation (related to the relative age effect), variations in development rates, and an emphasis on short-term performance over long-term development.

4.2. Variations in Development Rates: Uncovering Talent Takes Time

It is critical to understand that some talents may take several years to completely develop. The start of training and competitive participation might differ among elite bowlers in the same sport as well as among successful bowlers in other sports.

The Impact of Relative Age Effect: Birthdates and Bowler Differences

There are instances where young bowlers in the same selection year can be 11–12 months apart in age, which causes differences in *his* mental, physical, and emotional development. The "relative age effect" (RAE) is the name given to this phenomenon.

RAE has been seen in bowling among other sports. It alludes to the fact that elite sports teams have an excessive number of individuals who were born in the first few months of the selection year. It is commonly known that RAE has a significant impact on bowlers' growth, especially throughout the youth and junior stages of their careers. Bowlers' development is impacted by a variety of elements, including mental toughness, physical characteristics, technical proficiency, and strategic thinking. RAE, however, can also have a big effect on how they develop.

RAE may be common in bowling, particularly among younger and junior players. This indicates that, in comparison to players born later in the year, a disproportionate number of players born in the first few months of the selection year are selected for bowling teams. Numerous nations, including the United States, Australia, and Canada, have reported seeing this pattern.

The growth of bowlers can be impacted by RAE in bowling in a number of ways. First off, rather than being chosen for teams based on their true talent, younger players can be chosen only on the basis of their age. Because of this, players who were born later in the year may not get the opportunity to play and develop their skills, while players who were born earlier in the year may benefit more from more opportunities.

Secondly, younger athletes may have access to greater coaching and training options, which could help them develop their technical abilities and all-around performance. However, if the player is not yet physically mature enough to bear the demands of hard training and competition, this can also result in burnout and a higher likelihood of overuse injuries.

Thirdly, younger players may also be picked to play against lesser opposition more frequently, which could inflate their stats and give them an inaccurate impression of their skill. As a result, they could be overvalued and find it difficult to handle the pressures of competing at a higher level against stronger opponents.

In order to ensure that bowlers have a fair and equitable growth pathway and to maximize their potential for long-term success in the sport, it is imperative that the effects of variances in development rates and the relative age effect be understood and addressed.

Examples

Selection for Junior National Teams: December 31st may be the deadline set by a national bowling association to choose players for their U18 (Under 18) national squad. In comparison to their counterparts born later in the year, as in November or December, players born in January or February would be older. Their edge in terms of maturity—both physical and emotional—could make them more likely to be chosen for the national squad.

Access to Training Opportunities: January 1st may be the deadline for U12 (Under 12) bowlers to apply to a bowling academy's talent development program. Compared to athletes born later in the year, such in November or December, those born earlier in the year, like in January or February, would be able to enroll in the program earlier. They might benefit from having access to more possibilities for competition, specialized coaching, and training as a result, which could advance their skill development.

Competition in Age Group Tournaments: On September 1st, there may be an age group division just for U15 (Under 15) bowlers in a regional bowling event. The younger bowlers, born in October or November, would compete against the players born in January or February, who were born earlier in the year. They might have a comparative advantage in terms of emotional and physical development as a result, which could affect their output.

Scholarship and Sponsorship Opportunities: A bowling organization may have a scholarship program for U18 bowlers, and the cutoff date for eligibility may be December 31st. Players born earlier in the year, such as in January or February, would be eligible for the scholarship earlier compared to players born later in the year, such as in November or December. This could give them an advantage in terms of accessing financial support, sponsorships, or scholarships, potentially facilitating their talent development.

4.3. Balancing Early Performance and Long-Term Development

It's crucial to understand that senior bowling success does not necessarily require early specialization in any one sport. Rather of concentrating on just one activity as a child, many international bowlers have actually trained and competed in a variety of sports. Some young kids who were scouted and helped along the way didn't end up becoming good senior bowlers. Some senior bowlers, however, who are quite successful, did not take part in talent identification and development TID programs when they were younger. Given the complex nature of talent, the conventional methodology of TID programs may inadvertently leave out talented bowlers, particularly late players.

Consequently, putting too much focus on early success may limit the pool of talent and impede bowlers' long-term development. Since performance is influenced by a variety of interrelated and ever-changing elements, talent is a dynamic notion. Predictive talent models shouldn't be one-dimensional, according to several coaches. Although professionals who choose the best junior bowlers for a team appreciate the importance of psychological competencies in fostering growth, they might not have a thorough awareness of the psychological processes that go into developing a player's potential. Gaining a greater grasp of the psychological aspects influencing talent is essential to bridging the gap between theory and practice in talent identification and development. Thus, performance determinants (e.g., anthropometric, physical, and psychological characteristics), the talent development environment, and learning strategies and behaviors should all be taken into account in TID programs.

5. Fostering Competition Readiness

Young bowlers need to prepare for organized sports competitions during their formative years. As far as motivation is concerned, readiness is the degree to which kids play sports out of real interest and zeal. Parents' supporting involvement can help to improve motivational preparedness. From a cognitive standpoint, being ready means having the capacity for abstract thought as well as knowledge of the duties and responsibilities peculiar to the sporting environment. Role-playing and perspective-taking skills in children reach their peak development between the ages of 8 and 10. Consequently, young bowlers may become frustrated and lose interest in participating in sports if they are pressured by their parents, for example, to play sports before they are cognitively ready. This dissatisfaction is caused by a lack of cognitive talents necessary to deal with the difficulties and demands that come with playing sports. In addition, youngsters up until the ages of 10 or 12 may find it difficult to evaluate their own skills and frequently depend on adults for guidance and information. They start evaluating themselves against their peers as they get older. If bowlers have an ability-oriented perspective and believe they are not as good as their peers, then they are more likely to drop out. Consequently, the development of young bowlers in competitive sports is greatly influenced by motivation and cognitive maturation.

Furthermore, bowlers' goal orientation has a big impact on their growth and is directly related to how much they play and advance in the sport. The degree of satisfaction and confidence that bowlers have affects not just how much they participate in the sport but also how far they may go in their growth. Previous studies have distinguished between different motivational environments and how they impact goal orientation.

A young bowler who is just beginning to play in organized contests feels under pressure to do well. But rather than considering the child's cognitive and motivational preparation, his parents are pressuring him to compete and come out on top. The bowler becomes agitated and frustrated as a result, eventually losing interest in the game. Instead of concentrating only on winning, the parents might have promoted the bowler's growth by promoting involvement based on aptitude and interest.

Teenage bowler faces intense pressure from his friends and coach to perform well and win. The bowler continually compares himself to his classmates and has an ability-oriented goal orientation, which causes low self-esteem and feelings of inadequacy. This has a detrimental effect on his performance and motivation and may increase his chance of dropping out. To change his focus to a more task-oriented goal orientation, the bowler might find it helpful to work with a sports psychologist or coach. This would entail creating personal objectives and putting more emphasis on skill development than on comparing oneself to others.

5.1. Harnessing Goal Orientation for Success

In the bowling world, objectives greatly influence performance and results. There are two primary categories of goals: extrinsic goals and intrinsic goals. Extrinsic objectives center on things like fame, material gain, and attractiveness, whereas intrinsic goals center on things like physical fitness, community, affiliation, and self-acceptance. The self-determination hypothesis emphasizes that pursuing intrinsic objectives is directly tied to meeting the basic psychological requirements of relatedness, competence, and autonomy. However, chasing external objectives does not satisfy these fundamental psychological requirements.

There are three main types of achievement motivation: task-oriented motivation, ability-oriented motivation (also known as "ego" goal orientation in sport psychology), and social approval-oriented motivation (which has not gotten as much attention in the sports world as the other two). Bowlers are often encouraged to adopt competitive behaviors and beliefs by coaches, parents, staff, and teammates in a performance setting, which is defined by an ego-oriented motivating climate that tends to emphasize outcomes. On the other hand, by letting bowlers make mistakes and encouraging collaboration and peer engagement, a task-oriented or mastery climate environment promotes learning, personal development, and progress. The bowler's propensity to display task-oriented or ego-oriented motivation is greatly influenced by the motivational climate, regardless of whether it is mastery- or performance-oriented.

The two categories of goals, "task" and "ego," are intimately related to people's perceptions of their own abilities. Performance and mastery goals are two more categories under which achievement goals fall. Positive motivational constructs may be experienced more fully when mastery and performance approach goals are pursued together. Performance-oriented goals are strongly supported by those who exhibit high levels of mastery, performance approach, and performance-avoidance goals. It's noteworthy to observe that young bowlers don't just set performance objectives; this could be because mastery goals have a mitigating influence on the detrimental processes that result from pursuing avoidance goals. Four primary categories of achievement objectives have been recognized in the achievement goal approach: performance-avoidance, mastery-approach, mastery-avoidance, and mastery-approach. Enjoyment of physical education activities, perceived competence, and a sense of relatedness have all been connected to higher results in all four accomplishment goal categories.

Goals for achievement have a crucial role in influencing how people define and approach performance success. Athletes' motivation, conduct, and results are affected by the four primary categories of accomplishment goals: mastery-approach, mastery-avoidance, performance-approach, and performance avoidance. Bowlers can improve their motivation, concentration, and general performance in the pursuit of their bowling objectives by comprehending and utilizing goal orientation.

Intrinsic Goals:

Physical Fitness: To improve their overall performance on the lanes, bowlers may give themselves the intrinsic aim of becoming more physically fit. They might place more emphasis on strength training, conditioning regimens, flexibility exercises, and regular exercise to improve their physical endurance, coordination, and stamina—all of which can improve their bowling ability.

Community Feeling: Promoting a sense of togetherness and camaraderie among teammates and rivals may be a bowler's internal objective. To develop a welcoming and pleasant bowling environment that encourages respect for one another and pleasure of the sport, they might actively take part in team-building exercises, interact with other players, bowl in events, and assist their teammates.

Affiliation: A bowler may make it a personal mission to form deep bonds and associations with other bowlers, coaches, and bowling fans. He might look for ways to connect, work together, and form bonds with people who have similar interests in bowling, such as joining clubs, going to bowling events, and participating in social activities centered around the sport.

Self-Acceptance: Regardless of their performance results, bowlers can make it their core objective to develop self-acceptance and self-compassion, to embrace both their strengths and faults, and to keep a positive self-image. To develop a positive outlook on themselves and their bowling journey, they could engage in self-care practices such as self-reflection, mindfulness, and self-esteem boosting.

Extrinsic Goals:

Popularity: Becoming well-known or well-liked by their coaches, peers, or the bowling community can be an extrinsic objective for a bowler. He might be driven by the attention and validation he gets from others to concentrate on developing a strong social media presence, pursuing media attention, or aiming for high scores and accolades to improve his public image and reputation.

Financial Rewards: Bowlers may have as their extrinsic objective to win cash or other awards for their bowling accomplishments. They might be inspired by the material advantages and financial gains connected with their bowling performance to take part in high-stakes competitions, look for sponsorships or endorsements, or try to win cash prizes to meet their basic requirements.

Attractiveness: In order to draw others' attention or win their admiration, bowlers may have an extrinsic objective to enhance their physical attributes. To improve their outward look and perceived beauty, they can concentrate on their appearance, attire, grooming, or general presentation. This could be driven by a desire to be viewed favorably by others.

Different Types Of Goals In Elite Bowling

Within the intricate world of professional bowling, a bowler's journey towards success is deeply entwined with the diverse set of goals they choose, each goal carrying its own unique psychological impact. One pivotal category is **Mastery-Approach Goals**, where bowlers aspire not only for competence but also proficiency in specific skills. This goal orientation prompts a focus on personal improvement, setting individual records, and finding inspiration in the continuous process of refining techniques, leading to enhanced performance, ongoing learning, and heightened enjoyment. However, the long-term psychological impact of mastery-approach goals extends beyond performance improvement; it can cultivate a sense of personal satisfaction, increased self-esteem, and a resilient mindset that embraces challenges.

On the flip side, the psychological landscape of **Mastery-Avoidance Goals** unfolds with a fear of failure and a strong desire to avoid unfavorable outcomes. Bowlers driven by mastery-avoidance goals are primarily concerned with preventing mistakes and maintaining a performance level consistent with past achievements. However, this mindset can result in heightened anxiety, diminished self-assurance, and a reluctance to take risks or challenge oneself. The long-term impacts might include a persistent fear of failure, reduced motivation due to a focus on avoiding errors rather than embracing growth opportunities, and an overall stagnation in skill development.

Performance-Approach Goals introduce yet another layer of psychological intricacy. By emphasizing success and superior performance, bowlers with performance-approach goals strive to outshine their competitors and achieve higher scores, placing greater emphasis on the end result rather than the developmental process. This orientation fosters high motivation, a competitive spirit, and a relentless desire to succeed in bowling. The long-term psychological effects encompass heightened intrinsic motivation, increased perseverance, and a robust sense of accomplishment.

Contrastingly, the psychological landscape of **Performance-Avoidance Goals** presents its own set of challenges. Bowlers motivated by a desire to avoid failure and negative evaluations are primarily focused on preventing subpar performances. This goal orientation can lead to a heightened fear of making mistakes, decreased self-confidence, and a tendency to avoid challenging situations, hindering overall growth and development. Over time, bowlers with performance-avoidance goals might experience increased stress, a negative impact on their mental well-being, and a reluctance to take on new challenges.

When a coach decides on the type of goal setting for their bowler, they need to weigh the advantages and disadvantages of each. Mastery-approach goals are advantageous in fostering continuous improvement, self-satisfaction, and a resilient mindset. However, the potential disadvantage lies in a lack of competitive edge or external validation. Mastery-avoidance goals, while aiming to prevent mistakes, may hinder a bowler's confidence and willingness to take risks, resulting in limited growth. Performance-approach goals, with their emphasis on success and competition, can drive motivation but may lead to excessive focus on outcomes and peer comparisons. On the other hand, performance-avoidance goals, by aiming to avoid failure, might inadvertently stifle a bowler's creativity and willingness to take risks.

In coaching, selecting the most suitable goal orientation involves understanding the individual bowler's psychological makeup, strengths, and areas for improvement. A well-rounded approach might involve integrating mastery-approach goals to promote continuous improvement and resilience while balancing it with performance-approach goals to instill motivation and competition. However, steering clear of mastery-avoidance and performance-avoidance goals is crucial to avoid hindering a bowler's mental well-being and potential for long-term success. Coaches play a vital role in guiding bowlers towards a balanced goal-setting approach, ensuring optimal performance, sustained motivation, and a fulfilling journey in the competitive and demanding realm of professional bowling.

Performance-Avoidance Goals:

The main objectives of performance-avoidance strategies are to avoid failing and being outperformed by others. A bowler with a performance-avoidance aim in the context of elite bowling will be driven by a fear of failing and a desire to keep up with their rivals' performances. Rather than trying to outperform his rivals, he will be more concerned with staying out of trouble and making sure he don't perform worse. Anxiety, a lack of confidence, and decreased drive can result from such aspirations.

Mastery-Approach Goals: *To attain personal mastery and competence, a bowler who has a mastery-approach goal orientation may concentrate on improving and refining his bowling skills and tactics. He might establish objectives to become proficient in a particular bowling method, increase his accuracy or consistency, and improve his general performance. A bowler might decide to use the mastery approach to improve his spare shot, for instance, by practicing frequently, getting coach input, and reviewing their play to grow from setbacks and continue to improve.*

Mastery-Avoidance Goals: *A bowler who has a mastery-avoidance goal orientation could be driven by a fear of failing or making mistakes because he don't want to fail at a skill or technique. He could establish avoidance objectives pertaining to averting mishaps, errors, or subpar work. For instance, by concentrating on avoiding errors and being cautious when shooting spares, a bowler may establish a mastery-avoidance objective of not missing any single-pin spares in a game.*

Performance-Approach Goals: *A bowler who is oriented toward performance-approach goals could find motivation in outperforming other bowlers. He could establish objectives to beat rivals, emerge victorious in competitions, or attain high scores. A bowler might, for instance, set a performance-approach objective to win a regional bowling championship by consistently improving his craft, competing at a high level against other proficient bowlers, and practicing.*

Performance-Avoidance Goals: *The dread of doing poorly in comparison to others may serve as the driving force behind a bowler who has a performance-avoidance goal orientation. He might establish objectives aimed at preventing subpar work, errors, or failure. For instance, a bowler might focus on avoiding mistakes, errors, or bad performance outcomes and compare oneself to others in order to achieve the performance-avoidance aim of not finishing last in a tournament.*

Goal Type	Positive Affect Psychological Impact	Negative Affect Psychological Impact	Example Player
Mastery-Approach Goals	- Enhanced motivation, focusing on personal development and improvement.	- Ongoing learning and pleasure derived from the process.	Example: A young junior bowler sets a goal to improve his spare shooting technique, diligently practicing and enjoying the learning process.
	- Increased confidence and willingness to take chances.	- Potential overemphasis on personal performance.	
Mastery-Avoidance Goals	- Fear of failure may drive attention to detail and precision.	- Heightened worry, diminished self-assurance.	Example: A youth bowler, fearing mistakes, focuses on avoiding errors during competitions, leading to anxiety but also heightened precision in his shots.
	- Focus on maintaining performance standards already achieved.	- Reduced desire to take risks and push boundaries.	
Performance-Approach Goals	- High motivation, competitive spirit, and desire to outperform rivals.	- Potential for undue emphasis on external validation.	Example: An adult professional bowler sets a goal to consistently achieve high scores in tournaments, driven by the desire to be recognized as one of the top performers in the league.
	- Ambition for success and superior performance outcomes.	- Risk of increased anxiety due to peer comparisons.	
Performance-Avoidance Goals	- Drive to avoid failure and perform poorly in comparison to others.	- Anxiety, lack of confidence, and decreased drive.	Example: A pro bowler, fearing a drop in performance, focuses on avoiding mistakes during high-stakes competitions, leading to heightened anxiety and decreased overall motivation.

Goal Type	Positive Affect Psychological Impact	Negative Affect Psychological Impact	Example Player
	- Focus on maintaining a competitive edge to prevent being outperformed.	- Potential for negative impact on overall performance.	

Table 21 - These examples provide specific scenarios for each cell, illustrating the psychological impact of different goal types on bowlers across various age groups.

Psychological Characteristics For Elite Bowling Success

In order to achieve bowling excellence, bowlers must cultivate a variety of psychological traits that have been shown to be necessary for competing at the highest level. A number of psychological traits, including self-efficacy, goal-setting, dedication, and drive, have been found by researchers to set great bowlers apart from their colleagues and aid in their ascent to higher competitive levels.

The psychological traits that affect a bowler's total performance and growth are referred to as PCDEs, or Psychological Characteristics of Developing Excellence. These traits include mental abilities, attitudes, emotions, and desires. Coaches and academics have created frameworks and techniques to integrate psychological skills training into bowling training sessions, realizing the importance of these qualities.

The 5C Framework is one such framework that emphasizes five essential areas: concentration, commitment, communication, control, and confidence. For young bowlers who are just beginning their careers, this framework might be quite helpful. Let's examine the ways in which each of these elements can be utilized in the growth of young bowlers:

Commitment: For young bowlers to advance in the sport and realize their full potential, they must have a strong commitment to it. This entails making the time and effort to practice and get better in spite of obstacles or failures. Parents and coaches can help young bowlers by promoting patience and a positive attitude, as well as by setting clear expectations and goals.

A youthful bowler who is dedicated to the sport will be prepared to invest more practice time in order to elevate their performance. He will arrive early for practice and remain late to refine their style. By establishing clear expectations and goals and motivating young bowlers to persevere through difficulties and setbacks, parents and coaches may support this dedication.

Communication: Young bowlers must be able to communicate effectively both on and off the courts. It is essential to teach young bowlers how to interact with coaches, teammates, and other members of the bowling community. This entails speaking out, listening intently, and politely and clearly expressing oneself. Effective communication promotes growth and learning as well as healthy relationships.

Young bowlers must be able to communicate well in order to succeed both on and off the bowls. Young bowlers can learn excellent communication skills from their parents and instructors, as well as from other members of the bowling community. This entails asking questions, listening to criticism and counsel, and politely and clearly expressing oneself.

Control: For young bowlers, it's critical to develop emotional self-control and the capacity to use energy constructively. Essential abilities include developing self-control, controlling anger, and handling disappointment in a positive and healthy way. In addition to modeling positive conduct and offering constructive criticism, coaches and parents can foster a supportive environment that promotes self-control and emotional regulation.

It's important for young bowlers to develop emotional self-control and constructive energy focus. This entails gaining self-control and discipline as well as establishing constructive coping mechanisms for feelings of disappointment and annoyance. To help young bowlers acquire these abilities, parents and coaches can set a good example and offer helpful criticism.

Confidence: A young bowler's resilience, drive, and general performance are greatly influenced by his level of confidence. Setting reasonable and doable goals, giving constructive criticism, and acknowledging accomplishments are all part of developing confidence. Young bowlers need to know that learning, developing, and getting better are just as important factors in bowling success as winning.

Young bowlers who show confidence will be optimistic about both their skills and the sport. Young bowlers' confidence can be increased by parents and instructors by praising their accomplishments, offering helpful criticism, and creating attainable goals. It's critical that aspiring bowlers comprehend that learning, development, and improvement go hand in hand with winning in the bowling world.

Concentration: For young bowlers, the capacity to stay focused and mentally clear during practice and competition is essential. It can help them focus better if you teach them how to reduce distractions, practice mindfulness, and use visualization. Young bowlers can benefit from a disciplined and encouraging training environment that fosters mental focus and enables parents and coaches to assist them in coping with stress and anxiety.

During practice and competition, young bowlers must learn how to maintain their attention and alertness. Young bowlers can benefit from the guidance of parents and coaches in developing their attention abilities by receiving instruction in stress and anxiety management, being part of an organized and encouraging training environment, and being encouraged to practice mindfulness and visualization techniques. For instance, to help new bowlers stay focused during competition, a coach can advise them to picture their shots before taking them.

Bowlers who are successful have a variety of psychological traits and abilities that help them perform at their best. These elements include the capacity for sustained concentration, mastery of performance images, a dedication to perfection, practice goal-setting, mental preparation, simulation of competitive scenarios, creation of comprehensive competition plans, and preparation against distractions. Achieving optimal performance is also strongly correlated with mental competencies like goal-setting, self-regulation, self-assurance, motivation, commitment, coping mechanisms, goal-setting, and visualization. Even though they don't ensure success, these developing abilities are essential to bowlers realizing their full potential.

Furthermore, bowlers' psychological abilities are essential for overcoming changing times. Essential psychosocial skills, such as commitment, self-belief, motivation, goal setting, focus, distraction control, pressure management, imagery, realistic performance evaluation, and social and communication skills, are frequently possessed by teenagers who excel in sports and are able to balance their athletic endeavors with academic responsibilities. Research has indicated that successful professional bowlers who are acknowledged for their accomplishments exhibit greater levels of dedication, concentration, and mental training in comparison to less successful bowlers. Additionally, among high performers, motivation and self-assurance stand out as critical personal traits. The psychological qualities associated with mental toughness and its several dimensions are essential for bowling excellence.

5.2 Mental Toughness

It is often acknowledged that mental toughness, a complex idea, is necessary for success at the highest levels of competition. Bowlers who are mentally strong are able to handle pressure and setbacks well, and they are also devoted to pushing themselves to the utmost in their quest for achievement.

"Having the natural or developed psychological edge that enables you to generally cope better than other bowlers with the many demands (competition, training, and lifestyle) that sport places on a performer" is how a group of internationally seasoned bowlers defined mental toughness in the context of bowling. In particular, mental toughness refers to the ability to remain focused, resolute, confident, and in control under pressure, outperforming opponents on a more consistent basis." It's crucial to remember that each sport has its own particular requirements for how mental toughness might be displayed. In order to help athletes advance along the developmental pathway and achieve high performance, mental toughness is essential. Although there are many ways to define mental toughness, most bowlers agree that endurance, perseverance, and the capacity to overcome hardship are essential components. A framework identifying thirty attributes—belief, focus—that are divided into four dimensions— competition (pressure management, control of thoughts and emotions, sustained focus), training (long-term motivation, pushing limits), and post-competition (handling success or failure)—can be used to conceptualize mental toughness.

Myth: "Mental Toughness Is All About Suppressing Emotions"

Reality: Mental toughness is not about suppressing emotions but rather about managing them effectively. Successful bowlers acknowledge their emotions, both positive and negative, and use strategies to channel them in a productive manner. Mental toughness involves recognizing and regulating emotions to maintain focus and composure under pressure.

Myth: "Mental Toughness Means Never Feeling Pressure"

Reality: Even mentally tough bowlers experience pressure in competitive situations. Mental toughness helps them manage and thrive under pressure, not eliminate it entirely. Feeling pressure is a natural part of sports, and mental toughness equips bowlers with the tools to perform at their best despite the pressure.

Myth: "Mental Toughness Is a Fixed Trait"

Reality: Mental toughness is not a fixed trait. It can be developed and improved over time with training and practice. Bowlers can work on enhancing their mental toughness by continuously refining their mental skills, attitudes, and coping mechanisms, allowing them to adapt and excel in various situations.

Examples

Attitude/Mindset:

Belief: A bowler will approach each shot with confidence and work to achieve the greatest shot possible if he has faith in his own ability and keep an optimistic outlook despite difficult lane conditions.

Focus: A bowler who can keep his attention on his game plan and execution while blocking out outside distractions like crowd noise and competitive pressure will be able to make consistent shots and stay in the zone the entire game.

Training:

Long-term focus to promote motivation: Over time, a bowler who sets and persistently pursues long-term goals, such as raising his average score or perfecting a certain bowling technique, will remain inspired and dedicated to ongoing growth.

Pushing to the limits: A bowler can develop new talent skills and achieve new performance levels if he is prepared to push himself by attempting novel approaches, practicing frequently, and persistently going outside of his comfort zone with regard to lane circumstances, gear, and tactics.

Competition:

Cope with pressure: A bowler who can remain composed and execute shots with accuracy will be able to withstand the pressure of competition, such as that which arises in high-stakes tournaments or crucial times in a match, without succumbing to nerves or other distractions.

Belief control through feelings: A bowler who is able to control his emotions well during a match, for example, by controlling his frustration after a missed shot or his excitement after a strike, will be able to make composed decisions and keep his cool for reliable performance.

Stay focused: A bowler who can keep his attention on his game plan and strategy in the face of outside distractions like crowd noise or rivalry will be able to stay on course and make thoughtful decisions for maximum performance.

Post-Competition:

Handling success and failure: A bowler who can properly manage both kinds of situations—for example, by staying upbeat and learning from mistakes made during a high-scoring game or by remaining optimistic after a low-scoring one—will be able to sustain a positive outlook and keep getting better every time he plays.

Bowling excellence demands more than just technical proficiency. A key influence is played by psychological traits, and self-regulation abilities rank highly among them. Bowlers who possess self-regulation are able to master a set of psychological skills that govern their actions, thoughts, and feelings in order to accomplish their objectives. Elite bowlers need these abilities since they have to adjust to shifting circumstances and overcome unforeseen obstacles. The following essential self-control abilities can help bowlers compete at their best:

Self-Awareness: Self-awareness is the ability to identify and comprehend one's own feelings, ideas, and actions. Self-awareness aids bowlers in recognizing their advantages and disadvantages, enabling them to modify their strategy as necessary. For instance, practicing mindfulness can improve focus for a bowler who has trouble focusing.

Autonomy: The capacity to behave independently and make judgments without being unduly influenced by other forces is known as autonomy. When it comes to bowling, autonomy gives bowlers the ability to make strategic decisions based on their knowledge and experiences rather than just following the advice of others. This fosters a feeling of control and ownership over one's work.

Determination: Determination is the capacity to endure in the face of difficulties and disappointments. Determination in bowling aids players in keeping their motivation and concentration even under trying circumstances. This trait is particularly crucial in competitive settings where there may be a lot of pressure.

Persistence: Persistence is the capacity to keep pursuing objectives in the face of difficulty or sluggish progress. Persistence is a skill that bowlers use to keep up a regular practice schedule and focus on their areas of weakness, even when results are slow to show. This is essential for enhancing and perfecting technical abilities.

Examples

Self-Awareness:

Recognizing body mechanics: A bowler who can change his stance, approach, release, and follow-through according to his own physical limitations and strengths in order to maximize his performance.

Monitoring performance cues: A bowler who, throughout practice and competition, keeps an eye on indicators like ball speed, rev rate, and pin carry and uses that knowledge to make well-informed decisions and modifications to his technique and game plan.

Understanding mental state: A bowler who, during practice and competition, is conscious of his own mental state, including his degree of concentration, self-assurance, and emotions, and who takes action to control it for the best possible outcome, such as by practicing self-talk or relaxation techniques.

Autonomy:

Personalized training plan: A bowler who takes charge of his training program, including exercises, physical conditioning, and mental preparation, and creates his own personalized training plan suited to their individual needs, goals, and timetable.

Strategic decision-making: Bowlers who, without exclusively depending on outside counsel, make tactical decisions during tournaments, such as modifying their line, outfit, or pace, based on their own evaluation of the lane circumstances and opponents' performances.

Goal-setting and progress tracking: A bowler who establishes and maintains his own performance objectives, monitors his own development over time, applies his own standards of success, and accepts accountability for his own development by making necessary corrections and aiming for ongoing improvement.

Determination:

Resilience in the face of setbacks: A bowler who, by being optimistic, focused, and determined to turn the situation around, exhibits resilience in the face of setbacks, such as a string of missed spares or low scores.

Motivation to overcome challenges: A bowler who is driven to work hard, get advice, and never give up on their objectives in order to overcome obstacles and problems, such as technical shortcomings, physical restrictions, or mental barriers.

Mental toughness in competition: Bowlers who demonstrate mental fortitude in competition by being composed, remaining focused, and persevering through exhaustion or hardship in order to perform at their peak and meet their goals are admirable.

Persistence:

Consistency in practice: A bowler who maintains consistency in his practice regimen, by frequently turning up for practice sessions, especially when faced with distractions or competing priorities, and putting in the effort to continuously refine his skills and improve his performance.

Resilience in the face of failure: The ability of a bowler to bounce back from setbacks, stay motivated, and keep working hard to achieve objectives in the face of setbacks, such as a poor showing in a tournament or an extended period of difficulty.

Long-term focus on improvement: Bowlers who keep a long-term emphasis on improving themselves are those who set reasonable expectations, recognize that progress isn't always linear, and persevere in working toward their objectives over an extended period of time.

Self-generated ideas, emotions, and behaviors that support improved learning and skill development are all included in self-regulation. It also entails self-evaluation to gauge advancement toward predetermined objectives. People who possess self-regulation abilities are able to manage their emotions, concentrate on bettering themselves, and ask for help when they need it. Effective talent development and talent development environments heavily rely on self-reflection.

Success at the highest level of bowling requires a strong sense of discipline, dedication, perseverance, and the capacity to look for and make use of social support. Conversely, bowlers who have trouble transitioning have been found to lack self-determination. Self-control techniques can help separate young bowlers who succeed in making the transition to the elite level from those who don't. Bowlers can learn more effectively than their peers by reflecting on their learning process and applying self-regulation skills. Self-regulation, which includes elements like self-efficacy, reflection, effort, evaluation, planning, and self-monitoring, aids bowlers in controlling their ideas, behaviors, and emotions. In real life, self-regulating bowlers plot their course, evaluate where they are now, chart the course they want to take to get there, and stay motivated and focused over the long run. As a result, coaches and talent development programs should encourage emotional, mental, and behavioral self-control. It works better to promote preparation, introspection, and self-awareness than it does to give instructions.

Throughout the process of becoming an excellent player, individual traits can be cultivated, and specific tactics can help them do so. Young bowlers who receive mental skill instruction can develop the psychological traits needed to overcome challenges at higher levels of the sport. Intentional and planned challenges have also been proposed as a means of encouraging the development of desirable abilities and dispositions.

6. Developing Mental Skills In Bowling: A Pathway To Success

It is insufficient to concentrate only on technical abilities if you want to be a great bowler. The school system understands the value of teaching kids how to overcome obstacles, and it makes sense that sports should follow suit. Bowling success is strongly associated with psychological practices that enhance concentration and learning. Psychological tactics that are effective in developing mental skills and favorably influencing bowlers' dedication and persistence include goal setting, performance review, and planning. The development of life and psychological skills has become more commonplace in elite academies. It is advised that psychology consultants join the coaching staff as key members in order to support the development of fundamental psychological abilities. These consultants would advise on how to incorporate mental skills into training and assist bowlers in acquiring these skills via their experiences and instruction. In addition, those who have an impact on bowlers—like family members, coaches, and significant others—should be educated to help them acquire these vital psychological competencies. Failures and roadblocks on the route to development should be seen as chances for introspection, education, and further development. When used properly, both happy and bad experiences can aid in the growth of bowlers. Nonetheless, it's critical to take into account individual variations in the process, gender, psychological variables, and the degree of challenge.

Programs for developing mental talents should start early and offer a carefully thought-out educational experience. For instance, the pilot program "Developing the Potential of Young People in Sport" taught psychological characteristics and developmental experiences (PCDEs) in addition to physical obstacles. The program's instructors, parents, and coaches employed a variety of techniques to give the kids a consistent message. PCDEs were taught, supported, and ultimately evaluated using both direct and indirect methods. They were also exhibited by the coaches' actions and coaching methods. The kids stated that they were able to fulfill their goals by effectively implementing PCDEs in a range of situations, such as extracurricular activities and academic performance. Goal attainment in contexts other than sports has also been connected to the effective use of PCDEs. Bowlers' capacity to seize the chances presented by the talent development environment is based on their psychological makeup. As such, it is imperative that these qualities are emphasized from the very beginning of a bowler's career.

Challenges can help improve mental skills, which can help you advance in the sport more successfully. Intentional and structured challenges have garnered attention as a way to support the development of mental talents, even though some challenges may come at random. A certain amount of difficulty is a crucial component of the talent development path because it fosters the growth of psychological traits that support elite performance and the acquisition of abilities required to manage changes in the sport. A smooth and straight path to the top is frequently an indication of issues. All bowlers, regardless of their level of accomplishment, agree that facing difficulties has shaped both their personal and professional growth. They talk about feeling alone when they join a new team or category and helpless when faced with obstacles like injuries and being apart from friends and family. Nonetheless, they think that conquering these obstacles has strengthened them as people. Bowlers are likely to benefit from challenges as they develop. Furthermore, compared to teammates who may have started out less successful but persevered and enrolled in support programs later in their careers, bowlers who enjoy early success and excellent assistance at a young age have a lesser likelihood of achieving at the senior level. Setbacks can occur when a bowler does not receive early instruction and does not gain the confidence and abilities that come from difficult or challenging times in their career. This is especially true when the bowler is near the top of the performance pyramid and must overcome growing problems.

Young bowlers who have excelled in the sport frequently had more difficult circumstances, such as having more siblings and being a member of a minority ethnicity. It is important to remember that some sports-related groups might have gone through "trauma," such as the prevalence of single-parent households in the bowling community. Coaches have also stated that difficult bowlers present a daily challenge. Consequently, it is clear that life trauma-related abilities and information are crucial to the growth and effectiveness of bowlers in the game.

Bowlers can become more proficient by learning a variety of skills and using them well. Rather of emphasizing specific talents for a given difficulty, the idea of "learned resourcefulness" places more emphasis on developing a proactive coping strategy to get beyond obstacles. This method entails continuously improving and modifying abilities through a variety of techniques, such as assessment and adjustment through a variety of examinations. Developing these abilities can be very beneficial to bowlers' growth and development.

In addition to being essential for the development of skills and attitudes, overcoming obstacles gives people the fortitude and resiliency they need for new experiences. This idea states that one can change their response to stress and develop a solution-focused attitude by engaging in a training process that resembles stress inoculation or physical training with intentional rules and a causal progression.

Additionally, providing bowlers with challenges to assess and improve their skills in addition to Psychological Coping and Developmental Exercises (PCDEs) helps them adjust better to new training environments and universities. This blend of PCDEs and difficult events can serve as a catalyst, assisting bowlers in preparing for future difficulties.

Through the integration of a skill set, ongoing assessment and modification, and a willingness to take on new challenges, bowlers can effectively manage the demands of their sport and promote personal development. In addition to improving their performance, this all-encompassing strategy gives students important psychological and sport-specific abilities for long-term success.

Young bowlers may face pertinent challenges along their developmental path, such as competing in an older age group, playing out of position, having higher expectations of themselves than their teammates, being selected for international competitions or not, and having to endure training camps in unaccustomed or basic conditions.

Bowlers need to possess both cerebral and physical qualities to advance in their game. These personal qualities are essential for making the necessary advancements to the sport's elite level. Specifically, a bowler's surroundings, which include parents, coaches, and the broader cultural backdrop, can influence the mental components.

Understanding the differentiating model of giftedness and talent

There is a discernible difference between giftedness and talent according to the Differentiating Model of Giftedness and Talent (DMGT). Being gifted is defined as having and applying natural talents (gifts) in a certain area to the extent that one is ranked in the top 10% of one's age group among peers. However, talent is characterized as being able to master methodically cultivated skills and knowledge in at least one area, placing a person in the top 10% of their age group.

Natural abilities are the fundamental components of skill, according to the DMGT. However, when young people participate in methodical training, practice, and learning, talent growth becomes apparent. Two catalysts affect this process: environmental influences and intrapersonal elements.

Intrapersonal catalysts: motivation and volition

The two main intrapersonal catalysts that start the talent development process are motivation and volition. Bowlers advance on their path to realizing their maximum potential largely because to their own motivation and will to do better.

The factors and resources that surround bowlers are included in the category of environmental catalysts. These comprise social, cultural, geographic, and economic aspects. A bowler's development is also influenced by others including parents, siblings, teachers, and classmates. Furthermore, a particular environment's resources are a major factor in fostering talent development. Chance is another causal component that is related to the surroundings. A bowler's growth may be influenced by elements such as the family they are born into. The intricate interactions between personal traits and external factors that impact the development of talent are better understood when we acknowledge the significance of chance.

Investigating the characteristics of the environment surrounding bowlers is essential to understanding how talent development plays out in their journey towards the elite level. Bowlers who want to reach their maximum potential in the sport can greatly benefit from an understanding of and emphasis on the talent development environment.

The Differentiating Model of Giftedness and Talent (DMGT) Table:

Component	Description	Examples	Strategies	Level of Importance
1	Innate Ability	Hand-eye coordination, balance, strength	Maximize the use of natural attributes	High
2	Developmental Processes	Deliberate practice, coaching, training	Regular practice and structured training	High
3	Environmental Factors	Quality coaching, resources, support	Seek access to quality coaching and support	High
4	Personal Factors	Motivation, perseverance, commitment	Set goals, maintain motivation	High
5	Domain-Specific Factors	Lane conditions, equipment, rules	Adapt to different lane conditions	Medium

Table 22 - Differentiating Model of Giftedness and Talent (DMGT

According to this paradigm, bowling talent and giftedness are dynamic processes influenced by a variety of influences rather than permanent attributes. This talk will examine how the Differentiating Model of Giftedness and Talent (DMGT) relates to bowling, with examples to highlight the main ideas of the model.

Component 1: Innate Ability - Creating a Robust Basis according to the DMGT, giftedness and talent are based on innate ability, such as inherent physical characteristics. Certain people may naturally have advantages on the lanes due to their hand-eye coordination, strength, balance, and other intrinsic traits. Let's take the example of a bowler who, because of their natural physical characteristics, can produce powerful shots and balance with ease.

Hypothetical example

Young Alex is a bowler who uses his superb hand-eye coordination to effortlessly and precisely knock down pins. The basis for Alex's intrinsic skill and brilliance in this area is his bowling ability, which distinguishes him from other bowlers.

Component 2: Developmental Processes: The importance of not depending only on natural aptitude is emphasized by the DMGT. Rather, it emphasizes the participation of several developmental processes. These procedures include intentional practice, training, coaching, and competition for bowlers. Let's see how these procedures are used in practice using an example.

Hypothetical example

Maria, a gifted bowler whose constant improvement comes from intense practice and training. Her commitment, diligence, and persistence in improving her bowling techniques over time are essential growth factors that amplify her potential and gift for the sport.

Component 3: Environmental Factors - Nurturing Development through Support The importance of environmental influences in talent development is emphasized by the DMGT. When it comes to bowling, these include having access to good coaching, having resources available, having family and friends support, and having competition chances. Let us consider the example of a bowler who receives encouragement from family and friends as well as a committed coach and well-equipped training facilities.

Hypothetical example

Jamal is an outstanding bowler from an underprivileged background who does not have access to official coaching or training facilities. Jamal is naturally gifted, but he lacks the support he needs from his surroundings to realize his full potential. However, Sofia excels in her bowling endeavors because she has access to top-notch coaching, first-rate facilities, and encouraging family members. These instances demonstrate the importance of environmental elements in fostering talent and giftedness in bowling.

Component 4: Personal Factors - Harnessing Inner Drive and Resilience Individual elements that influence the development of talent include persistence, inspiration, and personality qualities. These elements are crucial to a bowler's dedication, perseverance, and drive in the bowling context. Take into consideration, for instance, a bowler who is incredibly persistent in the face of difficulty, has a positive outlook, and exhibits constant motivation.

Hypothetical example

Tim is an exceptionally talented bowler with a strong internal drive to succeed in the game. His ability to persevere in the face of obstacles and disappointments only serves to highlight his natural ability and skill as a bowler. Ben, on the other hand, is a skilled bowler who struggles to advance because he lacks ambition and gives up easily when things get tough. These instances demonstrate the influence that individual factors can have on the growth of bowling talent and giftedness.

Component 5: Domain-Specific Factors - Adapting to the Bowling Domain The DMGT acknowledges the importance of domain-specific aspects in talent development while acknowledging the distinctive qualities of many domains. These elements may include alley conditions, equipment specifications, rules, and strategies in the context of bowling. Let us look at a successful bowler who adjusts their game to changing lane circumstances, becomes proficient with various equipment, and uses rules and approaches wisely.

Hypothetical example

Jessica is a talented bowler who thrives in a variety of lane conditions and can quickly modify her game plan in response to changes in the oil patterns on the lanes. She stands out from other bowlers due to her domain-specific ability to adapt to various conditions, which further strengthens her talent and gifting. However, Mark, a gifted bowler, finds it difficult to adjust to shifting lane conditions and frequently has trouble with his plans, which has an impact on his game. This demonstrates how domain-specific variables might influence how giftedness and talent develop in bowling.

7. Talent Development Environments: Nurturing Bowlers' Growth

7.1. The Impact of TDEs on Bowlers' Progression

It's critical to establish an atmosphere that supports bowlers' successful progress. One constant and manageable element that has a big impact on the path of aspiring bowlers is the talent development environment (TDE). It's critical for young bowlers to start developing at the senior level as soon as possible. Setting long-term objectives requires seeing the junior level as a stepping stone to the senior level. For young bowlers, TDEs are excellent learning environments where instructors can support the development of their mental skills. Bowlers can succeed by efficiently encouraging and reinforcing the development of psychological traits within TDEs.

In addition to parents and peers, coaches are important micro-environmental elements that shape bowlers' development. The development of bowlers is greatly aided by loving families, a caring sport club environment, support from sport federations, and knowledgeable coaches that bowlers can rely on. It is within the power of coaches and parents to help children acquire the necessary psychological qualities for forward motion. Bowlers' confidence and drive can be increased by parents by fostering an environment that is goal-oriented and encouraging. These qualities are essential for success in the future. Coaches, on the other hand, have a big influence on bowlers' psychological growth because they emphasize discipline, hard work, and having traits that build trust. They also impart mental skills and offer support and encouragement. Additionally, a variety of settings and cultures have been investigated in order to determine the essential components of successful development.

Bowlers' growth can be greatly influenced by their thoughts, feelings, and emotions (TDEs), either positively or negatively. In this context, we will examine the detrimental effects that friends, parents, and coaches can have on a bowler's development and general well-being.

1. **Coaches: The Power of Words**

Bowlers are greatly influenced by their coaches, and they can be positively or negatively impacted by their words and deeds. Regretfully, a coach's bad actions might negatively affect a bowler's TDEs. A bowler's self-confidence can be undermined, anxiety and stress levels can rise, misunderstanding can arise, and a toxic team environment can result from harsh criticism, excessive expectations set, inconsistent feedback, and poor communication skills. A bowler may therefore experience a decline in performance and a decrease in desire to do better.

2. **Parents: Balancing Support and Pressure**

Although parents are extremely important in a bowler's life, if their influence is not appropriately controlled, it can also have unfavorable effects. Bowlers may experience negative effects from excessive performance pressure, excessive competitiveness, disregarding emotions, inappropriate behavior, and inflated expectations. Stress levels rising, low self-esteem, moral quandaries, and a lower sense of enjoyment from the sport can all result from such practices. These elements may ultimately impede a bowler's general growth and enthusiasm for the game.

3. **Peers: The Power of Social Dynamics**

Peers have the ability to influence bowlers' TDEs in both positive and bad ways. Sadly, a bowler's development can be seriously impacted by unfavorable interactions with others. Adverse impacts can be attributed to bullying, negative peer pressure, social exclusion, disruptive behavior, and an unsupportive environment. These toxic relationships can lead to low self-esteem, trouble focusing, increased annoyance, and a feeling of loneliness in the bowling community. As such, there may be significant effects on a bowler's drive and sense of community.

Positive Coaches:

a. *Positive Reinforcement: When bowlers play well, the coach gives them lots of praise and encouragement, which helps to build their self-confidence and drive for improvement.*

b. *Constructive Feedback: The coach helps bowlers find areas for improvement and cultivate a growth mindset towards their performance by giving them detailed comments on technique and strategy.*

c. *Goal Setting: The coach assists bowlers in creating attainable objectives that provide them with direction and a sense of purpose in their practice and competition. It also helps them control their emotions and thoughts in order to make improvements.*

d. *Mental Skills Training: The coach instructs bowlers on how to stay composed and focused during tournaments by teaching them deep breathing and visualization techniques.*

e. *Motivation Enhancement: The coach works with bowlers to pinpoint their intrinsic motivations, which they can use to stoke their enthusiasm and push for growth. Examples of these motivations include the love of the game or a sense of accomplishment.*

Negative Coaches:

a. *Negative Criticism: A coach continually degrades and criticizes their bowlers when they make errors or perform poorly, which saps their confidence and drives them to do better.*

b. *Unrealistic Expectations: Bowlers who are under excessive pressure to perform flawlessly and who are instilled with a dread of failing are subject to anxiety and stress as a result of this intense pressure.*

c. *Lack of Emotional Support: A coach ignores the worries and emotions of bowlers, putting all of their attention on their technical abilities. As a result, the bowlers and the coach don't feel emotionally connected or trusted*

d. *Inconsistent Feedback: A coach's inconsistent and contradictory comments to their bowlers cause confusion and aggravation, as well as hinder their ability to recognize their strengths and faults.*

e. *Poor Communication: A coach frequently uses harsh language and disparages their bowlers, which creates a toxic team environment and jeopardizes their mental and emotional health.*

Positive Parents:

a. **Parents:** *a.* **Emotional Support:** *Young bowlers receive unwavering love and support from their parents, which helps them develop resilience and self-worth while managing the highs and lows of competitive bowling.*

b. **Role Modeling:** *The parents are enthusiastic bowlers who play the sport often. As such, they provide their child with a positive example and encourage them to improve their abilities and follow their bowling love.*

c. **Encouragement:** *Another bowler receives constant support from his parents during competitions and celebrations of his accomplishments, which gives him a sense of accomplishment and inspires them to keep up his hard work.*

d. **Managing Expectations:** *A bowler's parents assist them in controlling his expectations and realizing that success in bowling requires time and work. This helps them keep a positive outlook on his performance and cultivate a realistic mindset.*

e. **Creating a Supportive Environment:** *Parents foster a supportive environment at home by giving their child access to the tools and practice opportunities they need and by fostering a positive and upbeat atmosphere that will aid in his bowling growth.*

Negative Parents:

a. **Overbearing Pressure:** *A bowler had significant levels of stress and anxiety as a result of his parents' relentless pressure to excel in bowling. They continually pushed the bowler to win and rank well.*

b. **Over-Competitiveness:** *Parents push bowlers to be too competitive by continuously contrasting their output and performance, which breeds resentment, competition, and a bad team environment.*

c. **Lack of Emotional Validation:** *Parents criticize their child for their feelings about bowling and advise them to be tough and not exhibit weakness, which causes them to repress their feelings and receive little emotional support.*

d. **Inappropriate Behavior:** *During contests, parents act aggressively and confrontationally with other bowlers, coaches, or officials, which negatively affects the environment and the bowler's mental health.*

e. **Unrealistic Expectations:** *A bowler experiences continuous stress and fear of failing because hi sparents place undue pressure on them to fulfill unrealistic dreams of becoming a professional bowler.*

Positive Peers:

f. **Friendly Competition:** *A bowler receives friendly competition from his bowling league mates, which encourages them to sharpen his skills and aim for greater scores.*

g. **Camaraderie:** *A member of a bowling team experiences a sense of camaraderie and teamwork among his teammates, increasing motivation and love for the sport.*

h. **Supportive Feedback:** *Peers provide encouragement and constructive criticism to a bowler, assisting them in finding areas for growth and fostering a sense of camaraderie among bowlers.*

i. **Motivation through Comparison:** *A bowler is motivated to work harder and perform better as they aspire to surpass friends who are at a comparable skill level.*

j. **Social Support:** *A bowler's classmates give them emotional support during competitions, helping them control fear and trepidation. This fosters an accepting and encouraging social atmosphere that allows the bowler to flourish.*

Negative Peers:

a. **Bullying and Teasing:** *Bowling alley classmates regularly make fun of a bowler's method or performance, which lowers his self-esteem and deters him from bowling as much.*

b. **Negative Peer Pressure:** *Peers push a bowler to partake in unethical behavior during competitions or use performance-enhancing drugs, which causes moral quandaries and affects his values and views.*

c. **Lack of Supportive Environment:** *Peers don't provide much encouragement or support, frequently disparaging or making fun of a bowler's efforts. This fosters a toxic peer environment that lowers self-esteem and motivation.*

d. **Distracting Behavior:** *During contests, friends frequently participate in distracting behavior that lowers a bowler's performance and increases frustration. Examples of such behavior include loud sounds and interference with attention.*

e. **Social Exclusion:** *A bowler experiences social exclusion from classmates, which negatively affects his sense of belonging and enjoyment of the sport in general. He feels left out and alone.*

7.2. Key features of effective talent development environments

For bowlers, an atmosphere that fosters skill development requires a number of essential components. These components include a long-term plan and strategy, efficient communication and assistance, adaptable procedures, transitional support, and an emphasis on the bowler's development. It is crucial that these initiatives are coordinated within an integrated system. Henriksen (2010) created the Athletic Talent Development Environment (ATDE) model, which offers a framework for comprehending the sports environment. It takes into account the past, present, and future and is divided into two levels (macro and micro) and two domains (athletic and non-athletic). The daily lives of young bowlers are included in the micro level, which emphasizes genuine communication and involvement inside the club setting as well as with peers, family, school, and related teams. The media, sports federations, the educational system, and other social and cultural contexts all have an impact on

Kristoffer Henriksen

bowlers; these elements are together referred to as the macro-environment. Supportive training groups, broader environmental support, varied training, the development of psychosocial skills, a strong organizational structure, a long-term focus, and the integration of efforts are important components of a successful talent development environment. By giving gifted bowlers the support, tools, and chances they need to grow, these components help them reach their full potential.

Examples:

Micro level - Athletic domain (Present): A coaching program for bowling that concentrates on helping young bowlers develop their technical abilities, physical stamina, and mental tactics. Regular feedback, individualized training programs, and competitive possibilities are all provided during the coaching sessions, which foster a tough yet encouraging environment for the growth of talent.

Micro level - Non-athletic domain (Present): A bowling academy that provides aspiring bowlers with extensive instruction and materials on subjects including sports psychology, sports nutrition, injury prevention, and time management. This non-athletic sector supports bowlers' general well-being holistically, which balances their athletic growth.

Macro level: Athletic domain (past): A bowling association with a track record of developing athletes through effective programs that have produced champions on a national and international level. A great legacy of athlete development in the sport has been established by the association thanks to its robust infrastructure of coaching, competitions, and talent identification procedures, all of which have been improved over time.

Macro level - Non-athletic domain (Past): The bowling facility that has made investments in cutting-edge equipment, training facilities, and resources to promote athlete development is an example of a macro level non-athletic domain (past). The venue has a track record of organizing global competitions, drawing elite athletes from all over the world, and fostering growth and talent development in a competitive atmosphere.

Macro level: Athletic domain (Future): The bowling federation has launched a nationwide campaign to find and develop young talent at the grassroots level. It offers possibilities for international exposure, mentorship programs, and scholarships. The initiative's goal is to establish a long-term talent development program that gets the next generation of bowlers ready for contests across the globe.

Macro level: Non-athletic domain (Future): Research on athlete development, injury prevention, and performance optimization will be conducted in conjunction with the bowling industry and academics. The results of the research are applied to facility design, training techniques, and coaching strategies, resulting in an evidence-based approach to talent development going forward.

8. The Role Of Culture In Bowler Talent Development

Culture is a major factor in bowlers' ability development. Bowlers' success and performance are greatly influenced by social, psychological, and cultural factors. When creating a talent development strategy, it is imperative to comprehend and take into account the country's culture.

8.1 National Culture

The common values, habits, beliefs, and practices that influence people's interactions and conduct are collectively referred to as national culture. It can significantly affect young bowlers' development in a number of ways:

1. Values and Beliefs: The values and beliefs that young bowlers absorb are shaped by their national culture. Different cultures could place more value on self-expression, personal growth, or winning. Young bowlers' motivation, objectives, and sense of self are influenced by these principles.

2. Training and Coaching Styles: The teaching and training methods used in bowler development are also influenced by national culture. Coaching philosophies can vary from authoritarian to collaborative, which can have an effect on how young bowlers learn, grow as players, and relate to the game.

3. Social Norms and Expectations: Cultural expectations and norms related to bowling varies between nations. Bowling is seen as a semi-formal recreational activity in certain cultures and as a fiercely competitive and esteemed sport in others. These social standards influence how young bowlers view themselves, their place in the sport, and the encouragement and acknowledgment they get.

4. Access and Resources: The national culture affects young bowlers' access to opportunities and the availability of resources. While some cultures have abundant training facilities, tools, and support services, others have few of them. The development and accomplishment of young bowlers' objectives might be influenced by the resources that are available.

5. Gender Roles: Cultural norms have an impact on gender roles and expectations in sports, which might have an impact on young bowlers' engagement and growth. While some cultures encourage gender equity and diversity in the sport, others may restrict chances for female bowlers due to conventional gender roles.

It is imperative to take into account the influence of national culture when establishing a nurturing and productive environment for talent development. It guarantees that development plans respect cultural values, offer suitable coaching methods, tackle societal conventions, grant equal access to resources, and encourage inclusivity for all bowlers.

Nations like Australia, Canada, Singapore, and Malaysia are a few examples of how national culture affects bowler development. The distinct cultural environments of each of these nations influence bowlers' growth and help them succeed in the sport.

Examples

Values and Beliefs:

Young bowlers may prioritize spending time with family and friends over intense training and competition in certain cultures where social connections and family ties are highly valued. This could have an impact on their degree of dedication and success in the sport.

Training and Coaching Styles:

Coaches in some cultures may use a more conventional, authoritarian coaching method in which bowlers are expected to do as they are told and not to ask questions or offer suggestions. This could have an effect on young bowlers' confidence and drive in the sport by limiting their capacity to voice their thoughts or opinions.

Social Norms and Expectations:

In certain societies, girls may be discouraged from engaging in activities like bowling that are typically associated with men. Young female bowlers may have fewer opportunities and assistance as a result, which could hinder their growth and advancement in the sport.

Access and Resources:

Bowling may be less accessible in some cultures because of a lack of money, infrastructure, or support for the sport. Young bowlers may have less opportunities as a result to practice, compete, and hone their abilities, which could hinder their overall growth in the sport.

Gender Roles:

Gender norms and expectations may exist in some societies, which restrict or deter girls from actively engaging in bowling. Young female bowlers may have fewer opportunities, less support, and lower participation rates as a result, which could hinder their growth and development in the sport.

Myth: "Talent Development in Bowling Is Universally Standardized"

Reality: Talent development in bowling is not universally standardized. It varies significantly based on national culture, social norms, and organizational structures. Different countries and regions have their own approaches to talent development, which are influenced by their unique cultural values and resources.

Myth: "Bowlers from Larger Cities Have an Inherent Advantage"

Reality: While there may be a birthplace effect in bowling, it does not guarantee an inherent advantage. Being born in a larger city may provide access to more facilities and opportunities, but it also comes with potential challenges such as higher costs and increased competition. Success in bowling is determined by a combination of factors, including dedication, coaching, and individual talent, rather than solely by birthplace.

Myth: "Gender Equity Is a Universal Standard in Bowling"

Reality: Gender equity in bowling is not a universal standard. While some countries prioritize gender equity and provide equal opportunities for male and female bowlers, others may have disparities in access to resources and support. Gender norms and expectations within each culture play a significant role in shaping the opportunities available to young bowlers.

8.2 The Influence of Social Culture on Bowler Development

Bowlers' growth can be impacted by a number of social and cultural influences. Young bowlers' development is influenced by various factors, including sport systems, social norms, place of birth, money and resources, cultural norms and values, gender norms, and organizational structures.

1. Sport Systems: The growth of bowlers can be greatly impacted by the various sport systems seen in different nations. The quality of coaching, training facilities, and general support for young bowlers vary depending on the financing and resource available. Some nations place a high priority on bowling and devote a lot of financing, while others can have less money and resources available, which could limit the opportunity for young bowlers to advance their careers.

2. Social Norms and Values: A society's cultural norms and values have an impact on bowler development as well. Bowling may be highly prized in some cultures when it is associated with fair play, sportsmanship, and teamwork. On the other hand, the importance of sports and the morals attached to them may differ in other cultures. These cultural disparities influence young bowlers' attitudes toward the sport, as well as their objectives, driving forces, and overall experience.

3. Birthplace Effect: It's interesting to note that a bowler's upbringing can have an effect on their professional trajectory. Research carried out in North America has indicated that there is a higher likelihood of becoming a professional bowler if one is born in a city with a population of 50,000 to 100,000. Though theories suggest that larger cities offer more facilities, possibly at higher costs or requiring significant travel time, the reasons for this phenomenon are still not entirely understood. However, smaller cities might have less expensive facilities and a friendlier atmosphere with less competition, which might increase the chances for young bowlers to play and get more help.

4. Gender Norms: Young bowlers' development is also influenced by gender norms and expectations. Gender equity in sports is highly prioritized in many nations, guaranteeing equal opportunities and assistance for athletes of both sexes. Gender discrepancies might, however, persist in other nations, where female athletes might encounter obstacles to competition, fewer options for training, and less financial assistance. Young bowlers' growth and development can be greatly impacted by these gender stereotypes, especially when it comes to opportunities and resource availability.

5. Organizational systems: Young bowlers' growth may be impacted by the organizational systems found in bowling clubs, leagues, and associations. A more consistent approach to teaching, training, and competition might be offered by centralized organizations with stringent standards. Decentralized institutions, on the other hand, can provide individual clubs and coaches more freedom and flexibility. The coaching style, training regimens, and general experience given to young bowlers are all impacted by the organizational structure.

It is essential to comprehend the impact of social culture while establishing a welcoming and encouraging atmosphere for the growth of young bowlers. Acknowledging the effects of social norms, funding, cultural values, gender norms, and sport systems, as well as organizational structures, can help improve opportunities and provide young bowlers the tools and support they need to succeed in their athletic careers.

Funding and Resources:

In certain nations, bowling might be considered a national sport with substantial financial backing from public or private institutions. This would lead to well-funded youth development initiatives that give young bowlers access to elite instruction, top-notch facilities for practice, and competitive opportunities.

Cultural Norms and Values:

Young bowlers may receive less emphasis on competitive training and more emphasis on leisurely enjoyment of the sport rather than severe performance-based training in cultures where bowling is largely seen as a recreational pastime.

Gender Norms:

Traditional gender roles in some societies may suggest that some sports, like bowling, are more suited for one gender than another. For young bowlers who don't fit these gender stereotypes, this can mean fewer opportunities or support, which can cause differences in their growth and involvement in the sport.

Organizational Structures:

In certain cultures, bowling associations' organizational structures may have constrained youth development initiatives or stringent rules that prevent young bowlers from participating or developing. This may have an effect on how young bowlers in that culture develop and mature.

THE IMPACT OF PSYCHOSOCIAL FACTORS ON YOUTH BOWLER DEVELOPMENT

Young bowlers who demonstrate extraordinary technical skill from an early age sometimes struggle to reach their full potential as their careers develop. Although technical proficiency is crucial, it takes more than technique to achieve exceptional accomplishment. Many gifted students and bowlers who had promised in their formative years are unable to realize their full potential and achieve notable success as adults. However, those who go on to become well-known might not have had their skills acknowledged at an early age. It becomes clear that psychosocial variables have a big impact on whether or not talent development occurs in different areas. The interaction between a person's psychological traits and the social factors that impact their behavior is referred to as "psychosocial".

Introducing the Talent Development Mega Model (TDMM)

Subotnik's Talent Development Mega Model (TDMM) heavily emphasizes the role of psychosocial elements in talent development. This paradigm states that talent is the result of the interaction between biological, educational, psychological, and psychosocial variables rather than being exclusively determined by biological or technical factors. It is domain-specific and frequently manifests itself in extraordinary achievements, especially as an adult. According to the TDMM, which investigates the long-term identification of gifted people, certain kids grow up with more talent than their classmates. It is still unknown whether these skills actually contribute to exceptional performance in the future, even though they may be able to anticipate significant consequences. In order to be acknowledged as gifted at the height of their profession, people who were previously classified as gifted—or not—need to show

Rena Subotnik

extraordinary performance or output in the future. Although broad ability is required, exceptional performance or creative production cannot be predicted just by it. Consequently, when attempting to explain high accomplishment, it is imperative to take into account both domain-specific abilities and psychosocial aspects.

Example of Talent Development Mega Model (TDMM) in Bowling

Stage	Element	Duration	Description	Application to Bowling	Roles and Responsibilities
1	Identification	6 months	Identifying Potential Talent	Use assessments, competitions, and scouting to identify individuals with the physical and mental attributes suited for bowling.	Coaches, federations, and schools collaborate to identify potential talents. Parents support by encouraging participation in sports activities.
2	Recruitment	3 months	Bringing in Talent	Develop recruitment strategies to attract identified talents, whether through local clubs, schools, or talent identification programs.	Coaches and federations actively recruit identified talents. Parents provide consent and support in the decision-making process.
3	Assessment	3 months	Skill and Performance Evaluation	Conduct comprehensive assessments of bowling skills, physical fitness, mental resilience, and strategic understanding to gauge the baseline of each player.	Coaches and specialized assessors conduct comprehensive assessments. Parents provide necessary information about the athlete. Schools may facilitate the assessment process.
4	Development Plan	1 year	Individualized Training Plan	Create personalized training programs that address specific areas for improvement based on the assessment results. This could include technical, physical, and mental training components.	Coaches, with input from parents, create personalized training programs. Federations support with resources and infrastructure.
5	Training	2 years	Skill Development and Conditioning	Implement a structured training regimen that focuses on refining bowling techniques, improving physical fitness, and enhancing mental toughness. Utilize coaches and specialized trainers.	Coaches lead training sessions. Parents ensure players adhere to training schedules and support overall well-being. Federations provide facilities and financial support.
6	Competition	1 year (Continious)	Exposure to Competitive Play	Provide opportunities for players to participate in various competitions to gain experience, learn from real-game scenarios, and build a competitive mindset.	Coaches and federations facilitate participation in various competitions. Parents provide emotional support and encouragement. Peers offer motivation.
7	Monitoring	Continuous	Performance Tracking and Feedback	Implement continuous monitoring of player performance, including data analytics, to track progress and provide timely feedback for adjustments to the training plan.	Coaches and federations continuously monitor performance. Parents stay informed and support adjustments to the training plan.
8	Mental Conditioning	6 months	Psychological Training	Incorporate mental conditioning techniques such as visualization, goal-setting, and stress management to enhance mental resilience during competitions.	Coaches and sports psychologists provide mental conditioning. Parents reinforce positive mental habits at home.
9	Education	Ongoing	Holistic Player Development	Provide educational programs covering aspects like sports nutrition, injury prevention, and sports psychology to ensure the holistic development of the athlete.	Schools and federations provide educational programs. Parents support academic and sports education balance.
10	Mentorship	1 year	Guidance from Experienced Players	Establish mentorship programs where experienced players or coaches guide and inspire younger talents, sharing insights from their own experiences.	Coaches and experienced players mentor younger talents. Parents encourage and facilitate mentorship.
11	Career Transition	1 year	Preparing for Post-Professional Life	Equip players with skills and resources for life after their professional careers, including education, career planning, or transition to coaching roles.	Coaches, federations, and parents guide players in career planning. Schools may offer education and training programs. Peers provide emotional support.

Table 23 - The Talent Development Mega Model (TDMM) in Bowling is a comprehensive framework for nurturing potential talent. It spans various stages, from identification to career transition, ensuring holistic player development.

Coaches, federations, schools, and parents play pivotal roles. The model emphasizes personalized training plans, continuous monitoring, mental conditioning, education, mentorship, and career transition support. This structured approach maximizes the potential of aspiring bowlers, fostering a well-rounded and successful athletic journey.

1. **Identification:** Use a combination of physical assessments, competitions, and scouting to identify individuals with the potential for bowling. Look for attributes such as hand-eye coordination, balance, and a competitive spirit.

2. **Recruitment:** Develop strategies to attract identified talents, whether through partnerships with local clubs, engagement with schools, or participation in talent identification programs.

3. **Assessment:** Conduct thorough assessments covering technical skills, physical fitness, mental resilience, and strategic understanding to establish a baseline for each player.

4. **Development Plan:** Based on assessment results, create personalized training programs that address specific areas for improvement, including technical aspects of bowling, physical conditioning, and mental toughness.

5. **Training:** Implement a structured training regimen that includes skill development, physical conditioning, and mental resilience training. Utilize coaches and specialized trainers to enhance player performance.

6. **Competition:** Provide opportunities for players to participate in various competitions to gain experience, learn from real-game scenarios, and build a competitive mindset.

7. **Monitoring:** Implement continuous monitoring of player performance, including data analytics, to track progress and provide timely feedback for adjustments to the training plan.

8. **Mental Conditioning:** Incorporate psychological training techniques such as visualization, goal-setting, and stress management to enhance mental resilience during competitions.

9. **Education:** Provide educational programs covering aspects like sports nutrition, injury prevention, and sports psychology to ensure the holistic development of the athlete.

10. **Mentorship:** Establish mentorship programs where experienced players or coaches guide and inspire younger talents, sharing insights from their own experiences.

11. **Career Transition:** Equip players with skills and resources for life after their professional careers, including education, career planning, or transition to coaching roles.

This hypothetical TDMM aims to provide a comprehensive framework for developing bowlers, covering various stages from talent identification to post-professional life. Adjustments can be made based on the specific characteristics and needs of the bowlers and the broader context of bowling development.

Understanding the Role of Psychosocial Factors in Talent Development

The Talent Development Model emphasizes that a plethora of empirical research on psychosocial aspects linked to talent development may be found in the psychological sciences. These elements include aptitude both broadly and in particular fields, originality, drive, attitude, dedication to a task, enthusiasm, curiosity, chance, opportunity, and mental toughness. They are crucial in determining how talent develops in a variety of fields, including bowling. A person's prospects of becoming eminent might be severely hampered by the underdevelopment of psychosocial characteristics, such as a lack of motivation or an unproductive goal-orientation style. Studies have revealed that students from lower-income backgrounds and underrepresented minorities are more susceptible to psychosocial hurdles, which include prejudices, limited chances, entrenched thought styles, and a lack of social support. In highly competitive situations like as bowling, it is vital to remove these hurdles and turn them into drivers of talent development.

Exploring Psychosocial Factors in the Bowling Environment

It is a relatively new field of study to examine psychosocial aspects in bowling environments utilizing talent development concepts. Chances for bowlers don't just fall into their laps; they need to be actively pursued. It is believed that having access to these opportunities is an essential psychosocial component for developing potential. In addition, the assistance that coaches and families offer is crucial in assisting young bowlers in acquiring the skills required for their future paths. The author's research with young bowlers shows that opportunities to develop a love for the sport, with coaches and family members playing crucial roles in supporting and fostering this passion, are often the driving force behind their decision to pursue mastery. The growth of bowlers is significantly aided by family support.

A gifted bowler's development depends heavily on social support because a lack of it can sabotage their goals. An examination of a failing bowling development program indicated that the program may not have helped bowlers advance to higher professional levels because of disorganized coaches who disregarded psychosocial skills and did the bare minimum to keep their jobs.

Moreover, the growth of bowlers' talents heavily depends on their thinking and their willingness to accept their own abilities. Believing in one's capacity to improve skills, or having a growth mindset, is a significant motivation for developing competencies in any discipline. Growth attitude, confidence in sport psychology, and bowlers' openness to psychological therapies are correlated. Another important component of the mindset of good bowlers is their goal orientation style. A mastery-oriented approach places a strong emphasis on lifelong learning and progress. Bowlers who possess this mentality—which is frequently seen in high achievers—are better able to bear pressure, regard setbacks as teaching moments, and consider successes as stepping stones toward personal growth. Long-term commitment to the sport and increased training intensity are similarly linked to mastery goal orientation.

Sports-related interventions that place a high priority on the development of psychosocial traits including psychological toughness, growth mindset, and stress management are regarded as essential. Tennis coaches like to point out that 80% to 90% of the game consists of mental components. According to interviews with the best bowlers in the world, success requires a number of essential qualities, such as extraordinary focus, pressure management skills, a strong drive to succeed, a compatible lifestyle, the ability to perform well under duress, acceptance of anxiety as a necessary component of the sport, stress management, resilience in the face of setbacks, self-belief, and the capacity to reach objectives. People with strong psychological traits are adept at managing stress, emotions, ideas, and actions under duress, which helps them shift between jobs with ease.

Talent development scholars have been looking to sports psychologists' methods in recent years for their insights. Some recommend using sport psychology methods to encourage the development of ability in several domains. Teaching children how to handle academic competition in a manner akin to that of athletes, musicians, or dancers may prove beneficial. According to the Talent Development Mega Model (TDMM), this kind of training ought to start early in the talent development process and could be beneficial for educational settings. Nonetheless, additional investigation is required to examine the circumstances and settings that result in peak performance in every discipline.

The Big Four Factors in Talent Development

1. Growth Mindset: This component affects how people view failure and success and is related to their views about their capacity to acquire technical and psychosocial skills. Ability Development Beliefs and Optimal Perception of Mistakes are two subcategories of a growth mindset, which is a potent talent development enhancer. Prominent bowlers constantly show that they have faith in their ability to grow as talent, believing that they can succeed in transitional times by building on their mental and technical development. They also see failures as chances to acquire important lessons that can help them overcome their shortcomings.

2. Ability Development Beliefs: A crucial quality that every bowler surveyed has in common is his steadfast faith in his ability to develop and learn to the point of preeminent talent. He has faith in his capacity to acquire technical and psychological abilities, and he knows how to turn setbacks into chances for growth that strengthen his areas of weakness.

Ten elite bowlers were asked a limited number of questions about their talent development, based on the majority of Elite bowlers that were interviewed. One of the bowlers stated that he became aware of his abilities and prospects at the age of 13:

A Dream of Excellence *"I always believed that I could be among the best bowlers, and playing professionally was something I had always wanted to do. My determination was fueled by my desire to succeed in the sport."*

Third Bowler said

Proactive Skill Development *"I approached skill improvement in a proactive manner. Whenever my coach gave me feedback, I had frequently previously given it some thought. Even before I got comments, I made it my mission to identify and fix any performance problems. I felt really accomplished to have qualified for the national adult squad and competed in an adult tournament at such a young age."*

First bowler said

Unwavering Belief *"Despite being fully aware of the enormous challenge that awaited me, I maintained an unwavering belief that I could qualify for the Youth championships." And I did fulfill that need."*

Fifth bowler said

Belief in Growth *"To compete in the Youth championship was my ultimate ambition. Even though I knew there was a big difference between my existing skill set and what was needed to qualify, I remained confident that I could succeed. I was resolved to take advantage of the chance and prove myself."*

Forth bowler said

Belief in Growth *"I've always had a great sense of self-worth and have been willing to learn new things, with a particular emphasis on improving my psychosocial aspects. With this mentality, I was able to seize the chance to learn and never stop trying to get better."*

Optimizing Mistakes for Growth

This topic looks at how bowlers handled errors and turned them into teaching moments and chances for growth. Remarkably, a few bowlers acknowledged that their prior preparations had been flawed since they had not used adequate psychological tools or routines before important matches. They saw these errors as signals that they needed to strengthen their emotional and mental fortitude, enlisting the help of a psychosocial support system and implementing fresh approaches. Two female bowlers used their panic attack experiences as a catalyst to seek out psychosocial support. Furthermore, a bowler admitted the necessity of psychological regimens during practice and matches, substituting mental patterns for previous irregularities. They accepted the ability of visualization to improve their motions. After a dismal World Cup in 2012, a bowler actively explored psychosocial support training to enhance their psychological resilience in preparation for the 2013 World Cup.

Commitment to the Task

All participants reported that task dedication is an important psychosocial aspect in the development of great bowlers when discussing their individual experiences.

Bowlers portrayed :

Relocating for Dreams *"In order to achieve my goals, I had to overcome many obstacles, such as persuading my parents to move to a busy city so I could train at a prestigious international club. Anxiety and adjusting to a hard lifestyle followed the voyage, but I persisted to get well over time."*

Balancing Act *"In spite of ongoing financial challenges, I was able to continue my intensive training and academic obligations. I did well on college admission tests when I initially got to the United States, and I won local tournaments my first semester. I was resolved to meet whatever problems that came my way, so I made it a practice to overcome daily obstacles and make sure I had access to training venues."*

Unwavering Commitment *"I showed an unyielding dedication to the sport that enthralled me, competing in multiple events and continuously looking for new challenges."*

A Young Journey *"I moved from my little rural home at the age of fourteen to attend one of the capital city's most prominent bowling academies for training. It was a difficult period since I had to learn how to live on my own even though I was too young to do so. I had to adjust to being apart from my family and stay with my grandparents. My attention was still on my training and my goal of playing for the national team in spite of the challenges."*

Enduring Challenges *"I had to suffer daily traveling to training facilities with poor accommodations and little food alternatives for about three hours for years. I was able to get past these challenges, though, because I had a strong psychological outlook. Though*

I was aware that these difficulties paled in comparison to the significance of mental preparation, I still didn't want to sleep on the floor or eat poorly before big events."

Seizing Opportunities

Three subcategories fall under the umbrella of "seizing opportunities": (a) identifying possibilities, (b) turning opportunities into success, and (c) pursuing serendipity. The first subcategory focuses on situations in which bowlers saw vital chances to further their careers. Their commitment to transforming these identified prospects into concrete accomplishments is the subject of the second subcategory. The third group encompasses the bowlers' endeavors to strategically arrange themselves at the appropriate moment or their tenacity in actively pursuing and seizing opportunities.

Bowlers portrayed :

Determined Training *"I realized my faults and made a commitment to train more in order to qualify for the Youth championship. I fully changed my training strategies and adapted to new routines in less than six months in order to compete in my ideal competition."*

Seizing Opportunities *"An important turning point occurred when I saw a chance to join a group that would eventually get me on the national squad. I took that opportunity and ran with it without hesitation."*

From Opportunity to Achievement *"I came across a big chance that ultimately made it possible for me to compete in the Beijing Olympics. Though I didn't really realize how big of a deal I was making until I pulled off an incredible performance in the finals. I won a US college scholarship thanks to my achievement in the WMC 2008 qualifying tournament in Thailand. When I competed in Thailand, I performed really well and didn't feel under pressure. My jaw dropped when I saw the outcome."*

Utilizing Social Support

Using social support looks at how people make the most of the different kinds of help that are accessible to them. Openness to Social Support and Social and Financial Support are its two subcategories. These sections investigate whether coaches, families, staff, and academies provided financial, emotional, or informational support to bowlers. The study's top bowlers underlined the value of having a variety of social and financial support networks, especially from sponsors, families, and coaches. They additionally showed that they were not only open to receiving help but also that they were determined to utilize it well.

Social and Financial Support

It is widely acknowledged that social and financial support are essential components of talent development, greatly impacting a person's capacity to turn potential into extraordinary achievement. These professional bowlers received invaluable instructional support from knowledgeable trainers who recognized their abilities and helped them advance to higher-level events during their developing stages. Their stories were significantly influenced by their families' support, particularly in the early going.

Bowlers portrayed:

The Crucial Role of My Mother in My Journey *"My mother was a crucial part of my trip. She reared me, looked after my medical needs, and was my steadfast support system. My father resided in a distant city, so we didn't have much contact until I reached eleven."*

Family Support *"One day I decided to concentrate on college because I didn't have the money to go from being an expert to being eminent. I made an effort to stick to my training regimen as closely as possible even though I was unable to train professionally. My brother frequently trained me as a child, so family support was crucial to this process."*

Managing Epilepsy *"My mother, a pharmacist, disapproved of the idea of medicating me for a condition for which we thought stress management would be sufficient. I was diagnosed with epilepsy. Both of us thought that problem-solving instruction and psychological support could aid in my ability to cope. Regrettably, my advancement was impeded by financial limitations. I didn't get much financial assistance or support. I had panic episodes and some doctors even suspected epilepsy before I started working with a psychologist. I was examined multiple times. All the same, my mother thought it preferable to explore non-pharmaceutical psychological treatment."*

Father's Sacrifices *"When I first started my job, I had financial difficulties, and my father helped me get through those. He sacrificed to pay for my competition gear and travel expenses even though he was working two jobs to maintain the family. It was a heavy financial load."*

Embracing Social Support

For people to develop their abilities and perform at extraordinary levels, they must not only get help but also embrace and accept that support. From an early age, all best bowlers showed a remarkable openness to social support. Their talents were recognized in nearby leagues and contests, and their trainers pushed them to take part in more difficult events.

Bowlers portrayed:

<u>Coach's Guidance</u> *"I kept an open mind about various kinds of assistance during my career. I got along well and trustedly with my head coach, and I always appreciated the counsel and direction the coaching team offered. I had total trust in my coach, and we had excellent communication, which led to a productive working relationship."*

<u>Strong Coach-Athlete Bond</u> *"My coach and I have a very strong relationship, and I completely trust him." We have a very strong relationship, and I really appreciate his advice. Our relationship transcends the just psychological and has been extremely important to my entire growth. I am appreciative of our excellent communication and how it has benefited my trip."*

<u>Invaluable Coach Relationship</u> *"One of the main factors in my success has been the bond I have with my coach. My current instructor and I have always gotten along really well, which has really helped me progress as a bowler. We are more than just psychologically connected, and his assistance has been priceless. Because of our great communication, we are always in agreement and collaborating to achieve my objectives."*

The Significance of the Four Factors

Elite bowlers owe much of their talent development to psychosocial issues. The Talent Development Mega Model (TDMM), which emphasizes the significance of psychosocial components and assistance, served as the foundation for this study. These results are consistent with recent research showing the significant impact of psychological factors on supporting or impeding talent development in a range of fields. Growth Mindset, Task Commitment, Opportunities Taken, and Social Support Usage are the four main characteristics that the TDMM identifies as being related to talent development.

The Power of a Growth Mindset

It was clear that bowlers had strong ideas about their capacity to improve their abilities and performance through commitment and perseverance, especially in trying situations. They agreed that throughout their careers, they needed to work toward skill development and ongoing progress. This way of thinking expresses the conviction that skills may be enhanced and developed. Despite hurdles that are getting harder to overcome on a technical, psychological, physical, and financial level, bowlers know they have the ability to learn the skills they need to overcome them. Resilience and the growth mentality are intimately related, both in athletics and academic endeavors. The bowlers' incredible rise to the top of the global rankings was attributed to their unwavering faith in their ability to improve their physical, psychological, and technical abilities.

Transforming Mistakes into Opportunities

Bowlers have shown time and time again that they are prepared to turn training or psychological errors into opportunities for valuable learning. They gave serious consideration to introspection and fault analysis. After recognizing their areas of weakness, bowlers showed a great desire to adjust and adopted new mental practices and training regimens. This mindset is a perfect example of another essential trait of growth mindset holders: the capacity to see failures and errors as chances for self-improvement and learning new coping techniques.

Understanding Brain Activity Patterns in Elite Bowlers

The way that professional bowlers think affects how their brains work both during practice and competition. Growth-minded bowlers had higher left-temporal activity for longer periods of time, especially when they were given coaching that called attention to their mistakes. Their superior outcomes on surprise retests show that this enhanced brain activity is linked to improved performance. As opposed to bowlers with a growth mentality, fixed mindset bowlers frequently exhibit attentional disengagement tendencies, which could account for their worse performance following errors.

Pro bowlers have an optimistic outlook on errors. Instead of seeing mistakes as roadblocks, they see them as challenges and devote a great deal of time and energy to learning how to overcome them. Their capacity to learn from their mistakes and keep becoming better is facilitated by this way of thinking.

Pro bowlers are incredibly passionate and committed to improving their physical and technical abilities, as well as their problem-solving abilities. This dedication is embodied in the psychosocial construct known as task commitment, which has long been acknowledged as a critical component in the development of ability across a range of fields. Within the sporting domain, Task commitment has been found to be an essential component in bowlers' talent development. The current study supports earlier findings by showing how bowlers exhibit constant commitment, hard work, and dedication throughout their careers. In the fiercely competitive world of athletics, success is frequently attained in youth or the early stages of adulthood. As a result, in order to match the demands of their sport, bowlers must devote countless hours to physical, technical, and psychosocial preparation, beginning at an early age.

The introduction of the Opportunities Taken component demonstrates its crucial role in talent development forecasting. Even the most gifted bowlers could find it difficult to realize their full potential in the absence of the right opportunities. At various points in a bowler's career, opportunities can make a big difference in how much or little they can develop their skills. In bowling, where achievement typically peaks early in life, bowlers must recognize and take advantage of opportunities to compete in higher divisions. These chances give students the perfect environment in which to hone their skills and expertise right away. The chances of being well-known in the sport are highly influenced by the opportunities that are accessible. Opportunities are especially crucial in the early phases of talent development when they are more plentiful, according to the Talent Development Mega Model (TDMM). As bowlers advance to the elite and skilled levels, there are fewer possibilities available. Talented bowlers therefore need to work even harder to get into national teams or elite bowling categories where they can be given the finest support for skill development within the sporting environment.

Bowlers don't just stumble into opportunities by accident or good fortune. Elite bowlers consistently search for and seize openings, showing unshakable commitment and tenacity in the process. They are aware of how crucial it is to take advantage of these opportunities by placing yourself in the ideal location at the ideal moment. Talented people must first create the conditions necessary for opportunities to flourish before taking advantage of them, according to the Talent Development Mega Model (TDMM). Whatever their initial socioeconomic situation, great bowlers have to overcome challenges and aggressively seek out chances, as seen by their biographies. These bowlers have shown from the beginning of their bowling careers that they can recognize and seize opportunities. They also show initiative in choosing the right competitions, divisions, and colleges to further their professional development.

Social Assistance Another important psychosocial component in bowlers' development is usage. Pro bowlers are adept at building deep connections with a variety of people in a variety of settings, and they understand the importance of these relationships throughout the duration of their careers. Talented bowlers have a lot of influence from their parents, coaches, peers, sponsors, mentors (such as psychologists and seasoned bowlers), and peers. Among the most important people who give bowlers concrete, informative, emotional, and self-esteem support are coaches. In the meantime, parents are essential because they provide information, emotional support, and financial support. Their impact on developing talent and key psychosocial skills is significant. But in the context of bowlers' growth, the value of peer and psychological assistance was not specifically mentioned. Nonetheless, bowlers' ability to progress is influenced by their openness to receiving assistance from a variety of sources. At various points in their careers, they actively seek out sources of financial, informational, technical, and emotional assistance. To become eminent, one must be willing to accept and make use of societal support. Bowlers understand that in order to advance, they require more than just technical proficiency, and in order to reach their greatest potential, they frequently look to seasoned instructors, mentors, or other bowlers for advice. Their choice to fully participate in their development is intimately linked to this acknowledgement. Over the course of their careers, bowlers have demonstrated an unwavering willingness to accept and actively seek out social support from instructors, families, and sponsors on a club and national level.

From an early age, elite bowlers demonstrate a strong passion for the game. In order to foster this desire and facilitate the shift from early involvement to competence, coaches and families are essential. Using social support is a crucial part of bowlers' growth as they advance from competence to higher levels. During this changeover period, psychosocial elements, including task dedication and the capacity to recognize and take advantage of pertinent possibilities, are important. In addition, bowlers' confidence in their ability to perform at greater levels serves as a driving force and a reflection of their growth attitude over time. Rather than viewing failures and mistakes as threats, they view them as chances for growth and challenge. These psychological elements play a part in the bowlers' progression from proficiency to mastery. Bowlers who advance from proficiency to prominence come to understand that technical skills alone are not enough. They are now more open to receiving psychosocial support to further their general psychosocial development, which can be given by professionals like sports psychologists and seasoned bowlers.

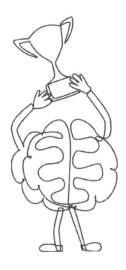

PSYCHOLOGICAL FACTORS TO BECOME COMPETENT IN BOWLING COMPETITION

Bowling is more than simply a physical activity; mental toughness and strategy are vital throughout a competition. Sadly, a lot of bowlers undervalue the role that psychological abilities have in their game. A bowler's game can be impacted by a variety of psychological elements, which is why psychological skills training (PST) is essential for improving overall sport performance. One of the most important things in helping people handle pressure and stress in any situation is effective competition preparation. Elite effective bowlers possess superior psychological qualities, such as focus, self-assurance, task-oriented thinking, reduced anxiety, positive thoughts and imagery, determination and commitment, that set them apart from their less successful peers. It is crucial to take into account the time, skill level, and experience in PST in order to comprehend the idea of psychological skill utilization more fully.

The Mental Aspect of Bowling

In bowling, the mental component of the game is very important. Many bowlers understand the importance of thinking correctly on the lane; some of the best bowlers even assert that 50% of a successful bowling shot is determined by mental toughness. They stress that in addition to mental toughness, a solid shot is made up of several components, including body mechanics, release, and swing. Coaches, bowlers, and team personnel have all embraced sport psychology, but there hasn't always been a direct correlation between psychological knowledge and peak performance. However, PST can dramatically increase bowling performance and improve emotional self-regulation abilities. Bowlers' psychological competency on and off the lanes can also be improved by using simple mental techniques like visualization and positive thinking. It is significant to remember that in order to become extremely effective in training and competition, these mental bowling skills—like physical bowling skills—require practice and patience.

Key Characteristics of Psychological Skills in Bowlers

There are noticeable variations in the way professional and amateur bowlers apply psychological techniques. When it comes to training and competition, amateur bowlers tend to rely more on imagery and relaxation, while elite bowlers use less automaticity, imagery, attentional control, and negative thinking than during training sessions. Instead, elite bowlers exhibit a higher percentage of goal-setting and activation during competition. In the same way, amateur bowlers use activation strategies more during matches than during training, but they use goal setting less frequently. Furthermore, the distinctions in psychological skill application between seasoned and novice bowlers during competition are largely attributable to PST experience. Proficient bowlers are more likely than less experienced players to use self-talk strategies among the eight psychological skills techniques.

Different Approaches to Psychological Skills Training

Regardless of their background in psychological skill development, professional and amateur bowlers exhibit different approaches and techniques when applying psychological skills. Even though their psychological makeup is similar, training and competitive periods differ from one another. The majority of professional bowlers get ready mentally by consulting bowling periodicals, coaches, parents, or sports psychologists. They then use these tactics in high-pressure training sessions. Elite bowlers, on the other hand, have personal mentors or sports psychologists who investigate different aspects and situations they may come into in the game. Both professional and recreational bowlers utilize their past psychological abilities during training and matches. But because training and competition include different circumstances, so do the bowlers' attitudes, sentiments, and reactions to things. Bowlers are under tremendous pressure to perform better than or on par with their rivals during tournaments. On the other hand, bowlers adhere to a structured training regimen during practice that is stress-free, entertaining and gives them a sense of accomplishment.

Example

When competing, a bowler who has never received psychological skills training finds it difficult to think negatively. The bowler learns how to utilize positive self-talk and reframe negative ideas to stay focused and confident during competition after training with a sports psychologist. The bowler uses relaxation and visualization techniques to reduce tension and anxiety during training, as well as goal-setting and activation exercises to help him get ready for competition. Consequently, the bowler experiences an uptick in his confidence and performance during practice and competition.

The Use of Psychological Skills During Training and Competition in the Elite Bowlers and the Amateur Bowlers

Even though the psychological talents of highly competent and low-skilled bowlers were comparable, amateur bowlers used goal-setting, visualization, and relaxation techniques much more frequently during training than their elite counterparts. Furthermore, compared to the Elite bowlers, the amateur bowlers exhibit much higher scores of imagery, relaxation, and negative thinking during the match. It is interesting to observe that amateur bowlers mostly employ imagery and relaxation techniques as part of their psychological skills, whereas elite bowlers primarily use a reduction in negative thinking. Thus, this could be the cause of elite bowlers' strong performance in matches. PST improves emotional control and results in better bowling performance.

Hypothetical examples

Example of an amateur bowler:

An illustration of an amateur bowler might be Tom, who is always looking to get better. He uses visualization techniques to see his shots, sets specific goals for himself, and engages in relaxation activities to help him stay focused and composed throughout training. But he has trouble with negative thinking during competitions, which hinders his effectiveness on the lanes. He frequently becomes frustrated and ruminates on his faults, which encourages him to make more mistakes. Nevertheless, he keeps using PST to hone his mental toughness in an effort to perform better in competition.

Example of an Elite bowler:

Sarah is an elite bowler with numerous championship victories under her belt. She establishes clear objectives for herself throughout her training sessions, concentrating on enhancing particular facets of her game. She uses visualization exercises to see her shots and gets ready for every

situation that could arise during competitions. She also practices relaxing to stay composed and concentrated during competition. She keeps her optimistic outlook and her goals in focus when competing. Her performance as a bowler has been greatly influenced by her usage of PST.

The Use of Psychological Skills during Training and Competition in the Elite Bowlers

In comparison to training, elite bowlers exhibit higher percentages of goal planning and activation during competition, but lower scores in automaticity, imagination, attentional control, and negative thinking. In terms of the psychological and psychomotor skills related to bowling performance, skilled bowlers are more mentally prepared, concentrate better when playing, experience fewer negative emotions and thoughts, have higher levels of psychomotor automaticity, and are more dedicated to the game than their less skilled peers. The Elite bowlers employ goal-setting and activation technique more in competition than in training. The percentage of negative thoughts during competition was lower among bowlers who showed a high level of goal-setting and activation during training sessions. It's probable that their competition is carried out in accordance with a process objective that emphasizes actions that can result in efficient performance. When it comes to psychological skills, elite bowlers have a higher percentage while training than competitors. Given their increased experience on a driving range and during a game of bowling, the Elite bowlers may be able to identify self-management on the lane and apply the images with ease in a real-world setting. But during the course of the match, the Elite bowlers' use of made-up talents rapidly declined.

Hypothetical example

Samantha bowls at the national level and is a talented bowler. She employs activation techniques and sets specific goals throughout her training sessions to help her learn with the proper mentality. To enable her to give her best effort, she also concentrates on strengthening her mental abilities, such as focus and optimistic thinking. Samantha use visualization to imagine her shots when she practices on a regular basis at the bowling driving range.

Samantha continues to use activation tactics and goal-setting strategies to get ready for her matches during the competition. She concentrates on process objectives, such as maintaining her composure and hitting every shot exactly on target. Samantha has had a lot of training and experience, which has helped her control her emotions and maintain her attention on the work at hand when driving.

Samantha can utilize her mental abilities to reinterpret her negative ideas in a good way, even though she occasionally has them during competition. She might tell herself, for instance, that it's only one shot and she can make it up in the next frame if she misses one. Because of this, Samantha is able to keep her confidence and compete well the entire time.

The Use of Psychological Skills during Training and Competition in the Amateur Bowlers

During the competition, amateur bowlers employ psychological skill activation techniques more than they do during training. One strategy that most bowlers employ to increase their self-confidence is the activation technique. Nonetheless, compared to training sessions, a smaller percentage of goal-setting strategies are employed during competitions.

The amateur bowlers could concentrate on the objectives and think about the outcome once the match is over. Bowlers who report being moderately or lowly motivated typically exhibit higher levels of competition anxiety, which is linked to a decrease in mental toughness. In the context of competitive sports, bowlers should emphasize the importance of automaticity in cultivating the experience of high performance.

Hypothetical examples

Examples of amateur bowlers:

Activation Technique: John, a novice bowler, usually uses self-confidence-boosting activation strategies before competition, like deep breathing and listening to inspirational music. He doesn't often employ this tactic during training sessions, though.

Goal Setting Technique: Jane, an amateur bowler, establishes objectives for every training session, such increasing her accuracy and striking a particular quantity of strikes. She can, however, fail to set clear goals and get overly preoccupied with the result rather than the process during a competition.

Examples of elite bowlers:

Activation Technique: Mark, a professional bowler, builds self-confidence in training and competition by using activation tactics including positive self-talk and visualization. He understands that reaching optimal performance requires mental preparation.

Goal Setting Technique: Sarah, an accomplished bowler, establishes clear goals for herself throughout practice and competition. Some examples of these goals include improving her technique and hitting a particular place on the lane. She understands that establishing process goals can help her feel less anxious and produce better results.

The Use of Psychological Skills during Training and Competition in the Elite and the in Elite Bowlers

Both Elite and Elite bowlers use comparable psychological techniques in practice and competition. When competing, the emphasis is on pre-shot routine, breathing control, visualization, relaxation, positive attitude, and shot focus. Because bowling is their vocation, elite bowlers employ a different set of psychological strategies to thrive in competition, unlike amateur bowlers. While amateur bowlers receive psychological instruction from a small number of sports psychologists and primarily watch movies and listen to music for mental relaxation, elite bowlers receive their mental skills training primarily from mentors, sports psychologists, and senior successful professional bowlers. Nonetheless, as the environment shifts from practice to competition, the majority of bowlers experience distinct thought processes and emotions. The bowlers are under pressure since there is a lot of responsibility on them to win the match or improve their bowling ranking at the end of the competition. Their regular workout routine, on the other hand, is stress-free and enjoyable. While the psychological capabilities of the Elite and the Elite bowlers were similar, the strategies employed during training and competition differed. While the Elite bowlers adhere to the sports psychologist's recommended regimen, various coaches may have different implementations of certain elements. They typically employ breathing exercises, visualization, relaxation, optimistic thinking, encouraging speech, a pre-shot ritual, and concentrating on the ball contact. Bowlers on the International Tour employ a range of psychological strategies, including self-talk, visualization, thinking-stopping, meditation, and breathing control.

The Individual Zones of Optimum Functioning Theory (IZOF Theory) is a psychological concept that suggests individuals have unique optimal zones of emotional and psychological functioning in which they perform at their best. This theory acknowledges that there is no one-size-fits-all optimal level of arousal or anxiety for everyone; instead, it varies from person to person and can even vary for the same individual depending on the task or situation.

In the context of bowling, IZOF Theory can be beneficial in the following ways:

Personalized Approach: IZOF Theory emphasizes the importance of recognizing that each bowler has their own optimal level of anxiety or arousal for peak performance. This means that coaches and athletes can take a more personalized approach to mental preparation and performance optimization.

Anxiety Management: By understanding their individual zones of optimal functioning, bowlers can work on managing their anxiety levels effectively. This may involve techniques such as relaxation exercises, visualization, or mindfulness to help them reach and maintain their ideal state of arousal during competition.

Consistency: IZOF Theory helps bowlers achieve greater consistency in their performances. By staying within their optimal zones, they are less likely to experience extreme fluctuations in performance due to anxiety or arousal levels that are too high or too low.

Improved Decision-Making: When bowlers are operating within their optimal zones, they tend to make better decisions under pressure. This can lead to more accurate shot selection and execution, which is crucial in bowling where precision is key.

Mental Resilience: Bowlers who are aware of their individual zones can develop mental resilience. They can better cope with challenging situations and recover quickly from setbacks, maintaining their focus and confidence throughout a competition.

To use IZOF Theory effectively in bowling, athletes and coaches can follow these steps:

Self-Assessment: Bowlers should engage in self-assessment to identify their individual optimal zones of functioning. This may involve reflecting on past performances and the emotional and psychological states associated with their best and worst games.

Psychological Skills Training: Once the optimal zone is identified, bowlers can undergo psychological skills training to develop strategies for managing their anxiety and arousal levels. This might include relaxation techniques, imagery, self-talk, and goal-setting.

Monitoring and Adjustment: During practice and competitions, athletes can continuously monitor their emotional and psychological states. If they notice that they are deviating from their optimal zone, they can employ the techniques they've learned to bring themselves back into that zone.

Coaching Support: Coaches and sports psychologists can play a vital role in helping bowlers understand and apply IZOF Theory. They can provide guidance, create personalized mental training programs, and offer support to ensure athletes are operating within their optimal zones.

Hypothetical examples

Examples of amateur bowlers:

Activation technique: As an amateur bowler, John finds it difficult to feel confident when competing. He employs activation techniques, including jumping jacks to get his adrenaline running before the game and listening to cheerful music, to enhance his confidence.

Goal setting technique: Sarah is a highly motivated amateur bowler who wants to get better. She sets quantifiable, precise goals for herself during her training sessions, such as hitting a certain amount of strikes or reaching a particular score. She does, however, place more of an emphasis on her overall performance than on particular objectives during competitions.

Examples of elite bowlers:

Imagery technique: Michael is a superb bowler who has taken home numerous international titles. During contests, he visualizes the ideal shot before taking it by using imaging techniques. This keeps him concentrated and enables him to continue performing at a high level.

Self-talk technique: For a number of years, Emily, a talented bowler, has received coaching from a sports psychologist. During competitions, she employs self-talk strategies to maintain her motivation and optimism. She can tell herself things like "I can do this" or "Stay focused" to help her stay focused and confident.

The use of Psychological skills training (PT) to control Anxiety Levels during Competitions

Numerous studies have been conducted on the connection between anxiety and performance. Bowling is seen as a tense and anxiety-prone sport that demands intense mental focus and precise movement to succeed. As such, it may be difficult to execute precisely when under a lot of stress or anxiety.

Bowlers' ability to perceive and manage their anxiety is one of the key components of their success. Pre-competitive anxiety levels can differ based on a number of variables, including age, sex, experience, and sport type. Due to the individual assumption of responsibility for the outcome, bowlers in solo games like bowling must exhibit higher degrees of anxiety than bowlers in team sports. Moreover, compared to fewer Elite bowlers, Elite bowlers have reduced levels of somatic and cognitive worry. While amateur bowlers continuously experience anxiety, elite bowlers experience anxiety during the lead-up to the event and during the tournament. Still, there appears to be a perfect amount of nervousness for every bowler. Performance might be hampered by levels that are either below or above ideal. According to the Individual Zones of Ideal Functioning Theory, an individual's ideal level of arousal may not always be at the middle of the arousal continuum. Unlike other sports that require gross motor skills, bowling requires fine motor control and is more sensitive to somatic changes. This could explain why optimal anxiety may be more significant. However, there has been evidence of a detrimental correlation between performance and overconfidence. As a result, overconfidence might impair performance and cause carelessness. Therefore, it would seem important to understand each bowler's ideal degree of anxiety separately.

Examples of how different bowlers may perform during high-pressure situations:

Pre-competitive anxiety levels: An amateur bowler who has never competed before may feel a lot of tension leading up to and during the tournament, which could have a bad effect on his performance. On the other hand, a skilled bowler who has participated in numerous competitions can have a better understanding of his anxiety levels and know how to take advantage of it.

Individual assumption of responsibility: *Bowling is an individual sport that places a great deal of responsibility on each bowler, which may cause anxiety. While an elite bowler who is accustomed to this pressure may have a more laid-back attitude, an amateur bowler may find it difficult to handle this duty.*

Optimal level of anxiety: The ideal amount of anxiety varies from bowler to bowler and is influenced by experience, personality traits, and other different factors. While an expert bowler with more experience may benefit from higher anxiety levels, an amateur bowler who is not accustomed to high-pressure conditions may benefit from lower anxiety levels.

Negative relationship between excessive self-confidence and performance: *An amateur bowler who is overconfident may make mistakes and perform poorly, yet a top bowler who is confident in his ability may perform better under pressure. There is a negative correlation between overconfidence and performance.*

Aspect	Description	Example in Competition	Steps to Obtain	Advantages
Elite Bowlers	Elite bowlers have lower cognitive and somatic anxiety levels, as they understand and control their anxiety effectively. They maintain an optimal level of arousal for peak performance.	Elite bowler remains calm and focused during competition, adjusting their anxiety levels to stay within their optimal zone.	1. Self-awareness: Identify their optimal anxiety level through self-assessment and performance analysis. 2. Psychological skills training (e.g., relaxation techniques, visualization) to control anxiety. 3. Practice maintaining composure under pressure.	1. Consistent performance under pressure. 2. Improved decision-making and execution. 3. Enhanced mental resilience.
Non-Elite Bowlers	Non-elite bowlers often struggle with managing anxiety levels, experiencing fluctuations in anxiety that can negatively impact their performance.	Non-elite bowler becomes overly anxious before a crucial shot, leading to shaky and inconsistent performance.	1. Self-assessment: Recognize their anxiety patterns and how they affect performance. 2. Seek guidance from sports psychologists or coaches. 3. Develop coping strategies to manage anxiety (e.g., deep breathing, positive self-talk).	1. Better control of anxiety-related performance issues. 2. Increased confidence and mental stability during competitions. 3. Reduced performance fluctuations due to anxiety.

Table 24 - Using The Individual Zones of Optimum Functioning Theory (IZOF Theory) in Bowling

Even elite bowlers can experience increased anxiety and anxiousness in pre-competition and competitive settings. Thus, it is generally acknowledged that physical therapy plays a significant role in athletic performance when it comes to mental preparation for both pre-competition and competitive sports. Regular physical therapy is linked to more consistent and successful performance, particularly at the top levels. Professional bowlers were always aware that they could have bowled more effectively in the past if they had developed their mental skills earlier in their careers.

There are two types of mental preparation: cognitive and somatic. Some bowlers in this line employ pre-competitive techniques including talking to teammates, playing music, or becoming quieter. These actions may help the mind avoid thinking negative thoughts and may be beneficial for motivation and relaxation.

Because of this, bowlers, coaches, and sports psychologists use cognitive or somatic coping strategies in addition to technical and physical training to decrease anxiety related to the pre-competitive state, maintain and focus concentration, regulate arousal levels, boost confidence, and maintain motivation and peak performance based on their modalities.

In order to help bowlers use physical therapy (PT) more effectively and perform better, professional psychological support (PPS) appears to be important. In addition to helping bowlers deal with the pressures of competition, modify their level of awareness, and stay focused amidst the numerous distractions of the competitive environment, sport psychologists may also educate bowlers on psychological skills and help them feel less anxious and depressed. In order to maximize performance, the sport psychologist must also be aware of the various sporting scenarios, the psychological resources available to the technical staff and bowlers, and their demands. For these reasons, PT—along with other training components—should be a crucial component of a bowler's overall training program.

Is stress during training a beneficial tool to simulate stressful situations during competition? A bad performance during competition can result from a lack of skill control while dealing with pressure. Training in a high-stress setting appears to be a useful strategy for reducing anxiety and enhancing performance.

PT Importance to Bowlers	Steps	Level of Importance	Example of PT	Cognitive and Somatic Techniques
Pre-competitive mental preparation	1. Identify stressors 2. Develop relaxation techniques 3. Develop visualization techniques	High	Deep breathing	Somatic
	1. Identify negative thoughts 2. Replace them with positive self-talk 3. Develop cue words	High	"I can do this"	Cognitive
	1. Establish pre-competitive routine 2. Stick to it 3. Repeat	High	Listening to music	Somatic
Competitive mental preparation	1. Identify the level of arousal needed 2. Develop techniques to regulate arousal 3. Establish focus cues	High	Physical warm-up	Somatic
	1. Develop positive self-talk for difficult situations 2. Practice visualization of successful performance	High	"I can handle this pressure"	Cognitive
	1. Stay focused on the present moment 2. Control thoughts and emotions 3. Develop coping strategies for distractions	High	Mindfulness meditation	Cognitive
Professional psychological support	1. Evaluate individual needs 2. Develop PT plan 3. Implement PT plan	High	One-on-one counseling	Cognitive and Somatic
Training in high stress environments	1. Simulate competitive environment during training 2. Develop coping strategies for high-pressure situations	Medium	Mock competitions	Cognitive and Somatic

Table 25 - Psychological Training (PT) is crucial for bowlers, enhancing performance and mental resilience. Key steps include identifying stressors, developing relaxation and visualization techniques, and establishing routines. Pre-competitive mental preparation involves addressing negative thoughts and creating focus cues. Competitive mental preparation focuses on arousal regulation, positive self-talk, and mindfulness. Professional psychological support tailors interventions, while training in high-stress environments simulates real competition. Both cognitive and somatic techniques, such as deep breathing and positive affirmations, contribute significantly to bowlers' success.

It's interesting to note that in order to achieve optimal learning, sensory inputs of voluntary actions during training should mimic the competitive environment. As such, practicing performance actions under duress may boost a bowler's context-specific confidence and ability. Furthermore, bowlers who believed they had the tools and ability to handle stressful situations saw worry as a boost to their game. Applying PT approaches that turn worry into a facilitator could be intriguing for coaches and bowlers, since anxiety can be viewed as both an additional stress factor and a facilitator.

Any of these high-stress scenarios can raise your chance of getting hurt. Bowling is one of the sports with the lowest risk of injury, but even with its low rate of injuries, there is a chance that it could affect performance. In addition to the physical restrictions, the pain from an injury can make it difficult for a bowler to concentrate and compete in ideal circumstances. However, pain can also be normalized and viewed as benign or usual. When it occurs, it may also have an impact on bowlers' mental health. As a result, bowlers may struggle with anxiety, sadness, low self-esteem, poor recovery feelings, low self-confidence, competitive insecurity, mistrust of their own level of skill, and failure fear. The rehabilitation process may also be impacted by this emotional state. It has been demonstrated that using mental techniques during recovery is quite successful. These explanations suggest that coaches and physiotherapists are essential to the psychological healing process following injuries. However, it is unclear if it is consistently incorporated, along with physiotherapists, in injury treatment programs, in spite of the scientific data.

One of the most crucial elements influencing a bowler's growth and development is their coach, although a diverse team may also have some positive effects on output. One of the key components of a bowler's success is the coach's capacity to enhance learning and maximize advancement. As a result, the coach serves as a leader, mentor, psychotherapist, friend, educator, people manager, administrator, and role model in addition to imparting knowledge and skills.

The bowlers' performance, competence, internal motivation, and level of satisfaction are all positively correlated with the instructors' rewards and compliments. As a result, the most demanding and well-liked coaches are those who exhibit the skills necessary to handle the requirements and issues of the bowlers while fostering a good rapport through friendship, trust, availability, and concern for the bowlers' overall wellbeing, including their mental health.

Are bowlers truly aware of the benefits of possessing PPS? Do bowlers know which PT is best suited for bowling? In what ways can anxiety affect performance, and what is the ideal amount? Does performance suffer from injuries? Can the psychologist be replaced by the coach? What qualities should one anticipate from a cherished coach? Which psychological factors, then, have an impact on bowlers' performance as seen from their own point of view?

Importance of PT

Approximately ten bowlers were asked a few psychological questions about anxiety, based on the majority of Elite bowlers who were interviewed. With the exception of two bowlers, every bowler stated that PT helped lower, manage, and regulate anxiety levels.

> *It was very expensive for me to handle my anxiety at first, but as I figured out how to unwind and reduce it,....*
> *It can be really beneficial for easing your competition-related anxiety. That's the reason I think PT is crucial.*

(Bowler 2)

Relationship Between Anxiety and Performance

Competition Anxiety Levels

It's crucial for bowlers 2, 3, 4, 5, and 7 to feel a little nervous before a match. Despite not being quantifiable, these anxiety states help bowlers stay focused and better prepared for competition. The frequency with which bowlers brought up this idea throughout the interview suggests that this subject is quite important:

> *"It depends on how well you manage your feelings, which might have a favorable or unfavorable effect. In my case, for example, it's the exact reverse. I do exceptionally well in emotional control during competitions, frequently matching or even exceeding my training level." (Bowler 4)*

Conversely, Bowlers 6 and 8 claimed that nervousness has a negative impact on their performance in competitions, whereas Bowler 1 claimed he do not feel anxious when competing. In these kinds of situations, he finds no need to feel anxious.

> *"I spend most of my effort on technical management during the competition, and I spend far less time worrying about the results. As a result, it seems that stress levels stay low and anxiety practically vanishes."*

(Bowler 1)

Competitive Experience and Its Influence in the Control of Anxiety Levels

With the exception of bowler 2, the competitive experience is crucial since it gives bowlers improved mental stability and lowers their anxiety levels over the course of their athletic careers.

"My competitive background has helped me manage my anxiety to the point where it completely disappears before and during competitions."

(Bowler 6)

Physiological Changes Related to Anxiety

For the entirety of their athletic careers, all bowlers admitted to experiencing some physiological changes (also known as "somatic anxiety") associated with the competition. These changes included an elevated heart rate, discomfort (burning, cold, or tightness), restlessness, nervousness, and agitation, muscle tension, tremors, and shallow breathing. Nonetheless, they were able to control their anxiety levels more effectively thanks to their competitive experience, PT, and PPS.

"I became a little anxious. These days, the competition is the only time my heart starts to race. However, I do recall an instance in the past when I would get nervous and tremble at the beginning of tournaments." (Bowler 5)

Changes in Anxiety Levels from the Previous Week to the Competition and During It. There are no discernible differences in anxiety levels before and during competition for bowlers 1 and 6.

"I have no doubt that competing has helped me control my anxiety to the point where I no longer experience anxiety before or during competitions." (Bowler 6)

Conversely, there is a progressive fluctuation in anxiety levels until competition for bowlers 2, 3, 5, 7, and 8. Anxiety rises for bowlers 2, 3, and 8 particularly when things go wrong in the competition, and it can also rise for bowlers 5 and 7 even when things are going well:

"The first part of the competition was when I was most nervous. It usually goes up when things don't go as planned, but it tends to go down when I perform well." (Bowler 2)

Bowler 4 expressed his desire for the tournament to begin as soon as possible, saying:

"I'm eager to start competing as soon as I can," despite trying not to worry about it during the week. I try not to think about the competition the week before it happens until I'm there. Ensuring I have everything I need for the event is my only priority." (Bowler 4)

Pre-Competitive and Competitive Mental Preparation

Bowlers 2, 3, 4, 6, and 7 stated that they employ mental preparation strategies like music listening, breathing exercises, and visualization during pre-competition and competing times. Additionally, bowlers 1, 2, 4, and 7 have a tendency to be more reserved the day before and on competition day. In addition, Bowler 7 enjoys watching videos, while Bowler 1 typically goes to bed sooner.

"I think visualization is also involved in this. I think that breathing is very important for helping our bodies relax. Our hearts beat more quickly the night before a competition, and we frequently have butterflies in the stomach." (Bowler 3)

Conversely, bowler 5 wants to converse with teammates, and bowler 8 is more focused on competition:

"Whether I'm by myself or trying to focus, I'd rather have a chat than listen to music. Speaking is what I like to do best." (Bowler 5)

Elite Psychological Support (PPS)

Bowlers 3, 4, and 6 reported having psychological support, which they said was crucial to their performance in terms of PPS. The subject of PPS and PT seems to be quite relevant for all bowlers, as seen by the interviewee's frequent mention of it:

"Yes, I'm working with a skilled psychologist." (Bowler 6)

"Yes, I'm currently working with a sports psychologist who provides me with assistance." (Bowler 3)

On the other hand, bowlers 1 through 8 reported not having PPS. Bowler 1 explained away his actions by saying he was ignorant and unnecessary, and Bowler 8 cited lack of time and knowledge in his justification:

"From my perspective, I don't do it because I lack the knowledge and it's not a necessity." (Bowler 1)

Bowlers 2, 5, and 7 stated that their federations provided them with very little help and that they received very little psychological support over the course of their careers. Bowler 5 added that most coaches don't think that's vital:

"I've received minimal psychological support throughout my entire career. In 1994, I had a (PPS), which was a worthwhile experience. But after that, it stopped happening frequently. I gained relaxation skills, discovered efficient breathing techniques, and even started to meditate as a result of that effort. I have been doing these routines since 1994, and they have become a way of life for me." (Bowler 7)

Furthermore, bowlers 2, 5, and 7 said that they would have finished their current results faster if they had received psychological support:

"I might have been able to learn these skills in a one-year journey with a psychologist, but it actually took me 10 years to reach this point." (Bowler 5)

Stress during Training

Two scenarios were taken into consideration with regard to this topic: the pressure that the instructor places on training and the pressure that the bowler puts on training when working alone. Out of all the interviewees, seven out of ten said that training alone is not as effective in simulating competition as stress applied by the trainer. Bowler 4 continued, saying that it really depends on your goals and how much emphasis you wish to put on the bowler's stress:

"Working with a coach makes it much easier to achieve that state, but training alone and simulating a stressful situation can be quite challenging." (Bowler 9)

Bowlers 1, 2, 3, and 6 also stated that having the team or other bowlers present during training can increase the amount of stress applied.

"During team training sessions, we often simulate finals, and I can't help but get excited because I always have a strong desire to win." (Bowler 10)

Conversely, bowlers 1 and 4, who typically train without a coach, stated that they make an effort to create a stress environment that mimics competition:

"I participate in training sims that imitate the competition setting prior to competitions. In accordance with the new rules, I play background noise, such music. I change the music's volume to mimic various settings because competing in complete silence isn't the same as competing to the tunes of music, which can greatly increase your energy levels." (Bowler 4)

Psychological Effects of Injuries

In this sense, bowlers 1, 3, 9, and 10 had no injuries during their athletic careers, bowler 5 suffered a slight injury to his elbow and shoulder, while bowlers 2, 6, and 7 had more severe injuries. Bowler 2 suffered injuries to his elbow and shoulder; bowler 6 had injuries to his elbow and shoulder, as well as to his cervical spine; and bowler 7 suffered injuries to his elbow and shoulder. Despite the varying degrees of injury, none of the four bowlers experienced psychological effects or performance impairments during competition. Bowler 6 experienced more physical pain during competitions, but she overcame it by reflecting on a recent family loss:

"Despite the injury, it was challenging for me to train, but it didn't affect my performance in terms of pain or physical limitations." (Bowler 7)

Psychologically speaking, I don't feel pain because I'm at ease in the bowling position. Even if I may feel more exhausted and react a little slower, I can still complete the tasks at hand correctly." (Bowler 5)

The Coach's Influence in the Bowler

According to all bowlers, the coach has a significant impact on them both personally and technically. The impact of the coaches' remarks, their position as friends, the value of timely praise, their capacity to help bowlers overcome difficult circumstances (in training and competition), and their capacity to optimize their performance were all emphasized by the bowlers:

"Yes, I think it's crucial that my coach congratulates me when I finish a tournament and do well. For me, it is really important that my coach be happy with how I performed." (Bowler 6)

"You could go chat to your coach during a competition if things weren't going well, and whatever he said may change how you were feeling at the time. His advice could stop the downward spiral and assist you in regaining your composure and attention so that you can perform better." (Bowler 2)

Aspect	Description	Number of Bowlers	Example Bowlers
Relationship Between Anxiety and Performance	Bowlers 2, 3, 4, 5, and 7 find initial anxiety important as it keeps them alert for competition.	5	Bowler 4: "I excel at emotional management during competitions."
	Bowlers 1, 6, and 8 do not see benefits in anxiety during competition.	3	Bowler 1: "I don't experience anxiety during competitions."
Competitive Experience and Anxiety Control	Competitive experience helps control anxiety levels (except Bowler 2).	9	Bowler 6: "Competitive experience helped me gain control over anxiety."
Physiological Changes Related to Anxiety	All bowlers experience physiological changes related to anxiety but can manage them through PT.	10	Bowler 5: "My heart used to race, now I manage it through PT."
Variation in Anxiety Levels Before & During Competition	Bowlers 1 and 6 have consistent anxiety levels.	2	Bowler 6: "I don't feel anxious before or during competitions."
	Bowlers 2, 3, 5, 7, and 8 experience increasing anxiety levels as competition approaches.	5	Bowler 2: "My anxiety peaks at the beginning of competition."
Pre-Competitive & Competitive Mental Preparation	Bowlers 2, 3, 4, 6, and 7 use mental preparation techniques.	5	Bowler 3: "Breathing and visualization are crucial for me."
	Bowlers 1 and 5 prefer other approaches (e.g., conversation).	2	Bowler 5: "I'd rather engage in conversation than use techniques."
Elite Psychological Support (PPS)	Bowlers 3, 4, and 6 consider PPS very important for their performance.	3	Bowler 4: "I'm working with a skilled psychologist."
	Bowlers 1 and 8 do not have PPS due to various reasons.	2	Bowler 1: "I lack the knowledge and don't see it as a necessity."
Stress During Training	Training stress with a coach simulates competition better.	7	Bowler 9: "Working with a coach makes it much easier to achieve that state."
	Bowlers 1 and 4 simulate stress when training alone.	2	Bowler 4: "I introduce background noise and adjust music volume."
Psychological Effects of Injuries	Bowlers 1, 3, 9, and 10 had no injuries and performed well.	4	Bowler 10: "I had no injuries during my career."
	Bowlers 2, 5, 6, and 7 had injuries but were not significantly affected psychologically.	4	Bowler 7: "I didn't experience psychological pain despite injuries."
The Coach's Influence in the Bowler	Coaches have a substantial influence on bowlers' performance and mental state.	10	Bowler 6: "My coach's words can break negative flow and help me focus."

These comments attempted to ascertain, from the Elite bowlers' own viewpoint, how important PT is. It's crucial to keep in mind that the participants were really skilled bowlers who had competed in international championships, despite the tiny sample size.

According to the current input, every one of the ten bowlers regarded PT as crucial to performance. Additionally, it was demonstrated that physical therapy (PT) could assist in controlling anxiety, managing stress, improving technique, increasing or maintaining a more regular performance, and avoiding anxieties. As a result, our findings concur with those of the majority of research that found physical therapy helps athletes perform at their best.

The bowlers are improving technically and putting themselves in a zone of optimal functioning by learning how to deal with difficult conditions and coping with pressure in an appropriate manner. As a result, PT aids in the development of effective training plans that enable the bowler to handle competition pressure more skillfully. Remembering that there isn't a perfect amount of anxiety is crucial. Because every bowler is different, each would have the ideal amount of anxiety. Finding this level and modulating and adjusting it to get the greatest performance should be a component of the training. As a result, PT could assist bowlers in determining and adjusting this level.

Bowlers generally reported being able to manage their anxiety levels during competition, outperforming their training results. Pro bowlers believe that in order to stay awake during competition, it's critical to experience little anxiety. It appears that the ideal degree of anxiety and excitement does not hinder performance, but rather enhances it. However, it may not occur in every bowler. Very few bowlers have the aforementioned anxiety-causing consequences on their game. Furthermore, it appears that other factors like the bowler's age and gender, the kind of sport, or the PPS are connected to the anxiety's effects on performance. As a result, depending on how the bowler perceives the changes and the ideal level of worry for themselves, the consequences of anxiety can be either positive and enabling or bad and crippling.

Remarkably, when compared directly to amateur bowlers, the majority of top bowlers expressed a reduced level of somatic and cognitive anxiety, indicating that their competitive experience has improved their ability to manage stress and maintain mental stability. More elite bowlers may experience anxious sensations as competitive facilitators, boost their confidence, and learn better-coping mechanisms. PPS, when combined with experience, may be able to regulate the physiological responses associated with worry, such as elevated heart rate, dyspnea, burning in the stomach, trembling, tense muscles, anxiety, and nausea. For both individual and group sports, the competitive experience has a major impact on how competitive anxiety is perceived and directed, as well as how confident one feels in oneself.

Competitive anxiety is experienced differently by elite bowlers. Until the start of the tournament, most bowlers experience a rise in anxiety that varies based on how the event is going. The pre-competitive expectations that bowlers appear to acquire for each competition could provide an explanation for these outcomes. As a matter of fact, anxiety may rise when causal attributions in sports lead to unfavorable or unexpected outcomes. As a result, PPS appears to be essential, with psychological training programs tailored to the bowlers' requirements based on their experience and skill levels. Pro bowlers practice visualization, breathing techniques, and music listening. These somatic methods used as part of pre-competitive routines may be crucial to the growth of bowlers, help to reduce anxiety and pre-competitive stress, and enhance athletic performance.

Every bowler thought PPS was significant. Bowlers without PPS and/or without PT practice cited lack of time, ignorance, carelessness on the part of instructors, absence of a high-performance framework, and lack of federation support as their main causes.

A lack of understanding of the procedure and the mechanism by which PT influences performance appears to be one of the causes of the non-use of PPS. Nonetheless, research has shown that using PPS enhances bowlers' understanding, leading them to appreciate its significance for bowling performance and include PPS in their micro-cycles as a result.

Bowlers may experience psychological impacts from sports injuries or limitations in their ability to concentrate on their game.

Generally speaking, the coach is quite important during the training process. In addition to technical and tactical skills, the relationship between the coach and the bowler appears to be founded on positive interpersonal interactions. Since his engagement tactics may affect the bowler's emotions, the coach needs to be aware of his actions in order to help the bowler adapt psychologically. This truth is evident in a variety of circumstances. For instance, bowlers believe that the coach's stress during practice is far more beneficial than their own. In particular, a bowler says that pressure-free training is ineffective and inefficient.

"EMBARKING ON THE MENTAL MASTERY ODYSSEY: A PERSONAL EXPLORATION OF PSYCHOLOGICALLY TAILORED PREPARATION FOR HIGH-STAKES BOWLING COMPETITIONS"

By Robi Godnic

The intricacies of preparing for a game or match on game day are central to the mental training journey, posing distinct challenges for youth players and those aspiring to shine on the international stage of bowling competitions. The entire day leading up to the game becomes a canvas where athletes strive for perfection, underpinned by the inherent pressure to flawlessly execute during the actual match.

In my experience as a coach, engaging with a diverse array of bowlers, each characterized by unique backgrounds spanning education, economic standing, social dynamics, and familial influences, has highlighted the delicate task of effecting meaningful changes in their gameplay without inadvertently triggering additional psychological complexities. This challenge is particularly pronounced in the crucible of high-stakes competitions.

In the minds of these athletes, a myriad of thoughts surfaces, ranging from the imperative need to secure a coveted "CUT" to aspiring for an average score exceeding the coveted 200 mark. Simultaneously, the desire to outshine friends, rivals in the club, or even national teammates emerges, creating a complex interplay of thoughts. Topping it off is the aspirational need for relaxation and a pressure-free state, believed to enhance the likelihood of clinching victory.

While these athletes may genuinely feel prepared and boast elevated self-confidence, an underlying "BUT" lingers. As an illustration, consider a scenario in tennis where the consumption of high-sugar substances provides a brief surge in energy but inevitably results in a more profound energy drain. This analogy underscores the importance of strategic mental nourishment.

In bowling, this principle holds sway. The rigorous demands of reaching a final match necessitate at least 24 preceding games across different days and blocks. Mental preparation emerges as a pivotal component, given that feeding the mind with destabilizing ideas can lead to a collapse in performance. The absence of correct mental training on how to approach such a critical game may result in failure.

Contrary to dedicating an entire day to preparation, the optimal approach involves a concise 30-minute preparation period. During this interval, athletes meticulously outline their intentions for the game and formulate a precise plan. This plan, meticulously documented on paper, might encompass specific objectives such as pacing with feet, staying on the outside lanes, and implementing a regulated breathing routine before each shot.

After completing the game preparation, a vital step involves taking personal time to engage in activities that bring joy and a sense of well-being. Before initiating the warm-up, revisiting the prepared notes serves as a powerful reminder of the strategic plan.

The subsequent step is crucial: athletes must be unequivocally clear with themselves. If they achieve the outlined points, success is defined. The sense of accomplishment is derived from adhering to the plan, irrespective of the actual game outcome. This mindset shift involves training the mind to prioritize the process over the outcome, cultivating positive feelings in a healthy manner.

This mental training emphasizes that winning is not the singular focus; instead, the emphasis lies in adhering to oneself, maintaining belief in the devised plan. This approach cultivates a positive mindset, even in the face of potential setbacks, positioning mistakes as integral to the journey without accepting them outright.

In adopting this nuanced approach to mental preparation, athletes embark on a journey of self-discovery, mastering the art of psychological readiness for high-stakes bowling competitions. This personalized method not only propels them toward their ultimate goal but also reinforces resilience, instilling a sense of pride in each step taken towards success. The metamorphosis from mere preparation to a profound mental mastery journey becomes the cornerstone of their success in the realm of competitive bowling.

Robi Godnic, Slovenia National Team Head Coach

MOTOR MENTAL - PRE-PERFORMANCE ROUTINES (PRE-SHOT) ON BOWLING

It has been discovered that motor-mental PPR improves bowling performance. According to studies, bowlers who routinely practice mental imagery before every shot have a tendency to produce more precise and consistent shots than those who don't. Research has shown that motor-mental PPR improves coordination, kinesthetic awareness, and muscle memory, which improves the way the physical motions used in the bowling shot are executed. Bowlers can strengthen the neural connections linked to their intended motions by mentally practicing and picturing them. This will result in more effective and efficient motor patterns during the actual shot. Additionally, it has been observed that motor-mental PPR helps bowlers feel more confident and less anxious during performances because they can mentally practice successful shots, anticipate obstacles, and mentally prepare for the next shot. This increases their self-assurance and belief in their abilities.

Psychological Factors:

Self-control

The technique through which a bowler deliberately guides and controls behavior toward predetermined goals is known as self-control. Anxiety, fear, pain, unsettling thoughts, and other internal processes can all be managed by a bowler who possesses a high degree of self-control. People with self-control take on duties, execute a variety of jobs, and are able to put up with discomfort, physical and mental stress, and delayed gratification in order to get the desired outcomes. Self-control promotes participation in the learning process, which leads to deeper learning. Additionally, elite bowlers with strong self-control are more likely to try out different tactics than amateur bowlers with weaker self-control, which will ultimately result in better performance and learning.

Self-Control: A bowler may use deep breathing exercises as part of his motor mental PPR to manage his emotions and keep his composure during competition. For instance, before every shot, the bowler can maintain composure, concentration, and emotional control by inhaling deeply and letting go of the air gradually.

After a string of missed shots, a bowler may experience frustration or anxiety; however, by using self-control strategies like deep breathing, visualization, or encouraging self-talk, he can maintain composure. This self-control can help the bowler avoid rash decisions or emotional outbursts that could affect his performance.

Self-efficacy

A cognitive psychological construct known as self-efficacy expresses a bowler's belief in his capacity to keep an eye on and control events that impact their surroundings and lives in order to meet their needs and find the drive, mental tools, and abilities necessary to succeed at a given task. The relationship between self-efficacy and athletic achievement is strong. Successful task completion, behavioral model observation, verbal persuasion, and positive levels of psychological and physiological stimulation are all effective ways to build self-efficacy. Behavior and emotions are influenced by one's feeling of self-efficacy. **Bowlers who have self-doubt typically put in less effort and quit easily when things get tough.** Situations that people believe they are ill-equipped to handle lead to worry and other depressing feelings. Furthermore, self-efficacy influences people's confidence in their skills just as much as or even more than their credentials or other people's opinions.

Self-Efficacy: To increase their sense of self-efficacy, bowlers can incorporate positive self-talk into their motor mental PPR. For example, talking to yourself repeatedly with affirmations like "I am a skilled bowler," "I am confident in my abilities," or "I can hit my target with precision" may help you feel more capable of yourself and increase your self-efficacy.

To help them believe that they are talented and capable of performing well, bowlers might engage in mental images and positive affirmations. Being confident in their talents and feeling assured of their own abilities will help them perform better on the lanes and increase their motivation.

Pre-performance Routine and Accuracy in Bowling (Pre-Shot Routine)

A Pre-Performance Routine (PPR) is a prearranged series of mental and physical exercises that are done before trying a shot in the sport of bowling. Bowling is a closed, self-paced motor skill activity in which players have plenty of time to practice shots and a generally steady setting. But there are guidelines that specify how much time can be spent getting ready.

A PPR has three essential components that support efficient performance planning. The first is readiness, where the bowler must be ready to make the shot both mentally and physically. The second is to avoid becoming sidetracked by unimportant details and concentrate on the pertinent stimuli needed to execute the skill. Finally, the PPR can be used as a tool to evaluate previous results and pinpoint areas in which work has to be done. Whatever their skill level, bowlers can improve their accuracy and performance by adhering to a regular PPR.

Professional bowlers are more likely than unskilled amateurs to consistently execute personal PPR, according to numerous prior research. Furthermore, both expert and beginner bowlers' accuracy in performing abilities is enhanced by motor and mental PPR. Bowlers in high school and college who execute a motor PPR are more accurate than those who do not, and the most accurate bowlers are those who follow set routines to get ready for a stroke.

Preparedness

PPR is crucial for closed, self-paced motor skills since it improves the body's readiness for elite bowling in the future. While it may be difficult for bowlers to wait the necessary two minutes between shots to regain their physiological and cognitive alertness, this period can still be crucial in maintaining their body's state of readiness.

Example 1: Before the match, make sure all the required gear is ready, including the shoes—making sure they fit well and are clean—and the bowling balls—polishing and cleaning.

Example 2: Accomplishing the necessary equipment modifications and showing up early at the bowling center to become acquainted with the lane conditions, including oil patterns and lane surface.

Example 3: Develop a pre-game checklist to make sure all gear, accessories, and personal belongings—such as an extra ball, towel, wrist support, and other necessities—are prepared and packed.

1. Preparedness:

Neurological Advantages and Benefits	Psychological Advantages and Benefits
Enhanced neural readiness for motor skills.	Increased confidence and a sense of readiness.
Improved neural connectivity and synchronization.	Positive psychological state contributing to overall performance.

Mental Rehersal

The second is mental rehearsal, which is the practice of visualizing and carrying out an action before really doing it. According to research by Cohen et al. (2005), PPRs can offer a framework for putting cognitive processes like self-feedback, imagery, and attention into practice. This can eventually improve athletes' performance outcomes and may have a favorable impact on bowlers.

Imagining a desired result or a certain movement pattern in the mind is a cognitive strategy known as imagery. Bowlers can utilize imagery to focus on the intended target, mentally practice the shot, and picture the ball's flight. Bowlers can improve their technique and confidence by using imagery in their PPR, which will improve their accuracy and performance.

Example 1: Using visualization techniques to picture the intended ball trajectory and pin reaction while mentally practicing every step of making a great shot throughout the PPR, from the approach to the release and follow-through.

Example 2: To strengthen positive muscle memory and boost confidence, go over mental notes or video recordings of successful shots from past games or practice sessions and mentally play them again.

Example 3: Using affirmations or cue words, such as "smooth release," "target focus," or "stay relaxed," to reinforce confidence, attention, and a good mindset while practicing positive self-talk during the PPR."

2. Mental Rehearsal:

Neurological Advantages and Benefits	Psychological Advantages and Benefits
Activation of mirror neurons during mental visualization.	Enhanced self-confidence through mental imagery.
Reinforcement of neural pathways associated with successful bowling techniques.	Improved mental resilience and belief in one's capabilities.

Attention

Another crucial cognitive ability that PPRs can help with is attention. The ability to tune out distractions and concentrate on pertinent stimuli is referred to as attention. Attentional methods are a useful tool for bowlers to help them stay focused on the ball as they approach it and release it. Bowlers might employ strategies like deep breathing exercises or reciting certain words aloud to help them concentrate and tune out outside noise.

Example 1: Establishing a regular pre-shot process that entails concentrating on the target, utilizing a certain visual target or area on the lane, and muting background noise and other players to prevent distractions.

Example 2: Maintaining a calm and concentrated state of mind, being totally present during every shot, and employing mindfulness practices to bring awareness to the breath, the body, and the surroundings.

Example 3: Applying concentration strategies, like focusing just on the bowling ball and the desired path to the goal, and preventing negative thoughts or mental diversion throughout the practice pitch and shot.

3. Attention:

Neurological Advantages and Benefits	Psychological Advantages and Benefits
Heightened focus through attentional control.	Improved focus and reduced distraction.
Strengthened neural circuits related to sustained attention and concentration.	Enhanced mental discipline and concentration.

Self-Feedback

For bowlers, self-feedback is also a crucial part of PPRs. Self-feedback entails keeping an eye on and assessing one's own work. Bowlers can see where they are lacking and can instantly modify by adding self-feedback into their PPRs. For instance, in order to make sure that their PPR technique is accurate and consistent, a bowler can concentrate on their footwork, release point, or grip.

Bowlers who employed PPRs that integrated cognitive processes like self-feedback, imagery, and concentration performed noticeably better than those who did not. PPRs give bowlers a structure to apply these cognitive processes, which can improve their physical and mental preparation and produce better results.

Example 1: Self-evaluation of execution, technique, and result, including identification of strengths and faults, based on reflection of each shot's performance during the PPR.

Example 2: During the PPR and following every shot, make notes in a bowling notebook or on a mobile device to record observations, insights, and opportunities for progress.

Example 3: Getting feedback from a coach, a teammate, or a reliable source and implementing the suggestions to modify the PPR and make the required adjustments to enhance accuracy and overall performance.

4. Self-Feedback:

Neurological Advantages and Benefits	Psychological Advantages and Benefits
Increased neural monitoring and self-awareness.	Greater self-awareness and a growth mindset.
Improved neural plasticity for real-time adjustments in technique.	Improved psychological adaptability and a proactive approach to improvement.

EXAMPLE OF PRE_PERFORMANCE ROUTINE

Here is an illustration of how a professional bowler might prepare for a shot by using mental imagery and psychological techniques:

Visualization of the Lane:

- *To defuse tension, the star bowler locates a peaceful area close to the lanes and inhales deeply.*

- *He begins to see the bowling lane in great detail when he closes his eyes. He makes up the lane's length, the arrows' locations, and the pin locations.*

- *He mentally goes down the lane, noting any surface transitions and oil patterns that could alter the trajectory of the ball.*

- *He visualizes the lane's boards clearly, building a mental map of the desired path for the ball to go.*

Imagining the Bowling Shot:

- *After the bowler has a clear mental image of the lane, he begins to visualize his bowling approach.*

- *He visualizes themselves retrieving the ball from the rack and experiencing its feel and weight in his hands.*

- *He mentally practices all of his movements, including his starting stance, approach, swing, and release.*

- *He visualizes the ball's trajectory down the lane, its response to the oil patterns, and its route to the pins as he works.*

Positive Outcome Visualization:

- *The accomplished bowler directs his attention to the pins situated at the end of the lane. He observes the pins and the shape of the trajectory as he stands.*

- *He pictures the ball precisely hitting the pocket.*

- *He pictures the pleasurable sound of a strike and the pins scattering.*

Psychological Steps:

- *The bowler concentrates on staying composed and self-assured while imagining. He reaffirms to himself his abilities and prior accomplishments.*

- *He speaks to himself positively, boosting his confidence in his skills. "I can hit my mark" or "I've trained for this" are examples of phrases that give him more confidence.*

- *The bowler inhales confidently and exhales any remaining stress or uncertainty as he takes another long breath.*

Transition to Reality:

- *The top bowler opens his eyes and advances to the approaching position. He carries the vibrant visuals and upbeat attitude.*

- *He senses the link between his mental image and the present as he grasps the ball. He knows they've practiced this shot endlessly in his minds.*

Execution:

- *He follows the mental pattern they've prepared, executing the shot with a seamless and unwavering focus.*

- *His body and mind are in harmony, collaborating to achieve the intended result.*

Elite bowlers can increase their mental preparedness and confidence, which can result in better performance on the lanes, by integrating psychological techniques and visualization.

VISUALIZATION TECHNIQUES IN BOWLING: A PROFOUND EXPLORATION OF MENTAL MASTERY *By Rick Vogelesang*

In bowling, we often focus extensively on our physical skills, perfecting our form and delivery, while the power of mental strength tends to be overlooked. But let me tell you, this mental side of the game is a game-changer. It's the secret that separates good bowlers from great ones. Just like legends in the sport like Jason Belmonte and EJ Tackett, you can harness the magic of visualization to elevate your game to new heights.

I personally discovered the incredible potential of visualization back in the 1980s when Team Canada graced my bowling center. Among their ranks was Craig Woodhouse, a celebrated coach in the bowling world. It was during their visit that I stumbled upon the "Play to Win" tape, which opened my eyes to the profound impact of mental preparation. This tape became my gateway into a world where the mind's power can transform athletic performance.

Since that eye-opening moment, I've been a strong advocate for integrating mental training into my coaching program. It's about unlocking the hidden potential within every bowler. With a strong mental game, you can rise above those who may have more physical skill but lack the focus and visualization prowess needed to seize victory.

So, I urge you to embark on this journey. It's a transformative path that will take your mental game to new heights, lifting you beyond the ordinary and towards the pinnacle of success.

Mastery of Visualization Techniques

To fully grasp the potential of visualization, you need to dedicate time and effort in a peaceful and comfortable environment, ideally in your own home. Whether you're lounging or sitting in a cozy chair, the key is to create a space where you can immerse your mind in visualization exercises. Start this process roughly 6 to 8 weeks before any significant event or competition.

During your actual bowling sessions, integrating a trigger word or phrase becomes crucial. This mirrors what professional bowlers do on TV as they approach the lane. These triggers act as anchors, instantly propelling you to your peak performance state. Your chosen trigger should fit seamlessly into your personalized pre-shot routine, one tailored to your unique needs. Imagine yourself confidently uttering that trigger word or phrase, conditioning your subconscious mind, and awakening the ideal mindset for success.

Furthermore, when you're at home, listening to that tape, pay careful attention to the unfolding visual and auditory tapestry of each shot. Immerse yourself in the sounds of the crowd, the satisfying crash of pins, and the electric atmosphere of competition. This mental image, known as your self-image, is a crucial aspect of your mental arsenal. Envision yourself in a championship showdown against your idol, delivering perfect shots with precision, and rehearse this scenario with enthusiasm and frequency. The emotions and sensations you'll experience during this exercise are extraordinary.

The Power of Repetition

Repetition is the key to mastery. In the weeks leading up to your next bowling encounter, visualize the perfect shot countless times during your practice sessions at home. However, don't just visualize everything while standing at the approach. Instead, mentally prepare in your designated bowlers' area, a tranquil space where you can immerse yourself in your pre-shot ritual.

This is where your trigger word or phrase comes into play with unwavering conviction, serving as the beacon to summon your best performance. By diligently following these visualization techniques and embracing the power of repetition, you'll rise above the ordinary and take your mental game to new heights, reaching levels of success that once seemed unattainable.

Strategic Plan for Visualization Techniques for Bowler: Peaking Program

The strategic plan for visualization techniques for bowlers is designed as a comprehensive peaking program leading up to a tournament. In the first stage, which begins eight weeks before the competition, bowlers are advised to create a dedicated visualization space—a serene corner with a comfortable chair and soft lighting. Additionally, acquiring relevant resources, such as mental training books or guided visualization apps, is recommended during this preparation period.

Moving into the second stage, taking place seven weeks before the tournament, bowlers are encouraged to study a "Play to Win" tape, observing professional bowlers executing perfect strikes to note posture, release, and pinfall sounds. Choosing a trigger word or phrase, like "precision," to focus on accuracy is another task during this familiarization phase. Maintaining a visualization journal to document experiences during the six-week period is suggested.

The third stage, six weeks before the tournament, emphasizes establishing a visualization foundation. Bowlers are advised to engage in daily visualization sessions for four weeks, imagining themselves at the bowling alley, feeling the ball's roll and smooth release. The use of a trigger word in visualization and expanding techniques, such as visualizing different lane conditions, is also encouraged.

Visualization refinement occurs in the fourth stage, five to four weeks before the tournament. Enhanced visualization exercises, like immersing oneself in challenging scenarios, are recommended. Incorporating competition elements, such as visualizing the final frame against a formidable opponent, is another task during this period. Practicing visualization under pressure, especially in high-stakes moments, is an ongoing aspect.

The power of repetition is highlighted in the fifth stage, three to two weeks before the tournament. Practicing with bowlers' area simulation, increasing visualization frequency, and consistently visualizing in the designated space are integral tasks during this phase.

Approaching the tournament week, the sixth stage, bowlers are advised to review their progress, reflecting on the evolution of their visualization techniques. Engaging in a visualization pep talk, where a trusted coach or mentor provides motivational encouragement, is suggested. Ongoing mental rehearsal, visualizing specific game scenarios, is also emphasized during this final preparation stage.

In the last stage, leading to the tournament days, bowlers are encouraged to incorporate a daily visualization routine, imagining themselves confidently walking to the lane and flawlessly executing each shot. Engaging in daily mental relaxation through deep breathing exercises and visualizing cues and tactics, such as adjusting approaches based on observed lane conditions, is ongoing throughout the tournament week.

Rick Vogelesang, Malta National Team Coach

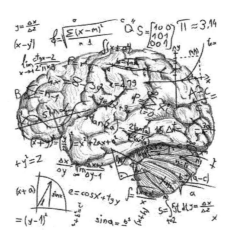

"DECODING THE 4 SECONDS: THE INTERPLAY OF THOUGHT BEFORE STARTING THE SHOT "

"What to THINK Before Taking My First Step"

In the complex world of sports thinking, especially in games like bowling, golf, and darts, athletes dive into a smart pre-movement thinking process. This acts as a mental warm-up before starting physical actions, playing a crucial role in improving performance by creating an ideal mental state. Athletes think about many things during this time, with a main focus on the powerful strategy of imagining success. The mental pictures of doing movements perfectly create a detailed plan, carefully showing the way to achieve desired results.

Also, big importance is given to the development of focus and concentration, where athletes direct their attention only to the upcoming task. This skillfully blocks out possible distractions and stops harmful thoughts from bothering them. A close look at technical execution is another important part, going through a complete mental check of stance, grip, alignment, and overall biomechanics. This planned mental practice makes sure future movements are done with the highest accuracy and efficiency.

At the same time, athletes do a careful check of how ready they are physically, thinking about things like posture, balance, and overall physical condition. This thinking time lets them see what adjustments they need to make, making their overall performance better. Building confidence is another important part of the pre-movement thinking. By using positive sayings and talking to themselves in a good way, athletes carefully remind themselves of their natural abilities, past successes, and the hard training they've done. This careful confidence-building creates a strong base for their upcoming journey to success.

Many athletes carefully follow specific pre-shot routines or rituals, acting as mental signals showing they are ready and focused. These planned routines often include a mix of breathing exercises, purposeful movements, or deeply ingrained mental signals, helping create a calm and centered state of mind. It's really important to understand that each athlete's thinking process is naturally different, with the specific things they think about before moving having some differences. The process of finding and improving a personal pre-performance routine becomes the key to unlocking one's best mental and physical abilities, making the way for achieving greatness in sports.

Bowlers' Mental Symphony

In bowling, the preparation before taking a shot holds a deep psychological meaning, weaving itself into the complex fabric of handling emotions and expectations. This detailed process acts as a guide for bowlers as they navigate the twists and turns of their own minds, carefully examining psychological factors to achieve the perfect state of readiness for upcoming shots. In this mental space, bowlers keep a close watch on their emotions, understanding how much it can affect their overall performance. They recognize the importance of maintaining a steady heartbeat, knowing that any changes can disrupt their focus and execution.

Rituals and pre-routines become essential tools in calming heightened heart rates, giving bowlers the tools to regain control and concentrate on consistently accurate shots. These rituals, whether involving deep breaths, visualization exercises, or the repetition of calming phrases, act as reliable anchors in the stormy sea of emotions. They empower bowlers to find their center, approaching each shot with a clear sense of purpose.

As bowlers step onto the lane, they embark on a mental journey that intricately weaves together psychological and physical readiness. With a comprehensive checklist in mind, they carefully get themselves ready, methodically checking off each item to make sure nothing is left to chance. Visualization plays a crucial role as bowlers picture the ball's path, imagining its smooth journey as it glides effortlessly towards the pins. This mental practice allows bowlers to use the power of their thoughts, aligning their intentions with precise actions and creating a strong connection between mind and body.

In the continuous pursuit of psychological readiness, bowlers deal with the subtle aspects of muscle tension. They understand that too much muscle stiffness can hinder performance, disrupting the fluidity and finesse needed for a successful shot. Therefore, they seek a delicate balance, refining their ability to control muscle tension and developing bodies that move with grace and agility. This detailed process requires a heightened sense of kinesthetic awareness, as bowlers fine-tune their physicality to enhance performance in the bowling alley.

In the intricate dance of mental and physical readiness, bowlers develop a well-rounded approach to the sport. They understand that achieving success goes beyond the technicalities of holding the ball or mastering the release; it involves gaining control over their own minds. By carefully addressing the psychological factors that affect performance, bowlers arm themselves with the necessary tools to navigate the complexities of the game. With each shot, they tirelessly aim for the elusive state of optimal mental and physical preparedness, recognizing that true greatness can be achieved within this delicate balance.

In the lively world of bowling, where every moment holds deep significance, a sophisticated psychological process unfolds within the brief 2.5 to 2.8 seconds it takes for a bowler to complete their footwork from the initial step to the fifth. This short timeframe becomes the testing ground where a harmony of skills, smoothly blending the physical and psychological aspects of the game, comes to life. As the bowler gets ready to start their approach, the fusion of mental readiness and physical skill takes center stage, determining the success of their shot.

In this fleeting moment, the bowler taps into a wealth of knowledge and experience gained through countless hours of practice. Their understanding of footwork, body positioning, and release techniques becomes embedded in their subconscious, creating a delicate balance between conscious thought and automatic execution. The main goal is to establish an environment where physical movements flow effortlessly, guided by the subconscious mind, eliminating any potential psychological errors that could hinder their skills.

The battlefield of the bowler's mental strength truly comes to light in those precious seconds before the approach. Holding the ball, they assess its weight and grip while simultaneously envisioning its path towards the pins. The mental preparation for precise footwork is crucial, ensuring that muscles are ready for automatic movement. Within just 4 to 5 seconds, the bowler must execute their approach with precision and finesse, turning this into a crucible where their thoughts converge to determine the sequence of actions leading to a perfect shot.

The detailed thinking process of a bowler revolves around finding the perfect mental state to start their approach, considering elements like mindset, focus, and emotional control. Some bowlers discover that reaching a calm and focused state helps them unlock their full potential, while others thrive on a carefully controlled surge of intensity, using emotions to boost their performance. At the same time, giving importance to different stages of the approach, such as the initial steps, arm swing, or release, becomes crucial. Each bowler might have their own way of doing things, but the common aim remains unchanged – achieving optimal consistency and precision in their shot.

Essentially, the heart of bowling lies in the delicate balance between mental and physical readiness. Managing through the complex web of thoughts and emotions, the bowler strategically uses these elements to enhance their physical skills. Through this continuous pursuit of synchronization, the bowler not only aims for perfection but also understands that aligning psychological and physical states is the key to consistently achieving their desired outcome on the bowling alley.

Pre-Movement Cognitive Process (PMCP)

The pre-movement cognitive process in sports is like the secret sauce for enhancing athletic performance across different games. This mental preparation goes beyond just the moments before a physical action; it's a comprehensive mental groundwork that athletes carefully go through. At its heart, this process involves a deep exploration of psychological factors to establish the perfect mental state for top-notch performance. Athletes consider a variety of elements, from visualizing success to maintaining focus, concentration, technical execution, and physical readiness. It's like a dynamic dance of mental skills, creating a mental state that sets the stage for peak performance.

In the larger sports context, athletes dive into the powerful strategy of success visualization during this cognitive process. This mental imagery acts like a detailed map, outlining the path to achieving desired outcomes. By mentally picturing flawless execution, athletes align their intentions with actions. Focus and concentration become crucial during this mental phase. Athletes learn to direct their attention solely toward the task at hand, skillfully blocking out distractions and avoiding harmful thoughts. The intricacies of technical execution are also in the spotlight, with athletes mentally reviewing their stance, grip, alignment, and overall biomechanics. This strategic mental rehearsal ensures that upcoming movements are executed with precision and efficiency.

At the same time, the pre-movement cognitive process includes a careful evaluation of physical readiness. Athletes reflect on things like posture, balance, and overall physical condition. This reflection helps them make necessary adjustments, optimizing overall performance. Building confidence is another vital aspect, with athletes strategically using affirmations and positive self-talk. This intentional confidence-building lays a strong foundation for the upcoming pursuit of success. It's important to note the uniqueness of each athlete's thought process, with the specific content of their pre-movement contemplations showing variations based on individual differences and sport-specific requirements.

Now, narrowing down to the world of bowling, the pre-movement cognitive process takes on profound importance. As bowlers navigate their own minds, a careful examination of psychological factors becomes crucial for getting ready for upcoming shots. Managing emotions is key to this process. Bowlers closely monitor their emotional states, understanding how emotions can impact their overall performance. The importance of maintaining a steady heartbeat is recognized, as any fluctuations could potentially disrupt concentration and execution.

Rituals and pre-routines become essential tools in the bowler's pre-movement cognitive process. These rituals, whether involving deep breaths, visualization exercises, or repeating calming phrases, act as steady anchors in the stormy sea of emotions. They empower bowlers to find their center, approaching each shot with a clear sense of purpose. As bowlers step onto the lane, they start a mental journey that intricately weaves together psychological and physical readiness. With a comprehensive checklist in mind, they carefully prepare themselves, checking off each item to make sure nothing is left to chance. Visualization plays a crucial role as bowlers imagine the ball's path, envisioning its smooth journey as it glides effortlessly towards the pins. This mental rehearsal allows bowlers to use the power of their thoughts, aligning their intentions with precise actions and creating a profound connection between mind and body. In the relentless pursuit of psychological readiness, bowlers deal with the nuanced aspects of muscle tension, understanding that too much muscle stiffness can hinder performance. Thus, a delicate balance is sought as bowlers refine their ability to control muscle tension, fostering bodies that move with grace and agility. Through this intricate interplay of psychological and physical readiness, bowlers cultivate a holistic approach to the sport.

- **Situation:** *Bowler D faces a critical moment in a high-stakes competition, requiring mental preparation for optimal performance.*

Pre-Movement Cognitive Process (PMCP):

- *Visualization for Success: Prior to approaching the lane, Bowler D engages in a focused pre-movement cognitive process. He mentally visualizes the entire shot process, creating a detailed blueprint of flawless execution. This involves picturing the ball's trajectory towards the pins and aligning his intentions with a successful outcome.*

- *Emotional Regulation: Recognizing the pressure of the situation, Bowler D actively monitors and regulates his emotional state. He consciously ensures a balanced and composed mindset, crucial for maintaining concentration and execution during the game.*

- *Strategic Confidence-Building: As part of his PMCP, Bowler D strategically implements affirmations and positive self-talk. This deliberate exercise in confidence-building erects a robust foundation for his pursuit of success, instilling belief in his abilities.*

Athletes leverage the pre-movement cognitive process as a cornerstone of their mental preparation. Through visualization, bowlers mentally picture successful outcomes, creating a detailed blueprint for flawless execution and aligning their intentions with precise actions. Emotional regulation is integral, with a conscious monitoring of emotional states to maintain a balanced mental demeanor crucial for sustained concentration and execution during the game. Technical precision involves a meticulous mental review of aspects like stance, grip, alignment, and biomechanics, ensuring movements are executed with utmost precision. Physical readiness is honed through an assessment of posture, balance, and overall physical condition, allowing for necessary adjustments to optimize performance. Managing muscle tension is nuanced, with an understanding that excessive rigidity impedes performance; thus, fine-tuning control fosters agile and graceful movements. Confidence-building is strategically integrated through affirmations and positive self-talk, laying a robust foundation for success. Rituals, including deep breaths and visualization, serve as psychological triggers to lower heart rates, regain control, and focus on accurate shots. The holistic significance of the pre-movement cognitive process lies in its ability to meld mental and physical readiness, enhancing decision-making, execution, and overall game performance. Beyond a single shot, it establishes a foundation for consistency, precision, and success, enabling bowlers to navigate mental complexities, harness thoughts' power, and achieve a profound mind-body connection. Ultimately, this process unlocks a bowler's optimal mental and physical potential, paving the way for sporting excellence on the bowling alley.

Pre-Movement Thinking Process (Pmtp)

The thinking process before making a move in sports is like creating a game plan, shaping the mental groundwork athletes go through before making a move. It's not just about the moments right before a move; it involves carefully thinking through different aspects for top-notch performance. Athletes consider things like planning, decision-making, and adjusting their strategies based on the game's dynamics. It's like a thoughtful dance of mental skills, setting the stage for their best performance.

In the bigger sports picture, athletes use a powerful strategy of visualization during this thinking process. This mental strategy acts like a detailed map, showing the path to achieve desired outcomes. By thinking about flawless execution, athletes align their intentions with a thoughtful approach. The focus on thinking strategically becomes really important during this mental phase. Athletes learn to direct their thoughts toward the strategic parts of the task, skillfully handling challenges and avoiding potential problems. The spotlight is on decision-making, with athletes thinking about and refining their approach to make sure it's a smart move.

At the same time, the thinking process includes carefully evaluating their readiness. Athletes reflect on their posture, balance, and overall readiness for the challenges ahead. This reflective process helps them make necessary adjustments, optimizing their overall performance. Building confidence in their strategy is another important part, with athletes using positive self-talk to reinforce their belief in their chosen strategies. This confidence-building sets a strong foundation for their pursuit of success. It's important to note that each athlete thinks differently, and what they think about before a move varies based on their own style and the specific requirements of their sport.

Focusing on bowling, the thinking process becomes crucial. As bowlers plan their approach, a close look at strategic factors is important for preparing for shots. Strategic decision-making is key, as bowlers closely monitor and adjust to lane conditions. Managing the strategic parts of their approach is crucial, with bowlers recognizing the importance of a thoughtful plan for managing the game's complexities.

- **Situation:** Bowler C enters a crucial frame in a tight competition, requiring strategic decision-making for optimal performance.

Pre-Movement Thinking Process (PMTP):

- Strategic Decision-Making: Before stepping onto the approach, Bowler C engages in a deliberate thinking process, analyzing the current lane conditions. He strategically plans his approach, considering factors like oil patterns and pin positions.

- Adjusting Strategies: Recognizing the dynamic nature of the game, Bowler C adjusts his initial strategy based on observed changes in the lane conditions. This involves a thoughtful decision-making process to ensure adaptability and precision.

- Visualization of Adjustments: As part of his PMTP, Bowler C envisions the adjustments he needs to make during his approach. He mentally rehearses the modified strategy, aligning his intentions with precise actions for the upcoming shot.

Routines and strategies become important tools in the bowler's thinking process. These routines, whether involving adjustments based on lane conditions, thinking through decision-making processes, or envisioning adjustments, act as anchors in the ever-changing game. They empower bowlers to find their strategic center, approaching each shot with a clear purpose. As bowlers step onto the lane, they start a journey that weaves together mental and physical readiness. With a checklist in mind, they carefully prepare themselves, checking off each item to make sure nothing is left to chance. Visualization plays a crucial role as bowlers imagine the ball's path, envisioning its journey as it moves towards the pins. This mental rehearsal allows bowlers to use the power of their thoughts, aligning their intentions with precise actions and creating a connection between mind and body. In the pursuit of readiness, bowlers deal with the nuances of decision-making, understanding that precision is crucial for optimal performance. Thus, a delicate balance is sought as bowlers refine their ability to make decisions, fostering approaches that navigate the intricacies of the sport with grace and agility. Through this interplay of mental and physical readiness, bowlers cultivate a holistic approach to the sport, managing the challenges of the alley with finesse.

Difference Between The Three

Aspect	Pre-Movement Cognitive Process (PMCP)	Pre-Movement Thinking Process (PMTP)	Pre-Shot Routine or Ritual (PSR)
Description	Involves mental activities and psychological preparation before executing a shot. Athletes engage in visualizing successful execution, regulating emotions, and strategically building confidence.	Focuses on strategic thinking, planning, and decision-making before initiating a movement. Bowlers analyze lane conditions, formulate shot strategy, and make tactical adjustments based on the evolving dynamics of the game.	Consists of a set sequence of mental and physical actions undertaken during the period of after his previous shot and prior the next one for consistency and focus. Bowlers engage in a specific routine involving deep breaths, visualization of the intended shot, and recitation of a calming mantra.
Example	Athletes visualize the entire shot process, creating a detailed mental blueprint of flawless execution. Emotional regulation involves monitoring and adjusting emotional states to achieve a balanced and composed mental demeanor. Confidence-building is strategically implemented through affirmations and positive self-talk.	Bowlers analyze lane conditions, considering factors like oil patterns and pin positions. They formulate a shot strategy, deciding on the approach, target, and adjustments needed for optimal performance. Tactical adjustments may involve choosing the right bowling ball or altering the angle of delivery.	After finishing his frame, , Bowlers rest analyze and stand again to take three deliberate deep breaths, visualizing the intended shot path. They then wipe their bowling ball with a microfiber cloth, a ritual they always perform for consistency. Finally, they recite a short, positive mantra to enhance focus.
Steps to Do It	1. Visualize successful execution. 2. Monitor and regulate emotional states. 3. Strategically build confidence.	1. Analyze lane conditions, 2. Formulate shot strategy. 3. Make tactical adjustments.	1. Take deep breaths, 2. Visualize the shot. 3. Recite a calming mantra.
When Athlete Does It	Before approaching the lane and while at stance position for a shot, athletes engage in the pre-movement cognitive process to prepare mentally. This occurs during the moments leading up to their turn.	Prior to stepping onto the approach, bowlers initiate the pre-movement thinking process to analyze lane conditions and formulate a strategic plan. This typically takes place during their opponent's turn.	As part of the pre-shot routine, bowlers perform these actions right after he finishes his previous shot, ensuring mental and physical readiness for the upcoming shot.

Aspect	Pre-Movement Cognitive Process (PMCP)	Pre-Movement Thinking Process (PMTP)	Pre-Shot Routine or Ritual (PSR)
Possibility to Change	Athletes may adjust elements of their pre-movement cognitive process based on personal preferences, coaching advice, or evolving game conditions. Flexibility is key to adapting to different situations.	Bowlers have the flexibility to modify their pre-movement thinking process as needed, considering changes in lane conditions, opponents' strategies, or personal performance feedback. Adaptability enhances their strategic approach to each game.	Bowlers often maintain consistency in their pre-shot routine for stability and focus. However, they may introduce minor adjustments if they believe it enhances their mental and physical preparedness. Balancing consistency with adaptability is crucial.
Components	Components include visualization, emotional regulation, and strategic confidence-building.	Components involve strategic analysis of lane conditions, formulation of shot strategy, and tactical adjustments.	Components consist of deep breathing, visualization, and recitation of a calming mantra.
Adaptability	Athletes can adapt elements based on personal preferences, coaching advice, or game conditions.	Bowlers can adapt their thinking process based on changes in lane conditions, opponents' strategies, or personal performance feedback.	Bowlers aim for consistency but may introduce minor adjustments for enhanced mental and physical preparedness.
Level of Difficulty to Learn	Moderate difficulty, as it requires mastering mental skills such as visualization, emotional control, and strategic confidence-building.	Moderate difficulty, involving the development of strategic thinking, decision-making, and adaptability to changing game dynamics.	Relatively low difficulty, focusing on the establishment of a consistent routine with specific mental and physical actions.

Table 26 - Aspect | Pre-Movement Cognitive Process (PMCP), Pre-Movement Thinking Process (PMTP), Pre-Shot Routine (PSR): Effective mental preparation before a shot. Athletes use visualization, emotion regulation, and strategic confidence-building in PMCP. PMTP involves strategic analysis, shot planning, and tactical adjustments based on lane conditions. PSR, a set routine, ensures consistency through deep breaths, visualization, and a calming mantra. Athletes adapt elements for personalized strategies and maintain a balance between consistency and flexibility for optimal performance.

Scenarios For Pre-Movement Cognitive Process (PMCP) Prior Initiating The Movements:

PMCP For Attaining Consistency And Flow State

Stage 1: Mental Preparation and Focus

"Clear the mind, find the quiet within." The bowler initiates the process with mental preparation, engaging in visualization to create a serene mental space free of distractions.

Stage 2: Establishing a Flow State

"Embrace the rhythm, become one with the approach." Through cue words like "fluidity" and "rhythm," the bowler focuses on feeling and acting. Visualization involves mentally dancing through each step, fostering a seamless connection.

Stage 3: Footwork and Approach Check

"Grounded steps, balanced flow." Attention shifts to footwork with a mental checklist, emphasizing thinking. Visualization encompasses feeling the ground beneath, ensuring precise and balanced steps.

Stage 4: Grip and Ball Visualization

"Feel the weight, sense the grip, embrace the ball." The bowler concentrates on the ball, engaging in thinking and visualization. Mental rehearsal includes envisioning the smooth motion of bringing the ball into position.

Stage 5: Alignment and Target Visualization

"Align body, ball, target – a direct path awaits." Alignment becomes crucial with a focus on thinking. Visualization involves mentally aligning elements and picturing the anticipated path and release angle.

Stage 6: Eliminating External Distractions

"Create a bubble of concentration, block out the noise." The bowler acts by creating mental focus, blocking external distractions, and maintaining concentration through visualization.

Stage 7: Ritual Check and Readiness

"Review the checklist, affirm readiness." The bowler conducts a mental ritual check with an emphasis on thinking. Visualization provides swift reassurance, affirming that footwork, grip, alignment, and target are in place.

Stage 8: Initiating the Shot

"Execute with precision, visualize the perfection." The bowler takes action by initiating the shot, combining acting and visualization. Visualization encompasses the entire approach – a cohesive, fluid movement leading to a perfect release.

Stage 9: Embracing Positive Anticipation

"Focus on the beauty of the shot, not the fear of error." The bowler consciously avoids negative thoughts, engaging in thinking and feeling. Positive anticipation replaces fear, fostering a mindset focused on the beauty and precision of the shot.

Stage 10: Stabilizing Initial Thoughts Throughout Approach

"Anchor the initial thoughts, ride the momentum." The bowler stabilizes initial thoughts with a blend of thinking, feeling, and acting. Mental and motor control elements come into play, focusing on balance, timing, and maintaining composure.

This comprehensive pre-approach thought process, enriched with quotes, positive anticipation, and the stabilization of initial thoughts, reinforces the bowler's ability to achieve a consistent shot. Mental and physical control elements, coupled with a focus on the beauty of the shot, contribute to the harmonious alignment of the bowler's mental and physical states, ultimately leading to a successful shot.

Training Session Template: Enhancing Working Memory Capacity for Elite Bowlers

Objective: The primary goal of this training session is to challenge and enhance the working memory capacity of elite bowlers. By incorporating drills that require the processing and integration of multiple sensory cues, including lane conditions, ball speed, and body positioning, this session aims to improve the bowlers' ability to use working memory effectively during competition, ultimately leading to improved repeatability and accuracy.

Duration: 2 hours
Session Components:

1. Warm-up (15 minutes):

- Brief physical warm-up exercises to prepare the bowlers' bodies for practice.
- Mental warm-up: Engage bowlers in a brief concentration and visualization exercise to focus their minds on the training ahead.

2. Lane Conditions Assessment (20 minutes):

- Bowlers will be asked to assess lane conditions, including oil patterns, dry areas, and transition zones.
- They will record their observations in notebooks and discuss their findings as a group to encourage teamwork and collective learning.

3. Sensory Integration Drills (40 minutes):

- Drill 1: Ball Speed Adjustment (15 minutes)
    - o Bowlers will throw balls at varying speeds and record their observations of lane reactions.
    - o The coach will guide discussions on how changes in ball speed affect lane conditions and pin action.
- Drill 2: Body Positioning (15 minutes)
    - o Bowlers will experiment with different body positions during their approach and delivery.
    - o They will analyze the impact of body positioning on shot accuracy and pin action.
- Drill 3: Real-time Adjustments (10 minutes)
    - o Bowlers will engage in a simulated competition scenario where they must adapt to changing lane conditions.
    - o They will practice making quick decisions and adjustments based on sensory cues.

4. Working Memory Challenge (30 minutes):

- Bowlers will participate in a memory challenge where they are presented with a sequence of sensory cues (e.g., lane condition, ball speed, body positioning) and must recall and replicate them in the correct order.
- The complexity of the sequences will gradually increase to stretch their working memory capacity.

5. Feedback and Analysis (15 minutes):

- Coach-led discussion to review the training session.
- Bowlers will share their observations, experiences, and challenges they encountered during the sensory integration drills and memory challenge.
- The coach will provide feedback, address questions, and offer insights for improvement.

6. Cool-down (10 minutes):

- Gentle stretching exercises to prevent muscle fatigue and promote relaxation.
- A brief mindfulness exercise to reflect on the session and reinforce mental focus.
- Homework Assignment: Bowlers will be encouraged to keep a journal to record their experiences, observations, and reflections on lane conditions and sensory cues during practice and competitions.

Session Notes: This training session is designed to progressively challenge and enhance the working memory capacity of elite bowlers by incorporating sensory integration drills and memory challenges. The goal is to help them become more adaptable and effective in using working memory during actual competition scenarios, leading to improved repeatability and accuracy in their shots.

PMCP For Technical Instability (E.G., Timing Issues):

Stage 1: Technical Awareness and Acknowledgment

"Recognize the timing challenge, acknowledge the issue." The bowler begins by thinking and feeling, acknowledging the technical instability. Visualization involves mentally dissecting the timing problem.

Stage 2: Focused Visualization on Timing Adjustment

"Visualize the corrected timing, feel the adjusted rhythm." The bowler prioritizes thinking and visualization, mentally rehearsing the corrected timing. Visualization focuses on feeling the rhythm with the adjusted timing.

Stage 3: Footwork and Timing Synchronization

"Sync steps with the corrected timing, feel the flow." Attention shifts to thinking and feeling, with the bowler ensuring each step aligns precisely with the adjusted timing. Visualization involves feeling the seamless flow of the adjusted rhythm.

Stage 4: Grip and Ball Release Coordination

"Coordinate grip with the corrected timing, visualize the release." The bowler concentrates on thinking and visualization, ensuring the grip aligns with the adjusted timing. Mental rehearsal includes picturing the release synchronized with the corrected rhythm.

Stage 5: Alignment and Target Visualization with Adjusted Timing

"Align body, ball, target – visualizing the new path." Alignment becomes crucial, with a focus on thinking. Visualization involves mentally aligning elements and picturing the adjusted path and release angle in sync with the corrected timing.

Stage 6: Eliminating External Distractions with a Focus on Timing

"Block distractions, maintain timing concentration." The bowler acts by creating mental focus, blocking external distractions. Visualization includes maintaining concentration on the corrected timing amid potential distractions.

Stage 7: Ritual Check and Readiness with Emphasis on Timing

"Review checklist with a focus on timing readiness." The bowler conducts a mental ritual check, emphasizing thinking and feeling. Visualization provides swift reassurance that footwork, grip, alignment, and target are aligned with the corrected timing.

Stage 8: Initiating the Shot with Priority on Timing

"Execute, emphasizing the corrected timing, visualize success." The bowler takes action, prioritizing thinking and visualization. Visualization encompasses the entire approach, ensuring the corrected timing leads to a successful release.

Stage 9: Positive Anticipation Emphasizing Timing Success

"Anticipate success, focusing on the perfected timing." The bowler consciously avoids negative thoughts, engaging in thinking and feeling. Positive anticipation replaces fear, emphasizing the beauty and precision achieved through the corrected timing.

Stage 10: Continuous Stabilization of Adjusted Timing

"Anchor the new timing, ride the momentum." Throughout the approach, the bowler stabilizes thoughts, focusing on the adjusted timing. Mental and motor control elements are crucial, maintaining balance, timing, and composure with the corrected rhythm.

This adapted thought process prioritizes correcting timing issues, emphasizing mental and visual elements to ensure a smooth, synchronized approach and release.

PMCP For Excessive Grip Pressure:

Stage 1: Recognizing Excessive Grip Pressure

"Identify the tension, acknowledge the grip challenge." The bowler begins by thinking and feeling, recognizing the excessive grip pressure issue. Visualization involves mentally acknowledging the tension in the grip.

Stage 2: Visualization for Optimal Grip Pressure

"Visualize a relaxed grip, feel the ideal pressure." Prioritizing thinking and visualization, the bowler mentally rehearses a relaxed grip. Visualization focuses on feeling the ideal pressure required for a successful release.

Stage 3: Footwork and Relaxation Synchronization

"Sync steps with a relaxed grip, feel the fluidity." Attention shifts to thinking and feeling, ensuring each step aligns with a relaxed grip. Visualization involves feeling the seamless flow of the approach with the ideal grip pressure.

Stage 4: Coordination of Grip and Release

"Coordinate grip with the ideal pressure, visualize the smooth release." The bowler concentrates on thinking and visualization, ensuring the grip aligns with the optimal pressure. Mental rehearsal includes picturing a smooth release synchronized with the ideal grip.

Stage 5: Alignment and Target Visualization with Controlled Grip

"Align body, ball, target – visualizing precision with a controlled grip." Alignment becomes crucial, with a focus on thinking. Visualization involves mentally aligning elements and picturing the controlled grip leading to precision and accuracy.

Stage 6: Eliminating External Distractions with Focus on Grip Control

"Block distractions, maintain grip control concentration." The bowler acts by creating mental focus, blocking external distractions. Visualization includes maintaining concentration on the controlled grip amid potential distractions.

Stage 7: Ritual Check and Readiness with Emphasis on Grip Control

"Review checklist with a focus on grip readiness." The bowler conducts a mental ritual check, emphasizing thinking and feeling. Visualization provides swift reassurance that footwork, grip, alignment, and target align with the controlled grip.

Stage 8: Initiating the Shot with Priority on Controlled Grip

"Execute, emphasizing the controlled grip, visualize success." The bowler takes action, prioritizing thinking and visualization. Visualization encompasses the entire approach, ensuring the controlled grip leads to a successful release.

Stage 9: Positive Anticipation Emphasizing Grip Success

"Anticipate success, focusing on the perfected grip." The bowler consciously avoids negative thoughts, engaging in thinking and feeling. Positive anticipation replaces fear, emphasizing the beauty and precision achieved through the controlled grip.

Stage 10: Continuous Stabilization of Controlled Grip

"Anchor the controlled grip, ride the momentum." Throughout the approach, the bowler stabilizes thoughts, focusing on the controlled grip. Mental and motor control elements are crucial, maintaining balance, timing, and composure with the controlled pressure.

This tailored thought process prioritizes addressing excessive grip pressure, emphasizing mental and visual elements to ensure a relaxed, controlled grip for optimal performance.

PMCP For Overcoming Fear Of Mistakes In An Important Shot:

Stage 1: Acknowledging Fear and Pressure

"Recognize the fear, acknowledge the pressure." The bowler starts by thinking and feeling, acknowledging the fear of making mistakes in this crucial shot. Visualization includes recognizing the pressure associated with the importance of the shot.

Stage 2: Visualization of Successful Past Shots

"Recall successful shots, visualize triumph." Prioritizing visualization and feeling, the bowler mentally revisits successful shots from the past. Visualization focuses on feeling the triumph and success associated with those moments.

Stage 3: Footwork and Breathing Synchronization

"Sync steps with deep breaths, embrace calmness." Attention shifts to thinking and feeling, ensuring each step aligns with controlled breathing. Visualization involves feeling the calmness that accompanies synchronized footwork and breathing.

Stage 4: Coordination of Shot Elements with Visualization

"Coordinate approach elements with positive visualizations." The bowler concentrates on thinking and visualization, ensuring all elements of the shot align with positive mental images. Mental rehearsal includes picturing a flawless release and pin action.

Stage 5: Alignment and Target Visualization with Confidence

"Align body, ball, target – visualize with confidence." Alignment becomes crucial, with a focus on thinking and feeling. Visualization involves mentally aligning elements and picturing the shot's success with confidence.

Stage 6: Eliminating External Distractions with Focus on Confidence

"Block distractions, focus on confident execution." The bowler acts by creating mental focus, blocking external distractions. Visualization includes maintaining concentration on the confident execution amid potential distractions.

Stage 7: Ritual Check and Readiness with Emphasis on Confidence

"Review checklist with a focus on confident readiness." The bowler conducts a mental ritual check, emphasizing thinking and feeling. Visualization provides swift reassurance that footwork, grip, alignment, and target align with confident execution.

Stage 8: Initiating the Shot with Priority on Confidence

"Execute, emphasizing confidence, visualize success." The bowler takes action, prioritizing thinking and visualization. Visualization encompasses the entire approach, ensuring the confident execution leads to a successful release.

Stage 9: Positive Anticipation Emphasizing Confidence

"Anticipate success, focusing on confident execution." The bowler consciously avoids negative thoughts, engaging in thinking and feeling. Positive anticipation replaces fear, emphasizing the beauty and precision achieved through confidence.

Stage 10: Continuous Stabilization of Confidence

"Anchor the confidence, ride the momentum." Throughout the approach, the bowler stabilizes thoughts, focusing on the confidence. Mental and motor control elements are crucial, maintaining balance, timing, and composure with the confident mindset.

This tailored thought process helps the bowler overcome the fear of mistakes in an important shot by emphasizing positive visualizations, confidence, and mental stability.

PMCP For Improper Finish Position Or Unbalanced Finish:

Stage 1: Awareness of Finish Position

"Mindful of the finish, acknowledge potential imbalance." The bowler starts by thinking, acknowledging the importance of a proper finish position and potential imbalance issues. Visualization includes recognizing the desired end posture.

Stage 2: Visualization of Ideal Finish Position

"Visualize the ideal finish, feel balance." Prioritizing visualization and feeling, the bowler mentally envisions the perfect finish position. Visualization involves feeling the balance and stability associated with the ideal conclusion of the shot.

Stage 3: Focus on Controlled Footwork

"Controlled steps for a balanced finish." Attention shifts to thinking and acting, emphasizing controlled footwork to ensure balance. The bowler visualizes each step with precision and the corresponding stability in the finish position.

Stage 4: Coordination of Arm Swing and Release with Visualization

"Coordinate arm swing with visualized finish." The bowler concentrates on thinking and visualization, ensuring the arm swing and release align with the mental image of a balanced finish. Visualization involves picturing a smooth release leading to stability.

Stage 5: Alignment and Target Visualization with Balanced End

"Align body, ball, target – visualize a balanced end." Alignment becomes crucial, with a focus on thinking and feeling. Visualization involves mentally aligning elements and picturing the shot's success with a balanced and stable finish.

Stage 6: Eliminating External Distractions with Focus on Stability

"Block distractions, focus on a stable conclusion." The bowler acts by creating mental focus, blocking external distractions. Visualization includes maintaining concentration on achieving a stable finish amid potential distractions.

Stage 7: Ritual Check and Readiness with Emphasis on Stability

"Review checklist with a focus on stable readiness." The bowler conducts a mental ritual check, emphasizing thinking and feeling. Visualization provides swift reassurance that footwork, grip, alignment, and target align with a stable and balanced finish.

Stage 8: Initiating the Shot with Priority on Stability

"Execute, emphasizing stability, visualize success." The bowler takes action, prioritizing thinking and visualization. Visualization encompasses the entire approach, ensuring stability in the finish position leads to a successful release.

Stage 9: Positive Anticipation Emphasizing Stability

"Anticipate success, focusing on a stable execution." The bowler consciously avoids negative thoughts, engaging in thinking and feeling. Positive anticipation replaces concerns, emphasizing the beauty and precision achieved through a stable finish.

Stage 10: Continuous Stabilization of Balanced Finish

"Anchor the balance, ride the momentum." Throughout the approach, the bowler stabilizes thoughts, focusing on the balance. Mental and motor control elements are crucial, maintaining balance, timing, and composure with the emphasis on a stable finish.

This tailored thought process helps the bowler address concerns about an improper finish position or unbalanced conclusion by emphasizing positive visualizations, stability, and mental control.

PMCP For Managing Anxiety In A High-Stakes Event:

Stage 1: Acknowledgment of Anxiety

"Recognize anxiety, accept the challenge." The bowler begins by thinking, acknowledging the anxiety associated with the high-stakes event and accepting it as a challenge. Acceptance becomes a crucial first step.

Stage 2: Visualization of a Calm State

"Visualize a calm mental space." Prioritizing visualization and feeling, the bowler mentally envisions a serene mental space, focusing on creating a calm internal state despite external pressures.

Stage 3: Breathing Control for Anxiety Reduction

"Controlled breaths to alleviate anxiety." Attention shifts to acting and thinking, emphasizing controlled breathing to reduce anxiety levels. The bowler consciously takes deep breaths, focusing on calming the mind and body.

Stage 4: Affirmations for Confidence Building

"Positive affirmations, bolster confidence." Engaging in thinking and feeling, the bowler employs positive self-talk and affirmations to build confidence. Visualization involves picturing successful shots and embracing self-assurance.

Stage 5: Controlled Focus on Immediate Action

"Focus on the present, one step at a time." The bowler thinks and acts by concentrating on the immediate action – the approaching steps. Visualization involves a step-by-step mental rehearsal with a focus on the present.

Stage 6: Eliminating External Distractions for Enhanced Focus

"Create a focused bubble, block external noise." Acting to block distractions and thinking to maintain concentration, the bowler creates a mental bubble, isolating himself from external pressures to enhance focus.

Stage 7: Ritual Check with Emphasis on Calm Readiness

"Review checklist with a calm readiness." The bowler conducts a mental ritual check, emphasizing thinking and feeling. Visualization includes swift reassurance – footwork, grip, alignment, and target – all in place with a calm readiness.

Stage 8: Initiating the Shot with Relaxed Confidence

"Execute with a relaxed confidence, visualize success." The bowler takes action, prioritizing feeling and visualization. Visualization encompasses the entire approach, focusing on executing each step with relaxed confidence.

Stage 9: Positive Anticipation with Calm Focus

"Anticipate success, maintain calm focus." The bowler consciously avoids negative thoughts, engaging in thinking and feeling. Positive anticipation replaces anxiety, emphasizing the beauty and precision achieved through calm focus.

Stage 10: Continuous Calming of Thoughts

"Anchor the calmness, ride the momentum." Throughout the approach, the bowler stabilizes thoughts, maintaining a focus on calmness. Mental and motor control elements are crucial, ensuring balance, timing, and composure in every step.

This tailored thought process assists the bowler in managing anxiety during high-stakes events, emphasizing visualization, controlled breathing, positive affirmations, and maintaining a calm and focused mindset.

PMCP For Managing Anger And Unfairness:

Stage 1: Acknowledgment of Emotions

"Recognize anger, acknowledge emotions." The bowler starts by thinking, acknowledging the presence of anger and unfairness. Acceptance is crucial for initiating a constructive thought process.

Stage 2: Visualization of Emotional Release

"Visualize releasing negative emotions." Prioritizing visualization and feeling, the bowler mentally envisions a way to release negative emotions. This might include imagining letting go of frustration and envisioning a clearer mental space.

Stage 3: Controlled Breathing for Emotion Regulation

"Breathe to regulate emotional intensity." Attention shifts to acting and thinking. The bowler engages in controlled breathing, focusing on exhaling tension and inhaling calmness to regulate emotional intensity.

Stage 4: Affirmations for Perspective Shift

"Positive affirmations for fairness." Engaging in thinking and feeling, the bowler uses positive self-talk to shift perspective. Affirmations might center around accepting the variability in pin action and focusing on personal improvement.

Stage 5: Reframing Perception of Unfairness

"Reframe unfairness as a challenge." The bowler thinks about the situation differently, reframing the perceived unfairness as a challenge. Visualization includes picturing overcoming challenges with composure.

Stage 6: External Distraction Elimination for Enhanced Focus

"Block external drama, enhance focus." Acting to eliminate distractions and thinking to maintain concentration, the bowler consciously creates a mental bubble, blocking external drama, and focusing on the upcoming shots.

Stage 7: Ritual Check with Emotional Control

"Review checklist with emotional control." The bowler conducts a mental ritual check, emphasizing thinking and feeling. Visualization involves swift reassurance – emotional control alongside footwork, grip, alignment, and target readiness.

Stage 8: Initiating the Shot with Controlled Emotions

"Execute with controlled emotions, visualize success." The bowler takes action, prioritizing feeling and visualization. Visualization encompasses the entire approach, emphasizing executing each step with controlled emotions.

Stage 9: Positive Anticipation with Emotional Balance

"Anticipate success, maintain emotional balance." The bowler consciously avoids dwelling on negative emotions, engaging in thinking and feeling. Positive anticipation replaces anger, focusing on the beauty and precision achieved through emotional balance.

Stage 10: Continuous Emotional Control

"Anchor emotional control, ride the momentum." Throughout the approach, the bowler stabilizes emotions, maintaining a focus on emotional control. Mental and motor control elements are crucial, ensuring balance, timing, and composure in every step.

This tailored thought process assists the bowler in managing anger and perceived unfairness, emphasizing visualization, controlled breathing, positive affirmations, and maintaining emotional balance to enhance focus and performance.

PMCP For Rebuilding Trust After Success:

Stage 1: Reflection on Past Success

"Recall success, acknowledge doubts." The bowler begins by reflecting on the successful shots in the previous frames, acknowledging the presence of doubt and the historical challenge in maintaining consistency.

Stage 2: Visualization of Positive Outcomes

"Visualize success, embrace possibility." Prioritizing visualization and feeling, the bowler vividly imagines a successful shot in the upcoming frame. This involves picturing the trajectory, the sound of pins falling, and the feeling of satisfaction.

Stage 3: Positive Self-Talk for Reinforcing Confidence

"Affirm capabilities, challenge doubt." Engaging in thinking and feeling, the bowler uses positive self-talk to reinforce confidence. Affirmations revolve around acknowledging his skill and challenging the doubt that arises.

Stage 4: Controlled Breathing for Calmness

"Breathe to calm nerves, reset focus." Attention shifts to acting and thinking. The bowler engages in controlled breathing to calm nerves, promoting a reset in focus. Controlled breathing serves as a tangible action to alleviate anxiety.

Stage 5: Analyzing Technical Aspects for Continuity

"Review successful mechanics, ensure continuity." The bowler thinks analytically, prioritizing the review of successful mechanics in the previous frames. This includes footwork, grip, and release techniques, ensuring a sense of continuity.

Stage 6: External Distraction Elimination for Enhanced Concentration

"Block external doubts, intensify focus." Acting to eliminate distractions and thinking to maintain concentration, the bowler consciously creates a mental bubble, blocking external doubts, and intensifying focus on the present shot.

Stage 7: Ritual Check with Confidence Boost

"Review checklist with renewed confidence." The bowler conducts a mental ritual check, emphasizing thinking and feeling. Visualization involves swift reassurance – confidence alongside footwork, grip, alignment, and target readiness.

Stage 8: Initiating the Shot with Trust

"Trust the process, visualize success." The bowler takes action, prioritizing feeling and visualization. Visualization encompasses the entire approach, emphasizing trust in the process and confidence in achieving success.

Stage 9: Positive Anticipation and Confidence Reinforcement

"Anticipate success, reinforce confidence." The bowler consciously shifts focus to positive anticipation, engaging in thinking and feeling. Positive thoughts replace doubts, with an emphasis on reinforcing confidence.

Stage 10: Continuous Confidence Control

"Anchor confidence, ride the momentum." Throughout the approach, the bowler stabilizes confidence, maintaining a focus on trust in his abilities. Mental and motor control elements are crucial, ensuring balance, timing, and composure in every step.

This tailored thought process aids the bowler in rebuilding trust after success, utilizing visualization, positive self-talk, controlled breathing, and continuous confidence control to enhance focus and performance.

PMCP For Adjusting Inconsistent Targeting:

Stage 1: Awareness of Consistent Misses

"Recognize the pattern, acknowledge adjustments." The bowler begins by acknowledging the consistent misses to the left side of the pocket. This stage involves thinking and feeling, recognizing the need for adjustments.

Stage 2: Visualization of Target Adjustment

"Picture the correction, feel the alignment." Visualization takes center stage, with the bowler picturing a corrected target to the right. Feeling the alignment involves mentally adjusting the position for the upcoming shot.

Stage 3: Positive Self-Talk for Alignment Reinforcement

"Affirm corrected alignment, trust the adjustment." Engaging in thinking and feeling, the bowler uses positive self-talk to affirm the corrected alignment. Trusting the adjustment becomes a crucial component at this stage.

Stage 4: Controlled Breathing for Calm Focus

"Breathe to ease tension, focus on correction." Action and thinking intertwine as the bowler engages in controlled breathing to ease tension. This serves as an action to refocus on the corrected target.

Stage 5: Analyzing Technical Aspects for Alignment Precision

"Review mechanics, emphasize precision." The bowler thinks analytically, reviewing mechanics such as footwork, grip, and release. The emphasis is on precision, ensuring the alignment is meticulous for the upcoming shot.

Stage 6: External Distraction Elimination for Enhanced Focus

"Block distractions, intensify concentration." Acting and thinking collaboratively, the bowler actively eliminates external distractions. Visualization involves creating a mental bubble, intensifying focus on the corrected target.

Stage 7: Ritual Check with Confidence in Adjustment

"Review checklist with confidence in the correction." The bowler conducts a ritual check, combining thinking and feeling. Visualization encompasses confidence in the corrected alignment alongside readiness in footwork, grip, and overall mechanics.

Stage 8: Initiating the Shot with Confidence in Correction

"Trust the correction, visualize on-target success." Action, feeling, and visualization merge as the bowler initiates the shot. Visualization involves a successful on-target outcome, reinforcing confidence in the correction.

Stage 9: Positive Anticipation of On-Target Result

"Anticipate on-target success, reinforce positivity." The bowler shifts focus to thinking and feeling positively. Positive thoughts replace concerns, and the anticipation centers around the expectation of hitting the target.

Stage 10: Continuous Focus on Alignment Precision

"Anchor precision, ride the momentum." Throughout the approach, the bowler stabilizes focus on alignment precision, ensuring a consistent application of the correction. Mental and motor control elements are vital for maintaining balance, timing, and composure.

This tailored thought process assists the bowler in adjusting targeting, utilizing visualization, positive self-talk, controlled breathing, and continuous focus on precision to enhance performance.

PMCP For Handling Psychological Distractions:

Stage 1: Recognition of Distraction Attempt

"Identify the intrusion, maintain focus." The bowler begins by recognizing the opponent's attempt at distraction. This stage involves thinking and feeling, acknowledging the potential disruption.

Stage 2: Visualization of a Focused Bubble

"Picture a shield of concentration, block the intrusion." Visualization becomes paramount. The bowler imagines a shield or bubble, mentally blocking out external distractions. Feeling the protective focus is essential.

Stage 3: Positive Self-Talk for Mental Fortitude

"Affirm mental strength, dismiss external influences." Engaging in positive self-talk, the bowler reinforces mental strength. This stage involves thinking and feeling confident, dismissing the impact of the opponent's attempt.

Stage 4: Controlled Breathing for Emotional Calmness

"Breathe for emotional control, stay composed." Action and thinking intertwine as the bowler practices controlled breathing. This helps maintain emotional control, ensuring composure despite the opponent's distraction attempts.

Stage 5: Analyzing Technical Aspects for Distraction Resilience

"Focus on mechanics, resilient to external attempts." The bowler thinks analytically about his mechanics. Emphasis is on being resilient to external distractions, ensuring a steadfast approach.

Stage 6: External Distraction Elimination for Enhanced Focus

"Block external influences, intensify internal concentration." Acting and thinking collaboratively, the bowler actively eliminates external distractions. Visualization involves creating an intensified internal focus, reducing susceptibility to opponent distractions.

Stage 7: Ritual Check with Confidence in Resilience

"Review checklist with confidence in mental resilience." The bowler conducts a ritual check, combining thinking and feeling. Visualization encompasses confidence in mental resilience alongside readiness in footwork, grip, and overall mechanics.

Stage 8: Initiating the Shot with Mental Resilience

"Trust mental resilience, visualize a focused approach." Action, feeling, and visualization merge as the bowler initiates the shot. Visualization involves a focused approach, reinforcing trust in mental resilience despite external attempts.

Stage 9: Positive Anticipation of Unaffected Performance

"Anticipate unaffected performance, reinforce positivity." The bowler shifts focus to thinking and feeling positively. Positive thoughts replace concerns, and anticipation centers around delivering an unaffected, optimal performance.

Stage 10: Continuous Focus on Internal Concentration

"Anchor internal concentration, ride the momentum." Throughout the approach, the bowler stabilizes focus on internal concentration, ensuring a consistent application of mental resilience. Mental and motor control elements are vital for maintaining balance, timing, and composure.

This tailored thought process empowers the bowler to handle psychological distractions effectively, utilizing visualization, positive self-talk, controlled breathing, and continuous focus on internal concentration to maintain optimal performance.

PMCP For Multitasking In Physical Game Enhancement:

Stage 1: Task Prioritization

"Identify primary focus, set priorities." The bowler begins by identifying the primary task among footwork, swing direction, and balance. This stage involves thinking and deciding which aspect requires immediate attention.

Stage 2: Visualizing Task Integration

"Picture seamless integration, envision the harmony." Visualization becomes key as the bowler envisions seamlessly integrating the identified tasks. This involves feeling the smooth coordination of footwork, swing, and balance.

Stage 3: Mental Checklist for Multitasking

"Establish a mental checklist, synchronize tasks." The bowler creates a mental checklist that includes footwork, swing direction, and balance. Thinking becomes crucial as they synchronize these tasks mentally, ensuring simultaneous execution.

Stage 4: Positive Affirmations for Confidence

"Affirm confidence in multitasking, banish doubt." Positive self-talk takes center stage as the bowler reinforces confidence in his ability to multitask. Thinking positively about his capacity to manage multiple aspects simultaneously is crucial.

Stage 5: Controlled Breathing for Focus

"Breathe for focused energy, maintain concentration." Action intertwines with thinking as the bowler engages in controlled breathing. This helps maintain focus on the multitasking process, ensuring energy is directed toward the integrated tasks.

Stage 6: Analyzing Mechanics for Task Harmony

"Analyze mechanics, ensure harmony in execution." Thinking analytically, the bowler assesses his mechanics. The emphasis is on ensuring the harmonious execution of footwork, swing direction, and balance to enhance the physical game.

Stage 7: Ritual Check with Multitasking Confidence

"Review checklist with confidence, affirm multitasking." The bowler conducts a ritual check, combining thinking and feeling. Visualization involves confidence in multitasking abilities alongside readiness in footwork, swing, and balance.

Stage 8: Initiating the Shot with Integrated Tasks

"Trust integrated tasks, visualize a coordinated approach." Action, feeling, and visualization merge as the bowler initiates the shot. Visualization involves a coordinated approach, trusting in the integration of footwork, swing direction, and balance.

Stage 9: Positive Anticipation of Seamless Execution

"Anticipate seamless execution, reinforce positivity." The bowler shifts focus to thinking and feeling positively. Positive thoughts replace doubts, and anticipation centers around executing footwork, swing, and balance seamlessly.

Stage 10: Continuous Focus on Task Integration

"Anchor task integration, ride the momentum." Throughout the approach, the bowler stabilizes focus on integrating footwork, swing, and balance. Mental and motor control elements are vital for maintaining this balance and coordination.

This tailored thought process equips the bowler to effectively multitask, integrating footwork, swing direction, and balance seamlessly for an enhanced and coordinated physical game.

THEORIES OF REPEATABILITY

Closed-Loop Theory

Furthermore, the significance of repeated performance under stable settings for skill learning and improvement is addressed by a number of traditional theories. According to the "closed-loop" theory of motor learning, the basis of the physical movement being performed and the memory trace that aids in selecting an appropriate motor activity are the basis of the physical movement that is regulated by feedback that is evaluated by a "reference of correctness" encoded in a person's memory system. In other words, a bowler retains a single fundamental source—a representation of acquired motor skills—for every physical action. Initially, the bowler compares newly acquired motor skills to this memory-stored source in order to assess *his* own performance. To produce a high-quality memory trace, skills also need to be exercised in stable, constant, and even the same conditions.

Closed-Loop Theory:

Closed-Loop Theory: According to this theory, when a skill is being performed, sensory receptors provide feedback that governs movement. This principle can be used in bowling in the following ways:

Example1: Upon releasing the ball, the bowler concentrates on the feedback gathered by the senses, including the sensation of the ball in the hand, the sound it makes as it hits the lane, and the visual of the ball's path as it approaches the target. The bowler can increase accuracy and consistency in subsequent shots by making adjustments based on this feedback.

Example 2: The bowler records a video of his shots during practice to provide himself a visual representation of his form and technique. The bowler can establish a closed-loop feedback loop that results in repeatable and consistent strokes by going over the recordings and comparing them to the intended result. This allows the bowler to make necessary adjustments to his approach, release, and follow-through.

Example 3: When a coach or colleague watches a bowler during practice or competition, the bowler takes into account his quick input. Advice on body alignment, arm swing, release, and follow-through are examples of input that the bowler can use to improve his performance in real-time.

Memory Drum Theory – Neuromotor Reaction

The "memory drum" theory of neuro-motor reaction posits that learning occurs through repetition. Its key points are as follows:

   a) Motor movements are independently stored in the memory as distinct units;

   b) The bowler develops action plans that are stored in the memory and use them to perform motor tasks;

c) As the bowler gains experience, the action plans necessary to perform a physical movement become solidified;

d) Motor skills must be repeatedly performed under identical conditions in order to be stored in the memory.

A theoretical model that explains the intricate cognitive and neuromuscular processes involved in bowling is called the Memory Drum Theory - Neuromotor Reaction. According to this view, memory and neuromuscular reactivity play two key roles in the capacity to repeat a good bowling action. In this sense, memory refers to the capacity to remember and reliably reproduce a good bowling motion. According to the Memory Drum Theory, effective bowling motions are stored in the brain's motor memory, which is then retrieved and repeated on subsequent tries. This memory, sometimes known as the "memory drum," is essential to the constancy of a bowler's performance. On the other hand, the physical procedures involved in carrying out the bowling action are referred to as neuromuscular reactions. This involves timing the ball release, coordination of motion, and the firing of particular muscle groups. According to the Memory Drum Theory, the brain receives the motor program required to perform an action from the memory drum, which facilitates neuromuscular responsiveness. According to the Memory Drum Theory, the combination of these two elements is necessary for a successful bowling performance. To recreate a good bowling movement, the bowler needs to be able to extract the appropriate motor memory from the memory drum and perform the appropriate neuromuscular reaction. Through repetition, the bowler may create a reliable and effective motor program that is saved in the memory drum and can be repeatedly retrieved and used.

Memory Drum Theory – Neuro-motor Reaction:

According to the Memory Drum Theory, proficient motions are automatically retrieved and carried out in response to particular stimuli after being stored as motor programs in the memory. This principle can be used in bowling in the following ways:

Example 1: The bowler establishes a pre-shot routine that includes the approach, arm swing, release, and follow-through that is reliable and repeatable. When a routine is repeated during practice and competition, the motor program linked to it gets embedded in the memory, enabling the execution of the same motions automatically in reaction to particular cues, like seeing the target or feeling the ball in the hand.

Example 2: To develop motor programs in the memory that can be retrieved and carried out automatically during competition, the bowler regularly trains in particular actions or techniques. To develop an automated and repetitive motor program that can be activated by the right cues, a bowler might, for instance, repeatedly practice the identical arm swing and release approach.

Example 3: The bowler programs motor programs in memory by using mental rehearsal or mental visualization approaches. The bowler can strengthen neural pathways and motor programs in the memory by vividly visualizing the intended movements and sensations connected to the bowling shot. This will result in more reliable and repeatable motions during real performance.

Cognitive Workload Through Quiet Eye Duration

There is more to performing successfully under duress than merely physical prowess. Cognitive psychology has advanced our understanding of the cognitive processes involved in various tasks over time. Scientists who study performance psychology apply psychological concepts to enhance athletes' and other high-stress situations' performance. It is now evident that having strong mental faculties is equally as necessary for success as having strong physical faculties. These mental skills include the capacity to focus while working on a task, filter out distractions, and regulate eye movements.

The Quiet Eye

A cognitive characteristic known as the quiet eye (QE) denotes the last fixation of the eyes before to executing a goal-directed motor action toward an ideal objective. It is described as the fixation that starts at least 100 milliseconds before the performance of a motor task (like a bowling shot) and lasts for more than 100 milliseconds, during which the eyes look away from the target by more than three degrees. It is proposed that during this interval, sensory data is integrated with cognitive processes to coordinate and organize the intended motor actions. Since the QE includes both the individual's motor behavior and internal gaze metrics, it can be considered a perception-action variable. The application of lightweight glasses attached on the head to monitor fixations in a variety of scenarios has revolutionized eye tracking technology, and QE research has had an impact on police enforcement and sports performance, particularly in bowling shots.

The actual performance improves with a longer QE period spent aiming at a target. Longer quiet eye duration (QED) is one of the three most significant cognitive characteristics of motor expertise, together with target fixation itself and the ability to regulate the number of fixations made, according to a 2007 meta-analysis in other sports like golf. It has been discovered that QED is a significant predictor of effective performance.

Similar to bowling, studies have found that elite athletes have longer QEDs than novices. Skilled bowlers are better at focusing their visual attention and allocating it to pertinent cues in their surroundings. In particular, great bowlers typically exhibit longer QEDs on the objective (three bowling targets) and shorter QEDs on other unrelated stimuli, like background distractions or their own body motions.

Moreover, amateur bowlers can be trained to perform better with QED. Amateur bowlers can enhance their capacity to allocate attention more effectively, leading to improved accuracy and consistency in their bowling performance, by employing targeted training techniques that concentrate on QED.

The following procedures provide examples of how to measure silent eye time and cognitive workload during bowling shot performance:

Step 1: Set up the experiment or assessment environment

Establish a regulated and authentic bowling environment, like a practice lane or bowling alley, complete with uniform lane setup and equipment.

Make sure everyone is comfortable using the bowling equipment and technique, and that they have had enough practice to play to the best of their abilities.

Step 2: Measure Cognitive Workload

To gauge the bowler's subjective cognitive workload during the shot, use a proven cognitive workload assessment technique, like the NASA Task Load Index (TLX).

Give the bowler the TLX questionnaire right away following a bowling shot.

Six dimensions—Mental Demand, Physical Demand, Temporal Demand, Performance, Effort, and Frustration—are used by the TLX to evaluate cognitive burden. Each dimension is rated by the bowler on a range of 0 to 100, where higher scores correspond to a heavier cognitive burden.

Example:

After bowling a shot, Bowler A uses the TLX questionnaire to rate his subjective cognitive burden. He gives himself a score of 70 for mental demand, 50 for physical demand, 60 for temporal demand, 40 for performance, 65 for effort, and 30 for frustration. The aggregate of these ratings, or 315 out of 600 in this instance, is the overall cognitive workload score.

Step 3: Measure Quiet Eye Duration

Measure the amount of time that your eyes are calm during the bowling shot by using eye-tracking equipment or video analysis software.

The last fixation or look on a particular target or area prior to the start of the shot is known as the quiet eye.

Examine the eye-tracking data or video recordings to find out how long the subject's eyes were quiet during the shoot.

Example:

After Bowler B finishes a bowling shot, the eye-tracking data reveals that he fixed his attention on the target pin for 0.5 seconds before releasing the ball.

Step 4: Analyze and Interpret the Results

To find patterns or trends, compare the quiet eye time and cognitive workload ratings between different bowlers or under different circumstances.

Investigate any relationships between silent eye length and cognitive workload, and how these relate to bowling shot performance.

Take into consideration additional variables that could affect the outcome, such as the bowlers' experience, skill level, and competence.

Example:

Data analysis reveals that bowlers with greater cognitive workload scores typically have quieter eyes for longer periods of time, whereas bowlers with lower cognitive workload scores typically have longer quiet eyes. This implies that a higher cognitive workload could result in a shorter calm eye period, which could have a detrimental effect on bowling shot performance.

Step 5: Draw Implications and Recommendations

Make recommendations for bowlers, coaches, and practitioners based on the results regarding how to maximize silent eye length and cognitive burden for better bowling shot performance.

Make suggestions for mental techniques, training methods, and interventions that can assist bowlers in controlling their cognitive load and maximizing the amount of time they have to maintain a silent gaze throughout a bowling shot.

COGNITIVE OVERLOAD: Extended QED improves the likelihood that the brain will have enough time to arrange the systems required to coordinate the planning and execution of a successful motor action. The Attentional Control Theory (ACT) states that both an individual's efficacy and the amount of cognitive effort they put into an activity impact its efficiency.

When someone is asked to comprehend too much information at once, they experience cognitive overload, which lowers their performance. When athletes must make snap judgments while under time constraints and juggling various sources of information, cognitive overload may result in sports. Decision-making and performance errors may result from this.

The **NASA Task Load Index (NASA-TLX)** is a widely used tool for assessing cognitive workload across various tasks, including sports like bowling. It helps individuals evaluate and quantify their mental workload during specific activities. Here are the steps to use the NASA-TLX for assessing cognitive workload in bowling, along with an example:

Step 1: Identify the Factors Identify the key factors that contribute to cognitive workload in bowling. These factors may include mental focus, decision-making, concentration, and emotional control.

Step 2: Select NASA-TLX Scales The NASA-TLX consists of six scales: Mental Demand, Physical Demand, Temporal Demand, Performance, Effort, and Frustration. Determine which scales are most relevant to bowling. For example, Mental Demand, Performance, and Effort scales are typically relevant.

Step 3: Define the Anchors Define the anchors for each scale. NASA-TLX uses a scale from 0 to 100, with descriptions at each end of the scale to represent low and high workload. For example:

Mental Demand: 0 (Very Low) - 100 (Very High)

Performance: 0 (Perfect) - 100 (Failure)

- Effort: 0 (Very Low) - 100 (Very High)

Step 4: Assess Cognitive Workload After a bowling session or during a specific event, ask the bowler to rate their workload on each scale. They should choose a point on the scale that best represents their perceived workload for each factor. For instance:

- Mental Demand: 70 (Moderately High)
- Performance: 40 (Good)
- Effort: 60 (Moderate)

Step 5: Calculate the Weighted Workload Calculate the weighted workload score for each factor by multiplying the chosen rating by its associated weight (from 0 to 5, indicating the perceived importance of that factor). For example:

- Mental Demand: 70 (rating) x 5 (weight) = 350

- Performance: 40 x 4 = 160

- Effort: 60 x 3 = 180

Step 6: Sum the Weighted Scores Sum up the weighted workload scores for all factors. For this example, it would be:

Total Weighted Workload = 350 (Mental Demand) + 160 (Performance) + 180 (Effort) = 690

Step 7: Normalize the Score Normalize the total weighted workload score by dividing it by the sum of the weights (5 + 4 + 3 = 12) to get the final NASA-TLX score:

- NASA-TLX Score = Total Weighted Workload / Sum of Weights = 690 / 12 = 57.5

Step 8: Interpret the Score The final NASA-TLX score of 57.5 indicates the cognitive workload experienced during the bowling session. A higher score suggests a higher cognitive workload, while a lower score suggests a lower workload.

Example Interpretation: In this example, a NASA-TLX score of 57.5 indicates a moderate cognitive workload during the bowling session. This means that the bowler perceived a moderate level of mental demand, put in moderate effort, and achieved a good performance during the session.

Repeat these steps for multiple bowling sessions to track changes in cognitive workload and identify areas for improvement in mental skills, concentration, and decision-making in bowling.

Attentional Control Theory (Act) For Elite Bowlers

According to the Attentional Control Theory (ACT), an athlete's ability to control their attention is a key component in determining their success. The capacity to ignore irrelevant cues in the environment and concentrate attention on pertinent cues is known as attentional control. While novice bowlers may find it difficult to focus and get sidetracked by unimportant cues, elite bowlers are able to sustain this attention for extended periods of time.

Elite bowlers' cognitive overload and attentional control have been linked by sport psychologists with expertise in establishing national teams. Bowlers at the top of their game are better equipped to control cognitive overload because they can selectively focus on pertinent cues and shut out distracting ones. Their excellent attentional control, which enables them to distribute attention precisely and efficiently, is linked to their ability to manage cognitive overload.

Mental skill training can also assist elite bowlers manage cognitive stress and enhance attentional control. Bowlers can lower their cognitive load during competition by using strategies like self-talk and visualization to help them concentrate on pertinent cues and block out distractions.

What does Attentional Control in Bowling means?

Attentional control in bowling refers to a bowler's ability to effectively manage and direct their focus and attention during the game. It involves the capacity to concentrate on relevant cues while ignoring distractions, ultimately optimizing performance. Here are some key aspects of attentional control in the context of bowling:

Selective Attention: Elite bowlers with strong attentional control can selectively focus on critical elements of the game, such as the positioning of the pins, the movement of the ball, or the condition of the lane. This skill allows them to tune out irrelevant information and concentrate on what's essential for a successful shot.

Cognitive Overload Management: Attentional control helps bowlers manage cognitive overload, especially in high-pressure situations. By directing their attention to pertinent cues and blocking out distracting elements, skilled bowlers can maintain focus and execute their shots with precision.

Goal-Directed Attentional System: The goal-directed attentional system involves actively focusing attention on a specific task or location. In bowling, this could mean concentrating on the alignment of the pins, the trajectory of the ball, or the release technique. Elite bowlers effectively use this system to stay focused on the task at hand despite external distractions.

Stimulus-Driven Attentional System: The stimulus-driven attentional system reacts to salient or unexpected stimuli in the environment. Professional bowlers can leverage this system to respond quickly to unforeseen changes, such as a sudden shift in lighting or the movement of other players. This is particularly crucial in dynamic and fast-paced situations.

Mental Skill Training: Techniques like self-talk and visualization are part of mental skill training that can assist bowlers in managing cognitive stress and enhancing attentional control. These strategies help them concentrate on relevant cues, maintain focus, and minimize cognitive interference.

The two attentional systems—the goal-directed attentional system and the stimulus-driven attentional system—offer the most compelling explanation for the underlying brain mechanisms of the silent eye in relation to the ACT. While the stimulus-driven system reacts to an emerging salient stimulus that may or may not be relevant to the work at hand, the goal-directed system concentrates on the pertinent task at hand.

The ability to actively focus attention on a certain place or task is a characteristic of the goal-directed attentional system in bowling. Pro bowlers can make use of this technique to focus on pertinent environmental signals, including where the pins are located or how the ball moves. This enables individuals to stay focused on the task at hand in spite of outside distractions.

Conversely, the stimulus-driven attentional system is distinguished by its innate capacity to react to salient or unfamiliar stimuli in the surrounding context. With the use of this technology, professional bowlers can react fast to unanticipated changes in their surroundings, including a rapid shift in illumination or the movement of other bowlers. This method is especially crucial in high-stress scenarios where athletes might have to react fast to unforeseen circumstances.

When it comes to the goal-directed attentional system in particular, elite bowlers have better attentional control than amateur bowlers. Pro bowlers are more adept at using this system to selectively pay attention to pertinent environmental cues, which helps them stay focused on the activity at hand. Furthermore, skilled bowlers possess the ability to efficiently utilize the stimulus-driven attentional system, which enables them to react promptly to unforeseen circumstances in their surroundings.

Attentional Control Theory (ACT):

According to the Attentional Control Theory, the accuracy and repeatability of a skill can be affected by how attention is allocated during its performance. The following are some ways that this principle can be used in bowling:

Example 1: The bowler concentrates on pertinent signals, such as the target, the intended ball trajectory, and the arm swing, throughout the pre-shot routine by using selective attention. The bowler can achieve repeatability and precision by making sure that the same movements are performed consistently in response to the same cues by tuning out unnecessary distractions and exercising excellent attentional control.

Example 2: During the approach, release, and follow-through, the bowler uses attentional focus to maximize timing and coordination of motions. For instance, in order to guarantee that the movements are coordinated and performed consistently, which results in accurate strikes, the bowler may concentrate on the timing of the push-off, the arm swing, and the release.

Example 3: Throughout the performance, the bowler maintains ideal attentional control by using self-regulation techniques. This could involve stress management, distraction reduction, and task-maintaining techniques like deep breathing, positive self-talk, or mindfulness. Through good attention management, the bowler can improve the consistency and precision of their throws.

An elite bowler's example of an attentional control plan:

Pre-Practice Routine:

To de-stress and clear your head, start with relaxation techniques like progressive muscle relaxation or deep breathing exercises.

- *Pay attention to your practice session objectives and picture yourself making* effective shots.
- *Talk to yourself to help you remember to tune out distractions and concentrate on pertinent* environmental clues.
- *Practice the proper form and technique in your mind for every shot by using* visualization techniques.

During Practice:

- Pay attention to pertinent environmental signals like the patterns changing or the shape of the ball by using your goal-directed attentional system.
- Use self-talk to tell yourself to ignore distractions and concentrate on the current work at hand.
- Visualize successful shots and proper form and technique by using visualization techniques.
- When needed, take pauses to refuel and refocus.

Pre-Event Routine:

- *To decompress and ease tension, start with relaxation techniques like progressive muscle relaxation or deep* breathing exercises.
- *Pay attention to your objectives for the competition and picture yourself making* winning shots.
- *Talk to yourself to help you remember to tune out distractions and concentrate on pertinent* environmental clues.
- *Mentally practice the proper form and technique for every shot during competition by using* visualization techniques.
- *Recognize possible distractions or unforeseen circumstances that might arise during the competition and get ready to respond rapidly by using the stimulus-driven* attentional system.

Elite bowlers can use this strategy to minimize cognitive overload during practice and competition, focus on pertinent environmental cues, and enhance their attentional control.

Myth: "Attentional Control Only Involves Blocking Out Distractions"

Reality: Attentional control encompasses more than just blocking out distractions. It also involves the ability to selectively focus on relevant cues in the environment and shift attention as needed. Elite bowlers excel in both aspects, allowing them to make precise adjustments during a game.

Myth: "PPRs Are Solely About Physical Preparation"

Reality: PPRs not only involve physical preparation but also mental preparation, including enhancing attentional control. Elite bowlers use their PPRs to optimize their attentional focus, ensuring they are mentally ready to execute each shot accurately.

Myth: "Attentional Control Can't Be Improved with Mental Skills Training"

Reality: Mental skills training, including techniques like imagery, self-talk, and mindfulness, can significantly enhance attentional control. Elite bowlers incorporate these strategies into their routines to improve their ability to focus on relevant cues and manage cognitive overload.

Myth: "Attentional Control Is Only Important During Competition"

Reality: Attentional control is crucial both during practice and competition. Elite bowlers understand the importance of maintaining attentional focus in practice to ensure that their skills are transferable to high-pressure competition settings.

Stroop Interference

A well-known cognitive test that assesses a person's capacity to suppress automatic reactions in order to concentrate on a particular activity is the Stroop interference task. People are given color words (such as "red," "blue," and "green") printed in various colored inks in the traditional Stroop task. Without considering the word meaning, participants are asked to identify the hue of the ink. The purpose of the activity is to assess the participant's capacity to suppress their natural tendency to read the word and instead concentrate on the ink's color.

Stroop interference in the bowling context can shed light on the mental processes that go into the game. Elite bowlers, for instance, might possess superior cognitive control than less skilled bowlers, enabling them to selectively attend to pertinent cues while blocking out extraneous information. This could be especially crucial in stressful situations or distracting settings.

When it comes to the Stroop task, bowlers at the top of the game show better cognitive control than bowlers at lower skill levels. Compared to inexperienced bowlers, they showed less interference from the word meaning; instead, they were able to suppress their automatic, conscious response and concentrate on the pre-shot preparation and execution.

Bowling-Specific Stroop Interference Test:

In a simulated bowling environment, participants are presented with cues related to the sport. These cues could include words or images associated with bowling, such as "strike," "spare," "lane," or visual representations of bowling balls and pins.

Color-Matching Task: Participants are instructed to identify the color of the presented cues while ignoring the bowling-related word or image. For example, if the word "strike" is presented in red ink, the participant would respond with "red."

Cognitive Control Assessment: The interference in this task arises when the word or image contradicts the color it is presented in. The participant's ability to suppress the automatic response (reading the word) and instead focus on the ink color reflects their cognitive control.

Bowling-Specific Distractions: To mimic real-world scenarios, the test might introduce distractions related to bowling, such as crowd noise, the movement of other players, or sudden changes in lighting. The bowler's ability to maintain attention on the color-matching task despite these distractions is evaluated.

Examples

Elite Bowler A: The camera intently studies Elite Bowler A's facial expressions and demeanor during a high-stress tournament finals. Elite Bowler A exhibits remarkable cognitive control even in the face of a large viewership and the potentially distracting presence of the camera. He demonstrates the ability to focus and maintain attention on the current work while disregarding other distractions.

Elite Bowler B: Bowling in a championship tournament, Elite Bowler B must contend with the pressure of doing well in front of a large audience. Concentration may be affected by a sizable live crowd as well as aural distractions. But it's clear that Elite Bowler B has exercised cognitive control. He demonstrates the capacity to keep his attention on performing his talents, blocking off outside distractions and audience pressure. This emphasizes how important cognitive resilience is to elite performance in these kinds of situations.

Elite Bowler C: While competing in a high-stakes bowling match, Elite Bowler C is embroiled in an unusual psychological conflict. He becomes aware of rumors and devious strategies from his rivals as he gets ready for his pivotal moment. Some opponents try to divert attention with subtly spoken statements or psych-outs. In this case, Elite Bowler C's cognitive resilience really shows. he stays in a constant state of mind, ignoring outside attempts to break his focus and making sure his opponents' psychological tactics have no effect on his performance. The importance of cognitive control in reacting to competitive mind games in bowling is demonstrated by this example.

Bowlers can also enhance *his* cognitive control and suppress automatic reflexes by practicing mental skills. Bowlers can enhance their performance by learning strategies like cognitive restructuring and mindfulness meditation, which can help them focus and block out distracting thoughts and inputs.

Working Memory Capacity (WMC)

Working memory capacity (WMC) is a measure of a person's ability to perform on the Stroop test. The term "working memory capacity" (WMC) describes the mind's short-term capacity to store and process information. It is a crucial cognitive skill that is necessary for many tasks, including competing in sports. WMC is measured by the traditional cognitive challenge known as the Stroop task. For instance, a list of color names written in various colors is given to the participants. The participant's job is to identify the ink's color without considering the word's meaning. The purpose of the activity is to assess the participant's capacity to block out unnecessary information while selectively attending to pertinent cues.

WMC has the potential to significantly impact performance in the bowling context, especially under pressure. It has been demonstrated that experienced bowlers have better WMC than inexperienced bowlers. This mental capacity to store and process information may be especially crucial when handling complex information, as in a bowling competition when competitors must keep score, lane conditions, and other details in mind.

Bowler Example: During each shot, a bowler with a high working memory capacity can more effectively process and incorporate sensory feedback, such as ball speed and lane conditions, into his motor program. His ability to make prompt adjustments and execute consistent shots leads to increased accuracy and repetition.

An example of a bowler with limited working memory would be someone who finds it difficult to interpret and apply sensory feedback, which could result in erratic shots and decreased repeatability. Lower accuracy could be the result of his inability to focus on various areas of his technique or adapt to changing lane conditions.

Coach Example: During practice or competition, a coach can evaluate a bowler's working memory capacity by having him takes cognitive ability tests or by watching him analyzes and applies sensory feedback. With the use of this information, the coach can modify training plans to increase the bowler's working memory capacity, which will enhance stroke accuracy and repetition.

Example of a Bowler and Coach: To increase a bowler's working memory, a coach and bowler may work together to create and use mental techniques like cognitive rehearsal and visualization. By mentally practicing and reinforcing his motor programs, bowlers can improve his execution and repeatability of actual strokes.

Example between Coach and Bowler: During practice and competition, a coach might offer advice and comments to help a bowler develop his working memory. To improve repeatability and accuracy and to assist the bowlers in making better use of his working memory, the coach could, for instance, encourage him to concentrate on particular cues or signals that are most pertinent to his performance.

Coach Example: By combining drills that force a bowler to interpret and integrate many sensory inputs, such as lane conditions, ball speed, and body positioning, a coach can create training sessions that test a bowler's working memory. This can enhance the bowler's capacity to employ working memory efficiently during a match, resulting in increased accuracy and repetition.

Theory	Description	Examples	Steps	Assumptions
Closed-Loop Theory	- Closed-Loop Theory suggests that movements are controlled by feedback from sensory receptors, allowing bowlers to make adjustments to achieve repeatability. - Bowlers assume that proper muscle memory and sensory feedback will lead to consistent performance.	Example 1: Bowlers aim to repeat a specific release technique consistently to achieve optimal results. Example 2: Bowlers use muscle memory to repeat their approach and delivery in a consistent manner.	- Bowlers need to learn and practice a specific release technique with proper muscle memory. - Bowlers need to focus on proprioception and kinesthetic feedback to repeat the desired movement pattern.	- Bowlers may struggle with developing proper muscle memory and kinesthetic awareness. - Bowlers may face challenges in translating sensory feedback into effective adjustments.
Memory Drum Theory	- Memory Drum Theory suggests that consistent performances can be achieved by building a "memory drum" of successful movements in the mind. - Bowlers assume that recalling successful performances will enhance repeatability.	Example 1: Bowlers use mental rehearsal and visualization to create a "memory drum" of consistent movements. Example 2: Bowlers rely on their past successful performances as a reference for repeatability.	- Bowlers need to learn and practice mental rehearsal and visualization techniques. - Bowlers need to analyze and internalize successful past performances.	- Bowlers may struggle with creating vivid mental images and recalling past performances accurately. - Bowlers may face challenges in transferring mental rehearsal to actual physical performance.

Theory	Description	Examples	Steps	Assumptions
Cognitive Workload	- Cognitive Workload theory suggests that cognitive resources are limited, and minimizing cognitive load can enhance repeatability. - Bowlers assume that reducing mental distractions and focusing on critical aspects of performance will lead to improved repeatability.	Example 1: Bowlers strive to minimize cognitive load by simplifying their approach and delivery to increase repeatability. Example 2: Bowlers use cognitive strategies to manage the complexity of the game and focus on the critical aspects of performance.	- Bowlers need to analyze and simplify their approach and delivery to reduce cognitive load. - Bowlers need to develop cognitive strategies to manage the challenges of the game.	- Bowlers may struggle with identifying and managing cognitive load during the fast-paced nature of the game. - Bowlers may face challenges in applying cognitive strategies effectively under pressure.
Attentional Control Theory	- Attentional Control Theory suggests that bowlers can enhance repeatability by effectively allocating attention to relevant cues and shifting attention when needed. - Bowlers assume that focusing attention on critical aspects of performance will lead to improved repeatability.	Example 1: Bowlers use selective attention to focus on relevant cues, such as the target and their own movements, for improved repeatability. Example 2: Bowlers use attentional shifting to switch focus between different aspects of the game, such as lane conditions and opponents' performance.	- Bowlers need to develop selective attention skills to filter out distractions and focus on relevant cues. - Bowlers need to practice attentional shifting to adapt to changing conditions during the game.	- Bowlers may struggle with distractions from external factors or internal thoughts during the game. - Bowlers may face challenges in effectively shifting attention between different cues and aspects of the game.
Stroop Interference	- Stroop Interference theory suggests that irrelevant cues can disrupt repeatability by causing interference in attention and cognitive processes. - Bowlers assume that inhibiting irrelevant cues and thoughts will lead to improved repeatability.	Example 1: Bowlers need to manage the interference caused by irrelevant cues, such as lane markings or opponent's performance, to maintain repeatability. Example 2: Bowlers practice inhibitory control to suppress irrelevant thoughts or distractions that can disrupt repeatability.	- Bowlers need to identify and manage the interference caused by irrelevant cues during the game. - Bowlers need to develop inhibitory control skills to suppress irrelevant thoughts or distractions.	- Bowlers may struggle with managing irrelevant cues and distractions during the fast-paced nature of the game. - Bowlers may face challenges in developing effective inhibitory control skills to suppress irrelevant thoughts or distractions.
Working Memory Capacity (WMC)	- WMC theory suggests that higher working memory capacity leads to better decision making and shot execution, resulting in improved repeatability. - Bowlers assume that their WMC level affects their performance in bowling.	Example 1: Bowlers with high WMC are able to hold and manipulate more information in their working memory, allowing for better decision making and shot execution. Example 2: Bowlers with low WMC may struggle with information overload and reduced ability to adapt to changing conditions on the lane.	- Bowlers need to assess their individual WMC level through cognitive tests or self-assessment tools. - Bowlers need to practice techniques to enhance their working memory capacity, such as cognitive exercises or memory training.	- Bowlers may face challenges in accurately assessing their WMC level and understanding its impact on their performance. - Bowlers may struggle with cognitive overload and reduced ability to adapt to changing conditions on the lane.

Table 27 - Closed-Loop Theory emphasizes sensory feedback for repeatability. Memory Drum Theory builds a mental record of successful movements. Cognitive Workload minimizes distractions for improved performance. Attentional Control allocates attention effectively. Stroop Interference tackles disruptive cues. Working Memory Capacity (WMC) correlates with decision-making and execution. Each theory requires specific steps and assumptions for bowlers to enhance their repeatability, with challenges like cognitive load and interference to manage.

DEVELOPING A CHALLENGE MINDSET – A KEY TO RESILIENCE

Better athletic performance has long been linked to a challenge mentality. But one of the most important things a bowler can do to strengthen their psychological resilience is to adopt this mindset. In other words, resilience sets the two types of people apart that the majority of researchers have mentioned. Because of this, psychological resilience is now widely acknowledged as a key component of success in both the sports and non-sporting domains. It is simple to recall instances in which tough bowlers have flourished under duress; consider EJ Tackett. winning a record five championships in the first half of 2023 despite losing to a number of bowlers in the championship match. It's also simple to recall instances in which less resilient bowlers have buckled under duress. It follows that coaches' desire to develop their bowlers' resilience makes sense. In order to do this, it appears that coaches need to be well-versed in the actions they may take to assist bowlers in cultivating this challenge mindset so they can smash records rather than disintegrate in the face of difficulty.

What Is A 'Challenge Mindset'?

A bowler who adopts a challenging attitude responds constructively to the pressures and misfortunes he faces; this approach does not entail controlling the course of events per sequence, but rather the bowler's perception of them. When bowlers find themselves in a stressful situation, they go through a first appraisal in which they assess whether or not the circumstance matters to them and how it might influence them. The bowlers then evaluates whether they think they have the resources to handle the circumstance in the secondary appraisal that follows. A danger appraisal occurs when the bowler feels they lack the resources necessary to meet the demands of the assignment; a desirable challenge evaluation occurs when they think they can meet the needs of the task. Furthermore, bowlers engage in a process known as meta-cognition and meta-emotion in which they assess their own ideas and feelings. We may establish this challenge mindset in bowlers by encouraging them to appraise their resources, ideas, and emotions favorably and to replace negative self-assessments with positive ones.

Why Do We Want A 'Challenge Mindset'?

There are various psychological advantages to viewing a situation as a challenge rather than a threat, including enhanced performance and more helpful ways to interpret anxiety. Having this challenge mentality is also one of the three things bowlers need to do to build psychological resilience. Psychological resilience encompasses two qualities: robust resilience, which is the ability of a bowler to maintain performance and well-being in stressful or pressure-filled situations, and rebound resilience, which is the ability of a bowler to return to normal functioning after performance and well-being are momentarily disrupted under pressure. It is nearly a given that bowlers will face these kinds of setbacks at some point; the real question is not if they will face difficulty, but rather, how they will handle it. Therefore, it is simple to understand why resilience is essential for success and why cultivating a challenge mindset is essential for boosting resilience.

Resilience Aspect	Explanation	Example in Bowler
What Resilience Is	The ability to utilize personal qualities to withstand pressure	A bowler remains focused and composed despite a series of missed shots in a high-stakes competition.
	The ability to maintain wellbeing and performance when under pressure	A bowler maintains consistent performance even in the face of intense competition and crowd pressure.
	A dynamic process resulting from the interaction of the player and environment	A bowler adapts his strategy and approach based on lane conditions and opponent's performance.
	A proactive approach to managing stress and maintaining functionality	A bowler engages in regular stress-management techniques such as deep breathing and visualization exercises.
What Resilience Is Not	A rare or exclusive quality possessed by extraordinary individuals	Resilience is not limited to only a few exceptionally talented bowlers; it can be developed by anyone.
	A fixed trait that cannot be developed or improved	Resilience is not something inherent; it can be cultivated through practice and learning.
	Limited to an individual and not influenced by external factors	Resilience is influenced by factors such as coaching support, team dynamics, and environmental conditions.
	The absence or suppression of emotions	Resilience does not mean suppressing emotions; it involves effectively managing and channeling them to perform better.

Table 28 - Understanding Resilience in Bowlers

How Can We Develop A 'Challenge Mindset'?

Bowling personal traits combined with their absorption in a supportive environment help shape their challenging attitude, and these elements all contribute to resilience levels. Therefore, it's critical to improve one's character and create a supportive atmosphere in order to foster a challenging mindset, which will ultimately result in more resilient bowlers. Personal qualities include a bowler's personality and psychological skills. Since psychological skills are far more flexible than personality traits, it makes sense to concentrate on developing these psychological skills in a resilience training program rather than trying to manipulate personality traits. A bowler's personality is very stable.

What conditions and mental abilities must a bowler meet in order to foster a challenging attitude, then? Making the bowler feel as though he has what it takes to meet the demands of a given circumstance is crucial. We need to either lower the perceived demands or raise their perceived resources in order to do this. Theoretically, the best strategies to influence these assessments and persuade a bowler to view a situation as a challenge rather than a threat include high self-efficacy, high perceived control over the situation, and adoption of approach goals, especially mastery approach goals. Therefore, it makes sense that while trying to establish a challenging mindset, the bowler's psychological skills and the surrounding environment would promote the evolution of these three variables.

While many **psychological skills** are recommended to be taught to bowlers, three core psychological skills have emerged as the most significant findings from the research and are utilized extensively in a variety of high-level sports. These three abilities are **self-talk, goal-setting, and visualizing**. These three psychological abilities are particularly useful in promoting self-efficacy, perceived control, and approach goals—all of which are prerequisites for a challenge mindset. While I will offer a brief explanation of how to apply these techniques, coaches who wish to train these skills should familiarize themselves with the established methods in detail or speak with a psychologist because these are all thoroughly researched and in-depth areas in and of themselves.

What assistance can we therefore give the bowler to foster a challenge mentality and a **facilitative environment**? Assistance has to be provided as a component of pressure inurement training, which basically entails escalating the quantity of challenge and help offered to the bowler to attain a setting with elevated frequencies of both. To truly impact a challenge mindset, we need to concentrate on the support offered, as the process of increasing challenge is very inflexible. What other measures can we take to support a bowler's increase in self-efficacy, perceived control, and approach goals—all of which were previously identified as critical to developing a challenge mindset—aside from teaching and training the psychological skills previously mentioned?

First of all, a bowler's adopted aims can be greatly influenced by their trainers. **Mastery approach goals**, as previously said, stimulate a challenge mentality. The main objective of the mastery approach is for bowlers to work on themselves rather than to compare themselves to other bowlers. It is crucial that bowlers' significant others—coaches, parents, or anyone else who works with them—model the desired goals for them. For example, they should ask questions about the bowler's performance rather than the result of the match, and he should refrain from comparing the bowler to other bowlers. Additionally, it is critical to collaborate with the bowler to set these mastery approach goals during goal-setting sessions. This way, coaches can be consistent in their self-improvement throughout training by referring to the bowler's goals and determining how he can better themselves.

Second, coaches ought to concentrate on helping bowlers find their sources of **self-efficacy**. This may be done both when speaking with a bowler and when motivating oneself to talk about these things. The following are these resources and ways that others can help to publicize them:

- **Performance Accomplishments**– Reminding bowlers of instances in which they have succeeded in the same or a related activity.
- **Vicarious Experiences**– Bowlers witness someone who resembles them do the same task, which instills in them the belief that "if they can do it, why can't I?"
- **Verbal Persuasion**: Just tell the bowler that you think he can succeed and that you believe in them. It also helps to project confidence in oneself.
- **Imaginal States**: Encouraging a bowler to visualize themselves winning
- **Physiological and Emotional States**: Bowlers who perceive their arousal as positive, coaches who only explain that arousal symptoms, such as elevated heart rate, are required for optimal performance, have shown to be somewhat effective, and arousal management strategies, like as relaxation, may be beneficial.

Perceived control is strongly correlated with self-efficacy. While perceived control refers to the conviction that a bowler will have the chance to demonstrate this skill, self-efficacy is essentially the level of confidence a bowler has in their capacity to achieve in a particular circumstance.

Focus on controllable aspects– Talk to the bowler about pertinent, under-your-control issues. Parents or coaches should concentrate on the bowler's controllables, like their own strategy or technique.

- **Attribute success to bowler's effort**– When positive changes (i.e., improvements) happen, the coach should credit the bowler's efforts rather than any outside influences. This will instill in the bowler the belief that he can affect the necessary change on his own if he puts in the necessary effort.
- **Generate a variety of solutions**– Provide a range of solutions: By helping the bowler come up with multiple approaches to the same issue, you can help them feel more in control of the situation by showing them that there are multiple strategies for overcoming hardship. This has to do with the current research showing that "Langerian Mindfulness" enhances perceived control in athletic and educational environments17.

Factors	Description	Example (Player)	Example (Coach)
Performance Accomplishments	Remind bowlers of past successful tasks	"I have consistently achieved high scores in previous tournaments."	"Remember when you scored a perfect game last month? You can do it again."

Factors	Description	Example (Player)	Example (Coach)
Vicarious Experiences	Bowlers observe similar individuals succeed	"If they can score a strike, so can I."	"Watch how John executes his technique flawlessly. You can learn from him."
Verbal Persuasion	Coach expresses belief in bowler's abilities	"I believe in your skills and know you can succeed."	"You have the talent and skills to excel in this game. Believe in yourself."
Imaginal States	Bowlers visualize themselves succeeding	"Imagine yourself throwing a perfect strike."	"Visualize yourself executing the perfect technique in your mind."
Physiological and Emotional States	Bowler views arousal as positive	"Feeling my heart rate rise means I'm ready to perform at my best."	"Your increased heart rate indicates your body is preparing for peak performance. Remember to use relaxation techniques to stay focused."
Focus on Controllable Aspects	Communication focuses on relevant controllable factors	"I will focus on improving my footwork and ball release."	"Let's work on refining your technique and developing effective strategies."
Attribute Success to Bowler's Effort	Acknowledge bowler's efforts for positive changes	"My hard work and practice have led to noticeable improvements."	"Your commitment and dedication to training have paid off. Your efforts are making a difference."
Generate a Variety of Solutions	Encourage bowlers to develop multiple solutions	"There are different ways I can adjust my approach to overcome challenges."	"Let's explore different strategies together and find the best approach to overcome this obstacle."

Table 29 - The table outlines psychological factors in bowling performance, offering insights for both players and coaches. It delineates strategies such as reinforcing accomplishments, promoting observational learning, expressing belief in abilities, encouraging visualization, managing physiological states, emphasizing controllable aspects, attributing success to effort, and fostering creative problem-solving. The examples illustrate practical applications for players and coaches to enhance mental approaches, contributing to improved bowling performance through a holistic coaching philosophy.

Strategic Plan for Developing a Challenge Mindset in Bowlers

Duration: *12 weeks (3 months)*

Stage 1: Assessment and Goal Setting (3 days)

- **Step 1:** Assess Current Mindset
  - Carry out evaluations to ascertain bowlers' present mindsets and pinpoint any obstacles or constraints that may exist.

- **Step 2:** Set Challenge Mindset Goals
  - Work together with players to establish clear objectives for cultivating a challenge mentality at competitions.

Stage 2: Enhancing Personal Qualities (4 weeks)

- **Step 3:** Psychological Skills Training
  - Introduce and instruct players in the three primary psychological techniques of goal-setting, self-talk, and visualization.
  - Explain to them how these abilities can improve their sense of control and self-efficacy..

- **Step 4:** Self-Efficacy Development
  - Assist players in increasing their self-efficacy by:
  - Reminding them of prior accomplishments.
  - Providing chances to watch successful bowlers who are comparable to them.
  - Making a verbal persuasive argument and exhibiting assurance.
  - Promoting the use of imagery to picture achievement.
  - Encouraging favorable perspectives on emotional and physiological arousal.

Stage 3: Creating a Facilitative Environment (4 weeks)

- **Step 5:** Pressure Inurement Training
  - Raise the difficulty and level of assistance in the training setting gradually.
  - Concentrate on enhancing the assistance offered to encourage a challenge mentality..

- **Step 6:** Mastery Approach Goals
  - Motivate bowlers to set mastery approach objectives, placing more emphasis on personal growth than winning or losing.
  - Set a good example for goal-setting and refrain from comparing yourself to other people..
- **Step 7:** Focus on Controllable Aspects
  - Ascertain that player communications center around factors that they have control over, such strategy and execution.
  - Give the players credit for their efforts, highlighting their capacity to effect change..
- **Step 8:** Generate a Variety of Solutions
  - Work together with players to come up with several answers for the problems they encounter.
  - Encourage "Langerian Mindfulness" in order to improve control perception..

Stage 4: Continuous Improvement and Support (3 weeks)

- **Step 9:** Regular Goal Review
  - Regular Goal Review Review and modify challenge mentality objectives on a regular basis.
  - Make sure the emphasis on personal development is constant..
- **Step 10:** Reinforce Supportive Environment
  - Keep up a training atmosphere that is encouraging and strikes a balance between challenge and support.
  - Maintain the provision of psychological skill training and support..

Stage 5: Tournament Implementation (1 week)

- **Step 11:** Tournament Mindset
  - Stress the value of using the challenge mindset in real-world competitions.
  - Motivate participants to view circumstances surrounding tournaments as challenges as opposed to threats..

Stage 6: Post-Tournament Evaluation (1 week)

- **Step 12:** Performance Review
  - Examine tournament results and contrast them with the objectives of the challenge mindset.
  - Determine the training plan's shortcomings and where it needs to be adjusted..

Stage 7: Ongoing Development (1 week)

- **Step 13:** Continuous Learning
  - Motivate participants to keep refining their challenge mindset after completing the first session.
  - Help participants identify new objectives for continued development

Stress And Under Pressure

Many benefits of this demanding structure in daily life are also available to professional athletes, such as the capacity to overcome the fear of failure, constancy in training, consistency in achieving life goals, and unwavering commitment. In fact, competing in bowling contests can put a bowler under pressure. Under extreme stress, a bowler's performance in sports may also suffer. Bowlers who have high-performance standards to meet may become overwhelmed by them. Additionally, bowlers may be under pressure from both on-field factors like injuries, and errors made by referees, and off-field factors like the competitive environment, and the sentiment of the media, fans, and sports executives. When under stress, bowlers should identify their level of stress and then select and apply coping mechanisms that will help them manage it. The bowler's ability to withstand psychological setbacks is intimately linked to this ability. It follows that a bowler with a high-stress threshold should be able to handle the competitive environment and crisis impact it creates more readily, feel less burnout, and have a high degree of success motivation, all of which are reflected in their success in sports. The following is an expression of the elite bowlers' psychological resiliency process:

A talented bowler with a high degree of psychological resilience can identify and mitigate societal, personal, and family-related risks in their life. Consequently, it is anticipated that there will be fewer swings in the bowler's performance brought on by potential risk variables. The bowler's performance is anticipated to be high because of the protective factors—both internal and external—that contribute to psychological resilience and promote the bowler's sense of safety in social settings. Because of psychological issues that the bowlers find difficult to manage, such as low motivation, stress, high anxiety, and issues with self-confidence, many successful top bowlers' careers end before the anticipated period.

Due to the strain of rigorous training and constant pressure to succeed, bowlers' performances can differ from tournament to competition. In order to reduce these performance swings, handle the difficulties unique to sports, and ultimately succeed, the bowler must increase their level of psychological resilience. In reality, given the current situation, it may be argued that the trainings conducted to improve bowlers' athletic prowess and resilience are inadequate given the intensifying competitive landscape. A bowler with strong psychological resilience is believed to have a high stress threshold, high subjective well-being, and self-esteem, which sets them apart from other bowlers in terms of performance. The greatest training techniques, dietary guidelines, and sporting facilities are now available to anyone. Because of this, the ability to combine the ideal qualities of aptitude, hard work, and the appropriate psychological and mental profile is what sets top bowlers apart from others. Because of their greater talent in a particular sport, professional bowlers should be able to put together the greatest possible team; in other words, their psychological toughness should match their performance level. Elite bowlers are held to high standards regarding their psychological resilience, but their self-resilience is only moderate. In contrast, their psychological resilience is below average in the areas of social competence, structural style, future, social resources, and family cohesion.

The bowlers who are regarded and valued most highly in society are considered elite bowlers. Consequently, according to Maslow's hierarchy of wants, these are the bowlers who have achieved a certain level of self-actualization and whose basic needs of love and respect have been largely satisfied. It is anticipated that the bowlers who achieve self-actualization will possess a strong psychological resilience that will allow them to go through challenging times. Still, there is a growing emphasis on coaches looking for younger bowlers instead of spending more time, money, and effort developing and nurturing older bowlers due to the changing regulations of many bowling federations. The need for quick skill acquisition and faster learning is what's causing this transition. A sports policy that minimizes sports to winning medals and views sports as a means of achievement results in insufficient funding for the development of elite bowlers and makes them feel like inanimate objects that are easily forgotten. Elite bowlers thus experience psychological resilience reductions related to their future as a result of being crushed by the pressure of achievement and lacking sufficient confidence.

In order to handle the psychological pressure they encounter before to the tournament, bowlers who possess poor levels of psychological resilience may require the assistance of their close relationships. Because the best integration of technical, tactical, and psychological factors is necessary for good performance in sports, bowlers who feel that their families do not support them enough may find that they need to engage in self-talk to fill the emotional void in their lives. The imagination that gives us influence over every aspect of physical performance is one of these psychological aspects. Although the skill is based on movement, the organization and coordination of all the components of movement take place in the mind. Imagination is a mental preparation that aids in the physical implementation of the learning process and skill, the reduction of time spent, and the establishment of links between the parts of the skill. The bowler who uses language magic to envisage achievement and engage in self-talk sees the specifics of the skill. As a result, one may argue that they lessen the strain brought on by the competitive environment. Thus, self-talk and creativity improve performance and aid in learning.

Strategic Plan for Bowlers: Handling Stress and Pressure Professionally

Duration: 12 weeks (3 months)

Stage 1: Assessment and Goal Setting (3 days)

- **Step 1:** Assess Psychological Resilience
  - To determine current resilience levels, administer psychological resilience evaluations.

- **Step 2:** Set Performance Goals
  - Work together with the player to establish precise performance objectives concerning stress reduction and enhancement of performance.

Stage 2: Building Psychological Resilience (2 weeks)

- **Step 3:** Awareness and Recognition
  - Inform players about the various pressures and how they affect their ability to perform.
  - Instruct players on how to identify and accept stress when it arises.

- **Step 4:** Coping Strategies
  - Provide players with a variety of coping mechanisms (such as deep breathing, mindfulness, and visualization) and assist them in selecting the best ones.
  - Give players access to resources so they can practice these tactics.

- **Step 5:** Support System
  - Motivate athletes to ask family, friends, and coaches for social support.
  - Address any stressors connected to the players' families that are compromising their resilience.

- **Step 6:** Self-Talk and Imagery
  - Explain to players how using visualization and positive self-talk can lower stress and improve performance.
  - Assist players in integrating images and self-talk into their routines.

Stage 3: Skill Integration (6 weeks) ongoing

- **Step 7:** Skill Development
  - Put equal emphasis on psychological training and the development of technical and tactical skills.
  - Establish practice regimens that combine mental and physical preparedness.

- **Step 8:** Pre-Competition Rituals
  - Assist athletes in creating rituals prior to competition, such as visualization and self-talk.
  - The purpose of these customs ought to be to lessen nervousness prior to competition.

Stage 4: Competition Preparation (2 weeks)

- **Step 9:** Mock Competitions
  - Set up simulated contests to mimic the pressure of an actual event.
  - Motivate participants to use coping mechanisms in these virtual settings..

- **Step 10:** Review and Adjust
  - Hold frequent meetings to discuss progress, hone coping mechanisms, and modify objectives as necessary..

Stage 5: Tournament Execution (1 week)

- **Step 11:** Tournament Mindset
  - Stress the importance of being focused and having an optimistic outlook during the competition.
  - Remind participants to employ visualization and self-talk strategies..

Stage 6: Post-Tournament Evaluation (1 week)

- **Step 12:** Performance Review
  - Examine the results of the competition and contrast them with the predetermined objectives.

- Determine where performance in general and stress management need to be improved.

Stage 7: Ongoing Development (1 week)

- **Step 13:** Continuous Improvement
  - Motivate athletes to keep up their stress-reduction and psychological toughness exercises.
  - Help participants establish new performance targets for the future.

Tactics for Handling Stress and Pressure:

1. **Self-Talk and Visualization:** Before and during competitions, teach players how to focus better and lower their anxiety levels by using positive self-talk and visualization.
2. **Coping Mechanisms:** Give players a toolbox including several coping mechanisms (such as mindfulness and deep breathing) and assist them in selecting the ones that work best for them.
3. **Social Support:** Foster an atmosphere on the team where players feel comfortable asking for assistance and motivation from their coaches and teammates.
4. **Pre-Competition Rituals:** To foster a sense of habit and comfort, establish pre-competition rituals that involve mental preparation strategies.
5. **Regular Assessment:** Evaluate and track players' psychological resilience over time, and modify the training schedule as necessary.
6. **Mock Competitions:** Provide athletes the chance to experience managing tournament pressure in a safe setting.
7. **Goal Setting:** Give players a clear sense of direction and purpose by establishing performance goals that are attainable, quantifiable, and explicit.
8. **Skill Integration:** To emphasize the value of psychological resilience, incorporate mental preparation into skill development exercises.

Bowlers can improve their performance and general well-being by adhering to this strategic plan and learning process, which will help them manage stress and pressure professionally throughout tournaments.

Enhance And Refine Personal Qualities

A bowler's personal attributes, or the psychological shields that shield them from unfavorable outcomes, form the basis of the mental fortitude training program. Within the domain of personal attributes, we distinguish between personality traits, psychological abilities and mechanisms, and desired results that shield a bowler from unfavorable outcomes in the mental toughness training program. The most important, empirically supported character traits for fostering bowling resilience are enumerated and categorized. It is significant to remember that these attributes' applicability and significance will change with time and place. For instance, in the context of elite sports, exhibiting resilience to training-related stresses will probably call for a distinct set of character traits than those required to endure competition-related stressors. It's also important to emphasize that psychological skills and personality traits are more malleable and contribute to desired outcomes. Therefore, certain parts of a bowler's mentality are more flexible than others in terms of the developing potential of bowler resilience. We use the term "resilience bandwidth" to describe a bowler's natural developmental trajectory in relation to their point of maximum potential with psychological intervention, based on this discovery.

Personality characteristics: Extraversion is one trait that could shield a bowler from unfavorable outcomes throughout the mental fortitude training program. An outgoing and aggressive personality may come naturally to an extroverted bowler, which could help him deal with the pressures of competition or training. His resilience and capacity to overcome obstacles may be attributed to this personality feature.

Psychological skills and processes: Emotional control is another example of a personal attribute in the mental fortitude training program. The stresses of competition may be easier for bowlers who are adept at controlling their emotions and preserving emotional stability under duress. Their psychological toolset may include emotional management strategies like cognitive reframing, deep breathing, or mindfulness to shield them from unfavorable outcomes.

Desirable outcomes: Self-efficacy, or the conviction that one can succeed in a given circumstance, is a third example of a personal trait that may support a bowler's resilience. High self-efficacy bowlers may be more able to overcome obstacles and maintain motivation in the face of difficulties or failures during practice or competition. A key result of the mental fortitude training program may be the development and maintenance of a sense of self-efficacy, which gives bowlers the confidence and self-belief to shield themselves from unfavorable outcomes.

The ability of bowlers to constructively assess and interpret the pressure they face, together with their own resources, thoughts, and emotions, is arguably the most important component of any resilience training program. Here, the emphasis is on bowlers' responses to pressures and hardships rather than the actual environmental events.

Personality Characteristics Of Challenge Mindset

The bowler, characterized by an outgoing and attention-seeking demeanor, actively seeks communication with coaches, teammates, and fellow players. This manifests in dynamic participation during team discussions, wholehearted support for teammates, and an infectious enthusiasm during gameplay. Displaying a conscientious approach to bowling, the bowler meticulously attends to details, adheres to established techniques and plans, and dedicates ample time to rigorous self-evaluation, embodying a relentless commitment to continuous improvement. This dedication to perfectionism sets the bowler apart, as they establish and uphold exceptionally high personal standards, persisting tenaciously and striving for excellence in the face of challenges and setbacks. The bowler consistently maintains a positive outlook on future performances, exhibiting an enduring optimism and hopefulness that bolsters unwavering confidence in their skills and the potential for success, even when confronted with formidable competition or adversities. It is crucial to acknowledge that a narcissistic disposition, characterized by a grandiose self-view and feelings of entitlement, may not seamlessly align with a healthy challenge mindset that emphasizes personal growth and team success over individual prominence. Notably, the bowler adeptly demonstrates emotional composure even under duress, efficiently controlling their emotions to ensure optimal performance, maintaining a consistently cool-headed demeanor on the bowling alley. Driven by an inherent competitive spirit, the bowler leverages comparisons with others as a motivational tool, viewing competition as an invaluable opportunity for self-improvement and surpassing rivals. The bowler further embraces a proactive playing style, skillfully anticipating and adapting to evolving circumstances, opponents' tactics, and various situational factors, consistently making calculated decisions to navigate these elements in their favor. Intrinsic motivation remains a cornerstone for the bowler, who genuinely revels in the game of bowling, deriving immense pleasure from the preparatory, practice, and competitive phases, finding intrinsic satisfaction rather than fixating solely on external rewards. While harboring a natural inclination to demonstrate competence over others, the bowler adeptly balances this with a healthy challenge mindset that prioritizes collaboration and personal growth over ego-oriented goals. Guided by a task-oriented mindset, the bowler's focus centers on self-improvement, with a deliberate concentration on personal growth and development, steering clear of rigid comparisons with peers. The adoption of a self-serving attributional style is evident in the bowler's maintenance of self-esteem by attributing success to personal abilities and efforts, coupled with an astute recognition that failure or setbacks may also be influenced by external or transient factors. Bolstered by a robust self-confidence, the bowler exudes a compelling sense of self-worth, showcasing unwavering assurance and belief in their ability to perform effectively despite obstacles or failures, thus fostering a positive outlook and a resilient tenacity to persevere through challenges in unwavering pursuit of their objectives.

The Origins of Bowlers' Mindset Characteristics

Best Personality Characteristics:

A bowler with outstanding personality characteristics in a challenge mindset often attributes his positive traits to a supportive upbringing and coaching environment. Growing up, he had parents and mentors who emphasized the value of collaboration, personal growth, and maintaining a positive outlook in the face of challenges. These influential figures instilled a sense of intrinsic motivation, teaching the bowler to find joy in the game for its own sake. The high personal standards and dedication to perfectionism stem from a nurturing environment that balanced expectations with encouragement. The bowler learned to regulate his emotions through constructive feedback and experienced a healthy competitive spirit that focused on self-improvement rather than individual glory.

Bad Personality Characteristics:

For a bowler displaying less favorable personality characteristics in a challenge mindset, his upbringing and coaching experiences may have contributed to a more individualistic and ego-oriented mindset. Parents or mentors who overly emphasized winning and individual achievements, without a balanced focus on collaboration and personal growth, could have influenced this attitude. A lack of emotional composure under pressure may result from a childhood environment that did not prioritize coping skills or provided unhealthy models of dealing with setbacks. The narcissistic tendencies might stem from an early emphasis on external validation and a failure to attribute setbacks to external factors. In this case, a lack of balance in parenting and coaching likely contributed to a mindset that struggles with resilience and positive outlook in the face of challenges.

Psychological Skill Of Challenge Mindset:

In the cultivation of the psychological skill of a challenge mindset, self-awareness plays a pivotal role throughout the game, where the bowler consistently maintains consciousness of their feelings, thoughts, and actions. This heightened self-awareness extends to recognizing personal strengths, weaknesses, and areas for potential growth, allowing the bowler to comprehend the impact of these factors on their overall performance. For instance, a bowler may strategically manage arousal levels, demonstrating a proactive approach to mitigate anxiety in high-pressure circumstances. Additionally, the integration of positive self-talk, visualization, and mental rehearsal techniques becomes instrumental in sustaining focus, motivation, and confidence throughout the game. As the bowler envisions making flawless deliveries, striking pins precisely, and reaffirming their abilities, these psychological tools contribute to enhanced mental preparation and overall performance. Attentional control emerges as another crucial skill, enabling the bowler to selectively focus on relevant cues while adeptly blocking out distractions. This skill empowers the bowler to remain fully present, resist the influence of background noise or crowds, and deliver each shot with unwavering dedication. Arousal regulation takes center stage, offering bowlers effective strategies to manage tension and anxiety levels during the game. Tactics such as arousal control, activation strategies, and relaxation approaches become integral, with bowlers employing coping mechanisms like progressive muscular relaxation, deep breathing, and mental plans to maintain composure under pressure. Goal-setting emerges as a guiding force, with bowlers setting both short- and long-term, realistic objectives to direct their performance and motivation. These goals serve as beacons of purpose and determination, ranging from achieving specific scores to refining accuracy or perfecting particular techniques. Preparation and planning form the foundation of a resilient challenge mindset, with bowlers meticulously following precise preparation procedures. This includes anticipating and planning for various circumstances, from changing lane conditions to unforeseen diversions, with contingency plans in place for swift adjustments. Moreover, bowlers assess the volatility, uncertainty, complexity, and ambiguity (VUCA) of the game, strategically developing plans to navigate such circumstances with adaptability and resilience. In essence, the psychological skill of a challenge mindset encompasses a holistic approach that integrates self-awareness, mental imagery, attentional control, arousal regulation, goal-setting, and meticulous preparation to elevate a bowler's mental fortitude and performance on the bowling alley.

Desirable Outcomes Of Challenge Mindset

Within the dynamic and multifaceted world of bowling, embodying a challenge mindset extends beyond a mere pursuit of athletic prowess, transcending the surface-level pursuit of victories and recognition. Rooted in intrinsic motivation, a bowler with this mindset discovers genuine passion, excitement, and fulfillment in the very act of engaging with the sport, fostering a sustained dedication over time. This intrinsic motivation becomes a potent driving force, with the bowler recognizing the inherent value in the relentless pursuit of bowling excellence, irrespective of external accolades such as victory or recognition. At the core of this mindset lies the cultivation of executive functioning abilities, providing the bowler with the nuanced capacity to regulate thoughts, mental images, and emotions throughout the entire duration of a game. Essential cognitive control techniques, positive self-talk, and imagery serve as indispensable tools, allowing the bowler to effectively manage and mitigate the negative thoughts or emotions that may arise from errors or setbacks during play, maintaining a clear and focused mentality that significantly enhances decision-making and skill execution.

Confidence becomes the hallmark of a bowler imbued with elevated self-efficacy, persisting steadfastly even in the face of mistakes or challenges. This unwavering confidence is reinforced through effective regaining techniques, including visualization, positive self-talk, and a focused concentration on personal strengths. The bowler, armed with robust coping and stress-reduction techniques, adeptly navigates the intricate web of pressure and distress, employing tactical approaches such as deep breathing, mindfulness, and relaxation to skillfully handle failures and unforeseen circumstances that may unfold during the course of the game. Beyond individual skills, the attainment of automaticity in executing a myriad of skills, processes, strategies, and routines characterizes a bowler who has honed techniques to the point of spontaneity, thereby elevating overall efficiency and effectiveness throughout the entirety of play. Additionally, the ability to recognize and value social support from coaches, teammates, and various stakeholders significantly contributes not only to the bowler's individual performance but also fosters a conducive environment of inspiration and appreciation within the broader bowling community.

Moreover, a bowler fortified with robust communication and emotional intelligence adeptly navigates relationships within and outside the bowling alley, fostering a positive team dynamic through effective emotional management and communication. The integration of political acumen, encapsulating the ability to comprehend and adeptly negotiate the intricate dynamics of the bowling environment, empowers the player to adapt and thrive in various circumstances. This adaptability is further leveraged through a profound understanding of the sport's laws, rules, and dynamics, allowing the player to optimize performance in collaborative synergy with equipment, surroundings, and the unique conditions of the bowling alley. In essence, the outcomes of a challenge mindset manifest in a holistic and expansive approach, seamlessly weaving together intrinsic motivation, emotional regulation, attentional focus, confidence, coping skills, automaticity, social support recognition, relationship management, and environmental adaptability. Collectively, these elements elevate the bowler's mental fortitude and performance to unprecedented heights within the dynamic tapestry of bowling.

Examples Desirable Outcomes of a Challenge Mindset in Bowling:

1. **Elevated Confidence and Steadfast Resilience:** A bowler with a challenge mindset showcases unwavering confidence and resilience, persisting even in the face of mistakes or challenges. This mental fortitude is reinforced through effective regaining techniques, such as visualization, positive self-talk, and focused concentration on personal strengths. The bowler adeptly navigates pressure and distress, employing tactics like deep breathing, mindfulness, and relaxation to skillfully handle failures and unforeseen circumstances during the game.

2. **Automaticity and Enhanced Efficiency:** Mastery of skills, processes, strategies, and routines to the point of spontaneity characterizes a bowler with a challenge mindset. This automaticity elevates overall efficiency and effectiveness throughout the entirety of play. The bowler seamlessly executes a myriad of actions, allowing for a heightened focus on critical aspects such as personal performance, lane circumstances, and strategic considerations.

3. **Positive Team Dynamics and Social Recognition:** Recognizing and valuing social support from coaches, teammates, and various stakeholders contributes significantly to the bowler's individual performance. Beyond personal achievements, this positive social dynamic fosters a conducive environment of inspiration and appreciation within the broader bowling community. Effective communication and emotional intelligence further enhance relationships within and outside the bowling alley, fostering a positive team dynamic.

Undesirable Outcome:

1. **Overwhelmed Performance Pressure:** In some instances, a bowler may succumb to the overwhelming pressure associated with a challenge mindset. Excessive focus on external recognition and victory may lead to heightened performance pressure, negatively impacting the bowler's mental well-being. The pursuit of excellence may become burdensome, overshadowing the intrinsic joy and passion for the sport. Coaches and mental health professionals may need to intervene to recalibrate the bowler's mindset for a healthier and more sustainable approach.

Create A Facilitative Environment

Coaches must pay attention to developing conditions where bowlers may thrive as individuals and performers, even if it may be easy to concentrate just on a player's capacity to handle pressure. The concepts of challenge and support are fundamental to creating high-performance environments. The challenge lies in everyone's having high standards for one another—bowlers, coaches, support staff, and leaders—which fosters responsibility and accountability. Support is the ability to assist others in growing into their unique selves, as well as to encourage learning and foster trust. The environments that leaders and coaches build can be divided into four groups based on the concepts of challenge and support: low-challenge low-support, high challenge-low support, low challenge-high support, and high challenge-high support. These four areas can be referred to as, in that order, comfortable, uncompromising, stagnating, and facilitative environments. Although the characteristics of each environment vary, a supportive environment must be established and kept up in order for resilience to be formed for long-term success and wellbeing.

Resilience Factors for Developing a Challenge Mindset	Examples for Bowlers	Psychological Impact on Bowler
Embrace setbacks as opportunities for growth	- Bouncing back quickly after a missed spare or a low-scoring frame and focusing on the next shot. - Using setbacks as motivation to practice and improve bowling skills. - Seeing losses or defeats as opportunities to learn from mistakes and come back stronger in the next game.	Cultivates mental resilience and fortitude, enabling the bowler to navigate setbacks with a positive mindset, fostering a continuous growth mentality.
Stay mentally strong under pressure	- Managing nerves and staying focused during high-stakes competitions, such as tournaments or league championships. - Practicing relaxation techniques, such as deep breathing or visualization, to stay calm and composed in pressure situations. - Maintaining a positive attitude and self-belief, even when facing challenging opponents or difficult lane conditions.	Enhances the bowler's mental strength, allowing him to perform optimally in high-pressure situations, promoting a composed demeanor, and reinforcing self-confidence in challenging circumstances.
Maintain a growth mindset even after failures	- Viewing failures or mistakes as a part of the learning process and not as a reflection of personal worth or ability. - Recognizing that failures provide opportunities to identify areas for improvement and make adjustments in bowling techniques or strategies. - Staying motivated and persistent in practicing and striving for improvement, despite setbacks or failures.	Fosters a resilient mindset that views failures as stepping stones for improvement, promoting adaptability, sustained motivation, and a commitment to continuous self-betterment.
Adapt to changing circumstances and conditions	- Adjusting bowling techniques, such as ball speed, angle, or rotation, based on changing lane conditions, oil patterns, or pin placements. - Adapting strategies and game plans during competitions, such as making timely adjustments in shot selection or targeting. - Being flexible and open to trying new approaches or techniques when facing different challenges or opponents.	Instills adaptability in the bowler, enabling him to dynamically respond to evolving game conditions, enhancing strategic versatility, and promoting a proactive approach to challenges.
Develop coping strategies for stress and adversity	- Having coping strategies in place, such as taking deep breaths, using positive self-talk, or visualizing success, to manage stress or adversity during competitions. - Seeking support from coaches, teammates, or mentors for guidance or advice when facing challenging situations. - Reflecting on past experiences of overcoming adversity and drawing strength from him during challenging times.	Equips the bowler with effective tools to manage stress, fostering emotional resilience, and encouraging a proactive approach to seek support, promoting mental well-being and enhanced performance.

Resilience Factors for Developing a Challenge Mindset	Examples for Bowlers	Psychological Impact on Bowler
Foster a resilient team culture	- Encouraging and supporting teammates to bounce back from setbacks or failures and maintain a positive mindset. - Promoting a culture of learning, improvement, and support within the team, where failures are seen as opportunities for growth. - Celebrating resilience and perseverance among team members and recognizing their efforts and progress.	Cultivates a team environment that emphasizes resilience, mutual support, and a positive outlook, contributing to the overall psychological well-being of the bowler within a cohesive and encouraging team culture.

Table 30 - The table outlines resilience factors for developing a challenge mindset in bowlers, providing specific examples and highlighting the psychological impact on the bowler, emphasizing growth-oriented responses to setbacks, mental strength under pressure, maintaining a growth mindset post-failures, adaptability to changing circumstances, coping strategies for stress, and fostering a resilient team culture.

Sport psychology practitioners can help coaches and support staff to provide an appropriate balance between challenge and support by engaging in pressure inurement training. Training for pressure augmentation entails progressively raising the pressure on bowlers through challenges and environment manipulation. It will be important for practitioners to keep a close eye on bowlers' psychological reactions to these treatments as well as other results (i.e., wellbeing and performance). Bowlers are prone to more crippling reactions and unfavorable results when pressure surpasses available resources; in such cases, more encouraging feedback and support should be given, along with the possibility of momentarily lowering the challenge. On the other hand, more developmental feedback and challenge should be applied when bowlers respond with greater facilitative answers and favorable outcomes, suggesting that they are/have responded to the pressure. The challenge-support matrix can be a helpful framework to audit the environment across teams/squads for requirements analysis reasons, according to the results of our impact study. Teams and squads have modified training in terms of communication limitations, auditory diversions, and competition simulation based on the concepts of pressure training. This has improved bowlers' awareness of their own behavior and reactions under pressure, developed and refined their personal resources (such as psychological techniques and problem-solving skills), encouraged team processes like enhancing team connectivity and fortifying leadership, and ultimately improved bowler and team performance under pressure. This has benefited coaches, support staff, and bowlers alike.

Strategic Plan for Pressure Inurement Training in Bowlers

Duration: 12 weeks (3 months)

Stage 1: Assessment and Goal Setting (1 week)

Step 1: Initial Assessment The first step involves a comprehensive evaluation of each bowler's current response to pressure scenarios. This assessment considers both psychological and performance factors, providing a holistic understanding of the individual's strengths and areas that require improvement.

Step 2: Goal Setting Collaborating with the athletes, specific objectives for pressure injury training are established based on the assessment findings. Clear and achievable goals focus on enhancing areas identified for improvement during the assessment.

Stage 2: Gradual Exposure to Pressure (4 weeks)

Step 3: Baseline Pressure Simulation Initiating the pressure inurement training with baseline pressure simulation activities, such as simulated competition scenarios, helps determine each player's initial reactions and behaviors under pressure.

Step 4: Monitoring and Evaluation A continuous monitoring and evaluation process observes how players react to pressure scenarios, assessing both their overall performance and psychological responses. Key markers of well-being are also tracked to ensure the safety and feasibility of the training.

Stage 3: Feedback and Adjustment (3 weeks)

Step 5: Debriefing and Feedback After each pressure simulation, debriefing sessions are conducted to provide players with insightful feedback on their performance and emotional reactions. This step helps identify areas for improvement and acknowledges instances where players handled pressure effectively.

Step 6: Individualized Support Tailored support, including motivational comments and specialized coping mechanisms, is offered to players facing challenges with excessive pressure. Those who respond well are rewarded with more challenging assignments and constructive criticism.

Stage 4: Progressive Challenge (2 weeks)

Step 7: Gradual Intensification The training incorporates elements like communication limitations and auditory distractions to progressively increase the difficulty of pressure scenarios.

Step 8: Adaptation Assessment Players' ability to adapt to heightened pressure is evaluated continuously. The difficulty level is adjusted based on their responses, aiming for an optimal balance between challenge and support.

Stage 5: Skill and Resource Development (1 week)

Step 9: Resource Enhancement Players are equipped with additional mental strategies and problem-solving abilities to enhance their capacity for pressure reduction.

Stage 6: Team Integration (1 week)

Step 10: Team Training The entire team is educated on pressure tolerance, fostering team behaviors such as improved communication and poised leadership.

Stage 7: Final Evaluation and Adjustment (1 week)

Step 11: Final Assessment The final assessment evaluates each player's response to pressure, comparing it with the initial evaluation. Player input is gathered to identify opportunities for performance enhancement and team chemistry improvement.

Step 12: Review and Recommendations The entire pressure inurement training process is examined, considering successful aspects and areas for improvement. Recommendations for ongoing pressure-reduction tactics are made.

Tactics for Pressure Inurement Training:

1. **Baseline Pressure Simulation:** *Introduce participants to progressively higher pressure levels by starting with scenarios that mimic common competition settings.*

2. **Monitoring and Evaluation:** *Continuously evaluate how players react to pressure using information on psychological reactions and performance outcomes.*

3. **Debriefing and Feedback:** *Provide insightful feedback after each pressure simulation, identifying opportunities for development and adaptation.*

4. **Individualized Support:** *Offer encouragement and coping mechanisms tailored to the specific requirements of players experiencing excessive pressure.*

5. **Gradual Intensification:** *Progressively add components like communication limitations and auditory distractions to raise the difficulty level.*

6. **Resource Enhancement:** *Arm players with more psychological strategies and problem-solving abilities to improve their capacity for handling pressure.*

7. **Team Training:** *Provide pressure tolerance training to the whole group to promote better teamwork and resilience.*

The Challenge-Support Matrix

The resilience development matrix, put forth by Fletcher and Sarkar in 2016, is a conceptual framework that shows how various combinations of support and difficulties can affect a person's capacity to build resilience. Each of the four quadrants in the matrix—High difficulty/High Support, High Challenge/Low Support, Low Challenge/High Support, and Low Challenge/Low Support—represents a distinct mix of difficulty and support levels. Let's go into more detail about each quadrant:

High Challenge/High Support: This quadrant denotes a circumstance in which a person has high levels of stressors or challenges, but he also gets high amounts of support from a variety of sources. In this case, the person is probably going to think that the difficulties are doable because there are sufficient support networks in place. Resilience can emerge when there is a high level of challenge and support together because the person is helped to overcome the difficulties and has access to resources to help them. Since it minimizes the chance of burnout or extreme stress while offering possibilities for learning and growth, this quadrant is said to be optimal for building resilience.

Hypothetical example

High Challenge/High Support:

Sarah bowls professionally and participates in national competitions. She has a lot of obstacles to overcome, such as fierce competition, stressful competitions, and rigorous training regimens. But Sarah also has a strong support network in place, which consists of her family, who cheer her on, a sports psychologist who assists with mental skill training, and a coach who offers advice and criticism. Because of the high challenge and great support, Sarah is able to grow resilient, learn from her experiences, and effectively manage her obstacles.

High Challenge/Low Support: *An individual in this quadrant is experiencing high levels of stressors or problems, but he is also receiving low amounts of support from a variety of sources. Because he don't have the tools or assistance he needs to deal with the pressures in this situation, the person could find it difficult to handle the difficulties. Increased stress, diminished coping skills, and diminished resilience may arise from this. High challenge and low support environments can negatively impact a person's mental and physical health, and they may call for interventions to offer enough resources and support to build resilience.*

Hypothetical example

High Challenge/Low Support:

John is an amateur bowler who just began participating in nearby competitions. He has several obstacles to overcome, such as poor self-confidence, technical issues with his bowling technique, and insufficient funds to hire a coach. Regretfully, John does not receive a lot of financial support, coaching, or mentoring. He consequently finds it difficult to handle the difficulties and feels overburdened. John's resilience is heightened by the absence of support, making it more difficult for him to recover from setbacks.

Low Challenge/High Support: *This quadrant depicts a scenario in which a person experiences few obstacles or pressures but a lot of assistance from a variety of sources. Even if there might not be many obstacles for the person in this situation, having strong support networks might help them become more resilient by creating a nurturing environment that encourages development. Low challenge circumstances cannot always result in the development of resilience, but strong support can foster an atmosphere that supports resilience-building elements including self-efficacy, social support, and coping mechanisms.*

Hypothetical example

Low Challenge/High Support:

Emma bowls at the junior level and participates in regional events. Compared to professional bowlers, she has comparatively less obstacles to overcome, yet she is well-supported. Emma has a supportive peer group of fellow bowlers, her parents provide steadfast support, and her coach conducts regular training sessions to help her develop her skills. Her perseverance and growth as a bowler are fostered by the high amount of support she receives, which also gives her drive and a confidence boost.

Low Challenge/Low Support: *Low levels of obstacles or stresses and low levels of assistance from several sources are represented by this quadrant for an individual. In this case, the person might not encounter many big obstacles, but he also might not have enough support networks, which can impede the growth of resilience. Lack of challenges and support can lead to a lack of learning, growth, and development chances, which can affect a person's capacity to develop resilience.*

Hypothetical example

Low Challenge/Low Support:

Michael bowls occasionally only for enjoyment as a recreational player. He doesn't have many difficulties when it comes to performance or competition, but he also doesn't have any coaching, mentoring, or social support. Michael doesn't really focus on competition or skill development while he bowls, and he doesn't have access to any helpful resources to help him get better. As a result of his lack of growth, development, or support, Michael's resilience as a bowler stays comparatively low..

The interplay between difficulties and support is crucial for the development of resilience, as the Challenge-Support Matrix emphasizes. It highlights that building resilience requires striking a balance between difficulties and assistance because both are essential to a person's capacity to manage stress and overcome hardship. In order to encourage the development of resilience, the matrix also emphasizes the necessity of interventions that offer sufficient support in high-challenge/low support scenarios and chances for growth and development in low-challenge/low-support situations.

Quadrant	Description	Psychological Impact	Advantages	Disadvantages	Rating (Out of 100%)
High Challenge/High Support	Pro Bowler A competes at the highest levels, facing challenging opponents and demanding tournaments with extensive support from coaches, teammates, and mental health professionals.	Thrives in a high-pressure environment, sees challenges as opportunities for growth, manages stress effectively.	Resilience, continuous improvement, minimized burnout risks, excels in adversity.	Potential for intense competition stress.	90
High Challenge/Low Support	Amateur Bowler B competes in demanding tournaments but lacks comprehensive support, resulting in increased stress and diminished resilience.	High stress levels, struggles with coping, diminished resilience.	Recognizing the need for intervention, identifies areas for support enhancement.	Risk of burnout, reduced capacity for learning and growth.	60
Low Challenge/High Support	Semi-Professional Bowler C experiences few obstacles but receives substantial assistance from various sources, fostering resilience through strong support networks.	Strong support networks provide a nurturing environment, encouraging development.	Support-driven resilience, positive environment, opportunities for personal growth.	Low challenge circumstances may not always result in resilience development.	75
Low Challenge/Low Support	Casual Bowler D faces minimal obstacles and experiences low levels of support, hindering the growth of resilience due to a lack of challenges and support networks.	Limited challenges and support may result in a lack of learning, growth, and development opportunities.	Potential for a comfortable but stagnant environment.	Lack of challenges and support can impede resilience development.	40

Table 31 - The rating is based on a subjective assessment considering the balance between challenges and support, psychological impact, and overall advantages and disadvantages in each quadrant.

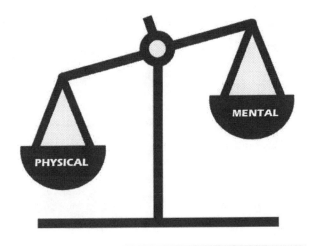

MINDSET & PHYSICAL DVELOPMNET IMBALANCE

In bowling, akin to any athletic pursuit, the delicate balance between mental and physical development is crucial for reaching the pinnacle of performance. Bowling is a unique sport, demanding a seamless fusion of physical prowess and mental acumen. Physical skills such as precise technique, coordination, and strength must harmonize with mental abilities like concentration, focus, and emotional control. A mismatch in the progression of these dimensions can have profound effects on a bowler's overall performance, leading to plateaus or inconsistencies in their game.

As bowlers navigate through different phases in their journey, they encounter a significant challenge that impedes progress on both the physical and mental fronts. In the early stages, bowlers focus on refining their mental and physical abilities. The subtle interplay between these aspects influences the trajectory of their overall game. With growing skill and experience, various factors come into play, influencing their holistic development. Athletes, admired across diverse sports like the iconic Muhammad Ali, often face analogous challenges that hinder their progress due to multifaceted circumstances.

A pivotal determinant shaping a bowler's trajectory lies in the physical environment where they train and compete. The conditions of the training ground and the presence of supportive structures play a vital role in determining a bowler's potential for growth. Suboptimal conditions or a lack of necessary support can significantly constrain their development, creating a situation where their inherent talent falls short of reaching full fruition, despite their unwavering determination. Over time, a bowler may encounter a juncture where physical progress plateaus, hindering the optimal acquisition of skills. This stagnation proves vexing for the bowler, who has invested considerable time and effort into refining their game.

In the face of tangible stagnation in physical abilities, doubt can gradually pervade a bowler's psyche, casting shadows on their self-belief and technical skills. This negative belief system, often termed "neutral triggers," manifests when limitations in the physical domain adversely reverberate into the mental game. The bowler's mental state, which is undeniably pivotal for optimal performance, becomes compromised, catalyzed by frustrations arising from seemingly insurmountable physical constraints. Extricating oneself from this complex and entangled cycle mandates a concerted effort to address both mental and physical dimensions in tandem.

Myth: Positive Mindset Emerges Spontaneously, Uninfluenced by Physical Plateaus

Reality: Dispelling the myth that a positive mindset emerges spontaneously, the journey reveals the intricate relationship between mental disposition and physical plateaus. The narrative emphasizes that maintaining a positive and resilient mindset is not automatic but requires intentional cultivation. Physical constraints can influence mindset, making it imperative for bowlers to consciously foster positivity to counteract potential negativity.

Myth: Mental Resilience Is Innate, Unaffected by Physical Challenges

Reality: Contrary to the myth that mental resilience is innate and impervious to physical obstacles, the narrative underscores the interconnected nature of mental and physical development. Stagnation in the physical realm can infiltrate a bowler's mental state, challenging their resilience. The reality is that mental fortitude requires deliberate attention and nurturing, especially when confronted with physical constraints.

To surmount this formidable hurdle, a bowler must confront not only the physical rigors of the game but also navigate the intricate nuances of mental fortitude. Concurrent attention to physical conditioning and skill refinement becomes imperative to transcend plateaus and propel towards new thresholds of performance. Simultaneously, the cultivation of a positive and resilient mindset proves indispensable to counteract any deleterious beliefs that may have taken root due to physical limitations. By holistically directing attention to both facets, the bowler endeavors to establish a harmonious synergy between their physical and mental prowess, ultimately unlocking the latent reservoirs of their true potential.

The journey of a bowler is inherently fraught with multifaceted challenges. The hurdles they confront, both physical and mental, possess the potential to significantly impede their development and stifle their growth. Grasping the intricate interplay between their mental and physical game is pivotal in managing these challenges with dexterity and poise. Through a concerted and simultaneous focus on both dimensions, coupled with the fostering of a positive mindset, the bowler aspires to break free from the pernicious cycle of neutral triggers, thus unlocking their full potential as a consummate bowler.

In essence, the bowler's journey serves as a microcosm of the broader human experience, where the synergy between the mind and body defines the path to excellence. The lessons learned on the bowling alley transcend the sport itself, offering insights into the delicate dance between perseverance and adaptability, between physical strength and mental resilience.

As bowlers strive for mastery, they echo the universal quest for balance in the face of challenges. It's a testament to the human spirit's ability to transcend obstacles, adapt to changing circumstances, and find equilibrium in the pursuit of excellence. The intricate interplay of physical and mental dimensions in bowling mirrors the intricate dance of life itself, where managing transitions and overcoming hurdles is not just a sporting endeavor but a profound journey of self-discovery and growth.

The journey of a bowler is a nuanced exploration of the symbiotic relationship between the physical and mental aspects of the game. From the early stages of skill refinement to the mature phases where external factors influence development, bowlers grapple with challenges that resonate beyond the bowling alley. The narrative of a bowler's quest for excellence encapsulates universal themes of resilience, determination, and the perpetual pursuit of balance. Through this holistic approach, bowlers endeavor to unlock their true potential, inspiring not only within the sporting arena but echoing the human spirit's capacity to triumph over adversity in the broader tapestry of life.

Examples

Example 1: A bowler whose journey reflects the delicate interplay between physical and mental development. In the early years, diligent work on refining technique and improving mental focus defined the approach. However, external factors such as suboptimal training conditions impeded growth. Despite undeniable talent, stagnation in physical progress cast shadows on mental resilience. Recognizing the need for a holistic approach, this bowler embarked on a dual journey—intensively addressing physical conditioning while cultivating a positive mindset. By managing the intricate dance between the mind and body, the aim is to break free from potential pitfalls and unlock full potential.

Example 2: Enter a bowler whose story echoes the broader human experience of managing challenges with perseverance and adaptability. In the initial stages, the focus was on refining both mental acuity and physical skills. However, as advancement occurred, a plateau in physical abilities led to doubts seeping into the psyche. These "neutral triggers" threatened to compromise the mental state, highlighting the symbiotic relationship between the mind and body. Determined to transcend these obstacles, a comprehensive approach was undertaken. Simultaneously addressing physical conditioning and fortifying mental resilience, the goal is to exemplify the universal quest for balance in the face of challenges and illuminate the broader path to excellence.

When Mental Game Is Better Than Physical Game

There are instances where a bowler's mental game takes center stage, overshadowing their physical skills. This phenomenon often arises during significant psychological transitions, leading to notable improvements in mental strength and resilience. Factors such as a nurturing environment and supportive parental or coaching guidance play a pivotal role in the development of this mental prowess.

Imagine a scenario where a young bowler grows up in a loving and supportive household. Recognizing their passion for bowling, the parents offer unwavering emotional and financial support. They understand the importance of nurturing their mental well-being, instilling a positive mindset and teaching the values of perseverance and resilience. This emotional backing forms a robust foundation for their mental game, enabling them to confront challenges with confidence and composure.

Simultaneously, the coach plays a crucial role in shaping their mental game, employing various techniques to enhance their psychological strength. Through visualization exercises, goal-setting strategies, and positive reinforcement, the coach helps establish a solid mental foundation. This training not only sharpens focus during crucial moments but also instills in them the ability to bounce back from setbacks, enhancing overall mental resilience.

Due to this nurturing environment and excellent coaching, the bowler's mental game flourishes, showcasing a profound understanding of the sport and remarkable psychological fortitude. The ability to remain calm under pressure and make strategic decisions sets them apart. This mental prowess extends beyond the bowling alley, positively impacting various aspects of their life. The resilience and problem-solving skills acquired through bowling become valuable assets in managing life's challenges.

However, despite their exceptional mental game, the bowler's physical skills do not progress at the same pace. The coaching they receive focuses more on basic techniques and overlooks the finer details required for technical excellence. While possessing natural talent and a deep understanding of the game, their physical game lacks the refinement and precision needed for the highest level of performance. This discrepancy underscores the importance of a balanced approach, where both mental and physical aspects receive equal attention for comprehensive skill development.

The bowler's story is not unique; bowlers worldwide face similar challenges. Possessing remarkable mental strength and wisdom, they may find their technical and physical skills not matching their mental prowess. This imbalance can be frustrating, excelling mentally while struggling to execute shots with precision consistently. The gap between mental and physical abilities may lead to disappointment and hinder overall performance.

To address this issue, bowlers need to recognize the importance of bridging the gap between their mental and physical game. While their mental game may be solid, prioritizing technical training and physical conditioning is essential for overall performance enhancement. Seeking coaches who can provide guidance in refining techniques becomes instrumental in achieving this balance. Bowlers can also benefit from incorporating mental strategies into their physical training routines, utilizing visualization techniques, positive self-talk, and mental rehearsal to enhance focus, confidence, and concentration during practice and competition. This integration of mental and physical training ensures a holistic approach to their development.

The separation between a bowler's mental and physical game can create imbalances that hinder progress. While excelling mentally due to nurturing environments and supportive coaching, their technical and physical skills may not reach the same level. Recognizing the importance of bridging this gap and incorporating both mental and physical training strategies is crucial for these bowlers to maximize their potential. With a balanced approach, they can unleash their full capabilities and achieve success in their bowling journey, both on the lanes and in life beyond.

Scenarios - Mental Game Leading Over Physical Game:

Scenario 1: Natural Mental Toughness

Early Stage: Starting bowling at 14, the bowler exhibits natural mental toughness, with a focus on technical training taking a secondary role.

Transition: As competitions intensify, the bowler's mental strength becomes the asset, allowing for consistent success despite occasional physical limitations.

Positive Impact:

1. The early development of natural mental toughness provides a solid foundation for handling high-pressure situations.
2. Consistent success boosts confidence, fostering a positive mindset that contributes to long-term resilience.
3. Enhanced overall satisfaction with the bowling journey, as mental prowess compensates for occasional physical limitations.

Negative Impact:

1. Over-reliance on mental toughness might lead to neglecting the refinement of technical skills.
2. Lack of focus on technical training could result in a plateau in overall performance.
3. The bowler may struggle in situations where mental resilience alone cannot compensate for technical shortcomings.

Scenario 2: Early Mental Conditioning

Early Stage: From a young age, rigorous mental conditioning prioritizes focus, emotional control, and resilience over technical skills.

Transition: Excelling mentally, challenges emerge when the physical game lacks precision and accuracy.

Positive Impact:

1. Rigorous mental conditioning builds a strong mental foundation, contributing to a high level of focus and emotional control.
2. Managing physical limitations with ease showcases the effectiveness of early mental training.
3. Confidence and passion for the sport remain intact, contributing to a positive and resilient approach to challenges.

Negative Impact:

1. Overemphasis on mental conditioning may lead to neglect of essential technical aspects.
2. Challenges in precision and accuracy may hinder the bowler's ability to adapt to varying conditions.
3. Occasional technical shortcomings might become more pronounced, affecting overall performance.

Scenario 3: Resilience in Adversity

Early Stage: Early training focuses on building mental resilience, learning to cope with setbacks while gradually refining technical skills.

Transition: Excelling mentally, occasional technical challenges are met with composure and a positive mindset.

Positive Impact:

1. Early focus on building mental resilience prepares the bowler to cope effectively with setbacks.
2. Excelling mentally contributes to composure and a positive mindset, enhancing overall enjoyment.

3. The ability to maintain satisfaction despite physical limitations underscores the value of mental resilience.

Negative Impact:

1. Overreliance on mental resilience may mask the need for continuous technical improvement.
2. Consistent enjoyment and satisfaction might be compromised when facing persistent technical challenges.
3. Long-term success could be hindered if technical skills are not given sufficient attention.

Scenario 4: Mastering the Mental Chess

Early Stage: Starting at 10, engagement in mental chess exercises emphasizes strategic thinking, focus, and decision-making prowess over technical skills.

Transition: Excelling mentally, hurdles arise in executing technically perfect shots consistently.

Positive Impact:

1. Engaging in mental chess exercises from a young age sharpens strategic thinking and decision-making prowess.
2. Despite occasional physical limitations, mental mastery allows effective strategizing, resulting in a high level of satisfaction.
3. The ability to overcome challenges in executing technically perfect shots showcases the power of mental strategies.

Negative Impact:

1. Excelling in mental mastery might lead to underestimating the importance of precise technical execution.
2. Inconsistencies in executing technically perfect shots may create frustration and hinder overall satisfaction.
3. The bowler might face challenges in translating mental strategies into consistent physical performance.

Scenario 5: Emotional Intelligence Triumphs

Early Stage: With a background in psychology, prioritizing emotional intelligence and mental well-being becomes the focus, with technical skills developed as secondary.

Transition: Excelling emotionally, challenges surface in maintaining technical precision under varying conditions.

Positive Impact:

1. Prioritizing emotional intelligence fosters a well-balanced and fulfilling bowling journey.
2. Excelling emotionally aids in overcoming physical limitations, ensuring consistent success.
3. The holistic approach enhances overall well-being, positively impacting various aspects of life beyond the bowling alley.

Negative Impact:

1. Relying heavily on emotional intelligence may lead to overlooking the importance of technical precision.
2. Challenges in maintaining technical precision could result in performance inconsistencies.
3. While emotional intelligence aids in overcoming obstacles, neglecting technical skills may limit overall success.

In the case of this bowler, the potential negative impacts that may arise from the plateau in his physical game and the widening gap between his mental expectations and physical reality:

Causes	Neurological Brain Asset	Psychological Impact
Frustration due to stagnant performance despite high mental standards	Neurological stress response, impaired memory consolidation	Decreased confidence, increased frustration, negative self-talk
Demotivation stemming from a lack of visible progress in skills	Neurotransmitter imbalances, reduced dopamine release	Lack of motivation, decreased enjoyment, potential burnout

Causes	Neurological Brain Asset	Psychological Impact
Strained relationships with family and friends due to disappointment	Increased cortisol levels, compromised emotional regulation	Social isolation, strained interpersonal relationships, heightened stress
Increased performance anxiety as expectations exceed physical capabilities	Heightened cortisol and adrenaline release, impaired neural communication	Performance anxiety, fear of failure, decreased self-efficacy
Negative impact on overall well-being and life satisfaction	Disruption of neurochemical balance, compromised mental health	Decreased life satisfaction, overall dissatisfaction, potential mental health issues
Tension and conflict with the coach as expectations are not met	Increased stress hormone levels, disrupted trust-related brain circuits	Strained coach-athlete relationship, heightened stress, decreased communication
Distorted self-perception and questioning of one's abilities	Altered neural pathways, negative cognitive biases	Negative self-image, self-doubt, distorted self-perception
Impact on other aspects of life as disappointment spills over	Disrupted emotional regulation, increased emotional contagion	Decreased performance in other areas of life, spill-over effects on relationships
Loss of passion and enthusiasm for the sport	Reduced dopamine release, decreased neural reward response	Loss of interest, diminished passion, potential withdrawal
Dissatisfaction with the overall bowling journey	Altered neurotransmitter levels, compromised reward circuitry	Decreased satisfaction, feelings of unfulfillment, potential burnout
Decreased motivation to continue training and competing	Diminished dopamine release, decreased neural reward response	Reduced motivation, lack of drive, potential withdrawal
Escalation of stress, anxiety, and potential depression	Dysregulation of stress-related neural circuits, altered neurotransmitter levels	Increased stress, heightened anxiety, potential development of depression
Potential withdrawal from the sport altogether	Disrupted neural pathways related to motivation and reward	Complete disengagement, loss of identity, potential negative impact on mental health
Impact on the bowler's identity and self-worth	Altered neural circuits related to self-concept, compromised self-esteem	Identity crisis, diminished self-worth, potential mental health issues

Table 32 - In such a scenario, it becomes essential for the bowler to seek a balanced approach that addresses both the mental and physical aspects of the game. Recognizing the need for technical training and refining physical skills is crucial, along with integrating mental strategies to enhance overall performance. Seeking support from coaches, mentors, and mental health professionals can help the bowler navigate these challenges and work towards a more harmonious development in both aspects of the game.

When Physical Game Is Better Than Mental Game

There are instances in the world of athletics where a player's physical prowess can outshine their mental acuity, emphasizing the delicate interplay between these two crucial aspects. To dig into this dynamic, let's explore the journey of a bowler who, unfortunately, found themselves lacking proper coaching and receiving subpar instruction throughout their formative years in the sport. This absence of adequate guidance resulted in a prolonged period of average performance, lasting nearly a decade from the age of 10 until their early twenties.

Conditioned by lackluster coaching, this bowler began to believe that their current skill level was the pinnacle of their potential, inadvertently accepting mediocrity as their norm. This self-limiting acceptance created a mindset where improvement became an alien concept, and the bowler settled comfortably into their perceived limitations, hindering any aspirations for growth. However, a pivotal turning point occurred when the bowler found themselves under the mentorship of a quality coach genuinely invested in their development.

With access to intensive training and a coach prioritizing skill acquisition, the bowler's physical game witnessed a remarkable transformation. Their technique became refined, and their accuracy soared, achieving near-perfect precision in their shots. Despite these significant physical advancements, the bowler's mental game struggled to keep pace. Years of believing in their limitations had taken a toll on their confidence and mental resilience. While their physical skills now ranked among the best, their mental game lagged behind.

The transformation in their mindset was a slow and gradual process, showcasing the intricate dance between the physical and mental dimensions in bowling. This example underscores the paramount importance of the mental aspect in bowling. Even with exceptional technical and physical skills, a bowler's inability to handle pressure, make strategic decisions, and maintain a winning mentality can profoundly impact their overall performance. This mental imbalance may manifest in missed shots, poor decision-making, and a lack of confidence during critical moments.

In essence, the bowler, despite possessing top-notch technical and physical capabilities, falls short in the mental game, lacking the mindset of a consistent champion. To address this challenge, the bowler must recognize the imperative of developing their mental game alongside improving their physical skills. Collaborating with a sports psychologist or mental skills coach proves highly beneficial in building mental resilience, confidence, and a winning mentality.

Techniques such as visualization, positive self-talk, goal-setting, and mindfulness can aid the bowler in overcoming mental obstacles and consistently performing at their best. Crucially, the bowler should surround themselves with a supportive network, including coaches, teammates, and family members who comprehend the significance of mental training. Establishing a positive and encouraging environment contributes to the bowler's mental growth and nurtures a winning mindset.

The example of a bowler whose physical game surpasses their mental game illuminates the importance of finding a delicate balance between these two aspects. While technical and physical skills are undeniably crucial for success in bowling, a robust and resilient mental game is equally indispensable. Recognizing the need for mental training, seeking guidance from sports psychologists, and cultivating a supportive environment are pivotal steps in bridging the gap between a bowler's physical and mental abilities. By integrating mental strategies into their training routine, bowlers can enhance their overall performance and unlock their full potential as champions in the sport of bowling.

Myth: Physical Skills Guarantee Mental Mastery

Reality: Dispelling the myth that exceptional physical skills automatically translate into mental mastery, the narrative highlights a bowler's journey where prowess in technique and precision soared while the mental game lagged behind. The reality underscores that despite achieving top-notch physical capabilities, the bowler struggled with confidence and resilience. The narrative serves as a reminder that mental prowess is a distinct facet, requiring intentional cultivation alongside physical development.

Myth: Acceptance of Mediocrity Is Irreversible

Reality: Challenging the myth that acceptance of mediocrity is an irreversible state, the narrative explores a bowler's transformation from a self-limiting mindset to one of growth. The reality reveals that under the guidance of a quality coach, the bowler broke free from the shackles of self-imposed limitations, emphasizing the potential for change and improvement. The narrative encourages recognition that mental shifts are achievable, contributing to overall development.

More Examples

Example 1: Consider a bowler managing a challenging journey where his physical prowess overshadows his mental acuity. Despite a decade of average performance due to inadequate coaching, a pivotal moment arrived under the guidance of a dedicated coach. The coach's focus on intensive training and skill acquisition led to a remarkable transformation in the bowler's physical game, achieving precision in shots. However, his mental game lagged due to entrenched self-limiting beliefs. This underscores the paramount importance of recognizing and developing the mental game alongside physical skills. Bowlers are encouraged to collaborate with sports psychologists, adopt techniques like visualization, and foster a supportive environment for optimal performance.

Example 2: Imagine a journey where a bowler's physical prowess outshines his mental acuity. Hindered by inadequate coaching and subpar instruction, a transformative moment occurred when a dedicated coach prioritized skill acquisition. Despite significant physical advancements, the mental game struggled to keep pace due to years of self-limiting beliefs. This example highlights the crucial interplay between physical and mental dimensions in bowling, emphasizing the importance of recognizing and developing the mental game alongside technical skills. Bowlers are urged to seek guidance from sports psychologists and cultivate a supportive environment for consistent champion-like performance.

Scenarios - Physical Game Leading Over Mental Game:

Scenario 1: The Overlooked Technique

Early Stage: Starting bowling at 12, intense focus on physical training becomes the hallmark of the journey. Technique and strength are honed meticulously, overshadowing attention to mental aspects like focus and emotional control.

Transition: As progression occurs, physical skills thrive, but a noticeable gap emerges in mental preparation, particularly evident during high-pressure situations.

Positive Impact:

1. Intense focus on physical training leads to the mastery of techniques and strength.
2. Meticulous improving of physical skills contributes to impressive early success.

Negative Impact:

1. Neglecting mental aspects like focus and emotional control creates a vulnerability during high-pressure situations.
2. Performance inconsistencies due to mental lapses lead to frustration and disappointment.

Scenario 2: The Technical Prodigy

Early Stage: A bowling prodigy, mastering technical aspects swiftly, neglects mental training during formative years, where flawless execution takes precedence.

Transition: Despite consistent strikes, challenges surface in maintaining concentration and adapting to varying lane conditions.

Positive Impact:

1. Swift mastery of technical aspects establishes the bowler as a prodigy.
2. Flawless execution leads to early acclaim and recognition.

Negative Impact:

1. Neglecting mental training results in challenges maintaining concentration and adapting to different conditions.
2. Increased anxiety and difficulty recovering from missed shots affect overall satisfaction.

Scenario 3: Neglecting Emotional Resilience

Early Stage: Starting young, rigorous physical training neglects emotional and mental aspects, omitting coping strategies from the equation.

Transition: As competition intensifies, the lack of emotional resilience becomes apparent, affecting confidence and motivation.

Positive Impact:

1. Rigorous physical training contributes to early skill development and competitiveness.
2. Early exposure to competition builds resilience in facing challenges.

Negative Impact:

1. Lack of emotional resilience leads to burnout and diminished enjoyment.
2. Absence of coping strategies hampers effective navigation through setbacks.

Scenario 4: Skill Mastery, Mental Struggles

Early Stage: Early years focus on perfecting technical skills, neglecting mental aspects like visualization and goal-setting.

Transition: Excelling technically, challenges arise in maintaining focus and positive self-talk during competitions.

Positive Impact:

1. Early focus on skill mastery leads to impressive technical proficiency.
2. Achieving excellence in technical skills contributes to early success.

Negative Impact:

1. Neglecting mental aspects results in persistent self-doubt during competitions.
2. Impact on overall satisfaction and motivation due to ongoing mental struggles.

Scenario 5: The Intense Physical Regimen

Early Stage: Intense physical training excels in mastering techniques and strength, placing mental aspects like resilience and strategic thinking on the back burner.

Transition: Excelling physically, struggles surface in decision-making under pressure and maintaining emotional composure.

Positive Impact:

1. Intense physical training results in exceptional mastery of techniques and strength.
2. Achieving physical prowess leads to early recognition and competitive advantage.

Negative Impact:

1. Struggles in decision-making and maintaining emotional composure under pressure affect overall performance.
2. Heightened stress and anxiety become constant companions, impacting well-being and enjoyment of the sport.

Causes	Neurological Brain Asset	Psychological Impact
Physical Game Leading Over Mental Game	Increased physical stress, neural fatigue	Lack of mental clarity, impaired decision-making, heightened physical exhaustion
When Mental Game Lags Behind Physical New Level	Cognitive dissonance, increased cortisol levels	Reduced mental resilience, heightened stress, potential burnout
Frustration due to unmet mental expectations despite high physical performance	Neural imbalance, impaired emotional regulation	Frustration, negative emotional response, potential mental health issues
Demotivation stemming from neglecting mental progress despite visible physical skills	Decreased neurotransmitter release, compromised cognitive function	Lack of motivation, diminished mental engagement, potential loss of interest
Strained relationships with family and friends due to neglecting mental well-being	Impaired social cognition, increased emotional reactivity	Social isolation, strained interpersonal relationships, heightened stress
Increased performance anxiety as mental preparation falls short of physical capabilities	Dysregulated neural circuits, heightened cortisol release	Performance anxiety, fear of mental failure, decreased self-confidence
Negative impact on overall well-being and life satisfaction	Disruption of mental health-related neural pathways	Decreased life satisfaction, overall dissatisfaction, potential mental health issues
Tension and conflict with the coach as mental expectations are not met	Strained trust-related brain circuits, impaired communication	Strained coach-athlete relationship, heightened stress, decreased cooperation
Distorted self-perception and questioning of mental abilities despite physical prowess	Altered neural pathways, negative cognitive biases	Negative self-image, self-doubt, distorted self-perception
Impact on other aspects of life as mental neglect spills over	Disrupted emotional regulation, increased emotional contagion	Decreased performance in other areas of life, spill-over effects on relationships

Causes	Neurological Brain Asset	Psychological Impact
Loss of passion and enthusiasm for the sport due to mental neglect	Reduced dopamine release, decreased neural reward response	Loss of interest, diminished passion, potential withdrawal
Dissatisfaction with the overall bowling journey due to mental neglect	Altered neurotransmitter levels, compromised reward circuitry	Decreased satisfaction, feelings of unfulfillment, potential burnout
Decreased motivation to continue training and competing without mental engagement	Diminished dopamine release, decreased neural reward response	Reduced motivation, lack of drive, potential withdrawal
Escalation of stress, anxiety, and potential depression due to mental neglect	Dysregulation of stress-related neural circuits, altered neurotransmitter levels	Increased stress, heightened anxiety, potential development of depression
Potential withdrawal from the sport altogether due to neglecting mental well-being	Disrupted neural pathways related to motivation and reward	Complete disengagement, loss of identity, potential negative impact on mental health
Impact on the bowler's identity and self-worth due to mental neglect	Altered neural circuits related to self-concept, compromised self-esteem	Identity crisis, diminished self-worth, potential mental health issues

Table 33 - The table elucidates the intricate relationship between neurological brain assets and psychological impacts in bowling. It underscores how imbalances, neglect, or discrepancies between the physical and mental dimensions can lead to diverse consequences. From diminished mental clarity and strained relationships to potential burnout and withdrawal, these insights highlight the profound influence of neurological factors on the psychological well-being of bowlers. It serves as a comprehensive guide for recognizing and addressing issues to optimize both performance and mental health.

MOTIVATIONAL DIFFERENCES
BETWEEN BOWLERS

Players try to show off their abilities and skills through their performance. In bowling, motivation is impacted by several objectives and actions that people think would result in success. Success in bowling depends not only on one's own motivation but also on external elements like the coaching approach.

Bowlers' intrinsic goal orientations and their understanding of the overall goal structure—which encompasses the coach's influence over the bowling environment—have an impact on their motivation. The motivating environment that bowlers encounter is greatly influenced by the coach's leadership style. Bowlers' individual or team motivational patterns are determined by the interplay between their own traits (personality, goal orientations, and self-perceived skill) and how they perceive the coach's motivational atmosphere.

The Self Determination Theory states that coaches have a big influence on how the motivating climate develops. Coaches can utilize strategies such as autonomy support, constructive feedback, and mastery-oriented setting to cultivate intrinsic drive in bowlers. These techniques improve bowlers' performance and increase their level of enjoyment.

It is often known that instructors play a crucial part in the development of bowlers. The personality qualities, abilities, qualifications, and communication skills of coaches vary, and they can all have an impact on a bowler's motivation in different ways. Coaches' consistent orientations, prevailing motives, the particular situations in which they operate, and their assessment of the motivation of their bowlers all have an impact on their behavior.

In bowling, instructors can take many different shapes and have distinct histories and traits. Their leadership styles, motivating structures, ages, educational backgrounds, coaching experiences, and personality qualities are all different. The self-esteem and intrinsic drive of bowlers may be impacted by these variations in coaches. By influencing their leadership style, coaches' methods of motivating their bowlers have an indirect effect on their motivation. This may lead to various patterns of motivation among teammates, which will ultimately affect the bowlers' entire experience with their instructor.

Myth: "Autocratic Coaches Are Inherently Ineffective in Motivating Bowlers"

Reality: While autocratic coaching styles may differ from democratic styles, they are not inherently ineffective. Some bowlers may respond positively to a more directive approach, depending on their individual preferences and needs.

Myth: "Democratic Coaches Only Prioritize the Well-Being of Bowlers"

Reality: Democratic coaches can also prioritize task accomplishment and winning, but they do so while maintaining a supportive and inclusive coaching style. They strike a balance between bowlers' well-being and achieving team goals.

Myth: "Motivation in Bowling Is Solely Influenced by the Coach"

Reality: Motivation in bowling is influenced by a combination of factors, including the coach, the bowler's inherent characteristics, the team environment, and the overall goal structure. It is a complex interplay of multiple elements.

Varied coaches have varied communication and behavioral styles, which may have varying effects on the motivation of bowlers. In bowling, leadership is a dynamic interplay between the coach, the bowler, and several contextual elements. The way a coach interacts with bowlers and makes choices shapes their leadership style, which in turn affects how the motivational climate develops. A coach's communication style has a direct impact on the motivated environment they foster.

The social contacts of a coach involve multiple procedures, such as providing instruction, offering support, and incentivizing conduct. The goal of instructionalness is to improve bowlers' performance by means of intense training, strategies, role definition, skill instruction, and efficient coordination. Being supportive means giving bowlers emotional support, consideration, and motivation. Offering positive reinforcement to bowlers—such as compliments, acknowledgment, and material prizes—in order to spur them on to greater effort is known as rewarding behavior.

A smart and successful coach always puts the welfare of each individual bowler first. This entails developing a supportive team atmosphere and solidifying personal ties with the bowlers. Acknowledging and appreciating the bowlers' excellent deeds, efforts, progress, and performances is a crucial part of coaching.

A coach's decision-making process is primarily composed of two components: social and cognitive processes. Rational decision-making is a component of the cognitive process. It involves problem identification and definition, alternative route evaluation, and choice selection based on desired results. Conversely, the degree to which the coach permits bowlers to engage in decision-making is a component of the social process of decision-making. Because bowlers understand and interpret the coach's direct and indirect messages differently depending on their leadership style and communication style, these procedures can have various effects on bowlers' motivation.

Task-oriented and people-oriented are two major categories into which bowling coaching leadership styles can be divided. Coaching philosophies that are autocratic and democratic are frequently seen. A democratic coach is more likely to put the players' welfare ahead of job completion. They give the bowlers encouragement, direction, and positive reinforcement. Bowlers who use this method report feeling more competent, independent, satisfied, and confident in themselves. Democratic coaches encourage players to handle problems that come up during practice or competition, use a less directive approach to leadership, and involve bowlers in decision-making processes.

Democratic coaches also emphasize giving each bowler individualized attention and care. They deal with team disputes and help bowlers find solutions. These coaches are more interested in developing positive relationships with the bowlers than they are in winning or other results.

If the bowler is not successful, a democratic coach will speak with them to assess their performance and offer consolation. Bowlers view these coaches as mentors, friends, or even a source of support, which fosters strong interpersonal bonds.

Conversely, autocratic coaches put more emphasis on results and task completion than on people. They are less encouraging, less educational, less results-oriented, and less likely to offer rewards. Bowlers have little say in decision-making under the directive and authoritarian leadership style of these coaches. Autocratic coaches frequently operate without consulting others when making choices. They are less adaptable, creative, and eager to try out novel teaching or training techniques than democratic coaches.

Furthermore, traits like great self-confidence and resistance to criticism are exhibited by autocratic coaches. They use rigid methods, strong leadership, and the use of their position of power to demand respect and compliance in order to influence bowlers. They frequently penalize subpar work, failure, or what is thought to be insufficient effort, but they show preference for extremely talented bowlers who are given star treatment. Autocratic coaches usually reserve their willingness to provide support or help for more serious issues, including sickness or injury. Because they believe that less proficient bowlers are not as valuable to the team, they are less likely to devote time and resources to them.

Conversely, coaches of bowlers who exhibit good traits have a more expansive definition of success than just winning or losing. Their bowlers respect and trust them because of their personality. These instructors create an atmosphere where failures are viewed as challenges rather than failures by pushing bowlers to be self-determined rather than controlled. Bowlers who are passionate, self-assured, and driven from inside are developed by coaches who exhibit these attributes.

In addition, effective coaches are defined as pragmatic, dependable, and trustworthy people who accept accountability for their activities. They exhibit creativity and help bowlers develop constructive motivational habits. These tendencies are especially well-nourished by democratic coaching, which results in more flexible behaviors as well as increased dedication, sportsmanship, and accomplishment. This leadership style is not often prioritized in the typical Western sport culture, which emphasizes the necessity for coaching behavior modifications to support bowlers' good motivational results.

Two broad categories of coaches can be distinguished in the context of team sports: authoritarian coaches and democratic coaches. A high ego goal orientation and a combination of inner and extrinsic motivation are common traits of autocratic coaches. This entails feeling a great sense of pleasure in and delight from coaching, as well as high pressure, moderate exertion, and a high sense of competence. Democratic coaches, on the other hand, take a bowler-centered, autonomy-supportive stance. Task goal orientation and high levels of intrinsic motivation define their motivational system. They are very competent and put up a lot of effort, love coaching, and feel less stressed and under pressure.

Moreover, bowlers' motivating frameworks vary based on the coaching profiles they work with. Bowlers who receive coaching that is democratic and focused on the needs of the bowler are typically more internally motivated and think they are more capable. They place a higher priority on task-oriented objectives and see their teams' mastery-oriented motivational environment. On the other hand, bowlers who receive coaching from less democratic, encouraging, informative, and positive coaches are more likely to be driven by external factors and believe they are less skilled. They view the motivational environment in their teams as performance-oriented and give priority to ego-oriented goals.

Myth: "Bowlers Are Passive Recipients of Coaching Styles"

Reality: Bowlers play an active role in shaping their motivation. They respond differently to coaching styles based on their personalities, goals, and perceptions of the coaching environment.

Myth: "Democracy Is Always the Best Coaching Style"

Reality: The effectiveness of coaching styles depends on the individual needs and preferences of the bowlers. What works best for one bowler may not work for another. Flexibility in coaching styles is essential.

Myth: "Coaches Can't Change Their Coaching Styles"

Reality: Coaches can adapt and evolve their coaching styles based on their bowlers' needs and the evolving dynamics of the team. Effective coaches are willing to adjust their approach as necessary.

Myth: "Bowlers' Motivation Is Predetermined by Their Inherent Characteristics"

Reality: While inherent characteristics can influence motivation, coaching, team dynamics, and environmental factors also play significant roles in shaping bowlers' motivation. It is a dynamic process.

Example 1:

A coach who solely concentrates on winning and losing and continuously berates his bowlers for falling short of expectations fosters a performance-oriented, drive-based environment. Bowlers who are trained in such an environment typically have low self-esteem, a strong ego-goal orientation, and are extrinsically motivated. They may experience pressure, anxiety, and a fear of failing as a result. These bowlers may also find it difficult to bounce back from defeats and view them as failures rather than chances for improvement.

Example 2:

In contrast, a coach who adopts a bowler-centered approach, democracy, and support fosters a mastery-oriented motivating environment. Bowlers who are trained in such an environment typically have a strong sense of competence, are task-goal oriented, and are genuinely motivated. They may experience an increase in self-reliance and competence as well as a growth attitude in relation to their performance as a result. These bowlers are more likely to bounce back from defeats fast, see setbacks as opportunities rather than setbacks, and grow deeply devoted to the game.

According to the bowlers themselves, the teams of bowlers function in a distinct motivating environment that combines task-oriented and ego-oriented effects. These teams' coaches place a high value on task-oriented elements and give bowlers' skill and ability development top priority. They do, however, also exhibit mild ego-oriented tendencies, suggesting that they place considerable significance on their own coaching performance.

The bowlers' ratings indicate that coaches are generally regarded as helpful and open to providing constructive criticism. They do, however, come across as less encouraging and behave in a less democratic manner. This shows that even though the coaches put the bowlers' talent development first, it's possible that they don't always create a welcoming and encouraging team environment.

In their coaching responsibilities, the coaches themselves exhibit high levels of intrinsic drive. They put in a lot of work, feel confident in their talents, love coaching, and are under comparatively little pressure. They believe that mastery is the main focus of the motivational climate in their teams, with less emphasis on competition among coworkers and results. Additionally, the instructors saw themselves as being very encouraging, educational, and prepared to give their bowlers constructive criticism. Nonetheless, their views of themselves are consistent with the bowlers' average appraisals, suggesting a lessened propensity for democratic conduct.

Coach	Leadership Style	Goal Orientation	Intrinsic Motivation	Review Score (out of 10)
Coach A	Directive	Task-oriented	High	8
Coach B	Supportive	Task-oriented	Moderate	7
Coach C	Participative	Ego-oriented	Low	6
Coach D	Autocratic	Ego-oriented	Moderate	5
Coach E	Participative	Task-oriented	High	9

Coach	Leadership Style	Goal Orientation	Intrinsic Motivation	Review Score (out of 10)

The coaches in this case have been categorized into various groups according on their scores for intrinsic motivation, goal orientation, and leadership style. The bowlers' evaluation of the coach's performance is reflected in the review scores (out of 10).

Coach A, for example, has been categorized as having a directive leadership style. This indicates that he is typically very task-oriented and may give his bowlers specific instructions and expectations. In addition, the bowlers believe Coach A has a high degree of intrinsic motivation, which indicates that he take pleasure in teaching and is confident in his abilities. The bowlers appear to largely approve of Coach A's coaching style, based on the review score of 8.

Conversely, Coach C is categorized as having a low intrinsic motivation and participative leadership style, meaning that while he typically involve his bowlers in decision-making, he might not be as passionate or motivated about coaching. The review score of six indicates that the bowlers may be wary of Coach C's methods of instruction.

Table 34 - **Example of how a cluster analysis could be used to evaluate bowling coaches based on reviews from their bowlers:**

THE POWER OF PRE-FEELING
THE SHOT (FORESIGHT)

Prominent psychologists and philosophers have acknowledged the tremendous significance of intuition throughout history. It is regarded as one of the basic mental processes, along with sensing, thinking, and feeling. The capacity to understand something instinctively, outside of the five traditional senses and without conscious thought, is called intuition. Intuition, sometimes called the "sixth sense," has been linked to paranormal experiences and psi phenomena. But the importance of intuition has frequently been overlooked in the field of athletic psychology.

Perceiving extrasensory information through clairvoyance, telepathy, and foresight is called intuition. Information can be sent between minds via telepathy without using sensory channels. People with clairvoyance are able to perceive information from sources that are out of reach for their normal senses. Perceiving information about future occurrences that cannot be deduced through conventional means is the essence of foresight. Premonition, or the perception of approaching bad things, and presentiment, or the pre-feeling or sensing of the future, are two examples of variations on foresight.

Certain types of intuition, especially foresight, seem to be important in the world of sports. Pro sportsmen have provided testimonies indicating a strong correlation between precognitive experiences and outstanding outcomes. Professional bowlers, for instance, have admitted in private that they frequently have a strong premonition of winning an event before it really happens. In addition, there are bowlers who know in advance of a tournament that they are going to make an unlikely stroke.

Although the recall of these incidents might be impacted by the result or ascribed to confidence, conversations with bowlers have revealed that these forecasts frequently occur during times of poor performance and low self-esteem. Imagine a bowler who is having trouble in a tournament because of bad timing or a weak grip, and he is losing confidence. Even though the bowler consistently misses pockets during a game, he feels a strange feeling and imagines that the unlikely shot will land in the pocket before it does. This inner understanding acts as a compass, overcoming the situation as it is and offering a glimpse of what might happen in the future.

Sportsmen with intuitive abilities have a distinct advantage in the fiercely competitive world of sports. Developing and applying intuition has the power to transform decision-making, improve performance, and reveal unrealized potential. Even though intuition is still a strange and elusive part of human cognition, athletes hoping to accomplish new heights in their sport have exciting opportunities as intuition develops and is incorporated into training and performance techniques.

Athletes can make snap judgments on the field, court, or lane thanks to the useful tool of intuition. It transcends reason; athletes are able to see opportunities and take acts before they even happen. This natural sixth sense turns into a compass that helps athletes perform amazing feats and react quickly to changing circumstances.

Even though the workings of intuition are yet unknown, athletes can actively develop and use this very useful skill. Athletes can improve their performance by adopting and utilizing intuitive training strategies, which can help them hone their intuitive abilities. This entails listening to their inner voice, following their instincts, and growing a strong sense of trust in their intuitive assessments.

Athletes can greatly benefit from incorporating intuition into their sports training and performance techniques. Sports psychologists and coaches are starting to understand how intuition affects athletic performance and has a transforming effect. Athletes can improve their intuitive abilities, increase their situational awareness, and obtain a competitive edge by combining intuitive exercises, visualization techniques, and mindfulness activities.

Athletes who start the process of developing their intuition become more open to a world of more possibilities. Through the use of this sometimes disregarded facet of human cognitive abilities, athletes can achieve unprecedented feats, realize their complete potential, and exceed their own constraints. Incorporating intuition into sports training improves performance on the field while also fostering personal development, resilience, and the creation of a well-rounded athlete.

Myth: "Pre-Feeling Is Merely a Superstition"

Reality: Pre-feeling, the ability to sense future outcomes, is not superstition. It is a phenomenon that challenges our understanding of how individuals can anticipate events, independent of external cues or influences.

Myth: "Self-Talk Is a Simple Mental Exercise"

Reality: Self-talk is not a simple mental exercise. It serves as a multifaceted tool for bowlers, influencing their attention, emotions, and performance. It can be a strategic and powerful aspect of mental preparation.

Myth: "Foresight Is Unrelated to Emotions"

Reality: Foresight is closely linked to emotions, especially during situations of significance. Emotions play a vital role in the foresight phenomenon, and heightened emotional states can influence athletic performance.

Examples of Scenarios

Scenario 1: The Unlikely Strike

During a highly competitive championship, a seasoned bowler finds himself struggling with poor timing and a weakening grip, leading to a significant dip in confidence. Despite consistently missing pockets during the game, an uncanny feeling grips the bowler. In an unusual twist, a strong pre-feeling emerges, and the bowler envisions an unlikely shot landing perfectly in the pocket before it even happens. This inner foresight acts as a guiding compass, transcending the current challenging situation and offering a glimpse into a future success. The bowler, drawing upon his intuitive ability, takes the shot with an unexplainable confidence, defying the odds and securing a remarkable strike that turns the tide of the championship in his favor.

Scenario 2: The Precognitive Victory

In another championship setting, a professional bowler privately admits to experiencing frequent premonitions of winning an event before it unfolds. Despite the skepticism surrounding such claims, conversations with the bowler reveal that these precognitive experiences often occur during periods of poor performance and low self-esteem. Imagine a bowler facing difficulties in a tournament, battling with issues like bad timing and wavering confidence. Despite the challenges, an unshakable premonition of victory emerges, becoming a beacon of assurance. The bowler, guided by this intuitive insight, delivers a stellar performance that aligns with his foresight, ultimately clinching the championship and validating the power of intuitive premonitions.

Scenario 3: The Unexpected Stroke

In the midst of a highly competitive tournament, a bowler encounters an unlikely scenario. Despite being aware of his weak grip and struggling with bad timing, the bowler experiences an unusual sensation, anticipating an improbable stroke that defies conventional expectations. This unique foresight emerges during a phase of the game characterized by poor performance and diminished self-esteem. The bowler, embracing this inner knowing as a valuable compass, decides to take the shot that, by all conventional measures, seems improbable. The result astounds both competitors and spectators alike as the bowler's intuition guides the ball with precision, landing an unexpected and extraordinary stroke that becomes the highlight of the championship.

Scenario 4: The Strategic Adjustment

In the midst of a challenging championship, a bowler faces a sudden shift in lane conditions, presenting an unexpected obstacle. Struggling to adapt to the altered environment, the bowler experiences a moment of intuitive insight. Foresight guides the bowler to make a strategic adjustment in his approach, anticipating the nuances of the changed conditions. Trusting this intuitive guidance, the bowler modifies his ball speed, angle, and rotation. As a result, the bowler not only navigates the challenging conditions effectively but also capitalizes on the strategic adjustment to secure crucial strikes. This intuitive adaptation proves instrumental in overcoming the unforeseen challenge and elevating the bowler's performance.

Scenario 5: The Resilient Comeback

In a high-stakes championship, a bowler encounters a series of setbacks, including consecutive missed spares and a string of low-scoring frames. Amidst the pressure and adversity, the bowler experiences a powerful intuitive pre-feeling—a sense of resilience and a belief in a comeback. Harnessing this foresight, the bowler reframes setbacks as opportunities for growth, using each missed spare as motivation to improve his bowling skills. With an unwavering positive outlook, the bowler makes a resilient comeback, turning the tide of the game. The intuitive pre-feeling becomes a driving force behind each successful shot, ultimately leading to a remarkable recovery and a triumphant finish in the championship.

A surprising phenomenon known as "confidence shots" emerged somewhat unexpectedly in an intriguing observation on the confidence levels of elite bowlers when observing them at tournaments or in finals. These incidents demonstrated that elite bowlers have the remarkable capacity to anticipate the exact path of the ball before they even enter the lane. Among top bowlers, there is a common observation of a remarkable unconscious reactivity to information that beyond their normal senses. The idea of foresight goes against traditional ideas of causality and the mechanical viewpoints that dominate contemporary scientific conceptions of the best possible sports performance.

Foresight Experiences - Cases

Case 1 - The Impact of Visualizing the Shot: Harnessing the Power of Prospective Imagery

Prospective vision, a compelling phenomenon, is extremely important to bowlers. Bowlers must have a clear and vivid mental image of their shot before they perform it. Unlike memories, these visual images appear spontaneously as thoughts.

The bowlers' descriptions of their encounters with future visuals shed more light on this intriguing topic. They frequently have a clear vision of the shot before it occurs, can visually predict the ball's trajectory, have a distinct feeling accompanied by a visual image just prior to executing the shot, believe in a link between mental images and self-talk, and envision what needs to be done before it manifests, making it a reality.

This topic focuses on bowlers' amazing ability to visualize and anticipate their shots with remarkable accuracy and clarity. The appearance of potential images spontaneously adds a layer of intuition and insight to their gaming, giving them a strategic advantage on the lanes. Bowlers can use the power of visual foresight to improve their performance by improving this skill and better understanding its relationship to self-talk and mental preparation.

How it originated: In the case of bowlers harnessing the power of prospective imagery, the experience of visualizing the shot is an intricate interplay between their mental processes and the actual execution on the bowling lanes. From childhood, these bowlers exhibit a unique cognitive ability to spontaneously generate clear and vivid mental images of their shots, a phenomenon known as prospective vision. This ability, deeply ingrained in their cognitive processes, allows them to foresee and anticipate the trajectory of the ball before it even leaves their hand.

The roots of this foresight can be traced back to their formative years, where early experiences and exposures to the sport contribute to the development of their visualizing skills. Perhaps, in their childhood, these bowlers engaged in consistent and focused practice sessions, improving their skills while mentally picturing each shot. Over time, this practice cultivates an innate connection between their mental imagery and the physical execution of the shot.

Early positive reinforcement and successes on the lanes further reinforce the effectiveness of this prospective vision, creating a powerful mental association between the imagined shot and the actual performance.

Case 2 - Pre-Feeling: Sensing the Future

A fascinating case has arisen in which bowlers have an extraordinary capacity to predict the future. These intuitive sensations give them a strong pre-feeling about the outcome of a specific block of games before it happens. These pre-feelings are especially noteworthy because they cannot be linked to external stimuli or environmental effects. Instead, they correspond to the concept of foresight.

The bowlers' descriptions of their pre-game feelings provide more light on this phenomenon. They describe a strange sense preceding the event, a specific feeling and visualization of the shot prior to its execution, an inside sensation indicating an upcoming remarkable feat, and an unexplainable, one-of-a-kind feeling.

These reports highlight the extraordinary character of pre-feelings, which appear to be spontaneous and internal, and show a close link to the concept of foresight. This subject calls into question our knowledge of how individuals might predict future occurrences without relying on external clues, offering new possibilities for research in the field of sports psychology.

How it originated : In this unique case, bowlers display an extraordinary ability to predict the future, termed pre-feelings. This intuition, not linked to external factors, aligns with the concept of foresight. From childhood, these bowlers develop a heightened sense of anticipation, describing specific feelings and visualizations before executing shots. This internalized foresight challenges conventional understanding, suggesting a learned or innate ability to predict outcomes without external cues. The spontaneous and internal nature of pre-feelings prompts further exploration in sports psychology, offering new perspectives on human cognition and performance in sports.

Case 3 - Harnessing Self-Talk

The bowlers' own experiences demonstrate how effective self-talk is for helping them focus, control their emotions, and perform at their best. Every quotation highlights the influence of self-talk on the bowlers' mental processes in a different way.

Bowlers utilize self-talk to tell themselves that their shots will strike, to focus intently and mentally repeat important phrases like "Just make it," to create a mental association with their self-talk, and to constantly remind themselves of what has to be done in order to succeed.

The various ways in which bowlers use self-talk to talk to themselves illustrate the intricate relationship that exists between intuition, feelings, and self-talk when it comes to foresight. It seems that self-talk influences different facets of the athletes' performance, acting as a tool for both instruction and incentive. Gaining insight into these complex relationships can lead to improved performance and the attainment of amazing feats on the bowling alley.

How it originated : In this case, the bowlers' foresight is closely tied to their skillful use of self-talk—a psychological technique influencing their mental processes and performance. From childhood, a connection forms, shaping their ability to employ self-talk effectively.

Bowlers use self-talk to affirm successful shots, maintain focus, and repeat key phrases, building a mental association over time. These practices, likely rooted in childhood experiences, contribute to the gradual development of their foresight.

The intricate relationship between intuition, feelings, and self-talk emerges as a versatile tool, impacting various aspects of their performance. Understanding these connections offers insights for improved performance and achieving extraordinary feats on the bowling alley, underscoring the transformative role of effective self-talk.

Case 4- The Emotional Tapestry of Foresight

Situations of great importance that elicit strong emotional reactions are intimately linked to the phenomenon of foresight. The bowlers who were interviewed gave detailed accounts of their feelings during experiences with foresight. They have stated that having foresight frequently happens when they are frustrated, under a great deal of stress during contests, unhappy with how they performed, or when they get a strange feeling that comes on before the actual event.

These bowlers' moving stories highlight the complex relationship between emotions and intuition in the sporting world. Elevated emotions during foresight imply that emotional states are essential to the phenomenon and have a major impact on athletic performance.

How it originated : In this case, the bowlers' foresight is closely tied to emotionally charged situations, forming an "emotional tapestry" that influences their intuitive abilities. Detailed accounts reveal that foresight often occurs amid frustration, high stress, dissatisfaction with performance, or a pre-event peculiar feeling. These emotional experiences, present since childhood, play a significant role in the development of foresight. The stories highlight the intricate link between emotions and intuition in sports, emphasizing the pivotal impact of heightened emotional states on athletic performance. Understanding and managing this emotional dimension can enhance foresight and overall athletic achievement.

Case 5- Foresights in Pressure-Packed Situations

Foresight is a quality that typically appears in extremely stressful and pressure-filled situations, which are referred described as "critical moments." Interviewee bowlers who have experienced foresight have responded in a number of ways to these dramatic and crucial events. Bowlers realize, more than ever, how much their performance can ultimately affect the result of the game at these pivotal moments. These bowlers' reports reveal a close relationship between precognitive experiences and peak athletic performance, with foresight frequently serving as a prelude to spectacular displays of ability and performance.

Bowlers have shared fascinating details about their experiences with intuition at pivotal moments. They talk about having a vision when they need a safe shot, especially when they see shots that look unachievable and are inspired to take on the task. Additionally, they usually exhibit foresight when they have to make critical shots to keep up their score or when they feel under pressure to perform exceptionally well. It seems that while making a spectacular shot, having foresight becomes the only practical course of action.

How it originated : In this case, the origin of foresight in pressure-packed situations seems to be closely tied to the heightened awareness and significance that bowlers attribute to critical moments. From childhood, bowlers have learned to recognize the pivotal nature of certain game situations, where their performance can singularly influence the game's outcome.

As these bowlers grow and accumulate experiences, the connection between critical moments and the emergence of foresight becomes more pronounced. The necessity to deliver under pressure, whether to secure a crucial shot or maintain a competitive score, appears to be a catalyst for the development of foresight. The interviews suggest that the need for a strategic and successful performance in these moments triggers a heightened intuitive response.

The intricate relationship between foresight and pressure-packed situations suggests that over time, bowlers learn to associate specific circumstances with the emergence of their precognitive abilities. The experiences shared by the bowlers indicate a learned or innate response to pressure, where foresight becomes a practical and effective tool for managing critical moments and achieving exceptional athletic feats.

Together, these bowlers' stories offer strong proof of the important part that anticipation plays at crucial moments. Athletes are given the insight and intuition needed to produce spectacular shots by these unusual moments, which appear to cause precognitive experiences. Athletes can have a great advantage if they can comprehend and use the power of foresight at these crucial times, which will drive them toward success and allow them to reach their full potential in the heat of competition.

Case	Description	Example in Bowler During Competition	Psychological Effect	Outcome
Case 1 - The Impact of Visualizing the Shot: Harnessing the Power of Prospective Imagery	Bowlers visualize shots before executing them, anticipating ball trajectory and connecting mental images with self-talk.	Bowler envisions a strike, mentally sees the ball's path, and believes in the connection between visualization and execution.	Increased confidence, strategic advantage	Enhanced performance, improved accuracy.
Case 2 - Pre-Feeling: Sensing the Future	Bowlers possess an uncanny ability to sense future outcomes independently of external cues.	Bowler experiences a unique, internal sensation and visualization that precedes a remarkable achievement.	Heightened anticipation, unique feelings	Enhanced performance, anticipation of outcomes.
Case 3 - Harnessing Self-Talk	Bowlers use self-talk to direct attention, regulate emotions, and optimize performance.	Bowler uses self-talk to maintain focus and repeat key phrases like "Just make it."	Improved concentration, emotional regulation	Enhanced performance, better execution.
Case 4 - The Emotional Tapestry of Foresight	Foresight is closely linked to emotionally charged situations, affecting performance.	Foresight occurs when bowlers are frustrated, stressed, or dissatisfied with performance.	Intense emotional responses, heightened awareness	Influence on athletic performance, emotional impact.
Case 5 - Foresights in Pressure-Packed Situations	Foresight manifests during critical, pressure-filled moments, often leading to exceptional performances.	Bowler experiences foresight when faced with challenging shots or the need for extraordinary performance.	Precognition, rise to the challenge	Exceptional shots, improved scores.

Table 35 - This table explores cases illustrating how specific mental strategies enable bowlers to unlock their full potential during competition. From harnessing the power of visualization and pre-feeling to leveraging self-talk and navigating emotional foresight, each case provides a unique psychological approach. Bowlers benefit from increased confidence, improved concentration, and the ability to rise to the challenge, resulting in enhanced performance, better execution, and improved scores. These cases offer valuable insights into optimizing mental approaches for success in the competitive world of bowling.

Potential Foresight Profiles of Elite Bowlers

The comprehensive table below, "Potential Foresight Profiles of Elite Bowlers" was meticulously curated through an exhaustive research process. The researcher, in a dedicated effort to ensure accuracy, collaborated closely with neurological specialists to understand the cognitive aspects associated with foresight in sports. Extensive analysis involved watching numerous videos of elite bowlers in action, observing their behaviors, and decoding potential indicators of foresight. In-depth internet research further contributed to the extraction of valuable insights and existing studies in the field of sports psychology. Additionally, interviews with the elite bowlers themselves played a pivotal role in capturing firsthand experiences and perceptions. The mixture of these diverse sources aimed to present as much depiction accuracy as possible of the foresight phenomena exhibited by these exceptional bowlers.

Bowler	Foresight Type	Why	Proof
Mika Koivuniemi	Prospective Vision	Critical for clear shot visualization	Descriptions of having a clear vision of shots before execution
Walter Ray Williams Jr.	Pre-Feeling	Strong pre-feeling about game outcomes	Reports of strange sensations and visualizations before events
Jesper Svensson	Harnessing Self-Talk	Utilizes self-talk for focus and control	Quotes demonstrating the influence of self-talk on mental processes
Jason Belmonte	Emotional Tapestry of Foresight	Foresight linked to strong emotions	Detailed accounts of emotional states during foresight experiences
Dominic Barrett	Foresights in Pressure-Packed Situations	Exhibits foresight in critical moments	Reports of having visions during pressure situations

Bowler	Foresight Type	Why	Proof
Norm Duke	Prospective Vision	Clear mental image crucial for success	Descriptions of vivid mental images preceding shots
Paeng Nepomuceno	Pre-Feeling	Strong pre-feeling before block of games	Descriptions of specific feelings and visualizations before events
Pete Weber	Harnessing Self-Talk	Utilizes self-talk for motivation	Instances of self-talk influencing performance
Kelly Kulick	Emotional Tapestry of Foresight	Foresight triggered by emotional states	Detailed accounts of emotional reactions during foresight
Chris Barnes	Foresights in Pressure-Packed Situations	Exhibits foresight in critical moments	Reports of having visions during pressure situations
Liz Johnson	Prospective Vision	Clear mental image crucial for success	Descriptions of vivid mental images preceding shots
Osku Palermaa	Pre-Feeling	Strong pre-feeling about game outcomes	Reports of strange sensations and visualizations before events
Shannon O'Keefe	Harnessing Self-Talk	Utilizes self-talk for focus and control	Quotes demonstrating the influence of self-talk on mental processes
Marshall Holman	Emotional Tapestry of Foresight	Foresight linked to strong emotions	Detailed accounts of emotional states during foresight experiences
Kim Yeau Jin	Foresights in Pressure-Packed Situations	Exhibits foresight in critical moments	Reports of having visions during pressure situations
Carolyn Dorin-Ballard	Prospective Vision	Clear mental image crucial for success	Descriptions of vivid mental images preceding shots
Parker Bohn III	Pre-Feeling	Strong pre-feeling before block of games	Descriptions of specific feelings and visualizations before events
Clara Guerrero	Harnessing Self-Talk	Utilizes self-talk for motivation	Instances of self-talk influencing performance
Diandra Asbaty	Emotional Tapestry of Foresight	Foresight triggered by emotional states	Detailed accounts of emotional reactions during foresight
Kim Terrell-Kearney	Foresights in Pressure-Packed Situations	Exhibits foresight in critical moments	Reports of having visions during pressure situations
Brian Voss	Prospective Vision	Clear mental image crucial for success	Descriptions of vivid mental images preceding shots
Shalin Zulkifli	Harnessing Self-Talk	Utilizes self-talk for focus and control	Quotes demonstrating the influence of self-talk on mental processes
Tore Torgersen	Emotional Tapestry of Foresight	Foresight linked to strong emotions	Detailed accounts of emotional states during foresight experiences
Rafiq Ismail	Foresights in Pressure-Packed Situations	Exhibits foresight in critical moments	Reports of having visions during pressure situations
Amleto Monacelli	Prospective Vision	Clear mental image crucial for success	Descriptions of vivid mental images preceding shots
Wu Siu Hong	Pre-Feeling	Strong pre-feeling before block of games	Descriptions of specific feelings and visualizations before events
Marshall Kent	Harnessing Self-Talk	Utilizes self-talk for motivation	Instances of self-talk influencing performance
Kelly Kulick	Emotional Tapestry of Foresight	Foresight triggered by emotional states	Detailed accounts of emotional reactions during foresight

Bowler	Foresight Type	Why	Proof
Shogo Wada	Foresights in Pressure-Packed Situations	Exhibits foresight in critical moments	Reports of having visions during pressure situations
Jazreel Tan	Prospective Vision	Clear mental image crucial for success	Descriptions of vivid mental images preceding shots
Anthony Simonsen	Pre-Feeling	Strong pre-feeling about game outcomes	Reports of strange sensations and visualizations before events
Bill O'Neal	Harnessing Self-Talk	Utilizes self-talk for focus and control	Quotes demonstrating the influence of self-talk on mental processes
Tommy Jones	Emotional Tapestry of Foresight	Foresight linked to strong emotions	Detailed accounts of emotional states during foresight experiences
Ildemaro Ruiz	Foresights in Pressure-Packed Situations	Exhibits foresight in critical moments	Reports of having visions during pressure situations
Sean Rash	Prospective Vision	Clear mental image crucial for success	Descriptions of vivid mental images preceding shots

Table 36 - This table profiles prominent bowlers and their distinctive foresight types, elucidating the significance and impact of various mental strategies on their game. From prospective vision and pre-feeling to harnessing self-talk and navigating the emotional tapestry of foresight, each bowler's approach is explored. The proof includes firsthand accounts, quotes, and descriptions, providing insights into how these mental techniques contribute to their success. The table serves as a comprehensive showcase of the diverse ways in which foresight positively influences the performance and outcomes of accomplished bowlers.

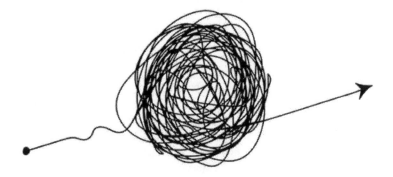

ANTICIPATION - THE SECRET OF CONTROLLING THE DIRECTIONAL MESS:

The Remarkable Skill Of Bowling

Anticipation is a fascinating quality in the thrilling sport of bowling that transcends mere physical skill. Bowlers can predict where the ball will go even before it leaves their palm thanks to this superpower-like capacity, which helps them achieve astonishing success rates.

It's comparable to what professional baseball player Theo Epstein found out when the conventional wisdom of "keep your eye on the ball" proved insufficient. The ball travels so quickly during a bowling game that it is difficult to observe with the unaided eye. Instead, adept bowlers watch the bowler's motions to predict the direction of the ball before it is launched.

The true secret to becoming a bowling star is anticipation. Pro bowlers may manipulate the direction of the ball with minute adjustments to their finger pressure. Their opponents are baffled by this talent and are unable to guess where the ball will end up.

However, this skill also involves cerebral agility; it's not simply about fast reflexes. Grandmasters of chess and bowlers both use their thoughts extensively. Not because they have superhuman memory, but rather because they can mentally arrange the pieces into meaningful groups that facilitate recall, these professionals can learn the layout of a chess board in a matter of seconds.

Pro bowlers are renowned for their exceptional ability to accurately foresee their shots; they can often predict the ball's trajectory before it leaves their hand. Years of practice, years of experience, and a thorough knowledge of the sport have all contributed to this extraordinary skill. These bowlers get important insights into their mental states and learn to control their emotions to prevent physical blunders during crucial situations by developing the ability to predict the result of their shots.

The ability to control emotions under duress is a crucial component of anticipatory skills. The bowler may feel a wave of uneasiness or worry as he pictures the approaching shot. However, he can stay focused and composed if he identifies these feelings and use useful coping mechanisms.

Chunking

In a similar vein, elite bowlers employ a method known as "chunking." Chunking, as used in bowling, is the mental process of organizing data or patterns into meaningful groups that help bowlers more accurately predict and anticipate future shots. Bowlers can absorb and simplify difficult knowledge using this cognitive talent, which helps them recall and use it during play.

Bowlers who chunk get a better awareness of the different aspects that might affect their strokes, including ball reaction, lane conditions, and their personal performance characteristics. Bowlers can more readily access and remember this information when needed, enabling them to make better educated decisions on the lanes, by arranging it into digestible portions. For example, a proficient bowler may mentally profile the present lane environment by piecing together certain lane conditions, such as oil pattern duration, volume, and breakdown. This enables players to change their shot before even starting the approach by foreseeing how the ball will behave.

Chunking is essential for deciphering the lane's body language, which includes pin carry and ball motion. Bowlers can modify their placement, speed, or release to get the desired pin action by identifying patterns in the way the pins respond to their shots and the movement of their bowling ball. To put it simply, chunking in bowling is the process of creating a mental database of observations, patterns, and experiences that bowlers can use to predict how their shots will turn out. It gives players the ability to take initiative during a game and make necessary modifications, which improves their capacity to predict the ball's future motions and produce the most efficient shots.

Training in this cognitive skill demands a distinct methodology. It won't be enough to just keep making the same motions in the bowling alley. Rather, the secret to anticipation is to learn to read the bowler's movements. Thus, keep in mind that successful bowlers rely on more than simply speed and repetitions the next time you watch them compete. They distinguish themselves as true masters of anticipation by predicting the ball's future trajectory in this mental game, which also involves perception and dance.

Anticipate The Error In Future

A bowler may make a number of mistakes or faults prior to throwing a shot, which could influence how the shot turns out. These errors may be caused by the bowler's lack of preparation, mental mood, or physical approach. Prior to a stroke being thrown, bowlers may commit the following typical errors:

Physical Errors During the Shot	Proactive Actions during Competitions (PRIOR THE SHOT)	Action Steps to Chunking the Error (AFTER THE SHOT)
1. Poor Ball Release	Take a deep breath, refocus on technique, and trust in the practice. Visualize a smooth release before stepping onto the approach.	1. Identify the specific aspects of ball release causing inconsistencies. 2. Break down the release into key components. 3. Develop mental cues or triggers for each component.
2. Misaligned Stance	Step back, reset, and realign the stance. Use pre-shot routines to ensure proper positioning before each shot.	1. Identify the key alignment checkpoints for the stance. 2. Create a mental checklist to ensure proper alignment.
3. Inconsistent Approach	Implement mental cues to maintain a consistent approach rhythm. Stay calm and composed to avoid rushing the approach.	1. Identify the phases of the approach (start, pushaway, steps). 2. Practice each phase separately, then link them together. 3. Create mental cues for a fluid approach.
4. Gripping the Ball Too Tightly	Shake out the tension in the hand and regrip the ball with a relaxed yet firm grip. Remind yourself to stay loose during the approach.	1. Be mindful of grip pressure during shots. 2. Practice releasing tension in the grip while maintaining control. 3. Develop a mental cue (e.g., "soft hands") to remind yourself to relax the grip.
5. Early or Late Timing	Use mental triggers to synchronize footwork and arm swing. Focus on the rhythm and timing of the approach.	1. Analyze the timing of your shots in various situations. 2. Identify the phases of the timing (backswing, release). 3. Practice each phase separately to achieve proper timing.
6. Overturning the Ball	Refocus on the target and visualize the desired ball path. Adjust the release if necessary to reduce excessive hook.	1. Study the ball rotation during shots. 2. Develop mental imagery of the desired ball motion. 3. Practice controlling the rotation to match the mental image.

Physical Errors During the Shot	Proactive Actions during Competitions (PRIOR THE SHOT)	Action Steps to Chunking the Error (AFTER THE SHOT)
7. Lack of Follow-Through	Concentrate on extending the arm fully and completing the follow-through after the release.	1. Pay attention to follow-through in practice. 2. Break down the follow-through into key checkpoints (release, balance). 3. Create a mental cue (e.g., "finish strong") for a complete follow-through.
8. Poor Balance at Release	Take a moment to stabilize and find your balance before starting the approach. Use balance drills during practice to improve stability.	1. Practice balance exercises and drills to improve stability. 2. Identify key moments of balance during the approach and release. 3. Develop mental cues for maintaining balance at those moments.
9. Drifting Off Target	Use visual markers on the lane to stay aligned with the target. Take a deep breath and recommit to hitting the mark.	1. Be aware of your target focus during shots. 2. Break down the target line into segments (arrows, breakpoint). 3. Use mental imagery to visualize hitting the target accurately.
10. Overthinking the Shot	Shift the focus to the process rather than the outcome. Trust in your training and let muscle memory guide the shot. Emphasize positive self-talk and confidence.	1. Recognize when you are overthinking or feeling stressed. 2. Develop a pre-shot routine to clear your mind and focus on the process. 3. Use specific cues or triggers to stay in the present moment.

Table 37 - This table highlights proactive actions and error chunking strategies to address physical errors during bowling shots. Bowlers can take steps before and after the shot to mitigate issues such as poor ball release, misaligned stance, inconsistent approach, gripping the ball too tightly, early or late timing, overturning the ball, lack of follow-through, poor balance at release, drifting off target, and overthinking the shot. Strategies include visualization, mental cues, pre-shot routines, and specific exercises to improve technique, maintain focus, and enhance overall performance. These techniques collectively contribute to refining the bowler's skills and optimizing their competitive experience.

Flow State (In & Out) Compared To Other Similar Sports

Reaching a state of flow in sports is frequently linked to peak performance, where players give their all, perform at their best, and have a sense of effortless control. Deep focus, a loss of self-awareness, and a fluid, nearly instinctive use of skills are traits of the flow state. While shooters, golfers, and bowlers can all feel flow, because of the special nature of bowling, bowlers may find it more difficult to stay in this condition during a game or match.

Myth: "Minor Errors Don't Affect Flow State in Bowling"

Reality: In bowling, even minor errors can disrupt a bowler's flow state, as the sport's outcome-focused nature can lead to self-consciousness and reduced immersion.

Myth: "Flow State Is Easier to Attain Over Time in Bowling"

Reality: Golfers and shooters may find it easier to enter the flow state over time due to the repetitive and consistent nature of their movements, while bowlers face the challenge of adapting to variable conditions.

Myth: "Muscle Memory Alone Leads to Flow State"

Reality: While muscle memory is essential, entering the flow state in bowling requires a focus on the process, mental adaptability, and embracing the sport's unique complexity.

Myth: "Achieving Flow State Is Impossible in Bowling"

Reality: Achieving the flow state in bowling is not impossible but may require a different approach and mindset due to the sport's inherent variability. Bowlers can increase their chances with the right mindset and preparation.

Because of the intricacy and unpredictability of the bowling environment, bowlers may lose their flow state more quickly than golfers or shooters. Every bowling shot requires a variety of modifications and potential outcomes, including body placement, ball selection, lane circumstances, and targeting. Bowling lanes may vary greatly from shot to shot, especially in a competitive environment, in contrast to shooting or golf, where the playing surface (shooting range or golf course) stays mostly constant.

The bowler's flow state may be disturbed by these frequent changes and variables, which increase the chance of errors or mistakes. An bad result might arise from a slight variation in approach, timing, or release, and this outcome-focused mentality can cause the bowler to lose focus on the current moment. The seamless and effortless execution of the flow state might be difficult to maintain when there is a sense of self-consciousness caused by the knowledge of possible mistakes.

In addition, bowling is more dependent on outside cues than shooting or golf. Bowlers must communicate with the crowd, opponents, and their teammates, which can cause distractions and make it harder for them to stay in the zone. Golfers and shooters, on the other hand, might perform more alone during their performance, which would minimize outside distractions.

One distinctive feature of bowling, though, is that players can return to their flow state in later frames or shots. Bowlers can utilize their prior successes or adjustments as reference points to recover focus and confidence because bowling games have an organized format. Bowlers may go back into the flow state and rediscover that feeling of effortless control by evaluating their performance, taking lessons from their errors, and quickly adapting.

The repetitive nature of the movements used by shooters and golfers may also contribute to their increased ease of entering the flow state over time. Shooting and golf both involve largely single motions that are repeated during a match or match. Both shooters and golfers regularly aim and fire their weapons, causing these actions to become very instinctive and imprinted in their bodies.

Players who shoot and golf are able to build a high degree of muscle memory and procedural expertise because of the repetition and simplicity of their movements. They can perform their talents with virtually easy precision thanks to this muscle memory, which increases the probability of them going into the flow state. Their minds can concentrate more on the process since the movements are constant, as opposed to constantly modifying their approach or adapting to changing conditions.

Bowling, on the other hand, requires a more varied and dynamic set of motions with many modifications for every shot. The bowler needs to adjust to the constantly shifting conditions of the lane, make snap judgments about which balls to hit in real time, and modify their approach and targeting depending on the results of prior shots. The unpredictable and intricate nature of these modifications may make it more difficult for the bowler to maintain a continuous flow state during the game.

It's important to understand that, because of the intrinsic variety of the sport, reaching the flow state in bowling is not impossible, but rather may call for a different strategy and frame of mind. Bowlers can still achieve a state of flow by maintaining process attention, drawing from their background and expertise, and approaching every shot as a fresh opportunity rather than thinking back on previous performances. Bowlers can improve their chances of reaching that elusive flow state and giving their best game by accepting the uniqueness of the sport and developing a more adaptable mindset.

Kawazoe's Journey To 2 Consecutive 300 Games On Television

Shota Kawazoe's remarkable achievement of scoring televised consecutive 300 games is a testament to his exceptional talent, mental fortitude, and an unwavering commitment to the sport of bowling. Let's dig into how he managed to accomplish this extraordinary feat.

To accomplish the remarkable feat of achieving two consecutive 300 games on television, Shota Kawazoe skillfully navigated a labyrinth of psychological challenges while maintaining a state of flow across all 24 frames. His success hinged on a profound ability to concentrate intensely, blocking out all distractions and remaining fully immersed in the present moment with unwavering focus. This flow state allowed him to synchronize his mind and body seamlessly, ensuring that every movement and decision felt instinctual and effortless.

Kawazoe's mental preparation was a critical element of his flow state. He engaged in extensive visualization and mental rehearsal, meticulously envisioning every aspect of his game. This not only instilled confidence but also helped him fine-tune his muscle memory, enabling him to regulate his muscle movements with precision and consistency.

Positive self-talk played a pivotal role in boosting his confidence and countering any self-doubt that may have arisen in the high-pressure environment. To manage the inevitable nerves and anxiety, he relied on relaxation techniques like deep breathing and mindfulness, ensuring that he maintained a calm and composed demeanor under the spotlight.

Amid mounting expectations from the audience and himself, Kawazoe shifted his focus to the process, rather than fixating on the outcome, to keep the pressure manageable. This mindset, combined with his flow state, allowed him to execute each shot with grace and poise.

As a seasoned bowler, he possessed the crucial skill of adaptability, swiftly adjusting his approach or ball selection in response to changing lane conditions while staying in his flow state. Embracing pressure as a challenge, he drew motivation and energy from it, rather than allowing it to overwhelm him.

Staying grounded and humble was key, despite the excitement of the moment. Kawazoe also benefited from a robust support system, including coaches, teammates, and family, who provided emotional support and guidance throughout the games.

Practice Vs Competition – Flow State

Bowlers frequently concentrate on improving their technical abilities and experimenting with various tactics during practice. There's usually less pressure to constantly perform at a high level and a more laid-back atmosphere. Bowlers might therefore have fewer psychological issues during practice sessions. When they are not afraid of facing instant repercussions, they can be more willing to try new things, make changes, and learn from their failures.

Nevertheless, the dynamic shifts dramatically when moving from cooperation to rivalry. Higher stakes, the urge to succeed, and the presence of spectators can all contribute to stress and anxiety. Bowlers who are more emotionally committed to the result face psychological obstacles that may not be present during practice. These worries can include self-doubt, performance anxiety, fear of failing, and trouble focusing in the face of distractions. Their mental stability may be affected, which could result in less-than-ideal performance, by the dread of making a mistake in front of others, or of falling short of expectations.

Furthermore, emotions like anticipation, trepidation, and excitement can be evoked in a competitive environment. These feelings have both positive and negative effects. While certain bowlers perform best under duress, others may find it difficult to control their emotions, which can cause inconsistent results.

Despite the several conditions covered above, regaining the flow state during competition calls for a combination of mental tactics and preparation. First and foremost, bowlers should establish a pre-shot routine that incorporates stress-reduction and anxiety-management tactics. They can maintain composure and concentration during every shot with the aid of breathing techniques and positive imagery. Prioritizing process-oriented goals over outcome-based ones can help move the emphasis from outside pressure to successful shot execution.

Bowlers should practice mindfulness to remain totally present and involved at the moment in order to regain the flow state. To swiftly regain focus following distractions or setbacks, this may entail the use of mental cues or trigger words. When things go tough, they must continue to have faith in their skills and preparedness and keep in mind their prior triumphs. They can feel more secure and perform at their best if you have faith in their instruction and tools.

Bowlers can work with mental coaches to build specific mental abilities and coping methods, or they can participate in sports psychology workshops to enhance their mental game during competition. These experts can help identify specific psychological issues and create solutions that are specifically designed to address them.

Aspect	Practice	Competition
Focus	Improving technical abilities, experimenting with tactics	Higher stakes, urge to succeed, presence of spectators
Atmosphere	Laid-back, less pressure	Intense, pressure to perform at a high level
Psychological Issues	Fewer psychological issues	Potential for self-doubt, performance anxiety, fear of failure, trouble focusing in the face of distractions
Risk-Taking	More willingness to try new things, make changes, learn from failures	Fear of making mistakes in front of others, falling short of expectations

Aspect	Practice	Competition
Emotional Response	Typically lower emotional intensity	Emotions such as anticipation, trepidation, excitement; varying effects on performance
Flow State Relevance	Easier to achieve flow state due to relaxed environment	Requires mental tactics, preparation, and mindfulness to regain flow state
Preparation Strategies	Focus on technical skills, experimentation	Establishing a pre-shot routine, stress-reduction, anxiety-management tactics, mindfulness, mental cues, positive imagery
Outcome Orientation	Emphasis on learning and improvement	Shift from outside pressure to successful shot execution, prioritizing process-oriented goals
Mental Stability	Typically less affected	May be impacted by fear of making mistakes or falling short of expectations
Faith in Skills and Preparedness	Generally high confidence in skills and readiness	Critical to maintain faith in skills, recall prior triumphs, and trust in training and tools
Performance Impact	Typically more consistent	Potential for inconsistent results due to emotional fluctuations and external pressures
Learning Environment	Primarily focused on skill acquisition and improvement	Balancing skill development with managing psychological challenges in a competitive setting
Post-Event Reflection and Improvement	Opportunities for analysis, adjustment, and learning	Post-competition reflection, identifying specific psychological issues, and working on targeted mental skills for improvement

Table 38 - This table succinctly differentiates practice and competition for bowlers, covering focus, atmosphere, psychological challenges, risk-taking, emotional responses, flow state relevance, preparation, outcome orientation, mental stability, faith in skills, performance impact, learning environment, and post-event reflection. Practice prioritizes technical improvement in a relaxed setting, while competition introduces higher stakes and psychological challenges, requiring the development of mental skills for consistent performance and targeted improvement post-events.

Practice Vs Competition - Muscle Movements Regulations

For a bowler to avoid mistakes or poor shots during competition, controlling muscle movements is essential. Achieving a stable and productive physical game requires striking the correct balance between tense and relaxed muscles. Bowlers need to concentrate on three main areas to do this: mental calmness, muscle memory, and bodily awareness.

Being conscious of one's body and its movements is referred to as body awareness. Bowlers should pay special attention to how their bodies feel throughout various shots during practice and training. They are able to determine the ideal level of muscular tension by developing an acute sense of proprioception. They can spot any muscle imbalances or excessive stress that can cause them to make bad shots during competition thanks to this knowledge.

Another important component in regulating muscle action is muscle memory. Bowlers can acquire muscle memory through regular practice and repetition, which makes their actions automatic when competing. Bowlers who have developed strong muscle memory are less likely to overthink or become overly aware of their motions in high-stress scenarios. To prevent creating negative habits, bowlers must make sure that their muscle memory is founded on proper technique.

Maintaining mental calmness is necessary to control physical tension during competition. While pressure and nerves are normal during competition, bowlers' ability to regulate their muscles can be greatly affected by how they handle these feelings. Effective muscle tension regulation and composure can be achieved by bowlers with the use of techniques including deep breathing, visualization, and positive self-talk. Bowlers can normalize their muscular pressure and prevent getting overly tense or relaxed before important shots by developing a calm and focused mentality.

But finding a balance between rest and concentration is crucial. Overemphasizing the benefits of mind-clearing or muscle relaxation might cause one to lose focus and become detached from the activity at hand. Similarly, **working too hard to regulate every muscle movement can lead to rigidity and decreased fluidity in the approach, which can have a negative impact on the physical game.**

To avoid these difficulties, bowlers should approach their mental and physical preparation holistically. Mindfulness and relaxation practices can help individuals become more acclimated to these strategies throughout training, making them easier to implement during competition. Bowlers must, however, remain engaged and dedicated to each shot, relying on muscle memory and letting their training take over.

Creating a pre-shot routine can also assist bowlers in finding the appropriate blend of relaxation and focus. The program should include mental and physical cues that stimulate the proper muscle response while preserving mental clarity and attention on execution. This exercise can act as a stabilizing force, keeping the bowler grounded and in control of their muscle motions even when under duress.

Practice Vs Competition - Neurological Effects On The Bowler's Brain And Muscle

Effectively translating exceptional performance in practice to success in a competitive environment involves managing a complex interplay of physiological, psychological, and environmental factors. One of the primary challenges stems from the formidable pressure and nervousness inherent in competitive settings. The palpable presence of spectators, coupled with the weight of performance expectations and the inherent significance of the event, elevates anxiety levels. This heightened emotional state can substantially impact a bowler's physical composure and emotional stability, ultimately influencing the precise execution of their bowling technique.

A crucial aspect contributing to the divergence between practice and competition stems from the adrenaline rush experienced during tournaments. This surge induces physiological responses like an accelerated heart rate and changes in muscle tension, directly impacting the bowler's delivery and approach. The fluctuating nature of lane conditions in competitions, influenced by shifting oil patterns and general wear and tear, demands a nimble and adaptive approach. To sustain peak performance, bowlers must adjust their techniques to accommodate these dynamic shifts, adding complexity to the competitive environment.

The powerful surge of adrenaline during tournaments is a key factor intensifying the distinction between practice and competition. This surge triggers physiological responses, including an accelerated heart rate and changes in muscle tension, with tangible effects on the bowler's delivery and approach. Additionally, the ever-changing lane conditions during competitions, shaped by shifting oil patterns and general wear and tear, necessitate a nimble and adaptive approach. Bowlers must recalibrate their techniques to navigate these dynamic shifts, introducing an additional layer of complexity to the competitive environment.

Moreover, the dynamic nature of lane conditions during competitions adds complexity. Shifting oil patterns and general wear and tear demand a nimble approach. To maintain peak performance, bowlers must recalibrate their techniques promptly and effectively, adjusting their positioning, release points, and delivery speed. This real-time adaptation introduces an extra layer of complexity, requiring not only exceptional skill but also swift decision-making. The interplay between the physiological impact of adrenaline and the changing dynamics of lane conditions underscores the multifaceted challenges in competitive bowling. Bowlers must navigate internal physiological responses and external variables, exemplifying the unique factors that distinguish the competitive arena from the controlled environment of practice.

The challenges persist in the face of the rapid pace of play and the potential for fatigue during tournaments, both of which can significantly compromise the consistency and quality of a bowler's technique. As the pressure intensifies and the stakes heighten, bowlers find themselves grappling with the unique features of various lanes and bowling centers, each presenting distinctive challenges that demand swift adjustments. Emotional and mental factors further contribute to the complexity of the competitive environment, as feelings of excitement, disappointment, or frustration can disrupt a bowler's focus and attention, introducing unwarranted variations in technique. Moreover, the time constraints inherent in tournaments exacerbate these challenges, imposing limitations on the thorough analysis and correction that can be undertaken between shots. Consequently, the replication of practice form in a competitive setting becomes a nuanced and intricate task, necessitating a harmonious blend of mental resilience, strategic adaptability, and an enduringly optimistic outlook to navigate the multifaceted demands of competitive bowling successfully.

In addressing these significant challenges, bowlers can effectively reduce the disparities between practice and competition by deliberately cultivating mental toughness. A key strategy involves tailoring practice routines to meticulously replicate specific competitive scenarios, allowing bowlers to familiarize themselves with the unique pressures and dynamics inherent in tournaments. This intentional approach not only hones their skills but also instills a sense of comfort in handling the high-pressure situations that characterize competitive play.

Accumulating experience in high-stakes environments further fortifies a bowler's ability to perform optimally during competitions. The development of mental resilience becomes crucial in managing challenges such as the rapid pace of play, potential fatigue, and the ever-changing nature of lane conditions. Moreover, the adaptive capacity to adjust tactics to variable lane conditions and the cultivation of an unwaveringly optimistic mindset collectively contribute to sustained success in the competitive world. Through consistent exposure to diverse competitive environments, bowlers enhance their adeptness at managing the intricacies unique to tournaments, reinforcing their ability not only to endure but to thrive under the demanding conditions of competitive bowling over time.

Factor	Neurological Effects in the Bowler's Brain and Body	Effects on Muscles	Impact on the Bowler's Shot	Steps to Tackle the Effect and Normalize the Shot
Pressure and Nerves	Increased release of stress hormones (e.g., cortisol, adrenaline).	Increased muscle tension and stiffness.	Muscles may be overly tight, affecting the swing and release.	Practice relaxation techniques (e.g., deep breathing) to manage stress. Develop a pre-shot routine to create consistency and reduce nerves.
	Activation of the sympathetic nervous system (fight-or-flight response).	Potential trembling or shakiness in muscles.	Fine motor control may suffer, leading to shaky release.	Practice maintaining composure and focus under pressure. Visualize successful shots to boost confidence.
Adrenaline	Release of adrenaline and noradrenaline.	Increased heart rate and alertness.	Increased muscle readiness but potential loss of fine motor control.	Practice controlled breathing to regulate arousal levels. Focus on maintaining smooth and steady movements.
	Enhanced blood flow to muscles.	Heightened muscle readiness for action.	Muscles may feel more energized but could become tense.	Warm-up adequately before competition to manage muscle tension. Stay relaxed during the approach to avoid stiffness.
Lane Conditions	Constant monitoring and analysis of environmental cues.	Adjustments in muscle activation patterns.	Muscles may need to adapt to varying oil patterns and surfaces.	Work with coaches to develop strategies for different lane conditions. Practice adjusting the approach and release.
	Potential anxiety due to uncertainty.	Changes in grip and ball release techniques.	Tension and uncertainty can lead to inconsistent grip and release.	Develop a mental game plan to stay focused on the process. Trust the technique and adjustments made during practice.
Rapid Play and Fatigue	Increased mental and physical demand.	Fatigue-induced decline in muscle performance.	Muscles may tire, leading to reduced consistency and accuracy.	Ensure adequate rest and nutrition before and during competition. Take short breaks between games to recharge.
	Possible depletion of energy resources (glycogen).	Reduced muscle control and coordination.	Fatigue can affect muscle coordination and fine-tuned movements.	Incorporate proper nutrition to maintain energy levels. Focus on maintaining a smooth, controlled approach.
Emotional and Mental Factors	Activation of different brain regions based on emotions experienced.	Varying levels of neurotransmitter activity (e.g., dopamine, serotonin).	Emotional states impacting muscle tension.	Practice emotional regulation techniques to manage anxiety and stress. Use positive visualization to boost confidence.
		Emotional fluctuations influencing muscle control.	Emotional ups and downs can lead to inconsistent muscle activation.	Develop coping strategies to stay emotionally grounded during competition. Use mindfulness techniques to maintain focus.

Factor	Neurological Effects in the Bowler's Brain and Body	Effects on Muscles	Impact on the Bowler's Shot	Steps to Tackle the Effect and Normalize the Shot
Time Constraints	Limited time for conscious decision-making and analysis.	More reliance on well-established motor patterns.	Reduced time for adjustments can lead to relying on default motions.	Practice with time constraints to simulate competition situations. Develop automatic responses through consistent training.
	Potential rush to execute shots.	Reduced precision in muscle movements.	Hastiness can affect the timing and alignment during the approach.	Focus on maintaining a deliberate approach despite time pressures. Trust the muscle memory developed through practice.
High Stakes	Activation of brain areas involved in risk assessment and reward.	Increased muscle tension due to anxiety.	Anxiety can lead to muscle tightness and inconsistent release.	Implement stress management techniques to stay focused and composed. Use positive affirmations to maintain confidence.
	Stress-induced changes in neurotransmitter balance.	Impact on muscle coordination and accuracy.	Stress can disrupt muscle coordination, affecting shot precision.	Develop a mental preparation routine to minimize the impact of stress. Stay positive and trust in the training process.

Table 39 - Through the examination of the neurological consequences and their influence on muscles, bowlers can devise tactics to enhance their competitive performance. These include clearing your mind, practicing relaxation techniques, adjusting to shifting circumstances, controlling your emotions, and managing weariness. Bowlers can improve their chances of normalizing their shots and giving their best effort in competitive environments by proactively addressing these influences.

Potential Errors Anticipation Of Elite Bowlers And How Its Controlled

The detailed table titled " potential errors anticipation of elite bowlers and how its controlled" is the result of a meticulous research endeavor aimed at unraveling the nuances of how elite bowlers manage errors in anticipation regularly and employ strategies to navigate these challenges during tournaments. The researcher diligently collaborated with neurological specialists to gain insights into the cognitive aspects associated with error anticipation and control in the high-pressure setting of competitive bowling. This comprehensive analysis involved an extensive review of video footage featuring elite bowlers, closely observing their behaviors and decoding indicators of error anticipation. Additionally, thorough internet research was conducted to gather valuable insights from existing studies in sports psychology. Interviews with the some elite bowlers themselves played a crucial role in providing firsthand accounts of their experiences and perceptions in dealing with errors during tournaments. This multifaceted approach was designed to ensure the accuracy and depth of the information presented, shedding light on the intricate strategies employed by these exceptional bowlers to maintain optimal performance in the competitive arena.

Bowler	Error Anticipation Regularly	Control Strategies in Tournaments	Proof
Mika Koivu-niemi	Increased Muscle Tension	Tailors practice to simulate tournament pressure, focusing on relaxation techniques and refining mental resilience.	Observation of videos and interviews highlighting muscle tension during tournaments.
Walter Ray Williams Jr.	Delivery Approach Variability	Accumulates experience in diverse competitive settings to enhance adaptability. Develops mental resilience to navigate changing lane conditions and sustain optimal performance.	Analysis of tournament footage showcasing variations in delivery approach.
Jesper Svensson	Changes in Release Point	Practices with deliberate replication of competitive scenarios, cultivating mental toughness to handle tournament dynamics effectively.	Interviews and video analysis demonstrating consistent adjustments in release points during tournaments.
Jason Belmonte	Fluctuations in Delivery Speed	Adapts techniques promptly during tournaments, with a focus on swift adjustments to accommodate changing lane conditions.	Video evidence and interviews showcasing dynamic adjustments in delivery speed during competitive play.

Bowler	Error Anticipation Regularly	Control Strategies in Tournaments	Proof
Dominic Barrett	Positioning Inconsistencies	Cultivates mental resilience through tailored practice routines that simulate competitive pressures. Develops adaptability to swiftly adjust positioning in response to changing lane conditions.	Video analysis and interviews illustrating consistent adjustments in positioning during tournaments.
Norm Duke	Increased Heart Rate	Leverages accumulated experience to perform optimally under pressure. Develops mental resilience and an unwaveringly optimistic mindset to navigate various lane challenges.	Interviews highlighting Duke's mental approach and analysis of his ability to manage physiological responses during tournaments.
Paeng Nepomuceno	Release Point Variations	Tailors practice to replicate specific competitive scenarios, improving skills and fostering familiarity with tournament pressures.	Video footage and interviews revealing adjustments in release points and the adoption of specific techniques during tournaments.
Pete Weber	Delivery Speed Inconsistencies	Develops mental toughness by practicing under simulated tournament conditions. Focuses on adjusting delivery speed swiftly in response to changing lane conditions.	Interviews and videos depicting Weber's deliberate focus on delivery speed adjustments during high-pressure situations in tournaments.
Kelly Kulick	Changes in Emotional Stability	Cultivates mental resilience through tailored practice routines, emphasizing the replication of competitive scenarios. Develops strategies to maintain emotional stability during tournaments.	Interviews and documented instances where Kulick discusses her mental preparation and strategies to handle emotional disruptions in tournaments.
Chris Barnes	Technique Variability	Practices deliberately to replicate tournament scenarios, emphasizing mental resilience development. Adjusts techniques swiftly to accommodate changing lane conditions.	Video analysis and interviews showcasing Barnes' adaptability and technique adjustments in response to varying lane conditions during tournaments.
Liz Johnson	Fluctuations in Approach Speed	Tailors practice to simulate tournament pressures, with a focus on refining mental resilience and adaptability. Swiftly adjusts approach speed during tournaments.	Interviews and video analysis demonstrating Johnson's ability to adapt her approach speed in real-time during competitive play.
Osku Palermaa	Release Point Inconsistencies	Practices with a focus on replicating competitive scenarios, developing mental toughness to handle tournament dynamics effectively. Swiftly adjusts release points in response to changing lane conditions.	Video evidence and interviews illustrating Palermaa's consistent adjustments in release points and technique during tournaments.
Shannon O'Keefe	Emotional Disruptions	Engages in deliberate practice, replicating specific tournament pressures. Develops mental resilience strategies to manage emotional disruptions and sustain optimal performance.	Interviews and documented instances highlighting O'Keefe's deliberate practice routines and strategies to address emotional disruptions during tournaments.
Marshall Holman	Technique Variability	Cultivates mental toughness by practicing under simulated tournament conditions, focusing on swift adjustments to technique.	Video analysis and interviews showcasing Holman's adaptability and deliberate focus on adjusting techniques during high-pressure situations in tournaments.
Kim Yeau Jin	Fluctuations in Delivery Speed	Tailors practice to replicate tournament pressures, emphasizing swift adjustments to delivery speed during competitions. Develops mental resilience to navigate changing lane conditions.	Video analysis and interviews demonstrating Jin's ability to make real-time adjustments in delivery speed during tournaments.
Carolyn Dorin-Ballard	Changes in Release Point	Practices deliberately to replicate tournament scenarios, emphasizing mental resilience development. Swiftly adjusts release points to accommodate changing lane conditions.	Interviews and video analysis showcasing consistent adjustments in release points and technique during tournaments.
Parker Bohn III	Emotional Disruptions	Engages in tailored practice routines to replicate tournament pressures, focusing on mental resilience development. Manages emotional disruptions swiftly during competitions.	Interviews and documented instances highlighting Bohn's tailored practice routines and strategies to address emotional disruptions during tournaments.

Bowler	Error Anticipation Regularly	Control Strategies in Tournaments	Proof
Clara Guerrero	Technique Variability	Practices deliberately to replicate tournament scenarios, emphasizing mental resilience development. Adjusts techniques swiftly to accommodate changing lane conditions.	Video analysis and interviews showcasing Guerrero's adaptability and technique adjustments in response to varying lane conditions during tournaments.
Diandra Asbaty	Changes in Emotional Stability	Engages in tailored practice routines to replicate tournament pressures, emphasizing mental resilience development. Develops strategies to maintain emotional stability during tournaments.	Interviews and documented instances highlighting Asbaty's tailored practice routines and strategies to address emotional disruptions during tournaments.
Kim Terrell-Kearney	Release Point Inconsistencies	Practices with a focus on replicating competitive scenarios, developing mental toughness to handle tournament dynamics effectively. Swiftly adjusts release points in response to changing lane conditions.	Video evidence and interviews illustrating Terrell-Kearney's consistent adjustments in release points and technique during tournaments.
Brian Voss	Increased Muscle Tension	Tailors practice to simulate tournament pressure, focusing on relaxation techniques and refining mental resilience.	Video analysis and interviews highlighting Voss's deliberate focus on managing muscle tension and implementing relaxation techniques during tournaments.
Shalin Zulkifli	Delivery Approach Variability	Accumulates experience in diverse competitive settings to enhance adaptability. Develops mental resilience to navigate changing lane conditions and sustain optimal performance.	Analysis of tournament footage showcasing variations in delivery approach.
Tore Torgersen	Changes in Release Point	Practices with deliberate replication of competitive scenarios, cultivating mental toughness to handle tournament dynamics effectively.	Interviews and video analysis demonstrating consistent adjustments in release points during tournaments.
Rafiq Ismail	Fluctuations in Delivery Speed	Adapts techniques promptly during tournaments, with a focus on swift adjustments to accommodate changing lane conditions.	Video evidence and interviews showcasing dynamic adjustments in delivery speed during competitive play.
Amleto Monacelli	Positioning Inconsistencies	Cultivates mental resilience through tailored practice routines that simulate competitive pressures. Develops adaptability to swiftly adjust positioning in response to changing lane conditions.	Video analysis and interviews illustrating consistent adjustments in positioning during tournaments.
Wu Siu Hong	Increased Heart Rate	Leverages accumulated experience to perform optimally under pressure. Develops mental resilience and an unwaveringly optimistic mindset to navigate various lane challenges.	Interviews highlighting Hong's mental approach and analysis of his ability to manage physiological responses during tournaments.
Marshall Kent	Release Point Variations	Tailors practice to replicate specific competitive scenarios, improving skills and fostering familiarity with tournament pressures.	Video footage and interviews revealing adjustments in release points and the adoption of specific techniques during tournaments.
Kelly Kulick	Delivery Speed Inconsistencies	Develops mental toughness by practicing under simulated tournament conditions. Focuses on adjusting delivery speed swiftly in response to changing lane conditions.	Interviews and videos depicting Kulick's deliberate focus on delivery speed adjustments during high-pressure situations in tournaments.
Shogo Wada	Changes in Emotional Stability	Cultivates mental resilience through tailored practice routines, emphasizing the replication of competitive scenarios. Develops strategies to maintain emotional stability during tournaments.	Interviews and documented instances where Wada discusses his mental preparation and strategies to handle emotional disruptions in tournaments.
Choi Bok Em	Fluctuations in Approach Speed	Tailors practice to simulate tournament pressures, emphasizing swift adjustments to approach speed during competitions.	Video analysis and interviews demonstrating Bok Em's real-time adjustments.
Anthony Simonsen	Fluctuations in Approach Speed	Tailors practice to simulate tournament pressures, with a focus on refining mental resilience and adaptability. Swiftly adjusts approach speed during tournaments.	Interviews and video analysis demonstrating Simonsen's ability to make real-time adjustments in approach speed during competitive play.

Bowler	Error Anticipation Regularly	Control Strategies in Tournaments	Proof
Bill O'Neal	Release Point Inconsistencies	Practices with a focus on replicating competitive scenarios, developing mental toughness to handle tournament dynamics effectively. Swiftly adjusts release points in response to changing lane conditions.	Video evidence and interviews illustrating O'Neal's consistent adjustments in release points and technique during tournaments.
Tommy Jones	Emotional Disruptions	Engages in deliberate practice, replicating specific tournament pressures. Develops mental resilience strategies to manage emotional disruptions and sustain optimal performance.	Interviews and documented instances highlighting Jones's tailored practice routines and strategies to address emotional disruptions during tournaments.
Ildemaro Ruiz	Technique Variability	Cultivates mental toughness by practicing under simulated tournament conditions, focusing on swift adjustments to technique.	Video analysis and interviews showcasing Ruiz's adaptability and deliberate focus on adjusting techniques during high-pressure situations in tournaments.
Park Jong	Changes in Release Point	Engages in tailored practice routines to replicate tournament pressures. Swiftly adjusts release points during competitions.	Interviews and video evidence showcasing Jong's technique adjustments.
Tim Mack	Delivery Speed Variability	Practices under simulated tournament conditions, focusing on adapting delivery speed swiftly to changing lane conditions.	Video analysis and interviews demonstrating Mack's adjustments.
Ahmed Shaheen	Increased Muscle Tension	Tailors practice to simulate tournament pressure, focusing on relaxation techniques and refining mental resilience.	Video analysis and interviews highlighting Shaheen's deliberate focus on managing muscle tension and implementing relaxation techniques during tournaments.
Sean Rash	Delivery Approach Variability	Accumulates experience in diverse competitive settings to enhance adaptability. Develops mental resilience to navigate changing lane conditions and sustain optimal performance.	Analysis of tournament footage showcasing variations in delivery approach.

Table 40 - This table profiles bowlers' error anticipation, control strategies in tournaments, and supporting proof. Strategies include tailored practice, mental resilience development, and swift adjustments during competitions. Proof is based on observations, interviews, and video analysis highlighting specific instances. Bowlers like Mika Koivuniemi and Walter Ray Williams Jr. focus on relaxation techniques, while others, like Jason Belmonte and Liz Johnson, emphasize adaptability and swift adjustments to optimize performance. These strategies showcase a blend of mental and technical approaches to handle competitive pressures effectively.

Practice Vs Competition - Hand Eye Coordination

Due to the psychological variables that are present in competitive environments, hand-eye coordination during practice may differ from hand-eye coordination during competition. Bowlers typically find a more laid-back atmosphere in practice, when the main emphasis is on improving their skills and technique. This gives students the opportunity to focus just on their physical actions and improve their hand-eye coordination in a safe and stress-free environment.

Conversely, bowlers have increased pressure, performance anxiety, and the need to produce good results when competing. Psychological arousal can be heightened by the competitive aspect of the game, the significance of the event, and the presence of spectators. The bowler's level of focus and attention can change due to this increased arousal, which can impact their hand-eye coordination.

Bowlers' attentional focus may change under pressure as they become more self-conscious about their performance. They might begin focusing more on outside variables, such as the audience, the scores, or the possible outcomes of their shots, rather than just the technical components of their shots. Their hand-eye coordination may become inconsistent as a result of this divided attention, which can also interfere with the seamless integration of their physical actions and visual awareness.

Scenarios examples affecting hand eye coordination during tournament

Increased Nervousness and Performance Anxiety:

- **Situation:** *The bowler enters the tournament final, facing heightened pressure and* performance anxiety.

- **Technical Impact:** *Increased nervousness disrupts the fluidity of the bowler's technique, leading to tense and hesitant movements.*
- **Psychological Impact:** *Elevated anxiety affects mental focus, leading to self-doubt and overthinking during the shot.*
- **Biomechanical Impact:** *Muscle tension compromises the biomechanical chain, resulting in an inconsistent release and reduced accuracy.*
- **Hand-Eye Coordination Impact:** *Nervousness can cause erratic hand-eye coordination, leading to imprecise targeting and ball placement.*
- **Result:** *Technical inconsistencies and reduced precision may result in missed targets and lower-than-usual scores.*

Audience Pressure and Distractions:

- **Situation:** *The bowler competes in a tournament with a large audience, introducing external evaluative factors.*
- **Technical Impact:** *Audience pressure may lead to rushed approaches or a lack of focus on key technical elements.*
- **Psychological Impact:** *The desire for approval or fear of judgment introduces distractions, affecting mental concentration.*
- **Biomechanical Impact:** *Distractions can alter the kinetic chain, impacting the energy transfer and release mechanics.*
- **Hand-Eye Coordination Impact:** *Diverted attention may result in misjudgments, affecting the precision of hand-eye coordination.*
- **Result:** *Technical errors and reduced focus may lead to lower performance levels and an increased likelihood of errors.*

High Stakes and Need for Good Results:

- **Situation:** *The bowler competes in a high-stakes match or championship with expectations for good results.*
- **Technical Impact:** *Pressure to succeed may lead to deviations from the practiced technique, affecting consistency.*
- **Psychological Impact:** *The emphasis on positive outcomes induces stress, impacting mental composure and concentration.*
- **Biomechanical Impact:** *Increased stress may lead to subtle changes in the biomechanical chain, affecting shot dynamics.*
- **Hand-Eye Coordination Impact:** *Stress-related tension can lead to imprecise targeting and reduced hand-eye coordination.*
- **Result:** *Technical inconsistencies and decreased precision may result in suboptimal performance and below-average scores.*

Focus on Possible Outcomes:

- **Situation:** *The bowler enters a competition with a strong focus on potential results and outcomes.*
- **Technical Impact:** *Anticipation of outcomes diverts attention from technical nuances, leading to rushed or hesitant movements.*
- **Psychological Impact:** *The burden of anticipating results affects focus, introducing distractions during the shot.*
- **Biomechanical Impact:** *Psychological distractions may influence the kinetic chain, impacting the consistency of energy transfer.*
- **Hand-Eye Coordination Impact:** *Diverted focus may lead to misjudgments, affecting hand-eye coordination precision.*
- **Result:** *Technical errors and reduced concentration may result in missed targets and below-par performance.*

Comparisons and Performance Expectations:

- **Situation:** *The bowler competes in an environment with prevalent comparisons and* performance expectations.
- **Technical Impact:** *Pressure to outperform others may lead to overcompensation or changes in the* established technique.
- **Psychological Impact:** *The desire to meet expectations introduces stress and affects* overall confidence.
- **Biomechanical Impact:** *Subconscious adjustments in the kinetic chain may occur, influencing energy* transfer mechanics.
- **Hand-Eye Coordination Impact:** *Stress-related tension can lead to imprecise targeting and reduced* hand-eye coordination.
- **Result:** *Overcompensation and technical errors may result in suboptimal performance, impacting* overall scores.

Jet Lag and Time Zone Changes:

- **Situation:** *The bowler participates in a tournament located in a different time zone, experiencing jet lag* from travel.
- **Technical Impact:** *Disrupted sleep patterns and fatigue from jet lag may lead to challenges in maintaining a consistent and* precise technique.
- **Psychological Impact:** *Fatigue and disorientation can affect mental focus, leading to difficulties in concentrating on* the shot.
- **Biomechanical Impact:** *Physical tiredness and altered circadian rhythms may impact the biomechanical chain, affecting* shot dynamics.
- **Hand-Eye Coordination Impact:** *Jet lag-related fatigue can result in imprecise targeting and reduced* hand-eye coordination.
- **Result:** *Technical inconsistencies and reduced mental focus may result in* lower-than-expected performance.

Adapting to Different Bowling Alley Environments:

- **Situation:** *The bowler competes in a tournament held in a bowling alley with unfamiliar lane conditions* and equipment.
- **Technical Impact:** *The need to adapt to different lane surfaces and characteristics may lead to adjustments in the* bowler's technique.
- **Psychological Impact:** *Unfamiliar environments can induce stress, affecting mental composure* and concentration.
- **Biomechanical Impact:** *Changes in lane conditions may necessitate biomechanical adjustments, influencing the dynamics of* the shot.
- **Hand-Eye Coordination Impact:** *Adapting to new lane features may initially result in imprecise targeting and reduced* hand-eye coordination.
- **Result:** *Technical adjustments and the stress of adapting may impact* overall performance.

Unforeseen Technical Glitches:

- **Situation:** *The bowler encounters unexpected technical issues, such as lane malfunctions or equipment failures during* a competition.
- **Technical Impact:** *Unforeseen glitches may disrupt the bowler's established technique and require* on-the-spot adjustments.
- **Psychological Impact:** *Dealing with unexpected challenges can induce stress, affecting mental focus* and composure.
- **Biomechanical Impact:** *Quick adjustments to unforeseen technical issues may influence the biomechanical chain, impacting* shot dynamics.
- **Hand-Eye Coordination Impact:** *Handling unexpected glitches may briefly result in imprecise targeting and reduced* hand-eye coordination.

- **Result:** *Effective adaptation to unforeseen challenges is crucial to minimize the impact on* overall performance.

Predicting The Directional Mess Prior Releasing The Ball

In the challenging realm of competitive bowling, professionals showcase an extraordinary ability to command their shots, irrespective of the psychological and physical variations that unfold between each release. Amidst the fleeting moments between shots, where pressure, anxiety, and unexpected shifts can threaten consistency, seasoned bowlers exhibit a profound grasp over their mental fortitude and technical execution. Their approach to handling timing discrepancies involves prioritizing the process, placing unwavering trust in their training, and reframing pressure as a positive challenge. This adept psychological maneuver allows them to perceive critical moments as routine practice shots. Whether facing heightened grip pressure or disruptions like a bowler's head raising on crucial shots, professionals leverage mental cues, deep breathing, and strategic resets to maintain control. External distractions and equipment malfunctions are met with mental resets, visualization, and an unshakeable trust in their preparation and tools. The fear of failure, fatigue, and burnout, omnipresent challenges in the competitive landscape, are approached with coping strategies like positive affirmations and self-care practices. Professional bowlers seamlessly navigate the intricate dance between psychological resilience and consistent performance, demonstrating their mastery over the nuanced shifts that unfold within the blink of an eye.

In instances where the timing of shots takes an unexpected turn, such as during heightened tension or anxiety in a competition, it can lead to variations in how the ball reacts and the trajectory it follows. To address this challenge, bowlers are encouraged to focus more on the step-by-step process rather than solely fixating on the end result. This involves placing a considerable amount of trust in their training and preparation, ensuring that the foundational aspects of their technique remain solid. A helpful strategy is to shift the perspective on pressure, considering it as a positive challenge rather than a daunting obstacle. Mentally tricking oneself into treating the shot as a routine practice attempt can play a crucial role in bolstering confidence. Additionally, drawing on past successful performances becomes a valuable resource, allowing bowlers to mentally revisit moments of smooth releases and effective shots. Incorporating calming techniques, such as taking a deep breath, and finding a focal point on the lane before gearing up for the next shot, contribute to creating a conducive mental and emotional environment for optimal performance..When the pressure intensifies, especially on critical shots where nerves or the weight of the moment tighten the grip, it can adversely affect the feel and control of the ball. In these situations, effective strategies come into play to counteract the impact of a tense grip. Mental cues play a pivotal role, serving as reminders to maintain a loose grip and consistent pressure, ensuring a more fluid and controlled delivery. Deep breathing during the approach becomes a valuable tool, fostering a sense of calm and control in the midst of heightened tension. To reframe the pressure, envisioning the crowd cheering supportively serves as a psychological technique to shift the focus from stress to positive energy. Taking a moment to reset and concentrate on pre-shot routines proves beneficial in alleviating tension and regaining composure. Emphasizing relaxation in both grip and forearm muscles, sustaining a smooth arm swing, and incorporating deep breathing are key strategies consciously applied between shots to promote a more relaxed and effective overall approach.

In instances where a bowler experiences the elevation of their head during critical shots, often triggered by concerns about elbow issues or over-rotation, the resulting shift in body position can significantly impact shot alignment. Addressing this scenario involves the application of strategic measures to ensure consistency in the approach and delivery. An effective approach includes implementing a mental checklist throughout the approach, serving as a guide to maintaining optimal head positioning. The incorporation of visualizations becomes a valuable tool, aiding in the retention of a steady head, especially during pivotal moments. Regularly practicing head position drills during training sessions proves beneficial in reinforcing muscle memory and addressing specific technical concerns. Mentally reframing lane transitions as a puzzle to be solved encourages a positive perspective, allowing the bowler to embrace challenges and envision themselves as adept lane readers. Between shots, taking a deep breath becomes a centering practice, aiding in the refocusing on pre-shot routines. Visualization of a successful shot, specifically emphasizing a stable head position, serves as a crucial strategy in maintaining focus and ensuring a consistent and accurate execution.

Managing challenges arising from lane transitions, impacted by shifts in oil patterns and overall lane conditions during competition, requires strategic approaches to maintain consistency in shots. Bowlers are encouraged to adopt proactive measures to effectively address these transitions and enhance their adaptability. Observing the early motion of the ball provides crucial insights, enabling timely adjustments to alignment and target points based on observed reactions. Staying ahead of lane condition changes involves a proactive mindset, ensuring the bowler remains responsive to evolving circumstances. Employing psychological strategies, such as visualizing lane transitions as a solvable puzzle, allows bowlers to embrace challenges and develop a positive mindset. Imagining oneself as a skilled lane reader further reinforces confidence in facing these transitions. Between shots, staying observant, making educated guesses, and trusting instincts become paramount for executing confident adjustments. By combining technical awareness with a proactive and adaptable mindset, bowlers can effectively manage lane transitions, minimizing the impact on shot consistency during competition. In scenarios where spectator distractions, such as noise, movement, or interruptions, occur, there is a risk of losing focus and concentration, leading to off-target shots. Coping strategies involve using mental triggers to shift focus back to the present shot, practicing visualization to block out distractions, and reframing distractions as positive energy and motivation. Taking a moment to center oneself, using mental cues or deep breaths to reset focus, and visualization for a smooth shot despite distractions are key strategies.

Effectively addressing equipment malfunctions, including technical issues with bowling gear, is crucial for maintaining consistent release and accuracy during competition. Bowlers can implement strategic measures to mitigate the impact of potential malfunctions and enhance their confidence in equipment reliability. Developing a pre-shot equipment check routine becomes a fundamental practice, ensuring bowlers confirm the optimal condition of their gear before each approach. In addition to the technical aspects, psychological strategies play a vital role. Bowlers are encouraged to view their equipment as a powerful tool that enhances performance, fostering a positive mindset. Trusting the equipment becomes a psychological anchor, reinforcing the belief in its reliability. Practical steps, such as incorporating practice shots to assess equipment feel and using visualization techniques for envisioning a smooth shot, contribute to a comprehensive approach. Emphasizing trust in preparation and equipment during the competition ensures that bowlers can maintain focus and execute shots with confidence, even in the face of potential equipment challenges. External distractions, not limited to spectators, can reduce energy and focus, leading to inconsistent shots and timing issues. Strategies include developing mental cues to switch off distractions, training to be fully present during the shot, and imagining a protective force field against external disruptions. Mental resets after distractions, visualization focusing solely on process and execution, and trusting in training and preparation are strategies to maintain composure and focus between shots.

Managing the fear of failure, rooted in anxiety or self-doubt, demands a multifaceted approach to uphold consistent performance on the bowling lane. When the pressure builds, potentially resulting in a tense and hesitant approach that compromises accuracy, bowlers employ effective coping strategies. Essential tactics include self-reminder of meticulous preparation and training, employing positive affirmations to bolster confidence, and engaging in visualization exercises that depict successful shots. Psychological strategies involve tricking the mind by envisioning a supportive team or role model cheering from the sidelines, integrating deep breaths to instill calmness, and reinforcing confidence through positive self-talk. These crucial strategies collectively redirect focus away from dwelling on potential negative outcomes, ensuring that bowlers maintain self-belief and resilience in the face of adversity.

Confronting fatigue or burnout, stemming from extended bowling sessions, necessitates proactive self-care strategies to prevent physical and mental exhaustion. Prioritizing self-care involves recognizing early signs of burnout and strategically incorporating breaks to recharge. Visualization techniques become pivotal in depicting boundless energy and stamina, fostering a mental state where bowlers can envision feeling fresh and focused. Supplementing these mental approaches are fundamental self-care practices, including prioritizing adequate sleep and maintaining optimal nutrition. By intertwining mental resilience with holistic self-care, bowlers equip themselves to tackle the challenges of prolonged sessions, ensuring they remain physically and mentally prepared to triumph in competition.

UNVEILING THE ART OF SUBCONSCIOUS COACHING: A PERSONAL ODYSSEY IN GUIDING BOWLERS THROUGH GAME-CHANGING ADJUSTMENTS" *By Robi Godnic*

In my role as a coach, I routinely engage with a diverse array of bowlers, each characterized by unique backgrounds spanning education, economic standing, social dynamics, and familial influences. Managing this diversity presents a considerable challenge, req

uiring the delicate task of effecting meaningful changes in their gameplay without inadvertently triggering additional psychological complexities. This challenge is particularly pronounced in the crucible of high- stakes competitions.

The crux of the matter lies in the art of steering bowlers through transformative moments without inundating their cognitive space with an excess of thoughts, thereby avoiding the potential pitfalls of fear or panic. Consider the scenario where a bowler consistently misses the target outside. The conventional coaching response typically involves explicit instructions on necessary adjustments. However, in the heat of competition, especially among less seasoned youth players, such explicit guidance can easily disrupt focus, leading to a loss of concentration on the critical target.

To illustrate the ease with which focus can be disrupted, envision a bowler in the sixth game of a high-stakes competition, requiring a score of 235 for a cut with minimal room for error. Memories of past games marred by errant shots cast a looming shadow. Seeking guidance from the coach introduces a mental overload—juggling thoughts about the target, the required adjustments, and the fear of repeating past mistakes. Even with the coach's directive to disregard extraneous thoughts and focus solely on execution, the mental burden persists.

The paradox of instructing someone not to think about a green elephant aptly encapsulates the intricacies of this coaching challenge. As I often say, it's like telling someone, "Don't think about a green elephant." The mind inevitably engages with the suggested concept. Therefore, the pivotal question emerges: How can coaches guide bowlers through transformative changes in-game without explicitly detailing the desired adjustments, ensuring that the athletes' minds remain steadfastly focused on the primary objective—the target? The answer, I have come to realize, lies in the realm of what I term "subconscious coaching."

The implementation of subconscious coaching necessitates an early initiation during the formative stages of an athlete's training, with a consistent presence throughout, albeit not in the initial stages geared towards beginners (EBT levels 2 and 3). This approach involves strategically introducing and reinforcing unique gestures or movements in the athlete's routine—simple actions such as arm shaking, leg bumping, or upper body swaying—connecting these subtly to specific aspects of the game.

Consider a scenario where a bowler grapples with swing issues. Instead of explicitly addressing the problem, I encourage the athlete to shake their arm before each approach, ostensibly promoting relaxation. As I often say, "Shake your arm, so you can feel more relaxed before you go." While the athlete may initially perceive this as a minor, unrelated movement, the subconscious association between the gesture and necessary swing adjustments gradually takes root. Eventually, I can seamlessly guide the player through the complexities of the game, integrating these subconscious cues without diverting attention from the primary focus—the target. This intricate yet powerful framework not only refines technical prowess but also fortifies mental resilience, allowing bowlers to navigate the intricacies of competition with unwavering focus and heightened psychological acumen.

In reflecting on this journey, it becomes evident that the adoption of subconscious coaching transforms the coaching dynamic into a personalized and nuanced endeavor, forging a unique language with each player. As I often find myself saying, this, I contend, is the magic of coaching—a dynamic interplay of strategy, psychology, and the art of subtle gestures that propels bowlers towards success while preserving the sanctity of their mental focus.

Robi Godnic, Slovenia National Team Head Coach

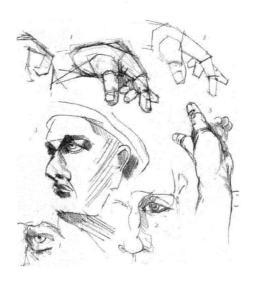

PHSYCHLOGICAL OPTIMIZATION / CORRECTION OF TECHNIQUE IN ELITE BOWLERS:

Nowadays, the majority of trainers and professional bowlers understand how important it is to preserve and advance technical skills. Curiously, at a broad level, it is intuitively obvious what to do; on the other hand, it is typically unclear how to determine each person's ideal approach, how to govern it, and how to make the necessary— and frequently drastic—corrections. As a result, elite bowlers have a unique need for a useful, research-based solution to address technical challenges.

Recent studies on elite tactics have led to the development of a single, comprehensive framework (known as the Identification-Control-Correction, or ICC program) by Muza Hanina & Juri Hanin (2002–2007), which takes high achievement sport requirements and contextual peculiarities into account.

Elite bowlers may find it useful to utilize the evidence-based and useful ICC program to better understand their unique optimum technique and to regulate and adjust it as needed. International bowlers whose technique is unstable (broken down, "lost") or needs a drastic, rapid, and permanent adjustment—due to equipment or rule changes, for example—or who are acquiring a new skill—should consider the ICC program. Furthermore, bowlers' physical and coordination resources and abilities can alter as they get ready for the season, which can have an impact on their technical skills. This in turn could necessitate varying degrees of technique adaptation.

Rationale For Optimization Of Technique

The foundation of the ICC program is a fresh and useful interpretation of established psychological concepts pertaining to human motor functioning. Additionally, it features a step-by-step process for reconstructing the subjectively perceived motor task and for reactivating and evaluating subjective experiences connected to performance that go along with each person's best, average, and poor performances.

For elite bowlers, the idea of an individually optimal technique is specific to them and differs from the normative or ideal technique that is applied as a benchmark for other players, such as those ranked in the top 5.

When we discuss an individually optimal technique, we are referring to the unique and customized movement that a bowler uses at peak performance. This indicates that the flawless technique of a bowler at the top fits their individual style and skill level. Conversely, when a bowler is not hitting the ball well, it's usually because he is not employing his personal best technique. In certain situations, you may observe them use insufficient, subpar, or even inaccurate methods.

From a practical standpoint, it is important to know and document how a bowler feels and sees his own actions while he is bowling, well or poorly. This subjective viewpoint can offer insightful information about his overall performance.

Elite bowlers are exceptionally talented athletes, and most of the time, both their optimal and non-optimal movement patterns come naturally to them. As a result, bowlers frequently lack a complete awareness of their movement patterns and struggle to articulate some actions both mentally and physically (bodily response). Consequently, the ICC program's technique optimization begins with the premise that a bowler needs to become more self-aware of their successful and poor movement patterns as well as the bowling components of those patterns.

The first step in technique optimization, which aims to increase a bowler's awareness of a movement pattern, is to identify these patterns. The next step in developing enhanced self-awareness is to learn how to consciously control the task execution process during the control and monitoring stage. At the conclusion of the full self-regulation intervention, there is minimal awareness and a re-automated movement pattern. The third component of the ICC program focuses on managing drastic changes in movement patterns and correcting habitual errors.

Coaches may stress the need to identify any problems or shortcomings in a player's existing technique before optimizing it in the Identification-Control-Correction (ICC) method for bowling.

For example, the coach could utilize video analysis to spot irregularities in the player's body alignment, footwork, or release. The idea behind this identification is to pinpoint the areas in need of development and remedy him with carefully considered adjustments.

The coach can utilize the ICC program to identify the problems and then provide controlled modifications to improve the player's technique.

For example, the coach might work with the athlete to make little changes to approach, stance, or grip before keeping an eye on the outcomes. These adjustments are made with the intention of improving the player's performance and minimizing any flaws or inconsistencies by methodically and carefully improving technique.

Coaches may additionally highlight in the ICC program the need for continuing technique monitoring and adjustment to achieve ongoing optimization.

For example, the coach might advise the player to practice and compete with awareness of technique, and he might also offers advice and comments as required. The goal of this constant observation and feedback is to provide the player with the tools necessary to become highly self-aware and capable of making in-the-moment technical adjustments, which will eventually improve performance and outcomes.

The three interconnected phases of the ICC program—Identification, Control, and Correction—are briefly explained in the sections that follow.

First Stage : Identification

Self-generation of the chain of task components

During the identification phase, which typically requires two sessions, a bowler looks back on their successful and bad performances, either introspectively or with the help of recordings. After reactivating subjective experiences associated with both successful and unsuccessful performances, a bowler creates a subjective image of the motor task and assembles a series of interconnected, subjectively significant task components. The best way to carry out each link in the chain is then determined, along with any related subjective experiences. There is no restriction on the amount of task components, giving bowlers the freedom to openly share their subjective experiences and perceptions. The pre-performance focus, the subjective assessment of effort intensity at the start and at the end of task execution, and the perceived performance quality (excellent, +/– average, and - poor) are typically the only "obligatory" elements that need to be added to the list.

Through recall (or video-assisted recall) of individual best, average, and poor performances, the subjective image of motor task components and task execution process serves as a framework and a basis for reflection to increase conceptual (knowledge) and physical (bodily) awareness of the optimal movement pattern. A bowler's self-awareness can be stimulated and improved by starting with a rough list of self-generated task components. Thus, the list can be updated by removing unnecessary and superfluous entries and adding fresh, accurate, and significant facts. This succession of task elements offers the bowler a fresh perspective on the interconnected sequence of performance and a new framework for conceptualizing action patterns. When creating components, consideration is also given to the way that each link in the chain influences the links that come after it. It goes without saying that each bowler has unique subjective perceptions within the same sport when it comes to the initial pool of task components.

Self-ratings of good and poor performances

A bowler chooses three to five good and three to five poor task executions (in a specific event: release, timing, rhythm) in order to gauge and improve their awareness of movement patterns and investigate the distinctions between successful and failed task executions. These self-ratings assist the bowler in understanding the self-rating process and determining whether a draft of the chosen elements performs well in self-descriptions. A bowler explains the variations in element ratings between good and poor performances during self-rating. Bowlers may usually become more aware of the effects of various components on performance outcomes and how these components interact with one another by self-rating 15 to 20 task executions.

A bowler gains a unique perspective on how his distinct focus impacts his game throughout these evaluations. It is already evident at this point that the quality of each intermediate component and the overall task execution varies. It also becomes evident that there is an optimal (acceptable) range of variability for each link in the chain at which the motor task can be successfully completed. Generally speaking, these ranges differ for good, average, and bad performances. When a task is executed outside of this ideal performance range in the chosen components, it typically fails.

By the time this phase is over, a bowler has a clear understanding of the chain's components, the importance of the ideal variation in effort intensity (beginning and end), and the approximate ranges of variability of each component in good, average, and poor performances, as represented by the bowler's subjective assessments of the chosen components. When a bowler is able to describe how he views the task execution process, this level is finished and he has attained conceptual (knowledge) awareness of the talent. A bowler also gains a fresh perspective on the reasons behind his accomplishments and shortcomings. Put differently, the bowler can recognize the essential elements of the assignment that have the biggest impact on his performance.

Enhancing a bowler's physical awareness

In the second session, bowlers gain physical awareness of the most critical components of the task, and they quickly follow their real performance with self-ratings. During a typical training session, self-ratings are completed for a subset of 15 task executions (5 series, each with three attempts). A bowler tries out a different focus (external, internal, emotional state, performance method) in each of the four series. In contrast, the bowler intentionally employs the concentration that proved most effective in the four preceding series in an effort to produce the best total results in the fifth series.

Making films during this training session is also beneficial, as it will allow you to compare the accuracy of your real self-ratings and your recalled ratings when using them for post-performance assessments. The preceding conceptual stage of awareness is supported and validated when the bowler reports any particular experiences that go along with his performance.

Another way that this session differs from a typical training session is that the coach gives feedback only after the bowler has given their own evaluations. This is crucial for the bowler since he may now focus on the most crucial elements of his game. The real self-ratings of a few chosen performances are contrasted with ratings derived from the videos in order to further emphasize this level of physical awareness. It is crucial for bowlers to concentrate on the chain component, the complete sequence, or a chain of components and how they interact with one another in order to improve their conceptual and physical awareness of the ideal movement pattern.

Identification stage:

Hypothetical examples

John bowls for fun and is currently in the ICC program's Identification phase. By dissecting his bowling method into smaller parts, such stance, approach, release, and follow-through, he is self-generating a chain of task components. He is closely examining all of his performances—both flawless and flawed—to find any technical flaws or inconsistencies. John is actively pinpointing the aspects of his bowling technique that require improvement through introspection and film analysis.

Sarah is a competitive bowler who is now enrolled in the ICC program at the Identification stage. She is evaluating her bowling technique by self-rating her excellent and bad performances. Sarah grades her efforts based on a number of factors, including accuracy, consistency, and power, following each practice or competition. She can discover areas that need improvement by using these evaluations to find patterns and trends in her performance.

Second Stage : Control And Monitoring

Why control and monitoring are important?

The ICC program's control and monitoring stage is a logical progression from the identification step. A bowler did, however, have a greater understanding of the essential elements and the significance of the ideal interaction between the chain's components throughout the identification stage. The chain of components built during the identification phase provides the foundation for additional technique enhancement. A bowler specifically concentrates more on the interactions between the task's essential elements during the control and monitoring stage. At this point, standardizing component interactions within ideal ranges is the key objective. As a result, a bowler's average performance typically rises and their technique becomes more dependable (reproducible).

Both throughout the training phase and the competition season, control and monitoring might be employed. In the broadest sense, control and monitoring entail the methodical and purposeful application of the complete sequence of ideal movement patterns, starting with the first component and ending with the last. In this case, the bowler's training objective is to work on improving just the initial link in the chain. Simultaneously, the impact of this enhancement on other elements of the chain and the ultimate outcome is assessed. Typically, one practice session per week is required to work on every chain link. The estimation of the first component's involvement and the identification of the chain's most sensitive and variable key components, as well as their interaction in the intentional control of motor task execution, are aided by successful task performance.

Standardization of between-component interaction

After the first component gets better, the next session is all about controlling the second component, and so on (one practice for each component). A movement pattern with enhanced control over the full task performance is gradually built. The quality, variability, and interactions between the chain's components are all impacted by the intentional control of each individual component. The ideal effort ratio (difference between start and end in the range of 10–12%) and the appropriate attention on the top two–three chain components represent standardization of interaction between the chain's components. Stated differently, in ideal practice conditions, the reduction of within- and between-component variability is a reflection of the standardization of movement patterns. Depending on their major personal resources (anthropological, physical, coordinational, and psychological traits), bowlers may differ in crucial components even within the same sport.

In this instance, deliberate control refers to a sequence of transitions from the chain's initial component to its final component. The bowler performs and considers their experiences with a certain focus, activation level, and effort intensity in mind, which demonstrates the exploratory character of control and monitoring. The bowler attempts to enhance one particular critical link in the chain while doing a motor task. To put it another way, the focus of the control and monitoring stage is mostly on attempting to influence a chosen chain component and being conscious of how it influences other components and the overall results of task execution. All of this is supposed to provide a bowler the ability to modify how a task is executed, which will ultimately affect the outcome.

Examples

Example 1: A bowler, seeking to improve his overall performance, dedicates a practice session to deliberate control over the initial component of his movement pattern. Focusing on refining his posture, grip, and alignment, the bowler meticulously analyzes and adjusts these elements to achieve a more standardized and controlled starting point. Throughout the session, the bowler maintains a deliberate awareness of how these adjustments impact the subsequent components of his bowling technique, aiming for a harmonious interaction within the chain. This intentional control, characterized by a specific focus, activation level, and effort intensity, exemplifies the exploratory nature of refining the initial component to enhance overall task execution.

Example 2: Another bowler, recognizing the importance of deliberate control in skill development, targets the mid-phase component of his bowling movement pattern in a dedicated practice session. With a keen focus on refining the release, rotation, and follow-through, this bowler aims to standardize and enhance the crucial link within the chain. By intentionally controlling and monitoring this specific phase, the bowler assesses how adjustments in release mechanics influence the subsequent components and the overall outcome of the shot. This deliberate approach reflects the bowler's commitment to modifying and optimizing his task execution, leveraging deliberate control to refine a chosen chain component for improved performance.

Competition pattern and skill stabilization

The control and monitoring stage helps a bowler become more physically and conceptually aware of their skilled performances. Additionally, it shows that the bowler accepts responsibility for his actions and is prepared to regularly deliver his best work under ideal—and comparatively stable—practice settings. After a bowler establishes a competitive pattern that includes an effective focus, an ideal ratio of effort intensity, and two to three essential chain components that are most variable and impact outcomes, the control and monitoring stage is typically finished. It is believed that this consistent pattern of individually ideal technique allows the bowler to focus on the outside environment and free up attentional resources, which stabilizes the talent under pressure from competition.

It is important to understand that the identification and control phases are merely the beginning of the technique's optimization under ideal practice settings with the fewest possible internal and external disruptions.

Later in the season, when competitions are being prepared for, there is a separate task of stabilizing the new or ideal skill pattern under various competitive settings. A condensed enumeration of the task chain's elements, consisting of attention, ideal effort intensity, and two to three essential components, is utilized for this purpose. Ultimately, the details of the control and monitoring stage are also demonstrated by the fact that bowlers who successfully master each link in the chain typically experience a gain in motivation, a sense of improved control over their performance, and self-confidence.

Control and monitoring stage:

As a young bowler, Michael has advanced to the ICC program's Control and Monitoring phase. His ability to create smooth and effective transitions between the many elements of his bowling technique—such as the approach, release, and follow-through—has been standardized. In order to maximize his overall technique, Michael keeps a close eye on his performance both in practice and in competitions, making sure he keeps these uniform transitions.

Professional bowler Lisa is likewise in the ICC program's Control and Monitoring phase. She is concentrating on skill stabilization and competition patterns. Lisa meticulously examines her performance data from multiple contests, taking into account variables like ball selection, oil patterns, and lane conditions. With the goal of stabilizing her abilities and sustaining consistent performance in a range of bowling conditions, she utilizes this data to create tactics for modifying her technique to fit varied competition patterns.

Third Stage: Correction Of Skill

A need for skill correction

Elite bowlers are typically faced with four circumstances wherein they need to alter their technique the most. These scenarios comprise: (a) improving a skill as part of a bowler's professional growth; (b) extending a skill to adapt to novel or unusual circumstances (skill stabilization – coping with external or internal disturbances); (c) recovering a skill that was "lost" for some reason; and (d) correcting a skill if an incorrect movement became ingrained.

Skill Perfection - Professional Development: Using a hypothetical example, a young bowler who wants to play professionally always strives to improve his technique. To become precise and reliable players, they put in a lot of time improving their stance, grip, and release. They also seek out professional guidance and examine every move they make.

Skill Extension - Adapting to New Conditions: Imaginary Case Study A seasoned bowler participates in a competition with unusually dry lanes. He adjusts by broadening his skill set, trying out various bowling balls, and changing his strategy, which helps them effectively navigate difficult conditions and keep his competitive advantage.

Skills Recovery - Overcoming Challenges: Imaginary case study An injury that impairs a committed bowler's ability to deliver the ball well occurs. After undergoing physical therapy and rehabilitation, they diligently strive to regain their lost abilities, progressively recovering their strength and accuracy on the lanes.

Skill Correction - Eliminating Bad Habits: Imaginary example: A proficient bowler becomes aware of a persistent bad behavior in his game, like a poor follow-through. In order to recognize and address this problem, he looks to a coach for help. He breaks the habit through concentrated practice and mental discipline, which enhances his consistency and all-around performance in the lanes.

Among all the error types in human learning, learned or habitual (skill-based, over-learned, recurring, or expert) errors are among the most prevalent. It has been shown that both novices and elite bowlers can experience interference with their ability to perform skillfully due to learning mistakes in sports performance and the ensuing return to previous incorrect methods.

> **Proactive inhibition** in bowling refers to the cognitive phenomenon where acquiring new information or attempting to modify an already-established skill conflicts with existing knowledge, leading to a hindrance in the learning process. In the context of skill correction, proactive inhibition plays a role in impeding the effectiveness of traditional drill-based approaches.
>
> In conventional skill correction methods, bowlers are often subjected to repeated drills focused on raising self-awareness and reinforcing the correct technique. The assumption is that the bowler needs a refresher on the skill, and repetitive practice of the correct method is believed to be the most effective approach. However, proactive inhibition comes into play when the bowler encounters conflicting information or attempts to change an automated, well-established skill.
>
> When faced with new information that contradicts what a bowler has already learned, proactive inhibition acts as a cognitive defense mechanism. It hinders the assimilation of contradictory concepts, maintaining the status quo of past knowledge and skills. Proactive inhibition does not discriminate between what is considered "right" or "wrong" in a particular situation; instead, it instinctively protects existing knowledge, making it challenging for bowlers to embrace and implement changes.

The effect of learned errors in sports is that, even with excellent coaching and extensive, intense, and highly motivated training sessions, learning from skill drills—the go-to method for overcoming learning errors—is frequently not well transferred to competition performance. Bowlers frequently appear to get better during skill exercises and training, but when left to their own devices—during intense training sessions and during competition—they seem to lose their way, make mistakes, and forget what they have learned. They fail to change, or change very slowly, and keep reverting to their old, flawed behaviors. As a result, it frequently takes a long time for bowlers to adjust to a new technique or skill. During this time, mistakes in technique become more common, and bowlers' emotional moods mirror these technical challenges. When bowlers experience technical difficulties despite being in good physical shape, they frequently experience disappointment, frustration, self-doubt, low self-confidence, a decrease in motivation, helplessness, fears, panic, and a loss of identity as an elite player. All of these frequently result in issues with relationships with the coach and the squad, as well as questions about a chosen preparation program.

Reversion to Old Habits in Competition: In bowling, it can be difficult for an elite bowler to resist going back to their old, ingrained habits during a high-stakes match if he has just made corrections to his stance and delivery technique during training. The strain and stress of competition can cause people to make mistakes he had worked so hard to avoid, even with excellent coaching and preparation.

Ineffective Transfer of Learning: A beginner bowler may find it difficult to put what he has learned into practice in real games after receiving intensive coaching and skill drills to increase his accuracy and spare shooting. Even when he makes progress in practice, he could struggle to apply his newly acquired abilities in competitive settings, which could result in repeated performance blunders.

Emotional Impacts of Learned Errors: A seasoned bowler who has been struggling with a recurring problem with his release method may feel a variety of unfavorable feelings. Even though he is physically strong and prepared, he may experience irritation, self-doubt, and disappointment if he is unable to correct this acquired mistake. His motivation and performance may be further hampered by these emotional reactions.

Prolonged-Term Adaptation to New Techniques: A bowler may need a considerable amount of time to get used to a new, more efficient technique. He might make more mistakes in his play during this shift, and he might find it difficult to remain composed. This protracted period of transition can be emotionally draining, which may have an impact on his motivation and self-assurance.

Strain on Coach-Athlete Relationships: When a bowler consistently makes learning mistakes in their performance, it can put a strain on their relationship with their instructor. While the coach may struggle to come up with fresh ideas to help the bowler avoid these mistakes, the athlete may grow irritated with their lack of improvement. The overall efficacy of the coaching relationship may be impacted by this tension.

Conventional Drill-Based Skill Correction

Traditional approaches to skill correction emphasize identifying the mistake, raising self-awareness, and then stressing the use of the proper skill or method. This method is predicated on the idea that the bowler was not retained from the initial coaching and practice sessions, necessitating a refresher of the talent. Skill drills are the foundation of almost all coaching techniques used today for skill development and technique correction.

Though practice is important and required for acquiring a new skill, experience demonstrates that practicing in the same manner as learning a new skill is significantly less helpful when attempting to modify or enhance an already-established, highly automated skill. Coaches and bowlers continue to practice the correct technique even though it is generally slow to produce results, time-consuming, resource-draining, and essentially ineffective. This is because there aren't many truly useful alternatives.

The Singapore National Bowling Team, renowned for its commitment to excellence, engages in a proactive and strategic approach to skill development and training. One notable facet of their comprehensive training program is the biannual pilgrimage to the Kegel Training Center in the United States. This initiative is a part of the Intensive Coaching Course (ICC) Program, an integral component of the team's training regimen.

The ICC Program operates on a multifaceted model that encompasses both regular, preventive interventions and emergency measures. In the context of preventive interventions, the team embarks on a journey to the Kegel Training Center in the U.S. twice a year. These preventive clinics serve as a cornerstone for discovering and evaluating each individual's ideal technique and the skill components that significantly impact stability. The primary emphasis during these sessions is on a meticulous assessment of stability and the quantifiable progress of each bowler's skills.

The Singapore National Bowling Team's choice of the Kegel Training Center reflects a commitment to excellence, as the center is renowned for its state-of-the-art facilities and expertise in bowling training. The preventive clinics not only allow the bowlers to fine-tune their techniques but also provide valuable insights into the stability dynamics within their skill development journey.

When someone acquires new information or a skill that goes against what they already know, this conflict leads to proactive inhibition, which speeds up the process of forgetting the new information they are trying to learn. Proactive inhibition (PI) shields all past knowledge, stops the association of contradictory concepts, and does not distinguish between what is "right" or "wrong" in a particular situation. It does not stop learning from happening. As a result, PI has a maintenance effect over past learning, preventing change and maintaining both accurate and incorrect knowledge and abilities. PI is an all-encompassing, instinctive system that is mostly out of one's control.

Example 1: A bowling great had a chronic problem with his follow-through. He tried innumerable drills and coaching sessions, but he was unable to fix the problem. His performance remained uneven, and he struggled to shake the habit of his erroneous follow-through.

Example 2: For years, a different proficient bowler had been adopting a particular stance technique. During practice, her coach pointed out a problem and stressed a different position. her struggled to give up her previous posture, though, and her coach and her were both frustrated that the new method was not working right away.

Example 3: A very good bowler had a special grip that wasn't like other bowlers' methods. In an effort to improve his accuracy, the team's new coach tried teaching him the more conventional grip. The bowler struggled to adjust to the new grip and sustain his prior level of performance despite great efforts and hours of practice.

Lyndon's Old Way-New Way In Educational Setting

The Old Way-New Way technique (Lyndon, 1989, 2000), which was created in an educational setting for the quick and permanent remediation of habitual (performance) faults, addressed the shortcomings of drill-based methods. The approach provides a four-step procedure (learning trial) for resolving this issue and is based on the necessity to deal with the maintenance effects of proactive inhibition. In summary, the OW-NW approach acknowledges the significance of prior knowledge and the necessity of managing proactive inhibition. To improve bodily self-awareness of both the old method (a mistake) and the new way (right pattern), it employs both positive and "negative practice," which is the purposeful performance of incorrect action. Ultimately, the mediation process—which involves conscious comparisons between the old and new ways—reinforces improved self-awareness by helping the learner unlearn habitual performance errors first. These elements highlight the particulars of skill re-teaching as opposed to traditional methods of teaching new skills, which focus primarily on intentional practice (drills) of the new method.

Correction of habitual performance errors in elite bowlers

Multiple experimental attempts to use a learning trial process and the Old Way-New Way paradigm in sports. But it's also important to take into account a few more theoretical and practical factors that represent the unique characteristics of elite sport.

- To start, coaches express athletes' subjective assessments of their performance using the concept of task components and the chain of components based on the idea of "kinematic chain" in error analysis (Old Way).

- Second, the greatest time to spot an error is during competition stress or when an athlete is purposefully pushing too hard during practice. A mistake can be a link in the chain or an interaction between links.

- Lastly, an error analysis identifies individually optimal and non-optimal techniques by analyzing an individual's best and worst performance (Identification step in the ICC program).

OW-NW in Bowling

To determine the best movement pattern for each bowler, their unique resources (strengths) are taken into account (New Way). In a number of situations, a bowler may require more practice to pick up a new movement pattern before making a change (skill replacement). A bowler and a coach should be able to identify the New Way as the optimum pattern with clarity. Until all parties are in agreement that the chosen New Way is the greatest alternative available, it is not advised to start a change in technique. To ensure that this new skill is standardized in practices and stable in competitions, several practices should be carried out following a skill correction utilizing the standard learning trial process to deal with proactive inhibition.

Correction stage:

David is an amateur bowler who has advanced to the ICC program's Correction stage. He has recognized that he has to correct his skills because he constantly finds it difficult to hit the intended target. David has been working with a coach who has exposed him to Lyndon's Old Way-New Way method in a classroom. This entails locating and fixing repetitive performance flaws in David's bowling technique by gradually breaking old habits and forming new ones.

Maria is a semi-professional bowler who has also advanced to the ICC program's Correction stage. She has recognized that she needs to improve her release technique because she frequently grips the ball too tightly, which leads to uneven shots. Maria is actively striving to improve her grip and release technique with the assistance of her coach. She is concentrating on keeping a relaxed grasp and a smooth release to maximize her overall performance.

1-Month Strategic Plan for Technique Optimization (Old/Way - New/Way) in Bowlers

Duration: *4 weeks*

Stage 1: Assessment and Goal Setting (3 days)

- **Step 1:** Initial Assessment
  - Evaluate each bowler's existing technique thoroughly, including performance evaluation and video analysis.

- **Step 2:** Goal Setting
  - Work with players to establish precise objectives for technique optimization, emphasizing areas that need work based on the assessment results.

Stage 2: Introduction to Old Way-New Way (OW-NW) Technique (3 days)

- **Step 3:** Understanding OW-NW
  - Introduce the Old Way-New Way technique to the players, along with its four-step process for fixing chronic mistakes.

Stage 3: Error Analysis and Identification (1 weeks)

- **Step 4:** Error Analysis (Old Way)
  - During the first week, assign bowlers to use the OW-NW technique to examine their previous performances in order to pinpoint chronic faults.
  - Motivate them to use the idea of the "kinematic chain" to deconstruct their technique into task components.

- **Step 5:** Identifying New Way (Correct Pattern)
  - Assist bowlers in determining their unique New Way movement patterns in the second week, taking into account their resources and areas of strength.
  - Verify that the instructor and bowler agree on the chosen New Way.

Stage 4: Skill Correction (1 weeks)

- **Step 6:** Skill Correction
  - Using the OW-NW method, walk bowlers through the process of unlearning old habits and forming new ones over the course of the following three weeks.
  - Apply the OW-NW four-step process, which consists of mediation, increased self-awareness, positive practice, and negative practice.

Stage 5: Standardization and Stabilization (1 week)

- **Step 7:** Standardization in Practice
  - To make sure the new skill pattern is standardized in training sessions, carry out multiple practices.
  - Give bowlers time to adjust to the new environment and improve under controlled circumstances.

- **Step 8:** Stabilization in Competition
  - Verify that the modified method remains stable and efficient in a competitive setting.
  - Offer assistance during contests so that the new skill pattern is maintained.

Tactics and Tasks for Each Stage:

1. **Initial Assessment:** To pinpoint areas where each player's technique needs to be improved, use performance evaluations and video analysis.

2. **Goal Setting:** Work with players to establish clear objectives for technique optimization, emphasizing areas that have been determined to need work.

3. **Understanding OW-NW:** Introduce players to the OW-NW technique and its four-step fix for persistent mistakes.

4. **Error Analysis (Old Way):** The "Old Way" of error analysis involves having players examine their previous performances to pinpoint recurring mistakes and dissect their technique into individual task components using the "kinematic chain" theory.

5. **Identifying New Way:** Assist players in determining their own best movement patterns (New Way), taking into account their resources and strengths, while making sure that the coach is in agreement.

6. **Skill Correction:** Guide players through the process of unlearning old habits and developing new ones using the OW-NW method, utilizing the four-step process employing the OW-NW approach and its four-step procedure, assist players in unlearning old habits and forming new ones.

7. **Standardization in Practice:** To guarantee that the new skill pattern is standardized in training sessions enable players to adjust to modifications, and conduct multiple practices.

8. **Stabilization in Competition:** Make sure the modified technique is stable and efficient in competitive settings, offering assistance to sustain the new skill pattern during contests.

Bowlers will improve their technique, eliminate bad habits, and be ready for competitions by placing this two-month strategic plan and learning method into practice.

ICC Program as an emergency Interventions

Additionally, the program can be applied to quick "emergency" interventions. Consequently, there are three packages that make up the ICC program:

1. *Preventive clinics* (Twice a year) are held to discover and assess each person's ideal technique and skill components that affect stability. Here, the primary focus is on assessing the stability and degree of skill growth.

Hypothetical Examples

Preventive Clinics:

a. *Professional bowler Jack lately saw a decline in his game, with erratic shots and less accuracy. He made the choice to go to a preventive clinic that his coaching staff was hosting. Jack got instant feedback on his technique in the clinic, with an emphasis on seeing and fixing any new mistakes or discrepancies. He also took part in exercises and drills meant to strengthen proper technique and stop any deterioration in performance.*

b. *Emily, a competitive bowler, was getting ready for a big competition and wanted to make sure she played with the best possible technique and performance. She went to a preventive clinic her coach was offering, and there she got one-on-one tutoring and technique criticism on bowling. In order to avoid possible performance setbacks, she also learned coping mechanisms for handling pressure and stress during contests.*

2. Immediate recovery of a "lost" skill (3-4 sessions) along with stability of performance in practice and competition. This intervention is comparable to a so-called "first-aid" strategy used to resolve a difficult circumstance and assist a bowler in getting "back on track" by regaining the proper concentration and maximum effort. In this case, the goal is to assist bowlers by helping them relive successful performances and activity patterns.

Immediate Recovery:

a. *During a match, Tom, a junior bowler, suddenly started to perform poorly, making several consecutive bad shots. He saw the problem right away and motioned to his coach for help right away. Tom received immediate feedback and direction from his instructor, which enabled him to see and fix the flaws in his technique. Tom managed to turn around his performance and end the tournament with better shots.*

b. *During a practice session, Samantha, a recreational bowler, was having trouble with the lane conditions, which caused her to make frequent mistakes in her shots. She went to her coach for assistance, who evaluated the problem right away and gave her advice on how to modify her strategy and release technique. Samantha was able to turn around her performance and have a productive practice.*

3. *Rapid error correction* (modified "learning trial" 1-2 training sessions) with the stabilization of a new movement pattern coming after (a modified "learning trial" lasting 1-2 training sessions).

The primary empowering consequence of using any package from the ICC program is that a bowler gains greater control over his technique and job execution. Furthermore, a bowler who understands his own ideal movement pattern is not only more conscious of it, but he also knows exactly how to regain the best movement pattern in the event of a spontaneous error by using a specific movement chain component.

Rapid Error Correction:

a. *During a match, semi-professional bowler Alex discovered a recurring problem with his release technique that was causing him to hit inconsistent shots and lose accuracy. He asked his coach for speedy error repair, and he recognized the problem right away and gave clear instructions on how to fix it. Alex was able to quickly remedy the mistake and get better at his shots with concentrated practice and tweaks.*

b. *Julie was having trouble regularly hitting the target when she was bowling in a friendly league. She went straight to her coach for assistance, and he saw right away that there was a serious problem with her alignment and targeting. Julie was able to fix the mistake and increase her accuracy in the games that followed with the use of quick error correction exercises and repetition.*

Strategic Plan and Learning Process for Technique Optimization in Bowlers

Duration: *Ongoing with periodic interventions*

Preventive Clinics (Twice a Year)

- **Step 1:** Identification and Assessment (1 day)
  - Completely evaluate each player's present technique and skill set as it relates to stability.
  - To find any problems, use performance evaluation and video analysis.
- **Step 2:** Skill Development Check-Up (1 day)
  - Pay close attention to the stability and extent of skill development.
  - Spot emerging mistakes or inconsistent techniques.
- **Step 3:** Feedback and Drills (1 day)
  - Give players quick feedback on their technique.
  - Create and carry out targeted drills and exercises to address new concerns and reinforce proper technique.

Immediate Recovery (As Needed)

- **Step 1:** Recognizing a "Lost" Skill (Immediate)
  - Assist players in identifying, in a timely manner, any abrupt decline in performance or "lost" skill during practice or competition.
  - When a player needs help right away, he should indicate to their coach.
- **Step 2:** On-the-Spot Feedback (Immediate)
  - Players experiencing setbacks in their performance receive immediate feedback and direction from coaches.
  - During the tournament or practice, spot and fix technique mistakes.
- **Step 3:** Re-Experience Success (1-2 sessions)
  - Assist players in reliving productive performances and behavior patterns.
  - Targeted practice sessions might help you regain confidence and concentrate on using the right technique..

Rapid Error Correction (As Needed)

- **Step 1:** Identifying Specific Errors (Immediate)
  - During practice or competition, players should quickly spot specific technique mistakes.
  - When mistakes are identified, ask the coach for help..
- **Step 2:** Quick Error Correction (1-2 sessions)
  - Coaches swiftly fix technical mistakes with a modified "learning trial" approach.
  - Offer detailed instructions and practical help to address the issues found.
- **Step 3:** Stabilization of New Movement Pattern (Ongoing)
  - In later practice sessions, players focus on stabilizing the adjusted technique.
  - Make sure the new movement pattern becomes dependable and constant.

Models For Accurancy Of Elite Bowlers

Accuracy stands as a cornerstone in bowling, defining the competence of elite bowlers and directly influencing their success on the lanes. In this intricate and precise sport, where the objective is to knock down all ten pins with a single delivery, precision becomes the differentiator between a good performance and greatness. The game's dependency on accuracy is profound, as every slight deviation in the release, angle, or speed can significantly impact the trajectory and eventual collision with the pins. Elite bowlers, aiming for consistent strikes and spares, understand the pivotal role that accuracy plays in their overall performance. To enhance and expedite the development of accuracy in bowlers, numerous coaches and researchers have formulated specialized models and methodologies. These models dig into the biomechanics, psychology, and tactics of the bowling approach, seeking to fine-tune each aspect to achieve pinpoint precision. Whether it's refining the release technique, perfecting the footwork, or cultivating a mental state conducive to accuracy under pressure, these models aim to make the process of attaining accuracy faster and more effective. Consequently, accuracy is not merely a skill but an art form in bowling, and the continuous pursuit of perfection in this regard is what elevates bowlers to the pinnacle of their game.

Pettlep

The process of creating or reproducing an experience in the mind through the use of most or all senses is known as imagery. When combined with psychological therapies, the program has demonstrated that, in comparison to other forms of mental training, imagery is a valuable and useful strategy for enhancing performance and achievement. Additionally, research findings indicate that visualization is a crucial psychological ability. The two main things that might affect a bowler's performance are the training methods and the imagery's qualities. As previously said, there aren't many formal protocols for making efficient use of the pictures.

The Physical, Environment, Task, Timing, Learning, Emotion, and Perspective (PETTLEP) is one example. Holmes and Collins (2001) created the training paradigm known as "imagery," which offers a set of recommendations for using imagery in athletic contexts. In particular, the term PETTLEP stands for crucial variables that must be taken into account prior to constructing an imaging intervention. Based on research from sports psychology, cognitive psychology, and neuroscience, the PETTLEP model of imaging athletes who practice with the PETTLEP imagery approach benefit from seven key components that set it apart from traditional imagery.

Three types of technologies are suggested for use in imaging training in relation to the application of physical and environmental elements in PETTLEP imagery: flotation, biofeedback, and video modeling. Based on the PETTLEP criterion, video modeling is the most effective approach to deliver visuals out of all of these ways. Applying imagery with video modeling has been proven to be simpler, more economical, and much more successful. Using this technique, an athlete watches a video recording and applies what he sees in the cognitive picture movie to their own motor performance. The bowler will be able to translate the model more successfully if it resembles the motor performance that he wishes to achieve. Two categories comprise the audio and the audio-video combination to convey imagery in the PETLEP imaging paradigm. The bowler receives a screenplay for traditional visuals to use in their residence. It has been discovered that imagery training can enhance bowlers' thought processes, and as a result, altering a bowler's perspective of success and boosting their drive is essential to producing their finest bowling performances. All bowlers, from amateurs to famous bowlers, enjoy using imagery in their play.

Key Element	Description	PETTLEP in Bowling Training	Example	Professional Steps
Physical	Refers to the physical actions required to perform a skill	Analyzing and improving the physical aspects of the bowling technique	Working on the bowling approach and release technique to maximize ball speed and accuracy	Conduct physical assessment and provide individualized training program
Environment	Refers to the physical and social environment in which the skill is performed	Modifying the environment to create optimal training conditions	Adjusting lane conditions to simulate different tournament environments	Evaluate the training facility and make necessary adjustments to improve performance
Task	Refers to the specific skills and techniques required to perform the skill	Breaking down the skill into smaller components to improve overall performance	Practicing spares to increase overall scoring ability	Analyze and breakdown individual bowling techniques to identify areas for improvement
Timing	Refers to the timing of the movements required to perform the skill	Focusing on the timing of the physical movements to optimize performance	Focusing on the timing of the push-away and release to maximize accuracy	Use technology to analyze and improve timing
Learning	Refers to the cognitive processes involved in acquiring and refining a skill	Encouraging learning through repetition and feedback	Practicing the same shot from different angles and positions	Provide individualized feedback and focus on specific areas for improvement
Emotion	Refers to the emotional and psychological state of the athlete	Emphasizing the importance of mental preparation and managing emotions	Teaching visualization and relaxation techniques to help manage competition nerves	Incorporate mental training and visualization techniques into regular training sessions
Perspective	Refers to the athlete's individual perspective on the skill and their performance	Encouraging a growth mindset and positive self-talk	Emphasizing the importance of self-reflection and identifying areas for improvement	Provide positive feedback and encourage athletes to set realistic goals for themselves

Table 41 - This table outlines key PETTLEP elements in bowling training. Physical aspects involve analyzing and enhancing techniques, while the environment is modified for optimal conditions. Breaking down specific skills and focusing on timing are crucial. Cognitive processes are improved through repetition and feedback. Emotional aspects are addressed with mental preparation, and individual perspectives emphasize a growth mindset. Professional steps include conducting assessments, adjusting environments, breaking down techniques, and providing feedback.

Comprehensive 1-Month Plan for Bowler Using PETTLEP Model

In this 1-month plan, we will follow the Physical, Environment, Task, Timing, Learning, Emotion, and Perspective (PETTLEP) model to enhance your bowling accuracy through the power of imagery.

Week 1: Introduction to PETTLEP Imagery

Stage 1: Understanding the PETTLEP Model

- **Steps to Do:** Attend a workshop to understand the PETTLEP model's seven components.
- **Cues and Thought Process:** Reflect on the role of each PETTLEP component in enhancing mental imagery.

Stage 2: Personal Imagery Assessment

- **Steps to Do:** Engage in self-assessment, identifying strengths and areas for improvement.
- **Cues and Thought Process:** Analyze the quality of mental images related to bowling.

Stage 3: Goal Setting with Imagery

- **Steps to Do:** Establish bowling-specific performance goals aligned with PETTLEP components.
- **Cues and Thought Process:** Visualize successfully achieving set goals.
- **Mental Drills:**
    0. Visualization of a Perfect Strike: Close your eyes and mentally walk through the steps of a flawless strike.
    1. Goal Visualization: Picture yourself achieving your set performance goals in vivid detail.

- **Technical Drills:**
  1. Stance Refinement: Work on achieving a consistent and balanced stance during practice.
  2. Release Technique: Focus on the smooth and controlled release of the ball, ensuring accuracy.

Week 2: Physical and Environmental Imagery

Stage 4: Physical Component Enhancement

- **Steps to Do:** Integrate physical sensations into imagery sessions.
- **Cues and Thought Process:** Emphasize muscle engagement and overall kinesthetic experience.

Stage 5: Environmental Component Application

- **Steps to Do:** Utilize video modeling to connect with the bowling environment.
- **Cues and Thought Process:** Picture the bowling alley, lane conditions, and surroundings in detail.
- **Mental Drills:**
  0. Kinesthetic Imagery: Imagine the sensation of a successful bowling motion, feeling each muscle's engagement.
  1. Alley Visualization: Use video clips or mental imagery to visualize the bowling alley environment.
- **Technical Drills:**
  1. Lane Adaptation: Practice adjusting your approach based on different lane conditions.
  2. Visual Alignment: Work on aligning your physical stance with the mental image of the target.

Week 3: Task, Timing, and Learning Imagery

Stage 6: Task-Specific Imagery

- **Steps to Do:** Break down the bowling task into key components for detailed mental rehearsal.
- **Cues and Thought Process:** Mentally visualize each task with precision.

Stage 7: Timing and Learning Integration

- **Steps to Do:** Fine-tune mental images to synchronize with the timing of a perfect shot.
- **Cues and Thought Process:** Pay attention to the rhythm and timing of movements.
- **Mental Drills:**
  0. Task Breakdown: Mentally rehearse each phase of your bowling approach separately.
  1. Temporal Alignment: Visualize your movements syncing perfectly with the desired timing.
- **Technical Drills:**
  1. Approach Consistency: Focus on maintaining a consistent approach during practice.
  2. Release Timing: Practice releasing the ball with precise timing for optimal results.

Week 4: Emotion and Perspective Imagery

Stage 8: Emotion Regulation

- **Steps to Do:** Incorporate emotional elements into imagery sessions.
- **Cues and Thought Process:** Cultivate a positive emotional state by visualizing confidence and focus.

Stage 9: Perspective Shifting

- **Steps to Do:** Experiment with different perspectives during mental imagery.
- **Cues and Thought Process:** Enhance adaptability by visualizing successful shots from various angles.
- **Mental Drills:**
  0. Emotional Resilience: Practice imagery sessions focusing on staying calm and confident under pressure.
  1. Multi-Perspective Imagery: Visualize successful shots from both first-person and third-person perspectives.

- **Technical Drills:**
  1. Emotional Stability: Work on maintaining focus and confidence during challenging practice scenarios.
  2. Angle Adaptation: Experiment with different angles of release during practice to enhance adaptability.

Final Thoughts:

Quotes to Inspire:

"Visualize your success, feel the motion, and become one with the perfect shot."

"In the lanes of your mind, create a masterpiece of every bowl."

"Imagination is your bowling ally; let it roll with precision, passion, and purpose."

Visual-Motor Behaviour Rehearsal (Vmbr) As Potential Approach

The utilization of psychological modalities, particularly imagery training, has proven to be a valuable tool for enhancing athletic performance among high-performance athletes. Imagery training involves mentally recreating scenes from sporting encounters, offering a range of benefits for bowlers, including improved training and competitive performance, increased self-confidence, motivation, and skill acquisition. It has also demonstrated efficacy in reducing anxiety and arousal levels. Despite its effectiveness, mental imagery training is underutilized in daily training regimens, particularly in local settings, and amateur bowlers often resort to traditional approaches that rely on increased effort through repetitive practice sessions without incorporating visual training.

Visual-Motor Behavior Rehearsal (VMBR), a cognitive-behavioral method, has shown promise in enhancing motor performance and accuracy in various contexts, including sports. Grounded in the idea that strengthening the integration between visual and motor systems through mental practice can lead to improved physical performance, VMBR presents a potential avenue for enhancing accuracy in elite bowlers.

Several applications of VMBR in bowling highlight its potential effectiveness:

Visualization of the bowling technique: By mentally practicing and visualizing the ideal approach, release, and follow-through, bowlers can adopt Visual Mental Bowling Rehearsal (VMBR), reinforcing proper movement patterns and improving precision.

Imagery for targeting: Using VMBR, bowlers can mentally aim for specific pins or sections of the bowling lane, enhancing accuracy during actual sessions by consistently visualizing hitting the target.

Mental rehearsal of competition scenarios: VMBR enables bowlers to mentally practice varied competition settings, preparing for changing oil patterns, challenging opponents, and diverse lane conditions to enhance performance under pressure.

Imagery for self-assessment and error correction: Bowlers can use VMBR for mental examination, pinpointing areas for improvement and mentally practicing adjustments to enhance their performance.

Visualization of performance goals: Utilizing Visualization of Bowling Recursion (VMBR), bowlers can mentally practice achieving specific goals, strengthening their drive, self-assurance, and concentration to improve overall performance.

The theoretical underpinnings of VMBR in bowling emphasize precision and consistency as crucial elements. VMBR models suggest that mentally practicing specific motor tasks strengthens neural circuits, contributing to enhanced accuracy and consistency. The training typically involves combining mental rehearsal with physical practice, allowing bowlers to receive feedback on their performance while executing the motor activity. Strengthening brain connections, reducing performance anxiety, and boosting confidence are key objectives of VMBR training, offering elite bowlers a potential avenue to improve accuracy performance. Mental rehearsal through VMBR can enhance their ability to visualize shots, adapt to input, and maintain focus during competition, ultimately improving accuracy and consistency.

Methods For Accurancy Through Psychological Enhancement In Bowling

1. Visual Focus Training:

Description: Visual focus training is a meticulous and comprehensive approach tailored for bowlers, placing a heightened emphasis on maintaining an unwavering focus on the target, specifically the bowling pins. This technique transcends the mere physical act of aiming and involves improving the bowler's concentration throughout the entire shot process, recognizing the profound impact of sustained focus on accuracy.

Steps:

1. **Stationary Drills:** Commence the training regimen with stationary drills designed to instill precise alignment of the gaze with the target pathway or the pins . This foundational step establishes a baseline for sustained concentration, laying the groundwork for advanced focus.

2. **Dynamic Drills:** Progress to dynamic targeting drills that seamlessly integrate the approach and release into the training. This phase challenges the bowler to maintain unwavering focus through the entire motion, simulating real-game scenarios and enhancing concentration during dynamic actions.

3. **Progressive Distances:** Gradually increase the distance between the bowler and the pins or the pathway width , introducing a dynamic element to the training that not only challenges but also enhances focus. This step is pivotal for adapting the bowler's concentration to varying shot distances, reinforcing the skill's applicability in diverse competition conditions.

To-Do Tasks and Cues:

- *Mindful Breathing:* Integrate mindful breathing exercises during stationary and dynamic drills to promote relaxation and sustained focus.

- *Visual Anchors:* Incorporate visual anchors, such as markings on the lane, to aid in maintaining a consistent visual focus during different phases of the shot.

- *Shot Visualization:* Encourage bowlers to visualize successful shots before execution, reinforcing the connection between focused visual attention and accurate shot delivery.

- *Eye-Target Synchronization:* Emphasize the synchronization of eye movement with the target, ensuring that the gaze remains aligned with the intended point throughout the shot.

Psychological and Neurological Impact: Visual focus training has a profound impact on both the psychological and neurological aspects of a bowler's performance. Psychologically, it enhances mental resilience by cultivating an ability to shut out distractions and maintain concentration under varying conditions. Neurologically, sustained focus is linked to improved neural efficiency, optimizing the brain's processing speed and accuracy in translating visual input into motor responses. This dual impact creates a holistic improvement in a bowler's accuracy, contributing to consistent and precise shot execution during competitions. Additionally, the enhanced concentration developed through this method positively influences decision-making under pressure, a crucial aspect of high-level competitive bowling.

2. Biofeedback Techniques:

Description: Biofeedback techniques represent an advanced and personalized approach for bowlers, leveraging cutting-edge technology to provide real-time information about physiological responses, including heart rate and muscle tension. This method is meticulously designed to enhance self-awareness and control, recognizing the intricate connection between physiological states and accuracy in bowling.

Steps:

1. **Wearable Sensors:** Initiate the process by equipping bowlers with wearable sensors designed to monitor key physiological indicators during shots. These sensors provide real-time data, offering bowlers invaluable insights into their physiological responses and establishing a foundation for heightened self-awareness.

2. **Immediate Feedback:** Implement immediate feedback mechanisms that relay information on changes in physiological responses directly related to accuracy. This instantaneous feedback fosters a profound

connection between mental states and performance, allowing bowlers to adapt and refine their approach in real-time.

3. **Breathing Exercises:** Integrate biofeedback into breathing exercises, emphasizing its role in managing anxiety and stress during the game. By incorporating biofeedback into these exercises, bowlers enhance overall composure, a critical factor for maintaining consistent and accurate shots, especially in high-pressure situations.

To-Do Tasks and Cues:

- *Baseline Measurement:* Begin with a baseline measurement of physiological indicators to establish a reference point for individual bowlers.
- *Calibration Drills:* Design calibration drills where bowlers focus on maintaining optimal physiological states while executing shots, using biofeedback to fine-tune their responses.
- *Stress Simulation:* Introduce stress simulation scenarios during practice, utilizing biofeedback to help bowlers navigate and regulate heightened physiological responses.
- *Biofeedback Integration:* Encourage bowlers to integrate biofeedback data into their mental routines, creating a seamless connection between physiological awareness and shot accuracy.

Psychological and Neurological Impact: The extended use of biofeedback techniques yields significant psychological and neurological benefits for bowlers. Psychologically, the real-time feedback enhances self-regulation and emotional control, crucial for maintaining composure during the ups and downs of a game. Neurologically, the integration of biofeedback refines the bowler's ability to synchronize mental and physical states, optimizing the neural pathways associated with accuracy. The tailored approach of biofeedback acknowledges the individuality of bowlers, contributing to a personalized journey of self-improvement in accuracy. As a result, bowlers develop a heightened sense of self-awareness, a key component in consistently delivering accurate shots in various competitive scenarios.

3. Mental Imagery Training:

Description: The extended approach to mental imagery training for bowlers digs into the realm of creating vivid mental images of successful shots, offering a comprehensive method to reinforce positive visualization and elevate overall performance. This technique transcends mere visualization, becoming a dynamic tool for shaping the bowler's mental framework and fostering a deeper mind-body connection.

Steps:

1. **Quiet Setting:** Commence mental imagery training in a focused and relaxed environment, providing bowlers with the ideal space to create clear and vivid mental pictures of successful shots. The quiet setting becomes the canvas where the bowler's mental images can take shape and gain clarity.

2. **Visualization Techniques:** Guide bowlers through visualization techniques that go beyond the basics, emphasizing not only the trajectory of the ball but also the nuances of the approach, the precision of the release, and the intricate dance of the pins. This detailed visualization fosters a positive mental association with each element of the shot.

3. **Positive Reinforcement:** Introduce positive reinforcement into the mental imagery process, associating uplifting emotions with the successful mental images created. This step is crucial in boosting confidence and laying the foundation for a resilient mental framework where success becomes an ingrained expectation.

To-Do Tasks and Cues:

- *Guided Imagery Sessions:* Facilitate guided imagery sessions where bowlers are led through a series of mental scenarios, emphasizing successful shots and positive outcomes.
- *Multisensory Visualization:* Encourage bowlers to engage multiple senses during mental imagery, incorporating touch, sound, and even the emotional thrill of success into their visualizations.

- *Progressive Complexity:* Gradually increase the complexity of mental imagery, challenging bowlers to visualize success in diverse scenarios, including high-pressure moments and varied lane conditions.
- *Reflective Journaling:* Introduce reflective journaling as a companion to mental imagery, allowing bowlers to articulate their thoughts, emotions, and insights gained during the visualization process.

Psychological and Neurological Impact: The extended mental imagery training not only refines the mind-body connection but also profoundly impacts the psychological and neurological facets of a bowler's performance. Psychologically, the positive reinforcement embedded in the mental imagery process contributes to heightened self-confidence and a resilient mindset. Neurologically, the brain's neural pathways associated with successful shots are strengthened through repeated mental rehearsal, paving the way for improved shot accuracy. This extended approach transforms mental imagery into a powerful tool for psychological resilience, confidence-building, and precision in bowling.

4. Progressive Target Drills:

Description: The extended approach to progressive target drills for bowlers elevates the training regimen by using targets of varying sizes and positions to not only challenge accuracy but also introduce adaptability into the bowler's skill set. This method transforms the training environment into a dynamic space where precision in targeting is honed under diverse conditions, enhancing the bowler's ability to make real-time adjustments.

Steps:

1. **Stationary Targets:** Initiate the extended target drill training with strategically placed stationary targets among the pins. This foundational step emphasizes precision in targeting, setting the stage for the bowler to master accuracy in a controlled setting.
2. **Moving Targets:** Progress to the inclusion of moving targets to simulate the dynamic nature of changing lane conditions. As the targets move, bowlers are compelled to adapt not only their targeting but also their release, fostering a heightened level of adaptability crucial in real-game scenarios.
3. **Game-Like Scenarios:** Integrate target drills seamlessly into game-like situations, creating a holistic approach that combines accuracy with contextual decision-making. By facing scenarios mirroring competition conditions, bowlers refine their ability to make precision-driven decisions under varying pressures.

To-Do Tasks and Cues:

- *Precision Calibration:* Begin with precision-focused calibration, where bowlers fine-tune their targeting skills with stationary targets, ensuring a meticulous approach to hitting specific pins.
- *Release Adaptation:* Emphasize release adaptation as the targets introduce movement, challenging bowlers to synchronize their release with the dynamic nature of the targets.
- *Strategic Decision-Making:* Incorporate strategic decision-making into the drills, encouraging bowlers to assess the changing scenarios and adjust their targeting and release accordingly.
- *Progressive Complexity:* Gradually increase the complexity of target drills, introducing additional challenges such as varied pin arrangements, unpredictable movements, and time constraints.

Psychological and Neurological Impact: The extended progressive target drills not only enhance accuracy but also significantly impact the psychological and neurological aspects of a bowler's performance. Psychologically, the drills foster adaptability, resilience, and strategic thinking, crucial elements for success in competitive scenarios. Neurologically, the brain's ability to make rapid calculations and adjustments during target drills strengthens, directly influencing precision in targeting. This extended approach transforms target drills into a comprehensive training method that not only hones accuracy but also prepares bowlers for the unpredictable challenges of real competitions.

5. Focus On Release Technique:

Description: The extended focus on the release technique for bowlers recognizes the critical role the release plays in achieving accurate shots. This method goes beyond acknowledging the importance of the release; it digs into refining and mastering this final stage of the shot for optimal pin action. By emphasizing the intricacies of the release, bowlers enhance their ability to control the ball's spin and angle, ensuring a precise and effective delivery.

Steps:

1. **Release Analysis:** Initiate the extended release technique training with a meticulous analysis of the release phase. Break down this crucial element into components, focusing keenly on hand positioning and timing. This step provides a detailed understanding of the nuances involved in achieving a precise release.

2. **Release Drills:** Incorporate specialized drills designed to target specific aspects of the release for improvement. These drills are tailored to enhance the consistency and precision of the release, addressing key areas identified during the release analysis. Each drill aims at refining the bowler's technique for optimal performance.

3. **Slow-Motion Repetition:** Progress to slow-motion repetitions as a method to refine the muscle memory associated with the release. This step ensures a controlled and consistent execution of the release, allowing bowlers to internalize the correct movements and positions. Slow-motion repetition is instrumental in perfecting the intricate details of the release.

To-Do Tasks and Cues:

- *Hand Positioning Mastery:* Focus on mastering hand positioning during the release, ensuring a solid and controlled interaction between the bowler's hand and the ball.
- *Timing Precision:* Fine-tune the timing of the release, emphasizing the synchronization of hand movements with the overall shot process for optimal precision.
- *Targeted Release Drills:* Integrate targeted release drills into the training, emphasizing specific improvements identified during the release analysis.
- *Visual Focus on Release:* Incorporate visual focus techniques specifically on the release phase, encouraging bowlers to maintain unwavering concentration on this critical aspect.

Psychological and Neurological Impact: The extended focus on the release technique not only sharpens the technical aspects of a bowler's performance but also significantly influences the psychological and neurological dimensions. Psychologically, mastering the release fosters confidence and mental resilience, knowing that the final stage of the shot is under control. Neurologically, the repetitive and focused nature of release drills enhances muscle memory, ensuring that the desired release becomes a natural and instinctive part of a bowler's technique. This extended approach transforms the release into a precision-focused skill, contributing profoundly to overall shot accuracy.

6. Lane Pattern Familiarization:

Description: The extended lane pattern familiarization method for bowlers recognizes the critical role of understanding and adapting to different lane patterns in achieving accuracy. This approach goes beyond mere acknowledgment of the impact of lane conditions on shot accuracy; it digs into an extensive training regimen aimed at developing adaptability. Bowlers engage in practicing on various lane conditions to ensure they can make quick and effective adjustments, fostering a heightened ability to navigate diverse conditions with precision.

Steps:

1. **Pattern Identification:** The extended familiarization begins with a comprehensive understanding of common lane patterns and their effects on ball motion. Bowlers learn to identify and interpret these patterns, establishing a foundational understanding that forms the basis of subsequent adaptations.

2. **Adaptation Drills:** Create specialized drills that simulate different lane conditions, requiring bowlers to make adjustments in targeting and release based on the identified patterns. These drills aim to hone

the bowler's adaptability, fostering the ability to make real-time adjustments in response to varying lane conditions.

3. **Consistent Pattern Practice:** Emphasize regular practice on consistent lane patterns to refine fundamental skills. Before tackling varied conditions, bowlers build a strong foundation through consistent practice on specific patterns, ensuring a deep understanding and mastery of the basics.

To-Do Tasks and Cues:

- *Pattern Recognition:* Focus on recognizing and interpreting common lane patterns, ensuring bowlers can anticipate and understand the effects on ball motion.
- *Adaptive Targeting:* Integrate adaptive targeting drills into the training, emphasizing the need to adjust targeting and release based on identified lane patterns.
- *Consistency in Practice:* Prioritize regular practice on consistent lane patterns to refine fundamental skills and establish a solid foundation for adaptability.
- *Real-Time Adjustments:* Encourage bowlers to make real-time adjustments during practice sessions, simulating the dynamic nature of competitions and diverse lane conditions.

Psychological and Neurological Impact: The extended lane pattern familiarization method not only shapes the technical prowess of a bowler but also profoundly influences the psychological and neurological aspects of performance. Psychologically, the ability to adapt quickly to changing lane patterns instills confidence and mental resilience, as bowlers approach competitions with a strategic mindset. Neurologically, the repetition of adaptive drills enhances cognitive flexibility and decision-making, ensuring that bowlers can make accurate and swift adjustments during the dynamic conditions of competitive play. This extended approach transforms lane pattern familiarity into a strategic skill, contributing significantly to overall accuracy.

7. Pressure Situations Simulation :

Description: The extended pressure situations simulation method for bowlers recognizes the intricate link between mental fortitude and accurate shots under competitive stress. Going beyond acknowledging the psychological component of accuracy, this approach digs into creating a comprehensive training regimen that prepares bowlers for the mental challenges of high-pressure situations. By recreating scenarios that mimic tournament pressure and complexity, bowlers develop the mental resilience required to maintain accuracy in the face of intense competition.

Steps:

1. **Mock Competitions:** Initiate the extended simulation with mock competitions, replicating tournament pressure and scoring conditions. This step prepares bowlers for the intensity and expectations of real-game situations, fostering a competitive mindset.

2. **Time Constraints:** Introduce time constraints for shot execution to simulate tournament pacing. Adding an element of urgency enhances mental resilience, ensuring bowlers can maintain accuracy even when faced with time pressure.

3. **Variable Challenges:** Combine pressure scenarios with additional challenges, such as lane adjustments, to replicate the complexity of real-game conditions. This step fosters adaptability, training bowlers to handle a variety of challenges during competitions.

To-Do Tasks and Cues:

- *Competition Mindset:* Encourage bowlers to adopt a competitive mindset during mock competitions, emphasizing the importance of accuracy under tournament-like pressure.
- *Urgency Awareness:* Train bowlers to execute shots within specified time constraints, promoting awareness of urgency and refining their ability to perform accurately under time pressure.
- *Adaptive Responses:* Integrate variable challenges into pressure scenarios, requiring bowlers to make adaptive responses to changes in lane conditions or additional complexities.

- *Performance Evaluation:* Conduct thorough evaluations of bowlers' performance in simulated pressure situations, providing constructive feedback to enhance mental resilience and accuracy.

Psychological and Neurological Impact: The extended pressure situations simulation method has a profound impact on both the psychological and neurological aspects of a bowler's performance. Psychologically, exposure to simulated high-pressure scenarios builds mental toughness, confidence, and the ability to stay focused under stress. Neurologically, the integration of time constraints and variable challenges enhances cognitive flexibility and decision-making, ensuring that bowlers can maintain accuracy in dynamically changing conditions. This extended approach transforms pressure situations into opportunities for growth, contributing significantly to overall accuracy in competitive settings.

8. Goal-Oriented Practice Sessions:

Description: The extended goal-oriented practice sessions method for bowlers epitomizes a meticulous approach that centers on specific accuracy-related objectives, ensuring deliberate and purposeful training with a clear direction. Going beyond routine practice, this approach involves identifying individual weaknesses, designing targeted drills, and progressively challenging bowlers to maintain a dynamic and goal-driven training regimen focused on accuracy enhancement.

Steps:

1. **Identify Weaknesses:** Commence the extended practice sessions by conducting a detailed analysis of individual weaknesses related to accuracy. This step involves identifying specific areas for improvement, such as spare conversions or targeting particular pins.

2. **Targeted Drills:** Design drills that specifically address the weaknesses identified in the analysis. These drills provide targeted training, improving in on accuracy improvement and systematically addressing individual challenges.

3. **Progressive Challenges:** Gradually increase the difficulty of drills as bowlers improve, ensuring a challenging yet achievable progression. This step maintains a purposeful training regimen, continually pushing bowlers to enhance their accuracy in a progressive and sustainable manner.

To-Do Tasks and Cues:

- *Individual Assessments:* Conduct comprehensive assessments to identify each bowler's unique weaknesses and areas requiring improvement in accuracy.
- *Drill Customization:* Design drills tailored to address the specific weaknesses identified, ensuring targeted training for accurate shots.
- *Progress Monitoring:* Regularly monitor bowlers' progress and skill development, adjusting the difficulty of drills to maintain an optimal balance between challenge and achievable goals.
- *Goal Setting:* Collaborate with bowlers to set clear and measurable accuracy-related goals for each practice session, fostering a sense of purpose and achievement.

Psychological and Neurological Impact: The extended goal-oriented practice sessions method significantly influences both psychological and neurological aspects of a bowler's performance. Psychologically, setting clear goals and addressing weaknesses enhances motivation, focus, and a sense of accomplishment. Neurologically, the deliberate and targeted nature of the drills strengthens neural pathways associated with accurate shots, facilitating the development of muscle memory. This extended approach transforms practice sessions into strategic opportunities for continuous improvement, contributing substantially to the bowler's overall accuracy.

9. Deep Practice Method:

Description: The Deep Practice Method for bowlers is a dynamic and adaptive approach that challenges bowlers to confront a variety of variables in every shot. Unlike traditional accuracy-focused training, deep practice introduces variations in speed, rotation, spin, axis tilt, and ball surface, creating a learning environment that promotes adaptability and quick decision-making. This method encourages bowlers to embrace the variability inherent in the sport, fostering a mindset of continuous improvement rather than fixating on avoiding errors.

Steps:

1. **Variable Adaptation:** Initiate deep practice by incorporating variables such as speed, rotation, spin, axis tilt, and ball surface in each shot. This step aims to expose bowlers to diverse conditions, requiring rapid adaptation and decision-making.

2. **Dynamic Shot Sequences:** Design practice sequences where each shot is intentionally different from the previous one. This dynamic approach challenges bowlers to develop versatility and refine their ability to adjust in real-time.

3. **Error Embrace:** Encourage bowlers to view mistakes as opportunities for learning and improvement. The deep practice method shifts the focus from avoiding errors to embracing them as integral components of the learning process.

To-Do Tasks and Cues:

- *Variable Implementation:* Systematically introduce variations in speed, rotation, spin, axis tilt, and ball surface during practice sessions, ensuring a comprehensive and diverse learning experience.

- *Continuous Adaptation:* Emphasize the importance of adapting to changing conditions in each shot, fostering a mindset of flexibility and versatility.

- *Error Analysis:** Incorporate error analysis as part of the learning process. Encourage bowlers to reflect on mistakes, understand the underlying causes, and implement adjustments for improvement.

- *Realistic Competition Simulation:* Design practice scenarios that simulate the unpredictability of competition, preparing bowlers for the dynamic nature of real-game situations.

Psychological and Neurological Impact: The Deep Practice Method not only enhances technical skills but also has profound psychological and neurological impacts. Psychologically, bowlers develop resilience, adaptability, and a growth mindset by embracing variability and learning from errors. Neurologically, the constant adaptation to different shot conditions strengthens neural pathways associated with decision-making and motor control. This method transforms practice into a dynamic and engaging process, contributing to the holistic development of bowlers' skills and mindset.

10. Progressive Lane Pattern Difficulty Method:

Description: The Progressive Lane Pattern Difficulty Method is a strategic training approach designed to build a bowler's confidence gradually while simultaneously challenging their adaptability to varying lane conditions. This method involves starting practice sessions with easier lane patterns and progressively advancing to more difficult ones. By doing so, bowlers can maintain a positive mindset and steadily improve their skills, fostering a neurologically adaptive response to increasingly complex lane patterns.

Steps:

1. **Pattern Gradation:** Begin practice sessions with well-known and easier lane patterns that align with the bowler's current skill level. This establishes a foundation for success and boosts confidence.

2. **Incremental Complexity:** Gradually increase the difficulty of lane patterns as the bowler demonstrates proficiency. This step introduces incremental challenges, encouraging continuous skill development.

3. **Challenge Milestones:** Set specific milestones for bowlers to achieve on each lane pattern. As they successfully navigate through easier and more challenging patterns, their confidence grows, and they become more adept at handling diverse conditions.

To-Do Tasks and Cues:

- *Pattern Familiarization:* Ensure bowlers are well-versed in the characteristics of each lane pattern. This familiarity aids in their ability to make effective adjustments as patterns become more challenging.

- *Positive Reinforcement:* Provide positive reinforcement and recognition as bowlers successfully navigate through progressively difficult lane patterns. This helps maintain motivation and a positive mindset.
- *Adaptive Strategy Development:* Encourage bowlers to develop adaptive strategies for each lane pattern, fostering a neurological response that enhances their ability to read and adjust to changing conditions.
- *Consistent Evaluation:* Regularly evaluate bowlers' performance on varying lane patterns to tailor the progression according to their evolving skill levels and challenges.

Psychological and Neurological Impact: The Progressive Lane Pattern Difficulty Method has significant psychological and neurological benefits. Psychologically, it ensures that bowlers consistently experience success, building and maintaining confidence throughout their training journey. Neurologically, the gradual exposure to diverse lane patterns enhances the development of neural pathways associated with pattern recognition, decision-making, and adaptive motor responses. This method contributes to a well-rounded skill set, preparing bowlers to confidently face the intricacies of different lane conditions in competitive settings.

11. Blind Execution Method:

Description: The Blind Execution Method is a distinctive training technique designed to shift a bowler's focus from the outcome of the shot to the precision and repeatability of their execution. This method involves blocking the view of the pins or the ball's trajectory, creating a scenario where the bowler can solely concentrate on the feel and mechanics of their shot without being influenced by the immediate result.

Steps: a. **Visual Obstruction Setup:** Introduce a curtain or screen that obstructs the bowler's view of the pins and the ball's path down the lane. b. **Execution Focus:** Encourage bowlers to focus solely on their execution, paying attention to their approach, release, and overall mechanics. c. **Feel-Oriented Practice:** Emphasize the importance of the bowler's kinesthetic awareness, urging him to feel the nuances of their shot without relying on visual cues.

To-Do Tasks and Cues:

- *Mechanical Awareness:* Guide bowlers to be acutely aware of their body movements during the execution, fostering a deep understanding of their mechanics.
- *Consistent Approach:* Reinforce the idea that each shot should be approached with a focus on consistent, repeatable execution, regardless of the immediate result.
- *Feedback from Body:* Highlight the feedback loop from the bowler's body to the arrows, emphasizing the importance of internal feedback for self-correction.
- *Mindful Repetition:* Encourage bowlers to engage in mindful repetition, refining their shot mechanics and enhancing muscle memory without being influenced by visual distractions.

Psychological and Neurological Impact: The Blind Execution Method has profound psychological and neurological effects on bowlers. Psychologically, it helps in breaking the misconception that every well-executed shot should result in a strike. Instead, it instills a mindset of focusing on the process rather than the outcome, reducing performance anxiety. Neurologically, the method enhances proprioception and motor control by fostering a deeper connection between the bowler's body and their shot execution. This approach contributes to a more resilient and adaptable bowler, capable of maintaining composure and executing precise shots under various conditions.

12. Three-Step Approach Method

The Three-Step Approach in bowling is a purposeful adaptation to traditional footwork, prioritizing efficiency, control, and accuracy. This method addresses the intricate dynamics of timing, swing control, and release precision within a simplified approach. Bowlers utilizing the Three-Step Approach position themselves for optimal execution from the beginning to the release, enhancing their overall game.

Starting Position and Alignment: Beginners and seasoned bowlers alike benefit from the clarity of the starting position. The stance is foundational, emphasizing stability and alignment with the target. This sets the stage for a controlled and deliberate approach.

Three-Step Movement Breakdown:

1. **Initial Movement (3rd Step):** The first forward movement with the dominant foot serves as the catalyst for the approach. Bowlers focus on initiating momentum while maintaining balance and stability.
2. **Second Movement (4th Step):** The subsequent slide with the non-dominant foot refines the positioning for the final release. This intermediate step allows bowlers to synchronize their body movements effectively.
3. **Release and Finish (5th Step):** The culmination of the approach involves the release during the final step. The bowler achieves a harmonious blend of balance, control, and accuracy as the ball is sent down the lane.

To-Do Tasks and Cues:

- *Balance Focus:* Instilling a keen awareness of balance throughout the approach is crucial. Bowlers are encouraged to find equilibrium in each step, ensuring a fluid and controlled movement.
- *Swing Management:* With a condensed footwork sequence, bowlers gain a heightened sense of swing control. The reduced number of steps allows for more efficient management of the swing's trajectory.
- *Timing Emphasis:* Precise timing is paramount in bowling, and the Three-Step Approach hones in on synchronizing foot movements with the release. This emphasis contributes to improved shot accuracy.
- *Lower Grip Pressure:* The streamlined approach leads to lower G-force, a key advantage in executing a relaxed and controlled release. Bowlers learn to minimize grip pressure, fostering a smoother and more consistent release.

Psychological and Neurological Impact: The Three-Step Approach carries psychological benefits by simplifying the bowler's mental checklist. The reduced complexity allows for increased focus on accuracy-related elements, boosting confidence. Neurologically, the method facilitates enhanced muscle memory development. Bowlers can ingrain precise movements more efficiently, translating to a quicker and more impactful learning process for accuracy improvement. The lower G-force during the approach contributes to a more relaxed neurological state, positively influencing the release mechanism. Overall, the Three-Step Approach offers a strategic and effective pathway for bowlers seeking mastery in accuracy.

13. Quiet Eye (QE) Method

The Quiet Eye (QE) method is a refined approach in bowling that places a deliberate emphasis on the bowler's visual attention during critical phases of the shot, particularly the release. It revolves around the concept of maintaining a focused, quiet gaze on the target, contributing to heightened concentration and control.

The QE Technique:

1. **Intentional Visual Focus:** Bowlers using the Quiet Eye method deliberately fixate their gaze on the target, specifically the pins, during the critical moments leading up to and following the release. This intentional focus is maintained for a specific duration.
2. **Release Control:** The release becomes a focal point during the Quiet Eye technique. As the bowler initiates the release, the sustained gaze on the target reinforces a sense of control over the shot's accuracy. This heightened awareness carries through the entire execution.
3. **Muscle and Fluidity Awareness:** Beyond target fixation, the Quiet Eye method encourages bowlers to maintain a heightened awareness of muscle engagement and the fluidity of their movements. This holistic approach aims to synchronize visual attention with the physical execution of the shot.

Benefits and Application:

- *Enhanced Concentration:* The intentional and prolonged focus on the target promotes enhanced concentration. This heightened level of attention minimizes distractions and optimizes the bowler's mental state for accuracy.
- *Controlled Release:* By emphasizing the release phase within the Quiet Eye method, bowlers develop a sense of control over their shot. This intentional control contributes to improved accuracy as bowlers align their visual focus with precise execution.

- *Reduced Performance Anxiety:* The Quiet Eye method assists bowlers in managing performance anxiety. The controlled and deliberate visual attention fosters a sense of calmness, reducing anxiety levels during critical moments.
- *Visual-Motor Integration:* The method strengthens the connection between visual perception and motor execution. By consistently practicing the Quiet Eye technique, bowlers enhance the integration of visual information with the physical act of releasing the ball, leading to more accurate shots.

To-Do Tasks and Cues:

- *Focus Duration:* Practice extending the duration of the focused gaze on the target, gradually increasing the length to improve concentration during critical moments.
- *Relaxed Execution:* Emphasize the importance of maintaining a relaxed and fluid execution while keeping the gaze fixed on the target. Tension in the body can counteract the benefits of the Quiet Eye method.
- *Post-Release Reflection:* Encourage bowlers to reflect on their visual focus post-release. Analyzing the connection between the gaze, muscle control, and the shot outcome provides valuable insights for improvement.

Psychological and Neurological Impact: The Quiet Eye method carries significant psychological benefits by instilling a sense of confidence and control in bowlers. The intentional focus on the target positively influences the neurological aspect by creating a clear and efficient pathway for information processing and execution. This method aligns the bowler's visual and motor systems, fostering a seamless integration that contributes to accuracy and overall performance improvement.

PSYCHOLOGICAL AND TECHNICAL PLAN TO OVERCOME TECHNICAL ERROR

EXAMPLES

Psychological And Technical Correction: Overextension Of The Bowling Arm

Issue: Overextension of the bowling arm during the bowler's swing results in balance problems and inconsistent release because the arm extends too far away from the body during the backswing.

Week 1: Self-Awareness and Analysis

Day 1: Self-Assessment and Goal Setting

- Task (3 hours): Spend three hours analyzing your bowling performance and establishing clear objectives.
- Tactics and Tasks:
    - Identify overextension of the bowling arm as a major technical fault.
    - Short-term objective: "Minimize overextension of the bowling arm for better balance."

Day 2: Video Analysis and Feedback

- Task (1.5 hours): Analyze videos to learn more about your methods and get comments.
- Tactics and Tasks:
    - Document bowling sessions from front and side perspectives.
    - Identify instances of overextension in the videos.
    - Show the videos to a coach or seasoned bowler for in-depth feedback.

Day 3: Video Analysis and Feedback

- Task (1.5 hours): Continue video analysis and feedback.
- Tactics and Tasks:
    - Review videos for overextension patterns.
    - Make notes on potential areas for improvement.

Day 4: Self-Awareness Development

- Task (3 hours): During practice, focus on raising your level of self-awareness.
- Tactics and Tasks:
    - Engage in mindfulness exercises for ten minutes before each training session.
    - Pay attention to the extension of your bowling arm during practice.

Week 2: Correction and Improvement

Day 5: Targeted Practice and Conditioning

- Task (3 hours): Schedule concentrated practice sessions to address overextension of the arms.
- Tactics and Tasks:
    - Perform the "Pushaway Drill" for twenty minutes:
        1. Without holding a ball, stand at the foul line.
        2. Push the fictitious ball forward in a bowling motion, keeping the bowling arm close.
        3. Repeat with a real bowling ball, progressively accelerating the pace.
- Work with a coach for quick feedback and corrections.

Day 6: Targeted Practice and Conditioning

- Task (3 hours): Continue concentrated practice sessions.
- Tactics and Tasks:
    - Repeat the "Pushaway Drill" with a focus on arm positioning.
    - Incorporate variations in the drill for added challenge.

Day 7: Adaptation to Lane Conditions

- Task (4 hours): Address arm overextension while cultivating adaptability.
- Tactics and Tasks:
    - Experience various lane circumstances.
    - Focus on maintaining corrected arm position in changing circumstances.
    - Use imagery cues such as "Keep the arm close to the body" before each throw.

Outcome: Bowlers can focus on fixing their swing problems by identifying the precise technical fault (arm overextension) and employing drills like the "Pushaway Drill." The strategy uses focused practice, fast feedback, and self-awareness building to progressively eliminate the overextension issue. Bowlers can enhance their performance and swing with regular practice and coaching.

Psychological and Mental Drills (Integrated into the Plan):

1. **Day 4 - Visualization Exercise**
    - Task (15 minutes): Practice visualizing a perfect bowling motion with ideal arm positioning.
    - Tactics: Imagine a smooth and controlled swing, focusing on keeping the arm close to the body.

2. **Day 5 - Positive Affirmations**
    - Task (10 minutes): Repeat positive affirmations related to arm positioning and overall performance.
    - Tactics: Use statements like "I maintain a balanced and controlled arm position in every throw."

3. **Day 6 - Progressive Relaxation**
    - Task (15 minutes): Engage in progressive relaxation to release tension and promote fluid arm movement.
    - Tactics: Focus on relaxing muscles associated with the bowling arm, promoting a natural swing.

4. **Day 7 - Goal Visualization**
    - Task (20 minutes): Visualize successfully executing the "Pushaway Drill" and other corrections during a game.

- Tactics: Picture achieving the set goals, reinforcing a positive mindset for the upcoming week.

Psychological And Technical Correction: Incorrect Number Of Steps

Issue: The bowler frequently approaches the ball with the incorrect amount of steps, which causes bad timing, unsteadiness in their balance, and inconsistent shots.

Week 1: Self-Awareness and Analysis

Day 1: Self-Assessment and Goal Setting

- Task (3 hours): Assess your bowling performance and establish clear objectives.
- Tactics and Tasks:
  - Identify the incorrect number of steps as a critical technical issue.
  - Short-term objective: "Consistently take the correct number of steps during the approach for better timing."

Day 2: Video Analysis and Feedback

- Task (1.5 hours): Analyze videos to learn more about your methods and get comments.
- Tactics and Tasks:
  - Document bowling sessions from front and side perspectives.
  - Spot occasions in the video when you counted steps incorrectly during your approach.
  - Show the videos to a coach or seasoned bowler for in-depth feedback.

Day 3: Video Analysis and Feedback

- Task (1.5 hours): Continue video analysis and feedback.
- Tactics and Tasks:
  - Review videos for patterns of incorrect step counting.
  - Make notes on potential areas for improvement.

Day 4: Self-Awareness Development

- Task (3 hours): During practice, focus on raising your level of self-awareness.
- Tactics and Tasks:
  - Engage in mindfulness exercises for ten minutes before each training session.
  - Intentionally count your steps during practice to ensure accuracy.

Week 2: Correction and Improvement

Day 5: Targeted Practice and Drills

- Task (3 hours): Set aside time for concentrated practice to adjust the step count.
- Tactics and Tasks:
  - Consult a coach to ascertain the ideal sequence of actions for your strategy.
  - Practice the "Step Count Drill" for twenty minutes every day:
    1. Assume the proper step count by practicing the first few steps while standing at the approach.
    2. Gradually add the entire technique while maintaining the correct step count.
  - Get prompt feedback and corrections from your instructor during these practice sessions.

Day 6: Targeted Practice and Drills

- Task (3 hours): Continue concentrated practice sessions.
- Tactics and Tasks:
  - Repeat the "Step Count Drill" with a focus on refining the step count.
  - Incorporate variations in the drill for added challenge.

Day 7: Adaptation to Lane Conditions

- Task (4 hours): Gain flexibility while keeping the right number of steps.
- Tactics and Tasks:
  - Practice on various lane conditions.
  - Pay attention to modifying your strategy without sacrificing the proper number of steps.
  - Use imagery cues such as "Count your steps" before each throw.

Outcome: Bowlers can focus on fixing their footwork problems by identifying the exact technical flaw (incorrect step count) and employing drills like the "Step Count Drill." The strategy uses focused practice, real-time feedback, and the growth of self-awareness to progressively solve the step count issue. Bowlers can enhance their performance by improving their footwork and general technique with regular practice and coaching.

Psychological and Mental Drills (Integrated into the Plan):

1. **Day 4 - Mindful Breathing Exercise**
   - Task (15 minutes): Practice mindful breathing to enhance focus and concentration during practice.
   - Tactics: Focus on each breath to stay present and attentive to your step count.

2. **Day 5 - Positive Affirmations**
   - Task (10 minutes): Repeat positive affirmations related to step counting and overall performance.
   - Tactics: Use statements like "I execute the correct number of steps with precision and confidence."

3. **Day 6 - Visualization Exercise**
   - Task (15 minutes): Visualize a flawless approach with accurate step counting.
   - Tactics: Imagine smoothly executing each step, reinforcing the correct sequence mentally.

4. **Day 7 - Goal Visualization**
   - Task (20 minutes): Visualize successfully incorporating the correct step count in various lane conditions.
   - Tactics: Picture achieving the set goals, reinforcing a positive mindset for the upcoming week.

Psychological And Technical Correction: Over-Rotation During Release

Issue: The bowler frequently overrotates the ball when releasing it, which makes it difficult to control, causes uneven ball motion, and increases the possibility of splits.

Week 1: Self-Awareness and Analysis

Day 1: Self-Assessment and Goal Setting

- Task (3 hours): Assess your bowling performance and establish clear objectives.
- Tactics and Tasks:
  - Identify the major technical error of over-rotation during the release.
  - Short-term objective: "Achieve a smoother and controlled release without over-rotation."

Day 2: Video Analysis and Feedback

- Task (1.5 hours): Analyze videos to learn more about your methods and get comments.
- Tactics and Tasks:
  - Take pictures of your bowling sessions from the front and the side.
  - Spot situations in the video where there was over-rotation during the release.
  - Show the films to a coach or seasoned bowler for in-depth feedback.

Day 3: Video Analysis and Feedback

- Task (1.5 hours): Continue video analysis and feedback.

- Tactics and Tasks:
    - Review videos for patterns of over-rotation during the release.
    - Make notes on potential areas for improvement.

Day 4: Self-Awareness Development

- Task (3 hours): During practice, focus on raising your level of self-awareness.
- Tactics and Tasks:
    - Perform ten minutes of mindfulness exercises before each practice session.
    - Concentrate on your wrist position and release technique during practice.

Week 2: Correction and Improvement

Day 5: Targeted Practice and Drills

- Task (3 hours): Set aside time for concentrated practice sessions aimed at resolving the over-rotation problem.
- Tactics and Tasks:
    - Collaborate with a coach to choose the appropriate release method.
    - Practice the "Release Control Drill" for twenty minutes every day:
        1. Start with a lighter ball to improve your control.
        2. Pay attention to keeping your wrist in a neutral posture when releasing.
    - Your coach will provide fast feedback and corrections during these practice sessions.

Day 6: Targeted Practice and Drills

- Task (3 hours): Continue concentrated practice sessions.
- Tactics and Tasks:
    - Repeat the "Release Control Drill" with a focus on refining control.
    - Incorporate variations in the drill for added challenge.

Day 7: Adaptation to Lane Conditions

- Task (4 hours): Gain flexibility while retaining authority over the release.
- Tactics and Tasks:
    - Practice on various lane circumstances.
    - Focus on modifying your release method while maintaining control.
    - Use imagery cues such as "Maintain wrist control" before each throw.

Outcome: Bowlers can concentrate on fixing their release problems by determining the precise technical fault (over-rotation during the release) and employing drills like the "Release Control Drill." The strategy uses focused practice, real-time feedback, and self-awareness building to eventually get rid of the over-rotation issue. Bowlers can enhance their release technique and get improved control and performance with regular practice and coaching.

Psychological and Mental Drills (Integrated into the Plan):

1. **Day 4 - Visualization Exercise**
    - Task (15 minutes): Visualize a smooth and controlled release without over-rotation.
    - Tactics: Picture the ideal release technique, reinforcing a positive mental image.

2. **Day 5 - Positive Affirmations**
    - Task (10 minutes): Repeat positive affirmations related to release control and overall performance.
    - Tactics: Use statements like "I release the ball with precision and control."

3. **Day 6 - Progressive Relaxation**
    - Task (15 minutes): Engage in progressive relaxation to release tension and promote a fluid release.

- Tactics: Focus on relaxing muscles associated with the release, promoting a natural motion.

4. **Day 7 - Goal Visualization**
   - Task (20 minutes): Visualize successfully executing the "Release Control Drill" in different lane conditions.
   - Tactics: Picture achieving the set goals, reinforcing a positive mindset for the upcoming week.

Psychological And Technical Correction: Wrong Body Angle Alignment From 1st Step To Finish Step

Issue: The bowler's body angle is always out of alignment from the first step of the approach to the last step, which makes it difficult to hit the target and causes uneven targeting and accuracy.

Week 1: Self-Awareness and Analysis

Day 1: Self-Assessment and Goal Setting

- Task (3 hours): Assess your bowling performance and establish clear objectives.
- Tactics and Tasks:
  - Identify the misalignment of your body angle as a primary technical mistake.
  - Short-term objective: "Achieve consistent alignment of body angle throughout the approach."

Day 2: Video Analysis and Feedback

- Task (1.5 hours): Analyze videos to learn more about your methods and get comments.
- Tactics and Tasks:
  - Take pictures (front, side, and rear) during your bowling sessions.
  - Spot times in the videos when there was misalignment during your approach.
  - Show the films to a coach or seasoned bowler for in-depth feedback.

Day 3: Video Analysis and Feedback

- Task (1.5 hours): Continue video analysis and feedback.
- Tactics and Tasks:
  - Review videos for patterns of misalignment during the approach.
  - Make notes on potential areas for improvement.

Day 4: Self-Awareness Development

- Task (3 hours): During practice, focus on raising your level of self-awareness.
- Tactics and Tasks:
  - Engage in mindfulness exercises for ten minutes before every training session.
  - Pay attention to how your body aligns from the first step to the last during practice.

Week 2: Correction and Improvement

Day 5: Targeted Practice and Drills

- Task (3 hours): Set aside time for targeted practice sessions to address alignment problems with body angles.
- Tactics and Tasks:
  - Determine the proper body alignment for the approach by working with a coach.
  - Practice the "Alignment Control Drill" for twenty minutes every day:
    1. Take a stance ensuring your body is facing the target.
    2. Maintain this alignment as you go through your strategy step by step.
  - Receive fast feedback and corrections from your coach during these practice sessions.

Day 6: Targeted Practice and Drills

- Task (3 hours): Continue concentrated practice sessions.
- Tactics and Tasks:
  - Repeat the "Alignment Control Drill" with a focus on refining body alignment.
  - Incorporate variations in the drill for added challenge.

Day 7: Adaptation to Lane Conditions

- Task (4 hours): Learn to be flexible while keeping your body in the right alignment.
- Tactics and Tasks:
  - Practice in various lane circumstances.
  - Focus on modifying your strategy while maintaining proper body alignment.
  - Use visualization cues such as "Maintain body alignment from start to finish" before each throw.

Outcome: Bowlers can focus on addressing their body alignment concerns by recognizing the exact technical error (misalignment of body angle) and employing drills like the "Alignment Control Drill." The strategy places a strong emphasis on focused practice, fast feedback, and increasing self-awareness to progressively solve the misalignment issue. Bowlers can achieve more precise and consistent shots by improving their body alignment during the approach with regular practice and coaching.

Psychological and Mental Drills (Integrated into the Plan):

1. **Day 4 - Visualization Exercise**
   - Task (15 minutes): Visualize a smooth and consistent approach with proper body alignment.
   - Tactics: Picture the ideal body alignment, reinforcing a positive mental image.

2. **Day 5 - Positive Affirmations**
   - Task (10 minutes): Repeat positive affirmations related to body alignment and overall performance.
   - Tactics: Use statements like "I maintain consistent body alignment for accurate shots."

3. **Day 6 - Progressive Relaxation**
   - Task (15 minutes): Engage in progressive relaxation to release tension and promote a fluid approach.
   - Tactics: Focus on relaxing muscles associated with body alignment, promoting a natural motion.

4. **Day 7 - Goal Visualization**
   - Task (20 minutes): Visualize successfully executing the "Alignment Control Drill" in different lane conditions.
   - Tactics: Picture achieving the set goals, reinforcing a positive mindset for the upcoming week.

Psychological And Technical Correction: Inconsistent Timing

Issue: The bowler has trouble timing his approach, which causes him to release the ball erratically and lose control of it.

Week 1: Self-Awareness and Analysis

Day 1: Self-Assessment and Goal Setting

- Task (3 hours): Assess your bowling performance and establish clear objectives.
- Tactics and Tasks:
- Identifying uneven timing as a critical technical fault is one of the tactics and tasks.
- Short-term objective: "Achieve consistent timing in the approach."

Day 2: Video Analysis and Feedback

- Task (1.5 hours): Analyze videos to learn more about your methods and get comments.

- Tactics and Tasks:
- Take pictures (front, side, and rear) during your bowling sessions.
- Point out any occasions in the videos when the timing is off.
- Show the films to a coach or seasoned bowler for in-depth feedback.

Day 3: Video Analysis and Feedback

- Task (1.5 hours): Continue video analysis and feedback.
- Tactics and Tasks:
- Review videos for patterns of inconsistent timing during the approach.
- Make notes on potential areas for improvement.

Day 4: Self-Awareness Development

- Task (3 hours): During practice, focus on raising your level of self-awareness.
- Tactics and Tasks:
- Engage in mindfulness exercises for ten minutes before every training session.
- During the approach, concentrate on your timing, paying special attention to your footwork and ball release.

Week 2: Correction and Improvement

Day 5: Targeted Practice and Drills

- Task (3 hours): Set aside time for concentrated practice sessions aimed at fixing timing errors.
- Tactics and Tasks:
  - Consult a coach to determine the best moment to make your move.
  - Practice the "Timing Control Drill" for twenty minutes every day:
    1. Take a stance and concentrate on your first ball push away.
    2. Observe how the ball moves and the timing of your steps.
    3. Use a metronome or ask a coach to give you quick-timing feedback.
  - Receive fast feedback and corrections from your coach during these practice sessions.

Day 6: Targeted Practice and Drills

- Task (3 hours): Continue concentrated practice sessions.
- Tactics and Tasks:
  - Repeat the "Timing Control Drill" with a focus on refining timing.
  - Incorporate variations in the drill for added challenge.

Day 7: Adaptation to Lane Conditions

- Task (4 hours): Learn to be flexible while keeping timing correct.
- Tactics and Tasks:
  - Experiment with various lane circumstances.
  - Pay close attention to modifying your strategy while maintaining appropriate timing.
  - Use imagery cues such as "Maintain consistent timing in all conditions" before each throw.

Outcome: Through self-awareness and focused workouts such as the "Timing Control Drill," bowlers can progressively refine the timing of their approach. Psychological drills, such as breathing techniques and encouraging self-talk, can assist practitioners in staying focused and confident. The strategy focuses on regular practice, fast feedback, and flexibility to adjust to various lane circumstances in order to improve timing and ball control.

Psychological Drills for Self-Awareness:

1. **Breathing Exercises (Week 1):**
   - Task (5 minutes): Practice deep breathing to maintain composure and focus before each practice session.
   - Tactics: Inhale deeply for a count of four, hold for four, exhale for four, and repeat.

2. **Positive Self-Talk (Week 2):**
   - Task (5 minutes): Replace negative self-talk statements concerning timing with affirmations such as "I have excellent timing."
   - Tactics: Repeat positive statements to reinforce confidence in your timing and approach.

Psychological And Technical Correction: Grip Pressure Inconsistency In Swing

Issue: The bowler has trouble maintaining a constant grip pressure throughout the swing, which causes changes in ball speed and release control.

Week 1: Self-Awareness and Analysis

Day 1: Self-Assessment and Goal Setting

- Task (3 hours): During practice, assess your grip pressure and set specific targets.
- Tactics and Tasks:
  - Identify inconsistent grip pressure as a technical fault.
  - Short-term aim: "Achieve consistent grip pressure throughout the swing."

Day 2: Video Analysis and Feedback

- Task (1.5 hours): Evaluate your grip pressure and get feedback using video analysis.
- Tactics and Tasks:
  - Document your bowling sessions, paying particular attention to your grip and hand position.
  - Point out any times in the videos where the grip pressure is inconsistent.
  - Show the films to a coach or seasoned bowler for in-depth feedback.

Day 3: Video Analysis and Feedback

- Task (1.5 hours): Continue video analysis and feedback.
- Tactics and Tasks:
  - Review videos for patterns of inconsistent grip pressure during the swing.
  - Make notes on potential areas for improvement.

Day 4: Self-Awareness Development

- Task (3 hours): Focus on raising your level of grip pressure self-awareness.
- Tactics and Tasks:
  - Include ten minutes of mindfulness exercises before every practice session.
  - Throughout the entire swing, be very aware of the pressure you use with your hands.

Week 2: Correction and Improvement

Day 5: Targeted Practice and Drills

- Task (3 hours): Set aside time for concentrated practice to address inconsistent grip pressure.
- Tactics and Tasks:
  - Work with an instructor to determine the proper grip pressure.
  - Practice the "Pressure Control Drill" for twenty minutes every day:
    1. Take the right stance and grip at the start.
    2. Pay attention to keeping your grip pressure constant throughout the whole swing.
    3. Use training tools or ask a coach to provide quick feedback on your grip.

- Receive fast feedback and corrections from your coach during these practice sessions.

Day 6: Targeted Practice and Drills

- Task (3 hours): Continue concentrated practice sessions.
- Tactics and Tasks:
- Repeat the "Pressure Control Drill" with a focus on refining grip pressure.
- Incorporate variations in the drill for added challenge.

Day 7: Mental Toughness and Focus

- Task (4 hours): Develop the mental fortitude necessary to keep a steady grasp under duress.
- Tactics and Tasks:
- Replicate competitive scenarios during practice to control grip pressure.
- Before each throw, use imagery cues such as "Maintain the perfect grip pressure."

Psychological Drills for Self-Awareness:

1. **Progressive Muscle Relaxation (Week 1):**
   - Task (5 minutes): To increase your awareness of grip pressure, take five minutes to relax your hand muscles before each practice session.
   - Tactics: Gradually tense and then release each hand muscle, focusing on maintaining a relaxed grip.

2. **Confidence-Building Affirmations (Week 2):**
   - Task (5 minutes): To bolster confidence, repeat encouraging statements to yourself, such as "I have perfect control over my grip pressure."
   - Tactics: Reinforce positive thoughts about your grip control and overall performance.

Outcome: Bowlers can improve their grip control during the swing by using the "Pressure Control Drill" and self-awareness to address grip pressure inconsistencies. Psychological drills, including progressive muscle relaxation and affirmations that boost confidence, can be included in practice to improve focus and self-assurance. To increase grip pressure consistency and overall performance, the strategy places a strong emphasis on mental toughness, rapid feedback, and constant practice.

Psychological And Technical Correction: Weak Ball Delivery And Low Ball Revolution

Issue: The bowler has trouble delivering a strong ball, which lowers the ball revolution rate, lessens the possibility of a hook, and reduces pin action.

Week 1: Self-Awareness and Analysis

Day 1: Self-Assessment and Goal Setting

- Task (3 hours): Assess your ability to deliver the ball and establish clear objectives.
- Tactics and Tasks:
  - Identify poor ball delivery and a low revolution rate as technical mistakes.
  - Short-term objective: "Increase ball revolution rate for a stronger delivery."

Day 2: Video Analysis and Feedback

- Task (1.5 hours): Evaluate your ball delivery with video analysis and get feedback.
- Tactics and Tasks:
  - Document your bowling sessions, paying particular attention to your ball rotation and release.
  - Point out instances of low ball revolution and weak ball delivery in the videos.
  - Show the films to a coach or seasoned bowler for in-depth feedback.

Day 3: Video Analysis and Feedback

- Task (1.5 hours): Continue video analysis and feedback.
- Tactics and Tasks:
  - Review videos for patterns of low ball revolution and weak delivery.
  - Make notes on potential areas for improvement.

Day 4: Self-Awareness Development

- Task (3 hours): Focus on increasing your awareness of the strength of your ball delivery.
- Tactics and Tasks:
  - Include upper body strength training activities to improve your delivery force.
  - Pay special attention to the way your fingers move and how you release the pressure.

Week 2: Correction and Improvement

Day 5: Targeted Practice and Drills

- Task (3 hours): Set aside time for concentrated practice sessions aimed at improving ball revolution and correcting weak ball delivery.
- Tactics and Tasks:
  - Work with an instructor to determine the best ball delivery method for maximizing revolution.
  - Practice the "Revolution-Boost Drill" for twenty minutes every day:
    1. Pay close attention to keeping your wrists in a firm position when releasing.
    2. Practice your follow-through motion to improve ball rotation.
    3. Strengthen your arms and wrists by practicing with a heavier ball.
  - Receive fast feedback and corrections from your coach during these practice sessions.

Day 6: Targeted Practice and Drills

- Task (3 hours): Continue concentrated practice sessions.
- Tactics and Tasks:
  - Repeat the "Revolution-Boost Drill" with a focus on refining ball revolution and delivery strength.
  - Incorporate variations in the drill for added challenge.

Day 7: Mental Toughness and Focus

- Task (4 hours): Develop mental tenacity to regularly deliver a stronger ball.
- Tactics and Tasks:
  - Simulate competing scenarios during practice to control delivery power.
  - Before each throw, use imagery cues such as "Deliver with power and spin."

Psychological Drills for Self-Awareness:

1. **Progressive Muscle Relaxation (Week 1):**
   - Task (5 minutes): To improve your awareness of ball delivery, relax your arm and wrist muscles for five minutes before each practice session.
   - Tactics: Gradually tense and then release each muscle, focusing on preparing your arms for a powerful delivery.

2. **Confidence-Building Affirmations (Week 2):**
   - Task (5 minutes): Use positive affirmations such as "I deliver with strength and spin" to reinforce confidence in yourself.
   - Tactics: Repeat affirmations to instill a positive mindset about your ball delivery and overall performance.

Outcome: Through self-awareness and the "Revolution-Boost Drill," bowlers can improve their weak ball delivery and low ball revolution, resulting in more strength and spin in their deliveries. Using a larger ball during practice and engaging in strength training activities both help to increase upper body strength. Psychological drills, like progressive muscle relaxation and affirmations that develop confidence, are included in practice to improve focus and self-assurance. The strategy places a strong emphasis on mental toughness, rapid feedback, and constant practice to improve ball delivery and boost overall performance.

Psychological And Technical Correction: Ball Speed Inconsistency

Issue: The bowler's inconsistent ball speed causes the ball to move erratically and makes it tough for him to hit target pins.

Week 1: Self-Awareness and Analysis

Day 1: Self-Assessment and Goal Setting

- Task (3 hours): Assess the speed of the ball and establish clear objectives.
- Tactics and Tasks:
  - Identify inconsistent ball speed as a technical fault.
  - Short-term objective: "Improve ball speed consistency for more accurate shots."

Day 2: Video Analysis and Feedback

- Task (1.5 hours): Evaluate your ball speed with video analysis and ask for comments.
- Tactics and Tasks:
  - Document your bowling sessions, paying particular attention to differences in ball speed.
  - Spot moments in the videos where the ball speed is irregular.
  - Show the films to a coach or seasoned bowler for in-depth feedback.

Day 3: Video Analysis and Feedback

- Task (1.5 hours): Continue video analysis and feedback.
- Tactics and Tasks:
  - Review videos for patterns of inconsistent ball speed.
  - Make notes on potential areas for improvement.

Day 4: Self-Awareness Development

- Task (3 hours): Spend three hours improving your self-awareness of ball speed.
- Tactics and Tasks:
  - Get comfortable using a radar-based speed measuring tool to monitor the speed of the ball.
  - Throughout practice, be mindful of the timing of your arm swing and release.

Week 2: Correction and Improvement

Day 5: Targeted Practice and Drills

- Task (3 hours): Set aside concentrated practice time to address inconsistent ball speed.
- Tactics and Tasks:
  - Work with an instructor to determine the perfect ball speed and timing for reliable shots.
  - Practice the "Speed Control Drill" for twenty minutes every day:
    1. Take a consistent approach at first, then release the ball.
    2. Vary the pace and timing of your arms while maintaining accuracy.
    3. Use speed control exercises to adjust the speed of the ball.
  - Receive fast feedback and corrections from your coach during these practice sessions.

Day 6: Targeted Practice and Drills

- Task (3 hours): Continue concentrated practice sessions.
- Tactics and Tasks:
  - Repeat the "Speed Control Drill" with a focus on refining ball speed consistency.
  - Incorporate variations in the drill for added challenge.

Day 7: Mental Toughness and Focus

- Task (4 hours): Develop mental tenacity to keep the ball moving at a constant speed.
- Tactics and Tasks:
- Construct practice scenarios that mimic competition settings to control ball speed under duress.
- Before each throw, use visualization cues such as "Maintain steady ball speed."

Psychological Drills for Self-Awareness:

1. **Breathing Techniques (Week 1):**
   - Task (5 minutes): To maintain composure and awareness of ball speed, do deep breathing techniques before each practice session.
   - Tactics: Focus on controlled, deep breaths to stay calm and focused during ball delivery.

2. **Visualization (Week 2):**
   - Task (5 minutes): During practice and competition, picture yourself constantly delivering the ball at the desired speed.
   - Tactics: Visualize a smooth and consistent ball release with the desired speed.

Outcome: Through self-awareness and the "Speed Control Drill," bowlers can overcome inconsistencies in ball speed and produce more accurate and consistent shots. Radar-based speed measuring equipment is used to monitor ball speed and track progress. For increased consistency, collaborative coaching and practice improve arm speed and timing. Psychological drills help athletes stay focused and composed throughout practice and performance. Examples include breathing exercises and visualization. The strategy places a strong emphasis on the value of constant practice, quick feedback, and mental toughness to improve overall performance and ball speed consistency.

ELITE BOWLERS: WHY DOES THE 'FIRE' BURN SO BRIGHTLY?

Coaches frequently claim that players who excel at the highest level are genuinely "driven," "hungrier," or fixated on winning, but why are some bowlers more driven than others? What are the supposed driving causes behind someone's desire to succeed in sports? What is it about these extremely driven bowlers that makes the "fire" burn so brightly?

Understanding the significance of motivation and how it affects people's thoughts, feelings, and behaviors is crucial. applications to sport and exercise environments, including the hierarchical model of motivation, accomplishment goal theory, and **self-determination theory (SDT)**. A solid theoretical foundation for analyzing the motivational processes of bowlers in sports has been made available by these three social-cognitive theories of motivation.

SDT is regarded as a framework for comprehending the social-contextual factors—also known as the motivational climate—that either support or contradict extrinsic and intrinsic motivation. SDT's fundamental premise is that people are naturally driven to take charge of their social surroundings. According to SDT, there are three main psychological demands that people must meet: relatedness, competence, and self-determination. Researchers have conceptualized intrinsic motivation by emphasizing the underlying demand for autonomy or self-determination. Behaviors that are self-determined are a reflection of how humans exercise autonomy or choice. One can freely decide to take part in a specific sport, for instance. In this instance, the sense of choice is internal to the person and is linked to an internal locus of causality. The innate inclination to seek out novel challenges, explore, and acquire knowledge is linked to intrinsic motivation. An internal locus of causality is linked to behaviors that are intrinsically motivated, according to SDT (e.g., the happiness obtained from playing sport). According to SDT, actions that are motivated by an external locus of causality that is seen to be there and that are linked to a sense of being powerless are typically connected with extrinsic motivation. Individuals who submit to the expectations and behaviors of others are seen as having an external locus of cause. For instance, parents may need to force their children to participate in a specific sport.

Sarah: Bowling is a self-determined activity that Sarah does for leisure and personal choice. She discovers intrinsic drive in taking on novel tasks, delving further into the game, and never stopping learning. Because she voluntarily chooses to play bowling in order to satiate her need for competence and self-determination, Sarah's involvement in the activity is motivated by her internal locus of causality. She establishes objectives for herself, works to get better, and evaluates success according to her own criteria rather than those of others.

Mark: As for Mark, he bowls with an extrinsic motivation. His parents' demands and coercion, in particular, are what spurred him to participate in the sport. Mark's participation is characterized by a lack of autonomy and choice because his behaviors are dictated by an external locus of causality that he perceives. Compared to Sarah, he might not like bowling as much because his motivation is mostly driven by outside factors rather than by a sense of personal fulfillment or pleasure..

According to SDT, there are two types of extrinsic motivation: self-determining and non-self-determining. Behaviors that are not self-determined and driven by external factors are linked to an external locus of causality that is recognized. These actions are linked to incentives and penalties (i.e., behaviors that are controlled externally) or more intra-personal behaviors (i.e., introjected regulated behaviors), like going to training because you feel bad about missing it. Though more internalized, imposed regulated behaviors lack self-determination. Individuals frequently display behaviors that they do not acknowledge as their own. Extrinsically motivated behaviors that are self-determined are distinguished by their choice. There are two categories of self-determined extrinsic motivation: integrated regulation and identified regulation. "Identification is the result of a deliberate evaluation of a behavioral objective or rule, making the action recognized or taken as personally significant." People adopt the rule as their own through identification. Bowlers who see training as a way to discover their potential and voluntarily practice to get better at what they do could be an example of an identified regulation.

> **Myth: "Highly motivated bowlers are always intrinsically motivated."**
>
> Reality: Bowlers can be motivated by both intrinsic and extrinsic factors. Their motivation can range from fully self-determined to non-self-determined, depending on individual experiences and perceptions.
>
> **Myth: "Extrinsically motivated bowlers lack enjoyment in the sport."**
>
> Reality: Extrinsically motivated bowlers can find enjoyment in the sport, but their motivation is primarily influenced by external factors or rewards.
>
> **Myth: "Extrinsic motivation always leads to a decrease in intrinsic motivation."**
>
> Reality: The impact of extrinsic motivation on intrinsic motivation depends on how the rewards are perceived. Rewards that enhance perceived competence can actually increase intrinsic motivation.
>
> **Myth: "Motivation is solely driven by internal factors."**
>
> Reality: The need for relatedness (social connection) is a significant factor in motivation, highlighting the importance of interpersonal relationships and belongingness in sports motivation.
>
> **Myth: "Achievement and competence are solely driven by intrinsic motivation."**
>
> Reality: The need to demonstrate competence, a part of SDT, can drive individuals to seek and conquer challenges, regardless of whether their motivation is intrinsic or extrinsic.

Flexible decisions based on values and consequences define integrated managed behavior. It "happens when recognized rules are completely assimilated to the self, meaning they have been assessed and brought into alignment with one's other needs and values." One of the most self-determined forms of extrinsic incentive is integrated regulation. Integrated regulating behaviors resemble those that are driven by internal motivation. The integrated controlled behavior, which is considered an extrinsically motivated behavior, is carried out to achieve some separable objective, which sets it apart from the other two categories of behavior. When performance or involvement brings inherent delight, behavior is considered genuinely driven.

Bowlers who regularly attend training can be considered an example of an integrated controlled behavior since they recognize that success in all facets of life is attainable through hard work and complete dedication, in addition to viewing the training as a means to an end. The bowler can feel more in control of their own destiny because of this internal perceived locus of causality.

The second principle of SDT is the demand for competence demonstration, which "leads people to seek and conquer challenges that are optimal for their capacities." People feel a sense of accomplishment when they engage with their surroundings in a successful manner, and they keep taking on new challenges in order to fulfill this need to show that they are competent. Boredom can result from learning activities that are too simple or unchallenging, and irritation and possibly a sense of inadequacy can arise from activities that are too hard or challenging.

Cognitive evaluation theory (CET), a mini-theory of SDT, assesses the social and environmental elements that support or contradict intrinsic drive in an effort to pinpoint reasons for the variability in motivation.

How does CET apply to the world of bowling? Let's explore a few examples:

Positive Reinforcement for Improvement: Imagine a bowler who consistently receives constructive feedback and encouragement from their coach and peers whenever they make progress in their technique or score higher. This recognition serves as a reward that informs them about their competence, according to CET. As a result, they are more likely to feel motivated to keep improving their skills and enjoy the intrinsic satisfaction that comes with bowling better.

Overemphasis on Winning: CET also suggests that an excessive focus on competition and the desire to win can have a detrimental effect on intrinsic motivation. In a highly competitive bowling league where the primary goal is winning at all costs, bowlers might shift their focus from the joy of the game to the external reward of victory. This shift can undermine their sense of self-determination and intrinsic motivation as they may start bowling primarily for the sake of winning rather than the inherent enjoyment of the sport.

Team Camaraderie and Relatedness: CET acknowledges the importance of relatedness, or the need to feel connected to significant others, in bolstering intrinsic motivation. In team sports like bowling, a supportive and cohesive team environment can enhance the sense of belonging and relatedness. Bowlers who feel accepted by their team members and share a strong bond are more likely to sustain their intrinsic motivation because they derive pleasure not just from the sport itself but also from the social connections it provides.

According to CET, rewards provided to an individual in the context of achievement have the potential to either strengthen or weaken intrinsic motivation. The impact of an incentive on intrinsic motivation is contingent upon the individual's perception of it. The reward is expected to increase intrinsic motivation if it is interpreted as offering information about competence. Rewards are expected to reduce an individual's sense of self-determination and, as a result, weaken their intrinsic drive if they are seen as exerting control over their behavior, or as an external locus of causality.

According to CET, environments in professional sports, which are marked by a concentration on winning and significant financial rewards, are likely to foster fewer levels of self-determination and, as a result, lower levels of intrinsic motivation. Research from both lab and field settings confirms CET's prediction that competition lowers intrinsic motivation. A concentration on winning (norm-referencing) is likely to be encouraged in competitive contexts. This leads to an increase in ego involvement and, as a result, a loss in intrinsic motivation due to its detrimental effect on self-determination.

The third basic human need put forth by SDT is the feeling of connection, or the sense of being a part of something bigger than oneself. A positive self-perception depends on having the need to fit in and be accepted by others as well as by groups (such as families and sports teams).

STRATEGIC PLAN USING SELF-DETERMINATION THEORY (SDT) FOR BOWLERS

In order to reach peak performance, an athlete needs motivation. Self-Determination Theory (SDT) can be used to create a strategy plan that will increase bowlers' motivation, which will result in better performance and tournament readiness. Three psychological needs—self-determination, competence, and relatedness—are the main goals of SDT. This is a stage-by-stage breakdown of the strategic strategy.

Stage 1: Assessing Intrinsic Motivation and Identifying Needs (Duration: 1 weeks)

- **Task:** Assess each player's intrinsic motivation, personal objectives, and bowling-related demands through one-on-one interviews and surveys.
- **Tactics and Tasks:**

- Interview players one-on-one to learn about their individual reasons for taking up bowling.
- Conduct surveys to determine the amount of intrinsic motivation of each participant and to pinpoint their needs and ambitions.
- Gather information and evaluate it to learn more about the motivating dynamics of the team.

- **Example:** Bowler Mark explains his intrinsic drive by saying he enjoys the challenge of raising his level of play and becoming an expert in the sport. He believes that in order to succeed at bowling, one must be dedicated and work hard.

Stage 2: Fostering Autonomy and Choice (Duration: 1 weeks)

- **Task:** Establish a setting that encourages each player's autonomy and decision-making..
- **Tactics and Tasks:**
  - Motivate athletes to establish personal season goals and objectives.
  - Give players options for workout regimens and training plans so they may select what works best for them.
  - Call open discussions about individual goals and motivations during team meetings.

- **Example:** Sarah, another player, Sarah, a different player, resolves to reach a personal target of 80% strike rate on a regular basis by the conclusion of the season. The freedom to choose her own goals inspires her.

Stage 3: Building Competence and Challenging Goals (Duration: 3 weeks)

- **Task:** Create training regimens that push players' skill levels and promote skill growth.
- **Tactics and Tasks:**
  - Adapt training exercises to the current skill level of each player, progressively raising the challenge.
  - Based on each player's evaluated level of competency, establish performance objectives that are demanding yet doable.
  - Offer helpful criticism and do frequent evaluations to monitor development.

- **Example:** Lisa, a coach, has been having trouble with her spare conversions. Tom creates a training schedule for her. As Lisa gets comfortable with the fundamentals, he progressively introduces more intricate spare combinations.

Stage 4: Fostering a Supportive Team Environment (Duration: Ongoing)

- **Task:** Enhance the team's sense of connection and relatedness.
- **Tactics and Tasks:**
  - Plan social gatherings and team-building exercises to foster comradery.
  - Motivate and assist one another as a team during practice and competition.
  - Foster an environment of acceptance where everyone is appreciated and contributes to the success of the team.

- **Example:** The team hosts a fun inter-squad bowling match and a team meal to honor their mutual love of the game.

Stage 5: Monitoring Progress and Adaptation (Duration: Ongoing)

- **Task:** Regularly evaluate and modify the motivational techniques in light of team and individual performance.
- **Tactics and Tasks:**
  - Check in with players on a regular basis to see how motivated they are and whether their needs have changed.
  - Modify goals and training schedules as players advance.
  - Deal with problems or obstacles as soon as possible to stay highly motivated.

- **Example:** The team observes after a few months that individual targets are being reached and player morale has increased. In an effort to increase intrinsic drive even more, they choose to implement more mental conditioning strategies.

Outcome: Bowlers can feel improved competence, a deeper sense of relatedness within the team, and increased intrinsic motivation by putting this SDT-based strategic plan into practice. Because they are more driven and focused on reaching excellence in the sport, their increased motivation and sense of fulfillment will better prepare them for tournaments.

Hierarchical Model Of Motivation (HMM)

A theoretical paradigm known as the Hierarchical Model of Motivation (HMM) places emphasis on how social elements, like coach behaviors and competitiveness, affect various forms of motivation. Three psychological demands are impacted by these social aspects in turn: relatedness, autonomy (or self-determination), and views of competence.

The feeling of independence and choice in one's actions and choices is referred to as autonomy. HMM contends that social circumstances have the power to either strengthen or weaken autonomy, which in turn has the power to affect motivation. Coaches that give their athletes the freedom to choose and contribute to their training regimens, for instance, may increase their sense of autonomy and consequently their motivation.

The term "perception of competence" describes a person's conviction that they can carry out activities satisfactorily. According to HMM, a person's sense of competence can be influenced by social circumstances like competitiveness. High levels of competition, for example, might boost motivation by giving people chances to show off and hone their talents, which can improve perceptions of competence.

Relatedness is a concept that deals with the need for belonging and social connection. According to HMM, social factors can improve relatedness, which in turn affects motivation. Positive coach actions that create a welcoming and supportive team environment are one example of these social elements. Athletes are more likely to be driven to perform well for the team if they have a strong sense of connection with their coaches and teammates.

Three types of intrinsic motivation are suggested by the HMM: intrinsic motivation for knowledge, intrinsic motivation for experience stimulation, and intrinsic motivation for accomplishment. The satisfaction derived from the process of learning or developing something (like perfecting a javelin technique) is linked to intrinsic motivation towards achievement. One's intrinsic drive to be stimulated is linked to the sensory delight derived from performing an activity (such as spinning the ball as fast as you can). Intrinsic incentive to know, the third sort of intrinsic motivation proposed by HMM, is the satisfaction that comes from discovering and/or learning something new (like a new tragic technique).

Motivational Level	Description	Example
Self-Determination	The highest level of motivation in HMM.	Bowler driven by personal improvement and learning. A player who participates for the sake of mastering skills.
Competence	The middle level of motivation in HMM.	Bowler motivated by the desire to achieve competence. A player aiming to improve his average score or accuracy.
Relatedness	The lowest level of motivation in HMM.	Bowler motivated by social connections and teamwork. A player who values the camaraderie of his bowling team.

Table 42 – This table outlines motivational levels in HMM. Self-determination is the highest, driven by personal improvement and learning. An example is a player participating for skill mastery. Competence is the middle level, motivated by achieving proficiency, like improving average score or accuracy. Relatedness is the lowest, driven by social connections and teamwork, as seen in a player valuing camaraderie in a bowling team.

The greatest level of motivation in the Hierarchical Model of Motivation is self-determination, where bowlers are primarily motivated by learning, mastery of the game, and personal progress. The intermediate level is competency, which focuses on the desire to master particular skills or performance criteria and feel competent in them. Finally, relatedness represents the lowest motivational level and highlights the value of interpersonal relationships, cooperation, and a feeling of community within the bowling group.

Amotivation

The third main motivational type, amotivation, is distinguished by the lowest degrees of self-determination. There are four main types of amotivation that have been proposed: capacity/ability beliefs, helplessness, capacity-effort views, and strategy beliefs. Amotivation is a multidimensional construct. It's a sign of not being motivated or interested in doing something.

1. **Capacity/Ability Beliefs:** People who feel they lack the aptitude, skills, or ability to excel in a given activity experience this kind of amotivation. They might believe that their efforts will be in vain if they hope to perform at a level that pleases them. This sense of personal inadequacy may make them unmotivated to take on the activity at all.

Example: A bowler may begin to question his ability if he has been continuously scoring lower than average in his league. "I just don't have the skills to compete with the others in my league," he may think. This capacity - or ability-based amotivation may result in a lack of desire to work out or play in league competitions.

2. **Strategy-Beliefs:** People become demotivated when they can't think of a clear or efficient way to approach and complete a task. This demotivation is linked to strategy beliefs. They can be confused and uninterested since they don't know how to approach the activity. If they don't have a clear plan for success, they can lose interest in the task at hand.

Example: Consider a bowler who finds it difficult to comprehend the tactics required to modify his throws in response to lane conditions. "I don't know how to read the lanes or adjust my technique properly," they could think, perplexed. Because of this strategy-based amotivation, the bowler may decide not to participate in competitions or in more difficult bowling situations.

3. **Capacity-Effort Beliefs:** This type of amotivation is defined by the conviction that exerting effort will not result in any notable advancement or achievement. People who hold capacity-effort beliefs could feel that their efforts won't change the result, which would deter them from devoting their time and energy to the work.

Example: A bowler who has worked hard to raise his game but hasn't experienced much improvement may become demotivated based on capacity rather than effort. It's possible he might think, "No matter how hard I practice, my scores don't improve," which would demotivate him to keep practicing or look for assistance.

4. **Helplessness:** People who experience helplessness lack drive because they believe they have no control over their circumstances. They may have had a history of recurrent failures or defeats, which has made them less confident in their capacity to change their situation. This sense of powerlessness that one has learned can result in an absolute lack of desire to try.

Example: Consider a bowler who has seen a string of defeats and disappointments in different contests. "I can't control my performance; it's always the same outcome," he can begin to feel hopeless. A person may become completely unmotivated to bowl recreationally or even to compete in future competitions as a result of this acquired helplessness.

Strategic Plan to Overcome Amotivation Causes in bowlers

An uninspired bowler can greatly reduce his excitement and performance in the game. A thorough strategic plan is required to address the four main forms of amotivation: capacity/ability beliefs, strategy beliefs, capacity-effort beliefs, and helplessness. The purpose of this plan is to help bowlers become more motivated and regain their sense of autonomy.

Stage 1: Identification and Assessment (Duration: 2 weeks)

- **Task:** Identify and evaluate individual players who show indicators of demotivation and determine the precise causes of their demotivation.
- **Tactics and Tasks:**
  - Have one-on-one conversations with athletes to learn about their issues and determine what motivates them.

- Give participants self-assessment surveys to see how they feel about their ability, strategy, effort, and powerlessness.
- List and classify each player's amotivational factors.
- **Example:** In a one-on-one conversation, bowler John expresses unhappiness with his recent performance and questions about his bowling talents. He shows signs of amotivation connected to capacity/ability views.

Stage 2: Individualized Motivation Restoration (Duration: 6 weeks)

- **Task:** Create specialized interventions to target the unique amotivation factors of every participant.
- **Tactics and Tasks:**
- Capacity/Ability Beliefs:
  - Assign athletes who are unsure about their abilities to work closely with a coach or mentor.
  - To increase confidence, offer individualized training programs and skill-building activities.
- Strategy-Beliefs:
  - Educate players on practical game strategies by holding strategy workshops.
  - Provide one-on-one coaching sessions to explain tactics according to lane circumstances.
- Capacity-Effort Beliefs:
  - Assign players attainable short-term objectives so they can observe noticeable progress.
  - Give constructive criticism and monitor advancement to show the results of their work.
- Helplessness:
  - Set up workshops or group discussions on mental toughness and resilience.
  - Inspire participants to share triumphs and methods for overcoming obstacles.
- **Example:** John receives mentorship from an experienced bowler who helps him with skill development activities and strengthens his self-belief as part of the capacity/ability beliefs intervention.

Stage 3: Regular Monitoring and Support (Duration: Ongoing)

- **Task:** Monitor players' motivation levels on a regular basis and offer assistance to address any recurrent causes of low motivation..
- **Tactics and Tasks:**
  - Arrange for frequent check-ins with players to talk about their development and mental health.
  - Modify interventions as necessary in light of players' reactions and changing difficulties.
  - Encourage a supportive and friendly environment among teammates to aid in the group's success in overcoming obstacles.

Outcome: Bowlers can progressively overcome amotivation factors and reclaim their intrinsic motivation for the sport by putting this strategic strategy into practice. With tailored interventions and continued support, players can address capacity, strategy, effort, and helplessness beliefs, increasing the likelihood of their enthusiastic and more self-determined return to the game. As a result, they are more motivated and have a more optimistic attitude on their bowling adventure, which helps them prepare for competitions.

Achievement Goal Theory (AGT)

Achievement Goal Theory (AGT) is the third social-cognitive theory of motivation that has garnered significant support in the literatures on sport and fitness as well as education. The main objectives of the individual for involvement as well as their perception of success and failure should be the focus of achievement motivation. Humans are driven to attain their goals, which makes goals a fundamental predictor of achievement behavior. AGT makes the assumption that each person is a purposeful, goal-directed creature that thinks rationally and that beliefs about success are shaped by objectives, which in turn influence behavior and subsequent decisions in situations related to achievement. The impact of personal objectives on an individual's thoughts, emotions, and actions during achievement scenarios is a topic of special interest.

Hypothetical examples of elite bowlers based on Achievement Goal Theory (AGT):

Task-Oriented Bowler: This outstanding bowler prioritizes skill improvement and personal mastery above everything else. The main motivation for participating is to keep getting better at what he does and how he does it. He establishes clear objectives, like raising his overall score or perfecting a difficult skill. When he competes, he is more concerned with whether he has achieved his personal objectives than with winning or losing. He sees victory as improving his own abilities, and he sees every game as a chance for development. The bowler is motivated by his inherent joy in perfecting the game rather than being influenced by outside forces like rivalry and societal comparison.

Ego-Oriented Bowler: This great bowler, on the other hand, is ego-oriented and heavily dependent on social comparison and outside validation. His main motivation for competing is to establish his dominance over others and earn the title of top player in his league or competition. He has a great desire to exceed his rivals and compare his performance to them frequently. His primary indicators of success are championships and honors. Despite his intense rivalry, he is driven primarily by outside forces such as the need to be accepted and establish superiority over his peers.

In contexts of achievement, people attempt to show high ability and avoid showing low ability. When it comes to achievement settings, there are two main objectives. The accomplishment of these individual objectives determines judgments of competence or ability, which in turn determines perceptions of success and failure.

Task objectives have to do with raising performance levels or learning new abilities. The main motivations of task-oriented performers are learning and personal growth. Self-identified motivations for taking part are linked to a task orientation. Because they are thought of as self-referent, whether or not personal performance requirements were met determines how successful or unsuccessful they are perceived to be (e.g., personal best 220 average in the whole season).

Enhancing oneself is linked to a feeling of accomplishment and, as a result, a higher sense of competency. Sport involvement motivated by cooperative and intrinsic factors is connected with task orientation. This is in line with SDT and HMM's forecasts.

Those who are primarily driven by the need to demonstrate their skill and competence to others are known as ego-oriented performers. Normative reference of ability refers to the tendency for people's sense of self-worth to be strongly correlated with how they perform, their abilities, and their talents compare to those of others. They often rely their assessment of their own skills on how easily and efficiently they can defeat opponents. Stated differently, their sense of accomplishment or proficiency is dependent on surpassing their peers and attaining a feeling of dominance.

The predictions of various motivational theories, such as the Achievement Goal Theory (AGT), the Hierarchical Model of Motivation (HMM), and the Self-Determination Theory (SDT), are supported by this viewpoint on ego-oriented performers. These theories contend that the motivation and behavior of ego-oriented performers are frequently influenced by outside forces like social comparison and competitiveness.

People who have a strong task disposition—that is, who prioritize learning new skills and developing their own abilities—also have higher levels of intrinsic drive. The internal desire and delight that result from doing something for its own sake instead of in response to outside pressures or incentives is known as intrinsic motivation. Conversely, people who have a high ego disposition and are more concerned with impressing other people with their skills are likely to be less intrinsically motivated. This implies that rather than deriving intrinsic gratification from the task at hand, ego-oriented workers might place a greater emphasis on extrinsic motivators like prizes or recognition.

It has been discovered that ego orientation is correlated with stronger extrinsic motivations for bowling involvement. Extrinsic incentives are those that originate from outside of oneself, including the desire for fame, awards, or social acceptance. This lends further credence to the theory that ego-oriented performers may place a higher value on approval and recognition from others and may be less driven from the inside to engage in activities such as bowling.

Achievement Goal Theory (AGT) proponents contend that participation in achievement contexts requires the capacity to exhibit competence. This is consistent with the viewpoints of the Hierarchical Model of Motivation (HMM) and Self-Determination Theory (SDT). A bowler's perception of their own abilities plays a vital role in how they perceive and analyze a competitive environment.

If a bowler has a task conception of ability, he is likely to see the competitive setting as a chance to learn and advance their own mastery. Put differently, he sees competition as an opportunity to grow and improve. Therefore, according to AGT, a task notion of ability will be linked to self-determined motivation, which denotes that the bowler is driven solely by their own desire and love of the activity.

A bowler with an ego view of talent, on the other hand, is more inclined to link the competitive environment to their sense of value. He could see winning as a means of demonstrating their dominance over others and validating their skills. As a result, according to AGT, an ego notion of ability will be associated with non-self-determined motivation. This suggests that the bowler's motivation may come from outside sources more so than from an internal sense of love for the sport, such as social comparison, prizes, or recognition.

The goal orientations of bowlers in sports differ in terms of disposition. "Differences in goal perspectives, or how people define success and assess their own abilities, are important precursors to differences in motivational processes." Competitive sports participation is neutral by nature; nevertheless, environmental and dispositional circumstances may encourage task- or ego-orientation, or a mix of the two. According to AGT, ego-involvement is a characteristic of elite sport because of the intrinsic focus on winning.

Task orientation and ego orientation are the two orthogonal aspects into which achievement goals can be divided. While ego orientation is defined by an emphasis on social comparison, external validation, and demonstrating one's superiority over others, task orientation relates to the goal of personal mastery, skill development, and improvement. Nicholls asserts that people might have different levels of task and ego orientation and that these two goal orientations are unrelated to one another.

Individuals can have both unique and coexisting task and ego orientations. Even for top athletes with a high ego orientation, task involvement can still be advantageous, despite some researchers' claims that ego involvement may be required for success in elite sports. To put it another way, even for those who also have a high desire for social comparison and outside validation, a task orientation that emphasizes personal mastery and skill development can nevertheless have a favorable effect on performance (ego orientation).

Form of Motivation	Description	Example for Bowler	Example for Coach
Intrinsic Motivation	Intrinsic motivation refers to motivation that comes from within, driven by personal enjoyment and fulfillment.	A bowler who practices regularly because he loves the game and find joy in improving his skills.	A coach who encourages bowlers to focus on personal growth and the joy of playing rather than just winning.
Extrinsic Motivation	Extrinsic motivation is motivated by external factors, such as rewards or recognition.	A bowler who competes to win cash prizes or gain social recognition for his achievements.	A coach who emphasizes winning tournaments and receiving awards as the primary goal of his bowlers.
Amotivation	Amotivation represents a lack of motivation or interest in an activity. It can result from various factors such as feeling incapable, seeing no value in the activity, or a sense of helplessness.	A bowler who practices reluctantly, feeling like they have no chance of improving or succeeding.	A coach who does not provide support, guidance, or encouragement to his bowlers, leading to a sense of hopelessness.
Task Orientation	Task orientation focuses on personal mastery, skill development, and self-improvement. Individuals with this orientation are driven by intrinsic satisfaction.	A bowler who aims to improve his technique and achieve personal best scores, regardless of others' performance.	A coach who encourages bowlers to focus on improving their individual skills rather than competing with others.
Ego Orientation	Ego orientation is driven by external validation, social comparison, and the desire to prove one's superiority over others. It often involves competing for external recognition.	A bowler who measures his success by outperforming others and constantly seeks to be the top scorer in tournaments.	A coach who emphasizes winning at all costs and values bowlers solely based on his competitive achievements.

Table 43 -- This table outlines bowling motivation. Intrinsic motivation is driven by personal enjoyment, while extrinsic motivation relies on external factors like prizes. Amotivation reflects a lack of interest or support. Task orientation focuses on personal mastery, and ego orientation seeks external validation. Coaches play a role in encouraging intrinsic motivation and personal growth or prioritizing external rewards and competition.

Despite their conceptual differences, SDT, HMM, and AGT share some common ground with one another as social-cognitive models of motivation. Firstly, bowlers' experiences from participating in sport are largely influenced by situational and dispositional elements. Through the psychological mediators of self-determination/autonomy, perception of competence, and relatedness, situational and dispositional factors impact motivation. Goal orientations affect a person's sense of relatedness, competence, and autonomy, all of which have an impact on motivation. Through their mediating effect on perceived locus of causality (i.e., self-determination) or sense of competence, differences in goal orientations may influence intrinsic motivation. Second, according to all three theories, motivation has multiple dimensions. As mentioned before, the multidimensionality of motivation must be taken into account for a thorough understanding of motivation. Third, differences in motivation have an impact on behaviors, affect, and cognitions in accomplishment situations.

Despite their conceptual differences, Self-Determination Theory (SDT), the Hierarchical Model of Motivation (HMM), and Achievement Goal Theory (AGT) have a number of things in common. These theories shed light on the various variables that affect professional bowlers' motivation and can help develop tactics for maximizing drive and output in this particular situation.

A prevalent concept among these hypotheses is that great bowlers' experiences in participating in sports are significantly shaped by both situational and dispositional elements. Elite bowlers' personal qualities, such as their needs, beliefs, and personality traits, are referred to as dispositional factors. Conversely, situational factors are those that have to do with the outside world that elite bowlers play in. These include things like coaching style, team dynamics, and the competitive landscape. Motivation is influenced by environmental and dispositional factors through psychological mediators such as relatedness, competence perception, and self-determination/autonomy. These psychological mediators operate as bridges between an individual's motivation in elite bowling and situational and dispositional factors.

Furthermore, goal orientations—which are essential to AGT—have an impact on elite bowlers' motivation. Goal orientations, such as task orientation (seeking personal mastery) or ego orientation (seeking social comparison and external approval), describe a person's overall orientation towards achievement. Elite bowlers' conceptions of autonomy, competence, and relatedness can be shaped by goal orientations, which in turn can affect their motivation. A bowler with a task orientation, for instance, may place high importance on mastering and personal growth. This would increase their sense of autonomy and competence and boost their motivation. Additionally, through their mediating effects on perceived competence or perceived locus of causality (i.e., self-determination), differences in goal orientations may potentially influence intrinsic motivation in elite bowlers).

Theory	Description	Example	Psychological Effect
Self-Determination Theory (SDT)	Emphasizes intrinsic and extrinsic motivation, with intrinsic motivation driven by internal factors and extrinsic by external rewards/pressures.	Competitive bowlers have lower intrinsic motivation but higher self-determined extrinsic motivation, like commitment to competitive bowling.	SDT predicts that competition can undermine intrinsic motivation but promote self-determined extrinsic motivation in elite bowlers. Successful bowlers may exhibit this pattern.
Hierarchical Model of Motivation (HMM)	Focuses on dispositional and situational factors influencing motivation. Psychological mediators, such as autonomy and competence, link these factors to motivation.	Dispositional traits and situational factors influence elite bowlers' motivation via mediators like self-determination/autonomy and competence.	HMM highlights the role of dispositional and situational factors and their mediation on motivation in elite bowlers.
Achievement Goal Theory (AGT)	Examines goal orientations, including task orientation (personal mastery) and ego orientation (external validation). Different orientations affect motivation.	Bowlers can have task orientation (seeking skill improvement) or ego orientation (seeking validation). AGT predicts intrinsic motivation is linked to task orientation and external factors to ego orientation.	AGT suggests that elite sport's emphasis on winning may promote ego involvement and extrinsic motivation over intrinsic motivation. Successful elite bowlers may exhibit this trend.

Table 44 - This table outlines bowling motivation theories. Self-Determination Theory (SDT) emphasizes intrinsic and extrinsic motivation, predicting elite bowlers may exhibit lower intrinsic but higher self-determined extrinsic motivation. The Hierarchical Model of Motivation (HMM) connects dispositional and situational factors to motivation through psychological mediators. Achievement Goal Theory (AGT) explores task and ego orientations, suggesting a link between intrinsic motivation and task orientation and extrinsic motivation and ego orientation in elite bowlers.

The idea that motivation is multifaceted is another element that these theories have in common. This indicates that motivation is a multifaceted concept with several facets rather than a single, monolithic one. A thorough examination of motivation in the context of elite bowling should take into account the multidimensionality of motivation and take into account the several psychological, cognitive, and emotional aspects that can have an impact on an elite bowler's motivation.

Moreover, these theories emphasize how motivational differences impact the interactions among behaviors, affect, and cognitions in accomplishment contexts. For instance, in the context of their bowling performance, a top bowler's motivation—whether it be autonomous or controlled—can alter their cognitive processes, affective experiences—such as emotions and mood—and behavioral responses—such as effort and persistence.

Winning is the main objective in competitive sports. According to SDT, HMM, and AGT, extrinsic motivation can be strengthened and intrinsic motivation can be undermined by the extrinsic or outcome focus (e.g., winning) that is frequently associated with elite athletics. Does someone who plays a high level sport always have external motivation? According to social-cognitive theories of motivation, competitive sport's framework will encourage a decline in self-determined extrinsic motivation and intrinsic motivation.

Interviewing Elite Bowlers: Gaining Insights into their Motivation

The Chosen Bowlers

We chose 11 extremely talented bowlers who had placed first in significant European Tour and world championship events throughout the previous six years in order to investigate the motivations of professional bowlers. The bowlers who were chosen were still involved in international competition. Ten of the eleven bowlers who were contacted volunteered to take part in the interview; the other two were unable to do so because of job obligations. Each bowler was personally called by the researcher (the author) to confirm their involvement.

The Interview Process

The first author conducted 45- to 60-minute individual semi-structured interviews with these best bowlers in order to obtain a deeper knowledge of their ideas, feelings, and behaviors. A series of open-ended questions (see Table 1) facilitated the interviews and allowed the bowlers to freely express their experiences and observations.

Interview schedule for elite bowlers

- ¿ How did you become involved in bowling?
- ¿ When did you start competing in bowling?
- ¿ Describe your initial level of interest in bowling when you first started competing.
- ¿ How much did you enjoy being involved in bowling?
- ¿ What aspects of bowling did you particularly enjoy? What aspects did you not enjoy?
- ¿ Has your level of motivation changed since then? If so, what has changed?
- ¿ How would you explain the reasons for your continued participation in bowling over the last few years?
- ¿ Has there been any change in these reasons? What specifically has changed? What factors do you think have caused these changes? What do you like about competing at the elite level in bowling?
- ¿ What aspects of competing at the elite level in bowling do you not enjoy?
- ¿ When faced with challenges, did you ever question your decision to compete at the elite level? Why did you continue despite difficulties?
- ¿ How do you define success in bowling? Do you consider yourself successful?
- ¿ How important is it for you to succeed in bowling? Why?

¿ What factors have contributed to your confidence in being successful in bowling? Where did you obtain the information that made you believe in your abilities?

¿ Have you ever doubted your ability? Were you able to overcome those doubts? How did you manage to do so? Regarding your participation in elite bowling, what is more important to you: financial gain, fame/glory, pleasing others (e.g., coach, parents, others), or enjoyment?

¿ How much do you enjoy training for bowling? What aspects of training do you like the most and why? What aspects do you like the least and why?

Insights from the Bowlers' Interviews

The interviews' qualitative analysis produced some amazing insights into the motives and state of mind of professional bowlers. Certain data details are left out of this part to protect confidentiality. We will talk about the main themes that came out of the interviews, though, and how they relate to the most recent theories of motivation that are social-cognitive. The bowlers were found to have the following traits:

1. **Driven by Personal Objectives and Achievement:** The top bowlers shown a strong desire to establish and meet personal objectives. The drive to consistently enhance their performance and achieve their goals propelled their motivation. These objectives included both personal development and sporting excellence in addition to winning titles.

2. **Firm Self-Belief:** The bowlers showed a resolute faith in their own skills. They were confident in their abilities and thought that success would come from their diligence and hard work. This confidence was essential to keeping them motivated and helping them get over obstacles.

3. **Bowling as a Way of Life:** For these professional players, bowling was more than simply a sport; it was a way of life. Their bowling responsibilities dominated their everyday activities, thoughts, and routines. They showed a great deal of dedication and passion by investing a great deal of time and energy into practicing, competing, and improving their talents.

These revelations offer insightful viewpoints on the driving forces behind professional bowlers. We can obtain a better knowledge of what motivates their performance and dedication by learning about their own objectives, strong sense of self, and the importance of bowling in their life. Coaches, trainers, and anybody else involved in helping great bowlers needs to have this understanding in order to be able to provide individualized assistance and establish an environment that supports and maintains the bowlers' motivation.

Personal goals and achievement: Pro bowlers are invariably extremely committed to achieving their individual objectives. A sense of accomplishment resulted from achieving these objectives, and this enhanced their motivation.

Bowlers needed to create and achieve personal goals in order to genuinely appreciate the game. Each time they reached their objectives, it was a noteworthy success that made them very happy. They wanted to be the best in the world, and achieving their goals was central to their notion of success.

According to the Achievement Goal Theory (AGT), the bowlers' strong motivation came from their own aspirations for success. Their drive came from both ego-driven objectives, like outperforming their rivals, and task-oriented objectives, like aiming for flawless performance.

In response to a question concerning what they prioritize during tournaments, the bowlers said that beating their opponents and hitting personal records were equally important. Reaching a personal best was considered a sign of progress and improvement for bowlers, and it was the benchmark for success in the sport.

All bowlers had ego goals mixed with a desire for mastery, although some were more focused on winning and showcasing their skills than others. They conveyed a great desire to be the greatest and to outperform everyone else in their endeavor.

In the talks and interviews, some bowlers showed a more task-oriented methodology. Their main priorities were developing their abilities and realizing their potential. They actually relished the challenge of competition and the chance to challenge themselves.

The bowlers had reasons for bowling that went beyond outside influences. Their drive came from an internal locus of causality, even if they aspired to win major international titles. They were motivated by self-determination, emphasizing their own motivation and the fulfillment that came from working for themselves. They understood the need for training and the worth of perseverance in order to develop their potential.

The bowlers knew at a young age that they had inherent athletic ability, but they also knew that in order to achieve their goals, they would need to put in a lot of work. They recognized the value of training diligently as well as pursuing the ultimate goal, which they called the "holy grail."

For these bowlers, the measure of success was their dedication to establishing and accomplishing individual objectives. It was crucial that they demonstrate the proper technique and give their best effort. They realized that they could accomplish amazing things if they used the proper method in conjunction with other elements.

Myth: "Elite bowlers do not exhibit intrinsic motivation to experience stimulation or acquire knowledge."

Reality: While intrinsic motivation for stimulation and knowledge acquisition may not be prominent, elite bowlers can still experience intrinsic motivation driven by the desire for accomplishment and mastery.

Myth: "The desire for recognition in elite sports is a superficial motivator."

Reality: Recognition and social acknowledgement are significant motivators for elite bowlers, as they seek validation for their competence and unique skills, which can enhance their motivation and drive for success.

Myth: "Medals and awards in elite sports are valued solely for their physical representation."

Reality: Medals and awards represent more than physical objects; they symbolize achievements, competence, and recognition, which are essential motivators for elite bowlers.

The bowlers demonstrated integrated regulation, meaning they opt for their own extrinsic motivation. They saw training as an essential part of their life and a way to keep their physical health, and they genuinely loved it. Their internal drive was also clear because they took tremendous pleasure in devoting themselves to the sport and working toward continual progress.

It was discovered in this qualitative interview with professional bowlers that reaching personal objectives improved their sense of competence, which in turn affected their intrinsic drive. They felt fulfilled and happy when they achieved their aims because of the gratification they felt. This result is consistent with a number of theories, such as the achievement goal theory (AGT), the hierarchical model of motivation (HMM), and the self-determination theory (SDT). Comparable results have been noted in elite soccer players, where success increases perceptions of competence and, consequently, intrinsic desire. People experience intrinsic drive when they perceive themselves as successful in their pursuits. The elite bowlers' healthy sense of competence was greatly influenced by the intrinsic gratification that comes from accomplishing personal goals. Their self-determined kinds of motivation, such as intrinsic motivation, were influenced by the influence of their personal goals on perceived competence.

A lot of people participate in activities just for the joy of learning a new ability, beating their own record, or creating something else. Their main concern is feeling like they've accomplished something. However, the Hierarchical Model of incentive's predicted intrinsic incentive to acquire knowledge and intrinsic motivation to experience stimulation were not evident among the elite bowlers in these talks and interviews.

A variety of motivations can be seen in elite bowlers; some may be self-determined, while others may not be. Competitive situations may reduce intrinsic motivation and boost non-self-determined extrinsic incentives, according to social-cognitive theories of motivation. The top bowlers in these talks and interviews, however, did not exhibit low levels of self-determined drive. One explanation could be that they view prizes like winning or money gained as effects on motivation rather than as elements that drive behavior because of how they make them appear competent.

These professional bowlers use their sporting accomplishments as a chance to forge their identities and win acceptance from others. Their stage, where they may express themselves and show off their abilities to the world, is the bowling facility. They saw themselves as entertainers, putting on a unique and captivating show. One of their main sources of motivation is the need for recognition that comes with being successful in professional sports. Their will to succeed is fueled by acknowledgment from others. Their want to be acknowledged as exceptionally talented people is clear evidence of their demand for individuality and recognition.

The capacity to function in a social setting and exhibit competence is directly related to one's sense of accomplishment, especially in competitive sports. Worthiness is correlated with a high sense of competence. Like people in many walks of life, elite bowlers have a strong desire to demonstrate their abilities. For instance, receiving a gold medal boosts their visibility from others in addition to providing them with a sense of personal fulfillment. It distinguishes them and denotes their unique skills. The desire for medals is motivated by much more than just the tangible item itself: the unquestionable evidence of one's abilities and accomplishments.

Bowler A stated that he wanted to be unique rather than just a competitor or a member of the team, expressing their strong desire for achievement and recognition. The desire for recognition and achievement served as their motivation. Similar thoughts were expressed by Bowler C, who emphasized the value of achievement and recognition. They acknowledged that their motivation came from the fear of being unimportant, of failing, and of not succeeding.

Adler's theory that human behavior is fundamentally motivated by a "striving for superiority" is consistent with the elite bowlers' reliance on social recognition. There's also the idea of effectance motivation, which emphasizes how important it is to show that you can navigate your surroundings. Individuals are naturally driven to take charge of their social environment. People feel a sense of accomplishment when they engage with their surroundings and overcome new problems, and they are motivated to show mastery all the time. Numerous disciplines, including education, sport psychology, and exercise psychology, support this drive to pursue competence, self-improvement, and mastery. People are frequently driven to improve their skills because they feel more accomplished and confident when they have a greater perceived skill level.

The competitive bowlers in these talks and interviews showed a great desire to prove their superiority, especially to validate their own value in the eyes of other bowlers and peers. While acknowledging the value of money, Bowler E emphasized that recognition was more important to them. According to Self-Determination Theory (SDT), one of the most basic human wants is the sense of connectedness to important persons, or relatedness. Because of their accomplishments in competitive sports, the great bowlers saw themselves as unique and belonging to a select group. They wanted the recognition that this membership entailed. For them to have a positive self-perception, they had to feel welcomed by others and that they belonged to different groups, such their family, their workplace, and sports teams.

Strong self-belief: It is not surprising that bowlers have a great sense of confidence in their abilities to meet their bowling objectives. Bowler G articulated their bold conviction that he is superior to all others. His sense of competence has been positively impacted by his accomplishment, which is consistent with the idea of learned optimism as opposed to learned helplessness. Although there were times when bowlers felt self-conscious, these were rare and fleeting.

The quest of mastering one's environment shapes one's concept of self, as stressed by the Hierarchical Model of Motivation (HMM) and Self-Determination Theory (SDT). Based on their performance in the sport at the highest levels, the bowlers in these discussions and interviews assessed their capacity to master their surroundings. The hierarchical model and the concepts of SDT were reinforced when it was shown that these elite bowlers had a substantial psychological demand related to their perception of competence. Bowlers knew at a young age that they had innate physical aptitude, which was reinforced by their early triumphs in spite of little coaching and little training. They also understood that in order to reach their full potential, hard effort and training are essential.

Elite bowlers' mindsets were largely influenced by their inner beliefs. Bowler F highlighted the value of self-belief, saying that believing he was better than his opponents kept them focused on the field. In a similar vein, Bowler I highlighted the importance of making use of one's skills and the sense of fulfillment it provides. These bowlers saw bowling as more than simply a passing passion or pastime; it was his vocation and their way of life.

Driven by high levels of self-determined motivation, bowling was the center of these great bowlers' lives. For them, bowling was more than just a sport; it was an integral part of their everyday lives and their personal growth. His decision-making was informed by his commitment to bowling, and they found identity in the game. His lives were consistent and fulfilled, and bowling became their identity. Bowler D talked about how much he enjoyed his workouts and how bowling has influenced his way of life. He valued the importance of leading an active and healthy lifestyle.

Understanding What Motivates Elite Bowlers: Our resources for understanding the motivation of great bowlers include social-cognitive theories of motivation. These theories offer an insightful framework for analyzing the mental processes that drive these remarkable athletes. Perception of competence is a key psychological mediator for these elite bowlers, in line with theories such as Self-Determination Theory (SDT), the Hierarchical Model of Motivation (HMM), and Achievement Goal Theory (AGT).

Motivation in Competitive Sporting Environments: Social-cognitive theories of motivation suggest that self-determined forms of motivation may be undermined in elite competitive athletic situations, particularly for bowlers with ego-oriented inclinations, as winning and financial rewards are frequently given priority. This implies that external factors replace internal ones as the source of their motivation. However, self-determined and intrinsic drive can still be strong if achieving personal goals in elite sports validates their sense of competence and self-determination. The center of causality in this instance is still internal. The professional bowlers we spoke with showed both task- and ego-oriented goal orientations. Their emphasis on enhancing performance and the assigned work encouraged self-regulated actions that resulted in independent motivation.

The Complex Motivations of Elite Bowlers: Our study's finest bowlers displayed a wide range of motives, but self-determined motivation stood out above the rest. It's important to remember that playing competitive sports doesn't automatically make people less motivated by themselves. These bowlers are motivated by more than just material gain. Although they can exert some control over their conduct and get information about their competence from external rewards, their self-determined motivation is strongly mediated by their judgment of competence. They believe that receiving outside rewards will improve their sense of competence and increase their intrinsic motivation.

Exploring Changes in Motivation Over Time: The desire to be exceptional becomes a stronger incentive with time, and financial benefits lose their controlling effect. This is another explanation for the motives of elite bowlers. This points to an apparent change in the perceived locus of causality—from outside to inside variables.

Understanding the motives of great bowlers also involves considering the impact that puberty plays. Because of the age range of the participants in previous studies, it's possible that integrated regulation—the most self-determining type of extrinsic motivation—did not emerge as a significant component. It's possible that the younger recreational bowlers in those studies first believed there was an internal locus of cause. However, their sense of causality may change from internal to external due to the competitive environment of adolescence. Adolescents look to their peers for validation and approval throughout this phase, which becomes essential to their positive self-perception.

The apparent locus of causality may change from external to internal as bowlers get older and consider why they sacrifice their social lives to participate in their sport and put in long training sessions. After a while, the perception of one's own competence and acceptability by others becomes a more potent motivator than money and success. When creating the training and competing environments for bowlers, coaches, and trainers need to take these changing motivations into consideration.

The Power of Personal Goals: A major source of motivation for elite bowlers is the sense of accomplishment they derive from accomplishing their many personal objectives. Their sense of competence is positively reinforced when they achieve their personal goals, which increases their motivation even more.

Implications for Coaches and Elite Bowlers: For coaches and other individuals who work with elite bowlers, the interview results have two significant ramifications. First and foremost, coaches need to be aware of the various motivational styles and the variables that affect them. Instead of imposing control over their conduct, financial benefits reveal information about the skill level of some great bowlers. Second, it is strongly advised that bowlers work with their instructors to create ambitious goals that aim to both improve and outperform their rivals, as exceptional bowlers are motivated by personal objectives. By helping people achieve their goals, coaches can significantly contribute to their perceptions of competence.

EXPLORING PERFORMANCE PLATEAUS, CHALLENGES, AND BREAKTHROUGHS IN SKILL DEVELOPMENT

Whether it's learning telegraphy, typing, programming, driving, or any other skill, we all want to get better at what we do. As bowlers, we know the value of training and the drive to improve our game every time. Experts in the early days of experimental psychology were distinguished not only by their rapidity but also by their well-honed routines, which allowed them to perform at a higher level than beginners. Remarkably, professionals observed that learning did not always follow a straight path and that there were times when progress stalled.

Plateaus: Where Progress Pauses

Performance plateaus are a typical part of learning any new skill. They stand for times when it feels like we're not moving forward as planned and we wonder why. In the game of bowling, despite our commitment and hard work, we could hit a wall where our scores don't move. These plateaus frequently result from a variety of circumstances, including lack of knowledge about the techniques needed to overcome performance hurdles, time limits, and personal priorities.

It's critical to understand that our perceived limitations do not always accurately represent our capabilities. Sometimes, either of outside influences or our own decisions, we unintentionally set boundaries for ourselves. For example, we may compromise on performance because we have other responsibilities that take precedence in our lives. In addition, some people could be discouraged by the time and effort that improvement calls for. Furthermore, how motivated and how much we care about going beyond our apparent boundaries depends largely on our own mindsets.

While it may be uncommon to achieve the ultimate peak of performance, it's crucial to recognize that there is frequently unrealized potential outside of our imagined boundaries. These boundaries are not set in stone; rather, they are shaped by both internal and external variables. Through developing an appropriate mentality, providing motivation, and learning more about the techniques required, we may be able to go beyond these boundaries and achieve greater levels of effectiveness and output.

Beyond Plateaus: Dips And Leaps

Although plateaus are well-known indicators of skill gain, dips and leaps are two more critical stages that are sometimes missed. Dips are times when we temporarily perform worse while we try out new techniques, evaluate various strategies, and decide whether to accept or reject them. These downturns might be difficult since we could experience disappointments and setbacks. They are, nevertheless, excellent chances for development and creativity.

Conversely, leaps are thrilling occasions when a novel approach or strategy results in a major discovery that raises our performance above earlier successes. These jumps encourage us to aim for even higher goals because they are marked by brief periods of success. To improve our understanding of skill development and competence, it is essential to comprehend the dynamics of plateaus, dips, and leaps.

As professional bowlers, we set out on a quest for ongoing development. It's critical to understand that this trip includes dips, plateaus, and leaps. Reaching a plateau forces us to reconsider our tactics and look for fresh ones. Dives serve as a helpful reminder that obstacles are transient and open doors for creativity. Leaps give us the will to overcome obstacles and reach new heights of performance.

Examples

Dip Example for Bowlers: A bowler who is at the top of his game may see a decline in performance throughout a competitive season. A new ball grip technique he believes could help him become more accurate leads him to try. But in the early stages of attempting this method, his scores do not improve, and he becomes frustrated since he is unable to adjust successfully. For the bowler, this slump is a difficult but worthwhile opportunity to hone his approach during a phase of skill development where he is experimenting with new techniques.

Leap Example for Bowlers: The bowler's performance takes a sharp turn after weeks of consistent practice and improvement of his new ball grip method. He makes a big breakthrough during a pivotal tournament when he hits spares and strikes with consistency and accuracy. Higher scores and possibly winning the competition are the outcomes of this improvement in his performance. His desire for even greater brilliance in the sport motivates him to keep improving his skills.

1. Understanding Performance Limits: Differentiating Spurious And Real Limits

It is crucial to understand the differences between various restrictions if you want to improve your bowling performance. These restrictions fall into two primary categories: false limits and actual limits.

Like plateaus, erroneous limits are surmountable with the appropriate modifications or advancements. They appear when an improved approach or plan is available to fulfill the existing objective. Stated differently, these boundaries are imposed by the employed techniques rather than being inherent to the work or environment. Bowlers can push past these erroneous boundaries and achieve new performance levels by recognizing them and implementing the required adjustments.

Real limits, on the other hand, resemble asymptotes. They stand for the intrinsic performance limitations of the task and its surroundings. These boundaries appear when the tactics and approaches being used are already the best ones available for the particular circumstance. Real boundaries are difficult to transcend unless there are notable modifications to methods, tools, or other outside variables.

Compared to many other activities examined in experimental psychology, bowling stands out. In contrast to typical psychological tests, which frequently concentrate on brief, repeated activities that isolate particular cognitive functions, our sport incorporates complex actions that develop gradually. It is important to view elite bowlers' performances through a hierarchical structure in order to better comprehend and analyze them.

There is a clear relationship between the many levels in this hierarchical framework, allowing us to examine the "why" and "how" of our performance. We can look at the inferior techniques at the following rung of the hierarchy to see how a bowler gets a specific outcome. On the other hand, we can look at the broad objectives at the top of the hierarchy if we want to know why a bowler performs a specific way. The local aim ("why") and its approach ("how") are the two levels of analysis that we can examine in order to learn a great deal about how elite bowlers execute.

As bowlers who strive for perfection, we come into a variety of performance thresholds along the way. By being aware of these boundaries, we may overcome obstacles and realize our full potential. Let's examine asymptotes, plateaus, dips, and leaps in more detail as some of the various performance restrictions we might run across.

Spurious Limit Example for Bowlers: An example of a spurious limit for bowlers would be someone who constantly has trouble picking up the 10-pin spare. He has been failing with a specific approach and been utilizing for a long time. He identifies his sparing shooting method as the reason behind his bogus limit after consulting with a coach and reviewing his strategy. He gets past this erroneous limit and greatly increase his spare conversion rate by modifying his posture and release.

Real Limit Example for Bowlers: A seasoned bowler competes in a difficult competition with difficult lane circumstances. Because of the intrinsic limits posed by the severe lane conditions, he struggles mightily to earn high scores despite his talent and knowledge. He can't regularly hit strikes with his finest methods and strategies because of the lanes' peculiar oil patterns. In this instance, the actual limit is the lane conditions' intrinsic difficulty, and beyond it would necessitate alterations to the equipment, lane upkeep, or other outside variables that are out of his control.

> **Chris Barnes:** Chris Barnes is a well-respected figure in professional bowling, having won multiple PBA titles and major championships. Throughout his career, Barnes has faced performance plateaus where he needed to adjust his game to maintain a competitive edge. His commitment to constant improvement and his willingness to explore new techniques have allowed him to overcome these plateaus and remain a top contender on the PBA Tour.

2. Asymptotes: Inherent Performance Limits

When it comes to bowling, an asymptote is a performance limit that is established by the task's and the environment's intrinsic limits. It represents the best possible performance that can be attained with the tools and techniques available at the moment. Limits on the ball's speed, accuracy, or other environmental or physical variables can be examples of asymptotes. It's critical to understand that exceeding an asymptote necessitates significant adjustments to methods, tools, or outside variables that affect the activity.

Let's take an example of a committed bowler who regularly bowls a 220 average in competition. Physical restrictions or lane circumstances can make it difficult for him to beat this number even with their constant attempts to get better. He has performed to the best of their ability with the techniques and approaches he currently employs, hence this is an asymptote of his performance.

Plateaus: Temporary Performance Limits

In contrast to asymptotes, plateaus are transient performance barriers that are surmountable. They appear when we seem to be at a standstill, resulting in a phase of inaction or gradual advancement. Plateaus are restrictions imposed by the techniques and strategies we use, not intrinsic constraints of the task or environment.

For instance, a bowler's scoring average may plateau because of a persistent technique fault, like having trouble with a certain spare.

Understanding Plateaus: Training And Performance Challenges In Bowling

In the game of bowling, plateaus are common and are defined as extended stretches of inactivity or slow advancement. Training plateaus and performance plateaus are the two different categories into which these plateaus fall. Despite their surface-level similarities, they differ in their underlying origins, traits, and approaches to overcoming them.

Training plateaus occur when bowlers, in spite of their constant dedication to regular practice and effort, reach a point where their skill growth plateaus. Bowlers sometimes become frustrated when they put in time and effort and don't see results. There are several causes that lead to these training plateaus. The lack of variety in their practice regimens is one of the contributing factors. Progress can be hampered by repeatedly performing the same exercises, methods, or approaches without adding new difficulties or changes. The body and mind grow acclimated to this monotonous routine, which limits the development of new skills. Incorrect form or technique is another thing that causes training plateaus. Advancement may be hampered by underlying defects that are not fixed. For example, problems with follow-through or release might negatively impact ball speed or accuracy. To go past plateaus, it is essential to recognize and address these flaws.

Training plateaus can also be caused by outside variables like motivation, exhaustion, or distractions. Making success during practice requires maintaining both physical and mental engagement. Adding variation and difficulties to practice routines is crucial for overcoming training plateaus. The bowler is forced to adjust and improve their skills when exercises are changed, new tactics and plans are investigated, or various lane conditions are used. Another effective tactic is to ask a coach or mentor for their opinion. These mentors can offer insightful advice and identify form or technique faults that might be preventing advancement. Resolving training plateaus requires making the required changes and adjustments.

Performance plateaus, on the other hand, describe a period of stable performance during which scores don't significantly improve or decline. Bowlers who compete and strive for constant improvement find these performance ruts frustrating. These types of plateaus can be caused by a number of things, such as the bowler hitting their natural talent limit or outside circumstances impairing their performance. An example of this would be a bowler who is at the peak of his physical capabilities and finds it difficult to improve upon his innate ability.

Performance can also be affected by outside variables, such as modifications to the equipment or the lane conditions, which can result in plateaus. To break through performance plateaus, it is essential to learn new equipment and adjust to these changes effectively. These plateaus can also be caused by psychological issues like stress brought on by competition, pressure, or trouble concentrating. Maintaining constant performance requires effective mental focus and stress management.

Reaching performance plateaus requires a diversified strategy. It entails a careful examination and management of outside variables that affect performance, such as adjusting to changing lane circumstances or equipment requirements. Furthermore, improving mental skills through practices like visualization, mindfulness, or relaxation exercises can greatly improve focus and performance in general.

Factor/Aspect	Description	Psychological Impact	Technical Impact
Training Plateaus	Skill development levels off despite practice.	Frustration, demotivation, and reduced self-confidence.	Reduced progress, limited skill improvement.
Lack of Variety	Repeating the same routines without new challenges.	Boredom, decreased engagement, and complacency.	Limited adaptability and skill refinement.
Improper Technique	Unaddressed fundamental flaws in bowling technique.	Frustration, self-doubt, and reduced self-efficacy.	Reduced accuracy, consistency, and ball control.
External Factors	Motivation, fatigue, or distractions during practice.	Reduced focus, motivation, and mental resilience.	Hindered skill development and consistency.
Performance Plateaus	Consistent performance without notable improvement.	Frustration, stagnation, and decreased motivation.	Limited score improvement and competitive challenges.
Skill Limit Reached	Maximum potential physical skills are achieved.	Contentment, acceptance, or realization of skill boundaries.	Limited scope for skill enhancement and innovation.
External Influences	Lane conditions or equipment changes affect performance.	Adaptation challenges, uncertainty, and mental stress.	Necessity for equipment adjustments and skill adaptation.
Mental Factors	Concentration, pressure, or competition-induced stress.	Anxiety, diminished focus, and decreased self-control.	Reduced consistency, accuracy, and decision-making.

Table 45 - This table discusses factors affecting bowling performance. Training Plateaus result in frustration and reduced progress. Lack of Variety leads to boredom and limited adaptability. Improper Technique causes frustration and decreased accuracy. External Factors like motivation impact focus and hinder skill development. Performance Plateaus lead to frustration and stagnation. Skill Limit Reached brings contentment but limits enhancement. External Influences create adaptation challenges. Mental Factors, such as stress, reduce consistency and decision-making.

Exploring Plateaus And Asymptotes In Bowling: Setting Realistic Goals For Performance

For the purpose of establishing objectives and controlling expectations along their bowling journey, bowlers should comprehend the notions of plateaus and asymptotes. Examining these terms and their connection to performance and training will help.

When a bowler's game levels out or stays largely unchanged without showing discernible growth or regression, it's known as a plateau. Training sessions and live performances may both cause this. It is possible, for instance, that despite training frequently, your skill level or scores do not appear to be improving. Analogously, there can be a phase in competitions where you maintain steady scores with little variation.

There are several reasons why bowling can reach a plateau. Incorrect form or technique, a lack of drive or concentration, monotonous practice sessions without adding new difficulties or variations, and even outside influences like altered equipment or lane conditions can be among them. In order to improve your performance, you must overcome your plateaus, which can be very irritating.

Unlike plateaus, asymptotes show the ideal or theoretical performance limit that a bowler may approach but never quite hit. They may be beyond your current capabilities, but he represents the best potential degree of performance. Like a goal you may strive for but not be able to fully accomplish because of physical limitations, innate skill level, or outside restraints, an asymptote is similar.

Establishing realistic goals requires an understanding of the distinction between asymptotes and plateaus. As long as training or performance tactics are modified, plateaus are transient and can be broken. They suggest that you can overcome a phase of inertia. Conversely, asymptotes stand for the maximum performance potential that might not be entirely reached. They represent the ideal standards that you may strive to meet but may not be able to do so for a variety of reasons.

Examples of Plateaus in Bowling:

Training Plateau: A bowler has been practicing regularly for several months, but in spite of this, his average score of 180 has not changed. Despite investing the time and energy, he is unable to observe any appreciable gains in his performance.

Performance Plateau: After years of competitive bowling, a seasoned player's scores have leveled off at about 200. There is a performance plateau evident in the comparable scores he continually attains without any discernible increases or decreases.

Examples of Asymptotes in Bowling:

Skill Asymptote: A bowler wants to score 300 to have a perfect game. But despite his best efforts to practice and get better, individuals eventually reach a skill asymptote where the task's inherent complexity and his own limits prevent him from regularly getting a perfect score.

Equipment Asymptote: A bowler spends money on the best equipment available, such as a bowling ball with exceptional performance. He first notices a notable change in his test results. He quickly, however, reaches an equipment asymptote where additional equipment improvements do not yield appreciable gains in performance since he has already attained the ideal level of equipment for his playing style and skill level.

Avoiding Plateaus by Setting Realistic Goals and Effective Methods

Plateaus can happen when players use inefficient techniques or set unattainable objectives for themselves when practicing and competing. Bowlers may encounter these plateaus and be unable to get to the level of ability and accomplishment they have set for themselves.

Erroneous goal setting is a common reason for bowling plateaus. If bowlers set too high of standards for themselves, or if their present skill level does not align with their ambitions, they risk hitting a plateau. For example, a bowler is likely to become frustrated and stagnate if they try to constantly score a perfect game of 300 without having the requisite abilities or expertise. A performance plateau can also result from concentrating only on score improvement while ignoring other factors like technique, precision, or consistency.

Additionally, picking ineffective tactics or approaches can sometimes result in plateaus. Bowlers may not make any more improvement if they stick to the same exercises and routines without adding any new difficulties or modifications. Similarly, bowlers may be stuck on a plateau for an extended period of time if they use poor form or technique, ignore coaching and feedback, or don't adjust to changing lane circumstances.

Bowlers need to rethink and modify their strategy in order to break through plateaus brought on by incorrect goals or approaches. Setting goals that are appropriate for the bowler's current skill level and developmental stage is essential. These goals should be reasonable and attainable. Bowlers can establish more realistic goals, such raising their average score by a certain number of pins per game, instead of obsessing about a perfect game of 300. It's also possible to stimulate development and avoid stagnation by introducing fresh challenges and diversity into training regimens. Getting advice and criticism from coaches or seasoned bowlers, examining and improving form or technique, and adjusting to shifting circumstances are all critical tactics for overcoming performance plateaus.

Breaking Through Plateaus with League-Stepping Methods

Using League-Stepping Techniques can assist bowlers break through and elevate their game when they reach a plateau in their performance, where they appear to reach a ceiling despite their best efforts. Three cognitive processes are involved in these methods: practice, method development, and method invention, discovery, or instruction. Bowlers can advance and succeed by doing these exercises and keeping an eye out for particular behavioral indicators.

1. **Method Invention, Discovery, or Instruction:** Developing a fresh strategy or method to improve performance is the first step towards breaking through a performance plateau. This can entail wondering if there's a "better way" to bowl or learning a new skill via guidance or observation. When bowlers see that their performance plateaus using their current approach, they might consider trying something different.

2. **Method Development:** Developing and improving a newly conceived or found method is the next stage. To effectively use the new strategy, bowlers need to practice and make necessary adjustments after learning how to do things differently. This is like a golfer giving up immediate rewards in order to learn a new swing. Although method development might not result in performance gains right away and might even cause short-term declines, these declines are a sign that the plateau is being broken.

3. **Practice:** The final step in the League-Stepping Methods is practice. Bowlers need to strengthen the new technique and elevate their game. They can perform noticeably better at first as they become used to the new strategy. This leap is an inspiring symbol of achievement and advancement. But with further practice, the performance gains can become less pronounced, setting up a new performance plateau.

It's important to remember that not every plateau calls for brand-new strategies. Improvements can occasionally be obtained by making minor changes or enhancements to the existing procedure. The secret is to deliberately practice on a regular basis, pushing your brain to learn new skills and strategies.

Example: John, a seasoned bowler, has been having trouble for a few months with a performance plateau. He has been following the same method on a regular basis, but he has not noticed a noticeable improvement in his scores. In an attempt to overcome the plateau, he chooses to use the League-Stepping Methods.

Hypothetical examples

Method Invention, Discovery, or Instruction: John begins recognizing that some proficient bowlers employ a distinct footwork method when he watches them play league games. His curiosity piques, and he begins looking up more information about this method online. Upon obtaining sufficient knowledge, he resolves to do it at his subsequent practice session.

Method Development: John starts working on the new footwork technique, getting his coach's input and modifying his strategy. His performance suffers at first as he tries to get the hang of the new skill, but he doesn't give up and keeps practicing.

Practice: John begins to see gains in his performance after a few weeks of focused practice. He can now produce greater force in his shots and has improved in precision and regularity. His performance takes a sharp turn for the better as his test results begin to rise above his prior plateau.

Two-Week Strategic Plan to Overcome Plateaus in Bowling

It's critical to move quickly to break past a plateau in bowling in order to increase performance. For quicker outcomes, this two-week strategic plan combines the League-Stepping Methods with intentional practice and brain training.

Week 1: Exploration and Refinement

Day 1: Evaluation and Goal Setting

- **Task:** Assess present performance, pinpoint reasons for plateaus, and establish clear objectives.
- **Tactics and Tasks:**
  - Evaluate your bowling abilities, concentrating on areas where advancement has stalled.
  - Establish short-term, attainable goals that focus on particular areas that need improvement.
- **Brain Training:** Start by focusing on working memory and attention in your brain training exercises.
  - Attention Training: Work on focusing and reducing outside distractions.

- Working Memory Training: Develop your mental information manipulation skills.

Day 2-4: Method Exploration and Research

- **Task:** Investigate novel approaches or strategies that might enhance performance.
- **Tactics and Tasks:**
  - Study proficient bowlers in league matches or practice sessions to get ideas.
  - Look up new bowling technique tutorials online, read books, or watch videos.
  - Try out various strategies throughout practice sessions.
- **Brain Training:** Keep up the brain training activities and incorporate tasks that test processing speed.
  - Processing Speed Training: Develop your capacity for swift information processing.

Day 5-7: Method Development and Refinement

- **Task:** Set aside time for concentrated practice sessions to hone the selected approach.
- **Tactics and Tasks:**
  - During regular practice sessions, continually apply the recently taught skill.
  - To make the required modifications, ask coaches or seasoned bowlers for their input.
  - Examine your performance information and contrast it with past results.
- **Brain Training:** Increase the difficulty of the activities and incorporate instruction in making decisions.
- **Decision-Making Training:** Become more adept at making accurate choices under time constraints.

Week 2: Implementation and Evaluation

Day 8-10: Method Implementation and Performance Evaluation

- **Task:** Use the improved technique in practice sessions and assess its results.
- **Tactics and Tasks:**
  - Utilize the recently acquired method while improving in on consistency.
  - Keep a thorough journal of your practice sessions, with special attention to your areas of weakness.
  - Constantly modify and improve the procedure in light of your practice experiences and input.
- **Brain Training:** Continue your brain training regimen while introducing new exercises.
  - To maintain the sharpness of your cognitive abilities, mix up your brain training activities.
- **Deliberate Practice:** Start intentional practice sessions in addition to your normal practice.
  - Goal-setting: Establish clear, difficult practice objectives.
  - Feedback: During focused practice, ask coaches or seasoned bowlers for their opinions.
  - Repetition: Pay attention to improving little by little with each repeat.
  - Variation: To encourage development, add variation to intentional practice sessions.

Outcome: This tactical plan combines method research and improvement, brain exercises for cognitive training, and purposeful practice in just two weeks. Bowlers can effectively break through plateaus and improve their overall performance by adhering to this method, which will give them newfound confidence and competitiveness before tournaments.

Two-Week Brain Training Program for Bowlers to overcome Plateau psychologically

WEEK 1 - Day 1

Training Aspect	Activity	Task	Focus
Attention Training	Mindful Breathing	Spend 10-15 minutes in a quiet space.	Train your mind to maintain concentration and block out distractions.
Working Memory Training	Memory Match Game	Create a set of cards with bowling terms or lane conditions.	Enhance your memory and recall skills.

Training Aspect	Activity	Task	Focus
Processing Speed Training	Rapid Release Practice	Focus on reducing your setup time and releasing the ball more quickly.	Enhance your overall bowling speed by reducing setup and execution time.
Decision-Making Training	Pin Configuration Analysis	Study different pin configurations and their implications for spare conversions.	Enhance your decision-making when faced with spare opportunities.

WEEK 1 - DAY 2

Training Aspect	Activity	Task	Focus
Attention Training	Single-Pin Focus	Set up a single pin on the lane.	Concentrate solely on hitting the target pin, blocking out any external distractions.
Working Memory Training	Number Sequences	List a series of numbers and have a partner read them aloud.	Strengthen your working memory by actively recalling and processing information.
Processing Speed Training	Speed Bowling Drills	Bowl with the goal of completing games within a specific time limit (e.g., 10 minutes per game).	Improve your ability to execute shots rapidly without sacrificing accuracy.
Decision-Making Training	Risk vs. Reward Analysis	Create scenarios where you have to choose between a safe play and a more aggressive approach.	Improve your ability to evaluate and select the most suitable strategy.

WEEK 1 - DAY 3

Training Aspect	Activity	Task	Focus
Attention Training	Visualization Exercise	Sit in a quiet area with your eyes closed.	Train your mind to stay focused on the visualization, excluding all other thoughts.
Working Memory Training	Lane Condition Analysis	Bowl on various lane conditions (e.g., dry, oily) during practice.	Improve your ability to assess and adapt to different lane conditions.
Processing Speed Training	Speed Reading and Reacting	Read and react to lane conditions more swiftly.	Enhance your ability to make rapid decisions based on lane conditions.
Decision-Making Training	Frame-by-Frame Planning	Bowl a practice game and plan each frame strategically.	Develop a habit of making decisions for each frame based on working memory.

WEEK 1 - DAY 4

Training Aspect	Activity	Task	Focus
Attention Training	Controlled Distractions	Have a partner or coach create distractions (e.g., making noise, talking) during practice.	Develop the ability to block out external distractions and maintain concentration on your shot.
Working Memory Training	Visual Memory Enhancement	Study different pin layouts and memorize their positions.	Enhance your visual memory for better pin positioning recall.
Processing Speed Training	Quick Spares	Practice converting spares as quickly as possible.	Hone your ability to quickly calculate angles and execute precise spare shots.
Decision-Making Training	Pressure Situations Simulation	Bowl under simulated pressure scenarios during practice.	Apply your enhanced decision-making skills under competitive conditions.

WEEK 1 - DAY 5

Training Aspect	Activity	Task	Focus
Attention Training	Tournament Scenario Visualization	Visualize being in a tournament setting.	Train your mind to stay focused and composed in high-pressure situations.
Working Memory Training	Rapid Decision-Making	Bowl a practice game with a limited time frame per shot (e.g., 15 seconds per shot).	Apply your improved working memory to rapid decision-making.
Processing Speed Training	Frame-by-Frame Speed Planning	Bowl a practice game and plan each frame quickly.	Develop a habit of making quick decisions for each frame.
Decision-Making Training	Rapid Decision-Making	Bowl a practice game with a limited time frame per shot (e.g., 15 seconds per shot).	Apply your improved decision-making to rapid shot execution.

WEEK 1 - DAY 6

Training Aspect	Activity	Task	Focus
Attention Training	Pressure Situations	Bowl under simulated pressure scenarios during practice.	Apply your enhanced attention skills under competitive conditions.
Working Memory Training	Speed Bowling	Bowl as fast as possible, simulating a rapid-fire tournament scenario.	Train your working memory to process information quickly and effectively.
Processing Speed Training	Scenario-Based Decision Drills	Create various challenging scenarios during practice sessions.	Enhance your ability to make quick and effective decisions in diverse situations.
Decision-Making Training	Speed Bowling Challenges	Bowl as fast as possible, simulating a rapid-fire tournament scenario.	Train your decision-making to process information quickly and effectively.

WEEK 1 - DAY 7

Training Aspect	Activity	Task	Focus
Attention Training	Breathing and Composure	Sit quietly and practice deep breathing.	Develop the ability to quickly regain focus after challenging shots.
Working Memory Training	Frame-by-Frame Planning	Bowl a practice game and plan each frame strategically.	Develop a habit of making decisions for each frame based on working memory.
Processing Speed Training	Tournament Simulation	Participate in mock tournament play with fellow bowlers.	Learn to make effective decisions under the pressure of real competition.
Decision-Making Training	Scenario-Based Drills	Create various challenging scenarios during practice sessions.	Enhance your ability to make rapid decisions in diverse situations.

WEEK 2 - DAY 1

Training Aspect	Activity	Task	Focus
Attention Training	Tournament Scenario Visualization	Visualize being in a tournament setting.	Train your mind to stay focused and composed in high-pressure situations.
Working Memory Training	Rapid Decision-Making	Bowl a practice game with a limited time frame per shot (e.g., 15 seconds per shot).	Apply your improved working memory to rapid decision-making.
Processing Speed Training	Frame-by-Frame Speed Planning	Bowl a practice game and plan each frame quickly.	Develop a habit of making quick decisions for each frame.

Training Aspect	Activity	Task	Focus
Decision-Making Training	Pin Configuration Analysis	Study different pin configurations and their implications for spare conversions.	Enhance your decision-making when faced with spare opportunities.

WEEK 2 – DAY 2

Training Aspect	Activity	Task	Focus
Attention Training	Pressure Situations	Bowl under simulated pressure scenarios during practice.	Apply your enhanced attention skills under competitive conditions.
Working Memory Training	Speed Bowling	Bowl as fast as possible, simulating a rapid-fire tournament scenario.	Train your working memory to process information quickly and effectively.
Processing Speed Training	Scenario-Based Decision Drills	Create various challenging scenarios during practice sessions.	Enhance your ability to make quick and effective decisions in diverse situations.
Decision-Making Training	Speed Bowling Challenges	Bowl as fast as possible, simulating a rapid-fire tournament scenario.	Train your decision-making to process information quickly and effectively.

WEEK 2 – DAY 3

Training Aspect	Activity	Task	Focus
Attention Training	Frame-by-Frame Planning	Bowl a practice game and plan each frame strategically.	Develop a habit of making decisions for each frame based on working memory.
Working Memory Training	Scenario-Based Decision Drills	Create various challenging scenarios during practice sessions.	Enhance your ability to make rapid decisions in diverse situations.
Processing Speed Training	Tournament Simulation	Participate in mock tournament play with fellow bowlers.	Learn to make effective decisions under the pressure of real competition.
Decision-Making Training	Frame-by-Frame Planning	Bowl a practice game and plan each frame strategically.	Develop a habit of making decisions for each frame based on lane conditions.

WEEK 2 – DAY 4

Training Aspect	Activity	Task	Focus
Attention Training	Rapid Decision-Making	Bowl a practice game with a limited time frame per shot (e.g., 15 seconds per shot).	Apply your improved attention skills to rapid shot execution.
Working Memory Training	Rapid Decision-Making	Bowl a practice game with a limited time frame per shot (e.g., 15 seconds per shot).	Apply your improved working memory to rapid decision-making.
Processing Speed Training	Quick Spares	Practice converting spares as quickly as possible.	Hone your ability to quickly calculate angles and execute precise spare shots.
Decision-Making Training	Pressure Situations Simulation	Bowl under simulated pressure scenarios during practice.	Apply your enhanced decision-making skills under competitive conditions.

WEEK 2 – DAY 5

Training Aspect	Activity	Task	Focus
Attention Training	Rapid Decision-Making	Bowl a practice game with a limited time frame per shot (e.g., 15 seconds per shot).	Apply your improved attention skills to rapid shot execution.
Working Memory Training	Rapid Decision-Making	Bowl a practice game with a limited time frame per shot (e.g., 15 seconds per shot).	Apply your improved working memory to rapid decision-making.
Processing Speed Training	Frame-by-Frame Speed Planning	Bowl a practice game and plan each frame quickly.	Develop a habit of making quick decisions for each frame.

Training Aspect	Activity	Task	Focus
Decision-Making Training	Rapid Decision-Making	Bowl a practice game with a limited time frame per shot (e.g., 15 seconds per shot).	Apply your improved decision-making to rapid shot execution.

WEEK 2 – DAY 6

Training Aspect	Activity	Task	Focus
Attention Training	Speed Bowling Challenges	Bowl as fast as possible, simulating a rapid-fire tournament scenario.	Train your attention to process information quickly and effectively.
Working Memory Training	Speed Bowling	Bowl as fast as possible, simulating a rapid-fire tournament scenario.	Train your working memory to process information quickly and effectively.
Processing Speed Training	Scenario-Based Decision Drills	Create various challenging scenarios during practice sessions.	Enhance your ability to make quick and effective decisions in diverse situations.
Decision-Making Training	Speed Bowling Challenges	Bowl as fast as possible, simulating a rapid-fire tournament scenario.	Train your decision-making to process information quickly and effectively.

WEEK 2 – DAY 7

Training Aspect	Activity	Task	Focus
Attention Training	Scenario-Based Drills	Create various challenging scenarios during practice sessions.	Enhance your ability to maintain focus and make decisions in diverse situations.
Working Memory Training	Tournament Simulation	Participate in mock tournament play with fellow bowlers.	Apply your enhanced working memory skills in a competitive environment.
Processing Speed Training	Tournament Simulation	Participate in mock tournament play with fellow bowlers.	Apply your enhanced processing speed in a competitive environment.
Decision-Making Training	Scenario-Based Drills	Create various challenging scenarios during practice sessions.	Enhance your decision-making skills in diverse and pressure-filled situations.

WEEK 2 – DAY 8

Training Aspect	Activity	Task	Focus
Attention Training	Review and Reflection	Review your progress over the past two weeks.	Reflect on how your attention and focus have improved.
Working Memory Training	Review and Reflection	Review your progress over the past two weeks.	Reflect on how your working memory has improved and impacted your performance.
Processing Speed Training	Review and Reflection	Review your progress over the past two weeks.	Reflect on how your processing speed has improved and how it has impacted your performance.
Decision-Making Training	Review and Reflection	Review your progress over the past two weeks.	Reflect on how your decision-making has improved and how it has impacted your performance.

Table 46 - This two-week brain training program for bowlers aims to overcome psychological plateaus. The program involves specific daily activities targeting attention, working memory, processing speed, and decision-making skills.

PERFECTIONISM ON ELITE BOWLING PERFORMANCE

Perfectionism is important in the world of competitive athletics. It is a personality trait that has both positive and negative consequences for athletes' psychological well-being. While unhealthy perfectionism has been linked to negative outcomes such as depression and eating disorders, it's also important to recognize that certain aspects of perfectionism can contribute to positive traits such as increased self-confidence, a goal-oriented mindset, high personal standards, and improved performance.

Researchers have made strides in comprehending perfectionism in recent years by employing multidimensional techniques. This transition has allowed for a more nuanced understanding of the term, moving away from a simplified interpretation that only focuses on the previously described negative associations.

Perfectionism is a multidimensional psychological phenomenon that has been researched from numerous perspectives. Here are some of the most influential multidimensional perfectionism models:

Hewitt And Flett's Multidimensional Perfectionism Scale (MPS):

(MPS) stands as a comprehensive and widely employed model developed by Gordon L. Flett and Paul L. Hewitt to assess various dimensions of perfectionism. This multidimensional approach seeks to provide a nuanced understanding of perfectionistic tendencies, acknowledging that perfectionism is not a monolithic construct. The MPS divides perfectionism into three distinct subscales, each shedding light on specific aspects of an individual's perfectionistic tendencies.

The first subscale is **Self-Oriented Perfectionism**, wherein a bowler exhibits unrealistically high expectations for their own bowling performance. Individuals with self-oriented perfectionism continually strive for a flawless game, setting stringent criteria for themselves. Consequently, when they fall short of these self-imposed standards, they may experience feelings of disappointment or frustration. This dimension emphasizes the intrapersonal aspect of perfectionism, delving into the internal expectations and demands individuals place on themselves within the context of their bowling pursuits.

Moving to the second subscale, **Other-Oriented Perfectionism**, this dimension explores the dynamics of perfectionistic expectations individuals may harbor towards their bowling partners or opponents. A bowler with other-oriented perfectionism sets unrealistically high standards for those around them, and feelings of dissatisfaction arise when these expectations are not met. This dimension highlights the interpersonal aspect of perfectionism, illustrating how an individual's perfectionistic tendencies extend beyond their personal goals and impact their relationships within the bowling context.

Lastly, the third subscale is **<u>Socially Prescribed Perfectionism</u>**, which captures the external pressures individuals may experience from external sources such as coaches, teammates, or others within the bowling community. Bowlers with socially prescribed perfectionism may feel compelled to perform flawlessly in every game due to external expectations. The fear of judgment and anxiety related to making mistakes or not meeting others' standards characterizes this dimension. Socially prescribed perfectionism underscores the impact of external influences on an individual's perfectionistic tendencies, adding a societal and contextual layer to the understanding of perfectionism in bowling.

In essence, the Multidimensional Perfectionism Scale provides a sophisticated framework for comprehending the multifaceted nature of perfectionism in the context of bowling. The three subscales collectively offer a nuanced perspective, encompassing the internal, interpersonal, and societal dimensions of perfectionistic tendencies, contributing to a more comprehensive understanding of how perfectionism manifests and influences individuals in the bowling domain.

Myth: Perfectionistic Striving Guarantees Success

Reality: Dispelling the myth that perfectionistic striving guarantees success, the narrative explores how high levels of perfectionistic striving (PS) can be accompanied by excessive concerns about mistakes (PC), leading to stress and self-criticism. The reality emphasizes that a balanced approach, incorporating both PS and PC in modest levels, can contribute to better overall well-being, motivation, and performance outcomes.

Myth: Worry-Free Perfectionism Leads to Optimal Performance

Reality: Addressing the myth that a worry-free approach to perfectionism leads to optimal performance, the narrative illustrates how excessive concerns about mistakes (PC) can detrimentally impact a bowler's game, even when coupled with high levels of perfectionistic striving (PS). The reality underscores the importance of a well-rounded strategy that acknowledges the learning process, combining high standards with a positive outlook on errors and setbacks.

Myth: Perfectionistic Concerns Are Inconsequential

Reality: Challenging the myth that perfectionistic concerns (PC) are inconsequential, the narrative highlights how excessive worries about making mistakes or falling short can impair a bowler's ability to perform at their best. The reality emphasizes the need for sports psychologists to work with athletes exhibiting high PC levels, helping them create a balanced perfectionism strategy to manage anxiety, cope with mistakes, and maintain high standards for improved performance outcomes.

Sample Multidimensional Perfectionism Scale (MPS) for Bowlers

Instructions: This assessment scale is designed to measure various dimensions of perfectionism in bowlers. Please rate each item on a scale of 1 to 5, with 1 being "Strongly Disagree" and 5 being "Strongly Agree." Be honest and reflective in your responses, considering how well each statement aligns with your experiences and tendencies in the context of bowling.

Self-Oriented Perfectionism:

1. *I set very high standards for my own bowling performance.*
2. *Falling short of my own expectations in bowling is disappointing to me.*
3. *I am constantly striving for a flawless game in bowling.*
4. *If I make mistakes in bowling, I find it difficult to forgive myself.*
5. *I feel a strong need to be perfect in every aspect of my bowling.*
6. *I often set goals for myself in bowling that are hard to attain.*
7. *I am my own harshest critic when it comes to my bowling performance.*
8. *I am rarely satisfied with my bowling, even when others praise me.*
9. *I have a strong desire to be the best bowler I can possibly be.*

10. *I find it challenging to accept imperfections in my bowling game.*

Other-Oriented Perfectionism:

1. *I expect my bowling partners to meet high standards during games.*
2. *I feel dissatisfied when my bowling partners or opponents don't meet my expectations.*
3. *I often find myself frustrated with the performance of others in bowling.*
4. *I set high standards for my teammates, and it bothers me when they don't meet them.*
5. *I believe that everyone on my bowling team should aim for perfection.*
6. *I feel a need for my bowling partners to be as committed to excellence as I am.*
7. *I get frustrated when others on my bowling team make mistakes.*
8. *I have a hard time accepting less than perfect performance from my teammates.*
9. *I expect everyone on my bowling team to give 100% effort in every game.*
10. *I feel responsible for the performance of my bowling partners.*

Socially Prescribed Perfectionism:

1. *I feel pressure from coaches to perform flawlessly in every game.*
2. *Teammates' expectations significantly influence my bowling performance.*
3. *I worry about what others will think if I don't perform well in bowling.*
4. *I often feel judged by my coach or teammates based on my bowling performance.*
5. *The fear of making mistakes in bowling can be overwhelming due to external expectations.*
6. *I feel the need to meet the standards set by my bowling coach.*
7. *I believe that my teammates expect me to be perfect in every game.*
8. *I often compare my bowling performance to the expectations of others.*
9. *I am anxious about not meeting the standards set by my coach or teammates.*
10. *External pressure significantly impacts my confidence on the bowling lane.*

Overall Perfectionism Rating:

- ***4-8:*** *Low Perfectionism Tendencies.*
- ***9-12:*** *Moderate Perfectionism Tendencies.*
- ***13-16:*** *High Perfectionism Tendencies.*
- ***17-20:*** *Very High Perfectionism Tendencies.*
- ***21-25:*** *Extremely High Perfectionism Tendencies.*

Note: Respondents should rate their agreement with each statement on a scale of 1 to 5, with 1 being "Strongly Disagree" and 5 being "Strongly Agree." The overall perfectionism rating is determined by summing the scores across all three subscales.

Frost's Multidimensional Perfectionism Scale (FMPS):

Frost's Multidimensional Perfectionism Scale (FMPS), devised by Randy O. Frost, stands as a significant and extensively employed model in the exploration of perfectionism within the context of bowling. This multidimensional framework comprises six distinct subscales, each illuminating specific facets of an individual's perfectionistic tendencies, thereby contributing to a nuanced understanding of perfectionism in the bowling domain.

The first subscale, **Concern over Mistakes**, digs into the cognitive and emotional aspects of perfectionism. A bowler characterized by concern over mistakes may be preoccupied with avoiding errors during gameplay. This preoccupation can manifest as continuous rumination on the possibility of making mistakes, leading to a heightened sense of discomfort or dissatisfaction when perceived errors occur. The dimension underscores the cognitive and emotional toll perfectionism may take on a bowler striving for flawlessness.

The second subscale, **Doubt about Actions**, explores the pervasive doubt that individuals may experience regarding their bowling technique or decision-making. Even after executing a shot, a bowler with doubt about actions may question their own judgment or performance, struggling to trust their abilities. This subscale sheds light on the persistent self-doubt that can accompany perfectionistic tendencies and its impact on a bowler's confidence in their skills.

Personal Standards, the third subscale, examines the internal expectations individuals set for themselves in their bowling performance. Bowlers with perfectionism in personal standards exhibit very high expectations, relentlessly pursuing a perfect score. The subscale highlights the internal standards that individuals with this dimension of perfectionism hold themselves to, and the resulting dissatisfaction or frustration when falling short of these self-imposed expectations.

Parental Expectations, the fourth subscale, introduces the external influence of parental or familial expectations on a bowler's perfectionism. Individuals with this dimension may feel pressured to excel in bowling, striving to meet the high standards set by their parents or family members. The need to perform flawlessly to fulfill these external expectations becomes a significant aspect of perfectionism within the familial context.

Parental Criticism, the fifth subscale, addresses the impact of past criticism or negative evaluations from parents or family members on a bowler's perfectionistic tendencies. Bowlers with parental criticism perfectionism harbor a persistent fear of not meeting expectations, and this fear may translate into dissatisfaction with their bowling performance. The subscale emphasizes the lasting influence of past critiques on an individual's current perfectionistic mindset.

The final subscale, **Organization**, shifts focus to the behavioral aspect of perfectionism. A bowler with perfectionism in organization exhibits a preference for an organized, neat, and tidy bowling environment. The discomfort or distraction experienced in a cluttered or chaotic setting highlights the behavioral manifestation of perfectionistic tendencies related to the organization of bowling equipment and the bowling environment.

In summation, Frost's Multidimensional Perfectionism Scale offers a comprehensive lens through which to examine the intricate dimensions of perfectionism in bowling. By exploring cognitive, emotional, behavioral, and external influences, this multidimensional model enhances our understanding of how perfectionism manifests in various facets of a bowler's experience and behavior on the lanes.

Concern over Mistakes:

1. *I often worry about making mistakes during my bowling games.*
2. *The thought of making a mistake in bowling bothers me even after the game is over.*
3. *I find it difficult to let go of mistakes I make in bowling.*
4. *I am preoccupied with the idea of avoiding errors in my bowling performance.*
5. *Mistakes in bowling create a heightened sense of discomfort for me.*
6. *I frequently ruminate on the possibility of making mistakes during gameplay.*
7. *I feel dissatisfied or frustrated when I perceive errors in my bowling.*

Doubt about Actions:

1. *Even after executing a shot, I often question my judgment in bowling.*
2. *I struggle to trust my own abilities and decisions in bowling.*
3. *Doubts about my bowling technique linger even when I perform well.*
4. *I find it hard to believe in my skills and decisions on the bowling lane.*
5. *I frequently second-guess my actions and choices during a bowling game.*
6. *Doubt about my performance in bowling affects my overall confidence.*
7. *Trusting my abilities in bowling is a persistent challenge for me.*

Personal Standards:

1. *I set very high standards for my own bowling performance.*
2. *Falling short of my own expectations in bowling is disappointing to me.*
3. *I am constantly striving for a perfect score in bowling.*
4. *If I make mistakes in bowling, I find it difficult to forgive myself.*
5. *I have internal expectations for my bowling that are hard to attain.*
6. *I often set goals for myself in bowling that are challenging to achieve.*
7. *I am rarely satisfied with my bowling, even when others praise me.*

Parental Expectations:

1. *I feel pressure from my parents or family to excel in bowling.*
2. *Meeting the high standards set by my parents is important to me in bowling.*
3. *I strive to fulfill the expectations my parents have for my bowling performance.*
4. *The pressure from my parents influences my approach to bowling.*
5. *Excelling in bowling to meet parental expectations is a significant goal for me.*
6. *I feel a sense of obligation to perform flawlessly to satisfy my parents' standards.*
7. *My parents' expectations significantly impact my confidence on the bowling lane.*

Parental Criticism:

1. *Past criticism or negative evaluations from my parents affect my bowling mindset.*
2. *I harbor a persistent fear of not meeting my parents' expectations in bowling.*
3. *Negative critiques from my parents influence my satisfaction with my bowling performance.*
4. *Criticism from my parents creates anxiety about making mistakes in bowling.*
5. *I carry the impact of past parental criticism into my current approach to bowling.*
6. *Dissatisfaction with my bowling performance is linked to past parental criticism.*
7. *I often worry about not meeting expectations due to my parents' previous evaluations.*

Organization:

1. *I prefer to have my bowling equipment and environment organized and tidy.*
2. *A cluttered or chaotic bowling environment makes me feel uneasy or distracted.*
3. *I spend time organizing my bowling gear before focusing on the game.*
4. *Maintaining an organized bowling space is important for my concentration.*
5. *I find it challenging to concentrate in a disorganized or cluttered bowling setting.*
6. *Order in my bowling equipment and environment is crucial for my performance.*
7. *I am uncomfortable or distracted when my bowling environment is not well-organized.*

Overall Perfectionism Rating:

- *4-8: Low Perfectionism Tendencies.*
- *9-12: Moderate Perfectionism Tendencies.*
- *13-16: High Perfectionism Tendencies.*
- *17-20: Very High Perfectionism Tendencies.*
- *21-25: Extremely High Perfectionism Tendencies.*

Note: Respondents should rate their agreement with each statement on a scale of 1 to 5, with 1 being "Strongly Disagree" and 5 being "Strongly Agree." The overall perfectionism rating is determined by summing the scores across all six subscales.

Slaney's Almost Perfect Scale (APS):

The Achievement Perfectionism Scale (APS), conceived by Robyn M. Slaney, represents a multidimensional model designed to illuminate various facets of perfectionism in bowling. Comprising three distinct subscales, the APS provides a nuanced framework for understanding the intricacies of an individual's perfectionistic tendencies, shedding light on the cognitive, emotional, and behavioral dimensions associated with their pursuit of bowling excellence.

The first subscale, **High Standards**, digs into the cognitive and emotional aspects of perfectionism. A bowler characterized by high standards perfectionism sets exceptionally high criteria for their bowling performance. This individual relentlessly strives for excellence and perfection, establishing a standard that is often challenging to attain. Consequently, when these lofty standards are not met, feelings of dissatisfaction and disappointment may permeate, emphasizing the internal expectations and demands that perfectionists impose on themselves within the context of their bowling pursuits.

The second subscale, **Discrepancy**, explores the emotional aspect of perfectionism, focusing on the discrepancy between an individual's actual bowling performance and their ideal standards. A bowler with discrepancy perfectionism frequently experiences dissatisfaction or frustration when their performance falls short of their idealized expectations. This subscale highlights the emotional toll that perfectionism may take, as individuals consistently grapple with a chronic sense of failure to meet their self-imposed standards.

The third subscale, **Order**, shifts the focus to the behavioral dimension of perfectionism. A bowler characterized by order perfectionism harbors a strong desire for organization and structure within their bowling equipment, gear, and overall bowling environment. The preference for order extends to an aversion to disorganization or chaos, and these individuals may feel uneasy or distracted in an environment that deviates from their need for orderliness. This dimension illustrates how perfectionism can manifest in tangible, observable behaviors related to the organization of the bowling experience.

In summary, the Achievement Perfectionism Scale provides a comprehensive and integrated understanding of perfectionism within the context of bowling. By dissecting the cognitive, emotional, and behavioral aspects, the APS enriches our comprehension of the intricate interplay of factors that contribute to an individual's perfectionistic tendencies in the pursuit of bowling excellence.

High Standards:

1. *I set exceptionally high criteria for my bowling performance.*
2. *Striving for excellence and perfection in bowling is a constant goal for me.*
3. *Attaining my self-imposed standards in bowling is often challenging.*
4. *Falling short of my high standards in bowling leads to feelings of dissatisfaction.*
5. *Disappointment arises when my bowling performance does not meet my lofty expectations.*
6. *I relentlessly pursue perfection in my bowling, even when it seems unattainable.*
7. *Internal expectations and demands significantly influence my approach to bowling.*

Discrepancy:

1. *I frequently experience dissatisfaction when my bowling performance falls short of my ideal standards.*
2. *Frustration accompanies the realization that my bowling doesn't meet my idealized expectations.*
3. *There is a chronic sense of failure when my actual bowling performance doesn't align with my ideals.*
4. *The emotional toll of perfectionism is evident when I reflect on my bowling outcomes.*
5. *I consistently grapple with feelings of not meeting my self-imposed standards in bowling.*
6. *Dissatisfaction or frustration lingers when my bowling doesn't match my idealized vision.*
7. *The emotional aspect of perfectionism significantly influences my overall bowling experience.*

Order:

1. *I have a strong desire for organization and structure within my bowling equipment and gear.*
2. *Maintaining order and structure in my overall bowling environment is crucial for me.*
3. *Disorder or chaos in my bowling equipment makes me feel uneasy or distracted.*
4. *I prefer a well-organized and structured bowling experience for optimal concentration.*
5. *The organization extends to my bowling routine, and deviations make me uncomfortable.*
6. *My preference for orderliness is observable in how I approach the tangible aspects of bowling.*
7. *A well-organized bowling environment positively impacts my overall bowling performance.*

Overall Perfectionism Rating:

- *4-8: Low Perfectionism Tendencies.*
- *9-12: Moderate Perfectionism Tendencies.*
- *13-16: High Perfectionism Tendencies.*
- *17-20: Very High Perfectionism Tendencies.*
- *21-25: Extremely High Perfectionism Tendencies.*

Note: Respondents should rate their agreement with each statement on a scale of 1 to 5, with 1 being "Strongly Disagree" and 5 being "Strongly Agree." The overall perfectionism rating is determined by summing the scores across all three subscales.

The Four Perfectionism Factors

The impact of four unique perfectionism characteristics on bowling performance has been studied: positive accomplishment striving, maladaptive evaluation concern, perfectionistic concerns (PC), and perfectionistic striving (PS).

Positive Achievement Strive:

Positive achievement striving is the desire to set exceedingly high standards, pursue excellence relentlessly, and work tirelessly to achieve one's goals. Individuals with a high level of positive achievement striving are extremely motivated to succeed and improve. Striving for positive results can be a valuable asset. Bowlers with this feature are more inclined to work on refining their techniques, improving their skills, and striving for constant excellence. They are driven to develop and meet performance goals, which can lead to higher scores, greater consistency, and a strong sense of personal accomplishment.

For example, a bowler with high positive achievement striving, for example, may continuously practice and work hard to enhance his skills, aiming for high scores and winning contests. Such players may be highly driven, resilient, and persistent in their pursuit of perfection, resulting in better performance outcomes.

Another example, a player who sets personal goals to enhance his accuracy and consistency in hitting particular pin targets is another example of positive achievement striving in bowling. To attain his goals, he may regularly assess his performance, seek input from instructors or teammates, and make improvements to his technique and strategy. Striving for high levels of achievement can lead to a sense of accomplishment, increased motivation, and higher performance.

Maladaptive Evaluation Concern:

Maladaptive evaluation concern refers to an excessive concern about how one's performance is perceived by others, as well as a fear of failure and high levels of self-criticism. This aspect of perfectionism can have a negative impact on players' performance and well-being in the context of bowling.

For example, a bowler with high maladaptive evaluation concern, for example, may be continually concerned about making mistakes, being assessed by others, or failing to fulfill his own or others' standards. This can result in heightened nervousness, self-doubt, and performance anxiety, all of which can impair his performance on the lanes.

Another example, a player who becomes extremely self-critical and frustrated when he does not meet his own high standards or receive critical feedback from coaches or teammates is another example of maladaptive assessment concern in bowling. This self-criticism can lead to a vicious cycle of anxiety, stress, and low confidence, all of which can hinder his performance and well-being.

Two-week plan to help bowlers overcome this challenge:

Week 1: Building Self-Confidence and Reducing Fear of Failure

Day 1: Self-Assessment

- Ask each bowler to evaluate his level of self-criticism and its impact on well-being and performance.
- Encourage reflective journaling on personal strengths and areas for growth.

Extra Task - Quotes:

- Bowler's Thought Process: "I am my own greatest ally, not my worst critic."
- Coach's Quote: "Self-awareness is the first step to self-improvement. Embrace it."

Day 2-3: Identifying Self-Criticism Patterns

- Instruct bowlers to document thoughts and feelings during preparation and competition.
- Facilitate a group discussion to help them recognize recurring patterns of self-criticism.
- Introduce cues for identifying negative thought patterns.

Extra Task - Quotes:

- Bowler's Thought Process: "My thoughts shape my reality; let's make them positive."
- Coach's Quote: "Awareness of negativity is the key to breaking free from its grip."

Day 4-5: Positive Self-Talk Training

- Define and discuss the concept of positive self-talk.
- Provide examples of positive self-talk specific to bowling scenarios.
- Encourage bowlers to create personalized positive affirmations.
- Engage in mental drills where bowlers practice positive self-talk during simulated gameplay.

Extra Task - Quotes:

- Bowler's Thought Process: "My self-talk shapes my performance; let's make it powerful."
- Coach's Quote: "Words have power; choose them wisely to uplift yourself."

Day 6-7: Visualization and Relaxation

- Teach relaxation techniques to reduce anxiety.
- Guide bowlers through visualization exercises, emphasizing successful and confident performance.
- Combine visualization with positive self-talk cues to reinforce a positive mindset.

Extra Task - Quotes:

- Bowler's Thought Process: "Visualizing success breeds confidence; I visualize my victories."
- Coach's Quote: "Relaxation is the gateway to peak performance; embrace it."

Week 2: Developing a Healthier Self-Evaluation Mindset

Day 1-2: Goal Setting and Focus on Process

- Shift focus to process-oriented goals rather than outcome-based ones.
- Guide bowlers in setting specific, measurable, achievable, relevant, and time-bound (SMART) goals.
- Incorporate cues for redirecting focus to the bowling process during practice and competitions.

Extra Task - Quotes:

- Bowler's Thought Process: "My goals drive my journey; let's make them SMART."
- Coach's Quote: "Process goals pave the way to success; focus on the journey."

Day 3-4: Self-Compassion

- Emphasize the importance of self-compassion in the learning process.
- Introduce self-compassion cues and affirmations.

Extra Task - Quotes:

- Bowler's Thought Process: "I am a work in progress; self-compassion fuels my growth."
- Coach's Quote: "Kindness to oneself opens the door to improvement."
-

Day 5-6: Exposure to Pressure Situations

- Create pressure scenarios during practice to simulate real-game situations.
- Introduce cues to help bowlers manage anxiety and refocus under pressure.

Extra Task - Quotes:

- Bowler's Thought Process: "Pressure is my ally; I thrive under its spotlight."
- Coach's Quote: "Pressure is a privilege; embrace it with confidence."

Day 7-8: Self-Evaluation Review

- Review progress in reducing maladaptive evaluation concerns.
- Discuss how the new mindset positively impacts performance.
- Introduce self-reflection cues for ongoing assessment and improvement.

Extra Task - Quotes:

- Bowler's Thought Process: "Progress, not perfection; every step counts."
- Coach's Quote: "A positive mindset fuels positive outcomes."

Day 9-10: Building Resilience

- Instill resilience by reframing setbacks as opportunities for growth.
- Provide cues for maintaining a resilient mindset in the face of challenges.
- Encourage bowlers to share personal experiences of overcoming setbacks.

Extra Task - Quotes:

- Bowler's Thought Process: "Setbacks are setups for comebacks; resilience is my strength."
- Coach's Quote: "Resilience turns challenges into stepping stones."

Day 11-14: Maintenance and Peer Support

- Continue practicing visualization, relaxation, and positive self-talk exercises.
- Foster a supportive team environment for open discussions.
- Encourage peer support through sharing individual successes and challenges.
- Emphasize the value of continual growth and maintaining a growth mindset.

Extra Task - Quotes:

- Bowler's Thought Process: "Together we rise; support and growth go hand in hand."
- Coach's Quote: "A team that grows together, excels together."

As part of regular training and competition routines, reinforce mental drills, cues, and positive self-talk strategies. Bowlers should observe a decrease in maladaptive assessment worries and an enhancement in overall well-being and performance over time. Stress the importance of ongoing self-improvement and maintaining a growth mindset for sustained success.

Perfectionistic Concerns (PC) And Perfectionistic Striving (PS):

Perfectionistic striving (PS) is the inclination to establish high standards and pursue excellence, but perfectionistic worries (PC) refer to the tendency to be excessively concerned about mistakes, fear of failing, and dread of making mistakes. These two aspects of perfectionism can interact to affect how well athletes perform in the bowling setting.

For example, Bowlers who exhibit high levels of perfectionistic concerns (PC) may be preoccupied with thoughts of making mistakes or falling short of others' or their own standards. This can lead to performance anxiety and have a detrimental effect on the bowler's game. Conversely, a player who exhibits high levels of perfectionistic striving (PS) might have high expectations for oneself, put in a lot of effort to develop his skills, and aim for excellence in each game. But when this is coupled with overwhelming worries about making mistakes and failing, it can cause stress and self-criticism, which can negatively impact his performance in the lanes.

A player who adopts a balanced approach to perfectionism, on the other hand, can exhibit modest levels of both perfectionistic striving and worries (PC and PS). He might sets difficult objectives and put up a great effort to meet them, but he also keeps a positive outlook on errors and setbacks as necessary components of the learning process. This well-rounded strategy can result in better overall well-being, more motivation, and better performance outcomes.

Favorable achievement striving encourages athletes to set high standards and put in great effort to reach their objectives, which can have a favorable impact on bowling performance. High positive achievement striving bowlers are probably driven, tenacious, and resilient, which can translate into better results on the lanes. Better accuracy, consistency, and overall performance may result from their constant practice, feedback seeking, and technique and approach modifications. Maladaptive evaluation concerns, on the other hand, might negatively impact a bowler's performance. Performers are more prone to suffer from performance anxiety, self-doubt, and a decline in confidence if they worry too much about other people's opinions of them, fear failing, and criticize themselves. Their performance on the lanes may suffer as a result, as they can be too preoccupied with not making mistakes as opposed to giving it their all. These athletes may require the assistance of coaches and sports psychologists in order to help them control their anxiety, create coping mechanisms, and adopt a positive outlook on errors and setbacks.

Bowling performance can potentially be impacted by the interaction between perfectionistic concerns (PC) and perfectionistic striving (PS). While having high expectations and aiming for perfection have their advantages, excessive worry about making mistakes and failing can lead to performance anxiety and have a detrimental effect on performance results. Bowlers who suffer from perfectionistic concerns (PC), which can impair their ability to perform at their best, include those who are excessively critical of themselves, fret about making mistakes, and fear failing. Sports psychologists might have to work with these athletes to help them create a more balanced perfectionism strategy so they can manage their anxiety about making mistakes and failing while still maintaining high standards. They may have better performance results if they take a balanced approach to perfectionism and have modest levels of both perfectionistic striving (PS) and perfectionistic concerns (PC). They might set difficult objectives and put up a great effort to reach them, but they also keep a positive outlook on errors and setbacks as necessary components of the learning process. Better general well-being, motivation, and performance outcomes on the lanes can result from this balanced approach.

Effects Of Perfectionism And Its Antecedents On Sporting Experience

The bowlers' perceived perfectionism had both adaptive and maladaptive effects on them, which is consistent with the aspects of perfectionism and what is thought of as PS and PC. In the section that follows, the causes and effects of perfectionism are examined in relation to the athletic experiences of elite bowlers who participated in the Perfectionism section of this book. Bowlers' differences are highlighted.

Perfectionist Striving. The adaptive qualities of *personal standards and organization* were highlighted by all bowlers when they identified a variety of traits linked to PS.

Personal Standards. All bowlers emphasized the advantages of having high personal standards and underlined them as a fundamental aspect of perfectionism. To encourage all bowlers to strive for perfection in their performances, high personal standards were proposed; one such example,

"I believe perfectionism makes you better because you want to keep going and try and perfect everything."

Another bowler suggested,

> "I set high standards for myself in training so that it shows in performances...You have something to attain if you have predetermined standards to follow, but nothing to aim for if you don't have anything beforehand.".

All bowlers experienced the adaptive effects of having high personal standards, which emphasizes the positive impact of perfectionism in bowling. **On the other hand, personal standards could also be detrimental. Bowlers with high personal standards were known to be excessively critical of others and to never be pleased with their own work. This result is consistent with the "Drive" theme**, which stands for a person's steadfast dedication to and concentration on continuously improving their performance or task.

Organization. All bowlers emphasized organization, emphasizing the efficient planning of routines and performances for various bowling components. Every bowler stated that improved performance resulted from the organization. For example

> ""My planning would have been less effective if I hadn't been so obsessed with perfection."

One bowler emphasized the value of performance preparation when talking about perfectionism in the context of competition. He linked this to perfectionism:

> "In order to ensure that I am competing at the greatest level, I always attempt to have a precise setup procedure so that I am aware of what conditions I am trying to create. I attempted to follow my meal plan, warm-up routine, and other regimens before a performance; it was like a rigid questionnaire to make sure I didn't stray from your definition of perfection."

Bowlers said that being well-prepared for a performance gave them confidence and comfort. As an illustration, one bowler proposed,

> "A positive aspect is that I feel ready and certain that I have done everything I could have done to ensure everything was flawless before entering the arena. It functions almost as a security blanket for me."

Another commented,

> "Knowing that there are certain things I've done correctly gives me confidence because of perfectionism."

The ability of a bowler to create and follow strategies or procedures that govern their conduct both before and during competition is referred to as organization. The improved attention that came from healthy perfectionists' adoption of structured routines is consistent with the positive impacts of organization and routines on performance. Organization and rituals can be beneficial for perfectionists in both good and pathological states.

Perfectionist Concerns. From the group of unhealthy perfectionists, characteristics linked with PC appeared, consistent with the maladaptive components of perfectionism, and bowlers suggested a possible negative impact on their sporting experiences.

Self-Critical Tendencies. It was believed that the bowlers' experiences were negatively impacted by their tendency toward self-criticism. All of the bowlers recognized potential maladaptive effects as a result of their self-critical tendencies, which were also affected by other bowlers. Most unhealthy perfectionists believed that having high standards for oneself encouraged traits of being too critical of oneself.

One bowler explained,

> "I tend to look at the negatives before the positives, and even if I had a good race, afterward I always think it didn't quite go right".

Another suggested,

> "I will actually say sometimes that judge hasn't been harsh enough... Additionally, "I don't understand why I was given that mark."

Dissatisfaction with Goal Progress. Unhealthy perfectionists also emphasized the potentially harmful outcomes of not being able to detach from performance or training goals and being unhappy with one's existing performance levels.

For example, in a training context one bowler stated

""I feel like the session is destroyed right away if I execute the first set poorly. Even before I begin, the session is destroyed."

The speaker proceeded to explain

"If things don't work out, I just tell myself to forget about it and try to move on, but no matter how hard I try, it will always come back.".

Another bowler explained how progress toward goals was impeded by high training standards:

"For example, I once spent a long time practicing a simple task like throwing a ball at a specific arrow. I realized afterward that I didn't need to be practicing, but I still stood there wasting time even though I didn't know how to do it. It's possible to devote excessive amounts of time to tasks that don't require it. It's as if you're not allocating your time between several disciplines sensibly or that you're spending too much time on one and not enough time on others."

When standards were employed to determine one's value, psychopathology was linked to high personal standards. This research has significant ramifications for unhealthy perfectionists whose sense of value depends on meeting their own expectations.

"It was proposed that worries about the requirement to meet high personal standards would be exacerbated by being a member of a team. For instance:

"You may find yourself in a bit of a dilemma if you concentrate on what your [teammate] is doing rather than what you are doing. Furthermore, you aren't accelerating the boat since you are focused on someone else's work. But you're only doing it because you want it to be flawless."

Concerns Over Mistakes. Each bowler's thoughts and actions before, during, and after a performance were impacted by concerns regarding mistakes, which were defined by fears of failure and making more mistakes. As an illustration, one bowler proposed:

"I get tremendously anxious before games; in fact, I get anxious before most games even when not much is at stake. I will be anxious even if it is just a simple game of pool. That sounds more like a dread of failing and things going wrong than a fear of "God that's going to hurt."

One bowler expressed feelings that many of the bowlers felt during a performance in reaction to an error:

"I would still be playing, but I would only be going through the motions. My performance will decline, and everyone will say things like, "You were having a good game then you played horrible in another game and you completely disappeared, you weren't even on the game anymore." Instead of desiring another chance to show that I am better, I would be afraid to make another error or play another poor game. I would think to myself, "Oh no, I can't go back there; I'll bowl well again. "As a result, I would be extremely cautious about what I did, which would lower my confidence and performance level."

Due to worries about errors made after the game, one bowler mentioned:

"When I'm playing a game, I can ignore my terrible behavior, but afterward, it consumes me until I've finished it piece by bit. When it comes to my performance, I believe I am most likely my own worst enemy because I will tear it apart. Others will say things like, "Yeah, you did that, which wasn't so great," and "But you did this and this, which was really good." But all I would feel is 'ugh!' It's probably because I wouldn't expect myself to do one or two horrible things, but I would expect to be able to do those things."

Excessive criticism of errors is a common trait of unhealthy perfectionists. Negative self-evaluations and the belief that anything less than a flawless performance is a failure are two specific consequences of PC. As bowlers in this interview put it, worries about making mistakes hindered learning, lowered self-esteem and motivation, and raised tension and anxiety levels. Due to the possibility of mistakes, bowlers stated that they are discouraged from learning as much in training:

Bowlers stated that they are sometimes a little bit afraid to make mistakes in training, which then leads to not learning as much as I could. This is because they are concerned about the possible consequences of their blunders.

These results align with the correlation between PC and a fear of failure syndrome and the drive for perfection, as well as studies that show the negative impact of fear of failure on performance.

Such worries have consequences that go beyond their detrimental influence on the pathological perfectionists' behaviors. More than half of the bowlers exhibited behavioral anger in reaction to an error. For instance, an unhealthy perfectionist once said:

> *"If I don't do well in training, all I want to do is go throw the balls far from my bag*
> *or really take my anger out on something to help me relax a little bit."*

Further, a bowler commented:

> *"I get a little irritated, my game suffers, and I start to go to fight after making a bad shot, and the*
> *other person scores. Like I'm going to punch him or take dumb shots and all that kind of stuff."*

Perfectionists are more likely to become angry when faced with criticism and dissatisfaction, and this rage might get in the way of task-relevant cognitive processes needed for expert performance. Research has indicated a connection between a maladaptive perfectionist mindset and a tendency to become angry when one performs poorly in a competitive setting.

Doubts About Actions.   Nearly all participants considered doubts regarding actions to be a crippling aspect of PC. "Overthinking" occurred as a result of the pathological perfectionists' uncertainties about taking action, especially when trying to avoid and correct mistakes before and during the tournament. It was therefore believed that a predisposition to mistrust one's actions would negatively impact performance.

For example, one bowler commented,

> *"I have had times when I have overanalyzed something so much in an attempt to get it perfect that*
> *when I got to the bowling center, I just kind of sat there and had a complete mental blank."*

Another explained,

> *""I believe that if someone is faster or has accomplished more than I have, they will defeat me. If their*
> *training has gone flawlessly, which is probably not the case, then mine training hasn't gone as well."*

These results are in line with studies that suggest performers' assessments of their own incapacity to carry out achievement-related tasks are the source of their reservations regarding actions.

External Pressure.   The study's bowlers named their parents, teammates, and rivals as outside pressure factors.

Half of the bowlers said that they felt pressure from their coaches and parents. As one illustration, a sick perfectionist proposed:

> *Although my parents don't visit me very frequently, I want them to see me perform to the*
> *best of my abilities when they do. I have negative thoughts like "That was bad, your whole*
> *performance was shocking" when I'm not performing to my full potential. If one small thing*
> *goes wrong, I'll believe the entire performance was subpar. Rather than thinking, "I didn't make*
> *that tackle," I'm more critical of myself, thinking, "That was bad, I let them down."*

In the same way, bowlers expressed feeling under pressure to perform well because they didn't want to disappoint their coaches;

> *"I feel like I let my coaches down because they have invested so much time in coaching me."*

Rather than believing that their significant others had high expectations of them, the bowlers felt pressure from their desire to disappoint them—coaches and parents, for example.

Coaches and/or parents assisted in lessening the impact of PC traits on certain bowlers. As an illustration, a bowler proposed:

> *"My coach occasionally has to tell me, "Yes, that wasn't quite as good, but look at these*
> *things that you did really well and those were quickest or as quick as the winner,"*
> *since I do have a tendency to focus on the negatives before the positives."*

Athletes who strive for perfection benefit from the positive motivational environment that coaches and parents may foster. The results generally showed that parents and coaches should avoid fostering motivational climates that generate worry-conducive environments that heighten maladaptive perfectionist cognitions, despite some subtleties in the outcomes regarding parent-athlete gender.

Perceived Teammate and Competitor Pressure. More than 50% of the bowlers emphasized the detrimental impact that perceived pressure from teammates or other players had on their bowling experience; the pressure from teammates was linked to social comparison and a feeling of betrayal. As far as social comparison goes, one bowler remembered:

> *"I would constantly compare myself to other individuals, saying things like "my shot needs to be better than that" or "their shots are better than mine." I used to think, "I need to be where they are at," when I looked at more accomplished people'."*

Another spoke on the social comparisons that occur prior to a game;

> *"...a lot of attention is paid to what other people are doing during their warm-up, such as 'are they warming up now?' and 'do I follow their routine or do I stick to mine?"*

Three bowlers mentioned pressure and worries about disappointing teammates in a team setting:

> *"You feel as though you have let your teammates down in huge team-open championships or important leagues, thinking, "Oh no, I haven't done that." You usually fail whether you strike or spare since no one else bowls after you, especially with me as the anchor. and others are telling you, "Don't worry, you'll get double (2 strikes)." However, you might wonder, "But what if I don't?" After that, you feel horrible and under a lot of strain."*

The bowler continued, implying that the additional pressure had an impact on other aspects of their game;

> ""It impacts all of your abilities because you are focused so much on the outcome that your rhythm and muscle tension aren't going to get you exactly what you want."

The important part teammates might play in the unhealthy bowling experience of a perfectionist. To put it another way, unhealthy perfectionists could worry about what their teammates were thinking and feel under pressure to do well for them.

Specificity and Level of Perfectionism. It is important to recognize that perfectionism is a domain-specific concept. Some pathological perfectionists made a distinction between perfectionism related to sports and more general perfectionism. One bowler said:

> *"During a competition, I want to know everything to the minute, but in general, I'm just a bit like 'Ah it's alright."*

Another emphasized this point in a similar way when they proposed:

> *"[Perfectionism] is something entirely different. "I'm not too great at this" or "I'm not too great at that" are statements I would happily make in my daily life and I don't find them bothersome at all. When it comes to bowling, I'll be all like "Whatever," but then I'll be like "No, that's not ok." It's just entirely divided. While I wouldn't consider myself a perfectionist in life, I do believe that I aim to be the greatest in bowling."*

Regarding the degrees of perfectionism exhibited in various settings, three bowlers indicated that their inclinations toward perfection were more pronounced during competition than during training. For instance:

> *"I believe that when I compete, I become more of a perfectionist."*

Two bowlers said that the significance of the competition had an impact on their degree of perfectionism. For instance, one bowler said the following while participating in a lower-level competition:

> *"I believe that as long as I succeed, it doesn't matter if it's flawless or if it takes me a few tries. I therefore typically fare fairly poorly in league competitions. However, I believe that it is irrelevant because it is a league competition and the only goal is to score points."*

When considered collectively, the results showed that fewer significant experiences could be linked to a decline in PS qualities like high personal standards. Due to the heterogeneity in perfectionism within and between persons and circumstances, these findings may have significant consequences for how perfectionism is conceptualized. Specifically, perfectionism may be better understood as context-specific.

BAD HISTORY - THE NEVER ENDING STORY

Like any other activity, bowling calls for a blend of technical mastery, mental toughness, and motor abilities. The ability to send the ball to the pins with accuracy, speed, and consistency is what defines a bowler's performance. Technical mishaps and ingrained behaviors, however, impede the development of many bowlers and keep them from raising their level of performance. This post will examine the reasons why bowlers struggle to improve their technique and overcome ingrained bowling habits.

The absence of appropriate coaching and assistance is a major factor in bowlers' inability to improve their technical faults. Bowling is an advanced sport requiring precise grip and release mechanics as well as complicated body movements. Bowlers may acquire bad habits or approaches without the right coaching, which can be challenging to break. Friends and other bowlers may occasionally offer informal advice to bowlers, but this advice may not always be precise or thorough enough to remedy technical faults. Bowlers may also lack a thorough understanding of the sport's mechanics, which could mean they are unaware of their technical mistakes. Inadequate coaching and direction can cause bowlers to unintentionally make the same mistakes repeatedly, which reinforces their technical flaws.

The Challenge Of Breaking Ingrained Habits And Muscle Memory In Bowlers

The fact that bowlers may have formed enduring habits that are firmly embedded in their muscle memory is another factor contributing to their difficulty in correcting technical faults. Bowlers may eventually acquire muscle memory for the repetitive motions required for the sport, even if they are performed incorrectly. It is difficult to intentionally alter or correct the movements since these muscle memories become involuntary responses. A bowler who has formed the habit of dipping their shoulder during the release, for instance, can find it challenging to deliberately maintain shoulder level since their muscle memory might instinctively go back to the previous behavior. It might be difficult for many bowlers to break old habits since it takes constant work and practice to retrain muscle memory.

Hypothetical example

Emma has been bowling as an amateur for a number of years. She's gotten into the habit of swinging her arm too far behind her body when she approaches the bowl. Her arm naturally reverts to the old habit despite her conscious efforts to maintain it in the proper position since it has been so deeply established in her muscle memory. Emma finds it difficult to fix this technological problem since her muscle memory keeps bringing her back to the wrong arm movement. Emma realizes she needs to practice and put in constant effort to retrain her muscle memory and create a new, proper arm swing in order to break this old habit.

Myth: Mastery Is Swift and Linear

Reality: Dispelling the myth that mastery in bowling is a swift and linear process, the narrative underscores the complexity of skill development. It highlights that progress in bowling involves navigating plateaus, setbacks, and nonlinear advancements. The reality is that achieving mastery requires patience, resilience, and an understanding that improvement is a nuanced journey.

Myth: Mental Toughness Can Compensate for Technical Shortcomings Indefinitely

Reality: Addressing the myth that mental toughness can indefinitely compensate for technical shortcomings, the narrative explores how, despite mental strength, consistent success requires a balance with refined technical skills. The reality emphasizes that over-reliance on mental toughness may lead to performance inconsistencies, showcasing the intricate interplay between mental and technical dimensions.

Overcoming Psychological Barriers In Correcting Technical Errors For Bowlers

Additionally, bowlers may encounter psychological obstacles when attempting to fix their technical mistakes. Like any sport, bowling may provide mental challenges. Bowlers may experience lack of confidence, performance anxiety, or fear of failing, all of which might impair their ability to concentrate and make the necessary adjustments. In certain situations, bowlers who have been following their old routines for a long time and feel comfort in familiarity may get emotionally tied to them. Even when bowlers are aware of their technical flaws, their emotional relationship to the game might generate resistance to change, making it difficult for them to break free of their old patterns. Bowlers may also experience peer or team pressure, as they may have become accustomed to their routines and be resistant to change. This psychological factor may be a major hindrance to bowlers' ability to improve their technical mishaps.

Hypothetical example

Although Michael is a skilled bowler, he has recently had trouble fixing a technical fault in his game. He has a tendency to rush his release under pressure, which makes him inaccurate. Performance anxiety and a fear of failing have resulted from this. Michael's psychological obstacles make it difficult for him to concentrate and make the required adjustments. Despite seeing that a change is necessary, he has grown emotionally attached to and at peace with his previous release strategy. The strain is increased by the fact that his peers and teammates are accustomed to his previous release and will not tolerate any modifications. These psychological factors make it difficult for Michael to get better at his technical errors.

Addressing The Lack Of Motivation And Dedication In Correcting Technical Errors For Bowlers

It's possible that bowlers lack the drive or commitment to fix their technical mistakes. Like any other activity, bowling demands constant practice and work to get better. To make adjustments, bowlers may need to devote time and resources to reviewing their technique, enlisting coaching, and practicing often. On the other hand, some bowlers might not be driven or committed enough to make the required effort. They might not perceive the immediate advantages of fixing their technical faults, or they might be happy with their existing performance level. This lack of drive may impede their development and keep them from implementing the required adjustments to raise their level of play.

Hypothetical example

Having been a bowler for a few years, Sophie is a gifted amateur. She has the ability, but she has been having trouble fixing a technical flaw in her footwork. Sophie isn't driven or committed enough to make the required effort. She does not see how improving her footwork will improve her performance right away and is happy with where she is at now. She lacks the motivation to spend time reviewing her technique, looking for assistance, and practicing consistently as a result. Sophie's lack of drive keeps her from moving forward and from making the required adjustments to better her game.

Overcoming The Challenge Of Lack Of Self-Awareness In Correcting Technical Errors For Bowlers

Lack of self-awareness is another thing that can prevent bowlers from fixing their technical mistakes. It takes a strong sense of self-awareness to evaluate one's own performance in bowling. Nonetheless, a lot of bowlers might not be able to assess their own technique objectively or pinpoint their technical mistakes. They might not fully comprehend the appropriate method, or their evaluation of themselves might be skewed. Sometimes bowlers overestimate their abilities and think their technique is perfect when it's not. Bowlers may be unable to identify and address their technical flaws due to a lack of self-awareness.

Hypothetical example

For many years, Alex has been a committed bowler who competes in league competitions. He frequently has trouble recognizing his own technical mistakes, though. He struggles to provide his technique with an unbiased critical evaluation. As far as identifying his technical mistakes goes, Alex is not very self-aware. When it comes to his technique, he tends to overstate its perfection and thinks it to be faultless. Alex struggles to take the required actions to fix his technical flaws because he lacks self-awareness, which keeps him from identifying and acknowledging them.

Addressing Physical Limitations In Correcting Technical Errors For Bowlers

In addition, bowlers may find it difficult to correct their technical flaws because of physical constraints. Strength, flexibility, balance, and coordination are all necessary for bowling. A bowler may find it difficult to make the required adjustments if he is not physically endowed with the proper traits for the technique. For instance, despite their best efforts, a bowler with restricted flexibility could find it difficult to maintain proper posture or release technique. Even with the right guidance and practice, physical restrictions can have a big influence on a bowler's ability to fix their technical faults.

Hypothetical example

Jake loves bowling and is an enthusiastic amateur player. However, he is limited physically, making it difficult for him to fix a technical mistake. Jake finds it challenging to maintain the proper arm swing and release technique due to his lack of shoulder flexibility. His physical limitations present difficulties despite his efforts to improve his technique through coaching and practice. Even with appropriate education and diligent practice, Jake recognizes that his physical constraints greatly affect his capacity to improve his technical faults.

Overcoming External Factors And Psychological Barriers In Correcting Technical Errors For Bowlers

A bowler's capacity to fix technical errors can also be impacted by outside variables like lane conditions or equipment constraints. A bowler's performance can be greatly impacted by their equipment, which includes their shoes, finger grips, and bowling ball. Technical errors can occur if a bowler is utilizing equipment that is poorly suited or does not fit their technique or style. A bowler's ability to execute their technique accurately can also be affected by lane conditions, such as lane topography or oil patterns. A bowler may need to modify their technique if the lane is too lubricated, for instance, and this might be difficult for someone who is not used to such conditions. A bowler's ability to enhance their game and repair technical faults may be further hampered by these outside influences. For many bowlers, it can be intimidating to put in the time and effort necessary to fix technical faults. Some people bowl only for fun; they might not have the time or energy to devote to rigorous practice and coaching to improve. Some bowlers may have competing interests, family obligations, or academic pursuits that take up time and energy that may be better spent improving their craft. Their technical faults might therefore continue, and they might struggle to make meaningful progress. Not to mention, some bowlers might not have access to the tools needed to correct their technical problems. Bowling may be a costly sport because of the expenditures associated with coaching, gear, lanes, and practice sessions. Bowlers from low-income families or those without access to bowling establishments could find it difficult to acquire the coaching or practice sessions they need to improve their technique. For bowlers looking to elevate their game, a lack of finances can be a major obstacle.

Furthermore, bowlers may find it difficult to overcome old habits and correct their technical flaws due to the psychological component of the game. Bowling is a sport that requires mental as well as physical skills. A bowler's ability to remedy technical errors and perform at their best can be significantly impacted by their emotional state. Bowlers may face psychological obstacles that prevent them from making technique adjustments, such as performance anxiety, low self-esteem, fear of failing, or other psychological issues.

For example, a bowler who, despite its flaws, has been employing a certain technique for a long time and becomes attached to it. He could be averse to change or uncomfortable with it, thinking that it would throw off his rhythm or cause his performance to suffer. An inability to let go of old habits might make it difficult for a bowler to be receptive to attempting new things or fine-tuning his current approach.

The inability of a bowler to improve their technical faults can also be impacted by performance anxiety and low confidence. A bowler may approach the game too cautiously or hesitantly if he is always concerned about doing poorly or failing. This may prevent him from using the proper technique or from making the required adjustments since he will be too preoccupied with not making mistakes instead of improving. Lack of confidence is another psychological barrier that might prevent a bowler from correcting technical faults. When faced with obstacles, a bowler who lacks confidence in his abilities to improve his technique may give up easily or not even try to make corrections. Insufficient self-confidence can lead to a pessimistic outlook and a self-fulfilling prophesy, wherein the bowler feels incapable of improving and, as a result, does not exert the required effort to bring about the required adjustments.

Psychological Barriers In Correcting Bowling Technical Errors: Anxiety, Confidence, And Self-Belief

Strong mental toughness and a positive outlook are necessary to get past these psychological obstacles. Bowlers must become more self-aware in order to identify any psychological barriers that might be preventing them from improving their technical faults. To address these issues, getting help from a sports psychologist or mental performance coach can be helpful. Bowlers can also enhance their technique and overcome psychological obstacles by fostering a growth mindset that welcomes change and challenges, as well as by boosting their self-confidence and positive outlook. Additionally, because bowling involves a lot of muscle memory, changing old habits can be difficult. The process known as muscle memory occurs when the body's muscles become used to performing a particular movement pattern through repetition. The bowler might not even be aware that he is committing technical mistakes because these movement patterns eventually become routine. Since the body has grown accustomed to the comfortable movement pattern, it can be challenging to alter this muscle memory, and doing so may feel awkward or uncomfortable.

Overcoming Technical Errors In Bowling

Bowlers must retrain their muscles and create new muscle memory in order to correct technical faults. This calls for deliberate practice, repetition of the right technique, and conscious effort. But it might be difficult and take some time to retrain muscles and break old patterns. Bowlers may first find it difficult to continuously use the proper technique, which could lead to frustration or setbacks during this period. It takes time, persistence, and commitment to practice the right technique again and over until the muscle memory is formed.

Bowlers occasionally may also have physical constraints that make it more difficult for them to fix their technical mistakes. A mix of strength, flexibility, balance, and coordination is needed for bowling. No matter how hard they try, a bowler may find it difficult to execute the proper technique if they lack the requisite physical qualities, such as wrist strength, shoulder flexibility, or approach balance.

For example a bowler with weak wrist strength would find it difficult to turn the ball sufficiently, which could result in uneven ball motion and accuracy. Alternatively, a bowler with limited shoulder flexibility would find it difficult to execute the correct arm swing and release, which would diminish his accuracy and power. In these situations, overcoming these restrictions and fixing technical mistakes could necessitate particular physical training and strengthening workouts, which could take some time and effort.

Moreover, a bowler's capacity to fix technical mistakes can also be impacted by the actual bowling environment. Lane conditions, oil patterns, and surface characteristics can all have an impact on how the ball behaves and how the bowler needs to modify their technique. A bowler may find it difficult to adjust their technique to new conditions if he is accustomed to bowling on a specific kind of lane condition or surface, which could lead to technical errors. A bowler may find it difficult to modify their release and rotation on a lane with heavy oil where the ball skids more if, for example, he is accustomed to bowling on dry lanes where the ball hooks much. This could lead to uneven ball motion and accuracy. In these situations, bowlers must learn to modify their technique to fit various lane conditions and surfaces, which calls for practice, education, and experience. Furthermore, outside elements like coaching and feedback can also be very important in a bowler's capacity to fix technical mistakes. A bowler may not be aware of his technical errors or how to fix them if he is not receiving the right coaching or feedback. Ineffective or inconsistent instruction might cause undesirable habits to stick around and keep the bowler from improving his technique. Furthermore, not every bowler has access to frequent coaching or feedback because of a variety of factors, including restricted practice opportunities, a lack of experienced trainers in his area, or budgetary limitations. Without the right assistance, bowlers could find it difficult to recognize and fix their technical mistakes and might have trouble raising their game.

Bowlers must be self-aware, patient, and committed to improving their technical weaknesses. It calls for a blend of mental toughness, physical practice, and an openness to change. Building a strong technical foundation and overcoming psychological obstacles can both be facilitated by seeking advice from certified coaches or sports psychologists.

Technical Errors Vs Psychological Errors (Triggering Each Other)

Technical errors and their interplay with psychological factors represent a fundamental aspect of sports performance, including bowling. The dynamic relationship between these two elements is a common occurrence in sports and can significantly impact a bowler's improvement trajectory. When technical errors persist, he can trigger psychological errors, such as frustration, self-doubt, and anxiety. For example, a bowler struggling with grip consistency or approach timing may become increasingly frustrated, which, in turn, affects their confidence and self-belief. Conversely, psychological errors, such as fear of failure or lack of confidence, can lead to technical errors as bowlers may alter their grip, timing, or other aspects of their technique in an attempt to compensate for their mental struggles. This cycle of technical and psychological errors can become self-reinforcing, ultimately hindering a bowler's progress and causing them to reach a plateau stage without realizing it.

Table below illustrates how technical errors can trigger psychological errors and vice versa, with examples for each:

Technical Errors	Psychological Errors	Examples
Grip Consistency	Fear of Failure	A bowler struggling with grip consistency may fear making mistakes and missing shots, leading to anxiety and apprehension.
Approach Timing	Lack of Confidence	Inconsistent timing in the approach can erode a bowler's confidence, causing him to doubt his ability to execute the shot effectively.
Release Point	Frustration	Difficulty in adjusting the release point can lead to repeated mistakes and frustration, affecting the bowler's mood and motivation.
Balance at Delivery	Self-Doubt	Inconsistent balance can make a bowler doubt his physical abilities, potentially leading to negative self-talk and reduced self-belief.
Ball Speed Control	Patience	Struggling to control ball speed can test a bowler's patience, as it takes time to refine this skill, potentially leading to impatience.
Accuracy of Targeting	Comfort Zone	Sticking to inaccurate targeting habits can be a comfort zone, where a bowler resists change due to familiarity with the existing style.
Hand Position	Peer Pressure	Resistance to changing hand position can result from peer pressure or expectations to conform to a particular technique within a group.
Lane Adjustment	Overthinking	Overthinking lane adjustments can lead to confusion, as a bowler might become too analytical, causing technical errors in the process.
Spare Shooting	Anxiety	Persistent errors in picking up spares can cause anxiety and nervousness during crucial moments, leading to more missed spares.

Table 47 - These examples demonstrate the interaction between technical and psychological components of bowling. Technical faults can lead to psychological issues, and vice versa, producing a complicated interplay that can affect a bowler's performance and mental state.

Table below explains how psychological errors can trigger technical errors and vice versa, with examples for each:

Psychological Errors	Technical Errors	Examples
Fear of Failure	Grip Consistency	Excessive fear of failure can cause a bowler to grip the ball too tightly, leading to inconsistency in his grip.
Lack of Confidence	Approach Timing	Low self-confidence can disrupt a bowler's approach, causing him to rush or hesitate and affecting his timing.
Frustration	Release Point	Frustration with performance may lead to changes in the release point as a bowler tries to force better results, causing inconsistency.
Self-Doubt	Balance at Delivery	Self-doubt can disrupt a bowler's focus on maintaining balance, leading to instability during the delivery and approach.
Patience	Ball Speed Control	Impatience to see results can cause a bowler to rush his shots, leading to difficulties in controlling ball speed.
Comfort Zone	Accuracy of Targeting	Staying within a comfort zone due to fear can lead to inaccurate targeting, as a bowler may avoid trying new techniques.
Peer Pressure	Hand Position	Peer pressure to conform to a specific hand position can cause a bowler to resist adjusting his technique, affecting hand position.
Overthinking	Lane Adjustment	Overthinking can disrupt a bowler's ability to make effective lane adjustments, leading to technical errors in targeting.
Anxiety	Spare Shooting	Anxiety during spare shots can cause a bowler to rush and make technical errors, resulting in missed spares.

Table 48 - These examples show how psychological factors can affect a bowler's technical execution and vice versa. The interaction between the two characteristics is dynamic and interwoven, and treating both is frequently required for total bowling performance improvement.

Sport psychologists and technical coaches are critical in dealing with this delicate interaction. Sport psychologists work with bowlers to help them develop mental toughness, handle stress, and develop strategies for overcoming psychological mistakes. They assist bowlers in understanding the underlying reasons for their mental issues and provide strategies to help them reduce their influence on technical performance. Technical coaches, on the other hand, use drills, practice, and feedback to refine and fix technical mistakes. By combining mental training and technical changes, these professionals can help bowlers break the cycle of technical and psychological errors. In doing so, they enable bowlers to identify and correct difficulties in real-time, enabling a more holistic approach to performance enhancement. Finally, the combination of mental and technical coaching can lead to breakthroughs in a bowler's game, allowing them to break through plateaus and reach new levels of skill and consistency.

Long-Lasting Error (Bad History)

A long-term error, whether it's a persistent technical flaw or an entrenched psychological obstacle, can severely hinder a bowler's capacity to progress and reach greater levels of performance. This constraint is frequently caused by the deeply ingrained character of these errors, which makes them tough to modify. It gets ingrained in the bowler's muscle memory, mental conditioning, and general approach to the sport. This endurance can be especially aggravating because the bowler may be unaware of how it affects their game.

Many bowlers around the world suffer this problem owing to a combination of reasons. First, the nature of bowling, like many other sports, necessitates constant and repetitive motions. This repetition can ingrain both correct and improper procedures over time. Second, self-diagnosis can be tough. Bowlers may lack the competence to identify and remedy their faults, or they may underestimate the severity of the problem.

Example 1: Bad Guidance or Coaching

In this hypothetical scenario, a bowler's long-lasting inaccuracy can be traced back to early tutoring that provided the wrong direction. The coach first taught the bowler a poor technique for releasing the ball, resulting in faults and inconsistencies in the bowler's game. Over time, the inaccuracy became embedded in muscle memory. The bowler, thinking the method to be perfect, continued to practice it frequently. Despite identifying the issue later, the deep-rooted behavior was exceedingly tough to break. The bowler battled with accuracy and consistency, and no amount of self-correction seemed to make a lasting effect. It was only after he sought professional advice from an experienced coach that he begins the laborious process of unlearning and relearning the appropriate technique.

Example 2: Environment and Facilities

In this case, a bowler's long-lasting inaccuracy might be linked to his environment and the limited facilities accessible to him. Growing up in a location with only a few antiquated bowling alleys, the bowler had limited access to good training and practice options. The lanes were badly maintained, and the equipment was often old. As a result, the bowler acquired routines to compensate for these weaknesses, such as adjusting his approach and release. When he eventually had the opportunity to practice in a high-quality facility with experienced instruction, he found it incredibly tough to unlearn his old habits and adapt to the right approaches. The engrained faults had become a part of his game, hampering his ability to execute at a competitive level.

Example 3: Psychological Issues from Parents and Bullying

In this fictitious instance, a bowler's persistent miscalculation is intricately linked to psychological problems originating from his childhood. The parent of the bowler put a lot of pressure on him and was always critical of his performance. He also experienced peer bullying while he was just starting out as bowlers. The bowler's surroundings became poisonous as a result of these encounters, leading to a serious lack of confidence and a fear of failing. These mental obstacles affected his shooting style, causing him to flinch and feel uneasy when he took his shots. Because of the psychological wounds from his childhood, the bowler struggled even after improving technically and obtaining coaching instruction. The hardest part of his path to recovery turned out to be resolving these pervasive psychological problems. In order to overcome his previous traumas, restore his confidence, and reach his full potential on the lanes, he required the assistance of a sports psychologist.

Example 4: Easy Home Center Patterns (House Pattern) and Lack of Competitors

In this case, a bowler's persistent mistake can be linked to the atmosphere of his neighborhood bowling alley. When compared to the patterns used in competitive settings, the home pattern utilized in this center was noticeably simpler. The bowler became used to this pattern's forgiving nature, which allowed for less concentration on technique adjustment and less accuracy in targeting. his skill development eventually reached a standstill as he grew dependent on the housing pattern's dependability. The center also had few real opponents, and most of his practice was with recreational bowlers. This absence of competition made the bowler even more complacent and demotivated to get better. The bowler found it difficult to adjust when he eventually entered more competitive settings with difficult lane conditions. Relearning his method, aiming, and ball selection to meet the demands of more difficult patterns and competition was necessary for him to overcome his enduring mistake.

Example 5: Wrong Hand Measurement and Bad Fitting

In this hypothetical instance, inaccurate hand measurement and poorly fitting equipment are the causes of a bowler's persistent mistake. In his early days in the game, the bowler's hand measurement was done incorrectly, which resulted in the ball being bought that didn't fit right. The grip, pitch, and span of the ball were all off, which made shots uncomfortable and difficult to control. The bowler unintentionally acquired a number of technical faults in his release and follow-through to make up for the inadequacies in the equipment. With time, these mistakes became second nature to him, and the agony of playing with a ball that didn't fit well further damaged his self-esteem. Despite his best effort to obtain professional help and equip himself with a properly sized and drilled ball, he found it extremely difficult to overcome the deeply rooted mistakes. The bowler attempted to overcome these persistent technical faults with perseverance and appropriate assistance, even though major adaptations were needed to accommodate to the new equipment.

Example 6: Low Tournament Participation Due to Lack of Support

In this fictitious scenario, low tournament participation is linked to a bowler's persistent inaccuracy, which is mostly the result of a lack of encouragement and support. The bowler had shown aptitude and love for the game at an early age, but he had to overcome many challenges before he could compete in the sport.

A notable obstacle he faced was the absence of assistance from his close relatives. Despite his good intentions, his parents were not completely aware of the potential and difficulties of bowling competitively. As a result, he failed to give the bowler the emotional or financial support required to frequently compete in competitions. Bowlers typically had feelings of loneliness and discouragement because they knew they were capable but lacked the tools to demonstrate his abilities.

The bowler received little exposure to competitive settings and tournament play as a result of this lack of assistance. His ability to grow and develop as a competitive bowler was severely hindered. He lacked the experience necessary to perform consistently under pressure and suffered from nervousness related to tournaments.

Example 7: Early Exposure to Difficult Oil Patterns and Persistent Performance Anxiety

In this fictitious case, a bowler's chronic inaccuracy is associated with early exposure to difficult oil patterns on the lanes, which resulted in dread of taking chances during shots and persistent performance anxiety. This bowler started his bowling career in *an environment where the lane conditions were significantly more demanding, even in his early years, in contrast to many other bowlers who start on simpler house patterns.*

He may have developed technically as a result of having to deal with challenging oil patterns early on, but there were also unforeseen repercussions. The bowler witnessed lots of splits and spares, but very few high scores. A lack of success coupled with the pressure to perform under these difficult circumstances increased performance anxiety.

The bowler consequently developed an excessive awareness of his shots, overanalyzed each action, and second-guessed his choices. He became afraid to take chances and try out various angles and ball selections because he thought that trying new things would end in failure. His nervousness was exacerbated by this fear of failing, and this vicious cycle continued into his later bowling years.

Example 8: Transitioning from Classic to Modern Bowling Style

In this fictitious situation, a bowler's persistent long-term inaccuracy is associated with his use of a traditional bowling technique in a sport that has transitioned to a more contemporary form. The bowler had studied and perfected the traditional bowling delivery, which usually consisted of a straighter delivery with less hook. He had found success with house patterns that fit his style, and this conventional method had served him well for many years.

But as bowling became a more popular sport, new methods emerged. These included creating a large hook, altering the shape and lane-play, and utilizing more sophisticated equipment. The bowler found it more difficult to adjust to these modifications. his traditional approach to play was no longer as successful with the increasingly difficult and intricate oil patterns that were developed in competitive environments.

Making the switch to the current style proved to be challenging. The bowler found it difficult to acquire the timing and muscle memory needed to produce the desired hook. Under duress, he frequently found himself falling back on his tried-and-true traditional style, even if it was no longer the most successful strategy. His inconsistent play developed into a chronic problem, and he observed as other bowlers adopted the contemporary approach and produced better results.

Example 9: "Straighter the Greater" No Longer Effective

In this hypothetical situation, a bowler's persistent mistake stems from his steadfast commitment to the "straighter the greater" philosophy of bowling, which progressively lost its efficacy in the dynamic environment of the game. Early in his bowling career, the bowler had developed a precise delivery technique that allowed him to regularly hit the pocket and leave reasonable spares.

But when alley conditions and bowling technology increased, the "straighter the greater" mentality started to demonstrate its limitations. Techniques with a large hook became more popular in the sport, enabling bowlers to raise his strike rates and produce more pin action. It was clear that the bowler's traditional straight style was no longer competitive at the highest levels, even if it had served him well in the past.

The bowler was aware that something had to alter, but he found it difficult to overcome his ingrained mistake. He discovered that it was difficult to build the muscle memory needed for a more hook-centric strategy. He frequently ended up frustrated and inconsistent after attempting to introduce a hook. He was afraid to embrace the current approach because he had grown accustomed to the straight manner.

For a bowler, a persistent, long-lasting error can be an intimidating and irritating foe, regardless of whether it stems from a mechanical defect or is wrapped in a complicated psychological barrier. It frequently calls for an unrelenting dedication to overtraining and several sacrifices, which ironically can make matters worse rather than better. To make up for the persistent mistake, some bowlers may focus their efforts on improving other technical areas of the game. Although this strategy is commendable for its tenacity, it may unintentionally produce a precarious equilibrium across skill sets, impeding a comprehensive improvement. The bowler feels utterly inadequate and their self-worth is questioned as a result of the error, which looms like a ghost. It turns into an incessant echo that muddles memories of successful strokes and traps the bowler in a vicious cycle of intense bewilderment, remorse, and self-blame.

Technically speaking, this mistake can set off a series of other problems that further damage the bowler's performance. If a seemingly insignificant error is not corrected, it might eventually result in negative behaviors that get engrained in muscle memory. These behaviors can have an impact on a number of game-related factors, such as ball speed and targeting as well as release and approach. The bowler may unintentionally reinforce the mistake through numerous repeats the harder they try to correct it.

Psychologically speaking, this persistent mistake frequently creates a widespread feeling of self-doubt. The bowler might start to doubt their skills, which would make them lose confidence. Doubt causes confidence to weaken and shots that were before made with poise and accuracy to slip. A succession of hesitant and unsure shots may replace the error, upsetting the bowler's flow state—a psychological state in which he performs at their peak.

In addition to technological improvements, breaking free from this cycle requires a significant mental makeover. It necessitates facing and reinterpreting harmful cognitive patterns that the error has caused to become deeply embedded. Sport psychologists are invaluable in helping bowlers recover their self-esteem, learn stress management techniques, and create coping mechanisms for performance anxiety. A more resilient and upbeat mindset can be developed by bowlers by reshaping their mental approach to the game using cognitive restructuring and visualization approaches.

Technically speaking, bowlers and coaches need to work closely together to pinpoint the mistakes' primary causes and make the necessary corrections. This could entail disassembling the motion into its component pieces, retraining the muscles, and performing targeted exercises to address the particular problem. It's a laborious procedure that requires patience and steadfast dedication.

Ultimately, correcting a long-standing mistake requires a whole process of self-discovery and transformation rather than just improving techniques or building mental toughness. It's about realizing that even though the mistake is severe, it is not unavoidable. With consistent work, the bowler can progressively rise beyond the shadows of their recurrent mistakes, prepared to accept a higher caliber of play and personal development on the lanes.

The frequency of these persistent mistakes among bowlers across the globe emphasizes the necessity of support and education in the sport. It is crucial to understand the technical and psychological components that underpin these problems. Coaches and governing organizations ought to stress to bowlers how important it is to get expert advice and offer resources to help them deal with these difficulties. Creating an environment where bowlers feel comfortable admitting and improving their shortcomings rather than letting them go unchecked is also essential. Bowlers can overcome ingrained mistakes and advance in their sport with the correct coaching, mental training, and a supportive atmosphere.

Strategic Plan To Overcome Old Habit

Objective 1: Diagnosis and Assessment

1. **Technical Analysis (Days 1-2, 4 hours):** Analyze gameplay videos from recent games, focusing on the exact moments when the persistent issue appears. Make notes and note any particular patterns associated with the error.

2. **Coach Discussion (Days 2-3, 2 hours):** Arrange a meeting to talk with a mentor or coach. Talk to them about your findings and analysis of the video. Ask them for their thoughts on the mistake and its possible reasons.

3. **Psychological Self-Awareness (Days 3-4, 6 hours):** Start a daily notebook to document your feelings, ideas, and actions associated with the mistake. Take note of the situations where the error frequently occurs.

4. **Professional Assessment (Days 5-6, 4 hours):** Find a sports psychologist or mental coach by doing some research. To talk about your observations and experiences regarding the inaccuracy, schedule a consultation.

5. **Complete Initial Assessment (Day 7, 2 hours):** To better understand the psychological components of the error, finish any early evaluations or questionnaires provided by the sports psychologist based on your conversation with them.

Objective 2: Technical Correction

1. **Deconstruction (Days 8-9, 6 hours):** Work with your coach to pinpoint the precise component of your bowling action that is causing the mistake. Dissect the motion into its component elements.

2. **Drills for Correction (Days 10-11, 4 hours):** Choose and start specific drills meant to address the identified problem in collaboration with your coach, taking into account the deconstruction. Retraining muscle memory is the main focus.

3. **Gradual Rebuilding (Days 12-15, 8 hours):** Keep using the revised strategy while progressively raising the bar on difficulty. Make sure that the new motion develops greater consistency and automaticity.

4. **Daily Video Analysis (Days 16-18, 6 hours):** Every day, record and examine the video from your practice sessions. Compare the error-prone movements from before with your improved method. Note the regions that still require repair and the advancements.

5. **Coach Feedback (Days 19-21, 6 hours):** Make time to check in with your coach on a regular basis to get their assessment of your development. Take care of any obstacles or failures you experience and modify the training schedule as necessary.

Objective 3: Psychological Transformation

1. **Cognitive Restructuring (Days 22-24, 8 hours):** Collaborate closely with the sports psychologist to pinpoint and disprove the error-related negative thought processes. Create plans to reinterpret these ideas in a positive light.

2. **Stress Management (Days 25-26, 4 hours):** To deal with performance anxiety, learn and put into practice stress management strategies such progressive muscle relaxation and deep breathing exercises.

3. **Mindfulness Training (Days 27-28, 8 hours):** Initiate a daily mindfulness routine to enhance your self-awareness and maintain present-mind awareness while taking shots. Focus and anxiety reduction are two benefits of mindfulness.

4. **Visualization (Days 22-24, 4 hours):** Keep doing the vision exercises, concentrating on visualizing the revised method being executed successfully. Imagine yourself acting with assurance and skill.

5. **Positive Self-Talk (Days 25-28, 6 hours):** Create a list of uplifting statements and constructive self-talk expressions. During training sessions and in difficult circumstances, practice saying these affirmations.

Objective 4: Overcoming Attachment to Old Technique

1. **Self-Reflection (Days 10-11, 4 hours):** Give some thought to the possible causes of your attachment to the outdated method. Determine any nostalgic or emotional ties to the earlier strategy..

2. **Visualize Letting Go (Days 12-13, 4 hours):** To psychologically let go of the previous method, employ visualization techniques. As a sign of your willingness to adapt, picture yourself letting go of it.

3. **Positive Reinforcement (Days 14-16, 6 hours):** Highlight the advantages of switching to the new method. Remind yourself of the advantages it might have on your performance as a whole and your game.

4. **Awareness in Practice (Days 17-20, 8 hours):** Pay close attention to and rectify any inclinations to regress to the previous method as you practice. Recognize the reasons behind these practices' recurrence.

5. **Coach Support (Days 21-22, 4 hours):** Talk to your mentor or coach about your challenges. Seek their advice and assistance in releasing yourself from the shackles of the outdated method. Talk about tactics to support the new strategy.

Objective 5: Building Confidence for Tournament Play

1. **Visualization of Tournament Success (Days 23-24, 4 hours):** Make use of visualization techniques to create a clear mental image of oneself using the new tactic in a competition. Envision accomplishment, gratifying responses, and assured performance.

2. **Practice Under Pressure (Days 25-26, 6 hours):** Set up practice sessions with time constraints and competitive pressure to resemble tournament settings. To gain confidence, gradually expose oneself to these situations.

3. **Positive Reinforcement (Days 27-28, 6 hours):** Keep highlighting the advantages of the novel approach. Remind yourself of your accomplishments and your ability to function successfully under duress.

4. **Mental Rehearsal (Days 23-24, 4 hours):** Practice your ability to confidently handle any obstacles that may come up during a tournament by mentally rehearsing yourself.

5. **Tournament Simulation (Day 29, 6 hours):** To put the new skill to use in a competitive environment, set up a practice tournament, sign up for a nearby competition. Make the most of this as a confidence-boosting and educational opportunity.

Objective	Timeframe	Concurrent Tasks
Objective 1: Identify Long-Lasting Error	Days 1-5	- Task 1: Self Reflection
		- Task 2: Video Analysis
		- Task 3: Discuss with Coach
		- Task 4: Identify Trigger Factors
		- Task 5: Set Clear Objectives
Objective 2: Address Root Causes	Days 6-10	- Task 6: Identify Technical Causes
		- Task 7: Explore Psychological Factors
		- Task 8: Consult with Sports Psychologist
		- Task 9: Analyze Past Experiences
		- Task 10: Develop Coping Strategies
Objective 3: Develop Corrective Habits	Days 11-22	- Task 11: Develop New Technique
		- Task 12: Practice Drills for New Technique
		- Task 13: Monitor Progress & Adjust
		- Task 14: Engage in Visualization & Mental Rehearsal
		- Task 15: Seek Continuous Feedback from Coach
Objective 4: Overcoming Attachment to Old Technique	Days 23-28	- Task 16: Self-Reflection
		- Task 17: Visualize Letting Go
		- Task 18: Positive Reinforcement
		- Task 19: Awareness in Practice
		- Task 20: Coach Support
Objective 5: Building Confidence for Tournament Play	Days 29-30	- Task 21: Visualization of Tournament Success
		- Task 22: Practice Under Pressure
		- Task 23: Positive Reinforcement
		- Task 24: Mental Rehearsal
		- Task 25: Tournament Simulation

In conclusion, bowlers may find it difficult to correct technical errors and overcome ingrained habits for a variety of reasons. These can include a lack of appropriate coaching and direction, deeply rooted muscle memory, psychological obstacles, a lack of drive or commitment, a lack of self-awareness, physical restrictions, outside variables like lane conditions or equipment limits, and time and resource constraints. It takes a mix of self-awareness, perseverance, appropriate coaching, practice, and patience to overcome these obstacles. Bowlers must acknowledge their technical faults, get expert advice, and invest time and energy into fixing them. Bowlers can increase their performance in the game and reduce their technical faults with constant practice and dedication.

LIFE AFTER SPORT: DEPRESSION IN THE RETIRED BOWLERS

A popular notion is that a professional athlete will experience two metaphorical deaths during their lifetime, the first of which will occur when he retires. This is a fascinating phenomenon that especially affects bowlers, whose lives are entwined with the sport they have dedicated their lives to. The question that follows is incredibly important: who really wins when the last frame is bowled and the raucous cheers are forgotten?

Pro bowlers spend the better part of their lives on an unrelenting path, committing years and years to the quest for perfection in a sport that requires unshakable dedication. These athletes frequently find themselves making significant personal sacrifices outside of the bowling center's lanes and alleys in their pursuit of fame. These include significant monetary outlays, time spent away from close family members to attend specialized schools, postponing academic endeavors, and even giving up romantic and emotional connections. With little room for reflection on the impending conclusion, the sum of these decisions depicts a life dedicated exclusively to the pursuit of perfection.

Retirement is an inevitable fate that all sportsmen must face, whether or not they achieve Olympic medals or reach the pinnacle of their sport. It's an eventuality that many bowlers would prefer to avoid. It can end because of time itself, the pain of crippling injuries, or just plain tiredness from years of nonstop work.

But after the intense training, nonstop travel, and adrenaline of competition end, what happens to bowlers? This is when depression could start to creep up on them. Every bowler has a different retirement experience, and it can be a difficult time full of emotional and psychological obstacles. Not every bowler gracefully transitions into retirement when the last frames are bowled and the crowd's applause wanes. Many find it difficult to adjust to living a more "normal" life away from the limelight. After years in the spotlight in the bowling world, they may be concerned about slipping into obscurity.

A bowler's personal, social, and professional lives alter significantly once he retires from professional bowling. A variety of psychological reactions may result from these alterations in his thinking, feelings, and behavior. Bowlers may find it difficult to transition emotionally to this new stage of life as they manage the social and professional changes that accompany retiring. After retiring from bowling, it's not uncommon for them to experience a sensation of emptiness. Their challenge now is to reconstruct their identities and get used to a new way of life that does not center around bowling. It is well known that the move from a full-time bowling career to retirement is difficult. It entails abruptly abandoning the rigorous demands of professional bowling competition, along with all of its benefits and recognition.

Dame Kelly Holmes, Neil Lennon, Ian Thorpe, and other well-known sportsmen have all openly discussed their struggles with depression after retirement. In order to increase awareness of depression in the community of retired athletes, other well-known individuals including Andrew Flintoff, Paul Gascoigne, and Frank Bruno have also openly discussed their struggles with this problem. Their personal accounts highlight the psychological costs associated with making the move from professional athlete to post-retiree.

Myth: All Athletes Easily Transition to a "Normal" Life

Reality: Another common misconception is that athletes seamlessly transition to a "normal" life after retirement. However, the reality is that this transition can be tumultuous for many athletes. The shift from a life entirely devoted to their sport to one where they must navigate different roles and responsibilities can be emotionally challenging. It's essential to understand that each athlete's retirement experience is unique, and not all of them adapt easily to this new phase of life.

One of the bowling world's greatest figures, Tomas Leandersson, who passed away in Sweden, was quoted as saying,

"There is nothing in life that can compare to becoming a world champion, having your hand raised in that moment of glory, with thousands, millions of people cheering you on."

Tomas had a tough time transitioning to retirement, and his battle with severe depressive episodes gained widespread attention. Due to this experience, he attempted several comebacks, highlighting the intense psychological difficulties that professional athletes may face after retirement. Tomas's tale is unfortunately not unique; over the years, heartbreaking examples have been reported of athletes who, unable to handle the change, ended their lives by suicide after retiring from professional athletics.

The late Tomas Leandersson

So what are the underlying causes that, when retired professional bowlers say goodbye to the days of rigorous training, the intense pressure of competition, and the glory of their prime athletic years, frequently leave them struggling with depression? The pieces of this complex puzzle must be put together by exploring the intricacies of their post-retirement existence, where they have to make their way across unfamiliar territory as bowling alleys are no longer their places of victory.

It may be quite difficult to go from a life entirely focused on bowling alleys and strikes to one where such activities are no longer the main focus. The loss of the activity that dominated their lives produces a hole that is difficult to fill for many retired bowlers. The intense rush of competition, the thunderous applause from the crowd, and the pursuit of excellence fade into the background, leaving behind a tangible sense of emptiness and longing.

Having to redefine oneself outside of the world of sport presents another significant barrier. For a long time, retired bowlers were seen as great athletes, with devoted fans and the media observing every move they made. They have to face the fact that, when their careers come to an end, they are no longer elite athletes but rather everyday people. This change can be confusing and cause feelings of worthlessness and extreme disorientation.

In addition, retired athletes' mental health may suffer significantly from the stresses of professional bowling, whether they come from internal or external demands for excellence. Emotional wounds that last long after retirement might result from the unwavering quest for perfection, the pressure to perform at the highest level, and the weight of society and personal expectations.

Loss Of Identity:

The dynamics of human identity are equally complex, with a particular emphasis often placed on athletic identity among bowlers. Athletic identity denotes the extent to which an individual identifies with their role as a bowler, seeking external validation within that sporting world. However, this exclusive focus on the bowler's identity may lead to the unintentional neglect of other roles in one's life, potentially giving rise to profound identity challenges. As retirement approaches for bowlers, the impending loss of this prominent athlete role may set in motion a cascade effect, impacting the bowler's overall self-concept.

Bowlers with a strong athletic identity, particularly as they approach retirement, may be more susceptible to experiencing emotional challenges during this transition. Renowned peak performance coach Bill Cole, celebrated for his expertise in guiding athletes through the nuanced journey from competition to retirement, underscores the significance of the intense sense of loss that bowlers often confront when their competitive days conclude. This insight digs into the intricate interplay between athletic identity and the broader spectrum of self-concept within the context of bowling, offering valuable perspectives on the emotional complexities that bowlers may navigate during this significant phase of their athletic journey.

Hypothetical example
The Reluctant Retirement

John had a bowling game and was totally committed to it. Bowling was his life, and throughout the years, he had solidified his identity as an athlete. He devoted endless hours to improving his craft, competing, and practicing. He was known as "the bowler" by his friends and family since it appeared to be the only role he accepted.

As John grew older, his performance began to suffer from injuries. He came to the conclusion that his professional bowling career was coming to an end and that he couldn't continue to compete at that level for very long. It was as though a piece of his identity was taken away when the time for him to retire had arrived. His identity as an "athlete" had been stripped from him, and he found it difficult to adjust to his new situation. John struggled emotionally to adjust to life without his strong athletic identity, feeling lost and alone in a world that no longer recognized him as "the bowler."

Tunnel Vision Syndrome:

Many professional bowlers encounter a phenomenon akin to "tunnel vision syndrome" at various points in their careers. While coaches, parents, and team managers often recognize this tendency, the athletes themselves may be unaware of its impact. Afflicted by tunnel vision, bowlers can become excessively fixated on the intricacies of their preparation, the competitive environment, and the outcomes of their performances. This intense focus, while beneficial for their sport, may inadvertently hinder the development of a more well-rounded perspective crucial for managing broader professional opportunities beyond the lanes.

The transition from a singular emphasis on bowling to a more expansive view that encompasses broader career prospects can be a daunting prospect. Athletes deeply committed to their sport may find themselves immersed in a pervasive self-centeredness that leaves them unprepared for life beyond the bowling alley. As retirement approaches, the once-occupied space filled with the routines and rituals of practice and competition can turn into a void, prompting a need for bowlers to broaden their perspective and embrace a more balanced approach to their professional lives. Recognizing and addressing tunnel vision in the context of bowling is vital for athletes to navigate successful transitions and embrace the diverse opportunities that await them beyond the lanes.

Example 1: The Consumed Competitor

One bowler developed tunnel vision, focusing only on his preparation and competitiveness. He frequently overlooked chances outside of the sport in favor of improving his bowling abilities every waking hour. Her or she was therefore ill-equipped to make the switch to a post-competitive career. He had thrown all of his efforts into bowling, leaving little opportunity for other job opportunities, so when retirement drew near, he left with an intimidating vacuum.

Example 2: The Well-Rounded Bowler

One bowler, however, was able to keep a more impartial viewpoint throughout his career. Despite his passion for sport, he understood the value of looking into professional options outside of the lanes. In addition to training and competition, he participated in networking, education, and personal growth. His adjustment to retirement was easier because he had developed a wider range of interests and abilities that could take the place of the hole created by the end of his competitive bowling days.

Potential Biological Factors:

The profound impact of biological variables on the challenges faced by athletes post-retirement cannot be ignored. Consider the consistent release of serotonin—a vital neurotransmitter crucial for mood regulation and overall well-being—that bowlers undergo throughout their competitive careers. The sudden reduction or cessation of this serotonin supply upon retirement can create substantial perturbations in the body's chemical equilibrium, presenting unique psychological challenges.

While the connection between serotonin levels and psychological well-being has been explored in various contexts, including retired athletes, there exists a compelling need for more extensive research specifically within the domain of bowling. Understanding the role played by biological factors in the psychological challenges faced by bowlers transitioning from active careers to retirement is crucial. Researchers have initiated investigations into potential links between imbalances in serotonin levels and conditions like depression, emphasizing the significance of tailored studies to address the unique demands of retired bowlers. This research not only enhances our comprehension of the psychological aspects of retirement in bowling but also paves the way for targeted interventions and support mechanisms for the well-being of athletes in the sport.

Example 1: The Serotonin Rollercoaster

A very successful career was led by a bowler who consistently felt the serotonin rush that comes with competition and success. But when he retired, his mood and general well-being suffered from the sudden stop of this serotonin release. He battled severe chemical imbalances in his bodies, which resulted in depressive and anxious feelings. The athlete's story emphasizes how biological variables, including serotonin imbalances, may have an effect on the psychological difficulties associated with retiring.

Example 2: The Uncharted Biological Terrain

Although he had a good career as a bowler, the other player was not aware that biological variables might be involved. After retirement, he suffered from mood swings and uneasiness, not realizing how much the sudden decrease in serotonin release affected his emotional condition. The experience of this athlete highlights the need for additional research to fully comprehend how biological elements impact the psychological difficulties faced by retired athletes, since many may have to traverse this unexplored biological territory without the necessary knowledge or assistance.

Managing Retirement: Strategies For Bowlers' Mental Health And Identity

Managing the transition into retirement is a crucial phase for bowlers, demanding consideration of strategies to mitigate the risk of depression and ensure a smooth shift in identity. In contemplating the conclusion of their athletic journey, bowlers are advised to dig into approaches that foster mental health and provide a foundation for a fulfilling retirement experience. A primary step involves **expanding one's self-identity** beyond the confines of the sport. While the identity as a dedicated bowler is undeniably integral, acknowledging the multifaceted nature of one's personality, interests, and skills is equally important. Embracing diverse facets of life, both within and beyond the sporting world, contributes to a more comprehensive sense of self. Another pivotal aspect is the **exploration of new avenues** post-retirement, offering bowlers the opportunity to acquire fresh skills and engage in hobbies that extend beyond the athletic arena. Roles such as coaching or mentoring other athletes can provide continuity and purpose, fostering a continued sense of participation and fulfillment. In the realm of personal development, **improving stress and time management skills** becomes essential for bowlers in their post-retirement years. Striking a balance between the demands of daily life and the recreational aspects of sports can be facilitated by these skills, promoting overall well-being and a smoother transition. Moreover, **nurturing supportive relationships** proves instrumental during this significant life shift. Establishing close bonds with management, coaches, family, and friends who genuinely care about personal development, rather than just athletic achievements, is invaluable. A robust network can offer guidance, encouragement, and a sense of security as bowlers explore alternative career options. Lastly, **engaging with a sport psychologist** emerges as a valuable resource for those managing retirement. Seeking counsel from experts in coping mechanisms and emotional support can aid in handling the psychological implications of leaving professional sports. By incorporating these multifaceted strategies, bowlers can approach retirement with resilience, cultivating a renewed sense of purpose and well-being in this transformative phase of their lives.

It's critical to recognize that bowlers, like other athletes, frequently exhibit mental toughness and are viewed as physically fit, healthy, and content. But these misconceptions and preconceptions are exactly what can make it difficult to ask for assistance when you need it. It's possible for athletes to be reluctant to disclose their difficulties out of embarrassment and shame.

It is therefore the responsibility of close friends, teammates, coaches, and family members to understand that depression does not always show symptoms. Athletes may decide to hide their mental struggles. The most important lesson is that retiring can be difficult, even for those who have achieved extraordinary success in their committed professions. Social support and honest communication are critical during this transitional period to help bowlers avoid the potentially crippling post-retirement blues.

Lifetime Strategic Plan for Retired Bowlers:

Stage 1: Pre-Retirement Preparation

1. **Self-Identity Exploration:**
   - Consider your identity in contexts other than bowling.
   - Determine your hobbies, other interests, and possible job options.
   - Start developing a more comprehensive view of who you are.

2. **Networking and Mentoring:**
   - Make contact with former bowlers who have made a smooth transition.
   - Look for mentors who can offer advice on what to do after retirement.

3. **Skill Diversification:**
   - Examine abilities and proficiencies that are not limited to bowling.
   - Think about enrolling in workshops or courses related to your interests.

Stage 2: Retirement Transition

4. **Embrace New Roles:**
   - Go into positions like mentorship, coaching, or sports administration.
   - These positions can offer consistency and meaning outside of competitive play.

5. **Stress and Time Management:**
   - Learn stress-reduction strategies, such mindfulness or meditation.
   - Establish a daily routine that strikes a balance between your hobbies, personal life, and any prospective duties you may have as a coach or mentor.

Stage 3: Building a Supportive Network

6. **Cultivate Supportive Relationships:**
   - Fortify ties with loved ones, close friends, and coworkers who appreciate your personal development.
   - Let them know about your retirement ambitions and goals.

7. **Professional Guidance:**
   - Speak with a sport psychologist or other mental health specialist.
   - Talk about coping mechanisms, adjustment methods, and emotional difficulties.

Stage 4: Post-Retirement Life

8. **Maintain a Healthy Lifestyle:**
   - For your health and wellbeing, keep up your physical exercise.
   - Give regular exercise, healthy eating, and rest top priority.

9. **Pursue Interests and Hobbies:**
   - Set aside time to investigate novel interests, whether or not they are connected to sports.
   - Join interest or social clubs to network and keep active.

10. **Community Involvement:**
    - Participate in community activities or volunteer work.
    - Giving to charitable projects unrelated to athletics can provide one a feeling of direction.

11. **Education and Personal Development**:
    - Take into account pursuing additional training or developing new skills in areas of interest to you or where you see yourself in the future.

12. **Open Communication**:
    - Be honest with close friends and family about your emotional state and difficulties.
    - If you require expert assistance, don't be ashamed to ask for it.

Stage 5: Ongoing Growth and Well-Being

13. **Set and Pursue Goals**:
    - Constantly establish and strive for new professional and personal objectives.
    - Retain your drive and feeling of direction.

14. **Regular Self-Assessment**:
    - Regularly assess your emotional and mental health.
    - Modify your tactics as necessary to keep a balanced, healthy lifestyle.

15. **Mentoring and Giving Back**:
    - Keep coaching or mentoring aspiring sportsmen or bowlers.
    - Give the younger generation support by sharing your knowledge and experiences.

Recall that retiring is a journey, and it could require some time to adjust. Have patience with yourself and give yourself space to develop and evolve. Retired bowlers can reduce their risk of depression, maintain a healthy lifestyle, and improve as people after retirement by adhering to this strategic approach.

FINAL WORDS

For the past three years, I have dedicated every waking moment to the effort of love that has been writing this extraordinary book. It has been a long road that has involved gathering data from global sources, interacting with coaches, bowlers, and industry experts, and overcoming many obstacles in the quest for collaboration and understanding. There were times when this felt like a huge undertaking, something out of the stories of Hercules and other myths because I had difficulty getting answers and acknowledgments from some people. Like many other sports, bowling has its own set of difficulties, such as dwindling support and enthusiasm. But it was in these trying times that I realized how important it is to persevere and how important it is to look for outside help in order to reignite my passion for the sport.

I would like to express my sincere gratitude to all of my fellow bowlers and coaches for voluntarily sharing their personal experiences and ideas, in addition to providing invaluable knowledge. Their constant assistance and collaboration have been invaluable in creating a book that I sincerely hope will be an everlasting light for future generations—a storehouse of wisdom and motivation that will breathe fresh life into the world of competitive bowling. We set out on a journey of transformation together, driven by the common goal of improving the sport, and I am incredibly grateful to everyone who went with me along the way.

The difficulties I encountered while researching this book included people I had long looked up to as mentors and regarded as the epitome of success in the bowling world. It was depressing to experience times when people who are generally considered the pinnacles of success in the sport ignored or rejected you. Still, these encounters highlighted the core of the expedition I embarked upon. They were heartbreaking reminders that even the most successful people have had difficult journeys to become the best versions of themselves. Even while the journey was often difficult, it served as a reminder of how important it is to be persistent and open to learning from everyone, no matter how they are regarded in the bowling community. In the end, these experiences strengthened my desire to write a book that crosses boundaries and provides a forum for bowlers and aficionados to develop, learn, and grow.

In this comprehensive work, I undertake a profound exploration of the intricate relationship between psychological abilities and the pursuit of excellence in the field of bowling. The book digs into the depths of the human mind, revealing the crucial role played by inner thoughts and emotions in the challenging journey toward achieving the highest level of performance. With meticulous attention to detail, I unravel the complex tapestry of psychological transitions that shape a bowler's path to excellence.

This is not merely a guide on navigating the mental aspects of the game during tournaments or practice sessions; it transcends conventional wisdom, addressing every facet of a bowler's existence. From the formative years under parental and educational guidance to the challenging ascent toward mastery, the book illuminates hidden patterns and profound truths underlying the pursuit of greatness. It underscores the fact that the foundation for mental fortitude and resilience is established long before a bowler steps onto the lanes.

Within these pages, readers will find a thorough investigation into the motives and dynamics that propel top-tier bowlers to reach their fullest potential. I dissect the essence of performance, shedding light on the obstacles and limitations that often impede progress. Through meticulous analysis, the book uncovers the secrets to unlocking the true potential that lies within every bowler.

As a former bowler and coach with experience on global and Asian tours, my game may not have always been flawless, but my unwavering determination to triumph and showcase a unique approach to the sport has never wavered. Having immersed myself in bowling literature and courses, I sought a fresh perspective that transcends the conventional, leading me on a three-year odyssey to create a literary masterpiece that redefines the landscape of bowling psychology.

As we come to the end of this fascinating tour through the world of professional bowling, we must consider how we may apply the understanding and information gained from this book to improve bowling competition standards across the globe, particularly for the bowlers of our younger generation. The teachings found within these pages are not artifacts from the past; rather, they serve as a guide for the sport's future. We can develop the potential of aspiring bowlers and take bowling to new heights by adhering to the values of commitment, resiliency, and a holistic approach to the game. The tales told here can serve as a source of motivation for mentors, parents, and coaches as they mold the next wave of bowlers who will push the envelope in the sport. We can make sure that bowling's legacy lives on and grows in the future by embracing the multifaceted nature of the game, cultivating a culture of growth, and relentlessly chasing excellence. It is my duty to carry the torch forward on the never-ending quest for bowling greatness and encourage upcoming generations to aim high on the lanes of competitive bowling.

This project is essentially more than just a book; it's a call to action, an invitation to all those involved in the bowling industry to work together to create a better future for the game. It's a recognition that the development of the sport depends not just on the abilities of individual bowlers but also on the community's combined efforts. Armed with the information and understanding necessary to take the sport to new heights, we find ourselves at a crossroads. The fundamentals of a more robust and dynamic bowling culture are commitment, resiliency, and a holistic approach. They are not just buzzwords.

Let us keep in mind that, as we set out on this trip, we are all threads in a beautiful tapestry that has been woven together by the experiences of innumerable bowlers, coaches, and enthusiasts who have committed their lives to the quest for greatness. Let us be the ones to set an example for the upcoming generation of bowlers by taking inspiration from their stories. The lanes are ready, and it is up to us to shape bowling's future. By working together, we can make sure that bowling endures and grows, capturing the interest of bowlers of all ages and making a lasting impression on the sports industry.

REFERENCES:

- Baxter, P., & Dole, S. (1990). Working with the brain, not against it: Correction of systematic errors in subtraction. British Journal of Special Education, 17, 19-22.

- Bernstein, N.A. (1947). On Construction of Movements. Moscow, USSR: MEDGIZ Publishers (In Russian).

- Buck, D., Hutchinson, J., Winter, C., & Thompson, B. (2016). The Effects of Mental Imagery with Video-Modeling on Self-Efficacy and Maximal Front Squat Ability. Sports, 4(23), 1–10. http://doi.org/10.3390/sports4020023

- Collins, D., Morris, C., & Trower, J. (1999). Getting it back: A case study of skill recovery in an elite athlete. The Sport Psychologist, 13, 288-298.

- Csıkszentmihályi, M. (1975). Beyond boredom and anxiety. In Book beyond boredom and anxiety (1975 edn). San Francisco, CA: Jossey-Bass.

- Csikszentmihalyi, M., & Csikszentmihalyi, I. S. (eds.). (1992). Optimal experience: Psychological studies of flow in consciousness. Cambridge University Press.

- Dawson, C., & Lyndon, H. (1997). Conceptual mediation: A new perspective on conceptual exchange. Research in Science Education, 27, 157-173.

- Fitts, P. and Posner, M.I. (1967) Human Performance. Brooks/Cole Publishing, Belmont, CA.

- Forlenza, S. T., Weinberg, R. S., & Horn, T. S. (2014). Imagery speed and self-efficacy: how fast (or slow) to go? International Journal of Golf Science, 2(2), 126–141. doi:10.1123/ijgs.2013-0012

- Hanin Y. (2007). Emotions in Sport: Current issues and perspectives. In G. Tenenbaum & R.C. Eklund (Eds.). Handbook of Sport Psychology 3rd ed. (pp. 31-58). Hoboken, NJ: John Wiley & Sons.

- Hanin, J., & Hanina, M. (2006). Correction of Habitual Performance Errors in Expert Athletes: Theory & Practice. In: K. Thomson, J. Liukkonen, & T. Jaakkola (Eds.). Promotion of Motor Skills in Sport and Physical Education. (pp. 89-97) Jyväskylä University, Department of Sport Sciences: Jyväskylä, Finland.

- Hanin, J., Hanina, M., & Rantanen, V. (2007). Käytännön malli lajitekniikan parantamiseksi. (Practical model for improvement of sports technique). HUU: Huippu-Urheilu-Uutiset, 3, 34-35.

- Hanin, Y. (2000). Emotion patterns in successful and poor performances. In Hanin, Y. L. (Ed.) Emotions in Sport. (pp.157-187). Champaign, Illinois; Human Kinetics.

- Hanin, Y., Korjus, T., Jouste, P., & Baxter, P. (2002). Rapid technique correction using old way / new way: two case studies with Olympic athletes. The Sport Psychologist, 16, 79-99.

- Hanin, Y., Malvela, M., & Hanina M. (2004). Rapid correction of start technique in an Olympic-level Swimmer: A case Study Using Old way/New way. Journal of Swimming Research. Vol.16, pp. 11-17.

- Holmes, P.S., & Collins, D.J (2001). The PETTLEP approach to motor imagery: A functional equivalanece model for sport psychologists. A Journal of Applied Sport Psychology, 13, 60-83.

- Hwang E. J., Link T. D., Hu Y. Y., Lu S., Wang E. H.-J., Lilascharoen V., et al. (2019). Corticostriatal flow of action selection bias. Neuron 104 1126.e6–1140.e6.

- Koehn, S., Morris, T., & Watt, A. P. (2014). Imagery Intervention to Increase Flow State and Performance in Competition. The Sport Psychologist, (2002), 48–59. http://doi.org/10.1123/tsp.2012-0106

- Lyndon, E. H. (1989). I did it my way! An introduction to Old way/new way. Australasian Journal of Special Education, 13, 32-37.
- Lyndon, E. H. (2000). Conceptual mediation: A new theory and new method of conceptual change. Australia: University of Adelaide. Unpublished doctoral dissertation.
- Maschette, W. (1985). Correcting technique problems of a successful junior athlete. Sport Coach, 9, 14-17.
- Morris, T., Spittle, M., & P.Watt, A. (2005). Imagery in sport. United States of America: Human Kinetics.
- Nordin, S.M., & Cumming, J. (2008). Types and functions of athletes' imagery: Testing predictions from the Applied Model of Imagery Use by examining effectiveness. International Journal of Sport and Exercise Psychology, 6, 189–206. doi:10.1080/1612197X.2008.9671861
- Orebro, Sweden: Orebro University Press.
- R.C. Eklund (Eds.). Handbook of Sport Psychology 3rd ed. (pp. 31-58). Hoboken, NJ: John Wiley & Sons.
- Rymal, A., Martini, R., & Ste-Marie, D. . (2010). Self-regulatory processess employed during self-modelling : A qualitative analysis. Sport Psychologist, 24(1), 1–15.
- Stambulova, N. (2003a). Symptoms of a crisis-transition: A grounded theory study. SIPF Yearbook (pp. 97–109).
- Stambulova, N. (2003b). Counseling athletes in crises. In R. Stelter (Ed.), New approaches to exercise and sport psychology. Proceedings of the XI-the European Congress of Sport Psychology (p. 161). Copenhagen, Denmark: FEPSAC.
- Subotnik, R. F., & Rickoff, R. (2010). Should eminence based on outstanding innovation be the goal of gifted education and talent development? Implications for policy and research. Learning and Individual Differences, 20(4), 358–364. https:// doi.org/10.1016/j.lindif.2009.12.005
- Subotnik, R. F., Olszewski-Kubilius, P., & Worrell, F. C. (2019). Environmental factors and personal characteristics iteract to yield high performance in domains. Frontiers in Psychology, 10, Article 2804. https://doi.org/10.3389/fpsyg.2019.02804
- Underwood, B. J. (1957). Interference and forgetting. Psychological Review, 64, 49-60.
- Underwood, B. J. (1966). Experimental psychology (2nd Ed.). New York: Appleton-Century-Crofts.

Index

Z

Made in the USA
Columbia, SC
02 February 2024

31006760R00243